ROUTLEDGE HANDBOOK OF NUCLEAR PROLIFERATION AND POLICY

D1709541

This new Handbook is a comprehensive examination of the rich and complex issues of nuclear proliferation in the early twenty-first century.

The future of the decades-long effort to prevent the further spread of weapons of mass destruction is at a crossroads today. If international nonproliferation efforts are to be successful, an integrated, multi-tiered response will almost certainly be necessary. A serious, thorough, and clear-eyed examination of the range of threats, challenges, and opportunities facing the international community is a necessary first step. This Handbook, which presents the most up-to-date analysis and policy recommendations on these critical issues by recognized, leading scholars in the field, intends to provide such an examination.

The volume is divided into three major parts:

- Part I presents detailed threat assessments of proliferation risks across the globe, including specific regions and countries.
- Part II explains the various tools developed by the international community to address these proliferation threats.
- Part III addresses the proliferation risks and political challenges arising from nuclear energy production, including potential proliferation by aspiring states and non-state groups.

This Handbook will be of great interest to students and practitioners of nuclear proliferation, arms control, global governance, diplomacy, and global security and IR in general.

Joseph F. Pilat is Project Manager at the National Security Office, Los Alamos National Laboratory and a Global Fellow at the Woodrow Wilson International Center for Scholars, Washington, DC, USA. He is the editor of *Atoms for Peace: A Future after Fifty Years?* (2007).

Nathan E. Busch is Professor of Government at Christopher Newport University (CNU) and Co-Director of CNU's Center for American Studies. He is the co-author of *The Business of Counterterrorism: Public–Private Partnerships in Homeland Security* (2014).

ROUTLEDGE HANDBOOK OF NUCLEAR PROLIFERATION AND POLICY

Edited by Joseph F. Pilat and Nathan E. Busch

LONDON AND NEW YORK

First published in paperback 2018

First published 2015
By Routledge
2 Park Square, Milton Park, Abingdon, Oxon OX14 4RN

and by Routledge
711 Third Avenue, New York, NY 10017

Routledge is an imprint of the Taylor & Francis Group, an informa business

British Library Cataloguing-in-Publication Data
A catalogue record for this book is available from the British Library

Library of Congress Cataloging-in-Publication Data
Routledge handbook of nuclear proliferation and policy / edited by Joseph F. Pilat and Nathan E. Busch.
pages cm
Includes bibliographical references and index.
1. Nuclear nonproliferation—International cooperation. 2. World politics—21st century.
I. Pilat, Joseph F., editor of compilation. II. Busch, Nathan E., 1971– editor of compilation.
III. Title: Handbook of nuclear proliferation and policy.
JZ5675.R69 2015
327.1'747—dc23
2014040250

ISBN: 978-0-415-87039-9 (hbk)
ISBN: 978-1-138-55499-3 (pbk)
ISBN: 978-0-203-70952-8 (ebk)

Typeset in Bembo
by Apex CoVantage, LLC

Printed and bound by CPI Group (UK) Ltd, Croydon, CR0 4YY

CONTENTS

FIGURES

TABLES

CONTRIBUTORS

Sun Young Ahn is currently working as a research assistant at the US-Korea Institute (USKI) at Johns Hopkins School of Advanced International Studies (SAIS).

Sibylle Bauer is the Director of the Stockholm International Peace Research Institute's (SIPRI) Dual-use and Arms Trade Control Programme. She has held positions with the Institute for European Studies at the Free University of Brussels, the EU Institute for Security Studies in Paris, and the International Security Information Service in Europe. Dr Bauer has a long record of research and publication on armaments and export control issues.

Jacques Bouchard has served as the Special Advisor to the Chairman and Chief Executive Officer of the French Atomic Energy Commission (CEA) since 2008. He has held positions as the Chairman of the Standing Advisory Group for Nuclear Energy of the IAEA, Chairman of the Generation IV International Forum (GIF), and President of the French Nuclear Energy Society.

Wyn Q. Bowen is Head of the Defence Studies Department, King's College London at the Joint Services Command and Staff College, UK Defence Academy. He is also Professor of Non-Proliferation & International Security and Co-Director of the Centre for Science & Security Studies at King's College. He served as a weapons inspector on several ballistic missile inspection teams in Iraq with the UN Special Commission in 1997–98. He has worked as a consultant to the International Atomic Energy Agency; as a Specialist Advisor to the House of Commons' Foreign Affairs Committee. He has also served on the Royal Society's Advisory Committee on the Scientific Aspects of International Security (2008–2011) and the Royal Society's Working Group on Nuclear Non-Proliferation. He is a Trustee of the Verification Research, Training and Information Centre (VERTIC) and a member of the Advisory Board of the Royal United Services Institute (RUSI) Journal. He was founding co-editor of the journal *Defence Studies*.

Matthew Bunn has held the position of Professor of Practice at the John F. Kennedy School of Government at Harvard University since 2013 and has held other positions at Harvard University since 2001. Previous other positions include advisor to the White House Office of

Science and Technology Policy, editor of *Arms Control Today*, and as a study director at the National Academy of Sciences. He has published widely on issues of nuclear security and terrorism, including *Securing the Bomb 2010: Securing All Nuclear Materials in Four Years* (2010).

Susan Burk has served as the Special Representative of the President of The United States for Nuclear Nonproliferation from 2009–2012. She has previously held positions as the first Deputy Coordinator for Homeland Security in the State Department's Bureau of Counter-terrorism, Acting Assistant Secretary of State for Nonproliferation, and Chief of the International Nuclear Affairs Division of the United States Arms Control and Disarmament Agency.

Nathan E. Busch is Professor of Government at Christopher Newport University (CNU) and Co-Director of CNU's Center for American Studies. He has held positions at the University of Georgia, Harvard University, and the Los Alamos National Laboratory. His previous publications include *The Business of Counterterrorism: Public-Private Partnerships in Homeland Security* (2014).

John Carlson is Counselor to the Nuclear Threat Initiative (NTI), Washington. His other current appointments include Advisory Council, International Luxembourg Forum; Associate, Project on Managing the Atom, Belfer Center, Harvard University; Nonresident Fellow, Lowy Institute; International Verification Consultants Network, VERTIC; Adviser, Asia Pacific Leadership Network for Nuclear Non-Proliferation and Disarmament. His previous appointments include Director General, Australian Safeguards and Non-Proliferation Office 1989–2010; Chairman, IAEA Standing Advisory Group on Safeguards Implementation (SAGSI) 2001–06; and founding Chair of the Asia-Pacific Safeguards Network 2009–12.

Ola Dahlman has been engaged for some forty years in disarmament negotiations and chaired for fourteen years the Scientific Expert Group at the Conference on Disarmament in Geneva and for ten years the work at the Preparatory Commission for the CTBT Organization to guide and oversee the implementation of the CTBT verification system. He also co-chaired a study on bio-terrorism conducted by European and Russian experts in 2004–2006. Ola is a former Deputy Director General of the Swedish Defense Research Agency (FOA) and has a long research career at FOA, including directing the FOA laboratories for Information Technology and Weapon and Weapon Systems. He has also worked at the EU research center in ISPRA, Italy, on resilience of complex systems. Ola is currently director of OD Science Application a consulting company on global security.

Anya Erokhina is a Nunn-Lugar Fellow at the Office of the Deputy Assistant Secretary of Defense for Threat Reduction and Arms Control where she conducts program oversight of the Cooperative Threat Reduction nuclear portfolios. Before joining the Department of Defense in November 2011, she was a research associate at the James Martin Center for Nonproliferation Studies, and interned both at the United Nations Office for Disarmament Affairs and Lawrence Livermore National Laboratory.

Christopher A. Ford has served as Republican Chief Counsel to the US Senate Committee on Appropriations since 2013. From 2008–13, Dr Ford was a Senior Fellow at Hudson Institute in Washington, DC, and before that, US Special Representative for Nuclear Nonproliferation, Principal Deputy Assistant Secretary of State, Minority Counsel and then General Counsel to the US Senate Select Committee on Intelligence, and Staff Director of the Senate's Permanent Subcommittee on Investigations. In addition to dozens of articles on international security topics, he is the author of *The Mind of Empire: China's History and Modern Foreign Relations* (2010).

Gregory F. Giles is a Senior Director with Science Applications International Corporation (SAIC), where he advises US Government decision makers on issues pertaining to Iran, nonproliferation, and deterrence. Mr. Giles has lectured at the US Air Force and Army War Colleges, the NATO Defense College in Rome, and at Saudi Arabia's Command and Staff College in Riyadh.

Alexander Glaser is Assistant Professor at the Woodrow Wilson School of Public and International Affairs and in the Department of Mechanical and Aerospace Engineering at Princeton University. He is a participant in the University's Program on Science and Global Security and works with the International Panel on Fissile Materials, which publishes the annual Global Fissile Material Report.

Rafael Mariano Grossi has been Chairman of the Nuclear Suppliers Group since June 2014. He previously served as Ambassador Extraordinary and Plenipotentiary of the Argentine Republic to the Republic of Austria as well as a Permanent Representative to the International Organizations in Vienna. Prior to that, he was Assistant Director General or Policy and Chief of Cabinet at the International Atomic Energy Agency as well as Chief of Staff for the Organization for the Prohibition of Chemical Weapons.

Arvind Gupta began serving as the Director General for the Institute for Defence Studies and Analyses (IDSA) in 2012. His former positions include holding the Lal Bahadur Shastri Chair on National Security at the IDSA, serving as the Joint Secretary for the Indian National Security Council Secretariat, and working with the Kargil Review Committee. His previous publications include *India in a Changing Global Nuclear Order* (2009).

Roger Howsley became the first Executive Director for the World Institute for Nuclear Security in 2008. His previous positions include Director of Security, Safeguards and International Affairs for British Nuclear Fuels Ltd, Chairman of the United Kingdom's Atomic Energy Police Authority, and serving on the International Atomic Energy Agency Director General's Standing Advisory Group on Safeguards Implementation.

Feroz Hassan Khan has been a Lecturer in the Department of National Security Affairs at the Naval Postgraduate School, Monterey California since 2008. He is a former Brigadier in the Pakistan Army, where he last served as Director Arms Control and Disarmament Affairs, in the Strategic Plans Division, Joint Services Headquarters. Khan had represented Pakistan in several multilateral and bilateral arms control negotiations and has served on numerous assignments in the United States, Europe, and Asia. He has published extensively on security issues and is author of *Eating Grass: The Making of the Pakistani Bomb* (2012).

Susan J. Koch is an independent consultant, specializing in policy issues regarding arms reduction and the proliferation of weapons of mass destruction. She is also a Distinguished Research Fellow at the National Defense University Center for the Study of Weapons of Mass Destruction, and an associate faculty member in the Department of Defense and Strategic

Studies at Missouri State University. From 1982 until 2007, Dr Koch held a series of senior positions in the White House National Security Council Staff, the Office of the Secretary of Defense, the Department of State and the US Arms Control and Disarmament Agency, focused on nonproliferation and arms reduction policy. Dr Koch began her government career in the Directorate of Intelligence of the Central Intelligence Agency, analyzing West European political issues.

Yusuke Kuno is Deputy Director and Prime Scientist, Department of Science and Technology for Nuclear Material Management, at the Japan Atomic Energy Agency (JAEA). He is also appointed Professor, Nuclear Non-Proliferation Research Laboratory of the Department of Nuclear Engineering and Management, the Graduate School of the University of Tokyo. Previously, was Head of Safeguards Analytical Laboratory (SAL) of the IAEA in Seibersdorf Austria in 1999, and had led the IAEA laboratory staff members in nuclear verification measurement and environmental sampling program of Safeguards for seven years. From 1993–1999, he was General Manager of the Analytical Laboratory of the Tokai Reprocessing Plant.

Luca Lentini is a Trainee at the European External Action Service (EEAS), working within the Weapons of Mass Destruction, Conventional Weapons and Space division. In his previous position as Data Quality Specialist at IHS Jane's. Lentini has conducted research activities on nuclear non-proliferation at the Stockholm International Peace Research Institute (SIPRI) and the Centre for Science and Security Studies (CSSS) at King's College London, where he co-authored the 2014 edition of the *Nuclear Security Briefing Book*.

Robert S. Litwak serves at the Woodrow Wilson International Center for Scholars as Vice President for Scholars and Director of International Security Studies. He also holds positions as an advisor to the Los Alamos National Laboratory and as an Adjunct Professor at Georgetown University's School of Foreign Service. He also served on President Clinton's National Security Council staff as Director for Nonproliferation. His recent publications include *Outlier States: American Strategies to Contain, Engage, or Change Regimes* (2012).

Klaus Mayer is the Action Leader for Forensic Analysis and Combating Illicit Trafficking at the European Commission's Joint Research Centre - Institute for Transuranium Elements (JRC-ITU). His previous positions include heading the Safeguards Programme of ITU and serving as Co-Chairman of the International Technical Working Group on Nuclear Smuggling.

Zia Mian is the Director of the Project on Peace and Security in South Asia at Princeton University's Program on Science and Global Security. He also holds positions as Co-Editor of Science & Global Security journal and as a member of the International Panel on Fissile Materials. He has held positions at Yale University, Quaid-i-Azam University in Islamabad, the Union of Concerned Scientists, and the Sustainable Development Institute in Islamabad. His recent publications include *Bridging Partition: People's Initiative for Peace between India and Pakistan* (2010).

Michael Nacht has been the Thomas and Alison Schneider Chair in Public Policy for the Goldman School of Public Policy at University of California, Berkeley since 2010. He also currently serves as the Chair of the Policy Focus Area for the Nuclear Science and Security Consortium. His previous positions include serving as the Assistant Secretary of Defense for

Global Strategic Affairs, Assistant Director for Strategic and Eurasian Affairs of the US Arms Control and Disarmament Agency, and as the Aaron Wildavsky Dean of the Goldman School. His publications include *Missile Defense and Strategic Stability: An American Perspective* (forthcoming).

Kapil Patil is a Research Assistant at the Indian Pugwash Society.

Benoît Pelopidas has been a lecturer in International Relations at the University of Bristol (GIC) and CISAC affiliate, Stanford University since 2012. He has held teaching positions at the University of Geneva and the Monterey Institute of International Studies.

Steven Pifer is director of the Arms Control Initiative at the Brookings Institution. He researches and writes on nuclear arms control, Ukraine and Russia. A retired Foreign Service Officer, his more than twenty-five years with the State Department included assignments as deputy assistant secretary of state, ambassador to Ukraine, and special assistant to the president and senior director for Russia, Ukraine, and Eurasia on the National Security Council.

Joeseph F. Pilat is Project Manager, National Security Office at the Los Alamos National Laboratory and a Global Fellow at the Woodrow Wilson International Center for Scholars where he co-directs the Nonproliferation Forum. He has held positions in the Pentagon and the Congressional Research Service, and has taught at Cornell University, Georgetown University, and the College of William and Mary. He has written numerous articles and opinion pieces for US and European scholarly journals and newspapers, and is the author or editor of many books, including *Atoms for Peace: A Future after Fifty Years?* (2007).

Dianne E. Rennack has been a Specialist in Foreign Policy Legislation with the Congressional Research Service since 1985. She writes on the use of economic sanctions in furtherance of foreign policy and national security goals for Members of Congress and their staff. Rennack has also written extensively on US sanctions legislation related to nonproliferation, human rights, religious freedom, trafficking in persons, international narcotics, and terrorism. She also serves as editor of Legislation on Foreign Relations, an annual joint committee print prepared for the Committee on Foreign Relations of the Senate and Committee on Foreign Affairs of the House.

C. Paul Robinson (Ambassador) has served in a variety of technical leadership positions in US national laboratories, industry, and government. He served as Chief Negotiator and Head of the US Delegation to the Nuclear Testing Talks under Presidents Ronald Reagan and G.H.W. Bush, and as President of Sandia National Laboratories from 1995–2005. He has led and authored many studies for a wide variety of government agencies and academies and has been honored with awards, prizes, and medals, including the Outstanding Public Service Award from the US Joint Chiefs.

Laura Rockwood became a Resident Senior Research Fellow with the Project on Managing the Atom at the Belfer Center in 2014. Her previous positions include serving as the Principal Legal Officer and Section Head for Nonproliferation and Policymaking with the IAEA's Office of Legal Affairs. She has been honored with the Distinguished Service Award of the Institute of Nuclear Material Management. Also, she is the principal author of the document which became the Model Additional Protocol.

Nickolas Roth is a research associate for the Project on Managing the Atom at the Harvard Kennedy School's Belfer Center for Science and International Affairs. He has held positions as a policy analyst for the Union of Concerned Scientists, the program director for the Alliance for Nuclear Accountability, and as a research assistant for the Center for International and Security Studies' Nuclear Materials Accounting Project.

Michael Rühle heads the Energy Security Section in NATO's Emerging Security Challenges Division in Brussels. Previously he was Head, Speechwriter, and Senior Political Advisor in the NATO Secretary General's Policy Planning Unit. He has published widely on transatlantic security relations, including nuclear matters, nonproliferation and missile defense.

Mohamed I. Shaker (Ambassador) is the Vice-Chair of the Board of the Egyptian Council for Foreign Affairs. He also serves as Chair of the Board of the Regional Information Technology Institute. His previous positions include serving as Egypt's ambassador to the United Kingdom, ambassador to Austria, and on the board of the IAEA.

Tatsujiro Suzuki is Vice Director of the Research Center for Nuclear Weapons Abolition at Nagasaki University. His previous positions include serving as Vice-Chairman of the Japanese Atomic Energy Commission, a member of the Pugwash Conferences on Science and World Affairs in Japan, and Associate Vice-president of the Central Research Institute of Electric Power Industry.

Abdullah Toukan is Chief Executive Officer of the Strategic Analysis and Global Risk Assessment (SAGRA) Center in Jordan. He was the Science Advisor to the Late King Hussein I of Jordan from 1978–1999. He has also been the Deputy Director of the National Security Council at the Royal Palaces and Secretary General of the Higher Council for Science & Technology. He served in the Government of King Abdullah II as the Minister of Telecommunications in 2000. He has been the head of the Jordanian Middle East Peace Negotiations Delegation to the Multilateral Arms Control and Regional Security Working Group, and a member of the Jordanian Bilateral Middle East Peace Negotiations Delegation in the Jordanian-Israeli Peace Negotiations.

Michito Tsuruoka became a Senior Research Fellow at the National Institute for Defense Studies (NIDS), Ministry of Defense, Japan in 2014. He also served as a Special Adviser for NATO and the Japanese Embassy in Belgium, Brussels (2005–2008) and Visiting Fellow at the Royal United Services Institute (RUSI), London (2013–2014). Tsuruoka has published widely on NATO, nuclear policy, deterrence, and Europe-Japan/Asia relations.

Frank N. von Hippel is a Senior Research Physicist and Professor of Public and International Affairs at Princeton University. He also co-founded, and is currently Co-Chair of the non-governmental International Panel on Fissile Materials. His previous positions include serving as Assistant Director for National Security in the White House Office of Science and Technology Policy, chairman of the Federation of American Scientists (FAS) and the FAS Fund. Also, in 1975, he co-founded what is now Princeton's Program on Science and Global Security and, in 1989, the journal *Science & Global Security*.

Andrew C. Weber became the Assistant Secretary of Defense for Nuclear, Chemical, and Biological Defense Programs in 2009. His previous positions include serving as an Adviser for Threat Reduction Policy in the Office of the Secretary of Defense, as a Professor at Georgetown University's Edmund A. Walsh Graduate School of Foreign Service, and as a United States Foreign Service Officer.

Joel S. Wit is a Visiting Scholar with the US-Korea Institute at Johns Hopkins University's Paul H. Nitze School of Advanced International Studies. He is also a Senior Research Fellow with the Weatherhead Institute for East Asian Studies at Columbia University. His previous positions include serving as Senior Adviser to Ambassador Robert L. Galluci, Coordinator for the US-North Korea Agreed Framework, and as a Guest Scholar with the Brookings Institute.

Amy F. Woolf is a Specialist in Nuclear Weapons Policy at the Congressional Research Service at the Library of Congress. She provides Congress with information and analysis on issues related to US and Russian nuclear forces and arms control and has addressed such topics as nuclear-weapon strategy, doctrine and force structure, the US-Russian arms control agenda, and ballistic missile defense policy. Before joining CRS, Ms Woolf was a member of the Research Staff at the Institute for Defense Analyses (IDA) in Alexandria, Virginia. She also spent a year at the Department of Defense, working on the 1994 Nuclear Posture Review.

Lyudmila Zaitseva works in the Division of Physics and Biophysics at the University of Salzburg. Her research interests include human rights, the European Union, and international criminal law.

ACRONYMS

A2/AD	anti-access/area denial
ABACC	Brazilian-Argentine Agency for Accounting and Control of Nuclear Materials
ABM	anti-ballistic missile
ACDA	US Arms Control and Disarmament Agency
AEC	Atomic Energy Commission (India)
AECR	Arms Export Control Act
AEOI	Atomic Energy Organization of Iran
AFCONE	African Commission on Nuclear Energy
AICMS	Automated Inventory and Control Management System
Am	americium
ANC	African National Congress
AP	Additional Protocol
ASEAN	Association of Southeast Asian Nations
AVSEC PMC	Aviation Security Management program
BARC	Bhabha Atomic Research Centre (India)
BMD	ballistic missile defense
BMDR	Ballistic Missile Defense Review
BTWC	Biological and Toxin Weapons Convention
BWC	Biological Weapons Convention
C/S	Containment and Surveillance
C2	command and control
C5	the five states of Central Asia
CANDU	Canadian deuterium uranium (reactor)
CANWFZ	Central Asian Nuclear Weapon Free Zone
CBM	Confidence Building Measures
CBRN	chemical, biological, radiological, and nuclear
CCP	Critical Capabilities and Practices
CD	Conference on Disarmament
CFS	Comprehensive Fuel Service
CIRUS	Canada-India-Reactor-US (India)

CNC	Computer Numerically Controlled
CPGS	conventional prompt global strike
CPPNM	Convention on the Physical Protection of Nuclear Material
CSA	comprehensive safeguards agreement
CSBM	confidence and security building measure
CTBT	Comprehensive Test Ban Treaty
CTBTO	Comprehensive Nuclear Test-Ban Treaty Organization
CTR	Cooperative Threat Reduction
CWC	Chemical Weapons Convention
DA	Destructive Analysis
DAE	Department of Atomic Energy (India)
DBT	design basis threat
DCI	Defense Counterproliferation Initiative
DDPR	Deterrence and Defense Posture Review (NATO)
DE	detection resource efficiency
DIQ	Design Information Questionnaire
DIV	Design Information Verification
DNDO	Domestic Nuclear Detection Office
DNI	Director of National Intelligence (United States)
DOD	Department of Defense (United States)
DOE	Department of Energy (United States)
DP	detection probability
DPRK	Democratic People's Republic of Korea (North Korea)
DRC	Democratic Republic of Congo
DSTO	Database on Nuclear Smuggling, Theft, and Orphan Radiation Sources
DUPIC	Direct Use of spent PWR fuel in CANDU
EBW	exploding bridge wires
EC	Executive Council (of the CTBTO)
EDD	extended deterrence dialogue
EDPC	Extended Deterrence Policy Committee
EEZ	Exclusive Economic Zones
ELWR	Experimental Light Water Reactor
ENDC	Eighteen Nations Committee on Disarmament
ENR	uranium enrichment and reprocessing of spent fuel
ENTC	Esfahan Nuclear Technology Center
EU-3	European 3 (Germany, France, and the United Kingdom)
EURATOM	European Atomic Energy Community
EXBS	Export Control and Related Border Security program
FATF	Financial Action Task Force
FBR	fast breeder reactor
FCA	Fast Critical Assembly
FMCT	fissile material cutoff treaty
FMT	fissile material treaty
FOM	figure-of-merit
FR	fast reactor
FSB	Federal Security Service (Russia)
FSU	Former Soviet Union
GCC	Gulf Cooperation Council

GCP	gas centrifuge uranium enrichment plant
GDP	gaseous diffusion uranium enrichment plant
GIF	Generation IV International Forum
GICNT	Global Initiative to Combat Nuclear Terrorism
GIRM	Graphite Isotope-Ratio Method
GLCM	Ground Launched Cruise Missile
GNEP	Global Nuclear Energy Partnership
GP	G-8 Global Partnership Against the Spread of Weapons and Materials of Mass Destruction
GR	graphite reactor
GTRI	Global Threat Reduction Initiative
HCoC	Hague Code of Conduct against Ballistic Missile Proliferation
HEU	highly enriched uranium
HTGR	high-temperature gas-cooled reactor
HTR	high temperature reactor
HWR	heavy water reactor
IAEA	International Atomic Energy Agency
IAG	Implementation and Assessment Group
IBG	Integrated Battle Group
ICAO	International Civil Aviation Organization
ICBM	intercontinental ballistic missile
ICP	International Counterproliferation Program
ICSANT	International Convention for the Suppression of Acts of Nuclear Terrorism
IDC	International Data Center
IFNEC	International Framework for Nuclear Energy Cooperation
IFR	integral fast reactor
IIV	Interim Inventory Verification
IMS	International Monitoring System
INF	Intermediate-range Nuclear Forces Treaty
INFA	International Nuclear Fuel Agency
INFCA	International Nuclear Fuel Cycle Association
INFCE	International Nuclear Fuel Cycle Evaluation
INFCIRC	Information Circular (IAEA)
INPO	Institute for Nuclear Power Operations
INPRO	International Project on Innovative Nuclear Reactors and Fuel Cycles
IRBM	intermediate-range ballistic missiles
IRGC	Islamic Revolutionary Guards Corps
ISAB	International Security Advisory Board
ISI	Inter-Services Intelligence Agency (Pakistan)
ISR	intelligence, surveillance, and reconnaissance
ITDB	Incident and Trafficking Database
ITT	intangible transfers of technology
IUEC	International Uranium Enrichment Centre
JPOA	Joint Plan of Action
JVE	Joint Verification Experiment
KEDO	Korean Peninsula Energy Development Organization
KEPCO	Korea Electric Power Corporation

KPI	key performance indicator
LEP	life-extension program
LEU	low-enriched uranium
LIBS	laser induced breakdown spectrometry
LTBT	Limited Test Ban Treaty
LWR	light water reactor
MAD	mutual assured destruction
MENA	Middle East and North Africa
MENWFZ	Middle East Nuclear Weapon Free Zone
MESP	Multilateral Enrichment Sanctuary Project
MEWMDFZ	Middle East Weapons of Mass Destruction Free Zone
MIRV	multiple independently-targetable reentry vehicle
MNA	multilateral nuclear approach
MNEPR	Multilateral Nuclear Environmental Programme
MNSR	Miniature Neutron Source Reactor
MOD	Ministry of Defense (Russia)
MOX	mixed oxide
MPC&A	Material Protection, Control, and Accounting
MRBM	mid-range ballistic missiles
MT	material type
MTCR	Missile Technology Control Regime
NAM	Nonaligned Movement
NATO	North Atlantic Treaty Organization
NDA	Nondestructive Analysis
NDPG	National Defense Program Guidelines (Japan)
NES	nuclear energy system
NFU	no first use
NNSA	National Nuclear Security Administration
NNWS	nonnuclear-weapon state
Np	neptunium
NPIA	Nonproliferation Impact Assessment
NPR	Nuclear Posture Review (United States)
NPT	Treaty on the Nonproliferation of Nuclear Weapons
NRC	National Research Council (United States)
NSA	National Security Agency (United States)
NSA	negative security assurance
NSC	National Security Council
NSG	Nuclear Suppliers Group
NSOI	Nuclear Smuggling Outreach Initiative
NSSC	nuclear security support center
NSSP	Next Steps in Strategic Partnership (United States/India)
NTI	Nuclear Threat Initiative
NTM	national technical means
NTNFC	National Technical Nuclear Forensics Center
NTT	Nuclear Testing Talks
NWC	nuclear weapons convention
NWFZ	nuclear weapon free zone
NWS	nuclear-weapon state

OAS	Organization of American States
OAU	Organization of African Unity
OECD	Organisation for Economic Co-operation and Development
OEG	Operational Experts Group
OPANAL	Agency for the Prohibition of Nuclear Weapons in Latin America and the Caribbean
OPCW	Organization for the Prohibition of Chemical Weapons
OSCE	Organization for Security and Cooperation in Europe
OSI	on-site inspections
P5	Permanent Five Members of the UN Security Council (China, France, Great Britain, Russia, United States)
PC	proliferation cost
PFBR	Prototype Fast Breeder Reactor (India)
PGS	Prompt Global Strike
PHRC	Physics Research Center (Iran)
PIV	Physical Inventory Verification
PMD	possible military dimensions
PMDA	plutonium management and disposition agreement
PNE	peaceful nuclear explosion
PNET	Peaceful Nuclear Explosions Treaty
PR	proliferation resistance
PR&PP	Proliferation Resistance and Physical Protection
PRADA	Proliferation Resistance: Acquisition/Diversion Pathway Analysis
PRC	People's Republic of China
PROSA	Proliferation Resistance and Safeguardability Assessment Tools
PSA	positive security assurance
PSI	Proliferation Security Initiative
PT	proliferation time
PTBT	Partial Test Ban Treaty
Pu	plutonium
PUNE	peaceful uses of nuclear energy
RAPS	Rajasthan Atomic Power Station (India)
RDD	radiological dispersal device
RevCon	Review Conference
RMC	roles, missions, and capabilities
RNFSWG	Reliable Nuclear Fuel Supply Working Group
ROK	Republic of Korea (South Korea)
ROX	rock-like oxide
SALT	Strategic Arms Limitation Talks
SBD	safeguards-by-design
SCCC	Common System of Accounting and Control of Nuclear Materials
SEAD	suppress enemy air defenses
SF	spent fuel
SIMS	secondary ion mass spectroscopy
SIPRI	Stockholm International Peace Research Institute
SLBM	submarine launched ballistic missile
SLC	state-level concept
SLCM	submarine launched cruise missile

SLD	Second Line of Defense
SNEPP	Study of Nuclear Explosions for Peaceful Purposes (India)
SNT	sensitive nuclear technology
SORT	Strategic Offensive Reduction Treaty
SQ	significant quantity
SQP	Small Quantities Protocol
SRBM	short-range ballistic missile
SSAC	State System of Accounting and Control
SSBN	ballistic missile submarine
SSO	Special Security Organization
SSP	stockpile stewardship program
START	Strategic Arms Reduction Treaty
SUA	Convention for the Suppression of Unlawful Acts Against the Safety of Maritime Navigation
TD	technical difficulty
TNRC	Tehran Nuclear Research Center (Iran)
TNW	tactical nuclear weapon
TRISO	tri-structural-isotropic
TRR	Tehran Research Reactor (Iran)
TS	Technical Secretariat (of the CTBTO)
TTBT	Threshold Test Ban Treaty
UAE	United Arab Emirates
UAV	Unmanned Aerial Vehicle
UF6	uranium hexafluoride
UNDC	United Nations Disarmament Commission
UNGA	United Nations General Assembly
UNSC	United Nations Security Council
UNSCOM	United Nations Special Commission (on Iraq)
UNSCR	United Nations Security Council Resolution
UR	User Requirement
USML	US Munitions List
(V)HTR	(very) high temperature reactor
VOA	voluntary offer agreements
WA	Wassenaar Arrangement
WANO	World Association of Nuclear Operators
WINS	World Institute for Nuclear Security
WMD	weapons of mass destruction
WMDFZ	Weapons of Mass Destruction Free Zone
WNA	World Nuclear Association
ZOPFAN	Zone of Peace, Freedom and Neutrality

Introduction

NUCLEAR PROLIFERATION

A future unlike the past?

Joseph F. Pilat and Nathan E. Busch

What is the threat of nuclear proliferation and terrorism today?[1] How is it likely to evolve in the years ahead? Is the international nuclear nonproliferation regime that was created during the Cold War capable of confronting the threats of today and tomorrow? Is the regime, the centerpiece of which is the Treaty on the Nonproliferation of Nuclear Weapons (NPT), in crisis? If so, what is the nature and cause of the crisis? Will we witness an end to the NPT regime, whether through its total collapse or gradual decline? Are other futures possible?

Nuclear proliferation at a crossroads

In the early 1960s, President John F. Kennedy predicted that, in addition to the current nuclear-weapon states – there were four at the time – fifteen or twenty nations would have nuclear weapons by the end of the decade. While the Cold War brought about an extended arms race, some instances of nuclear brinkmanship, and a few near misses, it came to an end without the predicted dramatic spread of nuclear powers or the cataclysmic nuclear exchange that many predicted.

The collapse of the Soviet Union and the Warsaw Pact also led to speculations about the changing role of nuclear weapons. It was held by many that these weapons, which had dominated military and strategic thinking during the Cold War, would become a diminishing element of the backdrop, or background, of international relations, with their role limited exclusively to deterring nuclear weapon use.[2] The belief that they might be abolished altogether – in an end of nuclear history – grew at this time in some quarters.[3]

Indeed, as late as 1997 or early 1998, the worst fears about the breakup of the Soviet Union – the prospect of four nuclear-weapon states emerging from the ashes – were not realized. An unprecedented problem had been managed via unprecedented efforts to deal with "loose nukes," the "brain drain," and so on. The list of proliferation's "usual suspects" was decreasing – Argentina, Brazil and South Africa gave up nuclear programs or weapons. The NPT was extended indefinitely in 1995. Efforts to strengthen IAEA safeguards resulted in the Additional Protocol, which was designed to fix the compliance problems that Iraq's illicit program revealed, and North Korea's reaffirmed, in the early 1990s. Other positive trends at this time could be noted. Serious problems remained, including NPT holdout states and a few states pursuing nuclear arms despite their nonproliferation obligations, but to many these problems appeared manageable.

1

Predictions today look very different. In the context of rising regional instability and conflict, along with increased incidents of global terrorism, in a dynamic, uncertain security environment, emerging nuclear and other weapons of mass destruction (WMD) threats – both state proliferation and terrorism – are seen as growing dangers giving rise to increasing global insecurity.

Many observers believe today that additional states as well as nonstate actors will obtain a nuclear-weapon capability or nuclear weapons, and that these weapons are more likely be used than in the past. So-called rogue states are seen as irrational, and possibly as undeterrable. It is widely believed that the terrorists are certainly not deterrable: "if they have them, they'll use them."

One scenario – first discussed in the 1940s and 1950s – invokes the notion of nuclear anarchy or a "nuclear-armed crowd."[4] It would postulate, taking into account the developments of the last sixty years:

- a climate of pervasive insecurity;
- widespread proliferation and a fear of nuclear terrorism, with overwhelming suspicions and threats and the prospect of use;
- the development as a "hedge" of latent nuclear capabilities by all states that can do so, with many states moving to develop and deploy nuclear weapons;
- the reversal of more than two decades of dramatic nuclear arms reductions and the emergence of new arms races;
- growth in the significance of defenses, both active and passive;
- the collapse of the NPT, the International Atomic Energy Agency (IAEA), and other elements of the nonproliferation regime or, more likely, their increasing irrelevance;
- the disappearance of the normative value of the treaty and associated regime along with questions raised about the authority and legitimacy of ad hoc, self-help actions including preemption, prevention, etc.; and
- concern about the dangers of utilizing nuclear energy, except under extraordinary security, with decisions to forego this option at a time when ensuring energy security and alleviating global warming are high priorities for leaders, which results in grave economic, environmental, and other consequences.

The developments and trend lines from which this scenario is extrapolated are familiar, and certainly worrisome. Following the 1998 nuclear tests in South Asia and the terrorist attacks in September 2001, there has been growing concern about increasing proliferation dangers.

What is the basis for current proliferation concerns? Areas of concern include Iran's suspicious and extensive WMD programs, especially its nuclear and missile activities. The discovery of the large enrichment facility at Natanz as well as other clandestine activities revealed two decades of Iran's noncompliance with its international obligations. North Korea's nuclear tests and its diplomatic brinkmanship highlight the dangers of its longstanding nuclear and missile programs and missile exports. Beyond the Iranian and North Korean crises, which dominate the debate, South Asia became a primary area of concern following the Indian and Pakistani nuclear and missile tests in the late 1990s. The region highlights the specter of dangerous nuclear arms and missile races on the subcontinent along with the prospect of battlefield and strategic use on the one hand, and the horrific prospect of thefts and use by extremists on the other.

In addition to the proliferation concerns of the present, there is a second tier of states that, it appears, might consider nuclear or other weapons of mass destruction in the future, including Egypt, Saudi Arabia, Turkey, Japan, South Korea, and Taiwan. After the annexation of

Crimea by Russia, Ukrainian and other observers speculated over whether it would have occurred if Ukraine had not given up the Soviet nuclear weapons it inherited. This may spur efforts in the future by Ukraine.[5]

The growing reality of cooperation among rogue states is especially troubling. The nuclear and missile cooperation between North Korea, Pakistan, and Iran has been examined in the open literature.[6] The question is whether that cooperation was limited to these or a few other states, or foreshadows an increasingly deadly future. Clearly, there are a growing number of states that now possess or are developing nuclear- and missile-related technological capabilities and expertise. Will these capabilities be shared, and under what, if any, constraints? Will they wind up in black markets? In either case, they will erode export control efforts like the Nuclear Suppliers Group (NSG).

To these country concerns may be added the following challenges:

- technology diffusion via globalization and the Internet;
- the security of nuclear and missile technology, materials, and expertise in Russia and the other Soviet successor states, as well as in such states as Pakistan, South Africa, Argentina, and Brazil, which could lead to loose nukes, materials leakage, and brain drain;
- the rise of nonstate actors like the A.Q. Khan network; and
- concerns about Chinese and Russian nonproliferation commitments and behavior.

The prospects of nuclear and radiological terrorism are seen to be rising – concern over a proliferation/terrorism nexus after 9/11 has never been higher. Speaking at The Citadel three months after the tragic events of September 11th, then President George W. Bush stated that, "almost every state that actively sponsors terror is known to be seeking weapons of mass destruction and the missiles to deliver them at longer and longer ranges ... we must keep the world's most dangerous technologies out of the hands of the world's most dangerous people."[7]

These problems are serious. However, the worst-case scenario outlined above is not the only – and not the most likely – outcome. New developments, actions, and measures are not fully factored into this assessment, including, among others, the impacts of:

- successful threat reduction and rollback cases over last fifteen years, including Libyan disarmament;
- Cooperative Threat Reduction (CTR) programs, the Proliferation Security Initiative (PSI), the Global Threat Reduction Initiative (GTRI) and other new initiatives, as well as proposed nonproliferation regime strengthening measures;
- growing concerns about the nuclear proliferation threat in the international community, including the growing realization that this is an issue of international peace and security and not merely a parochial US interest; and
- potential leverage in combating proliferation and terrorism that may come with new monitoring and verification as well as other technologies.

The worst-case scenario also fails to fully take into account other factors. Unanticipated developments, or surprises, that could change this picture for better or worse, include:

- geopolitical changes, both positive and negative;
- technological changes, particularly new ways to produce nuclear-weapon-useable materials; and

- proliferation or terrorism events, such as withdrawals from the NPT, further nuclear tests, sales of nuclear weapons or materials, interdictions and nuclear use by states or terrorists.

These and other factors highlight the complexity of the emerging security environment. While there may be differences over the level of danger we are confronting, under any realistic scenario we are living in a dangerous world. Faced with the prospect of nuclear proliferation and terrorism threats, what is to be done?

From a US perspective, proliferation has been seen from the beginning as a global problem. Responses to the threat in the nuclear realm have been primarily global in nature, including the Baruch plan (based upon the seminal Acheson-Lilienthal report),[8] which failed in the maelstrom of the emerging Cold War; and the Atoms-for-Peace initiative, a modest proposal that traded access to civil nuclear technology for restraints on military applications. In the nonproliferation realm, Atoms for Peace laid the framework for the IAEA and the NPT – the cornerstones of the international nuclear nonproliferation regime. The IAEA was created in 1958, and reflected in its Statute the twin Atoms-for-Peace objectives of the prevention of proliferation and the promotion of the peaceful uses of atomic energy. The NPT was concluded in 1968 and entered into force in 1970.[9] We have seen significant problems with both the NPT and the IAEA in the last two decades.

Revelations about Iraq's nuclear-weapon program after the 1991 Gulf War threatened the IAEA and its mandate to administer international inspections of peaceful nuclear activities to help ensure that diversions to military programs were not occurring. These revelations about Iraq's nuclear-weapon program resulted in intense criticism of the entire international nuclear nonproliferation regime, including the IAEA's safeguards system. To a large extent the Iraqi program was based on clandestine, undeclared nuclear facilities that were not covered and could not have been detected under the safeguards system that had developed during the Cold War.

In the last two decades, the IAEA has been transforming its safeguards system to address, in part, the limits of its verification mandate and the burden of noncompliance issues. In this context, the IAEA is adopting a fundamentally new approach to implementing safeguards based on the strengthening measures developed in the 1990s and the lessons learned from Iraq, North Korea, Libya, and Iran. Central to the transformation is the Additional Protocol (AP), which is an important new tool and needs to be universally accepted as the basis for safeguards and a condition for exports.

In addition to the NPT and IAEA, states have constructed a substantial political and legal framework to supplement nonproliferation efforts. These include various export control mechanisms; bilateral arms control and disarmament treaties such as the Strategic Arms Reduction Treaty (START) and follow-on treaties; treaties that establish regional nuclear-free zones; and multilateral treaties such as the Comprehensive Test Ban Treaty (CTBT), which has not yet entered into force, and a fissile material cutoff treaty (FMCT), for which negotiations have yet to begin. There have also been ongoing efforts to address these issues through ad hoc, extra-regime actions – ranging from the US-Russia Cooperative Threat Reduction program to rollback efforts in Iraq and Libya, interdiction efforts such as the PSI, and the Global Initiative to Combat Nuclear Terrorism (GINCT).[10] In the same vein, there has been renewed interest in a number of old ideas on how to address proliferation, including proliferation resistance and multinational approaches such as fuel banks and front- and back-end fuel cycle services.

Despite the potential benefits of these and other initiatives, significant challenges remain – not only with IAEA's safeguards system, but with the entire nonproliferation regime as a whole. The strengthened safeguards measures of the IAEA suffer from a lack of universal adoption and an incomplete implementation of IAEA's new and previously existing authorities. Moreover, even in instances where the IAEA has identified violations, nonproliferation efforts have been hamstrung by a lack of enforcement – owing primarily to disagreements in the IAEA Board of Governors and the United Nations Security Council (UNSC).

These problems will remain severe, complicated by geopolitics, the dynamics of an uncertain security environment, and the link between nuclear energy and weapons – all occurring at a time when, after the Fukushima Daiichi accident, nuclear energy is expected to grow globally (if not the nuclear renaissance some anticipated before the accident).

The future of the decades-long effort to prevent the further spread of weapons of mass destruction is therefore at a crossroads today. If international nonproliferation efforts are to be successful, an integrated, multi-tiered response will almost certainly be necessary. But a serious, thorough, and clear-eyed examination of the range of threats, challenges, and opportunities facing the international community is a necessary first step. That is what this *Handbook of Nuclear Proliferation* is intended to produce.

Outline of this book

This volume is divided into three major parts. Part I presents detailed threat assessments of proliferation risks across the globe, including specific regions and countries. Part II explains the various tools developed by the international community to address these proliferation threats – including the NPT, IAEA safeguards, and various international treaties and arrangements, as well as the military and political mechanisms for addressing existing nuclear programs, such as deterrence, counterproliferation, and arms control. Part III addresses the proliferation risks and political/technological challenges arising from nuclear energy production, including potential proliferation by aspiring states and nonstate groups. It examines the problems of nuclear security and terrorism, including risks of nuclear terrorism, potential loss of controls over nuclear weapons and materials, and the programs designed to improve nuclear security across the globe.

Part I. Identifying the threats

In the first section of the book, Michael Nacht, Adbullah Toukan, Gregory F. Giles, Michito Tsuruoka, Sun Young Ahn and Joel S. Wit, Feroz Hassan Khan, and Arvind Gupta and Kapil Patil provide detailed examinations of the nuclear proliferation risks across the globe; in specific regions (such as the Middle East or South Asia); and in specific "difficult cases" such as Iran and North Korea.

Michael Nacht begins this section by providing a general threat assessment of worldwide proliferation risks, especially in light of US President Barack Obama's 2009 goal of a worldwide move to renounce nuclear weapons. He argues that although the President's agenda has accomplished some positive outcomes, including in the US Nuclear Posture Review (NPR), overall it has received a cool reception by the other nuclear powers and had been challenged by ongoing nuclear activities in Iran, North Korea, and elsewhere.

Toukan and Giles focus on emerging risks in the Middle East. Toukan provides a regional assessment of the proliferation risks in the Middle East and North Africa, including the regional disruptions created by the prospect of a nuclear-armed Iran. He also examines potential steps that may be taken to address Iran's ongoing nuclear activities by the United States and the Gulf Cooperation Council States. Giles examines directly the status of the crisis over Iran's nuclear program. He discusses the history of this controversy beginning in 2002, the widely divergent claims made by Western states and by Iran about whether this program is peaceful, the threat that Iran's activities pose to the nonproliferation regime established by the NPT and IAEA safeguards, and what steps may be necessary to achieving a satisfactory resolution to the Iranian nuclear crisis.

Tsuruoka, and Ahn and Wit examine the ongoing proliferation concerns in East Asia, especially relating to China's military buildup and North Korea's growing nuclear arsenal. Tsuruoka provides an analysis of China's growing military presence and its impact on Japan and others states in the region. He addresses the prospects for extended deterrence; questions about a changing US nuclear posture; and whether Japan views the United States as a reliable ally, despite US claims about a "pivot" to Asia in US foreign policy. Ahn and Wit examine the status of the crisis over North Korea's ongoing nuclear-weapon program. They discuss the failure of the 1994 Agreed Framework and the beginning of the current crisis in 2002, the current state of North Korea's program, the progress and failures of the multilateral talks, and what options the United States and the international community have to help stop or slow North Korea's efforts to acquire nuclear weapons.

In the final two chapters of Part I, Khan, and Gupta and Patil provide Pakistani and Indian perspectives on the nuclear-weapon programs in South Asia. They address the respective motivations for these arsenals, the US and international responses to these nuclear programs, and such issues as the US-Indian nuclear agreement and its effects on the export control regime established by the Nuclear Suppliers Group and the implications of the A.Q. Khan nuclear smuggling network.

Part II: Nonproliferation, counterproliferation, and disarmament

Central to this volume, Part II is divided into three sections. In the first part, *The Nonproliferation Regime*, Christopher A. Ford, Joseph F. Pilat, Laura Rockwood, Sibylle Bauer, Ola Dahlman, Paul Robinson, and Zia Mian and Frank N. von Hippel examine the various nonproliferation mechanisms that have been developed by the international community to deter nuclear proliferation – or to detect it when it does occur – including the ongoing opportunities and challenges associated with the NPT, the verification authorities of the IAEA, and potential new mechanisms such as the CTBT and an FMCT.

Ford and Pilat examine the often-controversial role that the NPT has played in international nonproliferation efforts since its entrance into force in 1970. Although the NPT has served as a cornerstone for nuclear nonproliferation efforts, it has increasingly been subject to an array of criticisms, including the provisions of Article VI, which commit nuclear-weapon states to "good faith negotiations" with the goal of nuclear disarmament. Growing frustration among some member states (including states in the Nonaligned Movement) over perceived entrenched inequalities and obstacles to civilian nuclear technologies that are reinforced by the NPT, also threaten to undermine the treaty's effectiveness. Ford presents an overview of the history, goals, and primary challenges facing the NPT in the future. Joseph F. Pilat examines the debates and controversies associated with the NPT, especially relating to Articles IV and VI, and the decisive issues that will be relevant to the 2015 NPT Review Conference.

Rockwood examines the history and evolution of the IAEA and the international safeguards. For the last two decades, the IAEA has been transforming its safeguards system to address a new set of challenges to international safeguards – including the pre-Gulf War Iraqi nuclear program, the discoveries of additional NPT member-states developing clandestine programs, and the associated revelation of an extensive nonstate nuclear procurement network. This transformation includes efforts to implement the AP and more effectively integrate new and old safeguards measures. But the transformation remains a work in progress. She addresses the challenges to IAEA safeguards and discusses technological and institutional changes needed to meet those challenges. In similar fashion, Bauer examines the framework of agreements and treaties that make up the multilateral nonproliferation export control regime. She examines the strengths and shortcomings of current export control agreements and recommends steps that could be taken to strengthen the regime system.

In the remaining chapters in this section, Dahlman, Robinson, and Mian and von Hippel explore the prospects and challenges of negotiating, implementing, and verifying the Comprehensive Test Ban Treaty and a fissile material cutoff treaty. Dahlman and Robinson provide very different perspectives on the CTBT. The United States was the first country to sign the CTBT, but the US Senate subsequently failed to ratify the treaty in 1999. Although 157 countries have now ratified the CTBT (and an additional twenty-five have signed it), without the participation of the United States and eight other countries required for the treaty to become binding, the future of the CTBT remains in doubt. Moreover, there are debates over testing at low yields and whether undetectable tests could be particularly significant. Dahlman identifies and discusses some of the key issues that are likely to be addressed if and when the treaty is being considered again, including whether nuclear-weapon states (NWS) can maintain confidence in their nuclear-weapon systems without nuclear testing, whether the monitoring and verifying mechanisms envisioned in the treaty will be sufficient for detecting nuclear tests, and the potential nonproliferation advantages that would be provided by implementation of this treaty. Robinson, on the other hand, raises questions about the adequacy of the CTBT as envisioned. In particular, he discusses potential challenges for monitoring and verification, especially related to low-yield testing, and potential efforts by states to conceal nuclear tests by "decoupling" test devices from surrounding soil, and other efforts to disguise the tests. He suggests that it might be necessary to amend or even renegotiate the CTBT to address these and other issues.

Mian and von Hippel assess the prospects for successful negotiation of a fissile material cutoff treaty and their proposed fissile material treaty (FMT). Because the production of fissile materials remains the greatest challenge in nuclear weapon production, and because states such as Iran are suspected of taking advantage of a "loophole" in Article IV of the NPT to enrich uranium (which would have both civilian and military uses), an FMCT or FMT could therefore help the international community achieve nonproliferation and disarmament objectives – both by closing off an avenue for potential new proliferators, but also by effectively placing a cap on the size of the arsenals of countries such as India and Pakistan. Nevertheless, they argue, there remain significant obstacles to successful negotiation, owing in part to countries that may want to retain the capability for nuclear weapon production and other divisive issues. They examine the potential usefulness of an FMCT or an FMT, as well as the remaining challenges that may hinder or prevent the successful negotiation and entry into force of a treaty.

In the second section of Part II, *Deterrence, Counterproliferation, and the Use of Force*, Michael Rühle, Robert S. Litwack, Wyn Q. Bowen and Luca Lentini, Klaus Mayer and Alexander Glaser, Susan Koch, and Dianne E. Rennack address the steps that the international community could take to address ongoing proliferation activities throughout the world, including deterrence and the use of force, security assurances, nuclear forensics, interdiction and law enforcement, and sanctions.

In Chapters 16 and 17, Rühle and Litwak examine the role that force and the threat of force plays in US and international nonproliferation and counterproliferation policies. They examine the ongoing role of deterrence in US military planning; preventive and preemptive strike policies as iterated in official documents such as the 2002, 2006, and 2010 US National Security Strategies; the effectiveness of past interventions (such as the 2003 Iraq War); the use of cyber warfare to target nuclear facilities; and what place the use of force might hold in future US and international policies, including the case of Iran.

Bowen and Lentini examine the role of security assurances, or promises either to respect or ensure the security of other nations, as a method for enhancing deterrence or preventing the proliferation of nuclear weapons. In some instances, countries with nuclear weapons have been encouraged to offer "negative assurances," whereby they promise not to target nonnuclear-weapon states with nuclear weapons. In other instances, such as the extended nuclear umbrella offered by the United States during the Cold War, states have committed to defend certain nonnuclear-weapon states (up to and including with nuclear weapons) to deter attacks on those states. This chapter examines the advantages and disadvantages of security assurances for enhancing deterrence and preventing nuclear proliferation.

Mayer and Glaser examine the origins, types, and state-of-the-art of nuclear forensics in nonproliferation efforts. In the event of a discovery or use of a nuclear weapon or fissile materials, various states and international organizations are developing "nuclear forensics" capabilities, which could help identify the state of origin of the materials used in the weapon. These techniques have received increasing attention post-9/11, as the threat of nuclear terrorism has been taken more seriously. Mayer and Glaser explore the potential roles of nuclear forensics in supporting nuclear security; and what nuclear forensics can realistically achieve. They also chart a path forward, pointing at potential applications of nuclear forensic methodologies in other areas.

Koch examines international efforts to interdict suspect shipments of WMD-related materials, including the PSI and other related programs. She addresses what successes these programs have had, what legal and practical challenges they have and may yet encounter, and the role that interdiction will play in international nonproliferation and counterproliferation strategies in the future.

Rennack examines the use, effectiveness, and challenges of utilizing sanctions to discourage states from developing nuclear weapons. Often described as a "poor man's foreign policy," sanctions are widely and increasingly used to compel or discourage certain actions by states. Although they can be an important tool to discourage states from developing nuclear weapons, sanctions are often hamstrung by a host of factors, including a lack of consistent or uniform application or opposition by certain states, especially by the Permanent 5 (P5) of the United Nations Security Council. Rennack defines sanctions, examines how they work, and identifies the conditions in which they may be most effective.

In third section of Part II, *Arms Reduction and Disarmament*, Steven Pifer, Susan Burk, Rafael Mariano Grossi, Mohamed I. Shaker, Benoît Pelopidas, and Amy F. Woolf examine the role of arms reduction and disarmament in helping achieve nonproliferation objectives, the potential role of nuclear weapon-free zones (NWFZs), the prospects of rollback and restraint, and the mechanisms to verify disarmament.

In Chapter 22, Pifer examines the history and evolution of US-Soviet/Russian arms control and arms reduction treaties, including the Strategic Arms Limitation Talks (SALT) in the 1970s, the Intermediate-Nuclear Forces (INF) Treaty and Strategic Arms Reduction Treaty in the 1980s and 1990s, the 2002 Strategic Offensive Reduction Treaty (SORT) (or Moscow Treaty), and the 2010 New START. He also discusses potential further steps that the United States and Russia could explore, including further reductions of strategic weapons and a treaty to reduce nonstrategic nuclear weapons, as well as ongoing issues that may affect further nuclear reductions, such as ballistic missile defense, US conventional weapons capabilities, and the prospect of multilateral arms reductions.

In Chapters 23–25, Burk, Grossi, and Shaker assess the potential successes and verification challenges associated with NWFZs – specified regions in which countries commit themselves not to manufacture, acquire, test, or possess nuclear weapons. Burk provides a general overview of the history of NWFZs and identifies the potential advantages that NWFZs can play in nonproliferation, including avoiding internal tensions that have beleaguered the NPT, and examines the prospects of expanding NWFZs into other regions. Grossi discusses in detail the successes of the Treaty of Tlatelolco in establishing the first NWFZ in Latin America and the Caribbean, and assesses the prospects of applying the lessons of this treaty in expanding NWFZs in other regions. Shaker provides a sober analysis of the potential challenges of establishing a NWFZ in the Middle East.

Pelopidas critically examines "rollback" and "restraint" in the context of the nuclear proliferation debate, and proposes the "analytically and politically relevant" concept of "renunciation." He reviews the evidence and interpretations of the cases of Belarus, Ukraine, Kazakhstan, South Africa, Switzerland, and Sweden using the prism of the debates surrounding the Libyan case.

Woolf examines technologies for "monitoring and verification" that are used to verify a state's compliance with its nonproliferation obligations. She begins by describing the verification process, which includes collection of information about activities and facilities. She then analyzes several cases of monitoring and verification, including US-Soviet/Russian arms control, IAEA safeguards, and the experience of the IAEA and the United Nations Special Commission on Iraq (UNSCOM) to verify Iraqi disarmament. She concludes by arguing that technology will remain an essential part of monitoring and verification, though verification is essentially a political process that also relies on human judgment.

Part III. Nuclear energy and security

Part III is divided into two sections: *Nuclear Energy and Proliferation Risks*, which addresses the potential use for civilian nuclear programs to be used to support (and conceal) covert nuclear programs; and *Nuclear Security and Terrorism*, which examines the potential links between nuclear programs (both civilian and military) and nuclear terrorism, either as a potential target for nuclear attacks or as a source for materials that could be used in nuclear terrorist attacks.

Ever since the 1946 Acheson-Lilienthal report, it was recognized that military and civilian uses of nuclear power involve the same technologies and activities.[11] This recognition has been central to the development of US and global nonproliferation policies and approaches since that time, from the Baruch plan, to Atoms for Peace, to the IAEA and the NPT, to the current efforts to pursue multinational approaches to nuclear nonproliferation. In the first section of Part III, Jacques Bouchard, Tatsujiro Suzuki, Yusuke Kuno, and John Carlson examine the relationship between civilian and military nuclear programs in the context of future nuclear proliferation threats, and address the technologies and procedures that can simultaneously encourage the worldwide use of nuclear energy while minimizing proliferation risk.

Bouchard and Suzuki examine the inherently dual-use nature of nuclear energy and the subsequent proliferation risks arising from nuclear programs. Although the NPT guarantees member states the right to develop civilian nuclear programs, it remains the case that civilian nuclear programs pose some level of risk due to the dual nature of the atom. They argue that these programs can be used to develop latent nuclear weapons programs, create breakout capabilities, or provide cover for covert programs. They examine the likely increase of nuclear power as future worldwide nuclear energy demand rises, even after the 2011 Fukushima disaster, and the potential link between nuclear power and weapon programs. They also discuss possible ways to prevent civilian programs from supporting weapon programs – including a potential ban on enrichment and reprocessing, and multinational ownership of enrichment facilities.

There has been a dream since the dawn of the atomic age that there can be technical fixes to reduce the proliferation dangers inherent in civil nuclear technology. This prospect has continued to be of interest today. In Chapter 30, Kuno explains and assesses the array of new technologies (including the concept of safeguards by design) and new multinational approaches (including multinational and multilateral ownership of nuclear reactors, enrichment facilities, and other proliferation-sensitive facilities and technologies) as potential methods for preventing nuclear proliferation.

In Chapter 31, Carlson addresses multinational approaches to the nuclear fuel cycle. He begins by outlining the proliferation risks arising from civilian nuclear programs. He then assesses the range of proposals for multinational approaches to address these proliferation risks, including the 2005 IAEA study of the topic and other proposals to reduce or eliminate the need for independent state production. These options include assuring supplies of nuclear fuel, establishing nuclear fuel banks, and providing for multinational control over enrichment and reprocessing facilities.

In the second section of Part III, *Nuclear Security and Terrorism*, Matthew Bunn and Nickolas Roth, Roger Howsley, Lyudmila Zaitseva, and Andrew Weber and Anya Erokhina explore the connections between nuclear energy and nuclear terrorism. In the wake of the September 11, 2001 terrorist attacks, many analysts warned of the dangers of nuclear terrorism – including the possibilities of terrorists acquiring or building nuclear weapons, sabotaging nuclear reactors, or using nuclear materials in radiological dispersion devices. Although these risks may be less severe than often predicted in press reports, the risks of nuclear terrorism should be taken seriously. This section examines the changing perceptions of the threat of nuclear terrorism post-9/11; potential ways that terrorists (or their state sponsors) could acquire nuclear weapons or fissile materials; and some of the technical and diplomatic measures that can help address these threats, including such programs as the US-Russia Cooperative Threat Reduction and the use of nuclear summits.

Bunn and Roth provide an overview of the evolving perceptions of the threat of nuclear terrorism, especially in the aftermath of the September 11, 2001 terrorist attacks on the United States. They explore the motivations, strategies, and capabilities of certain terrorist groups that may lead them in this direction; what the different types of nuclear terrorism are (i.e., sabotage of nuclear facilities, what the risks are of use or threat of use of a stolen or assembled weapon, radiological attacks, etc.); and how terrorists might acquire nuclear weapons or materials.

Howsley discusses steps that the nuclear industry has taken to improve nuclear security and minimize risks of accidents or sabotage at civilian facilities. Although the nuclear industry initially devoted more attention to safety and operations, rather than security, this perspective changed significantly after the terrorist attacks of September 11, 2001. Following the attacks, the industry began exploring ways to collaborate and share best practices. Nevertheless, Howsley argues, the industry continued to encounter significant challenges in improving the discussion of security and sharing best practices. More recently, however, the industry has made rapid progress in these areas, including improved regulation, sharing of best practices, and the establishment of professional development and certification, including those sponsored by the World Institute for Nuclear Security.

Zaitseva analyzes nuclear material trafficking patterns observed since the collapse of the Soviet Union. The instabilities caused by the Soviet collapse created severe concerns that Russia's nuclear weapons, fissile materials, and related nuclear technologies and expertise could fall into the hands of proliferating states or terrorists. Ziatseva assesses the extent to which those fears materialized, discussing the global trends in illicit trafficking of all types of radioactive material, and concentrating on the incidents involving fissile nuclear material to assess their dynamics over the two decades. She then describes the impact of the international cooperative efforts to prevent and deter thefts and combat illicit trafficking, and concludes by addressing future challenges of illicit trafficking and steps that could be taken to address these challenges.

In the final chapter of this volume, Weber and Erokhina examine the collaborative programs between the United States and Russia that were designed to assist Russia in improving its nuclear controls, eliminating weapons systems, improving training of nuclear scientists, etc. They pay particular attention to the CTR and Material Protection, Control, and Accounting (MPC&A) Programs. After examining the successes and ongoing challenges of these programs, they assess the extent to which the lessons of cooperative threat reduction could be applied to other cases around the world.

Notes

1. These remarks are the authors' own and not those of the Los Alamos National Laboratory, the National Nuclear Security Administration, the Department of Energy, or any other US government agency.
2. Carl Kaysen, Robert S. McNamara and George W. Rathjens, "Nuclear Weapons After the Cold War," *Foreign Affairs*, Vol. 70, No. 4 (Fall 1991), pp. 95–110; McGeorge Bundy, William J. Crowe, Jr, and Sidney D. Drell, "Reducing Nuclear Danger," *Foreign Affairs*, Vol. 72, No. 2 (Spring 1993), pp. 141–155.
3. See, for example, the essays by Michael McGwire and Lee Butler in John Baylis and Robert O'Neill, (eds) *Alternative Nuclear Futures: The Role of Nuclear Weapons in the Post-Cold War World* (Oxford and New York: Oxford University Press, 2000).
4. Albert Wohlstetter, *Moving Toward Life in a Nuclear Armed Crowd?* Report to the U.S. Arms Control and Disarmament Agency (Los Angeles, CA: Pan Heuristics, 1976).
5. Paula Dobrianski and David Rivkin Jr, "Ukraine Must Wish it had Kept its Nukes," *USA Today*, March 6, 2004; Eric Posner, "Should Ukraine have Kept its Nuclear Weapons?" ericposner.com, March 25, 2014, ericposner.com/should-ukraine-have-kept-its-nuclear-weapons; Greg Myre, "What if Ukraine Still Had Nuclear Weapons?" *National Public Radio*, March 10, 2014, www.npr.org/blog/parallels/2014/03/10/288572756/what-if-ukraine-still-had-nuclear-weapons. For an earlier argument on this topic, see John Mearsheimer, "The Case for a Ukranian Nuclear Deterrent," *Foreign Affairs*, Vol. 72, No. 3 (Summer 1993), pp. 50–66, http://johnmearsheimer.uchicago.edu/pdfs/A0020.pdf.
6. For a fuller discussion of second-tier suppliers, see Chaim Braun and Christopher F. Chyba, "Proliferation Rings: New Challenges to the Nuclear Nonproliferation Regime," *International Security*, Vol. 29, No. 2 (Fall 2004), pp. 5–49.
7. George W. Bush, "President Speaks on War Effort to Citadel Cadets," The Citadel, Charleston, South Carolina, December 11, 2001, http://georgewbush-whitehouse.archives.gov/news/releases/2001/12/20011211-6.html.
8. *A Report on the International Control of Atomic Energy, Prepared for the Secretary of State's Committee on Atomic Energy* (Washington, DC: US Government Printing Office, March 16, 1946), http://universityhonors.umd.edu/HONR269J/archive/AchesonLilienthal.htm..
9. For a discussion of the legacy of Atoms for Peace, including the IAEA and the NPT, see Joseph F. Pilat, (ed.) *Atoms for Peace: A Future after Fifty Years?* (Baltimore, MD: Johns Hopkins University Press/Woodrow Wilson Center Press, 2007).
10. See, for example, US Department of State, "Office of Cooperative Threat Reduction (ISN/CTR)," US Department of State Website, N.D., www.state.gov/t/isn/58381.htm; US Department of State, "Proliferation Security Initiative 10th Anniversary High Level Political Meeting: Chairman's Summary." US Department of State website, May 28, 2013, www.state.gov/t/isn/c10390.htm; US Department of State, "The Global Initiative to Combat Nuclear Terrorism," US Department of State website, www.state.gov/t/isn/c18406.htm.
11. See *A Report on the International Control of Atomic Energy*.

PART I

Identifying the Threats

1

THE GLOBAL NUCLEAR ENVIRONMENT

President Obama's vision amid emerging nuclear threats

Michael Nacht

Concern about the proliferation and next use of nuclear weapons has been a central issue for the United States and other governments since the dawn of the nuclear age. After the United States detonated nuclear devices at Hiroshima and Nagasaki in August 1945 that led to Japan's surrender and the end of the Second World War, attention focused quickly on when the Soviet Union would acquire its own devices. When the Soviets detonated their first device in 1949, it was still a shock to Washington where most informed observers thought it would take another 5–10 years. The US leadership, of course, was unaware at that time of the extent of Soviet penetration of the Manhattan Project, espionage that permitted Soviet scientists to pursue effective paths to bomb design while avoiding dead ends. The British detonation in 1952 followed by the French in 1960 then led the famed British scientist and novelist C.P. Snow to predict that there would be a dozen countries capable of building atomic bombs within six years. Further, he asserted that if they did it was a "mathematical certainty" that, within ten years, some of these weapons would be exploded through "accident, folly, or madness."[1] While perhaps highly plausible at the time, these prognostications have proven incorrect and demonstrate the inherent difficulty in foreseeing accurately future trends in nuclear threats. This chapter focuses on the most apparent nuclear threats among states and nonstate actors and also considers the impact of new technologies and cooperation among current and potential proliferators.

A global nuclear threat assessment can begin with a review of the initiatives of the Obama administration to address these issues since 2009. President Obama inherited a nuclear threat "map" that included four declared nuclear-weapon states since Snow's prediction: China (1964), India (1998), Pakistan (1998), and North Korea (2006) where the dates indicate when each state detonated its first nuclear device and declared itself a nuclear weapon state.[2] This brings the official "nuclear club" to eight. But this number is inaccurate since Israel is widely believed to have developed and deployed a nuclear arsenal of perhaps one hundred or more nuclear weapons, dating back to the 1960s, although it has never detonated a device nor declared itself a nuclear weapon state.[3] Thus there were nine nuclear weapon states when President Obama took office in 2009.

Before Obama took office, in 2007 and again in 2008, four distinguished former US national security officials – former Secretaries of State Henry Kissinger and George Shultz, former Secretary of Defense William Perry, and former Chairman of the Senate Armed

Services Committee Sam Nunn – co-authored two widely noted opinion pieces in the *Wall Street Journal* endorsing the goal of a world free of nuclear weapons and offering several steps toward its realization.[4] These statements, at least in the eyes of many, legitimized the goal of a nuclear-weapon-free world for the first time in the nuclear age.

As a presidential candidate, Senator Obama endorsed the idea in a sweeping summary of his proposed approach to American foreign policy.[5] Once elected president, Obama delivered a major address in Prague in April 2009 laying out his vision once again, now with the force as the chief executive of the United States.[6]

The President has since followed up with two major addresses on nuclear-weapon policy. In April 2010, he spoke again in Prague, this time on the New Strategic Arms Reduction Treaty (START), and announced the issuance of the Nuclear Posture Review (NPR), which modified official US nuclear-weapon policy in conformity with his vision. Subsequently, in a speech in Berlin in June 2013, he specifically called for a one-third reduction in US- and Russian-deployed strategic nuclear weapons.[7]

Common features of these speeches include the President's acknowledgement that the transition to a nuclear-free world would be a long, arduous process perhaps not achieved in his lifetime, and that as long as nuclear weapons existed in the world, the United States was committed to maintaining a "safe, secure and effective deterrent." In short, unilateral nuclear disarmament was not likely to be part of the process. The NPR codified these positions and went on further to specify that the principal threats to US national security were now nuclear terrorism and nuclear-weapon proliferation, the latter leading to regional nuclear conflict as well as the promotion of nuclear terrorism.[8]

In the evolution of Obama's nuclear policy implementation, there were four initial pillars: the completion of the New START treaty as part of the US-Russia "reset" policy; the issuance of the NPR with its emphasis on the nuclear terrorism/nuclear proliferation threat; initiation of a set of nuclear security summits and associated activities intended to "lock up" as much of the world's vulnerable nuclear materials as possible within four years; and the achievement of a successful 2010 Nuclear Nonproliferation Treaty (NPT) Review Conference in which measures could be adopted to make it more difficult to withdraw from the NPT (as North Korea had done) and strengthen the safeguards regime of the International Atomic Energy Agency, in part through additional US funding.

The Russia "reset" policy was fundamental to the President's overall strategy. It was argued that US-Russia relations reached a dangerous low point after the Russian invasion of Georgia in the summer of 2008. The relationship had to be rebuilt for multiple reasons: to regain momentum in furthering deeper cuts in deployed strategic nuclear weapons, to forge closer bilateral strategic cooperation to enhance Russian support for US nonproliferation measures toward Iran, and to enlist Russian support for countering nuclear terrorism.

The NPR intended to emphasize the post-Cold War realities of the nuclear terrorism and nuclear proliferation threats, to downplay the US-Soviet nuclear arms competition, and to emphasize the need for US-Russia and US-China "strategic stability talks" that would increase transparency and promote cooperative measures. At the same time, it stressed the need to work closely with allies to ensure that "extended deterrence," i.e., the commitment of the US nuclear umbrella protecting the national security of key allies, especially the NATO alliance members plus Japan and South Korea, remained credible and persuasive to the elites of these countries.

The April 2010 Washington Nuclear Security Summit, which brought together more heads of state in the US than at any time since the founding of the United Nations in San Francisco in 1946, along with subsequent associated activities, was intended to put the spotlight on the need for broad international cooperation to "lock up" the vast amounts of fissile material (especially highly enriched quantities of Uranium-235, and separated Plutonium-239) that can be used to fabricate nuclear weapons. At the first summit, Chile and Ukraine pledged to turn over their fissile material to the United States. The central point behind these commitments was to deny terrorist groups access to the fissile material they needed for their own nuclear-weapon goals.

Finally, the 2010 NPT Review Conference was intended to showcase a strengthened NPT regime by promoting adherence to the Additional Protocol (AP) and comprehensive safeguards agreements (CSAs), which are intended to provide assurances about both declared and possibly undeclared activities. Under the AP, the International Atomic Energy Agency (IAEA) is granted expanded rights of access to information and sites.[9]

Although there have been some positive outcomes, the President's agenda has come up against a world with uncertain nuclear threats and risks. This chapter looks at the President's vision and the way in which it has influenced, and been influenced by, the emerging nuclear environment.

Changing the nuclear environment

Early positive outcomes

In the period since the President announced his vision, he has mobilized considerable support, especially in the United States and among selected elites in different parts of the world. First, senior members of his administration, including from the Departments of Defense, Energy, and State, as well as select groups within the military and intelligence community have dedicated countless hours to implementation of policies in support of this vision, aided by allies on Capitol Hill and in the media and think tanks.

The signing and ratification of New START in December 2009 and December 2010, respectively, renewed the US-Russia strategic arms reduction process, limiting each side to 1,550 deployed strategic nuclear weapons. Though a modest further reduction from previous agreements, it was nonetheless a very demanding treaty to achieve, with each element laboriously negotiated with the Russian negotiating team. It set the stage for the possibility of more comprehensive reductions involving nonstrategic and nondeployed weapons, the prospects for which were always uncertain even before the 2014 Ukraine crisis.

The NPR was greeted by many as a necessary refresher of US nuclear strategy and policy beyond its Cold War moorings, and a document highlighting the pressing threats of nuclear terrorism and nuclear proliferation. It triggered the start of strategic stability discussions with the Chinese leadership and a host of activities to shore up allied confidence in the US nuclear guarantee. It also succeeded in securing important financial support for the upgrade of the aging US nuclear-weapon complex, in support of the goal to retain a safe, secure, and effective nuclear deterrent, as long as nuclear weapons continue to exist.

The Nuclear Security Summits continued in Seoul in 2012 and The Hague in 2014. Many nations have joined in the venture to lock up fissile material. A notable achievement has been the decision by Japan, announced at The Hague, to return to the United States more than 700 pounds of weapons grade plutonium and a supply of highly enriched uranium that will be transformed into proliferation-resistant forms.

The NPT continues to be the principal legal means of restricting nuclear-weapon proliferation, and the IAEA has received some additional support to strengthen its safeguards and verification capabilities, remaining the principal internationally recognized body for conducting sensitive inspections of nuclear facilities.

Moreover, the Obama vision has spawned the "Global Zero" movement, endorsed by many notable figures, from former Vice Chairman of the Joint Chiefs of Staff James Cartwright to Mikhail Gorbachev, and including both Democrats and Republicans. The movement has raised funds to sponsor meetings, issue publications, and establish the goal of a nuclear-free world by 2030.

In the United States at least, there are many American policymakers who now doubt that nuclear weapons are the answer to today's national security threats.

A series of disappointments

Russia

One of the major disappointments since the Obama vision was unveiled has been Russian obstructionism over the President's arms control initiatives, with the situation now greatly exacerbated by the Ukraine crisis. Some might say that it was highly naive of the Obama administration to believe that a Putin-led government (even when he was prime minister before once again assuming the presidency), would be interested in cooperating with the tenets of American foreign policy. In any event, the President and his team worked assiduously to enlist Russian support on a host of issues, but with very little success.

First, with respect to the Russian nuclear force itself, there is no evidence, other than Russian ratification of New START, that Moscow is interested in diminishing the role of nuclear weapons in its national security policy. Indeed, just the opposite. Russia is embarking on a well-funded nuclear-weapon and delivery-vehicle modernization program and has announced its intent to replace the huge SS-18 intercontinental ballistic missile (ICBM) fleet with new, very large, liquid-fueled missiles that will carry a large number of multiple, independently targetable reentry vehicles (MIRVs).[10] This news is especially disturbing because large, liquid-fueled, land-based missiles armed with multiple warheads are considered "high value targets" that would be among the top priorities to destroy in the event of a nuclear exchange. In the parlance of strategic thought, these are "destabilizing weapons" because this means the Russian leadership would be forced to "use them or lose them" in the event of a crisis.

In addition to this development, Russia is thought to be carrying out an aggressive nuclear-weapon research and development program at its modern facilities in Novaya Zemlya and elsewhere. It continues to deploy a large arsenal of tactical or shorter range systems west of the Urals, and it shows little sign of accepting the Obama position that the world would be a much safer place if nuclear weapons were deeply reduced or eliminated altogether.[11] Since New START was ratified, the Obama administration has tried on numerous occasions and at multiple levels to engage Russia in a dialogue to outline the terms of the next phase of arms reduction negotiations including tactical and nondeployed weapons, yet no apparent progress has been made.

It is highly plausible that one reason for this stalemate is the fundamental asymmetry in which Washington and Moscow view the political and psychological utility of nuclear weapons. For the United States, with a defense budget larger than that of the next twenty biggest spending countries, nuclear weapons play a vital role to deter a nuclear attack on the United States while reassuring its allies that the US security guarantees pledged decades ago (especially for the NATO countries, Japan, and South Korea) remain credible. These forces supplement a very large and sophisticated conventional force posture based on land, at sea, under the sea, in the air, in space, and in cyberspace. Indeed, proponents of "going to zero" often note that US conventional military superiority is so pronounced that a world without nuclear weapons would be to the US strategic advantage.

For Russia, however, the reverse is true. Putin and his colleagues are still searching for ways to reclaim the superpower status that was lost when the Soviet Union collapsed more than twenty years ago. Russia's weak economic condition has precluded, until recently, spending huge sums to rebuild its once feared conventional forces. For Russia, its nuclear arsenal is the principal source of its geostrategic authority. The Russian Federation has many unresolved security issues, including finding itself with the NATO alliance right on its border in Poland and elsewhere. It seeks to sustain and enhance its influence over other states of the former Soviet Union, including Ukraine, Georgia, Moldova, and others. It sees an emerging Chinese juggernaut to the south with a gigantic disparity in border populations against which, it might reason, tactical nuclear weapons are a necessary safeguard. According to polling data, the maintenance of a large, modern nuclear force is well supported by the Russian people.

Another key bone of contention in the bilateral relationship concerns US ballistic missile defense (BMD) plans. When the Obama administration took office, it inherited a Bush administration plan to deploy ten large missile interceptors in Poland and a sophisticated radar system in the Czech Republic. After an extensive inter-agency review culminating in the issuance of the Ballistic Missile Defense Review in the fall of 2009, the US adopted what has been termed the "European Phased Adaptive Approach." This approach calls for the deployment of a mix of interceptors and sensors both on land and at sea, in Eastern Europe, the Eastern Mediterranean, Northeast Asia, and perhaps elsewhere by 2020 that would meet regional missile threats from Iran and North Korea but would not be capable of retarding the nuclear deterrent force of Russia or China.

However, neither Moscow nor Beijing has accepted this rationale. The military leadership of both countries appears to be convinced that these BMD plans are part of a long term US strategy to provide the capacity to inflict a disarming first strike on the nuclear retaliatory forces of Russia and China, and then to utilize BMD systems to minimize the likelihood of effective retaliation. They reason that once these systems are in place, both Russia and China would be forced to acquiesce to US policy demands in the face of almost certain strategic defeat. To counter these views, the United States has on numerous occasions briefed their Russian counterparts on the actual performance capabilities of the planned BMD systems, in order to convince them that the United States would not in fact possess the capabilities ascribed to them under these scenarios. Such efforts have also been conducted on a smaller scale with the Chinese – but to no avail. Russia instead has insisted on data exchanges and a virtual joint operation of the US systems to assuage their concerns. However, the United States has placed severe limits on the amount of BMD information it is willing to provide for fear of compromising its effectiveness, in the event of a serious deterioration in the relationship between Washington and Moscow. The net result of this deadlock to date is the pronouncements of Russian leaders that the failure to resolve the BMD problem could be the basis for a Russian withdrawal from New START (much as the United States under President George W. Bush in 2002 withdrew from the 1972 Anti-Ballistic Missile Treaty).

As if these differences were not sufficient, the United States and the Russian Federation are on opposite sides over a variety of regional and other issues. Their views of the annexation of Crimea and other threats to Ukraine and other neighbors could not be more different. They have also taken divergent positions on the Middle East. Russia, only with the greatest reluctance, finally acceded to some of the UN-sponsored economic sanctions against Iran over its unwillingness to comply with the NPT. For many years, it has provided vital technical assistance in the building of key Iranian nuclear facilities. In contrast to the American perspective, Russia apparently does not see a nuclear Iran as a threat to its core national interests. In the Syrian civil war, Russia has blocked UN Security Council resolutions to tighten sanctions against the Assad regime, and has seemingly turned a blind eye to the massive atrocities committed by the regime. Here again, however, Russia has its own strategic objectives that do not conform to American interests. Syria is the last foothold of Russian influence in the Arab world with important Russian naval forces utilizing Syrian facilities. Moscow, facing its own Islamist insurgency in Chechnya and Dagestan, is determined to support a Baathist, Alawite regime in its struggles against a mix of Sunni forces that include al-Qaeda and other jihadist elements.

The Snowden Affair has implanted a further wedge in bilateral relations. Moscow has granted asylum status to the American who leaked large amounts of information about US National Security Agency (NSA) data mining and electronic surveillance operations. This status was granted almost certainly with the explicit approval of President Putin over the repeated objections of the most senior Obama administration officials.

Despite these daunting challenges, President Obama has continued to pursue the dream "of a world without nuclear weapons – no matter how distant that dream may be."[12] He endorsed a further cut of US-deployed strategic nuclear warheads by up to one third, reductions of US and Russian tactical weapons in Europe, and the hosting of a nuclear security summit in 2016 to continue the goal of securing nuclear materials. He also expressed support for an effort to educate Congress on issues relating to the Comprehensive Test Ban Treaty (CTBT), which the US Senate failed to ratify in 1999, and sought to overcome opposition to an international fissile material cutoff treaty (FMCT), where Pakistan has been a principal obstacle to opening negotiations.[13]

All these proposed initiatives are now severely jeopardized by the Ukrainian crisis that started in March 2014 with Russia's seizure of Crimea and the destabilization of Eastern Ukraine. US-Russian relations have plunged into a deep freeze with the implementation of selected US economic sanctions against Russia followed by Russian refusal to allow its launch vehicles to be used for US space flight programs. How Ukrainian political instability plays out and whether Putin takes further aggressive steps will determine whether we are about to enter a new intense US-Russia nuclear weapons competition. Should this materialize, Russia's future cooperation to constrain nuclear proliferation will also be in doubt. This could produce a nuclear threat dimension not witnessed since the collapse of the Soviet Union at the end of 1991.

China and other nuclear powers

Russia is not the only country that has seemingly failed to join the Obama nuclear reduction and elimination movement. Consider the other nuclear-weapon states – recognized nuclear-weapon states under the NPT regime; nuclear-weapon states outside the NPT regime; and incipient nuclear-weapon states.

In the first category are Great Britain, France, and China. Great Britain, it appears, has moved to a minimum deterrence posture, with about 225 deployed nuclear warheads. Indeed, its senior officials endorsed the precepts of the Nuclear Posture Review in 2010, and its government seems to be searching for the smallest number it can have while convincing itself that such an arsenal would deter any rational adversary from attacking the British homeland with nuclear weapons.[14] There has long been a small but active anti-nuclear movement in Britain, although its influence has waned in recent years.[15]

The French situation, however, is markedly different. Although France claims to have about 300 deliverable nuclear warheads, its nuclear status is much more central to its body politic. There is no antinuclear movement to speak of, and conservatives and socialists agree on the need for the French arsenal. Perhaps they share the view that French nuclear weapons must compensate for conventional weakness against determined adversaries.[16] The French government was extremely displeased with the NPR in 2010, perhaps fearing it could ignite an antinuclear movement in France that would undercut support for its own arsenal. French officials also thought that the United States was very naive in thinking that US nuclear reductions would influence other key states such as Pakistan, Iran, and North Korea. It would thus appear that the nuclear stockpile landscape would have to change drastically for France to alter its position.

China, moreover, has continued to add to its nuclear arsenal since 2010. While some estimate China to possess about 300 nuclear weapons, these estimates are shrouded in uncertainty because of China's inherently opaque policies concerning its military capabilities. This lack of transparency has deep roots in China's strategic thought, dating back centuries to Sun Tzu, who argued that opaqueness is essential to conceal both China's strengths and its weaknesses. China has now agreed to participate in "strategic stability talks" that have centered on the North Korean nuclear problem and most recently on cyber issues. It steadfastly maintains an unwillingness to engage in nuclear arms reduction talks until the United States and Russia reduce to its levels. China has criticized US BMD plans and has increased investments in deployment of ICBMs that could reach at least the western portions of the United States. Chinese experts in Track II dialogues assert that in the event of a crisis in East Asia, China must have this capability to prevent potential intervention by the United States. Indeed, this is part of what Washington sees as Beijing's strategy of "anti-access/area denial" or A2/AD. In anticipation of a possible US surge in naval and air forces in the region during a crisis, China is investing in anti-ship missiles, anti-satellite weapons, cyber capabilities, and other means to deny the United States the ability to carry out its strategic objectives. The United States, in turn, is formulating an "Air-Sea Battle" that is intended to use advanced technologies and inter-operative capabilities on land, in and under the sea, in the air, in space, and in cyberspace to thwart this strategy.[17] China will certainly not be a leader in the Global Zero movement. Moreover, recent Chinese maritime assertiveness in the East China Sea and the South China Sea has raised tensions with all its neighbors, especially Japan. These geopolitical conditions could increase the prospects of nuclear proliferation in the region to counter China's growing strength, especially if the credibility of US security guarantees is in doubt.

The nuclear-weapon states outside of the NPT – India, Pakistan, and Israel – show even less enthusiasm for Obama's policies. India has now built up an arsenal approximating 100 deliverable warheads; the estimate for Pakistan is between 90–110 warheads; and the Israeli program, shrouded in secrecy from the outset, is estimated to have between 75 and 200 warheads.[18] The India-Pakistan strategic rivalry is well known and dates back to the founding of Pakistan in 1947. After several wars, crises, and threats of war, the rivalry continues unabated in its seventh decade: a Hindu dominant state (with a Muslim minority greater than the Pakistani population) against a Muslim dominant state with the territory of Kashmir an unresolved source of dispute. Not only are both countries adding to their arsenals, but there are some worrisome scenarios on the horizon. An attack by Pakistani terrorists against Indian civilians in Mumbai in 2008 failed to elicit an Indian military response, requiring enormous self-restraint by the government in New Delhi. A concern is that a replay of such events would make Indian retaliation a certainty, using conventional forces in a limited attack to destroy the perpetrators. Indian forces would be met by Pakistani conventional forces that could utilize short-range tactical nuclear weapons against them on Pakistani territory, out of fear that they would be defeated on the battlefield as in the three previous Indo-Pakistani wars. This use could trigger an Indian nuclear response, and the resulting escalation ladder would be catastrophic for both societies. The intensity of the rivalry is not waning, and Indian and Pakistani nuclear forces also command enormous domestic prestige. The motivation for Indian forces likewise reflects the

Sino-Indian rivalry (China defeated India in a previous border war). All these considerations suggest that a continued nuclear arms competition on the South Asian continent is far more likely than any embrace of Obama's policies. Whether the recent election of Indian Prime Minister Narendra Modi (with a reputation as a Hindu nationalist) exacerbates matters further remains to be seen.

Israel is unique among nuclear-weapon states in neither acknowledging nor denying its nuclear capability. This purposefully opaque posture seems to have produced an effective nuclear deterrent that has been sustained for more than forty years. Given recent regional trends since the start of the Arab Spring in 2011, especially the slaughter in the Syrian civil war and the pronounced instability in post-Mubarak Egypt, coupled with the intensity of Islamic jihadists in the region and the prospect of an Iranian nuclear-weapon program (as well as the unresolved Palestinian conflict), Israel faces national security threats from every direction. There is no evidence whatsoever that Israel would embrace the Obama movement even if significant progress were made with the declared nuclear-weapon states.

The incipient states, North Korea and Iran, are in a different category. North Korea withdrew from the NPT in January 2003. After more than two decades of development, North Korea is thought to have amassed between six and twelve nuclear weapons through both uranium enrichment and plutonium reprocessing paths to nuclear development, having violated a string of NPT requirements while still a party to the NPT. The North Korean case is important for several reasons: the nature of its closed, isolated society; the lack of resolution of the Korean War since 1953; the acts of aggression that the Pyongyang regime has periodically committed; and the consequent persistent threat that North Korea poses to both South Korea and Japan. If its intercontinental range missiles, long under development, reach deployment, they will pose a direct threat to the US mainland as well. North Korean weapons and launch vehicle tests and deployments have simply been unaffected by the Obama policy. More importantly, North Korea is the quintessential example of a state that uses its nuclear weapons to gain international attention, and, in the minds of its leadership, to deter US military intervention. In January 2002, North Korea was termed by then-President George W. Bush as part of the "axis of evil," together with Iraq and Iran, which were accused of supporting terrorism and seeking weapons of mass destruction. After the US invasion of Iraq in March 2003, Pyongyang probably believed that it too was a candidate for US intervention. By deploying credible threats to destroy Seoul (roughly 50 percent of the South Korean economy) and Tokyo, North Korea has validated the view of many in key countries that nuclear-weapon possession is essential to deter the United States. Iraq, for example, was invaded before it had a deployed capability and its leadership was overthrown. Libya's leadership suffered the same fate with the assistance of the US-led NATO no-fly zone, but only after it surrendered its WMD capabilities. Indeed, many US North Korean specialists now believe that Pyongyang wishes to be recognized as a nuclear-weapon state and seeks to negotiate with the United States on other economic and geo-political issues, a position rejected by Washington.

This is a fundamental shift in the role of nuclear weapons for the United States since the Cold War. During the decades of the superpower confrontation, the primary US objective was to use its nuclear arsenal to deter a Soviet conventional or nuclear attack on the American homeland or its allies' territory. Nuclear weapons are now used to deter US intervention. In short, the United States is judged by potential adversaries less in terms of deterring aggression and more as being deterred from committing aggression.

This reasoning seems to underlie the Iranian nuclear program. Iran has been an intense US adversary since the revolution of 1979, supporting terrorist organizations, including Hamas and Hezbollah; calling for the destruction of Israel; and promoting its aim to be a regional hegemonic power in the Middle East and Persian Gulf. While Iran continues to be a party to the NPT, it has violated its commitments on numerous occasions by preventing thorough inspections of suspected nuclear-weapon development facilities. According to recently published analyses, Iran may be able to produce a nuclear device before the end of 2014.[19] This has led to the P5+1 Geneva Interim Agreement, signed in November 2013, which consists of a short-term freeze of portions of Iran's nuclear program in exchange for the lifting of some economic sanctions.[20] Whether this agreement will lead to a tangible cessation or reversal of the program is highly uncertain at this time, leaving a US or Israeli military response still on the table.

An added unwanted complication has been the potential weakening of US extended deterrence guarantees, especially to Japan and South Korea in the shadow of the North Korean nuclear program. In recent times, parliamentarians in both countries have called for independent nuclear forces out of concern that US security guarantees are losing their credibility.

Nuclear realities and the Kissinger shift

A notable consequence of these actions by nuclear weapon states and aspirants has been a significant shift in former Secretary of State Kissinger's position on the goal of Global Zero. In an important statement co-authored with former US national security advisor Brent Scowcroft, Kissinger asserted that "nuclear weapons will continue to influence the international landscape as part of strategy and an aspect of negotiation."[21] They noted that "the global nonproliferation regime has been weakened to a point where some of the proliferating countries are reported to have arsenals of more than 100 weapons. And these arsenals are growing."[22] Kissinger and Scowcroft reiterated that work toward elimination of nuclear weapons must be accompanied by "a series of intermediate steps that maintain stability [i.e., no incentive to strike first] and that every stage of the process be fully transparent and verifiable … The precondition of the next phase of US nuclear weapons policy must be to enhance and enshrine the strategic stability that has preserved global peace and prevented the use of nuclear weapons for two generations."[23] The authors argued that the interrelationship between missile defense, tactical nuclear weapons, and precision guided large conventional warheads on long range delivery vehicles "must be taken into account in future negotiations."[24] Moreover, they asserted that "other countries need to be brought into the discussion when substantial reductions from existing START levels are on the international agenda."[25]

In the real world of real governments with the multiplicity of objectives described above, the Kissinger formula is a de facto rejection of the Obama approach, if not of the President's vision. There is simply no evidence that the numerous criteria proposed by Kissinger and Scowcroft, all of which are sensible from a strategic perspective, would be met by the full range of nuclear-weapon states and nuclear aspirants. Since Kissinger and Scowcroft are held in very high esteem by many serious students of these issues both within and outside government, their ideas underscore the enormity of the tasks to achieve greatly reduced reductions, not to mention a world free of these weapons (which would require exacting verification measures, since at very low numbers, even modest cheating could be highly significant).

Pursuing fissile material lock-up and a strengthened NPT

Another major area of disappointment has been the inability to make meaningful progress with those countries that house vast amounts of potentially vulnerable fissile material. Pakistan is particularly important. With a very active nuclear-weapon program, Pakistan has large stocks of fissile material, with perhaps 100 nuclear weapons in its possession, and it is working to acquire more. Domestically, it has a nominal democratic system but with a strong military leadership that appears to dominate foreign and defense policy. It is battling its own domestic terrorist groups led, among others, by the Pakistani Taliban, while simultaneously supporting the Afghan Taliban. Note that Osama Bin Laden lived in Abbottabad, in the shadow of Pakistan's West Point, for more than five years. Which is worse – the possibility that senior officials harbored the world's most notorious terrorist, or that the government was completely ignorant of his presence? Either possibility is a very damning statement on Pakistan's domestic security processes and its trustworthiness as a US ally.[26] Pakistan consistently claims that all of its nuclear material is safe and secure, yet it is the home of A.Q. Khan who spent fifteen years providing nuclear-weapon technical assistance, equipment, and materials to North Korea, Libya, and Iran. Its military headquarters were attacked for twenty-two hours by Pakistani Taliban in November 2009, and nuclear-weapon personnel were attacked in a bus by a suicide bomber in July 2009.[27] Is it believable that all its fissile material is secure, especially when considering the prospect of "insider threats" among its nuclear-weapon community, the Pakistan Army, and Pakistan's Inter-Services Intelligence Agency (ISI)?

To these concerns must be added the fissile material in Iran and North Korea, two states whose facilities are cordoned off from the President's Nuclear Security Summit initiatives by their own national policies. Yet these countries are the most likely to provide fissile materials willingly to other countries or terrorist groups, for political or financial reasons.[28] Thus while it is admirable that a large number of countries are cooperating fully with the Obama initiative, the most important and vulnerable sources of fissile material are not on the list. Russia and China have also been very slow to cooperate. Accordingly, there is little basis to conclude that the securing of the world's vulnerable fissile material will be achieved any time soon. The comprehensive implementation of the initiative, though well intentioned as a means to combat nuclear terrorism, is presently not feasible.

The pillar of strengthening the NPT, the 2010 Review Conference, also fell short of US expectations. The United States was required to endorse a future meeting on a Middle East Nuclear Weapons Free Zone conference in order to gain concessions in the wording of the final document (the conference, originally scheduled for 2012, was postponed). The Additional Protocol was approved by the IAEA in 1997 to rectify deficits in IAEA inspections and verification by improving its ability to detect undeclared nuclear material and activities. But NPT parties were unable to reach a consensus that the protocol should be an essential component of the Comprehensive Safeguards Agreement.[29] The IAEA has received less additional financial support than was expected, and the "teeth" of implementing challenge inspections are not as sharp as the United States hoped they would be.

State and nonstate proliferation collaboration and emerging technologies

Nuclear proliferation has been marked by collaboration among states since early in the nuclear age. The United States supported Great Britain; the Soviet Union aided China; France assisted Israel; China helped Pakistan; North Korea was probably aided by the Soviet Union, China and Pakistan; Pakistan also supported Iran and Libya; and North Korea helped Syria.

The entry into force of the NPT and its elaborate safeguards regime has limited proliferation and created an international norm of nonproliferation that has been respected by almost all states since it entered into force in 1970.

A key issue at present is whether an agreement can be reached with Iran, which keeps its program significantly distant from a nuclear-weapon capability, that it does not encourage further proliferation. Saudi officials have made statements claiming that the Kingdom will acquire nuclear weapons (presumably from Pakistan) if Iran's nuclear program is not stopped. This could trigger a "proliferation chain" including Turkey and Egypt. And a similar chain in East Asia could extend to Japan, South Korea and possibly Taiwan, should Chinese and North Korean assertiveness not be credibly checked by the United States in concert with its regional allies.

To date, there appears to be no evidence that any of the nuclear proliferators has been will-ing to share its technology and knowledge with nonstate actors – Al Qaeda and its affiliates; Hezbollah, Hamas, or Chechen separatists, for example. Each nuclear-weapon state – with the exception of A.Q. Khan's activities, which may or may not have been sanctioned by Islamabad – seems to have concluded that no more nuclear-weapon states serves their national interests.

The largest wild cards challenging this assumption are a deeply belligerent Russia, a completely isolated North Korea, and an Islamic fundamentalist sympathetic with Al Qaeda's global aspirations. That the history of nuclear-weapon proliferation reveals a pattern of coop-eration is not an encouraging precedent.

A vital additional consideration in offering an informed global nuclear threat assessment concerns the emergence of new technologies that could increase the obsolescence of our thinking about nuclear proliferation. The growing power of cyber technology is now readily apparent for civil society, with a wide variety of important military applications. The "Olympic Games" operation in which cyber systems were used to attack Iranian centrifuges and temp-orarily impede their nuclear-weapon development program was just the initial illustration of the role of advanced information technologies affecting nuclear-weapon proliferation. Cyber systems could be used to attack the command, control and communication of existing nuclear forces. They could impede space-based systems that are essential for early warning, tracking, surveillance, and numerous other missions essential to nuclear force operations. These applications could engage new nuclear states and aspirants such as North Korea and Iran with the United States, as both Pyongyang and Tehran are developing sophisticated cyber capabili-ties of their own.

Social media may also fit into this picture. Facebook and Twitter were used effectively in the overthrow of the Mubarak regime in Egypt in 2011. They can also be used to enhance the shar-ing of information that could undermine the security of nuclear materials, especially in countries with questionable nuclear security such as Pakistan.

Additive manufacturing, which encompasses but is not limited to "3-D Printing," is another technology that has revolutionary potential. This process enables the making of a three-dimensional solid object of virtually any shape from a digital model. Successive layers of material of different shapes laid down in an additive process are key to the approach, as distinct from traditional manufacturing that relies on the removal of material (e.g., cutting or drilling).

What is especially worrisome about this mix of new technologies is that they can empower nonstate actors to have access to knowledge and capabilities that could enhance the prospects of their acquisition of nuclear-weapon.

In sum, the global nuclear threat assessment is not encouraging. Existing nuclear weapons states are enhancing their capabilities. Potential nuclear weapon states see their acquisition as deterrence of US military intervention. Proliferation chains could materialize if existing nonproliferation measures fail. Collaboration between states and nonstates may accelerate. And new technologies are strengthening the access of nonstate actors to nuclear materials.

C.P. Snow was incorrect more than half a century ago about nuclear proliferation and nuclear-weapon use. We should know within ten years whether the trends cited above are as alarming as they appear to be.

Notes

1. Charles P. Snow, "The Moral Un-Neutrality of Science," *Science*, Vol. 133, No. 3448 (January 27, 1961), pp. 255–262, as cited by Harold Brown, "New Nuclear Realities," *The Washington Quarterly*, Vol. 31, No. 1 (Winter 2007–08), p. 8, http://home.comcast.net/~lionelingram/Nuclear_matters_08 winter_brown.pdf.
2. India detonated a "peaceful nuclear explosion" in 1974 near the border with Pakistan, but did not declare itself a nuclear-weapon state.
3. An incident in 1979 has been attributed to South Africa and Israel as a combined nuclear detonation, but this has never been verified. See Director of Central Intelligence, *The 22 September 1979 Event*, Interagency Intelligence Assessment, January 21, 1980, declassified June 2004, posted in the National Security Archive, George Washington University, p. 5, www2.gwu.edu/~nsarchiv/ NSAEBB/NSAEBB190/03.pdf.
4. George P. Shultz, William J. Perry, Henry A. Kissinger, and Sam Nunn, "A World Free of Nuclear Weapons," *Wall Street Journal*, July 4, 2007, http://online.wsj.com/news/articles/SB1167875 15251566636; George P. Shultz, William J. Perry, Henry A. Kissinger, and Sam Nunn, "Toward a Nuclear-Free World," *Wall Street Journal*," January 15, 2008, http://online.wsj.com/news/ articles/SB120036422673589947.
5. Barack Obama, "Renewing American Leadership," *Foreign Affairs*, Vol. 86, No. 4 (July/August 2007), pp. 2–16, www.foreignaffairs.com/articles/62636/barack-obama/renewing-american-leadership.
6. "Remarks by President Barack Obama, Hradcany Square, Prague, Czech Republic," The White House, Office of the Press Secretary, April 5, 2009, www.whitehouse.gov/the_press_office/Remarks-By-President-Barack-Obama-In-Prague-As-Delivered.
7. See Council on Foreign Relations, "Obama's Speech in Prague on New START Treaty," April 8, 2010, www.cfr.org/proliferation/obamas-speech-prague-new-start-treaty-april-2010/p21849. See also "Transcript of Obama's Speech in Berlin," June 19, 2013, http://blogs.wsj.com/washwire/ 2013/06/19/transcript-of-obamas-speech-in-berlin.
8. See US Department of Defense, "Nuclear Posture Review Report," Washington, DC, April 2010, pp. 9–22, www.defense.gov/npr/docs/2010%20Nuclear%20Posture%20Review%20Report.pdf.
9. See International Atomic Energy Agency, "Factsheets and FAQs: Nuclear Non-Proliferation: Chronology of Key Events (July 1945–Present)," IAEA website, www.iaea.org/Publications/ Factsheets/English/npt_chrono.html.
10. "Russia to Start Building Prototype of New Heavy ICBM in 2014," *Novosti*, June 18, 2013, http://en.ria.ru/military_news/20130618/181738737/Russia-to-Start-Building-Prototype-of-New-Heavy-ICBM-in-2014.html.
11. Note that the distinction between "strategic" and "tactical" is predicated on the ranges of the delivery vehicles. New START limits the number of warheads on deployed strategic delivery vehicles. But it may be possible to remove warheads on short range systems and redeploy them on long range systems. Thus, the very large Russian "tactical" force could in part be a reserve strategic force, giving Russia a major numerical advantage despite the limits of the treaty.
12. See Barack Obama, "Remarks by President Obama at the Brandenburg Gate   Berlin, Germany," June 19, 2013, www.whitehouse.gov/the-press-office/2013/06/19/remarks-president-obama-brandenburg-gate-berlin-germany.
13. The speech received decidedly mixed reviews in Germany and elsewhere. Even the pro-disarmament Stockholm International Peace Research Institute (SIPRI) offered that "given Russia's skepticism towards Obama's position … the likelihood of Russian-US alignment on reductions is slim." See Stockholm International Peace Research Institute, "SIPRI Statement on President Obama's Speech in Berlin," Press Release, June 19, 2013, www.sipri.org/media/pressreleases/2013/19-june-2013-sipri-statement-on-president-obama2019s-speech-in-berlin.
14. For unclassified estimates of the deployed numbers of nuclear weapon state arsenals, see Arms Control Association, "Nuclear Weapons: Who Has What at a Glance," April 2013, www.armscontrol. org/factsheets/Nuclearweaponswhohaswhat. The factsheet draws on estimates of the Federation of American Scientists, the International Panel on Fissile Material, the US Department of Defense, and the US Department of State.
15. If one visits the British Atomic Weapons Establishment (AWE), a few anti-nuclear demonstrators seem permanently encamped but do nothing to impede activities inside the facility.

16. More than three decades ago, I met with General Pierre Gallois, one of the intellectual fathers of the Force de Frappe. Gallois noted that France had fought many wars since 1870 – the Franco-German War, the First World War I, the Second World War, the Indo-China War, and the Algerian War – and had lost them all. For this reason, Gallois argued, nuclear weapons were essential to preserve the French state.

17. For some outlines of the Air-Sea Battle approach, see International Institute for Strategic Studies, "Anti-access/Area Denial: Washington's Response," *The Military Balance 2013* (London: International Institute for Strategic Studies, 2013), pp. 29–31.

18. See Arms Control Association, "Nuclear Weapons: Who Has What at a Glance."

19. See "Analysts Predict Iran Able to Produce Atom Bomb by mid-2014," *Jerusalem Post*, July 31, 2013, www.jpost.com/Iranian-Threat/News/Analysts-predict-Iran-able-to-produce-atom-bomb-by-mid-2014-321607. The report cites an analysis by the Washington-based Institute for Science and International Security.

20. See United States White House, "Summary of Technical Understandings Related to the Implementation of the Joint Plan of Action on the Islamic Republic of Iran's Nuclear Program," Office of the Press Secretary, January 16, 2014, www.whitehouse.gov/the-press-office/2014/01/16/summary-technical-understandings-related-implementation-joint-plan-actio.

21. Henry A. Kissinger and Brent Scowcroft, "Nuclear Weapon Reductions Must Be Part of Strategic Analysis," *The Washington Post*, April 22, 2012, www.washingtonpost.com/opinions/nuclear-weapon-reductions-must-be-part-of-strategic-analysis/2012/04/22/gIQAKG4iaT_story.html.

22. Ibid.

23. Ibid.

24. Ibid.

25. Ibid.

26. Note that the Pakistani medical doctor, Dr Shakil Afridi, who assisted US intelligence officials in locating Bin Laden, was convicted of treason and sentenced to thirty-three years in prison, which he is appealing. See Richard Leiby and Peter Finn, "Pakistani Doctor who Helped CIA Hunt for Bin Laden Sentenced to Prison for Treason," *The Washington Post*, May 23, 2012, www.washingtonpost.com/world/asia_pacific/pakistani-doctor-who-helped-capture-bin-laden-sentenced-to-prison-for-treason/2012/05/23/gJQApFVGkU_story.html.

27. On this last incident, see Salman Masood, "Attack in Pakistani Garrison City Raises Anxiety about Safety of Nuclear Labs and Staff," *New York Times*, July 4, 2009, www.nytimes.com/2009/07/05/world/asia/05pstan.html.

28. North Korea has demonstrated its willingness to sell missile parts and nuclear technology on several occasions, and Pyongyang and Islamabad have collaborated in the past in sharing nuclear and missile technology. Moreover, China provided important assistance in the development of Pakistan's nuclear program although it is alleged that this support was before China became a party to the NPT.

29. See Mark Hibbs, "The Unspectacular Future of the IAEA Additional Protocol," *Proliferation Analysis*, Carnegie Endowment for International Peace, April 26, 2012, http://carnegieendowment.org/2012/04/26/unspectacular-future-of-iaea-additional-protocol.

2

PROLIFERATION RISKS IN THE MIDDLE EAST AND NORTH AFRICA

Abdullah Toukan

The present situation surrounding the proliferation of nuclear weapons and the means for their delivery has become noticeably more complex. With the advent of globalization, and in conjunction with the emergence of international terrorism, the proliferation of nuclear and other weapons of mass destruction (WMD) has become the principal threat of the twenty-first century. Efforts by several countries to acquire WMD can be explained objectively by states' threat perceptions and security concerns, with little regard to the extent to which these efforts have undermined the security of their neighbors. This points to one of the main dilemmas on how a country can enhance its security without diminishing the security of its neighbors.

The position of many countries in the Middle East and North Africa (MENA) region is that they find it difficult to enter serious arms control negotiations until some form of regional peace is fully established. This stems from their perception that nations in the region still consider military force as the only viable source to achieve their policy objectives. The danger from this underlying reasoning, if perceived as the only alternative to preserving a regional security balance, is that it could give rise to an uncontrollable arms race and to a parallel proliferation of WMD.

Arms transfers to the Middle East are not the sole cause of the regional problems. In fact, the acquisition of arms has been the product of the unresolved political settlement of the Arab-Israeli conflict as well as other conflicts in the region. The continuing Arab-Israeli conflict has made it practically impossible to formulate and implement formal arms control agreements, resulting in a failure from the beginning. Over the past five decades, there have been a number of arms control proposals and attempts for the Middle East. One main weakness of these proposals was that they were not integrated into a political process. Therefore, in any move towards arms control and regional security in the region, the linkage between both conventional and nonconventional weapons and the ongoing peace process must be made.

Any massive rearmament will surely create an unrestricted arms race in the Middle East which will automatically be accompanied by the proliferation of weapons of mass destruction. The fear is that the proliferation of weapons of mass destruction could give rise to states announcing a so-called "in-kind" deterrence, or the right to retaliate in kind. Unless controlled, this arms race will give rise to another military conflict with catastrophic human and environmental consequences.

No single country can try to cope with the threat of proliferation alone or in isolation from a regional security arrangement. Thus the Middle East peace process is pivotal to any arms control and regional security process. Wider regional cooperation in controlling the proliferation of weapons of mass destruction and theater ballistic missiles will be very dependent on any ongoing Middle East peace process. If no progress is made in the peace process, then no effective regional cooperation can take place, consequently the risks of WMD proliferation, terrorist use of WMD, and ballistic missile proliferation will rise.

Achieving security is not a zero-sum game; in other words, a state or group of states cannot achieve security at the expense of neighboring countries' security. Nor can a state in the region any longer seek to gain military superiority with respect to individual states within the region, or a military posture of dominance versus neighboring countries. See Table 2.1 for a list of short-range ballistic missiles (SRBM), mid-range ballistic missiles (MRBM), intermediate-range ballistic missiles (IRBM), and intercontinental ballistic missiles (ICBM) in the Middle East and South Asia.

For a state to proliferate there must be two elements present: the capacity to do so, or nuclear capability, and the motivation based on the state's threat perceptions and security concerns. Are there countries in the region or adjacent that possess nuclear weapons and the delivery means? Are these states politically unstable, unfriendly, with internal violence? Are the economies stable

Table 2.1 Ballistic missile capabilities for countries in the MENA and South Asia

SRBM *<1,000km*	MRBM *1,000–3,000km*	IRBM *3,000–5,500km*	ICBM *>5,500km*
Iran			
Shahab-1	Shahab-3	Shahab-5	Shahab-6
Shahab-2	Shahab-4	–	–
Mushak-120	Ghadr-101	–	–
Mushak-160	Ghadr-110	–	–
Mushak-200	IRIS	–	–
–	Sajil	–	–
Syria			
SCUD-B	–	–	–
SCUD-C	–	–	–
SCUD-D	–	–	–
SS-21b	–	–	–
Israel			
–	Jericho II	–	Jericho II
Pakistan			
Shaheen I	Shaheen II	–	–
Hatf I	Ghauri I	–	–
Hatf II	Ghauri II	–	–
Hatf III	Ghauri III	–	–
M-11	–	–	–
India			
Agni I	Agni II	Agni III	Surya
Prithvi I	–	–	–
Prithvi II	–	–	–

and not on the verge of a crisis, with the prospect of becoming a failed state? Are they very much isolated from the international community, economically and diplomatically? Has an irreversible and definitive political decision to acquire nuclear weapons, no matter what the cost, been made? Are nuclear weapons looked upon as attractive alternatives to expensive modern conventional weapons for power projection and deterrence, as well as a means to increase status and prestige?

The other major element which increases the potential for a country to manufacture nuclear weapons is its nuclear capability, which consists of the inputs, technical know-how and resources. Resources include the necessary materials for a nuclear weapon and economic capacity.

Nuclear power and nuclear proliferation risks

The material that sustains nuclear reactions to produce nuclear energy can also be used to make nuclear weapons, and so the development of nuclear energy by a nonnuclear-weapon state is considered one of multiple pathways to potential proliferation and represents an important subset of issues within nuclear nonproliferation.

The technologies used in peaceful nuclear power programs overlap with those used in the production of fissionable material for nuclear weapons. Pathways from nuclear power to nuclear weapons include the following:

*   The theft of nuclear material;
*   The covert sale of nuclear material or enrichment and reprocessing technologies;
*   The diversion of uranium or spent fuel to a clandestine operation for conversion into weapons grade material; and
*   Break out, in which a signatory state of the Nuclear Nonproliferation Treaty (NPT) gains nuclear technology or stockpiles of fissile material, then renounces the NPT and pursues nuclear weapons.

The risk of proliferation through the nuclear energy development pathway on both horizontal proliferation (the spread of nuclear weapons to new states) and vertical proliferation (increases in the size and sophistication of nuclear arsenals within existing nuclear states) has become, in the words of United Nations Secretary General Ban Ki-moon, "one of the gravest challenges facing international peace and security."[1] Similarly, in his 2014 annual worldwide threat assessment to the US Congress, US Director of National Intelligence James R. Clapper observed that the proliferation of nuclear and other WMD, along with their delivery systems, constitute a major threat to US national security.[2] To respond to this threat, government officials devise policies to prevent the diffusion of the world's most dangerous weapons.

Israeli nuclear policy

A nuclear capability is needed to deter threats to Israel's existence. The possible acquisition of nuclear weapons by any Arab or other Muslim state in the region is considered to be a direct existential threat to Israel, which leads to an interest in preventing all states in the Middle East region from developing nuclear programs that it sees as threatening, or attempting to acquire nuclear weapons. Israel has deliberately maintained a nuclear policy of ambiguity about its own nuclear-weapon program.

The purpose of the nuclear ambiguity policy was based on the belief that it had introduced an effective "deterrent through uncertainty." Arab states were never sure whether Israel would use a nuclear weapon in retaliation in the event of a major war that put its survival at risk, or

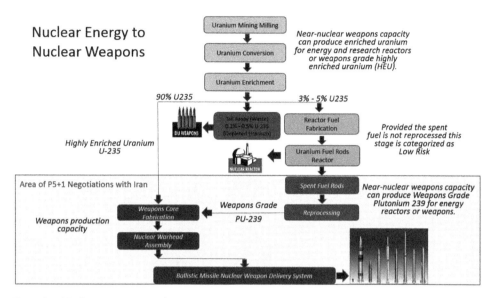

Figure 2.1 Nuclear energy to nuclear weapons

if any of the Arab states tries to acquire a nuclear capability. Israel's nuclear ambiguity policy has been articulated by a number of Israeli leaders in such statements as "Israel will not be the first to introduce nuclear weapons into the Middle East."[3] The Arab States' view is that such a nuclear doctrine can never be considered binding in case of war. Israel has never officially admitted that it possesses nuclear weapons and is not a signatory to the NPT. Many see the present status of Israel as that of an undeclared nuclear-weapon state. At the same time, it has come to be recognized as possessing a very sophisticated arsenal of nuclear weapons with the necessary delivery systems. (See Figure 2.2 for the coverage of Israeli ballistic missiles.)

Iran

Presently there exist no hard facts that Iran has or is developing a nuclear-weapon capability. However, it would be logical to assume that Iran sees nuclear weapons as a last resort and as a deterrent against two main threats that it perceives: the United States and Israel. The US war against the Iraqi regime and its occupation of the country is a constant reminder of the possibility that the United States might attack Iran even on a limited scale, since it was included in the "axis of evil."

Iran also perceives Israel as an enemy that might attack strategic targets within its boundaries, particularly its "peaceful" nuclear facilities, as on June 7, 1981 when sixteen Israeli warplanes bombed and destroyed Iraq's Osirak nuclear research facility near Baghdad, more than 600 miles from Israel's borders. To this end, Iran built and tested its Shahab-3 (range 990 km) and Shahab-3M (range 1,130 km) ballistic missiles and is reported to be developing the Safir and Seijjil ballistic missiles with ranges up to 2,000 to 3,000 km, emphasizing that the Israeli threat was the main impetus for developing such missiles and that they would be used in retaliation to any Israeli attack. Overall, Iran has been heavily investing in:

- Precision strike munitions;

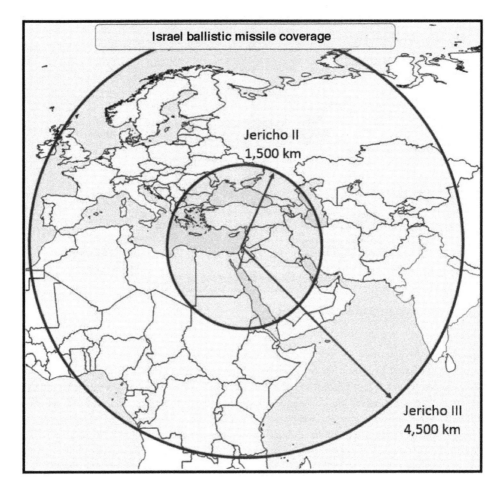

Figure 2.2 Israel ballistic missile coverage

- Naval anti-ship weapons such as the Chinese C802 that hit the Israeli Navy ship during the 2006 war in Lebanon and the Ra'ad 350 km anti-ship missile;
- Cruise missiles such as the Kh55 Russian land attack cruise missile; and
- Development of nuclear capabilities.

The arsenal of ballistic missiles possessed by Iran has been declared to be for defensive purposes against any foreign invasion, in particular by the United States. (See Figure 2.3 for the coverage of Iranian ballistic missiles). However, it has become very clear that it is an arsenal that is intended to inflict maximum casualties and damage. In essence, it is a major component for asymmetric warfare in the form of attrition and defense in depth, and is designed to compensate for any deficiencies in its air power.

According to Iran, there is a double standard in the International Atomic Energy Agency's (IAEA) treatment with regard to Iran who, as a member of the NPT, is being pressured to adhere to the Additional Protocol (AP), while countries such as Israel, India, and Pakistan have refused to even sign the NPT.

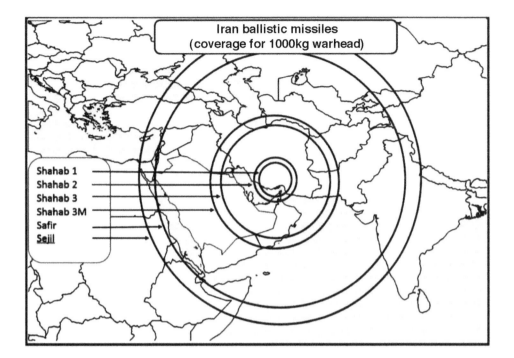

Figure 2.3 Iran ballistic missiles

The more there is an Israeli threat to the survival of the regime in Iran, the more Iran will be determined to acquire nuclear weapons. Iran would withdraw from the NPT based on the argument that it needs to acquire nuclear weapons to protect its sovereignty against further aggression by Israel and the United States. A strike by Israel on Iran could give rise to regional instability and conflict as well as terrorism, the regional security consequences of which would be catastrophic.

Israel views Iran as an existential threat to be dealt with in the immediate future with a military strike against its main nuclear facilities. Israel would rather see the United States join it in preventing Iran from developing the capability, rather than having the United States arm its allies in the region and provide a defense umbrella.

The United States recognizes Iran as having a sovereign right to peaceful civilian nuclear power, but does not have the right to nuclear weapons as stipulated in the NPT. To the United States, Iran is in violation of IAEA safeguards and United Nations Security Council Resolutions (UNSCRs). These are also becoming the findings of the international community and its institutions, and not those of the United States alone.

In a report on February 18, 2010, the IAEA wrote, "While the Agency continues to verify the nondiversion of declared nuclear material in Iran, Iran has not provided the necessary cooperation to permit the Agency to confirm that all nuclear material in Iran is in peaceful activities."[4] This statement has raised a great deal of concern in the international community.

Given the information available on nuclear weapons and the enrichment process, it is generally assumed that a simple implosion-type nuclear weapon does not need testing. The design is straightforward and has been tried by a number of countries. As a consequence, scientists and engineers can be confident that the weapon will work without undergoing multiple testing.

The capability to produce one nuclear weapon could also be considered as enough for a state to be considered a nuclear-threshold state.

There does not exist any publicly available information on whether Iran has made an irreversible and definitive decision to acquire nuclear weapons no matter what the cost, or if it is still in the "option" stage. Nor do we know if Iran has become self-sufficient and is in the process of completing a network of clandestine facilities, to either move the enriched uranium around from one to the other until it can produce a nuclear weapon, or if it will rely on one facility that can undertake the total conversion to highly-enriched uranium independently.

A possibility that has been talked about by Western analysts would be that Iran could produce 3.5 percent U-235 or 20 percent U-235 in these clandestine facilities, while at the same time continuing a diplomatic engagement with the P5+1 until it feels the political conditions are just right to give it the option to "breakout" from the NPT, and move towards the production of nuclear weapons in a short period of time. Moreover, once it comes on line, Iran's 40MWT Arak reactor could produce enough weapons grade PU-239 for one nuclear weapon per year. (See Figure 2.4 for the plutonium production capacity of Iran's Arak reactor.)

It is the view of many analysts that with the occupation of Iraq, Iran now sees new opportunities to enhance its strategic interests and to reemerge as the key power in the Gulf region. They have enumerated five threats to the region posed by Iran: Iran's ambition to acquire nuclear weapons and long-range ballistic missiles; its support for international terrorism; its opposition to the Middle East peace process and its rising political influence in the Middle East; its offensive military buildup and asymmetric warfare preparation; its threat to the stability of the Gulf States, including its annexation of the islands of Abu Musa, which dominate the entrance to the Straits of Hormuz.

It is evident that there will be a heavy economic burden on Iran if it decides to update its military forces and sustain a high operational readiness of its armed forces. Its air defense and military forces (air and ground) equipment are practically obsolete. These factors will lead the military to try to acquire what they presumably believe is a cheaper means of strategic deterrence, specifically nuclear weapons and ballistic missiles. Given these factors, the problem of

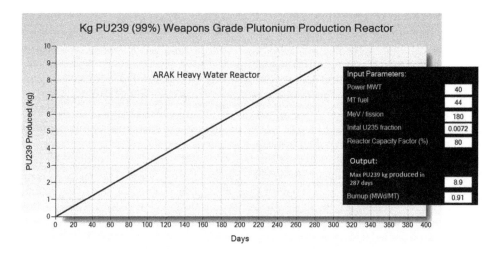

Figure 2.4 Plutonium production at Arak

proliferation will persist in the region. States such as Iran look upon nuclear weapons and ballistic missiles as attractive alternatives to expensive modern conventional weapons for power projection and deterrence, and as a means to increase regional status and prestige.

The Iranian National Security Doctrine is based on the perception that Iran possesses a leadership role in the Arab and broader Muslim world and should have a dominant role in the Gulf region, especially in any Gulf Cooperation Council (GCC) security arrangements.[5] Iran considers the occupation of Iraq by the United States and the presence of the US Fifth Fleet offshore in the waters of the Gulf, as well as the past US declared policy for "regime change" in Iran, to be a grave threat to its national security. Iran maintains that the United States is actually positioning itself to confront Iran and is building military bases to be used as launching pads for a possible strike against Iran's nuclear facilities. Iran also believes that Israel intends to destabilize Iran and attack its nuclear facilities, which Iran claims to be for the purpose of producing nuclear power. In addition, Iran is worried about unfriendly neighbors surrounding it, including a nuclear-armed Pakistan.

The Gulf cooperation Council States

The Gulf States have been investing heavily in modernizing and upgrading their force structures. The United States, France, and United Kingdom have been the major weapons suppliers. The Gulf Cooperation Council (GCC) member states also recognize that the assistance of outside regional powers will be required to deal with any military aggression in the region. As a result, they have signed bilateral defense agreements with their Western allies – the United States, United Kingdom, and France.

The two main considerations underlying the choice of a military doctrine by the GCC states have been the "balance of forces" and "strategic depth." In particular, for Kuwait, Bahrain, Qatar, the United Arab Emirates, and Oman, the main concern would be the lack of strategic depth to provide protection from an Iranian attack. A lack of strategic depth results in limitations on the area of operational maneuverability during conflict, the time available to respond, and the vulnerability of vital strategic economic centers due to their proximity to the borders. Saudi Arabia would be the only state that has strategic depth, and is looked upon to play a pivotal role in the security arrangements for the Gulf and a possible Arab-Israeli conflict. Saudi Arabia's oil resources, population and strategic depth make it a major and essential participant in any regional security arrangements.

In 2002, the GCC made a major security shift from a common security arrangement to a joint defense pact, which essentially is a collective security arrangement. A joint defense pact, or collective security arrangement, is directed against an aggressor coming from outside one's sphere. Participation in a collective security agreement entails a commitment by each member to join the coalition and an attack on one implies an attack on the other partners. This thinking is based either on defense in its traditional sense, or upon deterrence. In the foreseeable future, the GCC has to plan its defenses in order to deter Iran. What they can do is to build their collective and national assets to provide a military deterrent sufficient to make any direct confrontation as costly as possible to Iran or any other adversary. It is in this deterrent role that lies the ultimate rationale for any GCC joint defense pact and cooperation.

Iran's impact on the regional military balance

Iran's actions have already made major changes in the military balance in the Gulf and the Middle East. Iran may still be several years to half a decade away from becoming a meaningful nuclear power, if the decision is ever made, but even potential Iranian nuclear weapons has led Iran's neighbors, the United States, and Israel to focus on an Iranian nuclear threat.

For the United States and Israel, this focus has led to the serious consideration of preventive war. The United States, however, is also examining options for defense and extended deterrence. In this context, a key US policy objective has been to prevent the Arabian Gulf region to be dominated by a hegemonic Iran. The United States believes that Iran cannot try to dominate the Gulf region as long as a US military power is present. Washington would arm allies in the region and extend a ballistic missile-defense umbrella to protect its allies. Israel is also considering its options, with the fundamental difference that it sees Iran as a potential existential threat to Israel's very existence.

Iran's ballistic missiles cover the complete spectrum range from 150 km up to 5,500 km, from short to intermediate ranges. This arsenal of ballistic missiles possessed by Iran has been declared to be for defensive purposes against any foreign invasion, in particular against the United States. Iran believes that these missiles will compensate for any deficiencies in its air power. However, ballistic missiles can be used with success against soft targets in open areas and cities to inflict maximum human casualties and create terror. The missile arsenal is a major component for asymmetric warfare in the form of high attrition and defense in depth. In essence, a major component of Iranian asymmetric warfare would involve high civilian casualties.

Counterproliferation policies

Given the impact that Iran's nuclear activities may have on regional and international security, the primary objectives for the United States and the international community are getting Iran to end its uranium enrichment program, to comply with international agreements and laws, and to cooperate fully with the IAEA. The strategic policy options to achieve the aim are dialogue and diplomacy, economic and financial sanctions, deterrence and active defense, and military strikes. For each strategic policy option there are risks associated with the consequences for each policy option. Which strategic option or combination of these options does the United States and the international community need to adopt, to achieve the aim, while keeping risk consequences to the global economic and financial systems to a minimum?

Diplomacy, dialogue, and economic incentives

In this policy option, efforts are made to persuade Iran to not proliferate and to convince Iran that it does not face a sufficient threat to proliferate and cannot make major gains in power or security by doing so. The IAEA is granted full access for inspections to ensure that no nuclear-weapon program is being undertaken. Incentives can be in the form of economic and much-needed trade advantages to bring back the Iranian economy from a highly unstable level down to a more stable level.

How long will the international community tolerate the duration and depth (or even eventual shallowness in results) of dialogue and diplomacy with Iran? The perceived risk is that Iran just wants to exploit an open-ended dialogue to buy time and alleviate the pressure of sanctions, with no intention to terminate any of its nuclear activities. Additionally, this tactic would give Iran time to accelerate the process of further dispersing its enrichment facilities to locations buried deep underground. The possibility of dispersed facilities complicates the military strike option. Any assessment of a potential mission success would become uncertain, making it unclear what the ultimate effect of a strike would be on Iran's nuclear facilities.[6]

Sanctions and regime change

This option involves controls and measures designed to put economic pressure on Iran, limit its access to technology, and limit its access to arms. In addition, this option would involve efforts to change the regime and create one that will not proliferate. In general, this strategy would attempt to influence Iranian policy and promote a more positive Iranian regime, moving it from a confrontational to a cooperative foreign policy.

When it comes to sanctions, the key principle to be followed is that sanctions are multilateral and must be viewed as such when analyzed. The question becomes what defines an effective sanction, and can trade and financial sanctions help counter the proliferation of weapons of mass destruction? The policy of increasing the severity of sanctions could push a country such as Iran into the critical unstable region resulting in an economic collapse, which could have unknown regional implications. Would Iran then accelerate its nuclear program and decide to go nuclear as a means of defending itself? A multiplicity of dangerous moves here could be considered as an initial form of retaliation: Iran could stage attacks in the Straits of Hormuz in an attempt to disrupt the flow of crude oil through it, which will have serious consequences on the global economy.

Extended deterrence and active defense

This option involves a mix of measures, such as advanced technology combat aircraft, theater ballistic missile defense systems, asymmetric warfare capabilities, counterterrorism, civil defense, and passive defense that would both deter Iran and protect against any use it can make of its WMD capabilities and other war fighting capabilities. This option shows that any effort to use WMD weapons to intimidate or gain military advantage would be offset by the promised response.

Preventive or preemptive strikes before Iran has a significant nuclear force

This option would employ military force to destroy Iran's ability to proliferate or deploy significant nuclear forces. The United States and others would work to build an international consensus to allow the use of military force as a last resort when all other options absolutely fail. This option would also likely employ covert operations, sabotage of the main enrichment facilities and ballistic sites, and cyber warfare such as the Stuxnet attack with the goal of destroying as many centrifuges as possible in the Iranian fuel enrichment plant at Natanz and other enrichment facilities.

Within its unique perspective as a world power and the responsibility that entails, the United States is the only country that can launch a successful military strike of this nature. If all peaceful options have been exhausted and there are no other means to convince Iran to stop or change its course in pursuing nuclear weapons, then the United States alone bears the global responsibility and vision that should determine what the timeline would be if Iran does pursue the path to develop nuclear weapons.

The paramount question arising is what would be the objectives of a military strike? Would such a strike attempt to wipe out the program completely, delay it for five years, or even delay it one year? These criteria will define the force allocation required to achieve a successful mission against Iran's nuclear facilities. This is not merely a simple mission of bombers flying in and out of Iran. This is a complicated offensive air-to-ground operation that will involve many aircraft, each with its own role, such as combat aircraft whose role is to suppress enemy air defenses (SEAD) along the way, aircraft that fly fighter escort with the bombers, aircraft that carry specialized electronic warfare equipment to jam enemy radars and communications, and possibly air-to-air refueling along the way in and out of Iran. Depending on the forces allocated and the duration of the air strikes, it is unlikely that an air campaign alone could terminate Iran's program or prevent future hostility in the region once and for all.

The issue at hand is complex and bears lasting global consequences if not approached with adequate knowledge and awareness, particularly if the high risk tracks involved are not fully taken into consideration. The threat is perfectly understood: all are in agreement that Iran as a nuclear threshold state will be unacceptable to the security and stability of the region. The last thing this region needs is to become even more a part of the global arms race or of the heightened dangers of increased numbers of WMD, especially within the so far relatively stable GCC region that remains the global hydrocarbon reserve and has attained impressive and model levels of socio-economic development and globalization through oil revenues. The GCC has also been historically generous in crisis resolution throughout the region, as exemplified by the Gulf development funds set up in the 1960s, as well as extremely generous multilateral and bilateral aid to neighboring countries. The stability of Gulf countries is essential for any regional peace and socioeconomic development.

In the case of Iran, the direction of the United States and the international community has been one of adopting dialogue and diplomacy, sanctions, deterrence and active defense, carefully balancing their timing, duration, and the level of intensity of their implementation in each phase, with the goal of defusing the crisis with Iran, and inducing Iran to abide with all international agreements and to cooperate fully with the IAEA. With regard to a military strike, it should be made clear that it remains on the table as an option of last resort. It should be pointed out that the United States must put all its weight in not allowing any unilateral military strikes by Israel that can definitely push the presently volatile Middle East region into a war with far reaching global consequences and a high price for Israel itself. The issue has become an existential threat for the entire region rather than for any one country alone.

The ideal solution would be dialogue and diplomacy with economic incentives, if all agree, in particular Iran, to enter the negotiations with a serious political intention to find a solution and a workable plan. This is not a zero-sum game, where one side wins and the other side loses. All sides should come out feeling that they won with a strong set of confidence-building measures to resume dialog between the parties, increase transparency, and reduce the possibility of miscalculations. Such an approach is preferable to exchanges of threats and counter threats that most probably would lead to war.

A solution of this kind of a problem does not have a purely strategic solution. Rather, it will require a mixed strategy of policy options, which could involve a combination of some of the available strategic options.

Arms control and regional security

In conclusion, confronted with current and emerging risks of regional proliferation, there is a need to explore arms control and regional security. Arms control can be considered to be any measure that reduces the likelihood of war as an instrument of policy, or that limits the destructiveness and duration of war should it break out. It is not only technical, but is also of a political nature. Thus, arms control does not only mean arms reductions or disarmament, but also encompasses any measure that strengthens regional security and diminishes the use of military force as an instrument of national policy.

Conceptually, arms control can be broken down into structural and operational arms control. The structural component takes aim at scaling down manpower and military equipment, conventional and nonconventional (nuclear, biological, and chemical), ultimately producing agreements to implement major reductions in forces.

Operational arms control, on the other hand, are efforts carried out in the context of the Organization for Security and Cooperation in Europe (OSCE). These talks focus on confidence and security building measures (CSBMs), rather than on reductions in force structures.

CSBMs have the following objectives: preventing war owing to a misunderstanding or miscalculation; reducing the possibility of a surprise attack; and finally reducing the ability to use military forces for the purposes of political intimidation and carrying out an aggressive foreign policy. CSBMs thus require transparency and predictability to be effective.

We can further categorize CSBMs into two levels: technical-military CSBMs, which operate at the tactical operational level of military policy; and political-military CSBMs, including declarations of intent concerning the planned use of military force, which in effect is a declaratory posture regarding intentions. CSBMs are arrangements designed to enhance confidence and address security concerns at both levels of operational military planning and national security policy.

Within the context of arms control and proliferation, in particular WMD and their delivery systems – notably surface-to-surface ballistic missiles – each state's threat perception has become one of the determining factors of its own definition of the Middle East region, its national security objectives, force structure, and military doctrine.

There exist a number of criteria upon which the definition of the region is based. Typically they include the presence of military or political conflicts, geographic factors, natural boundaries, cultural, ethnic, demographic, and historic factors. To some, the region of the Middle East can be categorized into sub-regions based on conflict situations as:

- The central sub-region, referring to states directly involved in the Arab-Israeli conflict;
- The Gulf (GCC States) sub-region;
- The Maghreb sub-region; and
- The southern tip of the Arabian Peninsula sub-region.

In this type of categorization, one complicating factor is that states in the region have taken part in armed conflict in more than one sub-region.

With regard to the regional dimensions of the arms control process, it has been suggested that it could be more feasible in the initial stage to keep the geographic definition of the region as a flexible one. The regional parties that attended the multilateral negotiations addressing arms control and regional security, plus the states that were not initially invited (such as Iraq, Iran, Libya, and Sudan), could join in and be considered a group of states with political, security, and economic links that can be considered to define the region. In short, the region can then be defined to be from Morocco to Iran and from Syria to Yemen.

If stability and security can be achieved in a region by promoting arms control measures, this will have a positive effect on other regions. For this very reason, security concerns of peripheral states as well as other neighboring regions should be taken into consideration throughout the process. For instance, given the South Asia countries – Afghanistan, Bangladesh, British India Ocean Territory, India, Maldives, Nepal, Pakistan, and Sri Lanka – any arms control measures between the two nuclear states in this region, India and Pakistan, will have an effect on the Middle East region.

Notes

1. Ban Ki-moon, "The United Nations and Security in a Nuclear-weapon-free World," speech delivered at the East-West Institute, New York, October 24, 2008, www.un.org/sg/statements/?nid=3493.
2. James R. Clapper, "Worldwide Threat Assessment of the US Intelligence Community," statement for the record, Senate Select Committee on Intelligence, US Senate, January 29, 2014, p. 5, www.dni.gov/files/documents/Intelligence%20Reports/2014%20WWTA%20%20SFR_SSCI_29_Jan.pdf.
3. See, for example, Assaf Uni and Yossi Verter, "EU tells Israel to Clarify Olmert's Remarks on Nuclear Weapons," *Haaretz*, December 13, 2006, www.haaretz.com/news/eu-tells-israel-to-clarify-olmert-s-remarks-on-nuclear-weapons-1.207076; Nuclear Threat Initiative, "Israel: Nuclear," Country Profiles, May 2014, www.nti.org/country-profiles/israel/nuclear. For an extended discussion of Israel's policy of nuclear ambiguity or "opacity," see Avner Cohen, *Israel and the Bomb* (New York: Columbia University Press, 1998).
4. International Atomic Energy Agency, "Implementation of the NPT Safeguards Agreement and Relevant Provisions of Security Council Resolutions 1737 (2006), 1747 (2007), 1803 (2008) and 1835 (2008) in the Islamic Republic of Iran," Report by the Director General, GOV/2010/10, February 18, 2010, p. 9, www.iaea.org/Publications/Documents/Board/2010/gov2010-10.pdf.
5. United Arab Emirates, The Kingdom of Bahrain, The Kingdom of Saudi Arabia, The Sultanate of Oman, Qatar, and Kuwait. See The Cooperation Council for the Arab States of the Gulf, homepage, www.gcc-sg.org/eng/indexc64c.html.
6. Jim Zanotti, Kenneth Katzman, Jeremiah Gertler, and Steven A. Hildreth, "Israel: Possible Military Strike against Iran's Nuclear Facilities," Congressional Research Service, September 28, 2012, www.fas.org/sgp/crs/mideast/R42443.pdf.

3

IRAN

Gregory F. Giles

No nuclear proliferation controversy has consumed more international attention, diplomatic energy, and negotiating patience than Iran's. This ongoing saga reflects the vexing nature of Iran's multi-faceted challenge to the nonproliferation regime. At issue is whether the Islamic Republic can be coaxed by the international community back into compliance with its obligations under the Nuclear Nonproliferation Treaty (NPT) in a manner that balances each side's key security interests, namely, the Iranian regime's ability to construct a nuclear weapon should it be imperiled, and the West's ability to detect that construction early enough to thwart it, by use of force if necessary. In any event, serious consideration will need to be given to shoring up the nuclear nonproliferation regime in the wake of what may be called the Iranian proliferation model, for it appears that the current negotiating path will still leave Iran very close to the nuclear-weapon threshold. Other nuclear aspirants are likely to take note and potentially emulate Iran's behavior. By itself, an Iranian breakout from the NPT could lead to the unraveling of the nuclear nonproliferation regime. If other countries in volatile regions similarly build right up to the nuclear weapon threshold, collapse of the regime could come rapidly in the form of proliferation cascades.

As this chapter details, Iran's nuclear behavior has challenged the spirit and letter of the NPT, the treaty review process, the authority of the International Atomic Energy Agency (IAEA), and the nuclear export control regime. In discussing these challenges, the chapter addresses six themes: deception (including Iran's secret construction of sensitive nuclear facilities), denial (Tehran's refusal to admit to illicit nuclear activity, save when confronted with incontrovertible evidence to the contrary), defiance (such that in response to international calls for restraint and warnings, Iran accelerated its nuclear program), disruption (of the NPT review conference process to divert attention from its noncompliance), domestic politics (whereby the nuclear issue had become a political football among competing factions in Tehran), and diplomacy (the efforts since 2002 to negotiate a peaceful resolution of the Iranian nuclear controversy).

Background

The United States and a number of its allies and partners harbored suspicions of Iran's nuclear intentions well before Tehran's secret build-up of fissile material production facilities was publicly exposed in 2002. Indeed, US concerns about nuclear proliferation in Iran predate the founding of the Islamic Republic in 1979. The Carter administration feared that the Shah of Iran sought to produce nuclear weapons, causing it to draw out negotiations with Tehran on civil nuclear cooperation. US fears were stoked by the Shah's own comments indicating an interest in acquiring the bomb, as well as his formation of a nuclear-weapon design team.[1] The Shah was toppled before the issue of US civil nuclear cooperation was resolved.

As the mullahs assumed power in Tehran, the nuclear inheritance was but one of many issues they had to address. In such an unsettled and emotionally charged atmosphere, the revolutionaries condemned the Shah's investment in nuclear energy as a wasteful vestige of Western imperialism and cancelled Iran's contracts with Germany and France for construction of nuclear power plants at Bushehr and Darkhouin, respectively. The new regime opted to uphold Iran's adherence to the NPT. Behind the scenes, the situation was more complicated. The memoirs of Iran's current president, Hassan Rouhani, revealed that even before they assumed power, the mullahs were weighing their nuclear options. They called to Paris Iran's nuclear scientists and afterwards concluded that they would retain Iran's core nuclear research effort.[2] Within three months of Khomeini's triumphant return to Tehran as leader of the new Islamic Republic, Ayatollah Beheshti, a key Khomeini ally, summoned Iranian nuclear scientists and reportedly declared that the new regime was intent on acquiring nuclear weapons.[3]

Saddam Hussein's invasion of Iran in 1980 and his use of chemical weapons beginning in 1982 added impetus to the mullahs' atomic pursuits. Iran's current Supreme Leader, Ayatollah Khamenei, previously served as Iran's president beginning in 1981, after terrorist bombings killed a number of the fledgling republic's leaders, including Beheshti. Documents obtained by the IAEA by 2009 indicate that in 1984, then-president Khamenei advocated Iran's acquisition of nuclear weapons at a high-level government meeting, declaring that such weapons would be a deterrent in the hands of God's soldiers.[4] Iran at this time embarked on a major effort to expand its cadre of nuclear experts and to revive nuclear reactor deals with the West. The United States prevailed on its allies not to assist Iran in these efforts.

Frustrated in its attempts to restore nuclear cooperation with the West, Iran looked elsewhere. It found success with China. *Inter alia*, Beijing helped Iran develop the Esfahan uranium conversion facility, which played a critical role in preparing uranium for enrichment in gas centrifuges. In 1991, China also provided Iran with nearly 2,000 kg of uranium compounds that were used to secretly test conversion processes for the plant. Iran failed to declare these uranium imports at the time, as well as the conversion experiments, in violation of IAEA safeguards. By the late-1990s, US pressure caused China to attenuate its nuclear cooperation with Iran.[5]

Iran also turned to Russia, which in 1995 agreed to complete the Bushehr nuclear power reactor. A secret annex to the Russian-Iranian nuclear cooperation agreement called for Moscow to supply Tehran with a uranium enrichment facility. Under pressure from Washington, Russian President Boris Yeltsin announced that the enrichment proviso would be struck but otherwise, Russian nuclear cooperation with Iran would continue.

Much of the US effort to deny Iran technology that would support nuclear-weapon development focused on discouraging Chinese and Russian cooperation.[6] Washington was caught off guard, however, by Iran's dealings since the late-1980s with the nuclear black market being run out of the Pakistani nuclear complex by A.Q. Khan. The Khan network provided Tehran with critical uranium centrifuge technology and components, as well as nuclear-weapon-related design and production plans.[7]

A decade of nuclear crisis, 2002–2012

In August 2002, an Iranian opposition group claimed that the regime was constructing secret nuclear facilities in central Iran. Commercial satellite imagery lent credence to the claims in December, revealing a massive underground uranium enrichment facility being built at Natanz and a large-scale plant to produce heavy water, a moderator for reactors fuelled by natural uranium, at Arak. It was only after the cover was blown on these facilities that the Iranians officially notified the IAEA of their existence. A request by the IAEA to visit the sites was rebuffed by Iran, which cited "the need to prepare." It was not until February 2003 that IAEA Director General Mohammed ElBaradei and a team of agency inspectors was granted access to the sites. ElBaradei discovered an Iranian nuclear fuel cycle program far more advanced than expected.

The ElBaradei visit launched an IAEA investigation that uncovered numerous breaches of Iran's safeguards obligations. Under intense international scrutiny, Tehran shifted into crisis management mode. Some leadership figures sensed that the regime had to grant the IAEA greater access in order to allay fears that it was seeking to build nuclear weapons, a perception that could invite an attack on the Islamic Republic. Already, US military forces were massing on Iraq's border, determined to prevent Saddam Hussein from completing what was believed to be an effort to reconstitute his nuclear-weapon program. Other Iranian leaders, particularly from the military, resisted disclosure of the regime's nuclear-weapon work in order to save face and, presumably, retain the weapons option.[8] By fall 2003, with American troops having already toppled Saddam Hussein, Supreme Leader Khamenei personally called upon Hassan Rouhani, then-Secretary of Iran's Supreme National Security Council, to step in as the regime's nuclear trouble-shooter.

Rouhani focused on two efforts, externally allaying concerns that Iran was seeking nuclear weapons, and internally consolidating authority over the regime's nuclear activities. Regarding the former, Rouhani found willing partners in Europe and in IAEA Director General ElBaradei, who opposed the American invasion of Iraq and feared that the United States could launch an unsanctioned war against Iran next. Rouhani negotiated a deal in October 2003 with the so-called EU-3 (i.e., Germany, France, and the United Kingdom), whereby Iran would suspend its enrichment program and adopt a range of transparency measures, albeit on a strictly "voluntary, temporary" basis. Tehran understood that in return, the EU-3 would use their influence in the IAEA to ensure that Iran's nuclear portfolio was normalized and Tehran would not be referred to the UN Security Council and sanctioned.[9]

Internally, Rouhani had to coordinate the various institutional players in Iran's nuclear program, such as the Atomic Energy Organization of Iran (AEOI) and the Islamic Revolutionary Guards Corps (IRGC), Iran's radicalized military. He fully understood how challenging that would be:

> I could see the difficulties ahead … it was necessary that different organizations cooperate with the official in charge of the nuclear case and I wasn't sure at the time if all of them were willing to cooperate 100 percent. When the work started, 90 percent of the problems that I predicted came true. The problems included both disharmony and sabotage.[10]

Rouhani also presided over ongoing efforts to sanitize Iran's highly incriminating nuclear activities. Those efforts began in February 2003 when another secret facility was uncovered by the Iranian opposition, the Kalaye Electric Company in Tehran. Once publicly exposed, the regime immediately began to remove equipment and sanitize the site. The IAEA sought to take environmental samples at Kalaye in February but was rebuffed. Iran only acknowledged a nuclear connection for Kalaye under pressure, claiming that the site was a watch factory that also built centrifuge components. Tehran maintained that no nuclear material had been present at the site. It took months for the IAEA to obtain full access to Kalaye; even then, it was not permitted to take environmental samples until August 2003. The Agency discovered that Iran had not only removed equipment but also reconstructed the interior of the main building. Despite these deception efforts, the IAEA confirmed that nuclear material had been present at the site, a safeguards violation that forced Iran to divulge more details about its secret enrichment activities.[11]

By June 2004, Iran had completely demolished another suspect site, the Lavisan-Shian complex in Tehran, as documented by commercial satellite imagery, before allowing the IAEA access to it.[12] Lavisan-Shian housed the Physics Research Center (PHRC) which Iran subsequently acknowledged had been engaged in unspecified "nuclear defence" research.[13] Tehran maintained that no nuclear material or nuclear activities related to the fuel cycle had been present at the site. The IAEA was unable to detect the presence of nuclear material at Lavisan, but noted that "the detection of nuclear material in soil samples would be very difficult in light of the razing of the site."[14]

Sensing Iran's vulnerability, Rouhani was able, with the help of other key elite figures such as Ayatollah Hashemi Rafsanjani, to persuade the Supreme Leader to accept the enrichment suspension deal with the EU-3. He also appears to have halted the regime's weaponization work, the research, development, and testing of a nuclear explosive.[15] As the US Intelligence Community concluded in an unclassified summary to a National Intelligence Estimate in 2007, "We assess with high confidence that until fall 2003 [i.e., before Rouhani asserted control], Iranian military entities were working under government direction to develop nuclear weapons."[16]

Iran's enrichment suspension did not prove to be durable, however. The Iranian regime used ambiguities in the 2003 agreement to continue advancing its enrichment program, necessitating the deal to be renegotiated in 2004. Sensing that the Europeans were intentionally dragging out the negotiations to hold back Iran's nuclear development, the Supreme Leader directed in April 2005 that work resume on the Esfahan uranium conversion facility, effectively ending Iran's enrichment suspension. Notably, Iran's rejection of nuclear suspension preceded the election of firebrand president Mahmoud Ahmadinejad in June 2005.

Tehran's reactivation of its enrichment program triggered intense international diplomacy. In September 2005, the IAEA Board of Governors found that, based on the evidence gathered by IAEA inspectors, Iran was in noncompliance of its safeguards agreement. In February 2006, the IAEA Board voted to report Iran to the UN Security Council. In defiance of IAEA resolutions, President Ahmadinejad announced on April 11, 2006 that Iran had now enriched uranium. The UN Security Council followed with an ultimatum, Resolution 1696, demanding, *inter alia*, that Iran suspend all enrichment related activities by the end of August 2006 or face sanctions. Iran ignored the warning, and the Security Council passed Resolution 1737 in December, the first of many sanctions against Iran.

Under Ahmadinejad, and with the Supreme Leader's blessing, Iran embarked on a policy of nuclear defiance. Hassan Rouhani was replaced as the regime's lead nuclear negotiator. Tehran then made good on warnings that additional pressure on the regime would only trigger new advances in the nuclear program. The centrifuge program in particular witnessed rapid and sustained expansion. It went from about 200 IR-1 model centrifuges in late-2006 to 18,000 by early-2014. Tehran also continued to build out the IR-40 heavy water reactor at Arak. Another aspect of this defiance was to curtail cooperation with the IAEA to what Tehran determined was the bare minimum.

To forestall a preemptive military attack against its nuclear complex by Israel or the United States, Iran was careful all along to balance its nuclear defiance by professing a willingness to continue discussions with the international community. There were many attempts over 2005–2012 to test Iran's stated desire for a diplomatic solution.[17] After shunning the E3 process for years, the Bush Administration decided to join it, along with Russia and China, expanding it into the so-called P5+1 (or EU3+3) process in 2006. The P5+1 gained no traction with Tehran before President Bush left office in early 2009.

The incoming Obama administration was committed to engaging Iran in pursuit of a diplomatic settlement and dropped the Bush administration's insistence that Iran resume suspension of uranium enrichment as a prerequisite to negotiations. In September 2009, the Obama administration creatively proposed that Iran swap the low-enriched uranium it had produced by then for an equivalent amount of near-20 percent enriched uranium fuel that was now needed for the Tehran Research Reactor but which Iran was unable to manufacture by itself.

After Iranian negotiators accepted the "fuel swap" proposal in principle, the deal foundered on the shoals of Iranian domestic politics.[18] The Supreme Leader was still in no mood to compromise and factions opposed to President Ahmadinejad refused to hand him a diplomatic victory.

Doubts about Tehran's intentions where amplified at this time with the discovery that Iran was building another secret uranium enrichment site, this time beneath a mountain at Fordow to withstand air attack. Iran was forced to acknowledge the facility and to apply IAEA safeguards to it. Turkey and Brazil sought to resurrect the fuel swap deal with the Tehran Declaration of 2010 but Iran's last-minute enthusiasm was seen by the Obama administration as a cynical attempt to forestall another round of sanctions which was gaining momentum at the UN Security Council. Despite earlier encouragement of the mediation effort, President Obama set aside the trilateral deal and secured the passage of United Nations Security Council (UNSC) Resolution 1929, further tightening sanctions against Tehran. Iran responded by escalating its enrichment of uranium to near-20 percent to produce the research reactor fuel on its own. It also denied admission to certain IAEA inspectors and announced that it was preparing to build ten additional enrichment facilities.

Turning points, 2013

Following a dubious re-election in 2009, a popular uprising in protest, and its violent suppression by the regime, President Ahmadinejad proved to be a highly polarizing figure, even managing to alienate Supreme Leader Khamenei by the end of his tenure. Against this backdrop, the Iranian presidential election of 2013 proved to be a referendum on the regime's nuclear policy. The campaign pitted two nuclear negotiators against each other, President Ahmadinejad's appointee, Said Jalili, and Hassan Rouhani. The third televised debate among all eight candidates underscored elite dissatisfaction with Iran's nuclear defiance, particularly as US and European Union sanctions against the oil and banking sectors were exacting a harsh toll on Iran's economy. Rouhani openly questioned the regime's single-minded pursuit of enrichment, noting,

> All of our problems stem from this – that we didn't make the utmost effort to prevent the [nuclear] dossier from going to the UN Security Council. It's good to have [uranium enrichment] centrifuges running, providing people's lives and sustenance are also spinning.[19]

Rouhani promised to quickly resolve the nuclear dispute and get the sanctions lifted. He won the election decisively and took office in August 2013.

Having been marginalized politically during Ahmadinejad's eight-year presidency, Rouhani had ample time to strategize how to extract Iran from its nuclear predicament. He was receptive to secret back-channel negotiations with US officials to begin framing a deal.[20] Negotiations with the P5+1 resumed in October 2013, with Foreign Minister Javad Zarif being designated as Iran's new lead nuclear negotiator. A Joint Plan of Action (JPOA) was agreed on November 24, 2013. Under its terms,[21] Iran agreed for the first time in eight years to accept limits on its enrichment program. Indeed, key elements were to be rolled back. Specifically, Iran committed to:

- Convert half of its stockpile of uranium enriched to 20 percent to oxide form and down-blend the remainder to an enrichment level of no more than 5 percent;
- Suspend production of uranium enriched to above 5 percent;
- No further advances in nuclear activities at the Natanz Fuel Enrichment Plant, the enrichment plant at Fordow and the Arak heavy water reactor;
- Convert uranium enriched up to 5 percent produced during the six months to oxide form when the construction of the conversion facility is completed;
- No new enrichment facilities;
- Research and development practices, including on enrichment, will continue under IAEA safeguards;
- No reprocessing of spent plutonium fuel or construction of any facility capable of reprocessing; and
- Enhanced monitoring including: providing information to the IAEA on plans for nuclear sites and the Arak reactor; negotiating a safeguards approach for the Arak reactor; allowing daily IAEA access to Natanz and Fordow; and allowing managed access to centrifuge workshops and uranium mines and mills.

In return, the P5+1 committed to:

- No new nuclear-related sanctions from the UN Security Council, the EU, and the United States;
- Pause efforts to further reduce Iran's oil sales and partial repatriation of frozen Iranian assets from oil sales;
- Suspension of US and EU sanctions on petrochemical exports and gold and precious metals;
- Suspension of US sanctions on Iran's auto industry;
- Supply and installation of spare parts for Iranian civil airplanes, including repairs and safety inspections;
- Establish a financial channel for humanitarian goods using Iran's oil revenues that are frozen abroad, which can also be used for tuition payments for Iranian students abroad and payment of Iran's UN dues; and
- Increase of the EU thresholds for non-sanctioned trade with Iran.

The JPOA also included elements of a longer-term settlement, namely:

- An agreed upon duration;
- Reflection of the rights and obligations of all NPT parties and IAEA Safeguards Agreements;
- Lifting all multilateral and unilateral sanctions on nuclear-related measures;

- Defining Iran's enrichment program with agreed upon limits;
- Resolving concerns about the Arak reactor;
- Implementing agreed upon transparency measures, including Iran's ratification and implementation of the Additional Protocol of its safeguards agreement with the IAEA;
- Cooperation on civil nuclear projects, including a light water reactor for power, research reactors, and nuclear fuel.

The JPOA was a major breakthrough in the Iranian nuclear saga, coming within President Rouhani's first 100 days in office. Reaction to the deal was mixed in Iran and pointed to the gap between the people and the ruling elite. Supreme Leader Khamenei offered tepid support, expressing both his skepticism that these latest nuclear negotiations would lead anywhere, as well as his backing for the Rouhani negotiating team. IRGC Commander General Mohammad Ali Jafari warned that continued vigilance was necessary both against potential violation of the agreement by the United States and against Iran's negotiators conceding too much in a longer-term deal.[22] In contrast, the news was greeted with elation by the Iranian people and businesses that had been bearing the brunt of the sanctions; shortly after the JPOA was announced, Iran's stock market gained 14 percent, inflation decreased, and the national currency stabilized.[23]

In the West, the JPOA had a similarly mixed reception. Most nonproliferation and Iran experts found the deal to be surprisingly good, both for changing the trajectory of Iran's nuclear program and, potentially, Iran's relations with the outside world.[24] Hardliners, particularly in the US Congress, threatened to upset the agreement by calling for new sanctions, arguing that if economic sanctions had compelled Iran to negotiate, more were needed to ensure Iran complied.[25] Israeli Prime Minister Benjamin Netanyahu was categorically opposed to the deal, insisting that Iran could not be trusted and should have no enrichment capability. President Obama announced that he would veto such sanctions and, assisted by Senate Majority Leader Harry Reid, fended off a sanctions push in the Congress in early 2014.

Under the terms of the JPOA, the IAEA was invested with monitoring Iranian compliance. The Agency issued its first two such findings of compliance, in January and February 2014. The P5+1 and Iran resumed high-level talks in February 2014 to begin the push for the longer-term pact by the end of the year. Major divisive issues remained, including the future of the IR-40 reactor, the scope and nature of constraints on the centrifuge program, and lingering questions over the nuclear program's possible military dimensions.

Iran's challenge to the NPT

As the two sides drive towards a longer-term agreement, it is useful to reflect upon the nature of Iran's challenge to the NPT, to better understand potential tests of, and benchmarks for, compliance with such an agreement, as well as to inform thinking about how to strengthen the nuclear nonproliferation regime generally.

In retrospect, it seems doubtful that the Islamic Republic of Iran accepted its basic obligation under the NPT to not acquire nuclear weapons, at least prior to 2003. The entire thrust of its activity was to secretly develop the nuclear technology and infrastructure that would enable the regime to produce fissile material for nuclear weapons. Iran's nuclear program simply could not be justified on economic grounds,[26] and the evidence of weaponization, which the IAEA deems credible, is highly incriminating (see below). Indeed, a former Obama administration official recently noted that despite their differences, the United States and Russia have always agreed that the mullahs' nuclear program was intended to produce weapons.[27] The operative language of the NPT for the purposes of inhibiting the secret development of nuclear weapons resides in Article II, the obligation not to manufacture nuclear weapons, and Article III, the obligation to accept and comply with IAEA safeguards to ensure nuclear activities and materials are strictly for peaceful purposes.

With respect to the latter, the investigation mounted by the IAEA in 2002 revealed that Iran had been systematically violating its safeguards obligations for over two decades, as it secretly built up its ability to produce enriched uranium and plutonium, the two essential ingredients for nuclear weapons. These failures can be summarized as follows:

(a) Failure to report:
   (i)   The use of imported natural UF_6 for the testing of centrifuges at the Kalaye Electric Company in 1999 and 2002, and the consequent production of enriched and depleted uranium.
   (ii) The import of natural uranium metal in 1994 and its subsequent transfer for use in laser enrichment experiments, including the production of enriched uranium, the loss of nuclear material during these operations, and the production and transfer of resulting waste.
   (iii) The production of UO_2, UO_3, UF_4, UF_6 and ammonium uranyl carbonite (AUC) from imported depleted UO_2, depleted U_3O_8 and natural U_3O_8, and the production and transfer of resulting wastes (these unreported uranium conversion activities date back to 1981, two decades before Natanz was uncovered).
   (iv) The production of UO_2 targets at the Esfahan Nuclear Technology Center (ENTC) and their irradiation in the Tehran Research Reactor (TRR), the subsequent processing of those targets, including the separation of plutonium, the production and transfer of resulting waste, and the storage of unprocessed irradiated targets at the Tehran Nuclear Research Center (TNRC).
(b) Failure to provide design information for:
   (i)   The centrifuge testing facility at the Kalaye Electric Company.
   (ii) The laser laboratories at TNRC and Lashkar Ab'ad, and locations where resulting wastes were processed and stored, including the waste storage facility at Karaj.
   (iii) The facilities at ENTC and TNRC involved in the production of UO_2, UO_3, UF_4, UF_6 and AUC.
   (iv) TRR, with respect to the irradiation of uranium targets, and the hot cell facility where the plutonium separation took place, as well as the waste handling facility at TNRC. and
(c) Failure on many occasions to cooperate to facilitate the implementation of safeguards, through concealment.[28]

It was this systematic breach of its safeguards obligations relevant to NPT Article III that led the IAEA Board of Governors to refer Iran to the UNSC in 2006.

With respect to issues impacting Article II, the IAEA released in November 2011 a highly-detailed twelve-page annex on the possible military dimensions (PMD) of Iran's nuclear program. The report summarized material made available to the IAEA by its member states and developed by the IAEA itself pertaining to nuclear explosive development indicators in Iran, such as:

• A detailed program management structure for an undeclared nuclear program involving the PHRC and Iran's Ministry of Defense and Armed Forces Logistics. Operating under the so-called "AMAD Plan," the apparent aim of this work was to provide a source of uranium for an undisclosed enrichment program, develop high-explosives for a nuclear implosion device, and adapt a ballistic missile to carry the device.

- Procurement activities under the AMAD Plan targeting equipment, materials, and services that would be useful in developing a nuclear explosive device, such as high-speed electronic switches and spark gaps, high speed cameras, neutron sources, and radiation detection and measuring equipment.
- Acquisition of nuclear materials by the AMAD Plan, including kilogram quantities of natural uranium metal, and experiments aimed at the recovery of uranium from fluoride compounds.
- Preparation of components for an explosive device. Under pressure, Iran acknowledged that it had received from the A.Q. Khan network a fifteen-page document on how to convert uranium compounds into metal and then shape the metal into hemispheres, the tell-tale signature of a nuclear weapon. The Agency further believed that Iran had acquired sophisticated nuclear-weapon designs from the Khan network and may have undertaken early work to prepare natural and highly-enriched uranium metal components for a nuclear weapon.
- Detonator development. Iran asserted that it had been developing fast-acting detonators, so-called exploding bridge wires (EBW), for civil and conventional military applications. Material in the IAEA's possession indicated that the real purpose of this work was to develop a safer alternative to detonating a nuclear weapon.
- A 2003 experiment to initiate a high explosive charge in the shape of a hemispherical shell;
- Manufacture of simulated nuclear explosive components using high density materials like tungsten, and hydrodynamic high explosive testing possibly involving nuclear materials at the Parchin military complex—another site that Iran has extensively sanitized and kept off limits to IAEA inspectors.[29]
- Modeling and calculations conducted in 2008–2009 involving spherical geometries, consisting of the core of a highly-enriched uranium (HEU) device, which could only be related to a nuclear weapon.
- Development of a neutron initiator to spark a fission chain reaction in an implosion device, including work to manufacture and possibly experiment with small capsules in this regard. Notably, technical work in this area may have continued after 2004.
- Preparations to conduct a test of a nuclear explosive, including tests to see whether Iran's EBW equipment would function reliably over long distances between a firing point and a test device located down a deep shaft.
- Modification of Iran's Shahab 3 ballistic missile to integrate a new spherical payload.
- Development of a fusing, arming, and firing system for the missile payload modification. In the IAEA's assessment, the altitude of warhead burst for this system only made sense for a nuclear payload.

For all the documented safeguards violations and evidence of nuclear weapons intent, the Islamic Republic has been unapologetic and dismissive. Tehran maintains that it was only its inability to acquire peaceful nuclear technology on the open market, in violation of its "inalienable right" under NPT Article IV, that drove it to clandestine procurement. Iran even rejects the notion that it was constructing the Natanz enrichment facility in secret, claiming that the IAEA was well aware of the project. Behind the scenes, however, Hassan Rouhani lamented that the secrecy over Natanz had been breached.[30] Tehran maintains that it is prudently trying to develop nuclear energy to reduce its reliance on oil and natural gas, which it would prefer to export and which will not last indefinitely. According to the regime, it is the constant threat of attack from Israel and the United States that compelled it to build its enrichment plant underground at Natanz; the Fordow enrichment site was later added merely as part of Iran's overall strategy of passive defense, which calls for back-up facilities to be constructed to hedge against foreign attack.

Iran rejects out of hand the material in IAEA possession on PMD, calling it fraudulent, an argument that carries some sway with the international community following the Iraq WMD intelligence debacle. Iran also points out that it has been unable to review much of this material itself because the member states who contributed it have not authorized the IAEA to make it available to Tehran. Further, Iranian officials point to a religious decree, or fatwa, issued by Supreme Leader Khamenei which prohibits Iran's production, possession, or use of nuclear weapons. Officials such as President Rouhani contend that this fatwa is a more important impediment to nuclear weapons in Iran than even the NPT:

> My first negotiation with the European ministers [following the fatwa] was on December 13, 2004, a month after the fatwa ... I told the three European ministers that they should know about two explicit guarantees from our side, one of which is the fatwa of the [Supreme Leader]. He issued the fatwa and declared the production nuclear weapons *haram* [forbidden]. This fatwa is more important to us than the NPT and its Additional Protocol, more important than any other law.[31]

Yet, there is much ambiguity surrounding the fatwa, which appears to have been issued in response to international pressure. Skeptics, including a Shi'a scholar, point to the relative ease with which Khamenei's fatwa could be revoked.[32] Of course, the unintended implication of the regime's assertion is that if the Supreme Leader determined that possession of nuclear weapons was imperative to the longevity of the Shi'a theocracy in Tehran, not even the NPT could impede it.

Worrying as this is, the Iranian challenge to the nuclear nonproliferation regime extends beyond first principles and treaty articles. Tehran also demonstrated that it was prepared to reject IAEA authorities at will. After agreeing in 2003 to adopt the Agency's Modified Code 3.1 of the Safeguards Subsidiary Arrangement – which moved up the requirement to notify the IAEA of a new nuclear facility from 180 days before nuclear material was introduced at the site to as soon as the decision was made to construct it – Iran unilaterally abrogated this commitment in 2007, even though it arguably had no legal basis to do so, since mutual consent is required.[33] Iran also demonstrated in 2005 that it was prepared to jeopardize the crucial five-yearly review of the NPT by blocking consensus in order to avert attention from its suspect nuclear behavior.[34]

Iran poses an ongoing test to the nuclear export control regime. It managed to acquire illicitly the technology, plans, and components that gave rise to its now formidable enrichment program. Tehran procured from Russian institutes technology and design assistance for the IR-40 reactor at Arak before the United States interceded in the late-1990s.[35] It also succeeded on an individual basis, hosting from 1996–2002 a former-Soviet nuclear weapons expert, Vycheslav V. Danilenko, who appears to have provided critical information for Iran's development of a nuclear implosion device.[36] Indeed, the Islamic Republic has become quite skilled at evading nuclear export controls. As recently as mid-March 2014, a senior US official reported that Iran was still actively seeking to acquire illicitly components for its nuclear and missile programs, creating front companies and engaging in other activities to conceal its procurements.[37]

Meeting the Iranian Nuclear Challenge

Crafting an enduring arrangement to ensure the Islamic Republic honors its NPT obligations will thus be an arduous, if not heroic task. Success will hinge, in part, to the extent that:

- **The ruling regime, including the IRGC, believes its security needs can be satisfied with a latent form of nuclear deterrence, that is, a perceived ability to produce nuclear weapons in time to meet a dire threat.** There are indicators that President Rouhani subscribes to the notion of latent deterrence, but given his integral role in Iran's nuclear development since the '79 Revolution, he may be a fairly recent convert.[38] At the same time, the P5+1 must have what it judges to be an adequate margin of security, that is, confidence that it could detect an Iranian move to manufacture nuclear weapons far enough in advance to thwart it, including by military means. The JPOA does not provide that margin, as it would only move Iran back a matter of weeks from being able to produce enough highly-enriched uranium for a weapon, from about one month to two.[39] It will take a combination of restraints on the number and quality of centrifuges Tehran will be permitted to operate and the amount and purity of the enriched uranium it will be allowed to possess to achieve the West's desired security objectives. For example, a benchmark of six months of warning translates into an Iranian enrichment program of 4,000 IR-1 centrifuges and possession of less than 100 kg of near-percent enriched uranium.[40] To meet the West's margin of security as it applies to the plutonium rout to the bomb, Iran will need to significantly alter is plans for the Arak research reactor.
- **Iran demonstrates in a consistent, sustained fashion that it accepts the authorities of the IAEA, ambiguous as they might sometimes be, in ensuring that nuclear activities are strictly for peaceful purposes.** This will be a real challenge for a generally recalcitrant, yet highly legalistic regime. This acceptance will be measurable against major benchmarks, such as the regime's *ratification and sustained implementation* of the IAEA Additional Protocol, which it signed in 2003. For too long, Iran's cooperation with the IAEA has been "temporary and voluntary," a favor that could be withdrawn petulantly. Another measure of Iran's change of heart will be when it plays a constructive role in the NPT Review Conference process. Indeed, the 2015 Review Conference will be President Rouhani's first major test in this regard.
- **Iran shuts down its clandestine nuclear procurement network.** There can be no confidence in Iran's disavowals of nuclear weaponry so long as its purchasing agents aggressively scour the globe looking for key nuclear materials, components, and technologies. Of course, Tehran would counter that if the West lives up to its end of the bargain, Iran would not have any need to shop the black market. Western concerns about Iranian cooperation with North Korea in sensitive technologies also will need to be addressed.
- **Lingering questions about weaponization are resolved.** For the credibility of the IAEA and Iranian assurances, the lingering questions over PMD must be resolved. Presumably, this would involve some "bargain," whereby the Iranian regime makes restitution for nuclear-weapon-related research, development, and testing – e.g., in the form of confidential disclosures to the IAEA about the work and acceptance of highly intrusive monitoring to ensure it does not resume – while not being forced to publicly admit guilt or be further penalized. One can imagine a narrative wherein "unsanctioned activities" were discovered by Iranian authorities and then reined in under the Supreme Leader's fatwa. Granting IAEA access to the suspected nuclear-explosive-related test facility at Parchin will need to be part of such a bargain.

- **The P5+1 and Iran develop habits of cooperation to resolve disputes under the agreement.** Because of the deep and mutual deficit of trust, and historic patterns of megaphone diplomacy, Iran and the West will need to develop new approaches to resolving disputes, particularly in an agreement as complex as the long-term resolution is expected to be. The JPOA recognized this need by creating a Joint Commission of the EU3/EU+3 and Iran to monitor implementation measures and "address issues that may arise." The Joint Commission assigns responsibility for verification of nuclear-related measures to the IAEA and effectively links the P5+1 process to the IAEA's separate investigation of Iran's nuclear program. Presumably, the longer-term agreement will carry forward this mechanism and enable the parties to address their concerns with less risk of politicization.
- **More broadly, new efforts are needed to clarify and uphold the NPT Article II obligation by Nonnuclear-Weapon State parties not to manufacture nuclear weapons.** The framers of the NPT grappled with where to draw the line between permissible nuclear activity and prohibited nuclear weapons development. An early draft of the Treaty actually extended the Article II prohibition to "*prepare for* the manufacture of nuclear weapons." In the end, "prepare for" was dropped from Article II but the United States clarified in 1968 that, "facts indicating that the purpose of a particular activity was the acquisition of a nuclear explosive device would tend to show non-compliance [with Article II]."[41] Often overlooked is that this US interpretation was accepted by the Soviet Union and our European allies at the time.[42] In order to discourage Iran and those that would follow its proliferation pathway, it is necessary to reinforce Article II and uphold it. This could be done through retrospective analysis of NPT negotiating history, assessing the lessons learned from Iran, and fresh thinking about scientific, institutional, and normative approaches to build a higher barrier between nuclear energy and nuclear weapons.

The prospects for a successful and lasting diplomatic resolution of the Iranian nuclear challenge are uncertain. As of March 2014, the Rouhani Administration has indicated its willingness to be more forthcoming on issues like modification of the Arak research reactor and PMD, while at the same time drawing a firm red line around dismantling nuclear facilities, such as Fordow. The economic benefits of Iran's new-found spirit of cooperation are starting to flow into the regime's depleted coffers, enabling Rouhani to hold his nuclear critics at bay. Time will tell if the two sides' diplomats are able to produce a longer-term arrangement that brings Iran back into the NPT fold. What is clear is that Iran's nuclear activities will bear close watching for some time to come.

Notes

1. Shortly after India tested its nuclear device in 1974, the Shah was asked whether Iran would also possess nuclear weapons. He replied, "Without any doubt, and sooner than one would think." Quoted in Leonard S. Spector, *Going Nuclear* (Cambridge, MA: Ballinger, 1987), p. 259, n. 87. See also pp. 45–57.
2. Ray Takeyh, "What Will Iran's New President Do? His Memoir Offers Some Clues," op-ed, *The Washington Post,* July 5, 2013, http://articles.washingtonpost.com/2013-07-05/opinions/40382689_1_nuclear-program-iran-s-regime.
3. David Segal, "Atomic Ayatollahs," *The Washington Post,* April 12, 1987, p. D1.
4. Institute for Science and International Security (ISIS), "Internal IAEA Information Links the Supreme Leader to 1984 Decision to Seek a Nuclear Arsenal," April 20, 2012, http://isis-online.org/uploads/isis-reports/documents/Khamenei_1984_statement_20April2012.pdf.
5. "A History of Iran's Nuclear Program," *Iran Watch,* March 1, 2012, www.iranwatch.org/our-publications/weapon-program-background-report/history-irans-nuclear-program.

6. Robert J. Einhorn and Gary Samore, "Ending Russian Assistance to Iran's Nuclear Bomb," *Survival,* Vol. 44, No. 2 (Summer 2002), pp. 51–70.
7. International Atomic Energy Agency, "Implementation of the NPT Safeguards Agreement and Relevant Provisions of Security Council Resolutions 1737 (2006) and 1747 (2007) in the Islamic Republic of Iran," GOV/2007/58, November 15, 2007, pp. 3–5, http://iaea.org/Publications/Documents/Board/2007/gov2007-58.pdf. See also, International Atomic Energy Agency, "Implementation of the NPT Safeguards Agreement and Relevant Provisions of Security Council Resolutions in the Islamic Republic of Iran," GOV/2011/65, November 8, 2011, Annex, pp. 1–2, 7–8, http://iaea.org/Publications/Documents/Board/2011/gov2011-65.pdf.
8. Karl Vick, "Another Nuclear Program Found in Iran," *The Washington Post,* February 24, 2004, p. A1.
9. As recounted by Iranian nuclear negotiator at the time, Seyed Hussein Mousavian, in *The Iranian Nuclear Crisis: A Memoir* (Washington, DC: The Carnegie Endowment for International Peace, 2012), pp. 107–108.
10. Mehdi Mohammadi, "Nuclear Case From Beginning to End in Interview With Dr Hasan Rowhani (Part 1): We Are Testing Europe," *Tehran Keyhan,* July 26, 2005, translation available at http://lewis.armscontrolwonk.com/files/2012/08/Rowhani_Interview.pdf.
11. International Atomic Energy Agency, "Implementation of the NPT Safeguards Agreement in the Islamic Republic of Iran," GOV/2003/40, June 6, 2003, pp. 2–3, http://iaea.org/Publications/Documents/Board/2003/gov2003-40.pdf. See also, International Atomic Energy Agency, "Implementation of the NPT Safeguards Agreement in the Islamic Republic of Iran," GOV/2003/75, November 10, 2003, pp. 3–7, http://iaea.org/Publications/Documents/Board/2003/gov2003-75.pdf.
12. Institute for Science and International Security, "ISIS Imagery Brief: Destruction at Iranian Site Raises New Questions About Iran's Nuclear Activities," ISIS Report, June 17, 2004, http://isis-online.org/isis-reports/detail/isis-imagery-brief-destruction-at-iranian-site-raises-new-questions-about-i/8.
13. International Atomic Energy Agency, "Implementation of the NPT Safeguards Agreement in the Islamic Republic of Iran," GOV/2004/60, September 1, 2004, p. 8, www.iaea.org/Publications/Documents/Board/2004/gov2004-60.pdf.
14. International Atomic Energy Agency, "Implementation of the NPT Safeguards Agreement in the Islamic Republic of Iran," GOV/2004/83, November 15, 2004, pp. 21–22, http://iaea.org/Publications/Documents/Board/2004/gov2004-83.pdf.
15. Francois Nicoullaud, "Rouhani and the Iranian Bomb," op-ed, *New York Times,* July 26, 2013, www.nytimes.com/2013/07/27/opinion/global/rouhani-and-the-iranian-bomb.html.
16. National Intelligence Council, "Iran: Nuclear Intentions and Capabilities," Unclassified Executive Summary of a National Intelligence Estimate Office of the Director of National Intelligence, November 2007, www.dni.gov/files/documents/Newsroom/Reports%20and%20Pubs/20071203_release.pdf.
17. See Arms Control Association, "History of Official Proposals on the Iranian Nuclear Issue," Arms Control Association website, January 2014, www.armscontrol.org/factsheets/Iran_Nuclear_Proposals.
18. Nima Gerami, "Leadership Divided? The Domestic Politics of Iran's Nuclear Debate," *Policy Focus,* No. 134, Washington Institute for Near East Policy, February 2014, pp. 33–34, www.washingtoninstitute.org/uploads/PolicyFocus134_Gerami-2.pdf.
19. Scott Peterson, "Stalled Nuclear Talks Fuel Sharp Exchange at Iran's Final Presidential Debate," *Christian Science Monitor,* June 8, 2013, www.csmonitor.com/World/Middle-East/2013/0608/Stalled-nuclear-talks-fuel-sharp-exchange-at-Iran-s-final-presidential-debate.
20. Laura Rozen, "Three Days in March: New Details on How US, Iran Opened Direct Talks," *The Back Channel,* January 8, 2014, http://backchannel.al-monitor.com/index.php/2014/01/7484/three-days-in-march-new-details-on-the-u-s-iran-backchannel/.
21. Arms Control Association, "History of Official Proposals." The full text of the Joint Plan of Action is available at European External Action, "Joint Plan of Action," November 24, 2013, http://eeas.europa.eu/statements/docs/2013/131124_03_en.pdf.
22. See, for example, Annie Tracy Samuel, "Revolutionary Guard is Cautiously Open to Nuclear Deal," *Iran Matters,* Belfer Center for Science and International Affairs, Harvard University, December 20, 2013, http://belfercenter.ksg.harvard.edu/publication/23779/revolutionary_guard_is_cautiously_open_to_nuclear_deal.html.

23. Thomas Erdbrink, "New Emotion, Hope, Sweeps Across Iran in Aftermath of Temporary Nuclear Pact," *New York Times,* December 5, 2013, www.nytimes.com/2013/12/06/world/middleeast/new-emotion-hope-sweeps-across-iran-in-aftermath-of-temporary-nuclear-pact.html.
24. See, for example, Mark Fitzpatrick, "The Surprisingly Good Geneva Deal," *Politics and Strategy Blog,* International Institute for Strategic Studies, November 25, 2013, www.iiss.org/en/politics%20and%20strategy/blogsections/2013-98d0/november-47b6/geneva-deal-0ef2.
25. See, for example, Niels Lesniewski, "Schumer, Menedez Renew Calls for New Iran Sanctions," *#WGBD Blog,* Roll Call, November 24, 2013, http://blogs.rollcall.com/wgdb/schumer-menendez-renew-calls-for-new-iran-sanctions/.
26. Ali Vaez and Karim Sadjadpour, *Iran's Nuclear Odyssey: Costs and Risks* (Washington, DC: Carnegie Endowment for International Peace, 2013), pp. 13–17.
27. Gary Samore, "Negotiating with Iran: Prospects and Problems," International Institute for Strategic Studies, London, March 10, 2014, www.iiss.org/en/events/events/archive/2014-0f13/march-a2fd/negotiating-with-iran-9999.
28. International Atomic Energy Agency, "Implementation of the NPT Safeguards Agreement in the Islamic Republic of Iran," GOV/2003/75, November 10, 2003, p. 9 and Annex 1, http://iaea.org/Publications/Documents/Board/2003/gov2003-75.pdf.
29. David Albright and Serena Kelleher-Vergantini, "Changes Visible at Parchin Nuclear Site: Why Parchin Matters to a Final Deal," ISIS Report, February 25, 2014, http://isis-online.org/isis-reports/detail/changes-visible-at-parchin-nuclear-site/8. Iran maintains that no nuclear-related activity was conducted at the site and therefore the IAEA has no right of access. While Iran and the IAEA recently concluded a seven-point plan on inspections of nuclear facilities in February 2014, access to Parchin was not on the list.
30. Rouhani noted in a speech to Iran's Supreme Cultural Revolution Council that, "One of the [Council] members indicated here that all this [nuclear development] should have been done in secret. This was the intention; this never was supposed to be in the open. But in any case, the spies exposed it. We did not want to declare all this." Text of speech by Supreme National Security Council Secretary Hassan Rohani to the Supreme Cultural Revolution Council; place and date not given: "Beyond the Challenges Facing Iran and the IAEA Concerning the Nuclear Dossier," *Rahbord* (in Persian), September 30, 2005. Translation available at, http://lewis.armscontrolwonk.com/files/2012/08/Rahbord.pdf.
31. Muhammad Sahimi, "Former Iran Nuclear Negotiator: Bush Negotiation Bid was Rebuffed," Tehran Bureau, May 12, 2012, www.pbs.org/wgbh/pages/frontline/tehranbureau/2012/05/qa-formeriran-nuclear-negotiator-bush-negotiation-bid-was-rebuffed.html.
32. See, for example, Michael Eisenstadt and Mehdi Khalaji, "Nuclear Fatwa: Religion and Politics in Iran's Proliferation Strategy," Washington Institute for Near East Policy, September 2011, www.washingtoninstitute.org/uploads/Documents/pubs/PolicyFocus115.pdf.
33. The legal contentions over this issue are addressed by James Acton and Dan Joyner, respectively, at, "Iran Violated International Obligations on Qom Facility," Carnegie Endowment for International Peace, September 25, 2009, http://carnegieendowment.org/2009/09/25/iran-violated-international-obligations-on-qom-facility/6u2, and "The Qom Enrichment Facility: Was Iran Legally Bound to Disclose?" *Jurist,* March 5, 2010, http://jurist.law.pitt.edu/forumy/2010/03/qom-enrichment-facility-was-iran.php.
34. Observers point out that others, such as the United States, shared responsibility for the failure of the Conference to achieve consensus. See Harald Müller, "The 2005 NPT Review Conference: Reasons and Consequences of Failure and Options for Repair," Weapons of Mass Destruction Commission Report No. 31, 2005, www.blixassociates.com/wp-content/uploads/2011/03/No31.pdf.
35. Institute for Science and International Security, "Update on the Arak Reactor in Iran," ISIS Report, August 25, 2009, http://isis-online.org/uploads/isis-reports/documents/Arak_Update_25_August2009.pdf.
36. David Albright, Paul Brannan, Mark Gorwitz and Andrea Stricker, "ISIS Analysis of IAEA Iran Safeguards Report: Part II – Iran's Work and Foreign Assistance on a Multipoint Initiation System for a Nuclear Weapon," ISIS Report, November 13, 2011, http://isis-online.org/isis-reports/detail/irans-work-and-foreign-assistance-on-a-multipoint-initiation-system-for-a-n/.
37. William Maclean, "Iran Pursuing Banned Items for Nuclear, Missile Work – US Official," *Reuters,* March 16, 2014, http://uk.reuters.com/article/2014/03/16/uk-iran-nuclear-supplies-idUKBREA2F0KD20140316.

38. "…during a dinner in Tehran with visiting American [nonproliferation] experts in 2005, Iranian leaders Hashemi Rafsanjani and Hassan Rowhani flatly declared that the country's nuclear-weapon research had been halted because Iran felt it did not need the actual bombs, only the ability to show the world it could. 'Look, as long as we can enrich uranium and master the [nuclear] fuel cycle, we don't need anything else,' Rafsanjani said at the dinner, according to George Perkovich of the Carnegie Endowment for International Peace. 'Our neighbors will be able to draw the proper conclusions.'" Peter Baker and Dafna Linzer, "Diving Deep, Unearthing a Surprise," *The Washington Post*, December 8, 2007, www.washingtonpost.com/wp-dyn/content/article/2007/12/07/AR2007120702418.html.

39. David Albright, "The Rocky Path to a Long-Term Settlement with Iran," op-ed, *The Washington Post*, November 25, 2013, www.washingtonpost.com/opinions/reaching-a-final-iran-deal-will-be-a-tough-road/2013/11/25/dcc2f752-55ef-11e3-ba82-16ed03681809_story.html. For an illuminating football analogy, see Graham Allison, "The Red-Zone Theory of the Iran Nuclear Deal," *The Atlantic*, November 27, 2013, www.theatlantic.com/international/archive/2013/11/the-red-zone-theory-of-the-iran-nuclear-deal/281918/.

40. David Albright, Patrick Migliorini, Christina Walrond, and Houston Wood, "Maintaining at Least a Six-Month Breakout Timeline: Further Reducing Iran's Near 20 Percent Stock of LEU," ISIS Report, February 17, 2004, http://isis-online.org/uploads/isis-reports/documents/20_pct_stock_cap_17Feb2014-final.pdf.

41. "Extended Remarks by William Foster Regarding Possible NPT Article II Violations," July 10, 1968, in Paul K. Kerr, "Iran's Nuclear Program: Tehran's Compliance with International Obligations," Congressional Research Service, March 31, 2009, www.fas.org/sgp/crs/nuke/R40094.pdf.

42. George Bunn and Roland Timerbaev, *Nuclear Verification Under the NPT: What Should It Cover – How Far May It Go?* (Program for Promoting Nuclear Non-Proliferation, April 1994), pp. 4–5.

4

NUCLEAR PROLIFERATION, DETERRENCE AND STRATEGIC STABILITY IN EAST ASIA

The United States, China and Japan in a changing strategic landscape

Michito Tsuruoka

East Asia represents one of the most "proliferated" regions in the world when it comes to nuclear weapons. Four out of six stakeholders in the region are either nuclear weapon states recognized by the Nonproliferation Treaty (NPT) or the one widely thought to possess nuclear weapons – the United States, Russia and China are in the former category, while North Korea in the latter category. Only Japan and the Republic of Korea (South Korea) are nonnuclear powers, although the two have advanced civilian nuclear energy programs and not a small number of experts regard those countries as potential nuclear-weapon states given their nuclear expertise and the possession of fissile materials.

As China's nuclear arsenal develops both in quantitative and qualitative terms, the question of how to establish and manage strategic stability between the United States and China becomes more pertinent. At the same time, Japan and South Korea are under explicit US nuclear guarantee, which represents yet another characteristic of the region, not enjoyed (or needed) by other regions except Europe in the context of the North Atlantic Treaty Organization (NATO). In short, the role of nuclear weapons – and more specifically the role of extended nuclear deterrence – in the region is believed to be rising, unlike Europe and some other regions of the world, in light of North Korea's development and the rise of China's military power including its nuclear weapons.[1]

Related to this is the role of ballistic missile defense (BMD). East Asia is actually the region where the deployment of BMD is most advanced in the world. Japan is an active players of the US-led development and deployment of BMD, which has largely been driven by ballistic missile threats from North Korea for more than a decade. Beyond technical development, the issues being more intensively discussed include the role of BMD in the overall deterrence posture, particularly in relation to nuclear weapons, and its implications for strategic stability between the United States and China.

Current interest in East Asian security has tended to focus on maritime, territorial and diplomatic disputes in recent years, and Japan's security strategy and defense posture put increasing emphasis on what is called the "gray-zone" of low-intensity conflicts – somewhere between war and peace – strengthening, for example, amphibious capability and intelligence, surveillance and reconnaissance (ISR) in view of the tensions in the East China Sea. Nonetheless, this does not mean that high-end issues such as nuclear deterrence and strategic stability are less relevant in today's security environment in the Asia-Pacific. To the contrary, as the security situation becomes less predictable in overall terms, the value of ultimate guarantee of security – particularly nuclear deterrence – comes under a new light and becomes more important. Consequently, policy and academic interests in extended deterrence and the role of nuclear weapons have increased substantially recently, evidenced by a growing number of publications on those topics in the region.[2]

This chapter will focus on two of arguably the most significant aspects of East Asia's strategic landscape, namely the extended deterrence relationship between the United States and Japan, and strategic stability between the United States and China: the two are closely connected with each other in the sense that the direction of US-China strategic relationship inevitably influences Tokyo's views on its alliance with the United States as well as Beijing's strategic calculations, and Washington needs a delicate balance between its assurances to Japan – and to South Korea and other allies and partners in the region – and desirable strategic stability with China.

Another reason why the developments and debates in East Asia are relevant in a wider and global context lies with the fact that the region faces a set of questions regarding extended deterrence, BMD and strategic stability common to other regions in the world. In the Western strategic community, those are the topics that have been explored in the context of the Cold War and remain primarily understood in relation to Russia, such as in the context of US-Russia and NATO-Russia relations. However, East Asian issues – such as extended deterrence debates between the United States and Japan, the relationship between nuclear weapons and BMD, and strategic stability between the United States and China – are becoming a bigger factor in shaping US strategic thinking and more pertinent in the international security scene broadly.

The extended deterrence relationship between the United States and Japan

Evolution of Japan's debates

Tokyo's thinking on deterrence – particularly extended deterrence provided by the United States – is evolving to adjust to a changing context in which the US-Japan alliance is situated, not least in light of developments in North Korea and China. Japanese officials and experts are now seen to be more concerned about the effectiveness of deterrence. It may be easy to argue that the Japanese are losing their confidence in the US security guarantee. However, it is not just a matter of the credibility of the US commitment, but, probably more fundamentally, it has to do with the growing requirement for deterrence because of the deteriorating security environment surrounding Japan. In other words, it is not necessarily that "supply" of deterrence is declining, but that "demand" is increasing. And the real challenge is to increase the supply of deterrence at least to keep pace with increasing demand – and there should be no deficit of deterrence during that process, requiring the strengthening of conventional capabilities and more integration of efforts and operational cooperation between the two countries' forces.

While extended deterrence involves not only the nuclear element, but also conventional and even nonmilitary aspects, the fact remains that the US nuclear commitment is the ultimate guarantee of the defense of Japan. An explicit nuclear guarantee, as opposed to a more general nature of commitment from Washington, was something that Tokyo has tried hard to get since the early days of the alliance relationship. Prime Minister Eisaku Sato and his successors in the 1960s and 1970s repeatedly asked their US counterparts to come up with a clearer nuclear commitment, which finally materialized in the November 1975 Joint Statement between President Lyndon Johnson and Prime Minister Takeo Miki, which stated that: "the US nuclear deterrent is an important contributor to the security of Japan. In this connection, the President reassured the Prime Minister that the United States would continue to abide by its defense commitment to Japan."[3] In Tokyo's mind, China's first nuclear test in 1964 and the issue of joining the NPT loomed large. For Japan to decide to remain a nonnuclear weapon state in an increasingly nuclearized world then – in other words, abandon permanently the option of developing its own nuclear weapons – securing a clear US nuclear commitment was, after all, considered to be indispensable.[4]

The English literature on Japan's nuclear policy, which is published mainly in the United States, seems to be too much dominated by concerns about Japan's nuclear option – the question whether Japan will go nuclear or not – which is substantially different – almost out of touch – from the mainstream policy and academic debates in Japan. American academic interest in Japan's option of seeking its own nuclear weapons is understandable and clearly in line with the US national security interest of preventing nuclear proliferation. In the context of broader issues of nonproliferation, the Japanese case is often examined in parallel with the cases of Iran, Libya, North Korea, South Korea, South Africa, India, and others.[5] While it is true that most academic literature – actually many are written by Japanese experts – makes valuable contributions and presents balanced conclusions reflecting the actual state of affairs in Japan,[6] it is still worth questioning whether this sort of perspective, heavily focused on the possibility of Japan's going nuclear, is most appropriate and policy-relevant in thinking about what seems fundamentally to be a case of extended deterrence rather than that of proliferation. The basic reality remains that as long as the US nuclear commitment is perceived to be credible, Japan would not have to think about its own nuclear option. In fact, the issues that Washington and Tokyo need to address in managing their extended deterrence relationship are more similar to those that NATO and other US allies such as Australia face, rather than those common to the "rogue" cases such as Iran and Libya. Therefore, more comparative analysis between NATO and US allies in Asia – mainly Japan, South Korea, and Australia – seems necessary.[7]

Regarding Japan's policy on nuclear issues, while the most famous is the "Three Nonnuclear Principles" (1967) of not possessing, not producing, and not allowing the introduction of (US) nuclear weapons onto Japan's soil, it does not say anything about extended nuclear deterrence. What is more notable in relation to extended deterrence is Sato's "Four Pillars of Nuclear Policies" (1968) of upholding the three nonnuclear principles, promoting nuclear disarmament, relying on US nuclear deterrent for Japan's defense, and using nuclear energy for peaceful purposes. Japan's almost unique peaceful coexistence of seemingly incompatible positions on major nuclear issues – antinuclear weapon policy and sentiment including strong support for nuclear disarmament; reliance on US nuclear guarantees for security; and broad public support prior to the Fukushima Daiichi accident in 2011 for the government's policy of using nuclear energy – has emerged as a result.[8] One notable aspect of this is that antinuclear weapon movements and antinuclear energy movements have largely been separate and many of those in the former camp had not paid much attention to the use of nuclear energy for a long time – at least until Fukushima.

The notion of "relying" on US nuclear deterrent, first introduced by Prime Minister Sato, was repeatedly codified in government defense documents – most notably the 1976, 1995, and 2004 National Defense Program Guidelines (NDPG).[9] On the other hand, however, Tokyo, in fact, did not pay sustained attention to whether and how it could actually work when needed. As a result, the US-Japan alliance had long lacked substantial dialogue on deterrence, particularly on extended nuclear deterrence.

Enhancing extended deterrence through dialogue

It was only in 2010 that the two countries launched what is called an extended deterrence dialogue (EDD), the first-ever dedicated framework of talks on deterrence issues including the nuclear element. Its launch certainly reflected deteriorating security perceptions in Japan and the increasing need for a stronger US commitment. However, it can also be argued that it is just natural for allies in any normal alliance relationships to discuss deterrence issues, from which the US-Japan alliance should not be an exception. Therefore, the real question to be asked regarding the start of the deterrence dialogue between the United States and Japan is not why it became suddenly necessary in 2010, but why it had not been thought to be needed for such a long period.

James Schoff succinctly argues that "the details about how deterrence worked mattered little" for Japan during the Cold War.[10] First, the level of threat perception in Japan was relatively low throughout the Cold War. Moreover, because any Soviet aggression to Japan was thought to be part of a broader Soviet offensive and Japan was not likely to be the sole target, Tokyo did not have to think by itself about how to make deterrence credible to Moscow – it was thought to be something Washington would address. Second, the conventional balance has always been in favor of the US-Japan side *vis-à-vis* the Soviet Union or China, because of which, Japan, unlike NATO during the Cold War, did not have to rely too much on nuclear weapons. Third, constitutional and other domestic constraints in Japan prevented the government from engaging in deterrence discussions with the United States in substantial and operational terms. Because of this, it is said that Japanese officials were hesitant to engage in detailed discussions on the workings of extended deterrence for a long time.[11]

While not much information has been made available to the public on the US-Japan extended deterrence dialogue,[12] it is generally considered to have been successful so far.[13] For the United States, the overall purpose of the dialogue is to reassure Japan – maintain the credibility of its commitment in the eyes of the Japanese – covering three main functions: to tell the Japanese about US policies and thinking on deterrence; to address common problems together such as the situation in North Korea (including conducting table-top exercises); and to give the Japanese opportunities to actually see US capabilities supporting extended deterrence, such as intercontinental and submarine-launched ballistic missiles and strategic bombers. Given that Japan had not engaged in substantial discussions on those deterrence-related matters with the United States in the past, the initial phase of the new dialogue is said to have largely been an educational exercise for Japanese officials about US policies, thinking, posture, etc. The Obama administration has found this dialogue fruitful and decided to make it a permanent framework.[14]

For the dialogue to become more substantial beyond the initial "education" phase – and after all, for the credibility of the US commitment to be enhanced and the deterrence posture of the US-Japan alliance strengthened – the following three aspects need to be considered thoroughly. In addition to what officials discuss in their government-to-government talks, debates in the academic and policy community also need to be deepened.

The first question to be explored, simply put, is what Tokyo expects, particularly regarding the worst-case scenario involving high-intensity contingencies. There does not seem to be a consensus – or even an in-depth discussion – in Japan regarding under what circumstances Tokyo wants Washington to threaten to use or actually employ nuclear weapons, and this needs to be consciously complemented by examinations on under what circumstances Japan does not want the United States to resort to nuclear weapons. In the US-Japan extended deterrence relationship, while Japan certainly expects the United States to honor its nuclear commitment – in other words, to use nuclear weapons – it is also clear that Tokyo does not want to see any premature use of nuclear weapons by the United States in its vicinity. Western Europe faced a similar dilemma during the Cold War. After all, America's nuclear use, seen from its allies, should neither be too early, nor too late.

Second, there is still a question to what extent Washington is prepared to involve the Japanese – and other allies in the region for that matter – in its nuclear deterrence policy. It is undeniable that what Tokyo ultimately wants is to have a say in US policy, whether in operational or conceptual terms. The level of US preparedness in this regard is assumed to be determined by the degree of deterrence burden-sharing by Japan as well as by US domestic considerations. The United Kingdom's role as an independent nuclear power and NATO as a nuclear alliance exemplified by its unique nuclear-sharing arrangements are seen to be examples of the most advanced form of nuclear burden-sharing with the United States. Japan's challenge is to make its deterrence (including nuclear) dialogue with the United States substantial without such direct physical elements. The same challenge is shared by South Korea and other US allies outside NATO. While the idea of introducing a NATO-style nuclear-sharing mechanism to the US-Japan alliance is raised from time to time in the Japanese debates,[15] the likelihood of such an eventuality remains near zero. Rather, in view of a future possibility of the withdrawal of all US nuclear weapons from Europe, deterrence and nuclear dialogue without the physical element of nuclear-sharing could one day become a challenge for the NATO countries as well, which is a scenario much likelier than Japan's introducing nuclear-sharing with the United States.[16] Ultimately, the generic question is how to construct a mechanism for risk- and responsibility-sharing, which has constituted the very core of NATO's nuclear-sharing arrangements, without the physical element of nuclear-sharing.

The third question concerns Japan's operational role in strategic contingencies, involving the possibility of a threat or use of nuclear weapons. On the Japanese side, it has to do with constitutional and other issues particularly concerning the use of force, which Tokyo needs to address before tackling the ultimate operational aspects of extended nuclear deterrence. Without any realistic possibility of Japan's substantial operational military involvement in such contingencies, Tokyo's wish for more information sharing on nuclear matters or exerting influence would not make sense for Washington. In addition to BMD, how to incorporate conventional elements in deterrence discussions might be of increasing significance. The United States and Japan have been dealing with Japan's operational role in various contingencies and the division of labor between the two countries in the context of what is called roles, missions, and capabilities (RMC). In light of increasing tensions with China, particularly in the East China Sea, there needs to be more efforts to bridge between the high-end extended deterrence perspectives and the RMC discussions: as it now stands, the two do not seem to be fully connected with each other.

Being fully aware of those questions and challenges, Tokyo has from the outset intentionally favored a more inclusive and comprehensive approach to extended deterrence, without exclusively focusing on the nuclear aspect of it. Therefore, what has materialized is deliberately not a "nuclear dialogue."[17] This suited US thinking that emphasizes the comprehensive nature of extended deterrence as well.[18] In this context, Japan's role in BMD – including both its own deployment and a joint research and development program with the United States – is recognized as a contribution to the alliance's deterrence posture[19] – in other words, as a concrete example of deterrence burden-sharing by Japan.

Reflecting this, Japan's December 2010 defense document – the National Defense Program Guidelines – ceased the terminology of "relying" on US strategic deterrent. Instead, it states that as long as nuclear weapons exist, the extended deterrence provided by the United States, with nuclear deterrent as a vital element, will be indispensable. In order to maintain and improve the credibility of the extended deterrence, Japan will closely cooperate with the United States, and will also appropriately implement *its own efforts*, including ballistic missile defense and civil protection.[20]

The almost identical sentence is repeated in the latest 2013 NDPG and the first-ever National Security Strategy, both adopted in December 2013.[21] For Japan, beyond physical defense of its territory and the role in deterrence, BMD has been a catalyst of driving the transformation of the Self-Defense Forces in terms of legal structure, command and control, and US-Japan operational cooperation.[22]

Recognizing and addressing the gaps

In a broader account, for the purpose of strengthening the US-Japan deterrence posture and particularly enhancing Japanese confidence in the US extended deterrence commitment, it is not helpful to pretend that the two countries' perceptions on nuclear and deterrence issues are always identical. Given the substantial differences in geostrategic location, military power, strategic culture and history, the existence of gaps between the two allies is just natural. How to deal with such differences is always the most important task of alliance management.

Debates on the retirement of TLAM-N, nuclear tipped Tomahawk land attack cruise missile, in the run-up to the release of the 2010 Nuclear Posture Review Report (NPR) can be seen as one of the most typical of such gaps. Whereas the US position articulated by the NPR was that the role of TLAM-N could be substituted by other means including strategic bombers and nuclear-capable fighters, some Japanese, particularly before the release of the NPR, were reported as being worried about adverse implications its retirement would cause to the credibility of extended deterrence.[23] What these debates have raised is a generic question of whether the United States needs to possess a particular weapon system solely to reassure its allies regardless of its military utility. It is not surprising that Washington's view as an extended deterrence provider is often different from perceptions on the receiving end of US commitment. The TLAM-N debates were a timely reminder of that.

A related issue is the sometimes tricky relationship between the US deterrent capability in overall terms and the credibility of its extended nuclear deterrence commitment. Japan and other US allies cannot legitimately argue that the current US nuclear arsenal in terms of the number of warheads and the aggregate destructive power is too small: however, factors other than the numerical capability of the deterrent matter more in the real world. The question of how low the United States can go in terms of the number of strategic warheads in disarmament without undermining allies' confidence in US nuclear commitment is a case in point.[24] Mainly for political or psychological reasons, what is deemed sufficient for the purpose of US military planning including extended deterrence commitment might not be seen as sufficient in terms of reassuring the allies. This is a classic problem and will not go away.[25]

Second, the Barack Obama administration's goal of reducing the role of nuclear weapons cannot be said to be fully embraced even by US allies including Japan despite congratulatory comments on the NPR by a number of US allies, particularly when taking into account the accompanying notion that the nonnuclear elements or conventional capabilities need to be strengthened for the purpose of reducing the role of nuclear weapons.[26] As NATO's Deterrence and Defence Posture Review (DDPR) of April 2012 clearly stated, "Missile defence can complement the role of nuclear weapons in deterrence; *it cannot substitute for them*."[27] This represents a widely accepted understanding regarding the relationship between nuclear weapons and BMD. While it is partly a matter of definition and degree, what the NPR and other US documents appear to be strongly indicating is a direct link between the role of nuclear weapons and that of other (conventional) capabilities, which was repeated in June 2013 that, "As the role of nuclear weapons is reduced in US national security strategy, these nonnuclear elements [conventional weapons and missile defense] will *take on a greater share of the deterrence burden.*"[28]

For Japan, whereas BMD is mainly intended to address ballistic missile threats from North Korea, extended nuclear deterrence is not just about North Korea – it is certainly part of Japan's efforts to address challenges of China. Simply put, BMD and nuclear deterrence are essentially addressing different sets of concerns, which cannot be a basis for any substitutable relationship between nuclear weapons and missile defense.

Furthermore, while it is still debatable, the 2010 and 2013 NDPGs and the 2013 National Security Strategy seem to have elevated – rather than reduced – the role of US nuclear deterrent as part of Japan's deterrence and defense, at least as far as the text is concerned, by describing the nuclear deterrent as representing the "core" of extended deterrence.[29] Meanwhile, the conventional balance is shifting and the United States – and US-Japan – advantage is declining in the face of China's rapid conventional development. If these trends continue, Washington, in theory, may have to rely more – not less – on nuclear weapons in the East Asian theater in the years to come, as was the case during the Cold War in the European theater, despite the Obama administration's commitment to the contrary. While emphasizing the significance of the nuclear element of extended deterrence, this scenario would not be something that Tokyo really wants to see, given its long-held support for nuclear disarmament. What this indicates is the increasing relevance of Japan's conventional capability not only for actual operational considerations, but also for the overall deterrence posture of the US-Japan alliance. Deterrence in the real world cannot be based exclusively in the nuclear domain.

Strategic stability between the United States and China

Mutual vulnerability?

As the US-Japan alliance becomes more of a tool to address concerns about and challenges from China, the level of direct linkage between the US-Japan alliance and US-China security relations increases in both directions. China's recent assertiveness, not least in the East China Sea, often has had an effect of strengthening US-Japan security and defense cooperation, although this was never Beijing's intention. China in turn needs to address the outcome of the recent strengthening of the US-Japan alliance including the development of BMD. Simultaneously, however, Tokyo cannot escape from a nightmare scenario of a US-China condominium of the Asia-Pacific region achieved at the expense of Japanese interest, which is why many Japanese – and other Asians – are worryingly following China's proposal of a "new type of major-power relationship" with the United States, and Washington's reactions to it. The United States, for its part, cannot be free from the development of Japan-China relations, most notably in the East China Sea, because of its sheer scale of impact and the alliance commitment to Japan. There is no doubt that Washington would like to see more stable and cooperative relations between Japan and China and it is no secret that it does not want to be drawn into a possible armed conflict between the two countries, which raises in Japan the issue of the credibility of US commitment. While the Obama administration's decision to pivot to the Asia-Pacific region was a powerful message and warmly welcomed by Tokyo, its sustainability is now increasingly questioned.

One of the defining features of today's US-China relations is the increasing vulnerability of both countries to each other.[30] It is a two-way street and can be seen in various fields. Deep economic interdependence, for instance, means that both are vulnerable to each other, which represents arguably the biggest difference between the current state of US-China relations and the US-Soviet relations during the Cold War. On the security front, one of the most difficult questions is whether Washington is prepared to acknowledge the vulnerability – indefensibility – of the US mainland against Chinese nuclear attacks. While China has been consistently vulnerable to US attacks, Washington has been intentionally ambiguous in this regard.

Strategic stability

At the level of the strategic (nuclear) relationship, the issue of vulnerability is often understood in the context of strategic stability. The emphasis on strategic stability between the United States and China, presented in the NPR and Ballistic Missile Defense Review (BMDR), has raised some concerns and questions in the United States, China, and beyond. Those two documents have actually left the concept of strategic stability undefined. One of the main reasons why the use of the term strategic stability for Sino-American relations is controversial particularly in the United States and its allies in the region stems from the fact that the concept is thought to be based on mutual vulnerability – something called mutual assured destruction (MAD) – in a Cold War sense. While it may sound anachronistic, MAD still constitutes US-Russia strategic stability. As recently as in 2012, a US government document maintains that: "Stability in strategic nuclear relationship between the United States and the Russian Federation depends upon the assured capability of each side to deliver a sufficient number of nuclear warheads to inflict unacceptable damage on the other side, even with an opponent attempting a disarming first strike,"[31] repeating a very classic notion of strategic stability.

Regarding the US ballistic missile defense, the BMDR states it "does not have the capacity to cope with large scale Russian or Chinese missile attacks, and is not intended to affect the strategic balance with those countries."[32] The fundamental reason why BMD from time to time is still seen to be destabilizing stems from the Cold War understanding of the idea of strategic stability based on MAD. BMD – while not being capable of nullifying the first strike by a major power – might still undermine the MAD relationship by potentially threatening the second strike (retaliation) capability of an enemy, which could induce a first strike and thereby jeopardize strategic stability. The text of the BMDR is again intentionally ambiguous. First, neither it nor the NPR says anything about the future – as opposed to the current – capacity: indeed, the BMDR clearly states that the "Administration will continue to reject any negotiated restraints" on BMD.[33] Second, it keeps possibilities open for America's BMD to eventually cope with China's ballistic missiles without affecting the (undefined) strategic balance or stability, at least from the US perspective. As far as official pronouncements are concerned, therefore, as Bradley Roberts argues, Washington "has neither formally accepted nor formally rejected mutual vulnerability with China."[34] It looks close to the "neither confirm nor deny" policy of the United States regarding the location of nuclear weapons. On the other hand, however, this intentionally ambiguous statement could also be interpreted as indicating the US willingness to accept mutual deterrence with China.[35] Or, it can be pointed out that Washington at least does not emphasize the need for the United States to deny China's developing assured nuclear retaliatory – second strike – capability against the United States either.[36] Yet another way to approach this, is to conceive of a situation somewhere between two extreme positions of publicly accepting MAD, and rejecting any notion of vulnerability. Acknowledging some aspects of vulnerability is still certainly different from accepting MAD vis-à-vis China and it may rather be a matter of degree.

A close reading of the BMDR and NPR reveals, not surprisingly, that Washington's approaches to Russia and China are indeed different. Whereas Russia is regarded as the "only peer"[37] when it comes to nuclear weapons, Washington's aim as for China is essentially confidence-building, including enhancing transparency, which does not have to be based on mutual vulnerability and should not be controversial in substance from a US perspective. However, the terms strategic stability and transparency are not popular in the Chinese context and Chinese experts and officials are skeptical about – or more often than not openly hostile to – the US terminology.[38]

Meanwhile, China has been modernizing its nuclear arsenal, with more sophisticated penetration aids and Multiple Independently-Targetable Reentry Vehicles (MIRVs) for its intercontinental ballistic missiles (ICBMs) and a new generation of ballistic missile submarines (SSBNs) (the JIN-class) with improved submarine-launched ballistic missiles (JL-2). Those efforts are seen to counter BMD and ensure Beijing's second strike retaliatory capability.[39] Although Russia has been far more vocal in opposing the United States and NATO missile defense as something undermining its nuclear deterrent, China actually has more reasons to be concerned about negative implications of the US missile defense because of its limited number of nuclear weapons. What seems increasingly clear is that the development and deployment of BMD by the United States is now a major factor against which China's nuclear development is planned.[40] This is one of the reasons why some experts argue that the United States could avoid an unnecessary arms race with China by acknowledging mutual deterrence and vulnerability, therefore removing one of the main drivers of China's nuclear modernization.[41] The International Security Advisory Board (ISAB) of the Department of State, chaired by former Secretary of Defense William Perry, submitted a report in October 2012, in which it recommended that "mutual nuclear vulnerability should be considered as a fact of life for both sides."[42] The report goes on to argue that "neither the US ability to use conventional forces to protect our interests in the region nor the US 'nuclear umbrella' require the ability to negate China's nuclear forces."[43]

Politics of vulnerability

It remains, however, difficult for any US political leaders, not least the president, to acknowledge in public the US vulnerability for two major reasons. First, the American public does not seem to be prepared to accept the reality of vulnerability against China. The general public does not want to live under another MAD condition with China. Second, Washington needs to take into account the implications for its allies in the region, most notably Japan and South Korea. US acknowledgement of the mutual vulnerability between the United States and China would raise the issue of "de-coupling" as was seen during the Cold War between the United States and Western Europe when the Soviet Union became capable of attacking the US mainland. The argument goes – as it did during the Cold War – that if the US mainland is vulnerable to attacks, Washington would hesitate to honor extended deterrence commitment for fear of retaliation.

Because of this, the US government has so far maintained a policy of intentional ambiguity – neither confirm nor deny – regarding the mutual vulnerability between the two countries. Nevertheless, in light of the improvement of China's capability, one needs to think about the implications of the growing gap between the reality of the increasing vulnerability and the position of not acknowledging the vulnerability at least explicitly. When this gap continues to widen, the credibility of the government position would be questioned in the United States and abroad. It is in this context that a growing number of experts have started calling on the US government to acknowledge the existence of mutual vulnerability as mentioned above. In terms of military strategy, while it is no secret that China's nuclear forces increasingly constitute one of the benchmarks for determining the US nuclear posture,[44] it is still argued that China's nuclear development has yet to generate "any new deterrence requirements" for the US – therefore, "the United States has not so far adapted its strategic military posture in response to China's nuclear modernization."[45] The latter seems to be consistent not only with the assessment of the NPR, but also with the ISAB's view that the United States does not need to "negate" China's nuclear deterrent. Nonetheless, this by no means suggests that US deterrence posture should remain as it is despite the changing strategic landscape in East Asia, including China's nuclear modernization. The necessity for a constant review seems to be increasing.

One of the most significant developments that the United States – and its allies such as Japan and South Korea – need to take into account in terms of tailoring regional deterrence architecture is the shifting conventional balance mainly caused by China's rapid conventional development. While Beijing has been engaged in nuclear modernization in recent years, its priority has been on the conventional domain, particularly the air force and the navy. China's strategy of what the United States calls "anti-access/area-denial (A2AD)" has already forced the United States (and Japan) to adapt its posture. As long as the high-end strategic considerations are concerned, however, the dynamics are not only that the United States is reacting to China's development. As seen above, Beijing is seriously concerned about US BMD, and more than anything else, the idea of conventional prompt global strike (CPGS) is by far the biggest source of concern for China.[46] This suggests that in thinking about strategic stability between the United States and China (and its implications to Japan and other US allies in the region and beyond), not only nuclear weapons and missile defense, but also the conventional elements need to be taken into account in a broader picture.

Conclusions

Some of the major factors that are set to determine the future direction of the nuclear and deterrence relationships in East Asia, particularly among China, Japan and the United States include: evolution of US nuclear posture and prospects of US-Russia nuclear disarmament; development of America's BMD and other conventional capabilities, including most notably the conventional prompt global strike capability; China's nuclear modernization and possibilities for the country's involvement in multilateral nuclear disarmament; and Japan's role in BMD and conventional-weapon development.

In a broader picture, however, arguably the biggest challenge is how to connect the high-end nuclear and deterrence relationships to low-end daily security problems mainly involving maritime, territorial and diplomatic disputes in the region. Maintaining strategic stability is one thing, but it needs to be achieved without having an adverse impact on the low-intensity side of the picture – in other words, avoiding the situation called "stability-instability paradox," where stability at the strategic level makes instability at the lower level more likely. The need for a more comprehensive and operational approach to deterrence and a tighter conventional-nuclear linkage can be understood in this context, through which a new and broader concept of strategic stability would be expected to take shape.

Last but not least, another fundamental issue to be thought through regarding the future of nuclear and deterrence relationships in the region is to what extent the stakeholders – particularly the United States and Japan – are prepared to be deterred by China (and North Korea), in addition to deter it. Deterrence, after all, is mutual in nature. There are again two aspects – the military reality of the increasing US vulnerability against China, and political and public perceptions about this issue. During the Cold War, the United States had to accept the reality of being deterred by Moscow and it is undeniable that it constituted one of the basic foundations of strategic stability between the two countries. Accepting mutual vulnerability is essentially about agreeing to be deterred. BMD plays an important role here as it can be seen as a tool of not to be deterred – or at least a tool to lessen the degree of being deterred by others.[47] This raises an unresolved question of "how much [BMD] is enough."[48]

When it comes to the security environment in East Asia, concerns about a series of maritime, territorial, and diplomatic disputes in the region tend to dominate the scene. Nonetheless, the need to address the issues of nuclear deterrence and strategic stability will never go away as long as there are nuclear weapons in the region and world. Also, the questions and challenges that the region needs to address have various generic aspects shared by other regions, which provides a basis for more interregional comparative analysis of the issues of nuclear deterrence and strategic stability.

The views expressed in this chapter are solely of the author, and do not represent those of the National Institute for Defense Studies [NIDS], the Ministry of Defense, nor the Government of Japan.

Notes

1. See Andrew O'Neil, *Asia, the US and Extended Nuclear Deterrence: Atomic Umbrellas in the Twenty-First Century* (Abingdon: Routledge, 2013); Rod Lyon, "The Challenges Confronting US Extended Nuclear Deterrence in Asia," *International Affairs*, Vol. 89, No. 4 (July 2013), pp. 929–941.
2. Major examples include Andrew O'Neil, *Asia, the US and Extended Nuclear Deterrence*, Rory Medcalf and Fiona Cunningham (eds), *Disarming Doubt: The Future of Extended Nuclear Deterrence in East Asia* (Woollahra: Lowy Institute for International Policy, 2012).
3. Takeo Miki and Gerald R. Ford, "Japan-US Joint Announcement to the Press" Washington, DC, August 6, 1975, para. 4, www.ioc.u-tokyo.ac.jp/~worldjpn/documents/texts/JPUS/19750806.O1E.html.
4. Japan signed the NPT in February 1967, but ratified it only in June 1976. See Akira Kurosaki, *Kakuheiki to nichibei kankei: Amerika no kaku fukakusan gaikou to Nihon no sentaku, 1960–1976* [Nuclear Weapons and Japan-US Relations: US Nuclear Nonproliferation Policy and Japan's Choice, 1960–1976] (Tokyo: Yushisha, 2006).
5. See, for example, James J. Wirtz and Peter R. Lavoy (eds), *Over the Horizon Proliferation Threats* (Palo Alto: Stanford University Press, 2012); Jeffrey Knopf (ed.), *Security Assurances and Nuclear Nonproliferation* (Palo Alto: Stanford University Press, 2012); Toshi Yoshihara and James Holmes (eds), *Strategy in the Second Nuclear Age: Power, Ambition and the Ultimate Weapon* (Washington, DC: Georgetown University Press, 2012); Ashley Tellis, Abraham Denmark, and Travis Tanner (eds), *Strategic Asia 2013–14: Asia in the Second Nuclear Age* (Washington, DC: National Bureau of Asian Research, 2013).
6. See, for example, Katsuhisa Furukawa, "Japan's Nuclear Option," in *Over the Horizon Proliferation Threats*, James Wirtz and Peter Lavoy (eds) (Stanford: Stanford University Press, 2012), pp. 13–32; Yuki Tatsumi, "Maintaining Japan's Non-Nuclear Identity: The Role of US Security Assurances," in *Security Assurances and Nuclear Nonproliferation*, Jeffery Knopf (ed.), (Palo Alto: Stanford University Press, 2012), pp. 137–161; James Schoff, "Changing Perceptions of Extended Deterrence in Japan," in *Strategy in the Second Nuclear Age*, Toshi Yoshihara and James Holmes (eds) (Washington, DC: Georgetown University Press, 2012), pp. 99–114; James Holmes and Toshi Yoshihara, "Thinking about the Unthinkable: Tokyo's Nuclear Option," in ibid., pp. 115–132; Richard Samuels and James Schoff, "Japan's Nuclear Hedge: Beyond 'Allergy' and Breakout," in *Strategic Asia 2013–14: Asia in the Second Nuclear Age*, Ashley Tellis, Abraham Denmark, and Travis Tanner (eds), (Washington, DC: National Bureau of Asian Research, 2013), pp. 233–266; Michael Green and Katsuhisa Furukawa, "Japan: New

Nuclear Realism," in *The Long Shadow: Nuclear Weapons and Security in 21st Century Asia*, Muthiah Alagappa (ed.) (Stanford: Stanford University Press, 2008), pp. 347–372.

7. See Brad Roberts, "Extended Deterrence and Strategic Stability in Northeast Asia," NIDS Visiting Scholar Paper, National Institute for Defense Studies (Tokyo), No. 1 (August 9, 2013), pp. 15–16, www.nids.go.jp/english/publication/visiting/pdf/01.pdf; David Yost, "US Extended Deterrence in NATO and North-East Asia," in *Perspectives on Extended Deterrence*, Research & Documents, No. 3/2010 (Paris: Fondation pour la Recherche Stratégique, 2010), pp. 15–36, www.frstrategie.org/barreFRS/publications/rd/2010/RD_201003.pdf; Michito Tsuruoka, "Why the NATO Nuclear Debate is Relevant to Japan and Vice Versa," *Policy Brief* (Washington, DC: German Marshall Fund of the United States, October 2010). For a good example of the work on comparative extended deterrence (rather than proliferation) in the Asia-Pacific region, see O'Neil, *Asia, the US and Extended Nuclear Deterrence*.

8. See also Tatsumi, "Maintaining Japan's Non-Nuclear Identity," p. 140.

9. For a concise analysis of those documents, see National Institute for Defense Studies (ed.), *East Asian Strategic Review 2011* (Tokyo: Japan Times, 2011), pp. 257–264.

10. Schoff, "Changing Perceptions of Extended Deterrence in Japan," p. 101.

11. See Yukio Satoh, "Japan–US Alliance Cooperation in the Era of Global Nuclear Disarmament," in *The Japan-U.S. Partnership Toward a World Free of Nuclear Weapons*, Bryce Wakefield (ed.), Report of the Japan-US Join Public Policy Forum, Tokyo, October 21–22, 2009 (Washington, DC: Woodrow Wilson International Center for Scholars, 2010), p. 24.

12. The dialogue's low visibility is conspicuous, particularly compared to the more publicized US-South Korea Extended Deterrence Policy Committee (EDPC). It seems that the Korean side has wanted to highlight this new mechanism. See, for example, Cheon Seong Whun, "The Significance of Forming a ROK-US Extended Deterrence Policy Committee," *Online Series*, No. 10–39 (Seoul: Korea Institute for National Unification, 2010). In general, publicizing the fact that the allies conduct such dialogue serves deterrence purposes. The Japanese government, however, has been taking a low-key approach regarding the EDD.

13. The most detailed account (press report) regarding the dialogue is Yoshihiro Makino, "US Shows Nuclear Facilities to Reassure Japan, Allies on Deterrence," *Asahi Shimbun*, July 30, 2013, http://ajw.asahi.com/article/behind_news/politics/AJ201307300096.

14. "Bei no kakuyokushiseisaku kawarazu" [US Nuclear Deterrence Policy Remains Intact: An Interview with Bradley Roberts], *Yomiuri Shimbun*, July 6, 2013.

15. See, for example, Research Group on the Japan-US Alliance, "A New Phase in the Japan-US Alliance: The Japan US Alliance Toward 2020," Institute for International Policy Studies Project Report, 2009, p. 10, www.iips.org/en/research/data/J-US-SEC2009e.pdf.

16. Tsuruoka, "Why the NATO Nuclear Debate Is Relevant to Japan and Vice Versa," pp. 3–4. For the NATO debate on the future of nuclear-sharing without the physical presence of US nuclear weapons in Europe, see, for example, Karl-Heinz Kamp and Robertus Remkes, "Options for NATO Nuclear Sharing Arrangements," in *Reducing Nuclear Risks in Europe: A Framework for Action*, Steve Andersen and Isabelle Williams (eds), (Washington, DC: Nuclear Threat Initiative, 2011), pp. 13–32; George Perkovich *et al.*, "Looking Beyond the Chicago Summit: Nuclear Weapons in Europe and the Future of NATO," *The Carnegie Papers* (April 2012), pp. 1–54, http://carnegieendowment.org/files/beyond_chicago_summit.pdf.

17. Tsuruoka, "Why the NATO Nuclear Debate Is Relevant to Japan and Vice Versa," p. 4.

18. Roberts, "Extended Deterrence and Strategic Stability in Northeast Asia," pp. 16–17.

19. Condoleezza Rice, Robert M. Gates, Taro Aso, and Fumio Kyuma, "Joint Statement of the Security Consultative Committee – Alliance Transformation: Advancing United States-Japan Security and Defense Cooperation," Washington, DC, May 1, 2007, www.mofa.go.jp/region/n-america/us/security/scc/pdfs/joint0705.pdf.

20. "National Defense Program Guidelines for FY 2011 and Beyond (Provisional Translation)," approved by the Security Council and the Cabinet, Tokyo, December 17, 2010, p. 2 (emphasis added). For the change of terminology, see NIDS (ed.), *East Asian Strategic Review 2011*, pp. 257–264; Sugio Takahashi, "Ballistic Missile Defense in Japan: Deterrence and Military Transformation," *Asie.Visions*, No. 59/*Proliferation Papers*, No. 44 (December, 2012), pp. 20–24.

21. "National Defense Program Guidelines for FY 2014 and Beyond: Summary (Provisional Translation)," approved by the National Security Council and the Cabinet, Tokyo, December 17, 2013, www.mod.go.jp/approach/agenda/guideline/2014/pdf/20131217.e2.pdf.; "National Security

Strategy (Provisional Translation)," December 17, 2013, p. 16, www.cas.go.jp/jp/siryou/131217 anzenhoshou/nss-e.pdf.

22. Takahashi, "Ballistic Missile Defense in Japan," pp. 15–18.
23. See, for example, Nobuyasu Abe and Hirofumi Tosaki, "Untangling Japan's Nuclear Dilemma: Deterrence before Disarmament," in *Disarming Doubt: The Future of Extended Nuclear Deterrence in East Asia*, Rory Medcalf and Fiona Cunningham (ed.), (Woollahra: Lowy Institute for International Policy, 2012), pp. 25–27.
24. James Acton, *Deterrence during Disarmament: Deep Nuclear Reductions and International Security* (Abingdon: Routledge for IISS, 2011).
25. For the case of the US-Japan alliance, see Michael Keifer, Kurt Guthe, and Thomas Scheber, *Assuring South Korea and Japan as the Role and Number of Nuclear Weapons are Reduced* (Ft. Belvoir: Defense Threat Reduction Agency, January 2011), pp. 60–64, www.nipp.org/Publication/Downloads/Downloads%202012/2011%20003%20Assuring%20ROK%20and%20Japan.pdf.
26. For the Obama administration's view, see Department of Defense, "Nuclear Posture Review Report," Washington, DC, April 2010, pp. 15–17, 33, www.defense.gov/npr/docs/2010%20Nuclear%20Posture%20Review%20Report.pdf. For the Japanese Foreign Ministry's comment supporting the NPR, see "Statement by Mr. Katsuya Okada, Minister for Foreign Affairs of Japan on the release of the US Nuclear Posture Review (NPR)," Ministry of Foreign Affairs, Tokyo, April 7, 2010, www.mofa.go.jp/announce/announce/2010/4/0407_01.html.
27. NATO, "Deterrence and Defence Posture Review," Press Release No. 063, May 20, 2012, para. 20 (emphasis added), www.nato.int/cps/en/natolive/official_texts_87597.htm?mode=pressrelease.
28. Department of Defense, "Report on Nuclear Employment Strategy of the United States Specified in Section 491 of 10 USC," Washington, DC, June 19, 2013, p. 9 (emphasis added), www.defense.gov/pubs/reporttoCongressonUSNuclearEmploymentStrategy_Section491.pdf.
29. While the original Japanese expression remains intact from the 2010 NDPG, the English version of the 2013 NDPG and the NSS use different words. The term "core" is used in 2013 documents.
30. David Gompert and Phillip Saunders, *The Paradox of Power: Sino-American Strategic Restraints in an Age of Vulnerability* (Washington, DC: National Defense University Press, 2011).
31. US Department of Defense, "Report on the Strategic Nuclear Forces of the Russian Federation Pursuant to Section 1240 of the National Defense Authorization Act for Fiscal Year 2012," declassified in response to the Freedom of Information Act request made by Hans Kristensen, Federation of American Scientists, p. 6, www.fas.org/programs/ssp/nukes/nuclearweapons/DOD2012_Russian Nukes.pdf.
32. US Department of Defense, "Ballistic Missile Defense Review Report," Washington, DC, February 2010, p. 13, www.defense.gov/bmdr/docs/BMDR%20as%20of%2026JAN10%200630_for%20web.pdf, p. 13.
33. Ibid., p. 34.
34. Roberts, "Extended Deterrence and Strategic Stability in Northeast Asia," p. 30.
35. See, for example, Baohui Zhang, "US Missile Defence and China's Nuclear Posture: Changing Dynamics of an Offence-Defence Arms Race," *International Affairs*, Vo. 87, No. 3 (May 2011), p. 566.
36. Gompert and Saunders, *The Paradox of Power*, pp. 79 80.
37. Department of Defense, "Nuclear Posture Review Report," Executive Summary, p. iv.
38. Lora Saalman, "China and the US Nuclear Posture Review," *The Carnegie Papers* (Tsinghua: Carnegie-Tsinghua, February 2011), http://carnegieendowment.org/files/china_posture_review.pdf.; Saalman, "Placing a Renminbi Sign on Strategic Stability and Nuclear Reductions," in *Strategic Stability: Contending Interpretations,* Elbridge Colby and Michael Gerson (eds) (Carlisle: Strategic Studies Institute and US Army War College Press, 2013), pp. 343–382.
39. See, for example, United States Department of Defense, Office of the Secretary, "Annual Report to Congress: Military and Security Developments Involving the People's Republic of China 2013," Department of Defense, May 2013, pp. 29–32, www.defense.gov/pubs/2013_china_report_final.pdf.
40. Zhang, "US Missile Defence and China's Nuclear Posture"; Christopher Yeaw, Andrew Erickson and Michael Chase, "The Future of Chinese Nuclear Policy and Strategy," in *Strategy in the Second Nuclear Age*, Toshi Yoshihara and James Holmes (eds) (Washington, DC: Georgetown University Press, 2012), pp. 71–72.
41. See, for example, Yeaw, Erickson and Chase, "The Future of Chinese Nuclear Policy and Strategy," p. 74; Gompert and Saunders, *The Paradox of Power*, Chapter 4.

42. US Department of State, International Security Advisory Board, "Report on Maintaining US–China Strategic Stability," Washington, DC, October 26, 2012, p. 3, www.state.gov/documents/organization/200473.pdf.
43. Ibid., pp. 3–4.
44. Jeffrey Lewis, *The Minimum Means of Reprisal: China's Search for Security in the Nuclear Age* (Cambridge: MIT Press, 2007), pp. 143–144.
45. Roberts, "Extended Deterrence and Strategic Stability in Northeast Asia," p. 30.
46. See, for example, Saalman, "China and the US Nuclear Posture Review," pp. 9, 22–23.
47. See, for example, Jeremy Stocker, "The Strategy of Missile Defence: Defence, Deterrence and Diplomacy," *RUSI Journal*, Vol. 156, No. 3 (December 2011), p. 59.
48. Roberts, "Extended Deterrence and Strategic Stability in Northeast Asia," pp. 18–20.

5

NORTH KOREA'S NUCLEAR-WEAPON PROGRAM

Implications for the nonproliferation regime

Sun Young Ahn and Joel S. Wit

North Korea presents a significant challenge to international security due to its continued attempts to disrupt the global nonproliferation agenda. Pyongyang's activities also serve to undermine the peace and stability of East Asia, particularly the threat of attacks against the neighboring states.

International efforts to negotiate an end to North Korea's nuclear and missile programs over the past two decades have been replete with a pattern of impasse, deadlock, and progress. The United States and the international community have coordinated a variety of policy responses to deal with the challenges, including diplomatic initiatives, sanctions, and military cooperation.[1]

The 1994 US-North Korea Agreed Framework was designed to freeze and eventually dismantle Pyongyang's plutonium weapons program in return for aid, as well as an improvement in political and economic relations. But this first initiative collapsed after evidence of a clandestine uranium enrichment program was found in 2002, followed by Pyongyang's withdrawal from the Nuclear Nonproliferation Treaty (NPT) in 2003.[2] Despite a second diplomatic effort initiated in the Six-Party Talks among the regional states – China, Japan, North Korea, Russia, South Korea, and the United States – North Korea moved forward with two nuclear tests in 2006 and 2009.[3]

Pyongyang's hostility reached a high point in 2010, when it embarked on a series of provocative conventional military actions and the further development of its nuclear and missile programs. Despite sanctions imposed by the international community, Pyongyang moved ahead with its effort to improve its nuclear and long-range rocket capabilities, carrying out a successful long-range rocket launch in December 2012 and conducting a third nuclear test in February 2013.

In its continued push to develop nuclear weapons and modern ballistic missiles, North Korea has issued policy statements asserting its position as a nuclear-armed nation. In May 2012, Pyongyang released the text of a revised constitution declaring its nuclear-weapon status, further complicating international efforts to persuade the North to denuclearize. Furthermore, during a Central Committee of the Party plenary session on 31 March 2013, North Korea adopted the "Byungjin" line asserting that the development of its economy and nuclear weapons arsenal were closely linked. In early April 2013, Pyongyang announced that it would expand its entire nuclear-weapon program, including a plutonium-producing reactor at the Yongbyon nuclear facility, which had been disabled as part of the 2007 Six-Party Talks agreement.[4] Recent commercial satellite imagery suggests that Pyongyang subsequently restarted its plutonium production reactor that summer and also initiated new construction projects to develop larger space launch vehicles as well as mobile missiles.[5]

Although the precise future direction of the North's nuclear-weapon program remains unclear, based on public statements, it appears Pyongyang is interested in continuing to expand its nuclear and missile capability to develop miniaturized, light-weight, diversified, and precise nuclear weapons.[6] It believes that following such a course would accomplish important objectives, including increasing the credibility of its nuclear force, and expanding the regime's options for more flexible military responses.[7] Undoubtedly, nuclear weapons have become a fundamental component of North Korea's national security strategy.

Pyongyang's renewed vows to strengthen its nuclear-weapon program suggest that the road to denuclearize the Korean Peninsula is getting longer and more arduous. At the same time, North Korea's unbridled nuclear ambitions continue to pose one of the most complex dilemmas for the global nuclear nonproliferation regime, raising doubts about its adequacy and sustainability. Its extensive efforts raise a number of important questions including: how serious a threat does its development of a nuclear arsenal pose to its neighbors and to the international community; would North Korea transfer critical WMD-related information and technology outside its borders; are these two threats – the expansion of its forces and willingness to proliferate – related to each other; can this danger be reduced; and what are the implications of Pyongyang's arsenal for international security and the nonproliferation regime?

In addressing these questions, the first section of this chapter provides a brief overview of the North Korean challenge. The second examines North Korea's development of its nuclear-weapon capabilities, which include plutonium production and uranium enrichment programs. The third explores possible policy measures for engaging Pyongyang in response to its nuclear-weapon program.

Overview: North Korean proliferation challenges

The North Korean proliferation threat originates from two sources: the development of its nuclear weapons and missile capabilities (vertical proliferation), and the possible spread of related materials, know-how, and technology to other state or nonstate actors (horizontal proliferation).

Pyongyang's steady effort to quantitatively and qualitatively expand its nuclear and missile forces poses a direct security threat to regional stability. Moreover, its possession of short- and medium-range ballistic missiles capable of reaching targets in South Korea and Japan is of immediate national security concern to Seoul and Tokyo, and increases a risk of miscalculation leading to nuclear war on the Korean Peninsula or in the region. (In their efforts to counter Pyongyang, both are seeking to acquire preventive strike capabilities that may be highly destabilizing.) The North's recent successful launch of a satellite into orbit has demonstrated that it is striving to develop even longer-range ballistic missiles able to reach the United States, as confirmed by sightings of the KN-08 road mobile intercontinental ballistic missile (ICBM), which is now in development. However, it remains unclear whether Pyongyang will be able to successfully develop such a missile or a nuclear warhead that it could carry.

From the US policy perspective, North Korea's development of nuclear weapons and missile capabilities present a geopolitical and strategic challenge to its role in Northeast Asia. As Washington becomes vulnerable to a North Korean nuclear strike, such a development will undermine extended deterrence and call into question the US political commitment to defend its allies against the North's aggression. At the very least, this growing challenge to extended deterrence will require the United States to constantly reassure its allies through a wide range of measures from public statements to additional deployments of military capabilities. At worst, it might lead them to consider alternative security policies – including the pursuit of their own nuclear weapons – ending the US alliance structure that is the corner stone of its Asia policy and resulting in a significant breach in the international nonproliferation regime.

The danger of horizontal proliferation by North Korea poses another set of challenges in the regional and international security arenas, including the continuation of black market sales, the diversion of fissile materials to the highest bidder, and the collapse of regime control over its nuclear arsenals.

For many years, Pyongyang has been involved in supplying missiles as well as related components and technology to various countries, including Iran, Iraq, Syria, Pakistan, Egypt, Libya, and Yemen.[8] It has also engaged in providing nuclear reactor technology and related materials to Syria, Libya, and Myanmar. Pyongyang's transfer of nuclear reactor technology similar to its Yongbyon 5-megawatt (5 MWe) facility to Syria in the 2000s is considered one of the most serious cases of nuclear technology transfer.[9] Moreover, the North is believed to have provided Libya with uranium hexafluoride, the feed material used in the uranium enrichment process to produce fuel rods for nuclear reactors and nuclear weapons.[10] Recently, the North also has been suspected of having attempted to transfer nuclear-related items such as aluminum alloy rods to Myanmar.[11]

Concerns persist and are likely to grow that North Korea will continue its trade in nuclear-related expertise, technologies, components or materials for nonpeaceful purposes through a clandestine supply network. Pyongyang's proliferation activities are believed to have helped the North earn hard currency to develop its own weapon systems in the past.[12] To the extent that Pyongyang perceives that weapon proliferation is an effective way to accumulate financial resources, it will continue engaging in illicit arms trade and nuclear technologies. Moreover, the horizontal growth of the North's nuclear stockpile and expertise will only encourage the further vertical proliferation of this dangerous capability. The larger that North Korean nuclear stockpile is, the more it can afford to market capabilities abroad without adversely affecting its own nuclear strength. In short, a 2009 assessment by the Director of National Intelligence (DNI) that Pyongyang is less likely to sell weapon-grade fissile materials than nuclear technology or related equipment given its needs for fissile materials for its own deterrent may be increasingly irrelevant.[13]

North Korea will also have the necessary contacts with networks able to proliferate nuclear information, technology or materials abroad. In particular, the possibility that Pyongyang might sell or transfer fissile materials to state or nonstate actors is of a priority concern. Aside from its own overseas networks built up over five decades to engage in a variety of illicit activities, it is well known that North Korea received nuclear assistance from A.Q. Khan's nuclear network in the 1990s. Presumably, Pyongyang can utilize the remnants of that network as well as other foreign smuggling rings in any future effort intended to help nonstate actors in the acquisition of nuclear know-how and materials.

Moreover, Pyongyang continues to maintain its secret collaboration with other states, particularly Iran, on exchanging technical capabilities and sensitive information in order to reinforce each other's nuclear weapon and missile efforts. The extent of that cooperation remains unclear but the prospect of future cooperation between the two countries is certainly alarming in view of the potential damage they can do to the international nonproliferation regime.

Finally, the security of nuclear weapons and weapons-usable materials remains a key nonproliferation objective.[14] For instance, a proliferation risk could arise from an unwitting circumstance where domestic instability or a radical change in North Korea leads to the collapse of Pyongyang's control over its nuclear weapons or fissile materials. In particular, in the absence of a mechanism to track and locate Pyongyang's nuclear weapons, materials, components, and scientists, a 'loose nukes' crisis could have serious implications for East Asian and global security as well as for the international nonproliferation regime.[15]

The development of nuclear-weapon capabilities

Plutonium production

North Korea has taken a long, winding, and often perplexing road dating back over six decades to acquiring nuclear weapons. There are many explanations as to Pyongyang's motivation for its nuclear acquisition, ranging from an ideology of nationalism to external factors. These include US nuclear threats during the Korean War; the Cuban Missile Crisis, which demonstrated that Pyongyang could not rely on the Soviet Union in a confrontation with the United States; the example of China's nuclear program; and North Korea's rivalry with South Korea.[16] The conventional understanding has been that the primary logic for Pyongyang's pursuit of a nuclear-weapon capability is to provide meaningful deterrence of military attack against its homeland.[17]

From the 1950s until the early 1990s, North Korea engaged in a slow, steady effort to develop its own nuclear capability. Early on, the North took steps to build a nuclear infrastructure and to develop the institutional capability to train personnel for its program.[18] Like other proliferators, North Korea's nuclear program began under the guise of exploring the peaceful uses of nuclear energy with its major ally, the Soviet Union. Beginning with the establishment of its Atomic Energy Research Institute in 1955, Pyongyang signed an agreement with Moscow in 1959 for assistance in training in nuclear-related disciplines.[19] North Korea also received Soviet help in establishing a nuclear research center and constructing a 2-megawatt IRT nuclear reactor.[20]

Despite some Soviet and Chinese assistance, North Korea faced difficulties in securing the substantial foreign nuclear assistance necessary to build the bomb rapidly. Reportedly on at least two occasions – shortly after China's first nuclear test in 1964 and then after South Korea's decision to develop its own nuclear program in the early 1970s – Pyongyang requested help in building a nuclear weapon, both times rejected by the Chinese.[21] The Soviet Union and its East European allies also rejected Pyongyang's pleas for large-scale peaceful nuclear assistance, in part due to suspicions about the North's real intentions.[22]

Beginning probably in the 1970s, North Korea sought to pursue self-reliance in the development of its nuclear capability. While engaging in negotiations with the Soviet Union to acquire four Light Water Reactors (LWRs), Pyongyang conducted a separate effort to build a gas-graphite moderated reactor, using declassified British blueprints of the Magnox reactor designed to produce plutonium for nuclear weapons.[23]

In the 1980s, the North embarked on a major expansion of its indigenous program at the Yongbyon facility, including the construction of a 5-megawatt plutonium production reactor, a football-field-sized reprocessing plant, and a fuel fabrication facility. Photographs taken by a US spy satellite in 1980 identified components of what appeared to be a much larger reactor than the one provided by the Soviet Union. Located near a large hole dug for the reactor's foundation, the reactor components were part of what would become the 5-megawatt nuclear reactor.[24] Nine years later, the North's building of a reprocessing facility was discovered to the south of that reactor. Designed to separate fissionable plutonium from irradiated spent fuel rods through reprocessing, the plant would enable Pyongyang to extract a stock of separated plutonium that could be used for the production of nuclear weapons.

Since the 5-megawatt reactor became operational in 1986 until the freeze put in place by the 1994 Agreed Framework, the North is believed to have produced and separated enough plutonium for possibly one or two nuclear weapons, despite its signing of the NPT in 1985.[25] Moreover, North Korea simultaneously began a series of nonnuclear, conventional explosions at the Yongbyon facility in the late 1980s, which were believed to be intended to help design a nuclear device.[26] These developments indicated that Pyongyang's nuclear-weapon program had gathered steam.

North Korea's plutonium program remained operational until 1994 when Pyongyang agreed to freeze and eventually dismantle its existing nuclear program in exchange for two LWRs and fuel oil. The freeze of that program – which not only included the small reactor but also two larger facilities under construction – was implemented over the next eight years. The larger incomplete facilities were also gradually abandoned. In return, the United States, South Korea, and Japan agreed to provide two 1,000-megawatt LWRs and an annual shipment of 500,000 tons of heavy fuel oil to help offset the energy foregone due to the limits on its nuclear reactors.[27] In 1995, the Korean Peninsula Energy Development Organization (KEDO) was established to implement the Agreed Framework, providing financial as well as technical support for the LWR project and delivering heavy fuel oil to meet the North's electricity needs. The European Union and other countries later joined KEDO.

Despite the freeze of its nuclear program, however, the North restarted its plutonium produc-tion program by the end of 2002, following a confrontation with the United States over its secret uranium enrichment program and the escalation of tensions on the Korean Peninsula. The heightened concern over Pyongyang's withdrawal from the NPT in 2003 in the aftermath of the collapse of the Agreed Framework led to the Six Party Talks, which produced an agreement in 2007 on implementing actions aimed at disabling the North's restarted plutonium production program.[28] Several steps were taken at the 5-megawatt nuclear reactor and reprocessing facility, including the highly visible demolition of the reactor's cooling tower in June 2008. However, following the collapse of talks a year later, the North resumed operation of its separation plant to reprocess spent fuel rods from the 5-megawatt reactor, producing an estimated stockpile of 8 kg weapon-grade separated plutonium by October 2009.[29] Assuming that 2–5 kilograms of pluto-nium are used per weapon, eight kilograms is enough for 1–4 nuclear weapons.

In April 2013, Pyongyang announced that it would restart its 5-megawatt reactor for pluto-nium production as part of a plan to "readjust and restart all the nuclear facilities in Yongbyon."[30] That effort in fact seemed to be underway at the Yongbyon plutonium production reactor by late March 2013.[31] Rather than reconstructing the cooling water system destroyed under the 2007 agreement, the North appears to have connected the secondary cooling system to the pump house of the adjacent Experimental Light Water Reactor (ELWR) under construction since 2010.[32] The 5-megawatt reactor seems to have restarted operations by August 2013 although the secondary system may have experienced some operating problems by the end of the year.[33] Moreover, it appears Pyongyang began converting its old pilot fuel fabrication plant into a new facility for fabricating fuel rods for the 5-megawatt reactor after the Six Party agree-ment collapsed.

While the ELWR is designed to generate electricity for civilian purposes, there is a risk that it may be used to produce plutonium. Pyongyang previously claimed that it would use the facility for civilian electricity generation, but the design of ELWR may allow for the possibil-ity of the North's military use of civilian nuclear technology.[34] ELWRs are not typically used to produce weapons-grade plutonium, given the technical challenges and high costs associated with designing a different type of reactor core and making the operation successful. However, they could be operated to produce weapons-grade plutonium if the reactor core is specifically designed to use uranium enriched to a level greater than 3.5 percent as a driver fuel.[35] Although unlikely, the possibility that the North could optimize the construction of its ELWR to produce weapons-grade plutonium may provide Pyongyang with the capability to expand its nuclear-weapon arsenal.

Uranium enrichment

While North Korea's nuclear-weapon program started with its plutonium production from the beginning, Pyongyang also explored a second, alternative route to producing a nuclear weapon using uranium enrichment. The widely-held assumption is that Pyongyang received assistance from Pakistan in the 1990s through the A.Q. Khan network.[36] Deliveries of "nearly two dozen P-1 and P-2 centrifuges" from Pakistan to North Korea through the network were acknowledged in Pakistani President Musharraf's 2006 memoir, *In the Line of Fire*.[37] It was also revealed that North Korea was provided with a flow meter, special oils for centrifuges, and personnel training at A.Q. Khan's Research Laboratories as part of the government deal on missile technology.[38] Finally, there is a possibility that Pyongyang acquired the same highly enriched uranium nuclear-weapon design that was provided to Libya and Iran by Khan's network, which may have helped the regime miniaturize warheads for ballistic missiles.[39]

Nonetheless, there is also some evidence suggesting that North Korea began its research and development in uranium enrichment even earlier than generally known. The North's acquisition of enrichment technology appeared to have started in the late 1980s when it attempted to import vacuum pumps and valves from European companies.[40] Such uranium enrichment equipment was obtained through coordinated procurement efforts between the North Korean embassies and missions in East Berlin and Vienna, North Korean companies such as the Nam Chongang Trading Company and Korea Lyongaksan Import Corporation, as well as German and Swiss trading companies including Kohas.[41] It was only after these initial procurement activities that North Korea received P-1 and P-2 centrifuges, raw materials, and other equipment from the Khan's network in the mid-1990s.

In the late 1990s and early 2000s, North Korea sought to build a pilot plant based on the Pakistani P-2 centrifuge design.[42] In 1997, Pyongyang attempted unsuccessfully to procure large quantities of maraging steel, a critical raw material for manufacturing the rotor-tube of a centrifuge, from the All Russian Institute of Light Alloys in Moscow.[43] In 2002 and 2003, it successfully procured a large stock of high strength aluminum alloy from Russia and the United Kingdom, another vital raw material suited for use in gas centrifuges.[44]

By summer 2002, US intelligence estimated that North Korea had begun "seeking centrifuge-related materials in large quantities," and "obtained equipment suitable for use in uranium fed and withdrawal systems."[45] When then-US Assistant Secretary of State for East Asia and Pacific Affairs James Kelly confronted North Korea during October 2002 bilateral talks about a secret uranium enrichment program, First Vice Foreign Minister Kang Sok-Chu reportedly confirmed the existence of a program.[46] However, he later denied such acknowledgement and North Korea argued that it had only admitted to having a plan to deter a preemptive US military attack.[47]

The conflict led to the collapse of the 1994 Agreed Framework between Washington and Pyongyang. The Bush administration condemned Pyongyang for a "material breach" of the 1994 agreement and the 1992 North-South Joint Declaration on the Denuclearization of the Korean Peninsula, under which the North was committed to forgo the acquisition of uranium enrichment and nuclear reprocessing facilities.[48] In response to the North's failure to comply with its obligations, KEDO suspended the next shipment of heavy fuel oil.[49] Pyongyang retaliated by expelling the International Atomic Energy Agency (IAEA) inspectors monitoring the freeze at the Yongbyon nuclear facility, and resumed the operation of its reactor and reprocessing plant, leading to the end of plutonium production freeze in December 2002. Subsequently, the North announced its withdrawal from the NPT in January 2003.

While North Korea's NPT withdrawal and its two nuclear tests in 2006 and 2009 drew serious concerns from the international community, Pyongyang's public acknowledgement of its uranium enrichment program in June 2009 sharply elevated the level of significance of the issue.[50] In 2010, Pyongyang unveiled a previously unknown gas centrifuge uranium enrichment plant at the Yongbyon nuclear complex to a visiting group from Stanford University including Siegfried Hecker, the former Director of the Los Alamos National Laboratory. One former international inspector later observed his surprise at the "scale, level of sophistication, and brazenness for the North Koreans to have built a secret enrichment facility at the same site of a previously IAEA-monitored building."[51]

According to the November 2010 trip report by Hecker, the small industrial-scale uranium enrichment facility at Yongbyon housed almost 2,000 centrifuges at the time of his visit.[52] More recently, an analysis of satellite photos in August 2013 conducted by the Institute for Science and International Security suggested that the building housing the uranium enrichment facility had been enlarged to twice its original size, allowing the doubling of the number of centrifuges installed at the facility. This means that, in theory, North Korea could install up to 4,000 centrifuges in the plant, thus enabling the production of enough weapon-grade uranium for up to two atomic weapons per year.[53]

Pyongyang's new emphasis on the uranium enrichment path to building nuclear weapons raises a number of fundamental issues for regional and international security including: the development of a viable uranium enrichment program, a second path to producing fissile material, will allow the North to expand its nuclear-weapon stockpile; the appearance of one uranium enrichment facility at Yongbyon raises concerns of the likely presence of other clandestine facilities configured to produce highly enriched uranium;[54] it also raises important questions regarding the regime's domestic capability to produce components for these facilities, as well as how and when Pyongyang obtained equipment or materials, both of which are directly relevant to the effectiveness of sanctions and export controls;[55] and Pyongyang's uranium enrichment program revisits the issue of dual-use of nuclear technology.

First, North Korea's advancement in uranium enrichment technology is significant in that it has expanded the scope of Pyongyang's nuclear-weapon production capabilities by providing it with a second route to producing fissile material. This is of a serious concern because it implies that the regime has gained a technological and procedural advantage in manufacturing the bomb – it has become capable of developing its nuclear arsenals more easily and quickly than before, because the uranium route allows simple bomb design and easy fabrication.[56]

The North's increased capability to expand its nuclear arsenal and produce advanced nuclear weapons is well documented in an August 2012 paper published by David Albright and Christina Walrond at ISIS, which lays out three possible scenarios for North Korea's future fissile-material production. With both plutonium production and uranium enrichment programs, the North is projected to have approximately 14–25 nuclear weapons by the end of 2016 in the best possible scenario (where the North only produces low-enriched uranium for its ELWR without making any weapons-grade plutonium in the LWR).[57] However, in the worst possible scenario where the North optimizes the LWR for making weapon-grade plutonium, Pyongyang could produce almost 37–48 nuclear weapons by the end of the same year. As a result, Pyongyang's pursuit of an enrichment program has certainly lessened the prospect of achieving a denuclearized Korean Peninsula even further.

Second, based on their assessment of the Yongbyon facility and the relative speed at which it was constructed, experts believe that Pyongyang has additional clandestine uranium enrichment plants. The North may maintain at least one other smaller pilot facility at an unknown location that served as a stepping stone to the construction of a larger plant, a possibility suggested by the US intelligence community. The suspected locations so far have included Pyongyang, Pakchon, Taechon, Chonmasan, Hagap, and Yongjori.[58]

Aside from the obvious concern that the increased number of enrichment plants would allow Pyongyang to produce more highly enriched uranium (HEU), uranium enrichment facilities can be hidden more easily than plutonium facilities, making them more difficult to detect.[59] This reality in turn has important negative consequences for any future effort to achieve denuclearization, making it almost inevitable that verification will have to be based on full disclosure by Pyongyang as well as on-site inspections.

Third, North Korea's centrifuge program raises an important question about how it achieved such capability and whether its program has advanced far enough to make it relatively immune to international sanctions and export controls.[60] Evidence of North Korea's past procurement activities, which involve its deliveries of nuclear equipment and technology from Pakistan and other countries, suggests at least in its early stages the North was highly dependent on foreign assistance.

The key issue, however, is to what extent Pyongyang can domestically produce uranium enrichment centrifuges. If the North can successfully manufacture key components, ancillary equipment, and related materials – such as high-speed motors, frequency inverters, magnetic top bearings, vacuum pumps, aluminum-zinc alloys, and maraging steel – the likelihood of indigenous production of centrifuges would increase.[61] If Pyongyang is essentially self-sufficient in centrifuge manufacturing, the impact of export controls and sanctions systems on the North's uranium enrichment program may be significantly limited. If not, then those measures may still be able to slow Pyongyang's effort and have an impact on the growth of its HEU and nuclear-weapon stockpiles.

A recent debate among experts over this issue has focused on whether North Korea has the precision machine tools necessary to manufacture centrifuge parts, as well as whether it can indigenously produce maraging steel. Joshua Pollack and Scott Kemp have argued that the North has learned to produce key components of gas centrifuges, undermining policies based on export controls and sanctions intended to thwart the expansion of the North's uranium enrichment program. Citing photographs of Kim Jong-il and Kim Jong-un inspecting machine tools needed to make centrifuge rotors, as well as accounts of iron and steel making technologies in North Korean publications, Pollack and Kemp imply that North Korea is now likely to be self-sufficient in its mass production of centrifuges.[62]

David Albright and Ollie Heinonen argue against the idea that North Korea can produce centrifuges.[63] They believe that, while it is clear that the North has produced multiple generations of Computer Numerically Controlled (CNC) machine tools through a joint venture, the Huichon Ryonha Machinery General Plant,[64] the actual capability of such tools remains unclear. Albright and Heinonen agree that North Korea may be able to make centrifuge components domestically, but assert that Pyongyang still needs to import a wide range of materials and equipment necessary to make such components. They add that states seeking to build nuclear weapons have historically been unable to rely on domestic supplies to produce all of these components. Moreover, it is quite possible that Pyongyang could have acquired many of its centrifuge-related goods prior to the enforcement of export controls and sanctions. Therefore, the expansion of the uranium enrichment program does not mean that export control and sanctions systems have proved futile.

North Korea's domestic capability to produce maraging steel is another issue in this debate. As mentioned above, North Korea had previously sought to import maraging steel tubes as part of its early procurement efforts. Some experts believe that North Korea has an indigenous capability to produce maraging steel, referred to as "*juche* steel." Still others point to steel ingots visible in the photograph of Kim Jung-un's 2013 visit to Kanggye, arguing that these must have been domestically produced since previous imports of high-strength aluminum occurred in the form of tubes that could be directly flow-formed. Yet it still remains unclear whether Pyongyang maintains such capability.

The latest UN Panel of Experts report on North Korea, while silent on the HEU debate, provides a significant body of evidence suggesting that Pyongyang remains dependent on foreign assistance for other nuclear- and ballistic-related items. In particular, the panel assesses that "[North Korea] lacks sufficient domestic precision machine tool manufacturing capability and it purchases off-the-shelf items for its ballistic missile-related programs. The Panel also assesses that it will likely seek out foreign suppliers for components it will need to fabricate fuel rods for its reactors."[65] If North Korea is not self-sufficient in the production of nuclear-related components, it may continue to seek foreign assistance in developing that program, although it is uncertain how long that will be necessary. This suggests that further advances in the North Korean nuclear or missile programs can be limited through tightened export controls and sanction systems prohibiting the proliferation of related components and technology.

Finally, North Korea's emphasis on the uranium enrichment program touches on an essential aspect of proliferation concerns, i.e., how dual-use enrichment technology presents a danger of nuclear-weapon proliferation. Gas centrifuges create a proliferation risk because they can produce both low-enriched uranium, used for nuclear power reactor fuel as Pyongyang claims, and highly enriched uranium, suitable for nuclear weapons.[66] In short, this dual-use technology allows a plant to be reconfigured to produce highly enriched uranium for weapons.[67] Although Pyongyang has claimed that is enrichment facility is intended for peaceful civilian uses, its centrifuge program clearly has created opportunities for weapon-grade material production.

Also, as mentioned before, while LWRs are intended to generate electricity for civilian purposes, the North could optimize them to produce weapon-grade material if the reactor core is specifically designed to use uranium enriched to a level greater than 3.5 percent. This means that if the North enriches uranium to a level greater than 3.5 percent for ELWR use to produce weapon-grade plutonium, it could efficiently increase a total stock of plutonium for its nuclear arsenals while maintaining enough enrichment capacity to make weapon-grade uranium.[68]

Dealing with the North Korean challenge

North Korea's development of nuclear-weapon capabilities and proliferation activities presents an important challenge to regional and international security, as well as the global nonproliferation regime. Moreover, this challenge has only grown more severe over the past few years as the North's nuclear and missile programs have gathered momentum. Any chance of dealing with that challenge will require effectively utilizing a broad range of policy tools, from sanctions and military steps to diplomacy and incentives. Moreover, it will also require patience and lowering expectations. A solution, if one is possible, may take years to achieve and require moving forward step by step with no guarantee of success.

Moreover, any solution is going to have to deal with the fundamental problem embedded in the NPT, namely that members in good standing of the treaty are allowed to pursue peaceful nuclear development in the context of international inspections. That raises the issue of the implications of a possible decision by Pyongyang to rejoin the NPT while insisting on its right to develop nuclear energy for peaceful purposes. The same dilemma is playing out in the case of negotiations with Iran over its nuclear-weapon program. Although not as far advanced as Pyongyang's effort, the international community is confronted with the same problem: should Iran be allowed to maintain a peaceful capability in the context of any final agreement on its nuclear program? Whatever that solution may be, it will certainly have an impact on dealing with North Korea if diplomacy begins to gain traction.

While it may be unclear to the Obama administration, its current strategy of "strategic patience," which has combined the intensified sanctions and limited engagement aimed at changing Pyongyang's behavior and bringing it back to the negotiating table, has failed.[69] Indeed, critics of this "passive-aggressive approach" argue that it has allowed Pyongyang to continue to develop a uranium enrichment program while the United States and South Korea stand idly by.[70]

One approach to revising that strategy might include more active efforts intended to increase pressure on the North while also increasing diplomatic efforts. In this context, some of the steps could include the following:

Strengthen sanctions

Existing sanctions against Pyongyang may have had a limited impact on its WMD programs and proliferation activities, slowing down their development by drying up overseas funding and severing ties with potential customers. While the Obama administration has expressed its willingness to continue to press implementation of sanctions until significant progress on denuclearization is achieved, sufficient pressure has not been imposed on the North to impede progress on its nuclear and missile programs.

Strengthening existing measures, particularly UN Security Council Resolution 1874 (2009) is one option. That resolution commits all states to "inspect, in accordance with their national legal authorities and consistent with international law, all cargo to and from the DPRK [North Korea], in their territory, including seaports and airports."[71] Its implementation has proven difficult as a range of nations, particularly China, has not been fully cooperative in interdicting Pyongyang's shipments and preventing their financing.[72] The ability of the international community to prevent North Korea from proliferating its missiles and nuclear technologies, therefore, relies on the question of how to build greater collaboration in implementing the resolution.

More importantly, further efforts are required to impose financial pressure on the North. Impeding funding sources for its nuclear and missile programs should remain a key priority of sanctions. That will require, once again, greater multilateral action to identify those sources. Another key measure would be to increase pressure on Pyongyang's leadership by identifying overseas bank accounts. So far, insufficient progress has been made on this front. It also remains vital to take action against North Korean technology procurement efforts by focusing future measures on identifying fronts and entities based in third countries that are associated with the North's WMD programs, as well as constraining Pyongyang's use of sea and air routes for its proliferation.[73]

Step up diplomatic efforts

At the same time, the United States should either soften or even drop its stance that North Korea must meet a number of preconditions before Washington reengages in dialogue with Pyongyang. Its current position – that the North must meet a series of preconditions ranging from nuclear and missile test moratoria to disclosing the full extent of its uranium enrichment program – even before talks resume, while based on principle, has not been successful. Granted, there may be some reason to set preconditions for talks with Pyongyang given its recent lack of performance on the denuclearization front, but doing so is a prescription for having no dialogue at all. Neither Pyongyang, nor any country for that matter, would accept such preconditions.

Moreover, it is worth noting that dealing with Pyongyang is a three-dimensional chess match. North Korea may be the opponent but China is also a key player (as are the other countries who have participated in the Six Party Talks). It is quite clear that Beijing also finds Washington's position unacceptable, making the Obama administration's objective of securing China's support for more sanctions against the North even more difficult. A different position – perhaps even seeking to engage Pyongyang without preconditions – might help expose whether the North is serious or not about diplomacy, something that could help in this three-sided game.

A number of different approaches are possible. For example, both sides could demonstrate a willingness to take "confidence-building steps" very early in renewed contacts. In that context, North Korea might release Kenneth Bae, a Korean-American missionary held in prison. It might also reaffirm the Joint Statement of September 2005 that included Pyongyang's pledge to denuclearize, perhaps adding explicit language with regard to its uranium enrichment program. This will be essential since the United States will need to avoid the perception at home and abroad that it is accepting Pyongyang as a nuclear-weapon state. Other steps would include a moratorium on nuclear tests and a suspension of nuclear activities at Yongbyon accompanied by IAEA verification.[74]

While a moratorium on missile launches would also be worthwhile, that might prove to be a sticking point given Pyongyang's increasing attachment to its space launch program. Whether the North would be willing to consider possible alternatives remains unclear. For example, one option might be for the North to restate its right to peaceful space exploration but also express its willingness to forego launches for some temporary period.

As for the negotiations themselves, once again it is possible to devise a variety of roadmaps that might lead all participants down the road towards denuclearization and building peace and stability on the peninsula. One approach may be to make sure that any approach addresses core security issues on both sides, namely from the perspective of the United States and its allies, North Korea's WMD threat, and from the North Korean perspective, replacing the armistice ending the Korean War with a permanent peace treaty. Moreover, both sides will have to be willing to accept a process that moves forward in phases and that will mean not achieving denuclearization in the short or even medium terms. Rather, the benefit will be to prevent expansion of Pyongyang's nuclear and missile capabilities in the near term with the possibility over the long term of reversal and elimination. It will also mean in the near term, decreasing the possibility of horizontal proliferation of these capabilities to customers abroad.

Encourage better nonproliferation behavior by North Korea

In an environment of active diplomatic exchanges and perhaps even progress, a key component should be to bolster North Korea's adherence to nonproliferation norms. North Korea has made public commitments to maintain the security of its nuclear stockpile and not to sell dangerous technology abroad. Of course, there is reason to be somewhat skeptical about those commitments. However, they at least provide a starting point for securing Pyongyang's adherence to a menu of practical measures. These might include: obtaining Pyongyang's agreement to support international nonproliferation efforts to nonnuclear states, including technology and tacit knowledge related to WMD; securing its obligation to participate in the International Convention for the Suppression of Acts of Nuclear Terrorism, which would commit Pyongyang's assistance to nonstate actors as a crime; and beginning confidence-building measures through establishing presence of the Nuclear Supplier Group.[75]

Bolster export controls

North Korea's uranium enrichment capabilities would not have been possible without foreign assistance, while other countries also benefited from their back-door connections with Pyongyang in exchanging nuclear-weapon capabilities. Moreover, the level of North Korean development of its highly enriched uranium program remains a subject for active debate and some prominent experts still believe that tightened export controls can at least slow the program's growth.

An effective effort to tighten export controls must be pursued on two fronts. First, just as with sanctions, the role of China remains central as a conduit of materials and technology to North Korea. Therefore, a more effective regime will require greater Chinese cooperation in stopping the inflow of materials that might help North Korea's nuclear and missile programs. That, in turn will require, above all else, greater political cooperation between Beijing on the one hand, and the United States, its allies, and other international players on the other hand in a common overall effort to resolve this challenge. If the political context is right, then more narrowly focused export control measures might be more possible, although still probably limited by Beijing's overall economic ties with the North as well as concerns about destabilizing the regime in Pyongyang.

One possible measure would be to create a more comprehensive list of prohibited items and materials that are critical to the North's nuclear and missile program (such as maraging steel, high-strength aluminum alloys, and frequency changers) but are currently precluded due to Chinese opposition.[76] Furthermore, it is important to strengthen the existing multilateral export regimes by specifying the commitments and responsibilities of members as well as increasing transparency of information sharing on both export approval and denials, and establishing a dispute-resolution mechanism to allow for a collective decision process.[77]

A secondary but still important objective will be to tighten the existing international regime of export controls. For example, the Proliferation Security Initiative (PSI) – a US-led coordinating mechanism aimed to galvanize multilateral cooperation in carrying out WMD and missile-related interdictions – is a significant area where multilateral efforts can be coordinated to curb the Pyongyang's proliferation activities.[78] While increased surveillance would prove useful in the short term, greater collaboration under PSI with respect to land and sea routes would be necessary in the longer term.[79] Also, since some regional countries such as India, China, Indonesia, and Malaysia have expressed objections to the initiative and currently do not participate, promoting expansion of PSI membership in the region would be another key avenue to pursue. Furthermore, establishing clear authority and a coordination budget as well as cooperation with NATO and other countries may be some of the other measures to strengthen and expand PSI efforts, which would be fruitful in combating Pyongyang's proliferation activities.

Prevent nuclear leakage from North Korea

Such an approach might consist of a variety of measures tailored to essentially two different scenarios: the continuation of the current North Korean regime, and its collapse. The second scenario is relatively straightforward. Planning for dealing with North Korea's collapse has been underway since the demise of the Soviet Union in 1991 and has gone through much iteration. On the specific challenge of dealing with North Korea's WMD in the chaotic security environment likely to be found in the North after its collapse, the experience of trying to find and secure Iraq's WMD in the aftermath of the second Gulf War is likely to be the model for the future. Needless to say, the challenges will be enormous, not only because the United States probably does not know where Pyongyang's nuclear weapons and technologies are located, but also because securing them in a timely fashion before they are stolen or leak out of the country will be extremely difficult.

One way of addressing these challenges would be to attempt to coordinate advance planning with China as many experts have advocated. After all, Beijing also has an interest in preventing the leakage of nuclear materials, know-how and weapons given its proximity to North Korea and fears that nuclear items might find their way into the hands of domestic groups opposed to the Chinese regime. However, repeated attempts to build cooperation appear to have failed, in large part because Chinese participation in advance planning for collapse could seriously damage Beijing's touchy relationship with the North Korean regime.

As for seeking to build cooperation on nuclear security issues with the current North Korean government, that might be possible in the context of renewing dialogue with Pyongyang on the bigger challenge of denuclearization. Once again, North Korea has pledged to maintain tight control over its nuclear capabilities in an effort to appear responsible to the international community. Under the right circumstances, Pyongyang might be willing to go beyond just pledges and to establish a separate dialogue on nuclear security. While some might argue that security in a totalitarian state like North Korea should not be a concern, it would be in the interest of the international community, at the very least, to do a "reality check" on what measures the North has in place. That might lead to the discovery of deficiencies and even to limited cooperation in upgrading existing security measures. One delicate issue is to avoid the appearance of condoning the North's nuclear-weapon stockpile while negotiating for its denuclearization.

Notes

1. Arms Control Association, "Chronology of US-North Korean Nuclear and Missile Diplomacy," February 2014, www.armscontrol.org/factsheets/dprkchron.
2. Mary Beth Nikitin, "North Korea's Nuclear Weapons: Technical Issues," *Congressional Research Service,* April 3, 2013, p. 1, www.fas.org/sgp/crs/nuke/RL34256.pdf.
3. Arms Control Association, "Chronology of US-North Korean Nuclear and Missile Diplomacy."
4. Korean Central News Agency, "DPRK to Adjust Uses of Existing Nuclear Facilities," April 2, 2013, www.kcna.co.jp/item/2013/201304/news02/20130402-36ee.html.
5. For commercial satellite imagery analyses, see the US-Korea Institute, 38 North, Paul H. Nitze School of Advanced International Studies (SAIS), Johns Hopkins University, www.38north.org.
6. Chungang Ilbo, "북, '소형화, 경량화, 다종화, 정밀화' 핵무기 보유 주장 [North Korea claims its 'miniaturized, light-weight, diversified, and cutting-edge nuclear weapons']," May 21, 2013, http://money.joins.com/news/article/article.asp?total_id=11578004&ctg=1004.
7. Ibid.
8. Dick K. Nanto and Emma Chanlett-Avery, "North Korea: Economic Leverage and Policy Analysis," Congressional Research Service, January 22, 2010, p. 48, www.fas.org/sgp/crs/row/RL32493.pdf; see United States Department of Defense, Office of the Secretary, "Military and Security Developments Involving the Democratic People's Republic of Korea 2013," Annual Report to Congress, March 5, 2014, p. 20, www.defense.gov/pubs/North_Korea_Military_Power_Report_2013-2014.pdf; see also Arms Control Association, "Arms Control and Proliferation Profile: North Korea," April 2013, www.armscontrol.org/factsheets/northkoreaprofile.

9.   BBC News, "Syria 'had cover nuclear scheme'," April 25, 2008, http://news.bbc.co.uk/2/hi/ 7364269.stm.
10. Department of Defense, "Military and Security Developments Involving the Democratic People's Republic of Korea 2013," p. 20; also see Siegfried S. Hecker, "A Return Trip to North Korea's Yongbyon Nuclear Complex," Center for International Security and Cooperation, Stanford University, November 20, 2010, p. 5, http://iis-db.stanford.edu/pubs/23035/HeckerYongbyon.pdf.
11. United Nations Security Council, "Report of the Panel of Experts established pursuant to resolution 1874 (2009)," S/2014/147. March 6, 2014, p. 19, www.un.org/sc/committees/1718/poe reports.shtml.
12. Nikitin, "North Korea's Nuclear Weapons: Technical Issues."
13. Dennis C. Blair, "Annual Threat Assessment of the Intelligence Community for the Senate Select Committee on Intelligence," Office of the Director of National Intelligence, February 12, 2009, p. 25, www.intelligence.senate.gov/090212/blair.pdf.
14. Joseph Cirincione, "A Global Assessment of Nuclear Proliferation Threats," A Paper Prepared for the Weapons of Mass Destruction Commission, June 2004, p. 3, www.blixassociates.com/wp-content/ uploads/2011/03/No10.pdf.
15. Ibid.
16. Don Oberdorfer, *The Two Koreas: A Contemporary History* (Reading, MA: Addison Wesley, 1997), pp. 249–255; Jonathan D. Pollack, *No Exit: North Korea, Nuclear Weapons and International Security* (New York: Routledge, 2011).
16. Victor D. Cha and David C. Kang, "The Debate over North Korea," *Political Science Quarterly,* Vol. 119, No. 2 (Summer 2004), pp. 229–254.
17. Nuclear Threat Initiative, "North Korea," September 2013, www.nti.org/country-profiles/north-korea/nuclear/.
18. Olli Heinonen, "North Korea's Nuclear Enrichment: Capabilities and Consequences," *38 North,* June 22, 2011, http://38north.org/2011/06/heinonen062211.
19. Ibid.
20. Oberdorfer, *The Two Koreas,* pp. 252–253.
21. Walter C. Clemens, Jr., "North Korea's Quest for Nuclear Weapons: New Historical Evidence," *Journal of East Asian Studies,* Vol. 10, No. 1 (January–April 2010), pp. 127–154; Pollack, *No Exit,* pp. 43–77.
22. Heinonen, "North Korea's Nuclear Enrichment: Capabilities and Consequences."
23. Joel S. Wit, Daniel Poneman, and Robert L. Gallucci, *Going Critical: The First North Korean Nuclear Crisis* (Washington, DC: Brookings Institution Press, 2004), p. 1.
24. Jon Wolfsthal, "The Intelligence 'Black Hole' over North Korea," op-ed. *BBC NEWS,* July 17, 2003, available at http://news.bbc.co.uk/2/hi/asia-pacific/3073677.stm.
25. Nikitin, "North Korea's Nuclear Weapons," p. 1.
26. The Korean Peninsula Energy Development Organization, "Agreed Framework Between the United States of America and the Democratic People's Republic of Korea," October 21, 1994, www.kedo.org/pdfs/AgreedFramework.pdf.
27. Nikitin, "North Korea's Nuclear Weapons," pp. 18–20.
28. Siegfried Hecker, "The Risks of North Korea's Nuclear Restart," *Bulletin of the Atomic Scientists,* May 12, 2009, http://thebulletin.org/risks-north-koreas-nuclear-restart.
29. The announcement made by the Korean Central News Agency. See Korean Central News Agency, "DPRK to Adjust Uses of Existing Nuclear Facilities," April 2, 2013, www.kcna.co.jp/item/ 2013/201304/news02/20130402-36ee.html.
30. Nick Hansen and Jeffrey Lewis, "Satellite Images Show New Construction at North Korea's Plutonium Production Reactor: Rapid Start?" *38 North,* April 3, 2013, http://38north.org/2013/ 04/yongbyon040313.
31. Ibid.
32. Nick Hansen, "Major Development: Reactor Fuel Fabrication Facilities Identified at Yongbyon Nuclear Complex," *38 North,* December 23, 2013, http://38north.org/2013/12/yongbyon122313.
33. Nuclear Threat Initiative, "Experimental 25–30 MWe Light Water Reactor," *NTI.org* (Last modified on April 16, 2013), www.nti.org/facilities/769/.
34. David Albright and Christina Walrond, "North Korea's Estimated Stocks of Plutonium and Weapon-Grade Uranium," Institute for Science and International Security, August 16, 2012, pp. 1, 11–12, http://isis-online.org/uploads/isis-reports/documents/dprk_fissile_material_production_16Aug

2012.pdf; also see David Albright, "Challenges Posed by North Korea's Weapon-grade Uranium and Weapon-grade Plutonium: Current and Projected Stocks," *38 North*, October 24, 2012, http://38north.org/2012/10/dalbright102312.

35. International Institute for Strategic Studies, "Nuclear Black Markets: Pakistan, A.Q. Khan and the Rise of Proliferation Networks," *IISS Strategic Dossier*, May 2, 2007, www.iiss.org/en/publications/strategic%20dossiers/issues/nuclear-black-markets—pakistan—a-q—khan-and-the-rise-of-proliferation-networks—a-net-assessmen-23e1.

36. Pervez Musharraf, *In the Line of Fire: A Memoir* (New York: Free Press, September 2006), p. 296.

37. Ibid.

38. Nikitin, "North Korea's Nuclear Weapons," p. 17.

39. Olli Heinonen, "The North Korean Nuclear Program in Transition," *38 North,* April 26, 2012, http://38north.org/2012/04/oheinonen042612.

40. David Albright and Paul Brannan, *Taking Stock: North Korea's Uranium Enrichment Program* (Washington, DC: The Institute of Science and International Security, October 8, 2010), pp. 11–13, http://isis-online.org/uploads/isis-reports/documents/ISIS_DPRK_UEP.pdf.

41. Heinonen, "The North Korean Nuclear Program in Transition."

42. International Institute for Strategic Studies, "Pakistan and North Korea: Dangerous Counter-Trades," *IISS Strategic Comments,* Vol. 8, No. 9 (November 2002), pp. 1–2, http://carnegieendowment.org/pdf/npp/Pakistan-and-North-Korea.pdf.

43. Heinonen, "The North Korean Nuclear Program in Transition"; also see Albright and Walrond, "North Korea's Estimated Stocks of Plutonium and Weapon-Grade Uranium," p. 14.

44. United States Central Intelligence Agency, "Unclassified Report to Congress on the Acquisition of Technology Relating to Weapons of Mass Destruction and Advanced Conventional Munitions, 1 January – 30 June 2002," www.cia.gov/library/reports/archived-reports-1/jan_jun2002.html#5.

45. Richard Boucher, "North Korean Nuclear Program," US Department of State, Press Statement, October 16, 2002, http://2001-2009.state.gov/r/pa/prs/ps/2002/14432.htm; see also James A. Kelly, "US-East Asia Policy: Three Aspects," Remarks at the Woodrow Wilson Center, Washington, DC, December 11, 2002, http://2001-2009.state.gov/p/eap/rls/rm/2002/15875.htm.

46. Kelly, "US-East Asia Policy"; also see Selig Harrison, "Did North Korea Cheat?" *Foreign Affairs,* Vol. 84, No. 1 (January/February 2005), pp. 99–110.

47. US Department of State, "Adherence To and Compliance With Arms Control, Nonproliferation and Disarmament Agreements and Commitments," August 2005, www.state.gov/documents/organization/52113.pdf.

48. Ibid, p. 89.

49. Arms Control Association, "Chronology of US-North Korean Nuclear and Missile Diplomacy."

50. Heinonen, "North Korea's Nuclear Enrichment: Capabilities and Consequences."

51. Hecker, "A Return trip to North Korea's Yongbyon Nuclear Complex."

52. David Albright and Robert Avagyan, "Recent Doubling of Floor Space at North Korean Gas Centrifuge Plant," ISIS Imagery Brief, Institute for Science and International Security, August 7, 2013, http://isis-online.org/uploads/isis-reports/documents/Yongbyon_fuel_facility_7Aug2013.pdf.

53. Nikitin, "North Korea's Nuclear Weapons," pp. 7–9.

54. Ibid.

55. Ivan Oelrich and Ivanka Barzashka, "Centrifuges and Nuclear Weapons Proliferation," Federation of American Scientists, N.D., www.fas.org/programs/ssp/nukes/fuelcycle/centrifuges/proliferation.html.

56. Albright and Walrond, "North Korea's Estimated Stocks of Plutonium and Weapons-Grade Uranium."

57. Duyeon Kim, "Fact Sheet: North Korea's Nuclear and Ballistic Missile Programs," The Center for Arms Control and Non-Proliferation, Updated in July 2013, http://armscontrolcenter.org/issues/northkorea/articles/fact_sheet_north_korea_nuclear_and_missile_programs.

58. Nikitin, "North Korea's Nuclear Weapons," p. 11.

59. Ibid.

60. Oelrich and Barzashka, "Centrifuges and Nuclear Weapon Proliferation."

61. Choe-Sang-Hun, "North Korea Learning to Make Crucial Nuclear Parts, Study Finds," *New York Times,* September 23, 2013, www.nytimes.com/2013/09/24/world/asia/north-korea-learning-to-make-crucial-nuclear-parts-study-finds.html.

62. David Albright and Olli Heinonen, "In Response to Recent Questionable Claims about North Korea's Indigenous Production of Centrifuges," ISIS Reports, October 18, 2013, http://isis-online.org/isis-reports/detail/in-response-to-recent-questionable-claims-about-north-koreas-indigenous-pro.

63. See United Nations Security Council, "Report of the Panel of Experts established pursuant to resolution 1874 (2009)," S/2013/337, June 11, 2013, www.securitycouncilreport.org/atf/cf/%7B65BFCF9B-6D27-4E9C-8CD3-CF6E4FF96FF9%7D/s_2013_337.pdf.

64. Ibid., p. 4.

65. Ibid., p. 10.

66. Ibid., p. 9.

67. Albright and Walrond, "North Korea's Estimated Stocks of Plutonium and Weapons-Grade Uranium," p. 3.

68. Mark Manyin, "Kim Jong-il's Death: Implications for North Korea's Stability and US Policy," Congressional Research Service, December 22, 2011, p. 7, www.fas.org/sgp/crs/row/R42126.pdf.

69. Ibid.

70. United Nations Security Council, "Resolution 1874 (2009)," S/RES/1874 (2009), June 12, 2009, p. 3, www.un.org/en/ga/search/view_doc.asp?symbol=S/RES/1874(2009).

71. Nikitin, "North Korea's Nuclear Weapons," p. 29.

72. Joseph DeThomas, "Next Steps in Sanctions against Pyongyang," *38 North*, March 3, 2014, http://38north.org/2014/03/jdethomas030314.

73. Ibid.

74. Wit, Poneman, and Gallucci, *Going Critical*, p. 12.

75. Bruce Klingner, "Time to Go Beyond International North Korean Sanctions," *38 North*, April 29, 2014, http://38north.org/2014/04/bklingner042914.

76. Michael Beck and Seema Gahlaut, "Creating a New Multilateral Export Control Regime," *Arms Control Today*, Vol. 33, No. 3 (April 2003), pp. 12–18, www.armscontrol.org/act/2003_04/beckgahlaut_apr03

77. Ibid.

78. Sharon Squassoni and Fred McGoldrick, "Nonproliferation Policy towards North Korea," Nautilus Institute, November 24, 2009, p. 5, http://nautilus.org/wp-content/uploads/2011/12/SquassoniMcGoldrick.pdf.

6

SOUTH ASIA

Strategic competition and nuclear policies

Feroz Hassan Khan

With a plethora of new delivery systems and rising fissile material production rates, India and Pakistan continue to defy the global normative nonproliferation regime.[1] These nuclear investments are a symptom of the intense strategic competition that has embroiled India and Pakistan for decades and is now entering a third distinct phase. In the first phase (1974–1998), both states challenged the nonproliferation regime by developing and demonstrating their respective nuclear capabilities. In the second phase (1998–2013), both countries focused on developing operational deterrence force postures, doctrines, and command and control systems. In the ongoing third phase, nuclear capabilities are modernizing and expanding to encompass sea-based delivery systems, completing the third leg of the nuclear "triad."

Rivalry and distrust between India and Pakistan are the central drivers for this nuclear arms race, and lately, global power politics have been exacerbating these tensions. As the United States pivots to the Asia-Pacific, China feels threatened and increases its defense spending, which in turn spurs India to develop and modernize its own strategic and conventional forces, to include Agni intermediate-range ballistic missiles (IRBMs) and Sagarika submarine-launched ballistic missiles (SLBMs). Western powers tacitly endorse India's strategic ambitions and military investments as a means of "containing" China's rise, but meanwhile, Pakistan finds itself increasingly vulnerable. Pakistan is geographically exposed to Indian attack and lacks the resources to compete with India's superior conventional military. Islamabad relies on nuclear weapons to offset this imbalance and has most recently introduced battlefield-range systems, such as the 60 km-range Nasr. In essence, the Asia-Pacific rebalance is indirectly fueling the Indo-Pakistani rivalry and incentivizing the expansion of their nuclear arsenals.

As in the past, the international community does not desire an unhealthy arms race between India and Pakistan. Yet there is no discernable policy or visible involvement in the region that could mitigate regional tensions or resolve a conflict set in motion. The lack of coherent international effort to dampen Indo-Pakistani competition and integrate the two states into the nonproliferation regime has given them carte blanche to double-down on their efforts to expand and improve their strategic arsenals. South Asia therefore continues to fly in the face of the global nonproliferation regime in the twenty-first century.

The first section of this chapter will assess the current status and upward trajectories of Indian and Pakistani strategic forces. The second section examines the evolving military doctrines and command and control arrangements. The third section examines how regional political dynamics have aggravated the Indo-Pakistani arms race, with specific emphasis on the implications of the A.Q. Khan affair, the US-India nuclear deal, the US rebalance to the Asia-Pacific, and the lack of progress in regional confidence-building measures (CBMs). The final section concludes with some prospects for regional peace and stability and some recommendations for consideration.

Status of India and Pakistan's strategic arsenals

Overview of developments: 1998–2013

India tested its first nuclear device, known as "Smiling Buddha," in 1974. Despite New Delhi's attempts to characterize the test as a "peaceful nuclear explosion," the die was cast, and Pakistan began to aggressively pursue the bomb. By the mid-1980s, India and Pakistan had reached nominal nuclear capability and adopted a "recessed deterrence" posture wherein both states produced fissile material at a gentle pace, developed delivery means, and conducted several experiments and cold tests along the way. Nuclear weapons were not overtly declared but both sides tacitly understood one another's nascent capabilities. The 1998 nuclear explosive tests heralded the start of the overt nuclear era. By the turn of the century, conservative estimates of India and Pakistani nuclear weapons hovered around 40–50 weapons. Delivery was inordinately reliant on aircraft, as few ballistic missiles had been flight-tested. Nuclear weapons, in other words, were not fully operational and only notionally employable.

The fifteen years after the 1998 tests have witnessed unprecedented acts of terrorism, military crises, and intense international focus on South Asia. It is perhaps no surprise that during this same period, India and Pakistan have transitioned from a recessed deterrence posture to an operational one, characterized by a steady expansion of delivery systems and fissile material production infrastructure. Three events in particular give context to this momentous shift. First, India and Pakistan came to the brink of full-scale war in 2001–2002 when militants from Lashkar-e-Taiba and Jaish-e-Mohammed attacked the Indian parliament building in New Delhi. Second, the discovery and dismantling of the A.Q. Khan network in 2004 put Pakistan in the proverbial proliferation "doghouse," damaging its international standing and heightening its sense of isolation and insecurity. Third, the US-India nuclear deal, announced in 2005 and legislated in 2008 further heightened Pakistan's sense of isolation and grievances.

The abovementioned three events certainly did no favors for Indo-Pakistani relations. Instead, mutual mistrust and security anxieties have increased, and the stakes of conflict are higher than ever as both countries continue to invest in fissile production and delivery systems. Of note, observers have pointed out that India and Pakistan now possess more nuclear-weapon delivery vehicles – including families of cruise and ballistic missiles – than the United States.[2]

Status of fissile material development

India's nuclear program began a decade ahead of Pakistan's. According to the 2013 *SIPRI Yearbook*, the Indian arsenal comprises 90 to 110 warheads. Estimates in 2012 put India's highly enriched uranium (HEU) stockpile at 2.4 ± 0.9 metric tons, and its weapons-grade plutonium stockpile at 0.54 ± 0.18 metric tons.[3]

Pakistani security managers have long feared a fissile material gap with India, and this perception gained traction in the wake of the US-India nuclear deal, agreed upon in 2005 and set into motion in 2008. Under the terms of the deal, India was required to separate its civil and military nuclear installations and submit the civil sites to International Atomic Energy

Agency (IAEA) safeguards. In return, India was granted permission to import nuclear fuel and technology despite its not being a party to the Treaty on the Nonproliferation of Nuclear Weapons (NPT). This meant that India could now divert its domestic uranium resources toward the military nuclear program while relying on imported uranium to fuel the civilian component.

Pakistan has augmented its fissile production capacity in order to stay competitive with India and keep pace with the rapid induction of new delivery systems on the subcontinent. After the 1998 tests, Pakistan had only one plutonium production reactor at Khushab, but as of 2014, a fourth is in the works. As for HEU, Pakistan has expanded the uranium hexafluoride production capacity at the Chemical Plants Complex at Dera Ghazi Khan, and new-generation gas centrifuges (P-3 and P-4) have been installed at Kahuta.[4] Open-source analysis from 2012 estimated Pakistan to have 3 ± 1.2 metric tons of HEU and 0.15 ± 0.05 metric tons of plutonium – enough to produce one or two dozen weapons per year.[5] Pakistan is currently believed to have 90–110 warheads.[6]

In the coming years, Pakistan's fissile material output is slated to rise. Plutonium production will increase when the fourth planned Khushab reactor comes online later this decade. Feedstock for Khushab-IV may come from a new mine that is set to open at Shanawa in 2014, which will boost Pakistan's annual production of natural uranium from approximately 36 to 54 metric tons.[7] Increased fissile output means more weapons can be produced, and Pakistan can stretch its fissile stocks further if it adopts composite warhead designs or boosts its weapons with deuterium-tritium. On the other hand, as Pakistan's current uranium sources deplete, the nuclear program will suffer because unlike India, Pakistan does not enjoy the benefit of external supply. In any case, given Pakistan's strides in fissile material production and India's external supply advantage, it is no surprise that Islamabad continues to drag its feet in international negotiations on a Fissile Material Cutoff Treaty (FMCT).[8]

Strategic triad and force modernization

Indian strategic forces are modernizing under an ambitious program that demonstrates the country's burgeoning power projection capabilities. In April 2012, India conducted a flight test of the 5,000km Agni-V solid-fuelled ballistic missile. Declared as an intercontinental ballistic missile (ICBM), the Agni is expected to be operational by 2015. India claims it would be equipped with multiple independently-targetable reentry vehicles (MIRVs), designed to penetrate and defeat enemy missile defenses.[9] In early 2013, India carried out the maiden test of its 290-km range, supersonic submarine-launched cruise missile (SLCM) BrahMos, which was declared to be "ready for fitment on submarines in vertical launch configuration."[10] India also has plans to field submarine-launched ballistic missiles (SLBMs) such as the 700 km-range K-15 Sagarika, whose development trials were completed in January 2013.[11] Sagarika is designed to launch from the Arihant-class ballistic missile submarine (SSBN) and carry a 1,000 kg nuclear warhead. Each Arihant-class submarine would be able to carry 12 K-15 missiles which would later be replaced by the 3,500 km-range K-X. Three Arihant-class SSBNs are currently under construction – one at Visakhapatnam and two in Vadodara, India.[12] Prime Minister Manmohan Singh launched the first nuclear powered boat of this class in July 2009 at Visakhapatnam with great fanfare, with talk of India joining the elite club of nations equipped with nuclear submarines.[13] In tandem with these new offensive capabilities and delivery systems, India is also actively developing Ballistic Missile Defenses (BMD).

Pakistan's strategic forces comprise various types of short-range and medium-range ballistic and cruise missiles. These include the Hatf-1A, Hatf-II (Abdali), Hatf-III (Ghaznavi), Hatf-IV

(Shaheen-1, Shaheen-1A), Hatf-V (Ghauri), Hatf-VI (b-2), Hatf-VII (Babur), Hatf-VIII (Ra'ad), and Hatf-IX (Nasr).[14] Not content with the suite of delivery options at its disposal, Pakistan is reportedly developing sea-based delivery systems, as indicated by the 2012 inauguration of the Naval Strategic Forces Command. The sea-based deterrent will most likely comprise Agosta-class submarines armed with nuclear-tipped cruise missiles.[15]

The rapid development and deployment of delivery systems is not likely to slow down in the near term. India's BMD gambit threatens the integrity of Pakistan's nuclear deterrent (at least in theory if not in practice), thus Pakistan is compelled to diversify its delivery methods and develop penetration aids. For this reason, the possibility of a Pakistani MIRV, though technically complex, cannot be ruled out.

Doctrines and command and control

After the 1971 Indo-Pakistani War in which India successfully dismembered Pakistan and paved the way for creation of Bangladesh, new factors began to shape the rivalry. The advent of Bangladesh, for example, simplified the strategic landscape for India and Pakistan. India no longer had a Pakistani flank on both sides, and Pakistan no longer had to defend two fronts from India. Following a peace accord in 1972, a period of relative stability prevailed between the two states, despite India's 1974 nuclear test which inspired Pakistan's tenacious pursuit to obtain a nuclear-weapon capability.

New Delhi's strategic thinking began to transform by the early 1980s, however, when the Indian military started to contemplate how to defeat Pakistan in a conventional war before its nuclear deterrent became operational. As a means to this end, India's army chief General K. Sundarji reorganized India's army formations into a force that could fight a swift battle to sever Pakistan in two and destroy the country's nascent nuclear capability. The Indian army conducted several exercises in the mid-1980s to perfect this concept, one of which resulted in a major military crisis in 1986–1987 (Exercise Brasstacks).[16]

The 1990s were another time of major strategic shifts. The Soviet war in Afghanistan had ended, insurgency in Kashmir ramped up, and in 1998, the historic Indian and Pakistani nuclear tests took place. Thus by the end of the decade, the spectrum of war in South Asia was no longer solely conventional, but also had a sub-conventional and nuclear element. The nuclear tests theoretically restored the strategic imbalance and called for strategic restraint measures, but despite some high-profile political initiatives such as the 1999 Lahore memorandum, India and Pakistan were unable to agree to a formalized arms control and restraint agreement. Instead, a "mini-war" in Kargil in 1999 scuttled the prospect of a structured peace. The atmosphere deteriorated further in the post 9/11 environment when alleged militants from Lashkar-e-Taiba and Jaish-e-Mohammed attacked the Indian parliament building in New Delhi, resulting in a ten-month military standoff that lasted from 2001 to 2002.[17]

With the overt nuclearization of the subcontinent, India's military concept of the 1980s was due for a revamp, but India's botched response to the 2001–2002 crisis provided the true catalyst for the change. Stunned by the audacity of the parliament attack, India's political masters ordered the army to mobilize and move to the international border, but the process was painfully slow. The strike corps took nearly three weeks to reach their assembly areas. During this period, Pakistan managed to reinforce the border, India's political decision-makers hesitated, and the international community intervened to ease the crisis. Simply put, the Sundarji doctrine proved ineffective and sluggish. As a result, Indian military planners began to rethink their approach toward fighting and winning a war against a nuclear-armed adversary.

India ultimately decided that the only way to fight and win a war against Pakistan without triggering Islamabad's nuclear redlines was to keep the operation limited. India's military goals and tactics were calibrated to avoid deep strikes but use shallow maneuvers and heavy air–land firepower to degrade the Pakistani military. Yet Indian military also needed to overcome its problems of slow mobilization time, political indecision, and diplomatic intervention by the international community. India ultimately decided upon the so-called "Cold Start" doctrine, wherein India would muster division-sized forces known as Integrated Battle Groups (IBGs), which could strike across the international border within 72–96 hours of a crisis and create an opening for follow-on forces to exploit and consolidate. The objective would be to make shallow ingress, inflict maximum destruction of Pakistani military strength, and withdraw – all without triggering Pakistan's nuclear redlines. Operations would cease before the international community could intervene. Naturally, India began to calibrate its military procurement and nuclear policies to support the Cold Start concept.

Pakistan adapted and refined its own military concepts in response to India's doctrinal evolution. It reinforced its passive defenses by constructing a series of obstacles and reduced mobilization times in an attempt to defensively beat India to the punch. As the Pakistan army's 2011 doctrine "Comprehensive Response" points out, "With the possibility of Pakistan being drawn into a war at very short notice, all formations organise their administrative and routine activities in a manner that effective combat potential can be generated within 24 to 48 hours from the corps to unit level and two to three days at the Army level."[18] Decreased mobilization time also grants Pakistan the agility to mount a counteroffensive across the international border at the place of its choosing as a rejoinder to Indian attack.

Despite the changes to its conventional warfighting doctrine, Pakistan still faced inherent geographic handicaps in a conflict with India. Pakistan's main lines of communication are situated perilously close to the border and could be severed quickly by an Indian blitzkrieg. Furthermore, Pakistan's army is conducting counterinsurgency operations in the western tribal areas, drawing a large number of troops from the garrisons close to India's border, leaving the eastern flank somewhat exposed. Pakistani military planners sought a solution for these disadvantages.

In April 2011, Pakistan revealed the Hatf-IX, a 60km-range, road-mobile short-range ballistic missile (SRBM), otherwise known as Nasr. According to a press statement by Pakistan's Inter-Services Public Relations directorate, Nasr "carries nuclear warheads of appropriate yield with high accuracy, shoot and scoot attributes."[19] This system, in other words, is a tactical nuclear weapon (TNW). The revelation that Pakistan has added TNWs to its arsenal was widely seen as a riposte to India's Cold Start doctrine – an attempt to lower the threshold of credible nuclear use and thereby deny India the space to prosecute a conventional war under the nuclear overhang.

The advent of TNWs in South Asia raised a number of complex questions. First, would deploying the system successfully deter the Indians or incentivize preemption? Second, how would command and control (C2) be articulated for TNW? Centralized C2 would make the deployed weapon safe from accidental use but ineffective and vulnerable in the heat of battle. Third was the question of field security for the weapons. If deployed, they will be located in the midst of conventional forces operating under an entirely different chain of command.

Despite these complexities, however, Pakistan continues to defend the Nasr and attributes its development to the growing technological and quantitative conventional force imbalance with India, as well as the threat posed by India's limited war doctrine. India's answer to Pakistan's 2011 Nasr test was a test of its own SRBM, Prahaar. India is ambiguous whether or not Prahaar carries nuclear warheads, but given its 50–150 km striking range and its possible role as a replacement for aging Privthi missiles, a dual-use mission is probable – especially since India is believed to have tested compact warhead designs.[20]

India and Pakistan also have a differing approach to nuclear doctrine. India has officially endorsed a doctrine of no first use (NFU), but reserves the right to retaliate massively if Indian forces are ever attacked with nuclear, chemical, or biological weapons – regardless of whether the attack takes place on Indian soil or foreign territory. Islamabad's nuclear doctrine, meanwhile, maintains the right of first use and dismisses India's massive retaliation policy as not credible, knee-jerk, and disproportionate. Beyond that, Pakistan's doctrine is shrouded in ambiguity, and the country's exact redlines are undeclared. Pakistan believes an ambiguous nuclear doctrine and imprecise thresholds paralyze the Indians from embarking on a hostile course of action. In this formulation, deterrence stability rests on exploiting the adversary's fear of the unknown. In 2002, however, Strategic Plans Division Director-General Khalid Kidwai listed four broad conditions that could elicit a Pakistani nuclear response. Kidwai remarked that Pakistan would use nuclear weapons if India conquers a large portion of territory, cripples the armed forces, strangles the economy, or threatens regime survival through domestic destabilization.[21]

The implications of the Indo-Pakistani nuclear doctrinal mismatch are potentially grave. Imagine a scenario in which India initiates Cold Start and sends its IBGs across the international border into Pakistan. India believes that its massive retaliation policy will deter the Pakistanis from employing TNWs, but the Pakistanis doubt that massive retaliation is a credible response to a few low-yield tactical strikes – especially since Pakistan would be able to survive enough strategic nuclear assets to launch a retaliatory salvo of its own. To simplify, both India and Pakistan believe that their own second-strike capability deters the other side from using nuclear weapons, which in turn fosters a misplaced feeling of impunity and incentivizes brash behavior. And as the repertoire of Indian and Pakistani nuclear delivery capabilities expand, so does the mutual distrust between the two.

Regional politics

The nuclear and doctrinal competition between India and Pakistan is a symptom of their frayed bilateral relationship and mutual mistrust. Unfortunately, the diplomatic outlook in South Asia is not encouraging, as several factors have exacerbated Pakistan's sense of international isolation and its strategic anxieties over India. Specific factors include international opprobrium over the A.Q. Khan network and increased US-India strategic cooperation (apparent from the nuclear deal and the Asia-Pacific rebalance). Making matters worse, there has been a distinct lack of progress in confidence-building and arms control on the subcontinent. India seems to have little incentive for dialogues on peace and security with Pakistan, citing lack of satisfactory progress in bringing justice against the perpetrators of the 2008 Mumbai terror attack. The end result is a regional strategic environment that is politically prone to crisis and perhaps conflict.

A.Q. Khan fallout

In January 2004, Pakistani nuclear scientist and head of the Pakistani centrifuge program Dr Abdul Qadeer Khan admitted to running a proliferation ring that came to be known as the infamous "A.Q. Khan network." The illicit network spread nuclear technology not only to Pakistan but also to defiant regimes such as Iran, Libya, and North Korea. A decade later, Pakistan continues to suffer the consequences of the network's unraveling.

A.Q. Khan is viewed as a national hero in Pakistan and is considered to be the "father" of the Pakistani bomb. Pakistanis believe he has been unfairly castigated for providing Pakistan with the ultimate deterrent. In contrast, the western narrative views A.Q. Khan as a villain who established a proliferation ring composed of greedy businessmen who made a fortune by peddling dual-use technology. This narrative holds that Pakistan's enrichment capability is the product of stolen centrifuge designs.

Pakistan has steadfastly denied any official complicity in the proliferation network. As a gesture of good faith, Islamabad agreed to investigate A.Q. Khan and his accomplices in Pakistan and share information with the international community, but stopped short of permitting outside interrogation. In addition, Pakistan dismantled the network from its end and has subsequently taken major steps to improve and tighten its nuclear security and safety regime.[22] Yet these actions have failed to erase the blemish on Pakistan's reputation. Although a decade has passed since the A.Q. Khan network's unraveling, Pakistan's image remains tarnished, and allegations of state complicity continue.

US-India nuclear deal

While Pakistan has grappled with the aftermath of the A.Q. Khan fiasco, India has reaped the benefits of a nuclear deal with the United States, announced in 2005 and legislated in Washington in 2008 as the Hyde Act. The deal essentially granted India a waiver from the export controls of the Nuclear Suppliers Group (NSG), allowing the free importation of nuclear fuel and technology for civilian purposes. In return, India agreed to disaggregate its civilian and military nuclear installations and open the civilian sites to IAEA inspection and safeguards. The deal was controversial from the outset and once again made South Asia the center of the global nonproliferation debate.

Proponents of the nuclear deal argued that India was a responsible actor and the deal would yield substantial benefits. They hailed India's relatively clean external proliferation record – contrasting with Pakistan, whose record was irrevocably sullied by the A.Q. Khan affair.[23] They also pointed out India's status as an emerging power with democratic credentials. The benefits of the deal were primarily threefold for the United States. First, it would bolster the US relationship with India, a strategic partner and regional counterweight to China. Second, it made good economic sense, as it would provide the US nuclear industry with lucrative business deals, especially in the sale of power plants and other related services. Third, although the deal would not formally bring India into the NPT, New Delhi's acceptance of IAEA safeguards for its civil nuclear sites seemed to be a step in the right direction.

Skeptics of the deal voiced serious concerns over its consequences. They argued that the deal violates the very fundamentals on which the NPT is based, both in letter and spirit. It stands prejudicial to Article 1 of NPT; dis-incentivizes Article 4 for those NPT member states who received legal promise of access to peaceful technology by foregoing nuclear weapon ambitions; and makes a mockery of Article 6. The deal confers de facto nuclear weapon status on India, which is not a party to the NPT and has no legal obligation toward the treaty. Meanwhile, the deal undermines the United States' credibility to use the NPT as a legal basis for pressuring the North Korean and Iranian nuclear programs. Skeptics of the deal also argued that US businesses might not profit as envisioned because cost overruns and liability insurance problems in the US nuclear and defense industry would make Russia and France more competitive for contracts. Significant for Pakistan's strategic calculus, meanwhile, was that the deal explicitly exempted eight power reactors from IAEA safeguards and freed up India's domestic uranium resources entirely for military purposes. Several American experts on South

Asia testifying on the congressional hearings over the Hyde Act warned that it could aggravate the nuclear arms race in South Asia.

Five years have passed since the Hyde Act was signed into law, and it seems that many of the warnings on the hill are coming to fruition. The deal changed Pakistan's calculations over India's fissile stocks, compelling Islamabad to step up production of both plutonium and HEU. Sino-Pakistani nuclear cooperation has increased. Pakistan continues to oppose the FMCT and maintains an unattainable hope for a US-Pakistan nuclear deal. No lucrative Indo-American business deal came to pass, but Russia, France, and Australia have benefited.

Moving forward, Indian membership in the NSG appears likely. The United States, Russia, France, and the United Kingdom have thrown their support behind India's bid, though China remains opposed and several other countries have expressed reservations. Indian membership would be ironic considering the fact that the NSG was established in reaction to India's 1974 nuclear test. There is not even talk of Pakistani membership, however. The A.Q. Khan affair has tainted Pakistan's record, though Pakistanis feel that the West is exploiting the scandal to unfairly deny them the privileges of membership. Pakistan's accusations of discrimination could be blunted, however, if membership in export control regimes was based on a dispassionate, criteria-based approach instead of politics and favoritism. A legalistic approach toward membership would also strengthen global nonproliferation norms. As long as Pakistan feels discriminated against and isolated, it will continue to seek nuclear weapons to guarantee its security and punch above its weight.

Strategic cascade of the US rebalance

The US rebalance to the Asia-Pacific has been criticized as an exercise in rhetoric as opposed to substance. This analysis may be premature as the rebalance has barely entered its third year, but regardless of whether Washington underwrites the policy with a credible show of military and diplomatic force, China and other regional powers in Asia are taking it seriously. China's reaction to the rebalance will cause a strategic ripple effect that reverberates throughout South Asia, indirectly aggravating the Indo-Pakistani arms race.

Beijing perceives the rebalance as an attempt at containment despite Washington's claims to the contrary. Fearing encirclement, China has augmented its military spending and will continue to improve its naval reach and missile forces, which naturally threatens China's regional rival, India. India has responded by raising a new mountain corps (17 corps) to be headquartered in Panagarh with divisions in Assam and Bihar, not far from the disputed territory of Arunachal Pradesh. In addition, India continues to invest considerable sums in its military hardware. India plans to acquire hundreds of new T-90S main battle tanks to replace its aging T-72s, and several air platforms are on order, including Apache attack helicopters and the new Dassault Rafale fighter. India meanwhile continues to fine-tune its Agni, BrahMos, and Sagarika series of missiles. All of these acquisitions would be employable against Pakistan.

Unable to match India's conventional largesse, Pakistan has doubled-down on its nuclear program, which has most recently developed TNWs and the 60 km-range *Nasr*. Sea-launched delivery systems are also in the pipeline. The strategic cascade does not end with Pakistan, however. Pakistani military advancements – and its close relations with Saudi Arabia – cause anxiety in Iran; Iranian advancements threaten Saudi Arabia and Israel; and so on. Security among rivals, after all, is a zero-sum game. As the US rebalance continues into this decade, the security competition will heat up in South Asia and perhaps beyond.

Negligible progress in CBMs and arms control

Confidence-building and arms control in South Asia exist in a state of limbo. The 2008 Mumbai attack poisoned the well for a diplomatic breakthrough, and relations remain tense today. Although there are a number of confidence-building measures (CBMs) on the books, such as crisis hotlines between the prime ministers and Directors-General of Military Operations, as well as mutual notification of ballistic missile flight tests, there is a distinct feeling that the low-hanging fruit has already been plucked and both sides lack the political will to engage in more substantive arrangements. Another pervasive belief is that CBMs are ineffectual for easing crisis and dissuading conflict. The Lahore Declaration of February 1999, for example, was a celebrated bilateral agreement in which India and Pakistan promised to resolve disputes peacefully in good faith, improve bilateral dialogue, and avoid nuclear provocation, but three months later, Pakistani soldiers snuck across the line of control in Kashmir and occupied abandoned Indian posts, sparking the Kargil War. Beyond CBMs, there is also a noticeable dearth of arms control agreements. There is no agreement to limit conventional force expansion, nor is there any limitation against delivery system development or fissile material production. Thus fissile stocks, nuclear arsenals, and delivery systems in South Asia continue to expand unabated.

Many opportunities for arms control exist if only the Indians and Pakistanis would come to the bargaining table. Pakistan and India both have aging, obsolete SRBMs (the Hatf-I and Privthi-I, respectively) that are ripe to be decommissioned and dismantled. If India and Pakistan could agree to dismantle these missiles jointly and transparently, it could inspire mutual confidence and serve as a foundation for future arms control efforts.[24] Such an agreement, however, requires political will. So long as New Delhi and Islamabad lack the political will to make a diplomatic overture and accept the political risk that comes with doing so, the outlook for substantive arms control and diplomatic rapprochement in South Asia will remain gloomy.

Conclusions

South Asia continues to fly in the face of the global nonproliferation regime. Strategic arsenals are expanding, doctrines and command and control are shifting, and Indo-Pakistani relations remain tense. The situation is unlikely to improve as the United States rebalances to the Asia-Pacific. China will continue to invest heavily in its military, adding sophisticated missile systems and naval platforms. India will react accordingly with military investments of its own, which will naturally threaten Pakistan. Lacking the resources to match India conventionally, Pakistan will continue to invest heavily in nuclear weapons to deter Indian aggression. This strategic cascade will continue to intensify the security dilemma on the subcontinent.

South Asia lacks an effective safety valve to ease Indo-Pakistani strategic anxieties. Although a number of CBMs are on the books, no viable bilateral initiatives for arms control or strategic restraint exist. South Asia will therefore continue to pose a major challenge to the nonproliferation regime – even more now than in the early period of the NPT (1970s), wherein both India and Pakistan directly interpreted the treaty as a challenge to their respective national security. The motivations underlying the Indian and Pakistani nuclear programs are fundamentally more intense than was the case in the earlier phases of their nuclear history, and the lack of diplomatic progress makes détente or rapprochement unlikely.

The outlook for stability in South Asia is bleak. Unless regional leaders emerge that see wisdom in restraint over competition, any future crisis in the region is likely to escalate rather than be resolved positively. The international community should encourage India and Pakistan to construct a strategic restraint arrangement. A peace and security architecture of this sort would facilitate conflict resolution and help bring an end to the destabilizing security competition between these nuclear-armed rivals.

Notes

1. This chapter contains the author's personal views and does not represent US Department of Defense, the Naval Postgraduate School (NPS) or the Pakistani government. The author is grateful to Ryan French – NPS research associate, MA Security Studies – for his research assistance.
2. Michael Krepon and Julia Thompson, *Deterrence Stability and Escalation Control in South Asia* (Washington, DC: Henry L. Stimson Center, 2013), p. 9, www.stimson.org/images/uploads/research-pdfs/Deterrence_Stability_Dec_2013_web.pdf.
3. "Summary," *SIPRI Yearbook 2013: Armaments, Disarmaments and International Security* (Stockholm: Stockholm International Peace Research Institute, 2013); International Panel on Fissile Materials, "India," February 4, 2013, www.fissilematerials.org/countries/india.html.
4. Author's Interview with Dr Javed Mirza, former head of Khan Research Laboratories (KRL), June 2007, for the book *Eating Grass: The Making of the Pakistani Bomb* (Palo Alto, CA: Stanford University Press, 2012).
5. International Panel on Fissile Materials, "Pakistan," February 3, 2013, www.fissilematerials.org/countries/pakistan.html.
6. Daryl Kimball and Tom Collina, "Nuclear Weapons: Who Has What at a Glance," Arms Control Association, November 2013, www.armscontrol.org/factsheets/Nuclearweaponswhohaswhat.
7. International Panel on Fissile Materials, *Global Fissile Material Report 2010: Balancing the Books: Production and Stocks* (Princeton, NJ: Princeton University, 2010), p.127, http://fissilematerials.org/library/gfmr10.pdf.
8. Pakistan contends that the FMCT fails to address the asymmetry of existing stocks and would cement Pakistan's disadvantage vis-à-vis India. For details, see Tom Collina and Daniel Horner, "The South Asian Nuclear Balance: An Interview with Pakistani Ambassador to the CD Zamir Akram," *Arms Control Today*, Vol. 41, No. 10 (December 2011), pp. 8–13, www.armscontrol.org/act/2011_12/Interview_With_Pakistani_Ambassador_to_the_CD_Zamir_Akram.
9. Raja Pandit, "Agni-V, India's first ICBM test-fired successfully," *The Times of India*, April 19, 2012, http://articles.timesofindia.indiatimes.com/2012-04-19/india/31367147_1_agni-v-mirv-payload-targetable-re-entry-vehicles.
10. Press Trust of India, "India test-fires submarine-launched version of BrahMos missile," *Times of India*, March 20, 2013, http://articles.timesofindia.indiatimes.com/2013-03-20/india/37871259_1_underwater-pontoon-brahmos-missile-cruise-missile.
11. Defence News India, "DRDO to Test SLBM from INS Arihant by Early 2014," September 17, 2013, www.defencenews.in/defence-news-internal.aspx?id=vSuwgGIcah4=.
12. Naval-Technology.com, "Indian Navy's K-15 SLBM successfully completes development trials," January 29, 2013, www.naval-technology.com/news/newsindian-navys-k-15-slbm-successfully-completes-development-trials. Also see Kelsey Devenport, "India Moves Closer to Nuclear Triad," *Arms Control Today*, Vol. 42, No. 7 (September 2012), pp. 32–33, http://armscontrol.org/act/2012_09/India-Moves-Closer-to-Nuclear-Triad. For India's Strategic Force Modernization, see Hans M. Kristensen and Robert S. Norris, "Nuclear Notebook: Indian Nuclear Forces, 2012," *Bulletin of Atomic Scientists*, Vol. 68, No. 4 (July/August 2012), pp. 96–101, http://bos.sagepub.com/content/68/4/96.full.pdf+html.
13. "PM launches INS Arihant at Visakhapatnam," *The Economic Times*, July 26, 2009, http://articles.economictimes.indiatimes.com/2009-07-26/news/27650185_1_indigenously-built-nuclear-powered-submarine-ins-arihant-naval-dockyard.
14. Khan, *Eating Grass: The Making of the Pakistani Bomb*, p. 250.
15. For details of Pakistan's Strategic Forces, see Hans M. Kristensen and Robert S. Norris, "Pakistan's Nuclear Forces, 2011," *Bulletin of the Atomic Scientists*, Vol. 67, No. 4 (July/August 2011), http://bos.sagepub.com/content/67/4/91.full.pdf+html.
16. In the 1980s, Pakistan and the United States were jointly waging an asymmetric war in Afghanistan to defeat the Soviet occupation. Pakistan was therefore in a state of war at its western border when the Indian military initiated Brasstacks.
17. All militants that attacked the Indian parliament in December 2001 were killed in the fire-fight.

18. Government of Pakistan, Army Doctrine and Evaluation Directorate, "Pakistan Army Doctrine 2011: Comprehensive Response," December 2011, pp. 43–44.

19. Government of Pakistan, Inter-Services Public Relations Directorate, "Press Release No. PR94/2011-ISPR," April 19, 2011, www.ispr.gov.pk/front/main.asp?o=t-press_release&id=1721.

20. Vivek Raghuvanshi, "India Tests New Tactical Missile," *Defense News,* July 21, 2011, www.defensenews.com/apps/pbcs.dll/article?AID=2011107210309.

21. Paolo Cotta-Ramusino and Maurizio Martellini, "Interview of Pakistan's former Director-General of the Strategic Plans Division, Khalid Kidwai," Landau Network-Centro Volta, February 2002, www.pugwash.org/september11/pakistan-nuclear.htm.

22. See the latest National Threat Initiative Index of 2014.

23. In citing India's "clean" nonproliferation record, proponents of the US-India nuclear deal seem to gloss over India's abuse of Atoms for Peace and its subsequent 1974 test as a forgiven and forgotten episode of nuclear history.

24. For a detailed analysis, see Feroz Khan and Gurmeet Kanwal, "Building Trust in South Asia through Cooperative Retirement of Obsolescent Missiles," Centre for Land Warfare Studies, September 4, 2011, www.claws.in/Building-Trust-in-South-Asia-through-Cooperative-Retirement-of-Obsolescent-Missiles-Gurmeet-Kanwal.html. Also see Zachary Davis, "The Yin and Yang of Strategic Transparency," in *Deterrence Stability and Escalation Control in South Asia*, Michael Krepon and Julia Thompson (eds), (Washington, DC: Henry L. Stimson Center, 2013), pp. 175–185.

7

INDIA AND THE GLOBAL NUCLEAR NONPROLIFERATION REGIME

An assessment

Arvind Gupta and Kapil Patil

In the summer of 1998, India carried out five nuclear tests at Pokhran site on May 11 and two on May 13, thereby ending the prolonged restraint it exercised in acquiring the nuclear weapons. After declaring itself a de facto nuclear-weapon power, India promulgated a draft nuclear doctrine in August 1999 which outlined the rationale for nuclear weapons in the country's national security policy. The doctrine enunciated that India would build and maintain a credible minimum (nuclear) deterrent posture, and the policy of "no-first-use" of nuclear weapons against nonnuclear states. The draft nuclear doctrine once again reaffirmed India's long-standing commitment to the goal of universal nuclear disarmament. While the international community was critical of India's decision to acquire nuclear weapons, less than a decade later, India has been able to engage with the United States and the international community to end its isolation in the global nuclear nonproliferation regime.

After declaring itself a de facto nuclear-weapon power in 1998, India undertook additional measures to ensure fullest compliance with the existing nuclear nonproliferation norms. Despite not being a member of the Treaty on the Nonproliferation of Nuclear Weapons (NPT), India became more supportive of various nonproliferation measures and agreed to work with the United States and the global community to strengthen the nonproliferation regime. India took the lead in synchronizing its export controls with current international standards. It has extended its support to various global initiatives for safeguarding nuclear materials and technologies, as a means to enhance the nuclear safety and security.

After 1998, there were widespread fears and apprehensions that the possible India-Pakistan military clash over the Kashmir dispute, without proper command and control mechanisms, would escalate into a major nuclear exchange. In the absence of sustained cooperation and crisis management systems, the attainment of a mutually stable deterrent has proven to be difficult.[1] While terrorism has been one of the serious challenges to India's national security for over three decades, the country has shown considerable restraint and responsibility in responding to incidents of cross-border terrorism. Despite escalation of tensions after the terrorist attacks on the Indian parliament in 2001 and the Mumbai terrorist strikes in 2008, India chose to refrain from exercising the military option against terrorist groups across its border. Rather, India has preferred to engage with Pakistan through confidence-building measures on issues such as terrorism, nuclear stability and the Jammu and Kashmir dispute. India's overall strategic restraint in the use of force also guides its nuclear policy which has shaped its official thinking on nuclear escalation control and achieving the durable deterrence stability.

This chapter analyses the various motivations in historical context that shaped the Indian approaches to the use of nuclear weapons and subsequently its decision to cross the nuclear threshold in the late 1990s. The chapter is organized in three main sections. The first section analyses the motivations and decisions pertaining to India's nuclear-weapon program in three distinct historical periods, culminating in the May 1998 nuclear tests. The second section maps out India's engagement with the international community, particularly the United States on nuclear nonproliferation-related issues after Pokhran II, which facilitated its gradual integration into the global nuclear order. The final section evaluates the current proliferation challenges in South Asia from the Indian perspective and discusses the relevance of various nonproliferation alternatives.

India's nuclear history

Peaceful uses of atomic energy (1946–1965)

The idea of India's nuclear-power program was conceived well before the country achieved independence from colonial rule. Jawaharlal Nehru, India's first prime minister after independence, realized at a very early stage the potentially useful as well as destructive applications of nuclear power and the need to harness nuclear energy for peaceful purposes for India's development.[2] As early as 1948, Nehru appealed for limiting the use of atomic energy to peaceful purposes only and the elimination of atomic weapons from national armaments. The peaceful utilization of nuclear energy emerged as the cornerstone of India's nuclear policy and also the basis of her campaign for global nuclear disarmament.

India's indigenous efforts in nuclear science and technology were established remarkably early. On achieving independence, India launched an ambitious atomic energy program. On April 15, 1948, India's constituent assembly enacted the Atomic Energy bill and almost four months after, a three-member Atomic Energy Commission (AEC) was established with Dr Homi Bhabha as its first chairman. In 1954, Dr Bhabha became the Secretary of the Department of Atomic Energy (DAE). In the initial years, India's nuclear program was primarily aimed at achieving self-reliance in nuclear fuel cycle activities which, in the long run, has yielded substantial benefits. The technological self-reliance however, could not have been achieved without international cooperation as India lacked expertise in nuclear reactor design and construction. India thus became one of the earliest proponents of international cooperation towards harnessing nuclear energy for peaceful uses, which enabled the development of its nuclear-power program.

During the international conference on the peaceful uses of nuclear energy in 1956, Dr Bhabha welcomed the proposal for setting up an international agency to facilitate the use of "atoms for peaceful purposes." In his speech at the conference, Bhabha remarked that

> The purpose of it [the Agency] is to accelerate and enlarge the contribution of this great new source of energy to the peace, health and happiness of the world. We entirely agree that in carrying out this positive function the Agency should ensure, so far as it is able, that assistance provided by it does not directly further a military purpose.[3]

He further stated: "A military purpose, in our view, is the production, testing or use of nuclear, thermonuclear or radiological weapons. We shall be prepared to support any amendment which incorporates this idea in the statute."[4] However, Bhabha cautioned that while facilitating the peaceful uses of nuclear power, the proposed agency should enforce safeguards on the universal and nondiscriminatory basis, instead of targeting the countries from the developing world that received aid.[5] India thus became one of the earliest proponents of international cooperation in the peaceful uses of nuclear energy. India's nuclear diplomacy, thereafter, espoused the commitment to universally applicable principles to govern the international cooperation in the peaceful uses of nuclear energy, which later became the primary basis behind its objection to the Nuclear Nonproliferation Treaty (NPT) in 1968, calling it discriminatory.

In the early 1950s, India sought cooperation from countries such as the United Kingdom, France, the United States, and Canada to develop the nuclear reactor and fuel cycle facilities. In 1954, the United Kingdom offered to help India to build a "swimming pool-type" reactor fuelled with enriched uranium. This reactor, later named APSARA, became operational on August 4, 1956, became the first operating reactor in Asia outside of the Soviet Union.[6] Under the Colombo Plan, Canada offered to build an NRX 40 MW thermal research reactor in India at Trombay near Mumbai. The United States agreed to supply 20 tonnes of heavy water required for this reactor as moderator. This reactor, known as CIRUS (Canada-India-Reactor-US), for which the fuel rods were manufactured by the Indian scientists, went critical in 1960.[7] The CIRUS reactor and the heavy water were supplied to India under the contracts which specified the "peaceful uses."

While developing its indigenous nuclear-power program, India pursued its campaign for global nuclear disarmament in the United Nations and other international forums. Nehru particularly criticized the nuclear-weapon powers for their lack of restraint in conducting nuclear explosions in complete disregard of the hazards created by these tests. He strongly appealed to the nuclear-weapon powers for a "stand-still" agreement on nuclear testing.[8] Nehru's appeal went unheeded as the United States was not amenable to such an agreement. On July 12, 1956, India once again placed a proposal before the UN Disarmament Commission for "Cessation of All Explosions of Nuclear and Other Weapons of Mass Destruction."[9] Faced with criticisms and pressure from the international community to end the nuclear testing, the United States and the Soviet Union conducted several rounds of negotiations in the following years. The two great powers, however, could not agree on the comprehensive test ban treaty ostensibly due to problems of verification, and proposed a Partial Test Ban Treaty (PTBT), which was opened for signature on July 25, 1963.[10] India became one of the original signatories to the PTBT, although China never signed the treaty.

At the Second UN Conference on Peaceful Uses of Atomic Energy in 1958, Bhabha and N.B. Prasad outlined a three-stage fuel cycle for India's nuclear power program that would enable the country to produce electricity by making use of its abundant thorium resources.[11] As part of this plan, the AEC decided to build a plutonium reprocessing plant at the Trombay Complex. The Trombay Plutonium Plant, which became operational in June 1964, raised international concern that India might use this facility and the unsafeguarded CIRUS reactor for military purposes.[12] India nevertheless, maintained that its nuclear program is entirely for peaceful purposes. A few months later, the Chinese nuclear test at the Lop Nor site shifted the terms of debate in India's nuclear policy.

The Chinese nuclear test, which took place only two years after the Sino-Indian war of 1962, led to growing clamor in India's domestic political milieu for exercising the military option. It soon became evident that China had not only tested a nuclear weapon, but also aimed to acquire a range of strategic capabilities such as thermonuclear weapons, tactical nuclear weapons, and long-range delivery systems. Consequently, the Jan Sangh Party decided to bring a motion in parliament calling for the production of nuclear weapons. Nehru's successor Lal Bahadur Shastri rejected the calls for developing nuclear weapons. While outlining the policy of his government, Shastri maintained that, "we will not manufacture atom bombs in India. However, we will continue the development of our nuclear devices for peaceful purposes and we are going ahead with it."[13] The Indian scientists, therein, undertook a project called the "Study of Nuclear Explosions for Peaceful Purposes" (SNEPP), which culminated in India's peaceful nuclear explosion in 1974.[14]

From SNEPP to the PNE (1965–1974)

On January 11, 1966 Prime Minister Shastri passed away unexpectedly. In a separate incident, Dr Homi Bhabha died in a plane crash over Mont Blanc while returning from Geneva on January 24, 1966. The ensuing period witnessed a short phase of political uncertainty when Indira Gandhi, Nehru's daughter, succeeded Lal Bahadur Shastri. In July 1965, when the Eighteen Nations Committee on Disarmament (ENDC) was convened for negotiating a treaty on nuclear nonproliferation; India began to play a very active role in the negotiations. The resolution of the eight nonaligned countries, which included India, stated that the nonproliferation treaty should be "coupled with or followed by tangible steps to halt the nuclear arms race and to limit, reduce and eliminate the stocks of nuclear weapons and means of their delivery."[15]

During the negotiations, India strongly pitched for nonproliferation to be linked to nuclear disarmament measures. The nuclear-weapon powers not only rejected any formal link between nonproliferation and disarmament, but reluctantly agreed to include Article VI, which merely expressed a positive intent to pursue negotiations on measures relating to nuclear arms control and to pursue negotiations on a treaty for general and complete disarmament.[16] India's opposition to the draft treaty solidified when it became clear that the treaty would include a permanent division between nuclear-weapon states (NWS) and the nonnuclear-weapon states (NNWS). This division meant that China would be included among the NWS, while India would be excluded since it did not acquire nuclear weapons prior to January 1, 1967.

In order to make the NPT acceptable to NNWS, India insisted on concrete measures to be included in the NPT such as immediate enactment of a Comprehensive Test Ban Treaty (CTBT), a freeze on the development of nuclear weapons, substantial reductions in existing nuclear-weapon stockpiles, and security assurances for the nonnuclear-weapon states.[17] The Indian opposition to the NPT, at this point, was also driven by serious security concerns. China, which was perceived as a serious security threat by India, chose to stay outside the NPT. The Chinese decision to remain outside of the NPT regime without offering negative security assurances to nonnuclear weapon powers left India vulnerable to Beijing's nuclear coercion. Furthermore, the US and Soviet unwillingness to offer India any nuclear security guarantees, despite the latter's repeated entreaties, bolstered India's opposition to the NPT.[18] Realizing that none of the measures it suggested were acceptable to the NWS, India refused to sign the NPT in 1968 on grounds that the treaty was biased against the "nuclear have-nots" by preventing only horizontal proliferation as opposed to the vertical proliferation by the five "nuclear haves."[19]

The US–China rapprochement in the early 1970s, and the simultaneous emergence of the US-China-Pakistan axis in its neighborhood, posed new challenges to India's security. The Indo-Pakistani war in November–December 1971, which led to the creation of Bangladesh, saw a worsening of Indo-US ties and New Delhi gradually aligning itself with the Soviet Union. By the end of 1971, Indian scientists at the Bhabha Atomic Research Centre (BARC) had succeeded in developing a basic design of a nuclear explosive device.[20] When it became clear that India was seriously preparing to conduct a nuclear explosion, Washington conveyed that it did not view any real difference between peaceful nuclear explosions and the testing of nuclear weapons. The Canadian Prime Minister Trudeau also communicated to Mrs Gandhi that the Canadian agreement with India for the CIRUS reactor was strictly for peaceful purposes, although the agreement had hardly any specific details on what constituted peaceful uses or on possible end use of plutonium generated from the reactor. The Indian government, however, rejected both the US and Canadian contentions and argued that while India fully supports nonproliferation of nuclear weapons, it equally favors proliferation of nuclear technology for peaceful purposes. To the surprise of the international community, India conducted a "peaceful nuclear explosion" (PNE) on May 18, 1974. Although the nuclear test codenamed the "Smiling Buddha" infuriated the international community, India maintained that a PNE device was not a weapon and met a legal restriction of "peaceful use."

Prolonged nuclear restraint (1975–1998)

Through its PNE, India merely demonstrated its capability to build a nuclear device, but refrained from developing nuclear weapons. The PNE had evoked sharp reactions from the United States and Canada who threatened to terminate their nuclear cooperation contracts with India, if the latter refused to sign the NPT as NNWS and accept International Atomic Energy Agency (IAEA) safeguards on its nuclear facilities. India's refusal to accept either of the conditions eventually resulted in the termination of the nuclear cooperation agreements with Canada and the US. An era of nuclear isolation thus began for India, during which it was denied crucial technologies and fuel supplies, leading to a major setback for India's civil nuclear program. The US and Canadian opposition forced the Indian AEC to explore the possibility of obtaining fuel and heavy water supplies from the Soviet Union for the Rajasthan Atomic Power Station (RAPS). The Soviet Union demanded that India accept IAEA safeguards on RAPS I & II before the heavy water supplies could be fully delivered, which India accepted, albeit reluctantly. In the late 1970s, India also strongly objected to China's decision to provide clandestine assistance to Pakistan's nuclear program.

Throughout the 1980s, India was urged to either join the NPT or accept full-scope safeguards on its nuclear program. India rejected such pleas while reiterating its call for general and complete disarmament through successive governments. In 1988, Prime Minister Rajiv Gandhi proposed the time-bound action plan for nuclear disarmament.[21] However, much to India's dismay, the plan was rejected by the nuclear-weapon powers. During the late 1980s, India also experienced an uncertainty in terms of security assurances from the Soviet Union, especially after the 1986 Sino-Indian confrontation at the Sumdorong Chu valley, wherein Gorbachev chose not to endorse New Delhi's position.[22] But more importantly, the reports in 1989 that Pakistan had successfully acquired nuclear weapons were widely believed to have influenced India's decision to acquire nuclear weapons, which disrupted the long-standing Indian policy concerning peaceful uses of nuclear energy. The Indian government, nevertheless, remained indecisive about continuing restraint regarding nuclear testing, which had been practiced since the Pokhran test I, and about whether to declare its nuclear-weapon capability.

In 1993, India and the United States cosponsored a resolution to initiate negotiations for a Comprehensive Test Ban Treaty. In 1995, the Clinton administration decided to use the 1995 NPT Review Conference to extend the NPT for an indefinite period and in return the nuclear-weapon states, led by the US, agreed to adopt a CTBT, to be negotiated in the UN Conference on Disarmament (CD). Soon it became clear to Indian policymakers that the NPT that they had been opposing for being discriminatory had finally become a permanent structure in the international arena.[23] India reacted sharply to the indefinite extension of the NPT, which failed to impose any responsibility on nuclear-weapon states but permanently relegated India to the category of nonnuclear-weapon state. Despite being a cosponsor to the resolution on CTBT, India opposed the draft treaty since it did not include any definite time-frame for nuclear disarmament as proposed by Prime Minister Rajiv Gandhi's action plan in 1988.

Merely four days after the indefinite extension of NPT, China conducted nuclear tests, offering the gravest provocation to bomb supporters in India. The next year, India refused to sign the CTBT when it was opened for signature on September 24, 1996. Signing the CTBT would foreclose India's option to test its nuclear weapons while China would continue to aid Pakistan's nuclear program. The United States not only turned a blind eye towards China's clandestine assistance of Pakistan's nuclear program but in 1995, under the Brown Amendment, sanctioned military aid worth up to $386 million to Pakistan. The United States and the nonproliferation community also failed to check Pakistan's proliferation of uranium centrifuges to North Korea in exchange for North Korean missile technology which Pakistan tested in 1998. On numerous occasions, Pakistan publicly asserted the "India-centric" nature of its nuclear and missile capability. The mounting nuclear and missile threat from both China and Pakistan, together with the loss of security guarantees, severely tested India's nuclear restraint. Finally, on May 11 and 13, 1998, India ended its nuclear restraint and tested five nuclear devices at the Pokhran site. India's Pokhran II tests were followed by Pakistan's six nuclear tests on May 28 and 30.

Ending nuclear isolation

In the aftermath of Pokhran II in August 1999, India enacted the draft nuclear doctrine, which outlined the country's quest for achieving a credible minimum deterrence vis-à-vis its adversaries without giving up the larger quest for the general and complete nuclear disarmament. The Pokhran II tests were followed by a host of technological and economic sanctions on India. These posed a serious challenge to India's nuclear diplomacy in explaining to the global community its new nuclear posture and, more importantly, its commitment to the nuclear nonproliferation. India's post-1998 diplomacy thus mainly focused on changing the international and, especially, the US attitude towards India as a responsible nuclear power and not as a proliferator. This had been achieved mainly through the prolonged dialogue initiated by US Deputy Secretary of State Strobe Talbott and the Indian External Affairs Minister Jaswant Singh and continued under two different administrations in both countries. It was through the bilateral dialogue that India conveyed its long-standing commitment to the nuclear nonproliferation regime.

Post 9/11, New Delhi took the lead in engaging with the United States to counter the rising threat of nuclear terrorism globally. The Indo-US strategic dialogue further evolved into a bilateral strategic partnership in January 2004 when President Bush and Prime Minister Vajpayee unveiled the "Next Steps in Strategic Partnership" (NSSP), in which they reaffirmed their countries "are partners in the war on terrorism, and … are partners in controlling the proliferation of weapons of mass destruction and the means to deliver them."[24] India's willingness to work with the Bush administration to stem the new tide of global proliferation of nuclear and other weapons of mass destruction (WMD) reflected its determination to gradually enter into the new global nuclear order. India's reputation as a democracy with its growing economy and impeccable nonproliferation credentials encouraged it to take a burgeoning role in global nonproliferation efforts. India's approach to nonproliferation was outlined by Prime Minister Manmohan Singh in 2004:

> India is a responsible nuclear power … [it] will not be the source of proliferation of sensitive technologies. We will also ensure the safeguarding of those technologies that we already possess. We will remain faithful to this approach, as we have been for the last several decades. We in India are willing to shoulder our share of international obligations, provided our legitimate interests are met.[25]

The joint statement issued by Indian Prime Minister Manmohan Singh and the US President George W. Bush on July 18, 2005 reflected the depth of bilateral understanding on nuclear nonproliferation. This new understanding paved the way for intense negotiations between the two countries that resulted in Indo-US civilian nuclear agreement of 2008, and subsequently the India-specific waiver by the Nuclear Suppliers Group in 2009. Although, not a signatory to the NPT, India's responsible nuclear stewardship and commitment to fight proliferation by maintaining strict controls on its nuclear technology and not sharing it with any other country, unlike its neighbor Pakistan, was the driving force behind the agreement. Upholding its commitment to fight proliferation, in May 2005 India enacted the WMD Act, which criminalized the trade and brokering of sensitive nuclear technologies and materials.

As specified in the nuclear cooperation agreement, India agreed to separate its civilian and military nuclear facilities and to place all its civilian nuclear facilities under IAEA safeguards. By agreeing to place its civilian facilities under safeguards, India furthered its commitment, as it did in 1993, by voluntarily establishing new IAEA safeguards agreement on the Tarapur nuclear facility after the expiry of the original agreement. On February 2, 2009, it signed a safeguards agreement with the IAEA and soon afterwards it signed the Additional Protocol for its civilian nuclear facilities. While accepting the IAEA safeguards on its civilian facilities, India, despite being a nonsignatory to the NPT, became one of the unique de facto nuclear-weapon powers in the global nuclear order. The Indo-US nuclear cooperation agreement successfully accommodated India's security concerns while extracting new nonproliferation commitments from New Delhi.

India, Pakistan, and global nonproliferation regime

One of the major criticisms of the India-US nuclear cooperation has been that the agreement might heighten the nuclear rivalry between India and Pakistan, and potentially raise tensions in the region. Nonproliferation experts contended that the "deal" would free up domestic resources for its nuclear-weapon program whereas the absence of full-scope safeguards leaves the window open for diverting peaceful nuclear technology for nuclear-weapon purposes.[26] Another concern pertaining to India's nuclear program is related to its growing capability to produce weapons-grade fissile materials. While some of these concerns have been significant, the Indo-US nuclear cooperation agreement envisages realistic expectations from India to further the objectives of nuclear nonproliferation norms.

After declaring itself a nuclear power, India has maintained a unilateral and voluntary moratorium on nuclear testing. India has also expressed support for commencing negotiations on a universal, nondiscriminatory, and verifiable fissile material cutoff treaty (FMCT) in the Conference on Disarmament (CD). The Hyde Act, passed by US congress at the time of Indo-US cooperation agreement, clearly stipulates that United States must halt all nuclear exports if India resumes nuclear testing.[27] Although the Indo-US nuclear agreement does not specifically mention the termination of the agreement on resumption of nuclear testing, it appears unlikely that India will detonate in the near or distant future, unless compelled by any extraordinary changes in its regional security conditions triggered by nuclear testing by Pakistan or China.

One of the major obligations of the Hyde Act on the US president pertains to informing the appropriate congressional committees about any significant nuclear activities by India. This includes "significant changes in the production by India of nuclear weapons or in the types or amounts of fissile material produced; and changes in the purpose or operational status of any unsafeguarded nuclear fuel cycle activities in India."[28] In addition, as per Section 123 of the Atomic Energy Act, the President is required to submit a report within 180 days after the date of enforcement of the agreement with India, and annually thereafter, covering India's nuclear activities, its compliance with US policies and possible fissile material production.[29] There are no indications from the US administration which suggest that India has increased its fissile material production for weapon purposes. The concerns expressed over India's breeder reactor program and especially over the Prototype Fast Breeder Reactor (PFBR) which is yet to become operational, are also somewhat misplaced. The PFBR is expected to significantly increase India's plutonium production when it begins operation. The Department of Atomic Energy plans to use the plutonium produced in the PFBR to fuel the fleet of fast reactors in the future. One can, thus, reasonably conclude that India has neither shown any intent on enhancing its fissile material production for weapon purposes, nor does it aim to match Pakistan and China in their nuclear-warhead count.

On the contrary, numerous reports have suggested that Pakistan has significantly enhanced the fissile material production and has surged ahead of India in the race to build nuclear warheads. Pakistan's expansion of its nuclear arsenal appears to be driven by its quest to neutralize India's conventional military superiority. Pakistan has also embarked on the development of tactical nuclear weapons (TNWs) to achieve a full-spectrum of strategic capabilities. The successful test of a short-range ballistic missile, the Hatf *IX*, a battlefield nuclear weapon, is aimed at deterring India's conventional onslaught. Pakistan has also reportedly adopted a war-fighting doctrine that does not preclude use of nuclear weapons on its own territory in the event of any conventional onslaught by India.

The current nuclear dynamics in South Asia, thus, raises three important challenges: Pakistan's continuous opposition to an FMCT; the growing threats of nuclear terrorism; and the stability of the nuclear deterrent in light of the development of battlefield nuclear weapons. Pakistan is the only holdout state so far in proceeding with negotiations on an FMCT at the Conference on Disarmament in Geneva. As a result of Pakistan's intransigence, the CD is deadlocked even from initiating a program of action on an FMCT, let alone negotiations. Consequently, the international nuclear policy analysts have proposed granting a Nuclear Suppliers Group (NSG) exemption to Pakistan on par with India. Pakistani Ambassador to the CD Zamir Akram, in an interview with *Arms Control Today*, suggested that if Pakistan had an NSG waiver like India, it would be willing to enter negotiations on an FMCT with a clearer mandate.[30] Given the keenness of the international community to initiate negotiations on an FMCT, Pakistan needs to be brought on board. Thus, the appeal for granting an NSG exemption to Pakistan may likely grow, purely to eliminate its opposition to an FMCT. The NSG members are apparently divided over a possible NSG exemption to Islamabad, on account of its problematic proliferation history. Also, Pakistan's ongoing nuclear cooperation with China has been of considerable concern among many NSG members. The international community is, thus, confronted with the unique challenge of breaking Pakistan's intransigence over the FMCT.

Further, the concerns over the safety and security of nuclear materials in South Asia are often aggravated due to incidents of high intensity terror attacks. These concerns about the safety of Pakistan's nuclear arsenal have been heightened due to the series of attacks since 2007 by militants on various Pakistani military installations – some of them reportedly holding nuclear-weapon components.[31] Since 9/11, combating nuclear terrorism has been the foremost priority of the international community and the United States in particular. It would be nightmarish for the United States if some of the fissile materials in South Asia fell into the hands of terrorist groups. While this appears a probable scenario, both India and Pakistan have implemented a series of steps to safeguard their fissile materials.

Finally, Pakistan's quest to achieve a full-spectrum of deterrent capabilities has adversely affected strategic stability in South Asia. Pakistan's use of TNWs in a bilateral conventional conflict could trigger a potential chain reaction, leading to a full-fledged nuclear exchange. While India has a clearly stated "no first use" policy and views its nuclear arsenal purely as an instrument of deterrent, Pakistan ascribes potential wartime utility to its nuclear arsenal and refrains from formally outlining its nuclear doctrine. Deterrence stability is also affected due to proxy attacks against India by terror groups, such as the 2001 attack on the Indian Parliament building and the 2008 Mumbai attack. Pakistan's implicit support to various terror groups clearly does not bode well for stability in the region. A response to a terror attack could lead to miscalculation, resulting in a nuclear exchange, and is far more likely than terrorists stealing fissile material. Significantly, the odds of such an exchange increase with the deployment of battlefield nuclear weapons. Both India and Pakistan, thus, need to promote stability through mutually reinforcing confidence-building measures.

Conclusion

India's nuclear policy has historically evolved around two key principles of uses of nuclear energy and the pursuit of universal, nondiscriminatory, and verifiable nuclear disarmament. As early as 1948, India called for limiting the use of atomic energy for peaceful purposes and the elimination of nuclear weapons universally. In 1998, after declaring itself a de facto nuclear-weapon power, India reiterated its commitment to nuclear disarmament. India's post-1998 nuclear diplomacy has paved the way for Indo-US nuclear cooperation agreement and opened a new chapter in the international nonproliferation regime. The Indo-US nuclear cooperation agreement, signed in 2008, fostered the new arrangement to accommodate India in the existing nonproliferation framework. The deal strengthens existing nonproliferation principles by reinforcing India's responsibility towards unilateral moratorium on nuclear testing and its participation in the negotiations over an FMCT. The international community is, however, confronted with the challenges of ensuring nuclear safety and security in the region as well as maintaining optimum deterrence stability. While numerous efforts are being made to protect fissile materials in the region, more needs to be done to ensure deterrence stability in the region.

Notes

1.   In recent years, the array of technologies and platforms developed by India and Pakistan has caused serious concerns among analysts and policymakers alike all over the world. While India has been moving ahead with its ballistic missile defence (BMD) program, Pakistan, on the other hand, is fast-tracking the development of Short Range Surface to Surface Multi Tube Ballistic Missile Hatf IX (NASR). According to release by Pakistan's inter service public relations, the missile has a range of 60 km and carries nuclear warheads of appropriate yield with high accuracy, "shoot and scoot" attrib-

utes. See Inter Services Public Relations, Government of Pakistan, Press Release No: PR94/2011-ISPR, April 19, 2011, www.ispr.gov.pk/front/main.asp?o=t-press_release&id=1721, accessed on December 10, 2013.

2. The events during the Second World War such as the atomic bombing of Hiroshima and Nagasaki in 1945 had deeply distressed the leaders of Indian freedom movement. After the atomic bombing of Hiroshima and Nagasaki, Mahatma Gandhi publicly called for making the world free of nuclear weapons. See Mahatma Gandhi, "Atom Bomb and Ahimsa," *Harijan*, July 7, 1946, http://meaindia.nic.in/pmicd.geneva/?50031131.

3. United Nations, "Conference on the Statute of the International Atomic Energy Agency," Verbatim Record of the Seventh Plenary Meeting Held on Thursday, September 27, 1956, p. 44 www.iaea.org/inis/collection/NCLCollectionStore/_Public/42/061/42061197.pdf

4. Ibid.

5. Ibid.

6. N. Sarma and B. Banerjee, *Nuclear Power in India: A Critical History* (Rupa: New Delhi, 2008), p. 29.

7. Ibid.

8. Comprehensive Nuclear Test-Ban Treaty Organization, "Nuclear Testing 1945–Today," ND., www.ctbto.org/nuclear-testing/history-of-nuclear-testing/nuclear-testing-1945-today/.

9. Government of India, *Disarmament: India's Initiatives* (New Delhi: Ministry of External Affairs, External Publicity Division, 1988).

10. William Burr and Hector L. Montford, "The Making of the Limited Test Ban Treaty 1958–1963," *National Security Archives*, August 8, 2003, www2.gwu.edu/~nsarchiv/NSAEBB/NSAEBB94/.

11. Homi J. Bhabha and N.B. Prasad, *A Study of the Contribution of Atomic Energy to a Power Programme in India*, Proceedings of the Second United Nations International Conference on the Peaceful Uses of Atomic Energy, Geneva, 1958, pp. 89–101. The implementation of this plan required the Indian scientists to build a reprocessing plant, which would extract the plutonium from the irradiated fuel of the first stage, which would then be used in second stage and in turn facilitate the development of the third stage using thorium.

12. V.P. Kansra, "Status of Power Reactor Fuel Reprocessing in India," International Atomic Energy Agency advisory group meeting on status and trends in spent fuel reprocessing, 1999, www.iaea.org/inis/collection/NCLCollectionStore/_Public/30/047/30047648.pdf.

13. "Lal Bahadur Shastri Speech in the Lok Sabha on March 02, 1065, during the discussion on the President's Address," reproduced in Lal Bahadur Shastri, *Selected Speeches of Lal Bahadur Shastri, June 11, 1964– January 10, 1966* (Ministry of Information and Broadcasting, 2007).

14. Dr P.K. Iyengar, former Chairman of the Atomic Energy Commission, during an interview with the IDSA nuclear history project team, has confirmed the existence of the project on the Study of Nuclear Explosion for Peaceful Purposes (SNEPP).

15. United Nations, "Final Verbatim Record of the Conference of the Eighteen-Nation Committee on Disarmament [Meeting 244]," ENDC/PV.244, Palais des Nations, Geneva, March 1, 1966, http://quod.lib.umich.edu/e/endc/4918260.0244.001.

16. United Nations, "The Treaty On the Non-Proliferation of Nuclear Weapons," Department for Disarmament Affairs, March 11, 1995, www.un.org/en/conf/npt/2005/npttreaty.html.

17. United Nations, "Statement by the Indian Representative (Husain) to the Eighteen Nation Disarmament Committee (ENDC): Non-proliferation of Nuclear Weapons," US Arms Control and Disarmament Agency, *Publication 46*, December 14, 1967, released July 1968, www.un.org/disarmament/publications/documents_on_disarmament/1967/DoD_1967.pdf.

18. Two Indian envoys, L.K. Jha, secretary to Prime Minister Indira Gandhi, and Foreign Secretary C.S. Jha, pursued India's quest for nuclear guarantees in Moscow and Washington to no avail during 1965 and 1967. George Perkovich, *India's Nuclear Bomb: The Impact on Global Proliferation* (Berkeley, CA: University of California Press, 1999).

19. Indira Gandhi, "Non-Proliferation Treaty," Statement by Prime Minister Indira Gandhi during Lok Sabha debate on foreign affairs and Non-Proliferation Treaty, April 5, 1968, http://meaindia.nic.in/pmicd.geneva/?50031138.

20. Perkovich, *India's Nuclear Bomb*, pp. 140–141.

21. Rajiv Gandhi, "Speech on Disarmament at the Opening Session of Six-Nation Five-Continent Peace Initiative," January 21, 1988, http://meaindia.nic.in/pmicd.geneva/?50031142.

22. Andrew B. Kennedy, "India's Nuclear Odyssey: Implicit Umbrellas, Diplomatic Disappointments, and the Bomb," *International Security*, Vol. 36, No.2 (Fall 2011), pp. 120–153.

23. C. Raja Mohan, *India's Nuclear Diplomacy and the Global Order* (New Delhi: Academic Foundation, 2009).
24. George W. Bush, "Statement on the Next Steps in Strategic Partnership With India," January 12, 2004, www.gpo.gov/fdsys/pkg/WCPD-2004-01-19/pdf/WCPD-2004-01-19-Pg61-2.pdf.
25. Manmohan Singh, "PM's address at the Golden Jubilee function of the Department of Atomic Energy," Government of India, Office of the Prime Minister, October 23, 2004, http://pm india.nic.in/speech-details.php?nodeid=31.
26. Sharon Squassoni, "U. S. Nuclear Cooperation with India: Issues for Congress," CRS Report for Congress, Congressional Research Service, July 29, 2005, www.fas.org/sgp/crs/row/RL33016.pdf.
27. Henry J. Hyde, "United States-India Nuclear Cooperation," Sec. 104, January 3, 2006, www.gpo.gov/fdsys/pkg/BILLS-109hr5682enr/pdf/BILLS-109hr5682enr.pdf.
28. Ibid., Section 104 (g) (1) (C) and (D).
29. United States Congress, "Nuclear Regulatory Legislation," Atomic Energy Act of 1954 (PL 83–703), Sec.123, August 30, 1954, http://science.energy.gov/~/media/bes/pdf/nureg_0980_v1_no7_june 2005.pdf.
30. Tom Collina and Daniel Horner, "The South Asian Nuclear Balance: An Interview with Pakistani Ambassador to the CD Zamir Akram," *Arms Control Association*, Vol. 41, No. 10 (December 2011), pp. 8–13, www.armscontrol.org/act/2011_12/Interview_With_Pakistani_Ambassador_to_the_CD_Zamir_Akram.
31. Shaun Gregory, "The Terrorist Threat to Nuclear Weapons in Pakistan," European Leadership Network, June 4, 2013, www.europeanleadershipnetwork.org/the-terrorist-threat-to-nuclear-weapons-in-pakistan_613.html.

PART II

Nonproliferation, Counterproliferatiom, and Disarmament

The Nonproliferation Regime

8

AN NPT NET ASSESSMENT

Flawed, problematic, and indispensable

Christopher A. Ford

The global policy community concerned with arms control and nonproliferation matters are no strangers to controversy, and it has frequently been the case over the years that existing or proposed agreements and policies have engendered spirited argument and disagreement.[1] The Treaty on the Nonproliferation of Nuclear Weapons (NPT), however, is perhaps unique in that essentially all the relevant players claim to be deeply committed to its principles even while they feud bitterly over what that actually *means*. Arguably nowhere else does any treaty or institution receive such strong ostensible support from parties who quarrel endlessly over its meaning, and who proffer conclusions about this meaning that point in such very different directions. With the NPT now halfway through its fifth decade in existence, it is worth surveying the treaty's history and present-day controversies in search of some kind of "net assessment" of the institution.

Provisions and structure

The Treaty's nonproliferation core

In the early Cold War period, US officials predicted that the spread of technology would result in a huge expansion of the number of states possessing nuclear weapons. A US National Intelligence Estimate in 1957, for example, warned that "up to 10 countries" could produce nuclear weapons within a decade by means of exploiting their "civilian atomic energy program[s]."[2] Estimates prepared for Secretary of Defense Robert McNamara in 1963 similarly suggested that eight countries might conduct their first nuclear-weapon test within ten years, and that a further two could reach that stage thereafter. (The nuclear trajectories of four additional states were simply described as "unclear.")[3]

At a time when persistent Cold War tensions were coupled with rapidly-increasing super-power nuclear arsenals, the prospect of such a mushrooming cadre of nuclear-weapon "players" was alarming indeed, leading diplomats to talk increasingly about nonproliferation – a neologism for efforts to arrest the spread of atomic weaponry. In 1961, the United Nations General Assembly passed the so-called "Irish Resolution," which declared that "an increase in the number of States possessing nuclear weapons is growing more imminent and threatens to extend and intensify the arms race and to increase the difficulties of avoiding war and of establishing international peace and security based on the rule of law." Accordingly, the resolution called up on all states to secure the conclusion of

> an international agreement containing provisions under which the nuclear States would undertake to refrain from relinquishing control of nuclear weapons and of transmitting the information necessary for their manufacture to States not possessing such weapons, and provisions under which States not possessing nuclear weapons would undertake not to manufacture or otherwise acquire control of such weapons.[4]

Thereafter, a special negotiating committee was set up to address this issue, with the United States and the Soviet Union serving as lead drafters. The text it finally produced, the NPT, was completed in 1968 and entered into force in 1970. The treaty's first two articles closely tracked the original language of the Irish Resolution, the core principles of nondissemination and nonacquisition articulated therein having been picked up and carried forward by a US plan proposed in 1964, a draft treaty submitted by the United States in 1965, and a joint US/USSR draft in 1967.[5] The treaty's third article obliged non-weapon-possessing states party to accept safeguards on what nuclear technology and materials they possess pursuant to an agreement negotiated with the International Atomic Energy Agency (IAEA). These nonproliferation provisions constitute the foundation of the treaty.

Additional issues

Nevertheless, the NPT did not touch exclusively on nonproliferation issues, and much of the story of its subsequent contentiousness in international diplomatic circles is related to just how it dealt with additional matters. One such issue that could have proven quite problematic was the question of so-called "peaceful nuclear explosions" (PNEs), a notion which sounds oxymoronic to modern ears, but which in the 1960s was still taken seriously in some quarters. During the NPT's negotiations, a handful of countries urged that nuclear explosive technology be widely distributed so that it could be used for "peaceful purposes" such as excavating harbors or removing terrestrial overburden in large-scale mining operations.[6]

Given the obviously catastrophic damage that such distribution would do to the cause of nonproliferation – that is, in undermining the core principle of the treaty then being negotiated – this was recognized as being utterly inappropriate, and such efforts were rejected. Instead, the NPT's final text provided merely for the possibility that weapons-possessors might make the "potential benefits from any peaceful applications of nuclear explosions" available to nonnuclear states by, in effect, contracting for explosive services in ways that did not actually involve transferring relevant technology to anyone not already possessing it.[7]

Other contentious issues – notably disarmament and the question of peaceful uses of nuclear energy (PUNE) – could not be so easily sidestepped and are the basis of NPT debates and controversies over the succeeding decades. Additional matters also arose concerning the purportedly "discriminatory" nature of the treaty, what to do about non-signatories, and how long the NPT should remain in force.

Disarmament

As noted, the core provisions of the treaty draft focused upon what the Irish Resolution had described as "[p]revention of the wider dissemination of nuclear weapons."[8] Many governments also asked, however, what was to become of those weapons that were already in the hands of some states. This was the question of disarmament, and it became (and has remained) a very contentious diplomatic issue.

In the NPT negotiations, some countries proposed establishing an express connection between the nonproliferation obligations of nuclear-weapon nonpossessors and requirements for disarmament by possessor states. The US and Soviet negotiators, however – the lead drafters of the treaty – insisted (along with some other states) that these issues not be made reciprocally conditional, for fear that such linkage would prevent progress on either goal. Efforts to require specific disarmament steps as part of the NPT were rejected, failing to get support even from all the "nonaligned" members of the negotiating committee.[9] By 1965, as even the pro-disarmament Indian delegation explicitly recognized,[10] it was understood that disarmament requirements would not be made part of the nonproliferation treaty being negotiated.

At Canada's suggestion, the negotiators agreed upon the approach that produced the answer finally embodied in the NPT: instead of requiring disarmament steps, the draft instrument would merely signal the parties' intention to move toward nuclear disarmament. Wedded to Mexico's suggestion of language requiring at least an effort to "pursue negotiations in good faith" toward this end, this produced the final text of Article VI:

> Each of the Parties to the Treaty undertakes to pursue negotiations in good faith on effective measures relating to cessation of the nuclear arms race at an early date and to nuclear disarmament, and on a treaty on general and complete disarmament under strict and effective international control.[11]

The issue of what specifically to do about disarmament was thus explicitly put off for later, and not actually dealt with in the NPT. As even the "nonaligned" countries participating in the early negotiations had conceded as early 1965, the idea here was for a nonproliferation treaty to be "coupled with or followed by" limitations on nuclear weaponry. Nonproliferation, they hoped, would constitute "a step towards the achievement of general and complete disarmament and, more particularly, nuclear disarmament."[12] It was quite clear, however, that the NPT would not itself contain concrete disarmament provisions.

At a time when the United States was at, or just past, the peak size of its nuclear arsenal and the Soviet Union was still increasing the size of its own nuclear holdings, this outcome was hardly surprising. The Cold War nuclear arms race was in full swing, and arms limits (let alone reductions) were in fact still some years in the future. The drafters were surely correct that any more linkage in the NPT context than what little finally appeared in Article VI would have sunk the negotiations. Nevertheless, the issue of disarmament would haunt the treaty regime for years to come.

Peaceful uses

With the *idea* of nuclear technology-sharing given prominent encouragement by President Dwight D. Eisenhower's "Atoms for Peace" program, debates ensued about how to handle PUNE issues in the text of the NPT. A number of governments attempted to insert specific sharing requirements that would, in one form or another, have obliged technology holders to give information and materials to nonpossessors. These proposals, however, were rejected,[13] leaving the final language of the treaty somewhat ambiguous about the parameters of what was contemplated.

In its final form, Article IV of the NPT declared that nothing in it "shall be interpreted as affecting the inalienable right of all the Parties to the Treaty to develop research, production and use of nuclear energy for peaceful purposes without discrimination and in conformity with Articles I and II of this Treaty." It also called for "the fullest possible exchange of equipment, materials and scientific and technological information for the peaceful uses of nuclear energy."[14] Precisely what this means, or should mean, in practice has become an important area of contention in today's NPT and nonproliferation debates.

"Have/have not" structure

As presaged by the framework of the Irish Resolution in 1961, the structure of the NPT embodies a distinction between nuclear-weapon "haves" and "have nots," each of which are governed by different rules under the treaty's terms. Article IX of the treaty provides the distinction between two categories of state by defining a "nuclear-weapon state" (NWS) as one "which has manufactured and exploded a nuclear weapon or other nuclear explosive device prior to 1 January 1967."[15] This standard limited the universe of possible NWS to five – the United States, Russia (as the juridical successor to the Soviet Union), the United Kingdom, France, and the People's Republic of China (PRC). In effect, therefore – and with a sole exception[16] – the only option for NPT accession since its entry into force in 1970 has been for new signatories to join as "nonnuclear-weapon states" (NNWS), a category which is not expressly defined in the treaty instrument, but which clearly precludes possession of nuclear weaponry and is subject to different rules.

This structure is reflected in the NPT's text. As we have seen, the nontransfer obligations of Article I apply to the five NWS, whereas the nonacquisition rules of Article II – and the safeguards obligations of Article III – specifically apply to NNWS. Article IV's comment about the "exchange" of nuclear technology also calls out NNWS for special attention, while Article V's provisions on "peaceful nuclear explosions" speak to differences in the respective roles of NWS and NNWS parties. (Interestingly, however, the disarmament obligations of Article VI are phrased so as to cover all states party without distinction, though this is frequently forgotten today.) The treaty thus clearly embodies a structure that codifies the possessor/nonpossessor distinction; this has engendered no small amount of diplomatic controversy in subsequent years.

The NPT "Outliers"

As described above, the NPT's structural division into NWS and NNWS categories based upon the January 1967 nuclear test cutoff date ensures that the treaty, as written, prohibits joinder by any more recent weapon possessor except as a NNWS. For countries such as India, Pakistan, and Israel – countries which have not signed the NPT but are either known or presumed to possess nuclear weapons – this essentially precludes NPT accession except in cases of complete dismantlement. To be sure, South Africa took this approach, opting to destroy its small stockpile of independently-produced weapons before acceding to the NPT in 1991 as a NNWS. The path of relinquishment, however, has not been followed by other nuclear-weapon possessors. What to do about the three longstanding NPT "outliers" – joined, in 2003, by the Democratic People's Republic of Korea (DPRK) – has bedeviled nonproliferation diplomacy ever since.

Permanence

As it was originally written, the NPT did not have a precise termination date. Rather, pursuant to Article X, the parties were to convene twenty-five years after the instrument's entry into force in order to determine "whether the Treaty shall continue in force indefinitely, or shall be extended for an additional fixed period or periods."[17] This conference duly took place in 1995, and it was indeed decided to have the NPT extend in force indefinitely.[18] The NPT remains subject to reviews by Review Conferences (RevCons) of the parties to the treaty every five years "with a view to assuring that the purposes of the Preamble and the provisions of the Treaty are being realised,"[19] but the instrument has effectively been made permanent. The relationship between this extension and the issue of disarmament has been the source of much argument in the succeeding years.

History

Although counterfactual conclusions are notoriously difficult to draw, the imminent explosion of proliferation that was predicted in the 1950s and early 1960s has not yet occurred, and NPT proponents frequently give the treaty credit for limiting the number of nuclear-weapon possessors in the world. However, we cannot really know what would have happened had the NPT not existed, and it is hard to conclude this assessment with enormous confidence. Moreover, it seems clear that other factors were involved as well, including some that may have exerted a more powerful effect than the mere existence of the treaty itself.

The Cold War

During the Cold War, both superpowers had strong incentives to keep their allies in line, from a nonproliferation perspective, both in order to preserve their nuclear duopoly and to prevent the emergence of additional nuclear players whose behavior might prove strategically destabilizing. To be sure, the Soviets helped get the PRC's nuclear – and nuclear-weapon – program started in the 1950s, but Moscow came to think better of this, and assistance was eventually terminated. (A prototype nuclear weapon, ballistic missiles, and related technical data that the Soviets had promised to the Chinese under the two countries' October 1957 "New Defense Technical Accord" were never delivered.[20]) On the whole, the superpowers – and especially the United States – played an active role in seeking to dissuade other countries from developing nuclear weapons, and with some success.

The two superpowers' incentives to prevent allied proliferation, and the bloc-leadership tools that they were able to use to this end, thus had a nonproliferation impact that both predated and operated independently of the NPT. Factors related to the availability and relative cost of nuclear-weapon work – especially fissile material production – also affected the attractiveness of that path. Even as early at 1963, classified US assessments noted that "[m]ost of the countries able to undertake a [nuclear weapons] program have not done so," on account of a combination of factors such as high costs, lack of a clear military need, "legal restrictions," moral pressures, Soviet allies' lack of independence, and "concern for international repercussions." This "combination of motives," it was said, "has clearly been effective in such countries as Canada, Germany, India, Japan, Italy, and the European satellites [of the Soviet Union]."[21] The heterogeneity of the variables that serve to restrain proliferation behavior presumably did not lessen after the NPT entered into force.

It is hard to assess the relative contributions of such factors in comparison to whatever impact that the treaty itself may have had in helping prevent the great explosion of proliferation that had been expected. The NPT surely has played some role in making proliferation less prevalent than would otherwise have been the case.[22] Precisely how much impact the existence of the NPT has had relative to other factors in the aggregate, however, is hard to say.

The two cases of presumed or de facto nuclear weaponization by new players beyond the five NPT nuclear-weapon states during the Cold War period – Israel's likely development of nuclear weaponry in the late 1960s and India's "peaceful" explosion of a nuclear device in 1974 – are hard to assess in this respect. Presumably because they wished to develop and/or retain such capabilities, neither of these countries had signed the NPT, which could perhaps be read as a backhanded compliment to the compelling character of the NPT's legal regime, since neither power seems to have considered signing the treaty and cheating. Nevertheless, it is difficult to draw conclusions from this about the NPT's overall efficacy. Perhaps the only firm conclusions that one can reach about these outliers is that they demonstrate that the NPT regime is incomplete in important ways, even while the structure of the treaty makes it impossible to incorporate such states absent either their abandonment of nuclear weapons or a dramatic revision of the treaty instrument itself.

Transitional cases

It might be possible to get some window into the impact of the treaty itself – as opposed, for instance, to nonproliferation pressures from superpower alliance bloc leaders – by comparing such older precedents to the historical track record of the post-Cold War era, when such alliance-related pressures would presumably have become much attenuated. At the transition point into the post-Cold War world, both South Africa and the former Soviet republics of Belarus, Ukraine, and Kazakhstan all gave up nuclear weapons and joined the NPT, as NNWS, by 1994. Brazil and Argentina also both gave up covert weapons programs during this period and acceded to the treaty. The NPT's specific role in these important developments, however, is not entirely clear.

South Africa

South Africa dismantled its nuclear weapons in 1991, just prior to joining the NPT as a nonnuclear-weapon state. While treaty accession capped and codified this step, however, it appears to have been driven by factors unrelated to the NPT itself – not least, the desire of the white minority government there to get out of the nuclear-weapon business before handing over power to the black nationalists of the African National Congress (ANC). In this sense, the South African case is one of regime change as a driver for proliferation rollback.

Former Soviet Republics

For their part, the former Soviet republics also form an ambiguous case, inasmuch as they had simply inherited weapons "stranded" on their soil by the breakup of the USSR, and had not developed or acquired them "on their own" for any particular national purpose. As it was, lacking the infrastructure (and budgets) to produce or maintain such weapons and delivery systems themselves, these new governments were persuaded to give up "their" nuclear weapons as a way of building new post-Soviet relationships with Europe and the rest of the Western world. Offers of Western assistance contingent upon progress in relinquishment were also important: Ukraine received $5 billion in economic subsidies in 1993 alone, for instance, and Kazakhstan was promised a tripling of US aid in return for signing the NPT.[23] It is not clear that the NPT itself played a major role in this process on its own terms, except insofar as joining the treaty was regarded as a symbol of these republics' post-Soviet normalization, and that accession was urged by Western donors as a condition for their support.

Argentina and Brazil

Argentina had a secret nuclear program for many years, with basic research beginning in the late 1960s and being stepped up under military rule in the 1970s. With the return to civilian rule in 1983, however, this program was placed under civilian control. A joint nuclear inspection agency with Brazil – the Brazilian-Argentine Agency for Accounting and Control of Nuclear Materials (ABACC) – was established in 1991, and Argentina joined the NPT in 1995.[24] Brazil had a very similar trajectory, responding to Argentina's nuclear program with its own covert weapons effort. As had Argentina, however, Brazil began to reconsider this course after its own return to civilian rule in 1985; it joined the NPT in 1998. Here again, the role of local circumstances – specifically, the dissolution of military juntas in both countries, and the amelioration of their military rivalry – seem to have played the decisive role, with the NPT itself having been most significant merely as a symbol and codification of moves that had already been undertaken for other reasons.

Iraq

Another instance of proliferation rollback that took place at the time the world was making its transition from the Cold War into its current era of post-bipolarity is the case of Iraq, which after its defeat by US forces in 1991 was discovered to have been much closer to nuclear-weapon development than anyone had suspected. Saddam Hussein's defeat in that conflict – along with the intrusive regime of sanctions and multilateral inspections imposed upon Iraq thereafter – ensured the dismantlement of this effort, and despite Iraq's clear intention to reconstitute nuclear-weapon research (and other prohibited weapons of mass destruction and missile programs) as soon as this coercive international regime was ever relaxed,[25] the Iraqi program remained in abeyance until the Americans dismantled Saddam's government by force in 2003.

In the known cases in which weapon programs were ended, NPT accession repeatedly played an important role in symbolizing and codifying governments' strategic decision to abandon nuclear weaponry, but there is little sign that the treaty drove these outcomes in any significant sense. The NPT played a facilitating role, but local circumstances, especially those of domestic regime change and the waning of perceived security threats, appear to have been much more important.

Post-Cold War proliferation cases

India and Pakistan 1998

The record of the post-Cold War era is, if anything, even more ambiguous. Before their eventual overt weaponization, India and Pakistan had reportedly kept themselves on the brink of nuclear-weapon possession – to the point of keeping separate weapons components in a ready-to-assemble form,[26] a notably disingenuous way to remain a "nonpossessor" – for some time. India was the first to go further, however, abandoning its pretense of a "peaceful" explosion and openly announcing weaponization in May 1998 by conducting five underground nuclear tests in less than a week. Pakistan quickly followed suit, conducting five tests of its own before the end of the month, as the longstanding rivalry between these two countries shifted into its present, nuclear phase.

North Korea

North Korea, which acceded to the NPT in 1985 but declined to sign a safeguards agreement with the IAEA (as it was required to do by Article III of the treaty) until 1992, was apparently in continuous violation of its nonproliferation commitments from the moment it undertook them. The DPRK's nuclear-weapon program apparently began in the 1970s, and from the early 1980s involved efforts to develop a reactor-based plutonium production capability and research into implosion designs for a nuclear weapon.[27] Nor did Pyongyang's program ever really stop, irrespective of the country's NPT status: after secret plutonium reprocessing efforts were discovered by the IAEA in the early 1990s, North Korea agreed in 1994 to freeze its plutonium program in return for international assistance (and the promise of light water nuclear reactors), but undertook a secret new effort to develop a separate weapons pipeline based upon the enrichment of uranium, using technology acquired from Pakistan.[28] When the United States discovered this cheating and brought it to Pyongyang's attention, North Korea withdrew from the NPT entirely in 2003. It openly tested its first weapon in 2006, and conducted further tests in 2009 and 2013.

At the most basic level, the NPT seems to have been quite irrelevant to North Korea as it pursued its nuclear-weapon ambitions: it clearly put no stock in its nonproliferation undertakings to begin with. A more sophisticated analysis would note that the NPT regime *did* play a role in bringing DPRK cheating to light, insofar as it was IAEA inspectors who first visited the DPRK's plutonium reprocessing pilot plant at Yongbyon and discovered it to be what in fact it was. This positive NPT impact, however, must be set against the DPRK's degree of success in using nonproliferation negotiations and repeated agreements with international partners as cover for its ongoing weapons work.

The Khan Network

Although its activities began in the 1980s, one of the most important developments during the post-Cold War period, from a nonproliferation perspective, was the rise of the illicit proliferation technology network run by Pakistani nuclear scientist Abdul Qadeer Khan, which operated until its public exposure and (at least partial) dismemberment in 2003–04. The Khan network peddled uranium enrichment technology, fissile materials, and even Pakistani nuclear-weapon designs around the world, helping equip, and accelerate, emerging nuclear-weapon programs in several countries. Khan, apparently working closely with the Pakistani government, played an important role in helping the North Koreans develop their uranium program, and thus contributed enormously to proliferation and the escalation of tensions in Northeast Asia.

Libya

Khan's network also provided Libyan dictator Muammar Qaddafi with equipment and raw material for his nuclear-weapon program. The Libyan case is remarkable both for the suddenness of its development – in the sense that Libya acquired a nearly complete suite of weapons-making equipment and materials from Khan, including weapons designs, essentially from scratch – and for the striking strategic volte face that led Libya to the abandonment of this program.

The Libyan case of proliferation rollback seems to have been driven by a combination of the sanctions-stricken Qaddafi regime's desire for normalized relations with the Western world, and his personal fear of suffering the same fate as Saddam Hussein. The secret Libyan overtures to British and US intelligence officials that led to Qaddafi's ultimate decision began in March

2003, when a US-led coalition was massing on Iraq's border and was clearly about to crush the Iraqi army and unseat Saddam's government.[29] Qaddafi made his historic announcement about abandoning Libya's weapons of mass destruction programs, moreover, on December 19, 2003 – five days after Saddam Hussein had been dragged out of his underground hiding place and taken into custody by US forces in the Iraqi town of Tikrit.[30] As the Libyan dictator explained his decision several months later, he had sought to develop nuclear weapons during the Cold War, but since then it had been made clear that "now … if you built a nuclear bomb you would be in big trouble."[31] Having satisfied US, British, and IAEA authorities that its program had indeed concluded – and having permitted the constituent elements of this program to be shipped to the United States for analysis and safekeeping[32] – Libya was understood to have returned to compliance with the NPT.

The role of the NPT and related institutions in these developments is ambiguous. Clearly, compliance with the treaty meant essentially nothing to Qaddafi per se, and indeed the appearance of being a member in good standing – IAEA inspectors never detected Libya's clandestine nuclear work – may have helped allay foreign suspicions and create a false sense of security in the outside world. On the other hand, the "cover" of Agency involvement in helping verify dismantlement clearly lessened the political sting for the Libyans of turning over all their nuclear materials, equipment, and weapons designs to US officials, who quickly removed them from the country.[33] The existence of the NPT and the availability of the IAEA for this political cover thus surely made Libyan proliferation rollback easier to implement, but this step actually occurred for reasons largely independent of the treaty regime itself.

Iran

The Khan network also helped jump-start Iran's nuclear-weapon program, beginning in the 1980s and continuing at least until the exposure of Iran's previously secret enrichment facility at Natanz in August 2002. At the time of writing, international negotiations are underway in hopes of working out a comprehensive solution to the Iranian nuclear problem. Even if the current negotiations "succeed," it seems likely that Iran will be allowed to remain poised for a weaponization "breakout," with the continued ability to enrich quantities of uranium up to about the 5 percent level of purity, while construction proceeds on an Iranian heavy-water reactor at Arak. (Questions about the worrisome evidence of Iranian work on nuclear weaponization may or may not be answered as a result of these negotiations.[34]) In any event, Iran has done all of this nuclear work – and engaged in years of denial, deception, safeguards violations, and evasion of IAEA inspectors – from within the NPT, claiming to be in perfect compliance all the while. So far, at least, the Iran case is clearly not much of a success story for the NPT, though it is also true that IAEA inspectors have done a good job over the years, and particularly since 2009, in verifying at least the current state of Iran's declared nuclear activities, and of asking pointed questions about evidence of continued clandestine work.

Syria

In evaluating the proliferation case history of the post-Cold War era, one should also not omit Syria, which secretly constructed a plutonium production reactor in eastern Syria near the town of Al Kibar, with assistance from North Korean technicians. (The reactor was reportedly modeled upon the DPRK's own reactor at Yongbyon.[35]) This facility was bombed by Israeli warplanes in September 2007, before the Syrians could begin fueling operations at the facility, and there has been no publicly reported indication of ongoing Syrian nuclear work since that time. From the perspective of assessing the NPT's role, this is perhaps the clearest post-Cold War proliferation case: the NPT and its related institutions seem to have had essentially no positive impact upon Syrian behavior, nor did they play any role in the rollback of Syria's weapons program, which occurred at the hands of a nonsignatory for its own obvious strategic reasons. Syria had acceded to the NPT in 1969 and entered into a safeguards agreement with the IAEA in 1992, and it apparently violated these agreements for a considerable period prior to September 2007. Since the Al Kibar reactor's (former) existence was publicly revealed in 2008, Syrian authorities have not permitted IAEA inspectors all the access they have requested in order to assess the Syrian nuclear situation.[36]

Present-day controversies

The most important issues for the future are the basic challenges of nonproliferation policy itself – that is, how best to prevent and, if necessary, to respond to NPT and safeguards violations, and how to ensure that nuclear-weapon development is as unattractive and difficult as possible from the perspective of would-be proliferators. Many factors obviously contribute to shaping proliferator incentives, and to influencing the behavior of third parties whose own actions contribute to the strategic, political, and technological environment in which proliferation choices are made.

With regard to the NPT's contribution to these dynamics, however, the record seems to be generally positive, but mixed. A treaty regime such as the NPT is capable of influencing behavior in part by helping establish, codify, and symbolize a set of norms and policy priorities for states party and for the broader international community. To the extent, for example, that the NPT sets or contributes to the maintenance of clear and powerful international norms against proliferation, facilitates the early detection of (and, crucially, mobilization against) proliferation problems, and helps make proliferation seem unattractive, one can adjudge it a valuable instrument. By affecting the perceived availability of the proliferation path in the first place, and certainly by influencing how third-parties can be expected to respond to proliferation choices, the treaty can help shape how would-be proliferators consider the pursuit of nuclear weapons.[37]

To the extent that nonproliferation has been, and remains, a compelling norm in the international community, this is surely due in part to the existence and the influence of the NPT. What is less clear, of course, is the extent to which the NPT has contributed to keeping nuclear-weapon proliferation from having been as much worse as it was once expected to be. A clear net assessment of the treaty's positive or negative impact is, and is likely to remain, elusive.

The legal framework of the NPT regime has certainly seemed to mean at least something even to powers that do not wish to abide by it. The openly or presumptively nuclear-armed outliers of India, Pakistan, and Israel, for instance, were careful to avoid treaty accession, taking care to ensure that their own weaponization was not illegal in NPT terms. It is also probably of some significance that proliferators such as Iran, Iraq, Libya, and Syria – as well as, for a while, North Korea – sought to remain within the NPT even while violating its provisions. This may or may not imply any real respect on their part for the treaty's rules, of course, since maintaining the pretense of compliance is presumably helpful in reducing the likelihood of counter-mobilization by third parties. Either way, however, proliferators operating within the regime do seem to have wished to postpone the point of overt departure from Article II compliance for as long as possible. The existence of some kind of nonproliferation norm backed by a legally-binding and nearly universal treaty instrument thus appears to have helped have at least some constraint upon their perceived range of choices available to them.

In more concrete terms, moreover, by obliging nonpossessing states party to maintain safeguards agreements with the IAEA, the NPT also increases the cost and difficulty of violations and the likelihood that such work will be detected. The IAEA's work in Iran, at least, also eventually helped build a diplomatic constituency in favor of nonproliferation-promoting sanctions pressures, principally by documenting Iran's nuclear work (and raising questions about evidence of weaponization) in ways that it was much more difficult for naysayers to dismiss than if such warnings had issued solely from one or more national governments. These are certainly important factors, which are surely conducive to nonproliferation.

Part of the reason that proliferators may have sought to delay an overt break with the nonproliferation regime may be precisely that making a show of false compliance can help protect proliferators from adverse consequences even while they continue to pursue nuclear weapons. As the Iranian case suggests, it is surely easier to organize collective compliance pressures against an overt violator than one who insists upon his innocence and works to ensure that compliance assessments are hotly contested on factual and legal terrain that is as complex and arcane as possible.

The very existence of a legally binding treaty framework, moreover, focuses attention upon the question of "compliance" versus "noncompliance," helping make it more difficult to persuade third party states to support international pressures against a proliferator in the absence of some kind of "official" finding that a violation has occurred. Yet there is no international mechanism for finding a country in noncompliance with the NPT itself, and though the IAEA has express statutory authority to refer safeguards violators to the UN Security Council,[38] even this is a slow and cumbersome process. (It was not until more than two years after Iran's nuclear program was first publicly revealed, for instance, that a majority of the IAEA Board could reach agreement that Iran's secret nuclear work had violated its safeguards obligations.[39]) Individual national actors who care about such problems may decide to act on their own, of course, but anyone awaiting a formal finding of violation may wait a long time.

The NPT framework increases the cost and difficulty of noncompliance by NNWS, but for those among them willing and able to travel this path despite these challenges, certain aspects of the regime can arguably be turned to a proliferator's advantage. Violations that persist within the treaty regime, moreover, are perhaps more corrosive than ones that occur outside it, even in cases of withdrawal. The NPT has always contained a formal withdrawal mechanism,[40] and while the actual use of those provisions may present grave challenges to international peace and security, such use does not impugn the basic credibility of the treaty itself. In a sense, withdrawal could perhaps even be said to validate the NPT, with the alarm caused by a party's departure signaling the value of the instrument and the importance of its prohibitions.

By contrast, if it is possible for states party to develop nuclear weaponry within the treaty – or even to prepare themselves to take such a step on very short notice – the nonproliferation obligations contained within that document lose their meaning and significance. In addition to the immediate impact of proliferation in the violator state itself, such an erosion of the treaty's credibility would also undercut the ability of states elsewhere in the world to rely upon the NPT to restrain the potential nuclear ambitions of their neighbors, effectively terminating the security bargain among nonpossessors that gave them an incentive to accept the treaty's nonproliferation obligations in the first place. Such developments could thus encourage just the sort of proliferation "cascade" that was predicted before the treaty's negotiation.

These factors do not outweigh or fully counterbalance the positive impact of the NPT in reinforcing nonproliferation norms and increasing the difficulty of noncompliance; however, they are not negligible. It must also be noted that even though the net impact of the treaty is surely positive, the historical record does not permit very strong assertions about the relative weight of the NPT and its associated institutions, either in dissuading states that might otherwise have opted to pursue nuclear weaponry, or in inducing violators to return to compliance. Nor is it even clear that the NPT has had a very significant effect even upon the decisions of third parties, though one might expect the impact of general norms to be greater for them to the extent that, unlike proliferators themselves or their neighbors, such states' immediate security interests are not implicated. Other states' reactions to proliferation challenges seem more tied to their assessments of concrete local, regional, and geopolitical implications than to their judgments about compliance or noncompliance with any particular legal regime. North Korea's development of nuclear weaponry, for instance, has created widespread alarm, but Pyongyang's NPT status does not seem to have been a significant factor in such concern. The DPRK announced its withdrawal from the NPT in 2003, but no one seems to feel that the North Korean program is any less worrisome just because it is no longer "illegal."[41] The problem was clearly the prospect of overt weaponization, irrespective of its legalities.

Similarly, few countries have today been willing formally to identify Iran as a violator of the NPT – more than a third of the IAEA Board of Governors declining even to support the Board's initial finding of Iranian safeguards violations[42] – but many countries clearly worry greatly about the implications of the Iranian program. The locus of this concern seems to lie with the likely impact of Iran's program on security and stability in the Middle East much more than with whatever its particular legal status happens to be vis-à-vis the NPT or its IAEA safeguards agreement.

Some of this contextual distinction-making can also be seen in the international community's reaction to the Indian and Pakistani nuclear-weapon tests of 1998. Both were roundly excoriated for this move notwithstanding the fact that these detonations raised no NPT or safeguards compliance issues. In this sense, the two countries' refusal to join the treaty – and their implied (and presumably creditable) disinterest in behaving unlawfully – ended up "purchasing" India and Pakistan comparatively little. Their critics seem to have been concerned more about the substance of the actions in question, and the concrete implications of the tests for regional and global stability, than about the nature of their relationship to any international treaty regime.

As time went by, moreover, the gradual cooling of nuclear-related hostility toward India, and the relative degree of Pakistan's continuing nuclear isolation, also support the intuition that international reactions are more powerfully shaped by the complexities of real-world circumstance than by abstract principles of treaty propriety. If it were India, rather than Pakistan, for example, whose scientists had run an illicit proliferation network for two decades – and if it were India, rather than Pakistan, whose government from time to time seems to teeter on the edge of collapse to terrorist insurgents – one surely would not have seen India win itself an exemption from NSG rules ordinarily barring nuclear energy cooperation with countries not under full-scope IAEA safeguards.[43] Both countries remain equally "outliers," and both have policies that remain in some sense at odds with the values of the NPT regime, but states party treat them differently, giving more weight to actual behavior and circumstances than to either power's legal status. Their NPT status is hardly irrelevant in international eyes, but it is not dispositive, and it is clearly less important, for key third-party players, than other factors.

The "Big Three" disputes

Beyond the core issue of nonproliferation policy itself, the "big three" conflicts in NPT diplomacy revolve around the question of nuclear disarmament, peaceful uses, and what to do about treaty "outliers."

Disarmament

By its terms, the final language of Article VI requires no more than the mere pursuit of nego-tiations in good faith – and not merely by weapons possessors, but by all states party – with an eye to ending the arms race, achieving nuclear disarmament, and indeed establishing a treaty on general and complete disarmament.[44]

While the NPT's relative emptiness of disarmament content is certainly clear enough as a matter of law, the politics are more complicated. To begin with, one of the ways in which the treaty's drafters put off the issue of disarmament was to encourage states party to use the five-year NPT review cycle as a forum for assessing how well the treaty was contributing to the broad purposes envisioned for it – including its role as a "step towards the achievement of general and complete disarmament and, more specifically, nuclear disarmament."[45] Several of the delegations that had opposed the insertion of specific disarmament obligations, in fact, suggested that even though Article VI did not say very much, the treaty's periodic Review Conferences would be an appropriate venue for raising dissatisfaction with the pace of disar-mament by the NWS. Such complaints have been a staple of these meetings ever since.

Further impetus for injecting disarmament issues into NPT debates came with the treaty's indefinite extension. At the same time as the 1995 Review Conference extended the treaty to operate in perpetuity, it also agreed upon a resolution ("Decision 2") declaring the parties' support for the disarmament principles enshrined in Article VI and declaring that it was "important" for the realization of these principles that certain specific steps be taken – among them, a prohibition on nuclear testing, a ban on the production of fissile material for nuclear explosive purposes, and

> the determined pursuit by the nuclear-weapon States of systematic and progressive efforts to reduce nuclear weapons globally, with the ultimate goals of eliminating those weapons, and by all States of general and complete disarmament under strict and effective international control.[46]

Legally speaking, of course, such a mere political declaration by the assembled governments could add little to the thin gruel of Article VI. Politically, however, the specificity in Decision 2 about the importance of particular concrete steps was important. Many states today insist that whatever the legal situation, the 1995 extension of the treaty was made on the basis of a "polit-ical bargain" pursuant to which extension is to be repaid by accelerated progress toward nuclear disarmament. This is the real locus of much of the contentiousness of the disarmament issue in today's NPT debates, even to the point that some have tried to suggest that the possessor states' failure completely to disarm should justify NNWS in repudiating their own adherence to the treaty's disarmament obligations.[47]

Despite the superpowers' enormous progress in reducing their arsenals since the end of the Cold War, the possessor states' continuing failure to achieve complete abolition is the subject of much criticism and controversy. To the extent, therefore, that present-day strategic realities suggest that post-Cold War progress in nuclear reductions is likely to slow and to stop well short of "zero" in the near future – and indeed, to the extent that the goals of nonproliferation and nuclear disarmament ultimately work at cross purposes, inasmuch as too great a reduction in the remaining US nuclear arsenal could erode the "extended nuclear deterrence" it provides to its allies, potentially prompting one or more of them to undertake indigenous nuclear weaponization – one should expect that the contentiousness of disarmament in NPT fora will increase in the years ahead.

Peaceful uses

The view that there exists an "inalienable right" to the full nuclear fuel cycle irrespective of proliferation implications – that is, under IAEA safeguards but irrespective of how effective such safeguards actually are in reducing the danger of diversion, clandestine weapons development, or short-notice "breakout" – continues to gain strength in diplomatic circles. This has been occurring, moreover, while the cost and inaccessibility of enrichment and reprocessing technology have been dramatically reduced. Alternative interpretations of Article IV are available that do not so immediately permit its provisions to undermine the rest of the treaty, but such readings generally lack defenders in multinational fora and have been losing ground.[48] Though peaceful use issues may for this very reason be becoming progressively *less* controversial in NPT fora, the spread of dual-use capabilities is clearly a growing challenge for the nonproliferation regime.

To be sure, some scholars have suggested that an environment of "virtual" weapons states, each lacking nuclear weaponry but capable of building it on short notice, might actually be a stable one. Such thinkers hypothesize that the ability to build weapons might itself provide a sort of deterrence, inasmuch as potential aggressors would know that the victim of an attack could quickly assemble and deploy such devices in retaliation.[49] However, evidence points in just the opposite direction, suggesting that a world of virtual deterrence would be radically unstable in a crisis, for it would encourage actual or potential adversaries to race each other to the nuclear punch.[50] The spread of fuel-cycle technologies – aided and abetted by readings of Article IV that encourage the proliferation of the weapon "option" and discourage efforts to limit technology-sharing – present a structural challenge to the NPT regime.

Treaty outliers

Another of the major controversies that beset discussions in NPT fora today is what to do about the overtly or presumptively weapon-possessing treaty outliers – that is, the three countries that never signed the NPT in the first place (India, Pakistan, and Israel) and the one that withdrew from the treaty before conducting its first nuclear test (North Korea). The international community lacks any real option for dealing with these countries in strictly NPT terms, since formally incorporating them into the existing framework would require either its renegotiation or the complete elimination of their nuclear arsenals, neither of which seems even remotely feasible at this time. Efforts to develop middle-ground approaches such as the 2005 US-India deal,[51] however, have themselves proven controversial – not least because a good many countries regard any nuclear-related dealing with any of these outliers as some kind of betrayal of the NPT.

At the same time, the question of what to do about Israel's capabilities – and the closely-related topic of whether and how to establish "a Middle East zone free of nuclear weapons as well as other weapons of mass destruction," a goal endorsed by the 1995 NPT Review Conference[52] and a topic of much debate ever since – has increasingly preoccupied NPT diplomats and has periodically imperiled treaty-related negotiations.[53] One can expect that such "outlier" problems will continue for some time to come.

Conclusion

Supporters of the NPT are probably correct that the treaty has played a role in helping ensure that the explosion of nuclear-weapon proliferation predicted by analysts in the 1950s and early

1960s did not come to pass. At the same time, however, the treaty's impact may not be nearly as great as its supporters often claim, its record is somewhat mixed, the challenges it faces today are very significant, and its future is notably cloudy.

The NPT was born of expediency during the Cold War, as an attempt to help avoid an anticipated crisis of ballooning nuclear-weapon proliferation. It attempted to address the horizontal spread of weaponry, but carefully avoided taking clear positions on other issues of importance to the international players involved in the negotiations – in particular, the pre-existing but notably entangled questions of disarmament and peaceful nuclear use. Although the treaty was an appropriate and arguably much-needed response to an emerging crisis of potential proliferation, therefore, it was also, in a structural sense, merely a temporary measure. It was designed to mitigate the most immediately-addressable source of global danger and instability, but certainly *not* to solve all associated issues, and not necessarily to provide a *permanent* answer even on the points that it did touch.

The NPT was predicated upon the quite reasonable supposition that without addressing the problem of horizontal spread, issues such as disarmament and PUNE could certainly never be satisfactorily handled. Nonproliferation was both a conceptual and a practical *sine qua non* for real progress on other fronts – and indeed for peace and security in its own right – but the instrument was neither intended nor expected to represent a "solution" for the full spectrum of nuclear-weapon-related international security challenges. On top of the abiding difficulties of ensuring nonproliferation on its own terms, it is these entangled challenges which have continued to bedevil the NPT regime to the present day.

This is one of the reasons why the NPT has felt so unsatisfactory to so many participants. Essentially every participant in the treaty regime professes itself committed to the NPT's principles and faithful to its meaning and intent. Yet many of these same players in fact disagree continually on fundamental matters – not least about just what the treaty's meaning and intent is in the first place – and over issues that relate directly to the sustainability both of the NPT itself and the broader nonproliferation regime of which it is a part. Despite all but universal ostensible support for the treaty, therefore, there is surprisingly little meaningful or operationally useful agreement on NPT-related policy issues.

One *might* conclude a net assessment of the NPT pessimistically, by saying simply that the treaty is poorly suited to the contemporary world, not grounded in any strong policy-relevant consensus, and neither well-designed nor institutionally equipped for long-term coherence or success in the post-Cold War world that this regime had entered just before the NPT's provisions were extended indefinitely in 1995. And to some extent, all this would be true. At the same time, however, the NPT has played a role in helping forestall enormous problems by slowing the spread of nuclear weaponry. Even if its role to date has been only a modest one, moreover, any step away from its codification of the core principles of nondissemination and nonacquisition would be seen, correctly, as a very dangerous move indeed.

No one has yet offered any feasible replacement for this troublingly flawed instrument, much less a path for successfully navigating between today's complicated and contingent "is" to the "ought" represented by any such alternative vision. The NPT is deeply flawed, uncomfortable, "unfair," poorly suited to modern conditions, and ill-equipped for long-term survival – but it has also been relatively successful, is probably necessary for the maintenance of international peace and security, and is today essentially irreplaceable. This is a mixed record, to be sure, but the institution deserves support from its states party, especially at this juncture in humanity's struggle with the challenges and opportunities presented by the Janus-faced atom.

Notes

1. The views the author expresses here are entirely his own, and do not necessarily represent those of anyone else in the US Government.
2. United States Central Intelligence Agency, Office of the Director, "Nuclear Weapons Production in Fourth Countries: Likelihood and Consequences, NIE-100-6-57," June 18, 1957 (declassified version), pp. 1–3, www2.gwu.edu/~nsarchiv/NSAEBB/NSAEBB155/prolif-2.pdf.
3. Robert S. McNamara, "Memorandum for the President," February 12, 1963 (declassified version), p.6, available at www.fas.org/man/eprint/dod1963.pdf.
4. UN General Assembly, "Resolution 1665 (XVI)," December 4, 1961, http://daccess-dds-ny.un.org/doc/RESOLUTION/GEN/NR0/167/18/IMG/NR016718.pdf. [Hereafter "Irish Resolution".]
5. See, e.g., US Arms Control and Disarmament Agency (ACDA), "International Negotiations on the Treaty on the Nonproliferation of Nuclear Weapons, Publication 48," (Washington, DC: Government Printing Office, 1969), pp. ix–x, xiv, 9–10, 17, 78.
6. ACDA, "International Negotiations on the Treaty on the Nonproliferation of Nuclear Weapons," pp. 81, 84–86; ACDA, "Brazilian Amendments to the Draft Nonproliferation Treaty, October 31, 1967," *Documents on Disarmament 1967* (Washington, DC: Government Printing Office, 1968), p. 546.
7. United Nations, "Treaty on the Nonproliferation of Nuclear Weapons," July 1, 1968, Article V, www.un.org/en/conf/npt/2005/npttreaty.html.
8. Irish Resolution, p. 5.
9. ACDA, "International Negotiations on the Treaty on the Nonproliferation of Nuclear Weapons," pp. 8, 15–16, 20, 23–24, 44–45.
10. Ibid., pp. 8, 43–44.
11. NPT, Art. VI.
12. ACDA, "International Negotiations on the Treaty on the Nonproliferation of Nuclear Weapons," pp. 20–25.
13. See generally, Christopher A. Ford, "Nuclear Technology Rights and Wrongs: The Nuclear Nonproliferation Treaty, Article IV, and Nonproliferation," in *Reviewing the Nuclear Nonproliferation Treaty*, edited by Henry Sokolski (Carlisle, PA: Strategic Studies Institute, 2010), pp. 237, 308–9.
14. NPT, Art. VI.
15. Ibid., Art. IX(3).
16. As noted, the PRC did not accede until 1992; having first tested a nuclear weapon in 1964, however, it was able to do so as a NWS.
17. NPT, Art. X(2).
18. United Nations Office for Disarmament Affairs, "Decision 3: Extension of the Treaty on the Non-Proliferation of Nuclear Weapons," 1995 Review and Extension Conference of the Parties to the Treaty on the Non-Proliferation of Nuclear Weapons, New York, April 17–May 12, 1995, www.un.org/disarmament/WMD/Nuclear/1995-NPT/pdf/NPT_CONF199503.pdf.
19. NPT, Art. VIII(3).
20. John Wilson Lewis and Xue Litai, *China Builds the Bomb* (Palo Alto, CA: Stanford University Press, 1988), p. 41 (footnote).
21. McNamara, "Memorandum for the President," p. 2.
22. See, e.g., Jurg Stussi, "Historischer Abriss zur Frage einer Schweizer Nuklearbewaffnung" [Historical Outline on the Question of Swiss Nuclear Armament] (J. Wozniak, trans.), April 1996, available at http://nuclearweaponarchive.org/Library/Swissdoc.html.
23. See generally, e.g., Kevin Kiernan, "Why Do States Give Up Nuclear Arsenals?" *Bologna Center Journal of International Affairs*, Vol. 17 (2013), http://bcjournal.org/volume-11/why-do-states-give-up-nuclear-arsenals.html; Amy Woolfe, "Nuclear Weapons in the Former Soviet Union: Location, Command and Control," Congressional Research Service, November 27, 1996, www.fas.org/spp/starwars/crs/91-144.htm.
24. See, e.g., Nuclear Threat Initiative, "Argentina Overview," December 2013, www.nti.org/country-profiles/argentina/.
25. See, e.g., Special Advisor to the Director of Central Intelligence, "Comprehensive Report of the Special Advisor to the DCI on Iraq's WMD (Weapons of Mass Destruction)," September 30, 2004, www.cia.gov/library/reports/general-reports-1/iraq_wmd_2004. [a.k.a. "Duelfer Report"]
26. George Perkovich, *India's Nuclear Bomb: The Impact on Global Proliferation* (Berkeley, CA: University of California Press, 1999), pp. 335, 340 (quoting US intelligence conclusions).

27. See generally, e.g., Michael J. Mazarr, *North Korea and the Bomb: A Case Study in Nonproliferation* (New York: St Martin's Press, 1995), pp. 17, 24, 28–29, 44–45, 62.

28. See, e.g., David Albright, *Peddling Peril: How the Secret Nuclear Trade Arms America's Enemies* (New York: Free Press, 2010), p. 160; Larry A. Niksh, "North Korea's Nuclear Weapons Program," Congressional Research Service report IB91141, November 5, 2003, www.nautilus.org/publications/books/dprkbb/nuclearweapons/CRSIB91141_NKsNuclearWeaponsProgram.pdf; Mike Chinoy, *Meltdown: The Inside Story of the North Korean Nuclear Crisis* (New York: St Martin's Press, 2009), pp. 82–88, 90–91.

29. See, e.g., Nuclear Threat Initiative, "Libya Nuclear Chronology," February 2011, www.nti.org/media/pdfs/libya_nuclear.pdf?_=1316466791.

30. See, e.g., David E. Sanger and Judith Miller, "Libya to Give Up Arms Programs, Bush Announces," *The New York Times*, December 20, 2003, www.nytimes.com/2003/12/20/world/libya-to-give-up-arms-programs-bush-announces.html.

31. See, e.g., US Department of State, "Adherence To and Compliance With Arms Control, Nonproliferation, And Disarmament Agreements and Commitments," August 2005, p. 85 (quoting Qaddafi statement of March 2, 2004), www.state.gov/documents/organization/52113.pdf. [hereinafter "2005 Noncompliance Report"]

32. See, e.g., Brian Whitaker, "Libya Gives up Last Weapons Equipment," *The Guardian*, March 7, 2004, www.theguardian.com/world/2004/mar/08/libya.brianwhitaker.

33. By way of full disclosure, the reader should be aware that the author of this chapter was involved in this operation when serving at the US State Department.

34. See, e.g., IAEA, "Implementation of the NPT Safeguards Agreement and Relevant Provisions of Security Council resolutions in the Islamic Republic of Iran," GOV/20011/65, November 8, 2011, www.iaea.org/Publications/Documents/Board/2011/gov2011-65.pdf.

35. See, e.g., Dana Perino, "Statement by the White House Press Secretary on Syria and North Korea," April 24, 2008, www.cfr.org/syria/statement-white-house-press-secretary-syria-north-korea/p16102; US Central Intelligence Agency, "Syria's Covert Nuclear Reactor at Al Kibar," video, April 25, 2008, www.youtube.com/watch?v=yj62GRd0Te8.

36. See US Department of State, "Adherence To And Compliance With Arms Control, Nonproliferation, And Disarmament Agreements And Commitments," July 2013, pp. 29–32, www.state.gov/documents/organization/212096.pdf.

37. See generally, e.g., Christopher Ford, "The NPT Regime and the Challenge of Shaping Proliferator Behavior," in *Over the Horizon Proliferation Threats*, edited by James J. Wirtz and Peter R. Lavoy (Palo Alto, CA: Stanford University Press, 2012), p. 179.

38. Statute of the IAEA, October 23, 1956, Art. XII.C, www.iaea.org/About/statute.html.

39. IAEA Board of Governors, "Implementation of the NPT Safeguards Agreement in the Islamic Republic of Iran, GOV/2005/77," September 24, 2005, para. 1, www.iaea.org/Publications/Documents/Board/2005/gov2005-77.pdf.

40. NPT, Art. X(1).

41. Indeed, NPT States Party still cannot agree upon what North Korea's NPT status is in the first place. See generally, e.g., United Nations, *United Nations Disarmament Yearbook*, Vol. 30, 2005 (New York: United Nations, 2006), p. 3 (recounting initial decision to follow this model at 2003 NPT Preparatory Committee meeting).

42. See, e.g., Acronym Institute for Disarmament Diplomacy, "IAEA Resolution on Iran's 'non Compliance' with NPT Safeguards," September 24, 2005, www.acronym.org.uk/official-and-govt-documents/iaea-resolution-irans-non-compliance-npt-safeguards.

43. See, e.g., Wade Boese, "NSG, Congress Approve Nuclear Trade with India," *Arms Control Today*, Vol. 38, No. 8 (October 2008), pp. 27–28, www.armscontrol.org/act/2008_10/NSGapprove.

44. NPT, Art. VI.

45. Ibid., pp. 20, 25.

46. United Nations Office for Disarmament Affairs, "Decision 2: Principles and Objectives for Nuclear Non-Proliferation and Disarmament," NPT/CONF.1995/32, 1995 Review and Extension Conference of the Parties to the Treaty on the Non-Proliferation of Nuclear Weapons, New York, April 17–May 12, 1995, www.un.org/disarmament/WMD/Nuclear/1995-NPT/pdf/NPT_CONF199501.pdf.

47. See Daniel H. Joyner, *Interpreting the Nuclear Nonproliferation Treaty* (Oxford: Oxford University Press, 2011).

48. See Jonathan Schell, *The Abolition* (New York: Alfred A. Knopf, 1984); Michael J. Mazarr, "The Notion of Virtual Arsenals," in *Nuclear Weapons in a Transformed World*, edited by Michael J. Mazarr (New York: St Martin's Press, 1997), p. 3; Sidney D. Drell and Raymond Jeanloz, "Nuclear Deterrence After Zero," paper presented at the Conference on Deterrence: Its Past and Future at the Hoover Institution, November 11, 2010, www.cna.org/sites/default/files/news/2011/Goodby_DeterrenceCONF_FINAL_SCRIBD.pdf.

49. See generally, Ford, "Nuclear Technology Rights and Wrongs," pp. 247–72.

50. See Christopher Ford, "Nuclear Weapons Reconstitution and its Discontents: Challenges of 'Weaponless Deterrence'," in *Deterrence: Its Past and Future*, edited by George P. Shultz, Sidney D. Drell, and James E. Goodby (Palo Alto, CA: Hoover Institution Press, 2011), pp. 131–215; Christopher Ford, "Weapons Reconstitution and Strategic Stability," New Paradigms Forum, May 23, 2011, www.newparadigmsforum.com/NPFtestsite/?p=886.

51. See, e.g., US Department of State, "US-India Civil Nuclear Cooperation," N.D., www.state.gov/p/sca/c17361.htm.

52. United Nations General Assembly, "Resolution on the Middle East," NPT/CONF.1995/32, 1995 Review and Extension Conference of the Parties to the Treaty on the Non-Proliferation of Nuclear Weapons, New York, April 17–May 12, 1995, Annex, www.un.org/disarmament/WMD/Nuclear/1995-NPT/pdf/Resolution_MiddleEast.pdf.

53. See, e.g., Kelsey Davenport, "WMD-Free Middle East Proposal at a Glance," Arms Control Association, July 2013, www.armscontrol.org/factsheets/mewmdfz.

9

THE FUTURE OF THE NPT AND THE NUCLEAR NONPROLIFERATION REGIME

Joseph F. Pilat

A decades-long debate has been taking place on the question of whether the Treaty on the Nonproliferation of Nuclear Weapons (NPT) and the nuclear nonproliferation regime it anchors has been successful.[1] The global treaty approach has been important for setting norms concerning nuclear and other weapons of mass destruction (WMD) and missiles, and the treaties and other elements of the various nonproliferation regimes have been influential in redefining the problem and the manner in which it is perceived. In this context, international interest in strengthening the various global treaty regimes designed to control or eliminate WMD has grown, but the issues have been difficult and the results limited. For example, efforts to improve international safeguards are being undertaken by the International Atomic Energy Agency (IAEA). The IAEA is focusing in particular on enhancing the effectiveness and efficiency of safeguards for NPT parties. While these efforts are widely supported, expectations may be unduly high because of the inherent difficulties of detecting clandestine nuclear facilities and activities. Although all the nonproliferation regimes face similar, albeit clearly not identical, challenges, the debate may ultimately hinge on the fate of the NPT regime.

After the 2005 Review Conference (RevCon) of the Parties to the Treaty on the Nonproliferation of Nuclear Weapons, the future of the treaty looked bleak to many observers.[2] President Obama's 2009 Prague speech and the 2010 Nuclear Posture Review (NPR) report – with their focus on combating nuclear proliferation and terrorism, and support for the NPT – were elements in the successful outcome of the RevCon.[3] However, the 2010 RevCon by no means ended the Article VI debate or the challenges to the treaty, and the lead up to the 2015 RevCon will be challenging, with major noncompliance issues unresolved, uncertainties surrounding the convocation of the conference on a Middle East Weapons of Mass Destruction Free Zone called for at the 2010 RevCon and an effort by states and nongovernmental organizations to address the humanitarian consequences of nuclear-weapon use.[4]

In this context, this chapter addresses the following: What are the challenges faced by the nonproliferation regime centered on the Nonproliferation Treaty and the IAEA? What are the prospects for the NPT? Does it remain relevant to current and future efforts to deal with nuclear proliferation and terrorism threats? What improvements could ensure it can meet current and future challenges and be the foundation for the proliferation resistance and physical protection needed if nuclear power grows? What will make it a viable centerpiece of future nonproliferation and counterterrorism approaches?

The nonproliferation treaty

The NPT, which was concluded in 1968 and entered into force in 1970, was the boldest attempt in the post-Second World War era to use multilateral means to balance international concerns for global security with emerging national ambitions in the nuclear area. It sought to reflect the interests of the United States and the Soviet Union in ensuring a degree of stability in their relationship and in sensitive regions; to address the desires of developed industrial nations, especially in Europe and Japan, to exploit a promising technology for commercial use and advantage; and to meet the hopes of developing nations that transfers of nuclear scientific and technological capabilities might ameliorate their desperate economic and social straits. Accordingly, the operative articles of the NPT clearly evince a desire to balance the rights, obligations, and benefits of the states parties to the treaty.

What are the objectives of the NPT and the obligations of its parties? The fundamental objective of the treaty is to prevent the spread of nuclear weapons to states that do not possess them. The obligations of states parties to the NPT established in the first three articles of the treaty are designed to ensure the realization of this objective. Pursuant to Article I, each nuclear-weapon state (NWS) party undertakes not directly or indirectly to transfer nuclear weapons or other nuclear explosive device or the control over such weapons or explosive devices, and not to assist, encourage, or induce any nonnuclear-weapon state (NNWS) to manufacture or otherwise acquire nuclear weapons or other nuclear explosive devices, or the control over such weapons or explosive devices. Under Article II, each NNWS party to the NPT undertakes not to receive the transfer or direct or indirect control of nuclear weapons or other nuclear explosive devices, and not to manufacture or otherwise acquire nuclear weapons or other nuclear explosive devices and not to seek or receive any assistance in their manufacture. Article III provides that each NNWS party to the NPT is to accept international safeguards, as set forth in agreements to be negotiated with the IAEA, to be applied to all source or special fissionable material in all peaceful nuclear activities within its territory, under its jurisdiction or carried out under its control anywhere, for the purpose of verifying treaty obligations, with a view to preventing the diversion of nuclear energy from peaceful uses to nuclear weapons or other nuclear explosive devices.[5]

Another objective of the treaty is to ensure the fullest cooperation in the peaceful uses of nuclear energy, consistent with the objective of nonproliferation. While Article III provides for strict controls over peaceful nuclear activities to ensure they are not misused for proscribed military purposes, Articles IV and V provide a framework for peaceful cooperation. All the parties to the treaty undertake, in accordance with Article IV, to facilitate the fullest possible exchange of equipment, materials, and scientific and technological information for the peaceful uses of nuclear energy. Those parties to the treaty with an advanced nuclear capability are to cooperate in contributing to the further development of the applications of nuclear energy for peaceful purposes, especially in the territories of non-nuclear states parties to the treaty, with due consideration for the needs of the developing areas of the world. Article V affirmed the principle that potential benefits from peaceful nuclear explosions should be made available to nonnuclear states on a nondiscriminatory basis.[6] It is now a dead letter.

A third objective of the NPT is to encourage arms control efforts in the nuclear and non-nuclear arenas. Accordingly, under Article VI, each of the parties undertakes to pursue "good faith" negotiations on effective measures relating to cessation of the nuclear arms race at an early date, to nuclear disarmament, and to achieving a treaty on general and complete disarmament under strict and effective international control. And, in this vein, Article VII states that nothing in the treaty affects the right of any group of states to conclude regional treaties in order to ensure the total absence of nuclear weapons in their respective territories.[7]

The objective of nuclear nonproliferation embodied in the treaty is trumpeted by virtually all states, even those now seeking nuclear-weapon capabilities, and constitutes a "norm" of international behavior that has virtually silenced those who would advocate the possession of nuclear weapons as a symbol of prestige. But the NPT's structure, as well as what many critics see as a failure to adequately implement its key provisions, has been criticized throughout the twenty-year history of the treaty.

Enduring challenges to the treaty

From the time of its negotiation, the NPT has been regarded as structurally flawed. For nonparty states such as India, the treaty is viewed as structurally discriminatory because it distinguishes between nuclear and nonnuclear states on the basis of whether they had manu-factured or exploded a nuclear weapon or other nuclear explosive device before January 1, 1967. The problem, as perceived by critics, is that the NPT effectively freezes the status quo of "nuclear haves" and "nuclear have-nots" and provides for differing obligations on the part of each group, relegating the have-nots to permanent international inferiority.

Along with the critique of the structure of the NPT, during the last forty years, there has been almost constant criticism of the implementation of major provisions of the treaty, espe-cially Articles IV and VI. This critique is voiced not only by nonparties, but has appeared among parties themselves at the review conferences. At the review conferences, the often-contentious debates have addressed the manner in which the treaty's objectives were being fulfilled, focus-ing on the issues of nuclear disarmament, security assurances, and access to atomic energy for peaceful purposes. Dissatisfaction has been expressed by the parties in each of these areas, but it has been the debate over Article VI that has been most disruptive. Despite its negotiating history, the majority of the parties now perceive the treaty primarily as a disarmament effort, and has held that the nuclear states have not adequately implemented their Article VI obliga-tions. A majority of the NNWS parties have asserted that the nuclear states had not adequately fulfilled their obligations to negotiate effective measures to halt the nuclear arms race and achieve nuclear disarmament, and they urged the nuclear states to intensify their efforts in arms control and disarmament. And, in their view, the implementation of the treaty has unduly emphasized the obligations of the nonnuclear rather than those of the nuclear states.[8]

While the Article IV debate has not been as virulent and divisive, access to the peaceful use of nuclear energy has also been an issue in conference debates. Developing countries criticize restrictive export policies adopted by the suppliers of nuclear material, equipment, and tech-nology, as embodied in the Nuclear Suppliers Group (NSG) guidelines. They argue that the treaty had not assured them of access to the benefits of the peaceful atom, noting that non-parties to the treaty were able to obtain nuclear material, equipment, and technology more readily and under less stringent conditions than NPT parties. There have been demands by developing nations for greater access to nuclear materials and technology and calls for a tech-nical assistance fund to provide developing countries with the finances and technical resources necessary for nuclear power projects.[9]

Although these broad lines of criticism have persisted over decades, the challenges to the treaty have intensified as concern about increasing proliferation dangers grew following the 1998 nuclear tests in South Asia and the revelations of Iraq's, Iran's, North Korea's and Syria's nuclear programs and other activities. At the same time, the prospects of radiological/nuclear terrorism have been seen to be rising since 9/11.

In a world fundamentally different from that in which it emerged, the NPT-based nuclear nonproliferation regime is challenged by:

- new weapon states, which cannot be accommodated within the treaty and which affect the views of key nonnuclear-weapon states such as Japan and Brazil;
- North Korean withdrawal from the treaty and, more generally, by the NPT's Article X, which allows states to withdraw;
- North Korea's nuclear tests and the limited international response;
- Iranian programs, which are not compliant with the treaty's provisions and beyond that – directly related to the Atoms-for-Peace bargain, which is seen to allow a state, in principle, to obtain the entire fuel cycle while in full compliance with the treaty – opening up the possibility of using the treaty to develop a virtual weapon capability and then withdrawing from the treaty, all without violating its terms;
- concerns about growing noncompliance and limited consensus on compliance enforcement;
- the growing access of states (and nonstate actors) to sensitive materials and technologies and the rise of virtual weapon programs;
- the issue of the NPT's relevance to activities by nonstate actors, including black marketeers and potential nuclear terrorists;
- the tensions between reemerging commercial interest in the civil nuclear fuel cycle and nonproliferation aims, reflected in a revived debate over Article IV of the NPT;
- the increasingly bitter Article VI debate, involving the Comprehensive Test Ban Treaty (CTBT), a fissile material cutoff treaty (FMCT), concerns about progress in arms control efforts and perceptions of US nuclear-weapon policy.

Beyond regime problems, there may be "shocks" to the regime, which may or may not appear likely today. These may include:

- nuclear use in South Asia – with grave concerns in the last decade;
- Pakistani loose nukes, leaked materials and brain drain in a society with increasing extremism;
- possible new nuclear-weapon tests in South Asia or elsewhere; or
- the possible sale of fissile material or nuclear weapons by North Korea.

Other possibilities could be raised. There may also be other such shocks that we do not even have on our radar screens.

In addition to challenges to the treaty, other elements of the regime are also under pressure. When the NPT was concluded in 1968 and entered into force in 1970, the IAEA became the verification agency for the treaty. However, IAEA safeguards were not designed to verify fully the no-weapon pledges of the treaty, but only the misuse of peaceful activities, especially diversion of declared materials to proscribed military uses. This limitation was desired by the parties at the time, and was largely not seen to be a problem until the early 1990s, when Iraqi and North Korean violations of the treaty highlighted the shortfalls of these inspections. While the IAEA is transforming its safeguards to address these issues, the Agency remains hampered by restrictions and limits to implementation of its verification mandate and burdened by noncompliance issues, which raise questions about the value and effectiveness of international safeguards in some quarters. The Additional Protocol (AP) is an important new tool. Although most states with significant nuclear activities have now brought the AP into force, there remain a large number of states that have not yet ratified it. The Agency and member states are trying to remedy this situation.

The Nuclear Suppliers Group faces erosion. NSG rules need to be reinforced and strengthened. There is reason to be concerned about Russian and other countries' exports to proliferant states. The US-Indian agreement of 2005 required fundamental changes in the way that the NSG does business. Concerns have been raised that the arrangement will weaken the NSG's requirement of full-scope safeguards and open the door to similar trade with Pakistan and others. Technology diffusion, black markets and second-tier proliferation also raise questions about the long-term relevance of the NSG as these developments show that nuclear supply is no longer the preserve of a few advanced industrial states.

The United Nations Security Council was seen as the last great hope in addressing proliferation problems, including the North Korean crisis of the early 1990s. However, there was and is limited consensus within the Council on enforcement and none on the use of force. The Council was paralyzed in the 2002–2003 Iraq crisis. Until recently, it was also unable to act in Iran and North Korea. Will it ultimately be effective in dealing with noncompliant states?

Reforming the nuclear nonproliferation regime

All of the problems with, and stresses on, the regime pose real challenges and have been seen in some quarters as portending the regime's collapse or increasing irrelevance. It would be folly to act as if these problems did not exist, or to pretend that they could be adequately addressed using exclusively old measures and approaches, or resolved merely by muddling through.

Is it possible to create something better, however? There has, for example, been considerable interest in a revived (and revised) Baruch Plan for at least two decades, as well as some interest in a nuclear weapons convention (NWC).[10] There is reason to be skeptical of the prospects for such proposals or for any efforts to fundamentally alter the regime. Current institutions and treaties still command significant international support and consensus – such consensus as exists. But this consensus is largely limited on tough issues and difficult cases. Moreover, the specter of nuclear terrorism was not contemplated in the foundation of the regime, which was put forward in a world in which states were the only major actors. That is no longer the case today and the threat is seen as a greater concern today than at any time in the past due to the changing face of terrorism; the spread of technology relevant to nuclear-weapon production; potential access to nuclear materials and weapons through transnational black market networks or supportive states; and others.

This new reality raises questions about the value of the regime, but it also suggests little prospect that entirely new institutions would more effectively deal with these issues than the existing regime. It remains to be seen whether the regime will meet the challenges ahead. However, in the face of these challenges, the regime is being reformed. As it has in the past, the regime is evolving as threats have changed, as is evident in the case of safeguards.

The revelations of the Iraqi nuclear program after the Gulf War, the discoveries of Iranian, Libyan, North Korean, and Syrian clandestine programs and the associated revelation of an extensive nonstate nuclear procurement network, and the concerns raised by the terrorist attacks of 9/11 have presented new challenges to international safeguards and to the international nuclear nonproliferation regime.

In this environment, the IAEA is developing a new approach to safeguards based on the strengthening measures developed in the 1990s. The new approach is designed to provide an evaluation of the nuclear program of a state as a whole – including the possibility of clandestine facilities and activities – and not just each of its declared nuclear facilities. If they are to meet the demands of global growth in nuclear energy use, it is essential that safeguards be cred-ible and efficient.

In addition to strengthening safeguards and other traditional regime elements such as export controls, initiatives to address new and emerging threats, and unanticipated developments – from the end of the cold war to the rise of terrorism – have been especially prominent in the last twenty years. Among these are critical initiatives involving threat reduction, detection and interdiction, such as programs for Cooperative Threat Reduction; Material Protection, Control and Accounting; Second Line of Defense, including the Megaports Initiative; the Proliferation Security Initiative and the Global Threat Reduction Initiative; the Global Initiative for Proliferation Prevention and the Global Initiative to Combat Nuclear Terrorism; and UNSC Resolution 1540, the Convention on the Suppression of Nuclear Terrorism and the amend-ments to the Convention on the Physical Protection of Nuclear Material.[11]

The US-Indian Civil Nuclear Cooperation agreement was also an effort to deal with the current problems with the regime by bringing India into the nonproliferation fold to the extent possible. The deal is the first of its kind with one of only three nonsignatories to the NPT. Some fear that offering the benefits of Article IV to India makes the NPT "bargain" less valuable, and may lead states to rethink their commitments.[12] The ultimate impact on the regime and on arms control more broadly will be determined by its details and by the future actions of India and other states. If fuel supply provisions in the agreement lead to an expan-sion of India's nuclear arsenal, history will judge the agreement to have been a mistake. If, on the other hand, the agreement leads to a vested Indian interest in the nuclear nonproliferation regime and its constraints, and perhaps even draws China and Pakistan into regional arms control talks with India, it could produce valuable benefits to the regime.

A number of old ideas are also being revived and pursued, including assurances of supply, proliferation resistance, and multinational approaches. Offering an assured supply of fresh nuclear fuel and spent-fuel take back are old ideas that are receiving new attention. They have become central to thinking about addressing emerging challenges. Proposals by then International Atomic Energy Agency Director General Mohammed ElBaradei can be seen in the context of this long-standing desire. Multinational or multilateral ownership has been pro-posed by ElBaradei as a means of slowing, if not halting, the spread of enrichment and reprocessing (ENR) technologies (and other sensitive nuclear technology).[13]

The difficulties of realizing these or any of the other proposals that have been put forward to minimize proliferation and terrorism risks through reliable supply are significant and have bedeviled past efforts along these lines. Although such approaches have failed before, there are key differences in the situation today from that of the earlier considerations of various propos-als, including a more widespread sense of insecurity; the rise of new, illegitimate sources of supply, including black marketers; evidence of NPT noncompliance and the use of the so-called Article IV "loophole;" and the prospect of nuclear terrorism. In any event, the viability of current proposals depends ultimately on common interests (commercial, political, industrial, etc.). They cannot be imposed from the top down, nor should they interfere with market mechanisms.

Finally, new attention to another old idea – proliferation resistance – has grown and can be expected to grow in the years ahead.[14] Although the concept is not well defined and has at times been oversold – it does not mean "proliferation-proof" – there are benefits that can be realized from reactors and other facilities designed to minimize risks coupled with effective safeguards and other nonproliferation measures. The idea of proliferation-resistant small reactors with long-lived cores is among the new ideas for addressing underlying proliferation concerns, while expanding nuclear power to the developing world and increasing the attractiveness and acceptability of nonproliferation efforts. In this as in other cases, if proliferation resistance is to be real, it must be institutionally as well as technically based. There are no simple technological fixes or "silver bullets."

All of these responses to current and emerging threats are important, as efforts to reinforce and reform the global nonproliferation regime to address proliferation and terrorism risks. But not all are agreed or fully developed and implemented. Moreover, they may not be fully adequate (or be seen to fall short) in addressing specific regional problems and issues confronting the Middle East and North Africa. Additional measures may be required in the Middle East and North Africa.

Decisive issues for the 2015 RevCon

As we look toward the 2015 Review Conference, these reform efforts aimed at adapting the NPT to today's world may not be central to its outcome. Despite their importance, many are embroiled in debates over the meaning and future of the treaty, and in the diplomatic exchanges of the review cycle. From a US and Western perspective, the broad nonproliferation agenda for 2015 includes preserving the Action Plan agreed in 2010; pursuing progress on dealing with noncompliance and possible withdrawals from the treaty (Article X); and strengthening safeguards, fuel assurances, and multilateralization of the fuel cycle. The Nonaligned Movement is focused on ensuring the rights of NNWSs to pursue peaceful nuclear power programs, legally binding negative security assurances and disarmament. Moreover, uncertainties surrounding the convocation of the conference on a Middle East Weapons of Mass Destruction Free Zone called for at the 2010 RevCon and the fate of the interim agreement with Iran will be critical.

Article VI issues will likely once again be central, with predictable attention to US nuclear policy in the Obama administration, including the implementation of the 2010 Nuclear Posture Review, implementation of New START and the status of the proposed follow-on, ratification of the Comprehensive Test Ban Treaty, negotiations on a fissile material cutoff treaty, and other key issues.[15]

The US case for Article VI compliance is strong. The administration's declaratory policies and its commitment to diplomacy will continue to be welcomed, albeit with somewhat diminished enthusiasm given the impact of, and expectations created by, the Prague speech on April 5, 2009 and the 2010 Nuclear Posture Review report.

Reflecting the twin objectives of the Prague speech, the NPR outlined the Administration's approach to promoting the agenda put forward by President Obama in Prague for reducing nuclear dangers and pursuing the goal of a world without nuclear weapons while maintaining, as long as nuclear weapons remain, a safe, secure and effective arsenal, both to deter potential adversaries and to assure US allies and other security partners that they can count on America's security commitments.

For the first time, the 2010 NPR places US leadership of expanding efforts to strengthen the international nuclear nonproliferation regime at the top the US nuclear agenda. This attention underscores the fact that discouraging additional states from acquiring nuclear-weapon capabilities and stopping terrorists from acquiring weapon-usable nuclear materials or weapons are priorities of the United States. It also reinforced the view that positively influencing the 2010 RevCon of the Parties to the Treaty on the Nonproliferation of Nuclear Weapons was a key objective of the Obama administration.

The NPR was a key element in the successful outcome of the 2010 RevCon and provides a foundation for further progress toward disarmament. However, weapon funding and nuclear infrastructure modernization will be criticized, as will the fact that changes in US declaratory policy did not go far enough toward either a sole purpose or a no-first-use doctrine. In this context, details of implementation of the NPR will need to be developed as implementation will, in this NPT review cycle, focus on short-term actions that are related to stockpile stewardship, life-extension programs (LEPs), infrastructure modernization, and delivery system replacements. These actions are critical but will likely raise old criticisms again.

These issues will be all the more critical given the likelihood that the current stalemate of the Prague agenda will likely persist through 2015. It is widely believed that major progress in arms control and disarmament in the next few years is unlikely. The prospects for follow-on negotiations to New START, yet alone any movement to multilateralizing arms reductions, are not seen as high. CTBT ratification and the beginning of FMCT negotiations both appear unlikely.

On follow-on negotiations to New START, the Russians have been reluctant to engage and have very different ideas on the scope of the negotiations. The Russians have called for multilateral negotiations that address ballistic missile defenses as well as outer space and conventional strategic weapons. US priorities, which involve bilateral negotiations on strategic and nonstrategic, deployed and nondeployed nuclear weapons, are difficult technically and politically to achieve.

This stalemate is seen by some observers as an indictment of a step-by-step approach to disarmament and a rationale for a NWC, while others argue that efforts were ongoing, that an NWC was not possible and that an incremental approach to disarmament was the only one that is realistic. However, the growing effort by states and nongovernmental organizations to address the humanitarian consequences of nuclear-weapon use, and for some to utilize international humanitarian law to delegitimize nuclear weapons and deterrence interest, is being raised in the Article VI context. This will further complicate the debate in 2015, and is seen as likely to be a critical element in the lead up to, and during, the 2015 RevCon as expectations are high and NPT nonnuclear-weapon states are increasingly frustrated with the pace of nuclear disarmament and critical of the nuclear-weapon states.

In this context, the importance of dialogue among the P5 was widely recognized as critical to the future. The P5 process was a forum to advance the disarmament process, and although increasing engagement on substantive issues will be difficult because of significant differences among the P5 over key policy issues, it could promote work on transparency and verification. While P5 transparency is especially difficult, there is considerable interest in finding acceptable measures to promote transparency with Russia and China on nuclear-weapon and production facilities.

Conclusions

Created in a different time to deal with different threats, the treaty is clearly showing its age. However serious its problems and the challenges it confronts, the NPT has been the basis of international consensus; and it is likely to be with us as we think about dealing with today's and tomorrow's proliferation problems.

Given the stakes involved, in addressing terrorism as well as proliferation, the states with an interest in the existing regime – particularly the United States – must recognize regime problems and manage them. Safeguards, export controls and compliance enforcement will be critical. Efforts to strengthen the regime will be vital if the regime is to meet the challenges of the future. As noted, there are no silver bullets, however.

Challenged by new realities, the structure of the international nuclear order is being reassessed by the United States and other members of the international community. Everything from threat reduction efforts to the need for new burden-sharing involving diplomatic, economic, and other instruments to address noncompliance should be on the table. Rebuilding is necessary, but any lingering temptations to raze everything must be resisted. Over time, the actions of the United States and others can provide the foundation for new and reformed nonproliferation institutions and values that will ensure common security and, by enabling the growth of nuclear power, energy security and prosperity in the long term. From an American perspective, the pursuit of new nuclear institutions and norms is in the US interest. Greater diplomatic and other efforts are necessary to secure the support of the broad international community for what would, if realized, be the political structure or component of globalization that has been a missing piece in the emerging security mosaic. However, this project will be viewed more seriously throughout the US political spectrum if there is demonstrable international respect for efforts to ensure the credibility of, and compliance with, extant treaty-based norms and institutions. Unfortunately, there is not yet a consensus on dealing with this difficult matter.

Reform and strengthening efforts for the NPT regime are critical but, as suggested, they are only a part of the picture. All of these efforts can reinforce – and will be reinforced by – other counterterrorism and counterproliferation efforts, including possible efforts to deter, dissuade, and defend against nuclear proliferation and terrorism. The normative and legal weight of the regime is important for counterterrorism as well as nonproliferation, but it will probably not directly affect the behavior of rogue states and terrorists. Measures to prevent them from achieving their objectives if they attempt to employ nuclear or radiological weapons may deter and dissuade them, as may a credible prospect of punishment. The interaction of nonproliferation and deterrence so clear during the Cold War history of the NPT remains a crucial part of an increasingly complex picture.

With reforms, the regime can provide the foundation for future nonproliferation efforts, including the commitment to finding institutional means to enhance efforts to combat terrorism and to strengthen the proliferation resistance of civilian nuclear power programs. The United States and other states will need to continue efforts to strengthen the regime and will need to deal with difficult cases. It is imperative to ensure the regime is not further eroded, and that new difficult cases do not emerge out of flaws in regime.

Notes

1. These remarks are the author's own and not those of the Los Alamos National Laboratory, the National Nuclear Security Administration, the Department of Energy or any other US government agency.
2. See, for example, Harald Müller, "The 2005 NPT Review Conference: Reasons and Consequences of Failure, and Options for Repair," Weapons of Mass Destruction Commission, Report No. 31, August 2005, www.blixassociates.com/wp-content/uploads/2011/03/No31.pdf; and John Simpson and Jenny Nielsen, The 2005 NPT Review Conference: Mission Impossible," *Nonproliferation Review*, Vol. 12, No. 2 (July 2006), pp. 271–301.
3. Barack Obama, "Remarks by President Barack Obama, Hradcany Square, Prague, Czech Republic," The White House, Office of the Press Secretary, April 5, 2009, www.whitehouse.gov/the_press_office/Remarks-By-President-Barack-Obama-In-Prague-As-Delivered; US Department of Defense, "Nuclear Posture Review Report," Washington, DC, April 2010, www.defense.gov/npr/docs/2010%20nuclear%20posture%20review%20report.pdf.
4. See, for example, Scott D. Sagan and Jane Vaynman, "Reviewing the Nuclear Posture Review," *Nonproliferation Review*, Vol. 18, No. 1 (March 2011), pp. 17–37, www.tandfonline.com/doi/pdf/10.1080/10736700.2011.549169; Harald Müller, "A Nuclear Nonproliferation Test: Obama's Nuclear Policy and the 2010 NPT Review Conference," *Nonproliferation Review*, Vol. 18, No. 1 (March 2011), pp. 219–236.

5. For the text of the NPT, see United Nations, "Treaty on the Nonproliferation of Nuclear Weapons," July 1, 1968, www.un.org/en/conf/npt/2005/npttreaty.html.
6. Ibid.
7. Ibid.
8. Among the most vocal of groups to make these criticisms has been the Nonaligned Movement (NAM), consisting of 120 members and 17 observer states. For an extended analysis of the NAM, see William C. Potter and Gaukhar Mukhatzhanova, *Nuclear Politics and the Non-Aligned Movement: Principles vs Pragmatism* (Routledge, for the International Institute for Strategic Studies, Adelphi series, Vol. 427, 2012).
9. See, for example, Lawrence Scheinman, "Article IV of the NPT: Background, Problems, Some Prospects," The Weapons of Mass Destruction Commission, Paper No. 5, June 7, 2004, www.un.org/disarmament/education/wmdcommission/files/No5.pdf; John Simpson, "Is the Nuclear Non-Proliferation Treaty Fit for Purpose?" Report written for the United Nations Association of the UK, UNA-UK Briefing Report No. 1, August 2011, www.una.org.uk/sites/default/files/Is%20the%20Nuclear%20Non-Proliferation%20Treaty%20Fit%20For%20Purpose%20-%20Professor%20John%20Simpson.pdf; Mitchell B. Reiss, "Strengthening Nonproliferation: The Path Ahead," in *Atoms for Peace: A Future after Fifty Years?*, edited by Joseph F. Pilat (Washington, DC and Baltimore, MD: Woodrow Wilson Center Press and Johns Hopkins University Press, 2007), pp. 43–44.
10. See, for example, Randy Rydell, "LOOKING BACK: Going for Baruch: The Nuclear Plan That Refused to Go Away," *Arms Control Today*, Vol. 36, No. 6 (June 2006), pp. 45–48, www.armscontrol.org/print/2064.
11. See, for example, US Department of State, "Mission Statement," Office of Cooperative Threat Reduction (ISN/CTR), www.state.gov/t/isn/58381.htm; US Department of Energy, National Nuclear Security Administration, "Material Protection, Control and Accounting," http://nnsa.energy.gov/aboutus/ourprograms/dnn/impc/mpca; US Department of Energy, National Nuclear Security Administration, "Megaports Initiative," http://nnsa.energy.gov/aboutus/ourprograms/nonproliferation/programoffices/internationalmaterialprotectionandcooperation/-5; The White House, Office of the Press Secretary, "Proliferation Security Initiative: Statement of Interdiction Principles," Fact Sheet, Washington, DC, September 4, 2003, www.state.gov/t/isn/c27726.htm; US Department of Energy, National Nuclear Security Administration, "Global Threat Reduction Initiative," http://nnsa.energy.gov/aboutus/ourprograms/dnn/gtri; US Department of State, "Global Initiative to Combat Nuclear Terrorism," Office of Weapons of Mass Destruction and Terrorism, www.state.gov/t/isn/c18406.htm; US Department of State, "Joint Statement on the Contributions of the Global Initiative to Combat Nuclear Terrorism (GICNT) to Enhancing Nuclear Security," Office of the Spokesperson, Washington, DC, March 20, 2014, www.state.gov/r/pa/prs/ps/2014/03/223761.htm; United Nations Security Council, "Resolution 1540 (2004)," S/RES/1540 (2004), 495th meeting, April 28, 2004, http://daccess-dds-ny.un.org/doc/UNDOC/GEN/N04/328/43/PDF/N0432843.pdf; International Atomic Energy Agency, "The Convention on the Physical Protection of Nuclear Material," INFCIRC/274/Rev. 1, May 1980, www.iaca.org/Publications/Documents/Infcircs/Others/infcirc274r1.pdf.
12. Daryl G. Kimball, "Is the NSG Up to the Task?" *Arms Control Today*, Vol. 40, No. 6 (July/August 2010), p. 4, www.armscontrol.org/act/2010_07/Focus; Thomas Graham Jr., Leonor Tomero and Leonard Weiss, "Think Again: US-India Nuclear Deal," *Foreign Policy*, July 24, 2006, www.foreignpolicy.com/articles/2006/07/23/think_again_us_india_nuclear_deal; Sharon Squassoni, "US-India Deal and Its Impact," *Arms Control Today*, Vol. 40, No. 6 (July/August 2010), pp. 48–52, www.armscontrol.org/act/2010_07-08/squassoni.
13. See, Mohamed ElBaradei, "Toward a Safer World," *The Economist*, Vol. 369 (October 18, 2003), pp. 47–48, www.economist.com/node/2137602. See also the report of experts that followed up the original ElBaradei proposal (issued as INFCIRC/640), International Atomic Energy Agency, "Multilateral Approaches to the Nuclear Fuel Cycle: Expert Group Report submitted to the Director General of the International Atomic Energy Agency," INFCIRC/640, February 22, 2005, www.iaea.org/Publications/Documents/Infcircs/2005/infcirc640.pdf.
14. On the topic of proliferation resistance, see Robert A. Bari, "Proliferation Resistance and Physical Protection (PR&PP) Evaluation Methodology: Objectives, Accomplishments, and Future Directions," Paper 9013-final, Proceedings of Global 2009, Paris, France, September 6–11, 2009, http://cybercemetery.unt.edu/archive/brc/20120621022022/http://brc.gov/sites/default/files/mee

tings/attachments/bari_9013-final.pdf; Nuclear Energy Study Group, "Nuclear Power and Proliferation Resistance: Security Benefits, Limiting Risk," American Physical Society Panel on Public Affairs, May 2005, www.aps.org/policy/reports/popa-reports/proliferation-resistance/upload/proliferation.pdf; Jungmin Kanga and Frank N. von Hippel, "U-232 and the Proliferation-Resistance of U-233 in Spent Fuel," *Science & Global Security*, Vol. 9, No. 1 (2001), pp. 1–32; Matthew Bunn, "Proliferation-Resistance (and Terror-Resistance) of Nuclear Energy Systems," lecture for "Nuclear Energy Economics and Policy Analysis," Managing the Atom Project, Harvard University, April 12, 2004, http://ocw.mit.edu/courses/nuclear-engineering/22-812j-managing-nuclear-technology-spring-2004/lecture-notes/lec17slides.pdf.

15. For discussions of the challenges associated with negotiation and ultimate implementation of the CTBT and an FMCT, see Chapters 13, 14, and 15 of this volume.

10

THE IAEA AND INTERNATIONAL SAFEGUARDS

Laura Rockwood

The nuclear nonproliferation regime is a matrix of measures and mechanisms designed to address the threat posed to global peace and security by the possible misuse of nuclear material and technology for nuclear-weapon purposes. It has evolved as a function of shifting perceptions by states about the nature and source of that threat. These shifting perceptions have produced changes in international and national security policies and, as a consequence, in nuclear nonproliferation policy and demands for verification.

The regime as it currently exists is comprised of global and regional nonproliferation treaties, export controls, security assurances, physical protection, security measures designed to address the issue of nonstate actors, mechanisms to track and deter illicit trafficking in nuclear and other radioactive materials, and many other unilateral and multilateral initiatives. Although individually designed to address different aspects of that threat, these measures and mechanisms collectively contribute to the prevention of the proliferation of nuclear weapons.

International verification through International Atomic Energy Agency (IAEA) safeguards remains the cornerstone of nonproliferation efforts. This chapter addresses the origins and evolution of IAEA safeguards.

1945–1970: Creation of the IAEA and its safeguards

While it was clear, even at the outset, that the atom could be exploited for the benefit of mankind, it was equally clear that, without restraint and control, it could also destroy humankind. Among the first efforts to address this threat was the June 1946 Baruch Plan, which the United States proposed to the United Nations Atomic Energy Commission.[1] In exchange for the creation of a supranational organization responsible for inspecting, owning, controlling, and managing nuclear material and technology, and verified pledges by all other countries not to produce nuclear weapons, the United States would give up its nuclear weapons to the organization. However, by 1948, it was clear that this proposition was far too ambitious and, with the testing of a nuclear weapon by the Soviet Union the following year, had become all but impossible.[2]

Notwithstanding, there was significant demand for the new technology, and money to be made in its trade. It was clear, however, that if there were to be trade in nuclear technology, there was a risk that the supplied technology could be misused for the development of nuclear weapons unless there was some form of oversight. To address this possible threat, the states marketing the technology (initially nuclear material and small research reactors) to other countries did so through bilateral nuclear trade arrangements, many of which invested the supplier with the right to verify that the supplied items would not be used for proscribed military uses – in effect, bilateral national safeguards.

However, neither the early effort to ban the spread of nuclear weapons, nor bilateral controls on nuclear trade, was able to stem the tide of nuclear-weapon proliferation. By 1952, the United Kingdom had also tested a nuclear device and other states were already working on their own programs (including, among others, Belgium, Canada, France, and Italy). Moreover, while bilateral safeguards may have provided adequate assurance to the respective supplier that items supplied by it were not being misused, they did not provide the same degree of assurance to the broader international community.

What was needed was not bilateral verification of supply arrangements but independent verification by an international entity. At the 1953 United Nations General Assembly, US President Dwight D. Eisenhower introduced his Atoms for Peace proposal: to create an international atomic energy organization that could serve as a repository for nuclear material contributed by "the governments principally involved" (expressly including the United States and the Soviet Union) from which other states could make withdrawals for peaceful purposes.[3] The new organization would be responsible for promoting safe and peaceful uses of nuclear energy, and would be entrusted with verifying that nuclear technology was not misused.

This proposal resulted in the establishment of the International Atomic Energy Agency: an intergovernmental organization, headquartered in Vienna, Austria, independent from the United Nations, but with a unique relationship permitting direct access by the IAEA to the United Nations Security Council (UNSC).[4] The IAEA came into being with the entry into force of its Statute on July 29, 1957.[5]

It is the Statute of the IAEA (Article III.A.5) which authorizes the IAEA:

- To establish and administer safeguards to ensure that nuclear material, services, equipment, facilities, and information made available by the IAEA are not used to further any military purpose;
- To apply safeguards, at the request of the parties, to any bilateral or multilateral arrangement; and
- To apply safeguards at the request of a state to any of that state's nuclear activities.[6]

Article XII of the Statute reflects what the drafters anticipated that IAEA safeguards would include, measures that were novel and far-reaching for their time: extremely broad rights of access at all times to all places and data, and to any person dealing with items required to be safeguarded; examination and approval by the IAEA of the design of specialized equipment and facilities to ensure that they would not further any military purpose, that they complied with applicable health and safety standards, and that they would permit effective application of safeguards; reporting and record-keeping by the state; and reporting of noncompliance to the Security Council by the Board of Governors.[7]

However, since the Statute was not crafted so as to make safeguards mandatory simply by virtue of membership in the IAEA, the implementation of safeguards in a state required the crafting of agreements whereby the state would consent to accept them, i.e., safeguards agreements.[8] Safeguards agreements are treaties concluded between the IAEA and a state or states.[9] They are drafted by the IAEA Secretariat, negotiated with the other parties to the agreement, approved by the Board of Governors and signed by the Director General and by the head of state, head of government, or foreign minister of the state(s) concerned (or by representatives with full powers to do so). Depending on the state's domestic requirements, the agreement enters into force either upon signature, or upon receipt by the IAEA of written notification that the state's statutory and constitutional requirements for entry into force have been met.

In 1961, the IAEA established its first "safeguards system," consisting of procedures for safeguarding small research reactors, the technology that was being traded at that time. These procedures were published in IAEA document INFCIRC/26.[10] As time went by, and trade expanded beyond small reactors, the IAEA's safeguards system was also expanded, and in 1964 was extended to cover large reactors (INFCIRC/26/Add.1). Over the period 1964 to 1965, the system was thoroughly revised (INFCIRC/66), and included detailed procedures for safeguarding principal nuclear facilities[11] and nuclear material at other locations. Within the next few years, the IAEA's safeguards system underwent further revision: in 1966, special provisions were included for safeguards at reprocessing plants (INFCIRC/66/Rev.1), and in 1968 additional provisions were included for safeguarded nuclear material in conversion and fuel fabrication plants (INFCIRC/66/Rev.2, the "Safeguards Document"). Neither the Safeguards Document nor its predecessor documents were *model* agreements; their provisions only acquired legally binding force when, and to the extent, they were incorporated into safeguards agreements concluded between the IAEA and the state or states concerned.

While the safeguards agreements concluded on the basis of these documents (often generically referred to as INFCIRC/66-type agreements) share common procedures, the agreements themselves frequently varied from one to another in form, content, and duration. However, the state's undertaking in all of these early agreements – not to use the safeguarded items for any military purpose – consistently tracked the language of Article III.A.5 of the Statute.

In terms of scope, INFCIRC/66-type safeguards agreements evolved over time to cover the ever-increasing circumstances where safeguards were required (in connection with IAEA projects for the supply of nuclear material and/or facilities) or requested (in connection with bilateral supply arrangements). Some of the later agreements went beyond nuclear material and facilities and required the safeguarding of equipment, nonnuclear material and even a nonnuclear facility (a heavy water production plant). But they remained limited in scope, requiring the application of safeguards only in connection with the items specified in the agreement (and the nuclear material produced, processed or used in connection with those items). These agreements later came to be known as "item specific agreements," to distinguish them from "comprehensive" (or "full scope") agreements.

By the 1960s, states' perception of the risks associated with nuclear trade had started to shift. It was becoming increasingly clear that, as a natural consequence of the growing interest in nuclear energy and other applications of nuclear research and development, states were beginning to develop their own indigenous capacities to produce nuclear material without having to rely on external suppliers of nuclear technology. And the march toward the possession of nuclear weapons continued. By 1967, two more countries had developed and tested nuclear weapons: France (1960) and the People's Republic of China (1964).

Clearly, to prevent the proliferation of nuclear weapons, it was not enough to safeguard individual supply arrangements. What was needed were legally binding commitments by states to foreswear nuclear weapons – nonproliferation commitments – and a mechanism for verifying compliance with those commitments through international safeguards.

This shifting perception of the threat, compounded by the threat of nuclear Armageddon during the Cuban missile crisis, fuelled the next major development in the nuclear nonproliferation regime – two landmark multilateral nonproliferation treaties:

- The 1967 Tlatelolco Treaty: the first treaty prohibiting nuclear weapons within a populated region, Latin America, and requiring the acceptance of IAEA safeguards on all nuclear activities;[12] and
- The 1968 Treaty on the Nonproliferation of Nuclear Weapons (NPT).[13]

1970–1990: Comprehensive safeguards

The NPT was opened for signature in 1968 and came into force in 1970. It was the first global treaty to prohibit the spread of nuclear weapons by countries which had already exploded a nuclear device – the nuclear-weapon states (NWS),[14] and a commitment by those who had not yet done so – the nonnuclear-weapon states (NNWS) – not to develop or acquire nuclear weapons or nuclear explosive devices and to accept IAEA verification on all nuclear material in all peaceful nuclear activities to ensure that the material was not used for such purposes.[15]

The basic premise of NPT verification was that, without nuclear material, a state could not produce a nuclear weapon. Therefore, if all nuclear material – whether imported or produced domestically, and regardless of its location – were subject to safeguards, the nonproliferation of nuclear weapons could be assured.

Thus, Article III.1 of the NPT obliged each NNWS party to the treaty to

> accept safeguards, as set forth in an agreement to be negotiated and concluded with the [IAEA], in accordance with the Statute of the [IAEA] and the [IAEA's] safeguards system, for the exclusive purpose of verification of the fulfilment by [the state] of its obligations under [the NPT] with a view to preventing diversion of nuclear energy from peaceful uses to *nuclear weapons or other nuclear explosive devices*.[16]

Under the NPT, safeguards are to "be followed with respect to source or special fissionable material whether it is being produced, processed, or used in any principal nuclear facility or is outside any such facility," and they are to be applied on "*all* source and special fissionable material in all peaceful nuclear activities within the territory of the state, under its jurisdiction, or carried out under its control anywhere."[17]

Because of the nature of the NNWS' commitments under the NPT, a new approach to safeguards, and a new type of safeguards agreement – different from the earlier type, not only in form, but in undertaking, scope and duration – had to be developed. Accordingly, the IAEA's Board of Governors established a Safeguards Committee (Committee 22) to advise it on the form and content of these new agreements. By early 1971, the Committee had developed a document entitled "Structure and Content of Agreements between the Agency and States Required in Connection with the Treaty on the Non-Proliferation of Nuclear Weapons," which was approved by the Board of Governors in April 1971 and published as INFCIRC/153 (Corr.) (hereafter referred to as INFCIRC/153). In approving the text, the Board requested the Director General to use the material reproduced in INFCIRC/153 as the basis for negotiating safeguards agreements between the NNWS party to the NPT and the IAEA.

Like the Safeguards Document, INFCIRC/153 was not a model agreement. However, it spelled out in much greater detail what an agreement based on its provisions was to include.[18] As a result, unlike agreements concluded on the basis of INFCIRC/66, INFCIRC/153-type agreements were to be highly standardized. And, since the purpose was to cover *all* nuclear material of a state, rather than only the items which the state(s) concerned chose to submit to safeguards, these new agreements came to be known as "full scope" or "comprehensive" safeguards agreements (CSAs). These agreements were to remain in force for so long as the state was party to the NPT.

In anticipation of the possibility of non-proscribed military nuclear activities (specifically, nuclear naval propulsion), the basic undertaking of NNWS under the NPT only prohibited the use of nuclear energy for "nuclear weapons and other nuclear explosive devices." That same undertaking was reiterated in INFCIRC/153. Thus, unlike the earlier item-specific safeguards agreements, the NPT safeguards agreements did not prohibit all military uses of nuclear material.

To address that possibility, INFCIRC/153 included a provision, paragraph 14, requiring that, if a state "intends to exercise its discretion to use nuclear material which is required to be safeguarded [under the Agreement] in a nuclear activity which docs not require the application of safeguards under the Agreement," it must agree with the IAEA in advance on an arrangement so that "only while the nuclear material is in such an activity, the safeguards provided for in the Agreement will not be applied." The language of that provision makes it clear that the material to be used for such purposes would first have to be declared by the state and then withdrawn from safeguards.[19]

INFCIRC/153 reflected the collective perception of its drafters that the focus of these new agreements should be on nuclear material (wherever located), and on the facilities used for its production, processing, and storage. Based on assumptions about the amounts of nuclear material necessary for a nuclear device, the objective of safeguards, reflected in paragraph 28 of INFCIRC/153, was articulated as "the timely detection of diversion of significant quantities of nuclear material from peaceful nuclear activities to the manufacture of nuclear weapons or of other nuclear explosive devices or for purposes unknown, and deterrence of such diversion by the risk of early detection."[20]

INFCIRC/153 also reflected the prevailing perception that small quantities of nuclear material were not a problem: the "cost" of following such material (both in terms of the real cost to the IAEA and the feared cost of interference with scientific research and development) would not be worth the safeguards benefit, since a nuclear weapon required more than small quantities of material. Thus, states would be permitted to exempt specified quantities from safeguards. This also explains why, shortly after the Board approved INFCIRC/153, it permitted states that informed the IAEA that they had little or no nuclear material,[21] and no nuclear material in a nuclear facility, to conclude protocols that effectively precluded IAEA verification in those countries (the so-called "Small Quantities Protocols," or "SQPs").[22]

INFCIRC/153 also included a requirement, not reflected in the early item-specific agreements, for the state and the IAEA to conclude Subsidiary Arrangements to the CSA detailing how the procedures in the agreement were to be implemented. Although not specified in INFCIRC/153, Subsidiary Arrangements came to include a General Part, addressing procedures applicable to the state in general, and Facility Attachments, which detail the safeguards procedures for each individual facility (or other location where nuclear material is customarily used).[23]

INFCIRC/153 also served as the basis for agreements concluded by the NWS pursuant to voluntary offers to place certain nuclear activities under safeguards. Although these so called voluntary offer agreements (VOAs) used INFCIRC/153 as a point of reference, and they contain many of the same provisions as in CSAs, the scope of the VOAs is much more limited, covering only those facilities and material that the state chooses to offer to the IAEA.

At the time of the negotiation of INFCIRC/153, it was recognized that many states already had in place item-specific safeguards agreements with the IAEA. Accordingly, a provision was included that provides for the suspension of the application of safeguards under other safeguards agreements concluded by the state for so long as the INFCIRC/153 agreement remained in force.[24] Over time, the application of IAEA safeguards under most of the item-specific agreements was suspended in favor of NPT safeguards agreements (today, INFCIRC/66-type agreements are implemented only in India, Israel, and Pakistan).

Another event occurred in 1974 which had a significant impact on IAEA safeguards, although under item-specific agreements: India's testing of a so-called "peaceful" nuclear device, using nuclear material from a reactor which had been supplied to it under a bilateral trade arrangement with Canada which, like the INFCIRC/66-type agreements of that time, contained only a "no military use" prohibition. All INFCIRC/66-type safeguards agreements concluded by the IAEA after that contain a basic undertaking of the state which expressly precludes the use of safeguarded items not just for any military purpose, but for use in nuclear weapons and *any* other nuclear explosive devices.

Despite the Indian nuclear explosion, the 1981 bombing by Israel of an Iraqi reactor and, a few years later, the bombing by Iraq of an Iranian reactor, the "nonproliferation mood" at the beginning of 1990 was generally upbeat – the Cold War was ending, the Berlin Wall had been brought down, and the United States and the Soviet Union had made substantial progress in arms control and disarmament. And by the end of 1990, 141 states had become party to the NPT, including China and France, the two remaining NWS that had long stayed outside the NPT.

But the NPT safeguards system, as it existed at the close of the 1990s, had limitations – as a matter of law and practice – the consequences of which were soon to become apparent. As a matter of law, while safeguards were now implemented at the key choke points of the nuclear fuel cycle, CSAs did not provide for routine access to or information about the entire nuclear fuel cycle of a state. In addition, routine access was limited in terms of frequency and location, and had to be agreed upon with the inspected state. As indicated above, these agreements also permitted states to remove nuclear material from safeguards through exemption or termination, and paid little heed to small quantities of such material.

As a matter of practice, the implementation of safeguards was based on prescriptive and quantitative nuclear material accountancy driven safeguards criteria which concentrated on the quantity and type of nuclear material, and the type of nuclear facilities, placed under safeguards in a state. The safeguards criteria defined the frequency, scope and intensity of safeguards activities to be undertaken at declared facilities. In determining the inspection effort, little consideration was given to the state as a whole.

Of even greater consequence, however, was that, as a practical matter, and notwithstanding the legal authority granted to the IAEA in accordance with INFCIRC/153, safeguards activities of the IAEA had come to be focused primarily on the verification of nuclear material and facilities declared to it by the state(s) concerned.

The negotiating history of INFCIRC/153 makes clear that the drafters of INFCIRC/153 had actually anticipated the possibility that a state might try to evade safeguards by not declaring nuclear material or activities. In recognition of that possibility, paragraph 2 of INFCIRC/153 was drafted to provide for the IAEA's *"right and the obligation* to ensure that safeguards will be applied … on *all* source or special fissionable material."[25] This formulation was agreed upon by the drafters after due consideration – and after explicit rejection of a proposal that IAEA verification be limited to nuclear material declared by the State.[26]

The provisions related to special inspections are even more explicit. Paragraph 73 of INFCIRC/153 authorizes the IAEA to carry out special inspections if, inter alia, it "considers that information made available by the State, including explanations from the State and information obtained from routine inspections, is not adequate for the IAEA to fulfil its responsibilities under the Agreement."[27] Paragraph 77 provides further that an inspection shall be deemed to be special when it is "either additional to the routine inspection effort provided for in paragraphs 78–82 [of INFCIRC/153], or involves *access to information or locations in addition to the access specified in paragraph 76 for ad hoc and routine inspections, or both.*"[28]

However, as a result of a combination of member states' frequently reiterated fear of the IAEA carrying out "fishing expeditions," and the Secretariat's cautiousness in pressing the boundaries of its legal authority, comprehensive safeguards were, for the first twenty years, largely focused on verifying declared nuclear material and facilities (i.e., the correctness of states' declarations), and not on providing assurances about the absence of undeclared nuclear material or activities in the state (i.e., the completeness of states' declarations). That was about to change.

1990–2005: Strengthening safeguards

The years between 1990 and 2005 were characterized by dramatic challenges to the IAEA's safeguards system which resulted in fundamental shifts in states' perceptions of the nature of the proliferation threat and, as a consequence, in their demands for verification.

The IAEA Secretariat and its member states had already begun to contemplate the need to strengthen IAEA safeguards in the summer of 1990. Although no final document was agreed at the 1990 NPT Review Conference in Geneva, the text reported by Main Committee II (the Safeguards Committee) included language welcoming a study by the IAEA of the possible scope, application, and procedures for special inspections in NPT states where uncertainty existed about whether a state had declared to the IAEA all of the nuclear material required to be subject to safeguards.[29] In addition, in his address to the General Conference in September 1990 immediately following the Review Conference, the Director General also raised the prospect of measures to improve the safeguards system, including the use of unannounced inspections.[30] However, there still remained strong resistance by some member states to expanding the IAEA's verification role, whether by practice or by law.

1991–1993: Correctness and completeness

Over three short, but very intense, years, member states were compelled to reassess their security needs, and to reconsider the inherent weakness in restricting the IAEA's focus to verifying only declared nuclear material. Member states now demanded that the IAEA provide assurances that there were *no undeclared nuclear material and activities* in a CSA state: in other words, that a state's declarations were not just correct, but complete.

It started in April 1991, when the IAEA uncovered undeclared nuclear material and activities in Iraq, much of which had been co-located on the site of three safeguarded nuclear facilities just a short ride from Baghdad. Iraq's clandestine nuclear program exposed all too clearly the limitations of a safeguards system that focused almost exclusively on declared nuclear material, and one which disregarded small quantities of nuclear material and dual use items.

Member states of the IAEA, and the world community at large, questioned how it had been possible for Iraq to have developed an undeclared enrichment program, effectively "under the nose of the IAEA." The answer was as simple as it was unfortunate.

As already indicated, it was not a question of the lack of legal authority: paragraph 2 of INFCIRC/153 already provided not only for the right, but the obligation, of the IAEA to ensure that "safeguards will be applied, in accordance with the terms of the Agreement, on *all* source or special fissionable material."[31] Unfortunately, however, over the years, the IAEA and its member states had bought into the idea that the IAEA's authority was limited to verifying declared nuclear material, and that efforts to ensure that there was no undeclared nuclear material in the state would be rebuffed. Even if the IAEA had been amenable to carrying out inspections to ensure the absence of undeclared nuclear material and activities, the Secretariat could not have done so without information indicating the need for such inspections, information that it was not generally able to acquire in the course of routine inspections and was not routinely available from other sources. And unless that information were compelling – unless the case was strong – it was even less likely that, in the event of a challenge by the state concerned, the support of the Board of Governors could have been secured.

The world community had already developed solutions to address the threat to peace and security posed by the possible misuse of supplied nuclear material and technology, and other solutions to address the threat of misuse of declared indigenous nuclear fuel cycles. It was time now to address the clear and present danger attributable to a newly perceived threat: that of a state concealing nuclear material and activities in contravention of its international obligations.

That same year, South Africa, a long-time NPT "hold out," became party to the NPT and concluded a CSA. If Iraq had raised member states' awareness of the threat posed by undeclared nuclear material and activities, South Africa provided them with another, much more positive, but equally clear, case in point. In September 1991, both the Board of Governors and the General Conference of the IAEA adopted resolutions requesting the Secretariat to verify the correctness and completeness of South Africa's initial declaration of nuclear material which, with the cooperation of the South African Government, the IAEA was able to do.[32]

The Board took a number of other actions between 1991 and early 1993 with a view to strengthening IAEA safeguards, among which were:

*   *Special inspections*: The Board reaffirmed the IAEA's right to undertake special inspections to ensure that all nuclear material in all peaceful nuclear activities is under safeguards in CSA states, and reaffirmed "the IAEA's rights to obtain and have access to additional information and locations in accordance with the Statute and all [CSAs]."[33]
*   *Early provision of design information*: The Board called upon all parties to CSAs to provide early and complete design information for new nuclear facilities, and modifications to existing facilities, in accordance with a proposal by the Secretariat, and to request the Secretariat and all parties to CSAs to adapt, where appropriate, the related Subsidiary Arrangements.[34]
*   *Voluntary reporting scheme*: The Board endorsed a proposal for the establishment of a voluntary reporting scheme whereby states would provide more information on exports, imports and inventories of nuclear material, and exports of nuclear related equipment and non-nuclear material, not otherwise required to be reported under safeguards agreements.[35]

In February 1993, the Director General of the IAEA reported to the Board an anomaly the Secretariat had discovered in the Democratic People's Republic of Korea (DPRK) that had given rise to doubts about the completeness of the DPRK's initial report of nuclear material under its NPT CSA. In his report, the Director General made clear that, while the IAEA had identified the anomaly through its own verification activities (in particular, environmental sampling), the IAEA had utilized satellite imagery obtained through "national technical means" (i.e., intelligence information) to identify locations access to which it believed would be helpful in resolving the outstanding issues concerning the DPRK's failure to declare nuclear material. Based on that report, and a detailed briefing by the Secretariat, the Board adopted a resolution in which it decided that access under special inspections to the additional information and locations was "essential and urgent in order to resolve differences and to ensure verification of compliance [by the DPRK with its CSA]".[36]

In adopting that resolution, it in effect confirmed the IAEA's right and obligation to verify correctness and completeness of a state's declarations under a CSA; the IAEA's right to take into account all information available to it, including intelligence information, in fulfilling that obligation; the IAEA's right to use of environmental sampling; and the IAEA's right of access, through special inspections, to undeclared locations and information under a CSA.[37]

1993–1997: Program 93+2 and the model additional protocol

In June 1993, the Board of Governors requested the Director General to submit to it concrete proposals for the assessment, development, and testing of measures for strengthening safeguards and improving its cost-effectiveness. In December 1993, the Secretariat introduced to the Board "Program 93+2," the goal of which was to evaluate the technical, financial, and legal aspects of a comprehensive set of measures and to present, in early 1995, proposals for a strengthened and more efficient safeguards system.

Over the following two years, the Secretariat carried out extensive consultations with member states, provided the Board of Governors with a number of progress reports and, in February and May 1995, submitted its final reports on the results of Program 93+2.[38]

In summary, the approach proposed by the Secretariat involved a comprehensive set of measures related to: increased access to information and its effective use by the IAEA (including improved analysis and evaluation of all relevant information available to the IAEA about a state's nuclear material, facilities, and activities); increased physical access for IAEA inspectors; and optimal use of elements of the present system. Fundamentally, it involved a profound shift away from a "facility-level" approach to a "state-level" approach; that is, one involving the visualization of all of a state's nuclear program in a coherent and connected way by looking at the state as a whole.

The measures were identified in two parts: those which could, in the Secretariat's view, be implemented under the IAEA's existing legal authority (the "Part 1" measures) and those which it believed would be useful to implement under complementary legal authority (the "Part 2" measures, which subsequently served as the basis for the Model Additional Protocol).

By June 1996, the Board had endorsed the general direction of Program 93+2 for a strengthened and cost-effective safeguards system; reiterated that the purpose of CSAs was to verify that "all nuclear material in all nuclear activities within the territory of a State party to such an agreement" is not diverted to nuclear weapons or other nuclear explosive devices and that, "to this end, the safeguards system for implementing [CSAs] should be designed to provide for verification by the IAEA of the correctness and completeness of States' declarations, so that there is credible assurance of the nondiversion of nuclear material from declared nuclear activities and of the absence of undeclared nuclear activities."[39] The Board had also taken note of the Director General's decision to implement the Part 1 measures[40] and determined that complementary legal authority should be developed in the form of a model protocol, based on a first draft prepared by the Secretariat,[41] to provide the IAEA with more routine broader access to information and locations necessary for the IAEA to improve the effectiveness and efficiency of safeguards.

After a year of deliberations, the committee established by the Board in 1996 to negotiate a model text for complementary legal authority (Committee 24) completed its task, and agreed on a "Model Additional Protocol to the Agreement(s) between State(s) and the IAEA for the Application of Safeguards" (the Model Additional Protocol, published as INFCIRC/540 (Corr.)).[42] The Model Additional Protocol included measures designed to provide the IAEA with new tools for better achieving the objective of safeguards: verifying the correctness and completeness of states' declarations under CSAs. In a special session held in May 1997, the Board approved the text, and requested the Director General to use it as the standard for additional protocols (APs) to be concluded in connection with CSAs. The Board also requested the Director General to negotiate APs with other states, incorporating those measures that such other states were prepared to accept.

1997–2002: Integrated safeguards

As described in the reports on Program 93+2, the level of verification effort on declared nuclear material under a CSA alone was based on the assumption that undeclared nuclear activities necessary to produce nuclear-weapon-usable material may exist undetected (e.g., undeclared reprocessing or enrichment facilities). If, using the new state evaluation process of looking at the state as a whole, and the measures available to the IAEA under a CSA and an AP, the IAEA were able to conclude that a state's declarations were correct *and* complete (commonly referred to as "the broader conclusion"), in particular, that there were no undeclared enrichment or reprocessing activities, the IAEA could consider modifying some of the safeguards implementation parameters for less sensitive nuclear material (i.e., depleted, natural, and low enriched uranium and irradiated fuel) and reduce its inspection effort on declared nuclear material. The result of this process was called "integrated safeguards," an optimized combination of all safeguards measures available to the IAEA to maximize the effectiveness and efficiency of safeguards implementation within available resources – the first wide scale implementation of the state-level approach.

The implementation of integrated safeguards should not be confused with what is simply one part of the process of implementing safeguards on a state level basis, i.e., the collection and evaluation of all available safeguards relevant information for the state as a whole (including inspection results) with a view to drawing annual safeguards conclusions. While integrated safeguards were developed having in mind states for which the broader conclusion had been drawn (because they offered the greatest opportunity for optimizing safeguards implementation), the process of collecting and evaluating information is relevant to all states that have a safeguards agreement with the IAEA.

As foreseen in the May 1995 report to the Board on Program 93+2, implementation criteria that fully integrated the new measures with elements of the then existing system had to be developed.[43] The Secretariat provided the Board with two progress reports on the development of integrated safeguards in 2000,[44] before submitting to the Board a report on "The Conceptual Framework for Integrated Safeguards" in February 2002.[45]

As reflected in those reports, integrated safeguards involved the development and implementation of a state level "integrated safeguards approach" tailored to the state concerned. Each of these approaches was based on consideration of state-specific features and characteristics; adaptation of model integrated safeguards approaches for different types of facilities for application at specific facilities in the state (facility level integrated safeguards approaches); and a plan for the implementation of complementary access.

As noted in the February 2002 report, the IAEA had been implementing integrated safeguards since January 2001, but elements of the framework would be further developed or refined in the light of experience gained in implementation, further evaluation and available technology.[46]

2003–2010: The further evolution of safeguards

Even as the IAEA took steps to implement safeguards at the state level, another crisis was looming which would demand a further reassessment of states' perceptions of the nature of the proliferation threat.

In the first few months of 2003, the IAEA uncovered in Iran previously undeclared nuclear material and activities associated with conversion, uranium enrichment and reprocessing, much of which had been fueled by a clandestine international market in nuclear technology, equipment, and material. At the end of 2003, Libya publicly announced that it had had a program intended for the production of nuclear weapons, and that it had been engaged for more than a decade in the development of a uranium enrichment capability, including the import of undeclared uranium and centrifuge and conversion equipment and the construction of pilot scale centrifuge facilities. Over the following two years, it became clear that much of the information, equipment, and materials acquired by Libya for its clandestine nuclear program had been acquired through the same illicit nuclear trade network that had supplied Iran's enrichment program. Neither country had an AP in force.

Another concerning aspect of these undeclared activities was the role played by nonstate actors. Until this point in time, the measures taken to deter the proliferation of nuclear weapons had been premised on the assumption that the nuclear activities of a state were controlled by the state itself and that, if proliferation were to occur, it would be because the state had decided to do so. However the IAEA's findings in connection with the nuclear black market which had contributed to the programs of Iran and Libya, and the tragic events of 9/11, forced states to come to grips with the very real likelihood that states might not be the only potential proliferators: nonstate actors were now perceived as players on the world stage.

In an effort to try to address that aspect of the threat, the IAEA instituted a program for outreach to member states who were willing, on a voluntary basis, to provide pertinent information on international nuclear activities and trade (including nuclear supply and procurement data) relevant to improved safeguards implementation. It was hoped that the analysis of such information would contribute to the state evaluation process, and provide early indications of undeclared nuclear activities. In September 2005, the General Conference welcomed the Secretariat's activities in verifying and analyzing such information and invited all states to cooperate with the IAEA in this regard.[47]

These more recent findings, and expectations of growing demands on the IAEA's resources, also led to a re-examination of how safeguards were being implemented and to their eventual further evolution.

In late 2005, the Board decided, on the advice of the Secretariat, to modify the eligibility criteria for and the substantive requirements of SQPs. Now, in order for a state to qualify for an SQP, it would not only have to have limited quantities of nuclear material, but it must also not have taken a decision to construct or authorize construction of a facility.[48] In addition, the revised model SQP would now require the submission by the state of an initial report on nuclear material and modification as soon as a decision has been taken to construct or to authorize construction of a nuclear facility, and permits the IAEA to carry out ad hoc inspections in the state.

The other action that was taken was to consider whether, using state–level approaches, the implementation of safeguards could be further improved. Although some considerations relating to the state as a whole had been reflected in the state-level approaches involving integrated safeguards, the primary basis for determining safeguards activities at declared facilities in these states remained the safeguards criteria (although adjusted to take into account that the broader conclusion had been drawn for the state).

In 2005, the Board was informed that the implementation of safeguards based on state-level approaches developed using safeguards objectives common to all states with CSAs and taking into account state specific factors, what was for the first time referred to as the state-level concept (SLC), was being implemented for states with integrated safeguards and would eventually be extended to all other states with CSAs.[49]

The present and beyond: Current debate and future prospects

While the SLC was not new – it was simply the next logical step in the evolution of state-as-a-whole safeguards – the name was new. And so was its description as "fully information driven,"[50] which caught the attention of some, who erroneously misinterpreted it as a euphemism for "intelligence driven safeguards." As a consequence, the SLC has been subject to close scrutiny by the member states of the IAEA.

At the insistence of the General Conference in 2012, the Secretariat submitted to the Board of Governors in September 2013 a report on efforts to further strengthen the effectiveness of safeguards and increase their efficiency, "The Conceptualization and Development of Safeguards Implementation at the State Level."[51]

As described in that report, the SLC involves no changes to the IAEA's legal authority, but is geared towards improving both the effectiveness and efficiency of safeguards implementation – which should benefit both the IAEA and its member states. It is a holistic approach to safeguards implementation that considers a state and its nuclear activities and capabilities as a whole, rather than being focused on individual facilities. The intention is to implement safeguards in a more focused manner by investing verification effort and resources where they are most needed, making less predictable to states the timing and nature of IAEA verification activities and increasing the adaptability of safeguards to changing circumstances, thereby optimizing IAEA resources.

As contemplated in the SLC, in order to verify a state's compliance with its safeguards obligations, the IAEA pursues generic state-level safeguards objectives that are common to all states with similar types of safeguards agreements. In applying the SLC, the IAEA conducts continuous state evaluation, making full use of all safeguards relevant information available to the IAEA about a state. The idea is then to develop and implement a customized state-level safeguards approach for each state, taking into consideration relevant state-specific factors (such as the nuclear fuel cycle and related technical capabilities of the state). Based on an acquisition path analysis,[52] a state-level approach identifies technical safeguards objectives for a state and the applicable safeguards measures to address those objectives. The measures are executed though annual implementation plans which identify the safeguards activities to be conducted for a given calendar year. The effectiveness of safeguards is evaluated on the basis of the extent to which these activities achieve the generic and technical objectives. Safeguards conclusions are then drawn for, and reported individually, for each state.

Although the Secretariat's paper focused on the applicability of the SLC to states with CSAs, the SLC can be applied to all states with safeguards agreements in force, taking into account the objectives deriving from their respective safeguards agreements and the rights and obligations of the parties to those agreements.

Rather than being received as had been intended – as the next logical step in the evolution of safeguards – the report, and the concept it described, triggered a debate in the Board during which not only was the SLC challenged, but important measures to strengthen safeguards that had been put in place in the early 1990s were called into question by some member states. Most disconcerting were challenges – as likely prompted by unrelated external political factors as a lack of knowledge about the history of strengthening safeguards – to the IAEA's authority under CSAs to verify the nondiversion of declared nuclear material and the absence of undeclared nuclear material and activities – a right and obligation which has not been seriously challenged by any member state for the last twenty years, with perhaps the singular exception of Iran. As a result of this debate, the Director General undertook to provide a supplementary document for the Board of Governors before the 2014 General Conference.

At the time of this writing, the Secretariat is in the process of consulting with member states through a series of technical meetings with a view to drafting the supplementary report for submission to the Board in September 2014. While there may certainly be legitimate differences in how aspects of the SLC are viewed, hopefully these close consultations will offer an opportunity for the Secretariat to better clarify the concept where there are misunderstandings, and to take into account member states' concerns.

Ideally, this process will not, however inadvertently, result in erosion of the significant progress made by the IAEA and its member states in strengthening safeguards over the past twenty years. That could set the clock back by two decades and have unpredictable consequences.

Notes

1. See United States Department of State Office of the Historian, "The Acheson-Lilienthal & Baruch Plans, 1946," http://history.state.gov/milestones/1945-1952/baruch-plans.
2. George Bunn, *Arms Control by Committee: Managing Negotiations with the Russians* (Palo Alto, CA: Stanford University Press, 1992).
3. Dwight D. Eisenhower, "Atoms for Peace Speech." Address to the UN General Assembly, December 8, 1953, www.iaea.org/About/atomsforpeace_speech.html; National Archives and Records Administration, "Atoms for Peace," www.eisenhower.archives.gov/research/online_documents/atoms_for_peace.html.
4. International Atomic Energy Agency, "The Statute of the IAEA." October 23, 1956, Articles III.B.4 and XII.C, www.iaea.org/About/statute.html.
5. Ibid., Article XXI.
6. Ibid., Article III.A.5.
7. Ibid., Article XII.
8. While consent to accept safeguards has been manifested largely in the form of safeguards agreements with the IAEA, consent has also been expressed through voluntary undertakings (e.g., South Africa's permission to grant the IAEA any time, any place access to verify the completeness of its initial declarations), or as a consequence of prior consent by a state party to the United Nations Charter to be bound by decisions taken by the Security Council under Chapter VII (e.g., Iraq's obligation under UNSC resolution 687 (1991) to cooperate with the IAEA in mapping out and dismantling its nuclear-weapon program).
9. And sometimes regional organizations, such as the European Atomic Energy Community (EURATOM) and the Brazilian-Argentine Agency for Accounting and Control of Nuclear Materials (ABACC).
10. An "INFCIRC" is an information circular published by the IAEA either on its own initiative or at the request of a member state or states. INFCIRCs are publicly available at www.iaea.org.
11. "Principal nuclear facility" means a reactor, a plant for processing nuclear material irradiated in a reactor, a plant for separating the isotopes of a nuclear material, a plant for processing or fabricating nuclear material (except a mine or ore processing plant), or a facility or plant of such other type as may be designated by the Board, including associated storage facilities. See International Atomic Energy Agency, "The Agency's Safeguards System," INFCIRC/66/Rev.2, September 16, 1968, para. 78, www.iaea.org/Publications/Documents/Infcircs/Others/infcirc66r2.pdf.
12. United Nations Office for Disarmament Affairs, "Treaty for the Prohibition of Nuclear Weapons in Latin America." February 14,1967, http://disarmament.un.org/treaties/t/tlatelolco/text.
13. United Nations Office for Disarmament Affairs, "Treaty on the Non-Proliferation of Nuclear Weapons (NPT)," July 1, 1968, www.un.org/disarmament/WMD/Nuclear/NPTtext.shtml.
14. The People's Republic of China, France, the Soviet Union (now the Russian Federation), the United Kingdom, and the United States.
15. An excellent resource for those interested in an in-depth analysis of the history of the NPT negotiations is the book by the former General Counsel of the US Arms Control and Disarmament Agency and one of the US negotiators of the NPT, George Bunn, *Arms Control by Committee*.
16. United Nations Department for Disarmament Affairs, "NPT," Article III.1, emphasis added.

17. Ibid., emphasis added.
18. The model text for CSAs is set out in International Atomic Energy Agency, "The Standard Text of Safeguards Agreements in Connection with the Treaty on the Non-Proliferation of Nuclear Weapons." GOV/INF/276, February 22, 1974, annex A http://ola.iaea.org/ola/documents/GINF 276.pdf.
19. Any arrangement made pursuant to that paragraph would have to be reported to the Board of Governors, and it would be for the Board in each case to take the appropriate action. The IAEA has never concluded any such arrangement. While Canada initiated discussions with the Secretariat to that end in the late 1980s, it terminated its program to acquire nuclear powered submarines before concluding any arrangement with the IAEA.
20. Although not defined in INFCIRC/153, "significant quantity" is defined in the IAEA Safeguards Glossary, 2001 Edition, as the approximate amount of nuclear material for which the possibility of manufacturing a nuclear explosive device cannot be excluded. Significant quantities take into account unavoidable losses due to conversion and manufacturing processes and should not be confused with critical masses. See International Atomic Energy Agency, "The Structure and Content of Agreements Between the Agency and States Required in Connection with the Treaty on the Non-Proliferation of Nuclear Weapons," INFCIRC/153, June 1972, www.iaea.org/Publications/Documents/Infcircs/Others/infcirc153.pdf.
21. Specifically, less than the quantities of nuclear material specified in IAEA, INFCIRC/153, para. 37.
22. The text of the 1974 model SQP is set out in International Atomic Energy Agency, "Standard Text of Safeguards," annex B.
23. IAEA, INFCIRC/153, para. 39.
24. Ibid., para. 24. The item specific agreements remain in force, however. Only the application of safeguards under those agreements is suspended; the basic undertaking not to use the items subject to safeguards thereunder for *any* military purpose is not.
25. Ibid., para. 2, emphasis added.
26. See, for example, David Albright, Olli Heinonen, and Orde Kittrie, "Understanding the IAEA's Mandate in Iran: Avoiding Misinterpretations," Institute for Science and International Security, November 27, 2012, p. 3, http://isis-online.org/uploads/isis-reports/documents/Misinterpreting_the_IAEA_27Nov2012.pdf.
27. IAEA, INFCIRC/153, para. 73.
28. Ibid., para. 77, emphasis added.
29. International Atomic Energy Agency, "Fourth NPT Review Conference," GC(XXXIV)/INF/291, September 19, 1990, www.iaea.org/About/Policy/GC/GC34/GC34InfDocuments/English/gc34inf-291_en.pdf; International Atomic Energy Agency, "Extracts Appearing in Fourth NPT Review Conference," NPT/CONF.IV/DC/I/Add.3(A), September 19, 1990, para. 28, www.iaea.org/About/Policy/GC/GC34/GC34InfDocuments/English/gc34inf-291_en.pdf.
30. International Atomic Energy Agency, "Fourth NPT Review Conference," General Conference, Record of the 323rd Plenary Meeting, 34th Regular Session, held on September 17, 1990, GC(XXXIV)/OR.323, published March 7, 1991, www.iaea.org/About/Policy/GC/GC34/GC34Records/English/gc34or-323_en.pdf.
31. IAEA, INFCIRC/153, para. 2, emphasis added.
32. GOV/2547/Rev.1, September 11, 1991, as referenced in International Atomic Energy Agency, "The Conceptualization and Development of Safeguards Implementation at the State Level," GOV/2013/38, August 12, 2013, para. 5, footnote 5, reproduced in www.isisnucleariran.org/assets/pdf/GOV201338.pdf; International Atomic Energy Agency, "South Africa's Nuclear Capabilities," GC(XXXV)/RES/567, September 20, 1991, www.iaea.org/About/Policy/GC/GC35/GC35Resolutions/English/gc35res-567_en.pdf.
33. International Atomic Energy Agency, "Organization of Work under 'Programme 93+2,'" GOV/2784, February 1995, reproduced in International Atomic Energy Agency, "Strengthening the Effectiveness and Improving the Efficiency of the Safeguards System," Report by the Director General, GC(39)/17, August 22, 1995, annex 1, www.iaea.org/About/Policy/GC/GC39/GC39Documents/English/gc39-17_en.pdf; GOV/OR.776, February 25, 1992, paras 48, 83 and 84, as referenced in IAEA, GOV/2013/38, para. 5, footnote 6.
34. GOV/2554/Att.2/Rev.2 (1 April 1992); GOV/DECISIONS 1991-92, 91-92/22 as referenced in IAEA, GOV/2013/38, para. 5, footnote 7; GOV/OR.777, February 26, 1992, paras. 71–76, as referenced in IAEA, GOV/2013/38, para. 5, footnote 7.

35. GOV/2629 (22 January 1993); GOV/DECISIONS 1992-93, 92-93/21 as referenced in in IAEA, GOV/2013/38, para. 5, footnote 8; GOV/OR.803, paras 1–33, February 24, 1993, as referenced in IAEA, GOV/2013/38, para. 5, footnote 8.
36. International Atomic Energy Agency, "Report on the Implementation of the Agreement Between the Agency and the Democratic People's Republic of Korea for the Application of Safeguards in Connection with the Treaty on the Non-Proliferation of Nuclear Weapons," GOV/2636, February 25, 1993, http://ahlambauer.files.wordpress.com/2013/03/gov2636.pdf.; GOV/DECISIOS 1992–93; 92-93/19, as referenced in IAEA, GOV/2013/38, para. 5, footnote 5.
37. Unfortunately, the DPRK denied the IAEA's request, which was reported to the Board. The Board, in turn, decided to report the DPRK's noncompliance to the Security Council. See International Atomic Energy Agency, "Report by the Director General on the Implementation of the Resolution Adopted by the Board on 25 February 1993 and of the Agreement Between the Agency and the Democratic People's Republic of Korea for the Application of Safeguards in Connection with the Treaty on the Non-Proliferation of Nuclear Weapons," GOV/2645, April 1, 1993, www.security councilreport.org/atf/cf/%7B65BFCF9B-6D27-4E9C-8CD3-CF6E4FF96FF9%7D/Disarm%20GOV2645.pdf. For more detail on the history and status of the DPRK case see also International Atomic Energy Agency, "IAEA & DPRK," www.iaea.org/newscenter/focus/iaeadprk/index.shtml.
38. GOV/2784 (February 21, 1995) and GOV/2807 (May 12, 1995), reproduced in IAEA, GC(39)/17, annexes 1 and 4.
39. GOV/OR.864, paras 49–75 and GOV/OR.865, paras 1–57 (March 1995), reproduced in IAEA, GC(39)/17, annex 3.
40. GOV/OR.872, paras 7–10 (June 1995), reproduced in IAEA, GC(39)/17, annex 6.
41. GOV/2863 (May 6, 1996), Annex III, reproduced in International Atomic Energy Agency, "Strengthening the Effectiveness and Improving the Efficiency of the Safeguards System," GC(40)/17, August 23, 1996, annex 1, www.iaea.org/About/Policy/GC/GC40/Documents/gc40-17.html.
42. International Atomic Energy Agency, "Model Protocol Additional to the Agreement(s) between State(s) and the International Atomic Energy Agency for the Application of Safeguards," INFCIRC/540 (Corrected), September 1997, www.iaea.org/Publications/Documents/Infcircs/1997/infcirc540c.pdf.
43. GOV/2807 (May 12, 1995), Part II, Section D, reproduced in IAEA, GC(39)/17, annex 4.
44. International Atomic Energy Agency, "The Development of International Safeguards," GOV/INF/2000/4, March 9, 2000; International Atomic Energy Agency, "The Development of International Safeguards," GOV/INF/2000/26, November 17, 2000.
45. International Atomic Energy Agency, "The Conceptual Framework for Integrated Safeguards," GOV/2002/8, February 8, 2002.
46. Ibid., para. 49. See also International Atomic Energy Agency, "Strengthening the Effectiveness and Improving the Efficiency of the Safeguards System and Application of the Model Additional Protocol," GC(45)/23, General Conference, 45th regular session, August 17, 2001, Section B, http://iaea.org/About/Policy/GC/GC45/GC45Documents/English/gc45-23_en.pdf.
47. International Atomic Energy Agency, "Strengthening the Agency's Technical Co-operation Activities," GC(39)/RES/14, September 30, 2005, para. 21, www.iaea.org/About/Policy/GC/GC39/Resolutions/gc39r14.html.
48. International Atomic Energy Agency, "The Standard Text of Safeguards Agreements in Connection with the Treaty on the Non-Proliferation of Nuclear Weapons," GOV/INF/276/Mod.1, February 21, 2006, http://ola.iaea.org/ola/documents/ginf276mod1.pdf; International Atomic Energy Agency, "The Standard Text of Safeguards Agreements in Connection with the Treaty on the Non-Proliferation of Nuclear Weapons: Revision of the Standardized Text of the "Small Quantities Protocol,"" GOV/INF/276/Corr.1, February 28, 2006, http://ola.iaea.org/ola/documents/ginf276mod1corr1.pdf.
49. IAEA, GOV/2013/38, para. 12.
50. Prior to 1991, the safeguards relevant information available to the IAEA about a state was largely limited to that declared by the state, and that derived from IAEA verification activities, with respect to declared nuclear facilities. Since the early 1990s, the IAEA has also availed itself of information from a variety of other sources as well, including non-safeguards databases of the IAEA (e.g., the IAEA's Illicit Trafficking Database), open sources (e.g., scientific literature, commercial satellite imagery) and third parties (e.g., nuclear supply and procurement data). While safeguards have always

been "information driven," the phrase "fully information driven" was intended to convey the idea of the greater use by the IAEA of information about a state in developing individual state-level approaches and in the planning conduct and evaluation of safeguards activities.

51. IAEA, GOV/2013/38.
52. "Acquisition path analysis" is an analysis of all technically plausible paths by which the state concerned could pursue the acquisition of nuclear material for the development of a nuclear weapon or other nuclear explosive device. It does not involve judgments about the state's intention to pursue any such path.

11

EXPORT CONTROLS

Sibylle Bauer

Exports controls on goods and technology with both civilian and military applications (dual-use items) are a key instrument to prevent or reduce the proliferation of nuclear, biological and chemical weapons and their delivery systems, as well as conventional weapons. Even within the weapons of mass destruction (WMD) dual-use spectrum, there are differences between those who produce, trade with, and use the items; research communities and regulatory authorities; and national and international legal frameworks. This chapter focuses on nuclear aspects and its specificities, but will also explore the broader export control context and relevant connections to other WMD areas.

It should also be noted that the term dual-use has at least two meanings, and in this chapter refers to both civilian and potential military applications of materials, equipment and technology. In the nuclear community, it also refers to items that have both nuclear (whether civilian or military) and nonnuclear uses.

Trends and changes in export control

Over the past decade, controls on the cross-border movement of dual-use items have expanded from the traditional focus on exports to encompass controls on transit, trans-shipment, brokering, and financing. While this shift in trade control realities has not been fully reflected in a corresponding shift in terminology from "export control" to "trade control," the term "strategic trade control" is increasingly used. The persistence of the limited term export controls can be attributed to a number of factors: habit; strategic trade controls not easily translating into all languages; the fact that the name is included in existing names of programs, budget lines and institutions; and the argument that export control remains the core concept around which an increasing number of associated activities revolve.

To date, there are no standard international definitions of the terms "transit," "transhipment," and "brokering." Broadly speaking, transit refers to the movement of internationally traded goods through the territory of a state that is neither the port of origin nor the destination port. In some definitions, it refers only to cases where the goods stay on the same means of transport and is contrasted with "transshipment," in which the goods are transferred from one means of transport to another. "Brokering" can include different aspects of facilitating transactions. While the scope is often limited to transactions between other countries, some states include activities conducted on their territory in their legal definition of brokering. In the area of proliferation financing, the Financial Action Task Force (FATF) in 2007 developed guidance which was updated in 2013.[1] Differences in definitions can have important legal and practical implications; for example, the European Union (EU) defines transshipment as a form of transit or as part of the export process, whereas many countries give it a separate legal status.

In addition to the expanded range of actors and activities subject to control, the range of items has also broadened to include both tangible and intangible transfers of dual-use technologies. An increasing control challenge is posed by intangible transfers of technology (ITT). There are two main forms of ITT, transfer of know-how by a person, and the transfer of technical data in nonphysical form, for example through telephone, email or when technology on a server is accessed from another country.

The increased scope of controlled activities and items has also multiplied the number and type of public and private-sector actors affected by control provisions. Not only producers but also shippers, traders, freight forwarders and banks can be subject to laws regulating controls, as well as academia and research institutions.

Increasingly complex procurement patterns for illicit WMD programs and technological developments make proliferation-sensitive flows more difficult to control through the application of traditional legal concepts and enforcement methods. The use of intermediaries, front companies and transshipment – and thus potential diversion – points has multiplied. In addition, the increased complexity of regular production and trading patterns has made it easier for illegal procurement efforts to disguise the actual end-use and end-user of transactions.

One consequence of these developments has been a substantial increase in the number of countries and actors potentially involved in or used for proliferation activities. Therefore, not only producer countries are required to establish control systems. This has resulted in changed approaches to trade control, including a stronger focus on cooperative efforts. A number of actors have been involved in the delivery of technical assistance and other cooperation to establish and strengthen systems to control cross-border flows of dual-use items. The United States has the longest history of export control assistance programs, which originated in the immediate post-Cold War context of the early 1990s and initially focused on the Soviet Union and its successor states. These have since developed into the global Export Control and Related Border Security (EXBS) program, which is complemented by other US Government initiatives.[2] While the EU has provided technical assistance relevant to dual-use export control since the 1990s, it established a dedicated program in 2005 which now includes partner countries in Europe, Africa, Asia, and the Middle East, which is based on the EU WMD Strategy of 2003.[3]

While the EU and the United States have the only major dedicated programs with international scope, there is also engagement by a few other states with a regional, and WMD-related, focus: Japan and, to a lesser extent, Australia in the Asia-Pacific region, and some EU member states through bilateral cooperation.[4] Outreach activities are also conducted by the export control regimes and by the Proliferation Security Initiative.[5] A number of nongovernmental and international organizations have also been engaged in capacity building.[6]

Export control systems are implemented at national level and in the EU, also at the supranational, regional level. They comprise: a range of laws and implementing regulations, including foreign trade and customs acts, and penal codes; a policy-making mechanism with interagency involvement to make decisions on precedent-setting or difficult cases and give guidance to the licensing and enforcement system; a licensing system to process and risk-assess applications; an enforcement system to detect, investigate and prosecute suspected export control violations; and outreach to stakeholders such as producers, traders, and brokers of controlled items. The precise shape of each of these key elements varies from country to country, and it can safely be said that there are no two identical systems.

International legal framework

The 1968 Treaty on the Nonproliferation of Nuclear Weapons (Nonproliferation Treaty, or NPT), the 1972 Biological and Toxin Weapons Convention (BTWC), and the 1993 Chemical Weapons Convention (CWC) provide the rationale for WMD-related dual-use controls.

The perception that the main security threats were posed by an opposing bloc of countries, has since the end of the Cold War been replaced with shared international concerns about certain states seeking to acquire WMD and the possibility that nonstate actors could carry out terrorist acts with WMD or conventional arms. This shift is reflected in export control policies of states, as well as in several UN Security Council resolutions. In particular, a number of resolutions have been adopted imposing embargoes on the export of nuclear and missile-related items to North Korea and Iran.

Additionally, UN Security Council resolution 1540 (adopted in 2004) obliges states to "take and enforce effective measures to establish domestic controls to prevent the proliferation of nuclear, chemical, or biological weapons and their means of delivery," with particular emphasis on the need to prevent proliferation to and by nonstate actors. These resolutions were all adopted unanimously under Chapter VII of the UN Charter, and are therefore binding on all UN member states.

Resolution 1540 specifically obliges all states to establish strategic trade controls. States must:

> establish, develop, review and maintain appropriate effective national export and transshipment controls over such items [nuclear, chemical, or biological weapons and their means of delivery], including appropriate laws and regulations to control export, transit, transshipment and re-export and controls on providing funds and services related to such export and transshipment such as financing, and transporting that would contribute to proliferation, as well as establishing end-user controls; and establishing and enforcing appropriate criminal or civil penalties for violations of such export control laws and regulations.[7]

It also calls on member states to develop national control lists.

Another important aspect of Resolution 1540 is that it explicitly acknowledges that these threats can only be tackled cooperatively and invites "States in a position to do so" to "offer assistance as appropriate in response to specific requests to the States lacking the legal and regulatory infrastructure, implementation experience and/or resources for fulfilling the above provisions."[8] Over the past decade, Resolution 1540 has become the main driver for the establishment and enhancement of strategic trade controls by nonmembers of the international export control regimes, and for the mobilization of funding for capacity building for this purpose.

The multilateral export control regimes

Overview and cross-regime issues

Four informal, non-legally binding, consensus-based export control regimes – the Australia Group, the Missile Technology Control Regime (MTCR), the Nuclear Suppliers Group

(NSG) and the Wassenaar Arrangement on Export Controls for Conventional Arms and Dual-use Goods and Technologies (WA) – aim to strengthen export controls. Of these four, the NSG is the oldest, dating back to 1978.[9]

The Australia Group was set up in 1985 to prevent the inadvertent supply of dual-use items to initially chemical, and later also biological, weapon programs. The Wassenaar Arrangement was established a decade later to address conventional arms and dual-use items. This chapter focuses on the NSG since it deals with nuclear items, and also covers the MTCR which addresses delivery systems. However, while each of the regimes has a specific purpose, technical scope, membership, and internal dynamics, they have many structural, substantial, and procedural features in common.

Cross-regime features and functions

The common purpose of all four regimes is to strengthen the national transfer control systems of participating states. Thus, a primary cross-regime function is the setting of common standards and principles, and agreement of control lists, which are subsequently translated into national laws, regulations and other provisions. National implementation and enforcement systems are therefore key to making the regimes relevant. A second key function is the information exchange and facilitation of networks for policy, licensing and enforcement practitioners and technical experts. While the information exchange at the meetings encompasses a broad range of issues such as procurement matters, sensitive end-users and national approaches, specific information is also exchanged throughout the year, in particular regarding denials of license applications.

In addition, the regimes increasingly have an external function that reaches beyond the participating states, through the establishment of international standards and benchmarks which nonparticipating states can voluntarily adopt. These include control lists, guidelines, and effective national implementation practices. For example, a number of nonparticipating countries in Eastern Europe and Asia have adopted the EU control list intern, which consolidates the control lists agreed by the four export control regimes. The regimes have also had shaped internationally binding standards, for example through incorporation of the then-MTCR control list in UN Security Council resolutions 1718 and 1737 in 2006, which thus made it binding with regard to transfers to Iran and North Korea.

The participating states meet every year in a plenary session to exchange information and national practice, to agree new documents, and to update the control list(s). Working groups take place either during the year or right before the plenary. At these, licensing and enforcement officers and intelligence staff discuss specific implementation and enforcement issues. Additionally, technical experts meet to review the lists of controlled items. Three of the regimes (including MTCR and NSG) have an annually rotating chair, whereas from its establishment the Australia Group has been chaired by Australia.

Over time the regimes have expanded their scope in terms of issues, from an initial focus on control list definitions to discussions, guidelines, and best practice guidance, as well as engagement with nonparticipating states. And although export controls remain the regimes' main organizing principle, associated trade activities are increasingly becoming the focus of discussion. Other cross-regime themes include procurement methods and proliferation trends, national licensing and enforcement approaches and challenges, the risk of acquisition through terrorists, industry outreach, and technological developments.

Ongoing efforts by the regimes seek to address the challenge of emerging technologies of concern and keep pace with advances in research and innovation, easier access to technology and sophisticated procurement methods, through amendments of the common control lists. The control lists are annually reviewed and amended through clarifying, deleting, and adding entries. In addition to listing specific goods, equipment, and technology, all regimes also agreed on complementary catch-all provisions, which have become a standard element of modern and effective export controls. In essence, these catch-all or end-use clauses permit national authorities to impose licensing requirements or prohibitions on items that are not included on control lists if there is information indicating a WMD-related end-use.

The Zangger committee

The Zangger Committee emerged from a series of meetings between 1972 and 1974 of an informal group of countries to discuss export-control issues related to the NPT. Named after its first chairman, Claude Zangger, its purpose was to find a common interpretation of Article III.2 of the NPT, in particular of the term "equipment or material especially designed or prepared for the processing, use or production of special fissionable material."[10] The committee's most important achievement has been the development and maintenance of the so-called trigger list. The export of these items defined as 'especially designed or prepared' for nuclear use, trigger IAEA safeguards as a condition of supply. Its currently thirty-nine members meet on an annual basis.[11]

Cross-regime relevance of regime initiatives and documents

While the Australia Group, the MTCR and the NSG focus on WMD and their delivery systems, the Wassenaar Arrangement promotes transparency and the exchange of information and views on transfers of conventional arms and related dual-use goods and technologies. It encourages responsible behavior and seeks to prevent "destabilising accumulations" of such items.[12] The Wassenaar Arrangement has been particularly active in adopting and publishing best practice guides, for example on end-use, industry engagement, and international compliance programs. The relevance of such documents however extends beyond the technical scope of items subject to control in a given regime.

For the past decade, the international debate, policy decisions, and legal provisions have gradually been expanded to brokering, transit, and transshipment, as activities related to export controls. Before 2012, however, international export control regimes had not moved beyond discussions and exchanges of experience on these issues. The 2012 amendment of the Australia Group's guidelines to comprise brokering controls therefore marks a significant step towards it becoming a trade control regime. According to the new wording, its members "should have in place or establish measures against illicit activities that allow them to act upon brokering services" related to controlled items, and agreed to "make every effort to implement those measures in accordance with their domestic legal framework and practices". In addition, the factors to be taken into account when assessing license applications were amended to include

> the role of distributors, brokers or other intermediaries in the transfer, including, where appropriate, their ability to provide an authenticated end-user certificate specifying both the importer and ultimate end-user of the item to be transferred, as well as the credibility of assurances that the item will reach the stated end-user."[13]

It remains to be seen if and when the other regimes will take similar steps.

The missile technology control regime

The MTCR was established in 1987, with the original purpose to control ballistic missiles capable of delivering nuclear weapons. In 1993, the focus was expanded to include missiles for the delivery of chemical or biological weapons. In line with threat perceptions in other regimes and internationally, the regime's focus was broadened in 2002 to include preventing terrorists from acquiring missiles and missile technology.[14]

The MTCR Guidelines are to be applied to the export of an agreed list of items needed for the production, development, and operation of WMD-capable unmanned systems, which are compiled in the MTCR Equipment, Software and Technology Annex. The scope of the MTCR was expanded in 1992 to include Unmanned Aerial Vehicles (UAVs) in the MTCR's Category I of most sensitive items. Category I items can only be authorized for export on rare occasions and under specified conditions. Further, the transfer of Category I production facilities is not to be authorized at all. Category I items include systems capable of delivering a payload of at least 500 kilograms to a minimum range of 300 kilometers, as well as the production facilities and major subsystems for such items. For their export, "particular restraint" is to be exercised and a "strong presumption to deny" applies. In contrast, Category II systems, which are items capable of flying at least 300 kilometers but below Category I's payload size parameters, require an export license based on criteria specified in the guidelines, but are not subject to Category I's presumption to deny.[15]

Which UAVs to include in the Annex, and whether in Category I or II, has been contentious within the MTCR for a number of years. While many larger UAVs would be capable of delivering WMD, UAVs have significant conventional military and civilian applications. The UAV dilemma reflects the difficulties inherent in seeking to keep up with proliferation-related trends while protecting trade and market competitiveness.

At the 27th MTCR plenary held in Rome in 2013, membership issues were discussed but no new members admitted.[16] The most recent admission goes back to 2004 (Bulgaria), which brought the number of participating countries to thirty-four. While the regime is not derived from an international treaty, UNSCR 1540 refers to WMD delivery systems, and a static reference to the MTCR list was also included in country-specific UN Security Council resolutions, as mentioned above. At least five countries have officially declared their unilateral adherence to MTCR guidelines: India, Israel, Macedonia, Romania, and Slovakia.[17]

The MTCR is complemented by the Hague Code of Conduct against Ballistic Missile Proliferation (HCoC), which was formally launched at a conference in The Hague, The Netherlands in 2002. As of January 2014, it comprised 136 countries. Annual meetings are held in Vienna. Austria serves as the Immediate Central Contact and facilitates the information exchange. The initiative is based on a set of guidelines and confidence-building measures.[18]

Nuclear suppliers group

The NSG aims to prevent the proliferation of nuclear weapons by controlling transfers of nuclear and nuclear-related material, equipment, software, and technology "without hindering legitimate trade and international cooperation on peaceful uses of nuclear energy."[19] The NSG's June 2013 plenary in Prague brought together the forty-eight participating states – for the first time including Mexico and Republic of Serbia as new members, as well as the European Commission and the Chair of the Zangger Committee, both of which are permanent observers.[20]

The fundamental review of NSG control lists initiated in 2010 was finalized at the 2013 plenary. As with all public NSG documents, the revised trigger and dual-use lists were published by the International Atomic Energy Agency (IAEA) as information circulars.[21] The revision considered the applications of materials, equipment, and technology in relation to the processing, use, or production of special fissionable material and to the design, testing, and development of nuclear explosive devices.[22]

The NSG guidelines

The NSG has developed guidelines requiring suppliers to base decisions on the export of specified nuclear and nuclear-related items on certain conditions. The NSG first published its guidelines in 1978, and has revised them several times since.[23] Major amendments were made in 2011 which imposed additional conditions on the transfer of sensitive nuclear fuel cycle technologies, equipment and technologies for use in uranium enrichment and reprocessing of spent fuel (ENR).

The guidelines foresee that the recipient implements a comprehensive safeguards agreement with the IAEA and guarantees that the items will not be used for a nuclear explosive device. The supplier should make provisions regarding future arrangements for the physical protection of nuclear materials and facilities and regarding re-transfer controls, and be "satisfied that the transfers would not contribute" to nuclear proliferation or nuclear terrorism.[24] Suppliers should also have "in place legal measures to ensure the effective implementation of the Guidelines, including export licensing regulations, enforcement measures, and penalties for violations."[25] The guidelines include control lists of items to which specific restrictions apply and require catch-all controls. A "safety clause" states that transfers may be made to a nonnuclear-weapon state without a safeguards agreement with the IAEA "only in exceptional cases when they are deemed essential for the safe operation of existing facilities." In these cases, the nuclear supplier should "inform and, if appropriate, consult in the event that they intend to authorize or to deny such transfers."[26]

The debate on revising the NSG guidelines regarding ENR can be traced back to a US initiative in 2001, in response to Russia's invoking of the safety clause when exporting nuclear fuel to India.[27] However, the clause was not affected by the 2011 guideline revision as the discussion changed course. The public disclosure in 2003 of the A.Q. Khan network, which had sold uranium enrichment technology, gave momentum to the debate on ENR export restrictions. In 2004 US President George W. Bush proposed that the NSG should ban the spread of ENR technology to countries that do not already possess it.[28] While this proposal failed to secure consensus within the NSG, it prompted a discussion on revising the ENR guidelines, and a draft revision was circulated in 2008.[29]

Agreeing a list of specific criteria that countries would have to meet to be eligible to receive ENR transfers proved difficult.[30] A fundamental underlying issue is the justification for limiting ENR supplies and the scope for allowing legitimate civilian uses of highly enriched uranium and plutonium. Several countries were concerned that some proposed criteria might limit their option to develop a civil nuclear program in the future.[31] Argentina's and Brazil's concerns regarding the "objective" requirement for an additional safeguards protocol relates to neither of these countries having an Additional Protocol (AP) with the IAEA. Instead, the Brazilian-Argentine Agency for Accounting and Control of Nuclear Materials (ABACC), Argentina and Brazil signed a safeguards agreement with the IAEA, which in these countries' view made signing of an AP unnecessary.[32] The resulting revised text on safeguards provides a compromise. While an additional safeguards protocol is not an absolute condition of supply, the text indicates that efforts to sign an additional safeguards protocol should be evident even where a regional safeguards agreement is in place.

The 2011 revision focused on paragraphs 6 ("special controls on sensitive exports") and 7 ("special arrangements for export of enrichment facilities, equipment and technology"). The previous version only required suppliers to "exercise restraint in the transfer of sensitive facilities, technology and material usable for nuclear weapons or other nuclear explosive devices", but did not define the term "restraint." The 2011 revision for the first time further specifies conditions for the transfer of ENR technology, both regarding the decision on whether such a transfer can take place, and if so, how.[33]

Specifically, it requires that the recipient: is (a) party to and "in full compliance" with the NPT; (b) has not been identified in a report by the IAEA Secretariat as currently being in breach of its safeguards obligations; (c) adheres to NSG guidelines and has reported to the UN Security Council that it implements "effective export controls as identified in" Resolution 1540; (d) has "concluded an inter-governmental agreement with the supplier including assurances regarding non-explosive use, effective safeguards in perpetuity, and retransfer"; (e) has "made a commitment to the supplier to apply mutually agreed standards of physical protection based on current international guidelines"; (f) has "committed to IAEA safety standards and adheres to accepted international safety conventions"; and (g) "has brought into force a Comprehensive Safeguards Agreement, and an Additional Protocol ... or, pending this, is implementing appropriate safeguards agreements in cooperation with the IAEA, including a regional accounting and control arrangement for nuclear materials, as approved by the IAEA Board of Governors."[34]

The subjective criteria were kept rather vague. The revised guidelines require NSG suppliers to take "into account at their national discretion, any relevant factors as may be applicable". The term "restraint" was maintained, while adding that this should apply in particular to countries that include entities subject to active denials relating to Part 2 of the guidelines (on nuclear-related dual-use goods) from more than one NSG participant.[35]

The revised paragraph 7 reinforces the previous requirement on the recipient to seek the consent of the supplier before using the transferred facility or technology to enrich uranium beyond 20 percent. The supplier should now seek a "legally-binding undertaking" from the recipient state that transferred ENR facilities, equipment, or technology would not be used or modified for enrichment beyond 20 percent. An additional new requirement placed on suppliers is to "seek to design and construct" facilities and equipment in a way that precludes the possibility of enrichment beyond 20 percent "to the greatest extent practicable."

The new version of paragraph 7 also provides that the transfer of "enabling design and manufacturing technology" should be avoided and specifies that suppliers should seek acceptance from recipients of transfer conditions that "do not permit or enable replication of the facilities". However, an exception permitting cooperation to develop potential new enrichment technologies is included, and the wording falls short of the black box proposals put forward.

The NSG's relationship with India

One issue emerging from the guidelines revision was how this affected India's eligibility to receive ENR transfers, and its possible membership of the NSG. The NSG's relationship with India has been a key factor driving and shaping supplier cooperation, discussion, and action. The first Indian nuclear explosive test, in 1974, provided the raison d'être for the creation of the NSG. Based on India's position outside the NPT, and its refusal to allow comprehensive IAEA safeguards covering all of its nuclear activities and facilities, NSG participants agreed not to supply India with nuclear materials, equipment, facilities, and technology. This agreement in principle lasted until 2008 when, in a move spearheaded by the United States following the Indian–US Civil Nuclear Cooperation Agreement, the NSG agreed a country-specific exemption from the guidelines. Specifically, the NSG waived the full-scope safeguards requirement of paragraph 4 of its guidelines and allowed ENR exports, subject to paragraphs 6 and 7.[36]

As a result, bilateral agreements with a range of countries were concluded, such as Canada, France, Russia, the UK, the United States, and South Korea.[37] India has an interest both in receiving equipment and technology from advanced nuclear suppliers to implement its nuclear energy expansion program, and in offering equipment and expertise to countries seeking to begin or to expand nuclear energy. Since the 2011 revisions of the guidelines, Indian observers have voiced concern that these effectively eliminated the "clean waiver" that India claimed to have received in 2008, and India may be not eligible to receive enrichment and reprocessing technology since it is not a party to the NPT.[38]

During his November 2010 visit to India, US President Barack Obama announced his support for Indian membership of the NSG and the other export control regimes, thus initiating an international debate on the issue.[39] In a 2011 "food for thought paper" circulated by the United States to other NSG members, two options for pursuing Indian membership were presented: either revising the membership criteria or recognizing that not all of the criteria for NSG participation had to be met.[40]

No decision had been taken on Indian membership by January 2014, although NSG statements have referred to discussions on the issue. According to reports, France, Russia, the United Kingdom, and the United States favor Indian NSG membership, while China was opposed.[41] It was also reported that Japan and some European countries, including the Netherlands, Switzerland, and Ireland, were "'not particularly favorable to the idea,' but did not publicly express intent to block membership."[42] The Turkish Foreign Minister supported Indian NSG membership but stated that the issue of NPT membership had to be resolved first.[43]

The NSG's relations with Pakistan

The NSG's relationship with India has direct repercussions for its relation to Pakistan, since Pakistan has subsequently demanded similar exemptions as well as regime membership. Pakistan met with the NSG Troika in January 2013 in Ankara, and received an outreach visit from the MTCR in February 2013.[44] Some observers have expressed concern that the NSG's exemption for India had set a precedent for other countries – in particular, that it had paved the way for further nuclear cooperation between China and Pakistan.[45]

In 2010 China indicated that it would proceed with the supply of two new civil nuclear power reactors to Pakistan.[46] China had previously supplied two reactors to Pakistan under a bilateral civil nuclear cooperation agreement concluded in 1991.[47] The reactors are to be supplied under a bilateral agreement concluded in 2003, about which China informed the NSG when it joined the group in 2004. China claims that implementation of the 2003 deal did not need NSG approval since China did not join the NSG until 2004. While some NSG participants agreed with this, the United States maintained that this so-called grandfather clause was not applicable based on the information China provided to the NSG at accession.[48] In mid-2013 China agreed to provide Pakistan with a 5th and possibly 6th nuclear power reactor. There are concerns that although civilian, this may "contribute to Pakistan's nuclear-weapon program and increase the risk of proliferation in the region," but also "may be designed to apply pressure on NSG members to open the way for Pakistan to achieve a global nuclear market access agreement similar to that achieved by New Delhi in 2008."[49] This debate illustrates both ambiguities in the grandfather clause and the general difficulty of enforcing voluntary NSG provisions.

Challenges of export control and the way ahead

A range of factors has made the implementation of effective export controls a challenging task. These include the increase of international intra-company transfers, both in tangible and intangible form; the complexity of trade flows, typically involving multiple transit and transshipment movements and multiple actors; technological developments; risks of terrorist access to sensitive items; and effective enforcement, which requires matching policy priority with operational resource in a time of budgetary constraints.

Effective nuclear export control systems must facilitate legitimate trade and support those who seek to comply, while deterring those who are hesitant, negligent, or easily swayed by proliferators, and deter and punish those who have no intention to comply. To balance trade and security in today's economic reality, the focus of industry and government needs to be on the difficult cases and combine individual licensing with a form of license allowing multiple shipments for trusted companies and end-users, which in turn must be coupled with ex-post control through specialized audits. Moreover, the focus needs to be expanded from the exporter to include other stakeholders.

South Korea's retrieval of a rocket launched by the DPRK in December 2013 offered some insights into DPRK procurement and production, and illustrates both the limitations of dual-use export controls in curbing proliferation and the importance of catch-all provisions. According to reports, the majority of the parts were manufactured inside the DPRK. The foreign-made parts were produced in five countries. These converters, temperature sensors, and other electronic devices were 'made for everyday use' and not listed by the MTCR.[50]

And while the establishment of effective trade control systems is a necessary foundation for slowing down or preventing proliferation, it is only one element of an effective nonproliferation approach, and has to be seen in the broader context of the NPT. An issue at the very heart of nuclear nonproliferation is the relationship between suppliers and those states with nuclear weapons who are outside of the framework of the NPT and the NSG.

A factor to consider in future will be the expected wider availability of nuclear materials and technology due to increasing reliance on nuclear energy, and the probable resulting demands for an increase in NSG membership. While advanced nuclear technology has been within the control of a small number of suppliers for many years, this exclusivity has been continually eroded. In addition to the emergence of new countries with nuclear-weapon capabilities, the modus operandi of illicit procurement networks has adapted to restrictions on the direct export of dual-use items from producing countries by using increasingly complex transactions. Consequently, decisions and participation in nuclear export controls will have to further adjust to consider relations with non-NSG members and the full range of nuclear trade activities including brokering, transit, transshipment, and finance, as well as intangible technology transfers, and thus move beyond the classical supplier-recipient paradigm.

Notes

1.   Sibylle Bauer, Aaron Dunne, and Ivana Mićić, "Strategic Trade Controls: Countering the Proliferation of Weapons of Mass Destruction," *SIPRI Yearbook 2011: Armaments, Disarmament and International Security* (Oxford: Oxford University Press, 2011), pp. 441–443; Financial Action Task Force, "Financing of Proliferation," FATF website, www.fatf-gafi.org/topics/financingofproliferation/.

2. Sibylle Bauer, "Enhancing Export Control-Related CTR (Cooperative Threat Reduction) Programs: Options for the EU," Background Paper No. 6, Conference on Strengthening European Action on WMD Non-proliferation and Disarmament: How Can Community Instruments Contribute? Brussels, December 7–8, 2005, www.sipri.org/research/disarmament/dualuse/publications/papers_publications/BP6; US Department of State, "The EXBS Program," US Department of State website, n.d., www.state.gov/t/isn/ecc/c27911.htm.

3. Bundesamt für Wirtschaft und Ausfuhrkontrolle (BAFA), "EU Cooperation in Dual-use Export Control." German Federal Office of Economics and Export Control, n.d., www.eu-outreach.info; Council of the European Union, "Fight against the Proliferation of Weapons of Mass Destruction: EU Strategy against Proliferation of Weapons of Mass Destruction," doc. no. 15708/03, December 10, 2003, www.consilium.europa.eu/showPage.aspx?id=718.

4. Bauer, "Enhancing Export Control-Related CTR Programs"; Sibylle Bauer, "Arms Trade Control Capacity Building: Lessons from Dual-Use Trade Controls," *SIPRI Insights on Peace and Security*, No. 2013/2 (March 2013), http://books.sipri.org/files/insight/SIPRIInsight1302.pdf.

5. Aaron Dunne, "The Proliferation Security Initiative: Legal Considerations and Operational Realities," SIPRI Policy Paper no. 36 (Stockholm: Stockholm International Peace Research Institute, May 2013).

6. Mark Bromley and Paul Holtom, "Implementing an Arms Trade Treaty: Mapping Assistance to Strengthen Arms Transfer Controls," *SIPRI Insights on Peace and Security*, No. 2012/2 (July 2012), http://books.sipri.org/files/insight/SIPRIInsight1202.pdf.

7. United Nations Security Council, "Resolution 1540 (2004)." S/RES/1540 (2004), 495th meeting, April 28, 2004, p. 3, www.un.org/en/ga/search/view_doc.asp?symbol=S/RES/1540%20(2004).

8. Ibid., p. 3.

9. Ian Anthony, Christer Ahlström, and Vitaly Fedchenko, *Reforming Nuclear Export Controls: The Future of the Nuclear Suppliers Group*, SIPRI Research Report No. 22 (Oxford: Oxford University Press, 2007).

10. United Nations, "Treaty on the Nonproliferation of Nuclear Weapons," July 1, 1968, Art. III(b), www.un.org/en/conf/npt/2005/npttreaty.html.

11. Anthony, Ahlström, and Fedchenko, *Reforming Nuclear Export Controls*; Zangger Committee, N.D., www.zanggercommittee.org.

12. Wassenaar Arrangement, "Initial Elements," Wassenaar website, July 11–12, 1996, amended December 2001, p. 1, www.wassenaar.org/guidelines/docs/Guidelines%20and%20procedures%20including%20the%20Initial%20Elements.pdf.

13. Australia Group, "Guidelines for Transfers of Sensitive Chemical or Biological Items," June 2012, www.australiagroup.net/en/guidelines.html.

14. Missile Technology Control Regime, "Plenary Meeting of the Missile Technology Control Regime," Rome, Italy, October 14–18, 2013, www.mtcr.info/english/press/Italy2013.htm.

15. Missile Technology Control Regime, "Guidelines for Sensitive Missile-Relevant Transfers," N.D., www.mtcr.info/english/guidetext.htm; Missile Technology Control Regime, *MTCR Annex Handbook*, MTCR/TEM/2012/Annex, October 23, 2012, www.mtcr.info/english/annex.html.

16. Missile Technology Control Regime, "Plenary Meeting of the Missile Technology Control Regime."

17. US State Department, "Missile Technology Control Regime (MTCR)," Fact Sheet, Bureau of International Security and Nonproliferation, March 4, 2009, www.state.gov/t/isn/rls/fs/120017.htm.

18. *The Hague Code of Conduct against Ballistic Missile Proliferation (HCOC)*, HCOC website, N.D., www.hcoc.at/; Camille Grand, "The Hague Code of Conduct: 10 years of Combating Ballistic Proliferation," *Non-Proliferation Monthly*, No. 74 (Special Issue, January 2013), p. 1, www.cesim.fr/documents/onp/eng/74.pdf.

19. Nuclear Suppliers Group, "Public Statement (Final)," Plenary Meeting of the Nuclear Suppliers Group, Prague, Czech Republic, June 13–14, 2013, p. 1, www.nuclearsuppliersgroup.org/A_test/press/NSG%206%20PUBLIC%20STATEMENT%20HOD%20final.pdf.

20. Ibid.

21. Revised versions of the IAEA documents, INFCIRC/254/Part 1 (the trigger list) and INFCIRC/254/Part 2 (the dual-use list) are also available on the NSG website www.nuclearsuppliersgroup.org.

22. Nuclear Suppliers Group, "Updated Control Lists as Agreed by the 2013 Prague Plenary," n.d. www.nuclearsuppliersgroup.org/A_test/01-eng/13-list.php.

23. International Atomic Energy Agency, "Communication Received from Certain Member States Regarding Guidelines for the Export of Nuclear Material, Equipment or Technology," INFCIRC/254, February 1978, www.iaea.org/Publications/Documents/Infcircs/Others/infcirc254.shtml.

24. International Atomic Energy Agency, "Communication Received from the Permanent Mission of the United States of America to the International Atomic Energy Agency regarding Certain Member States' Guidelines for the Export of Nuclear Material, Equipment and Technology," INFCIRC/254/Rev.11/Part 1, November 12, 2012, Paragraph 10, www.nuclearsuppliersgroup.org/A_test/doc/infcirc254r11p1.pdf.
25. Ibid., par. 11.
26. Ibid., par. 4(b).
27. Ian Anthony, "Multilateral Export Controls," *SIPRI Yearbook 2002: Armaments, Disarmament and International Security* (Oxford: Oxford University Press, 2002), pp. 752–755.
28. The White House. "President Announces New Measures to Counter the Threat of WMD," Washington, DC, February 11, 2004, http://georgewbush-whitehouse.archives.gov/news/releases/2004/02/20040211-4.html; Mark Hibbs, *The Future of the Nuclear Suppliers Group* (Washington, DC: Carnegie Endowment for International Peace, 2011), p. 29.
29. Fred McGoldrick, *Limiting Transfers of Enrichment and Reprocessing Technology: Issues, Constraints. Options* (Cambridge, MA: Harvard Kennedy School, May 2011), appendix 2.
30. Hibbs, *Future of the Nuclear Suppliers Group*; Andrea Viski, "The Revised Nuclear Suppliers Group Guidelines: A European Union Perspective," EU Non-proliferation Consortium, *Non-proliferation Papers*, No. 15 (May 2012), www.sipri.org/research/disarmament/eu-consortium/publications/nonproliferation-paper-15.
31. Hibbs, *Future of the Nuclear Suppliers Group*.
32. Argentina, Brazil, ABACC and IAEA, "Agreement between the Republic of Argentina, the Federal Republic of Brazil, the Brazilian–Argentine Agency for Accounting and Control of Nuclear Materials and the International Atomic Energy Agency for the Application of Safeguards (Quadripartite Agreement)," signed December 13, 1991, www.abacc.org.br/?page_id=150&lang=en; Viski, "Revised Nuclear Suppliers Group Guidelines."
33. International Atomic Energy Agency, "Communication received from the Permanent Mission of the Netherlands Regarding Certain Member States' Guidelines for the Export of Nuclear Material, Equipment and Technology," INFCIRC 254/Rev.10/Part I, July 26, 2011, www.iaea.org/Publications/Documents/Infcircs/2011/infcirc254r10p1.pdf.
34. Ibid.
35. Ibid., par. 6.
36. Nuclear Suppliers Group, "Statement on Civil Nuclear Cooperation with India, Extraordinary Plenary Meeting," September 6, 2008, Attachment to IAEA, INFCIRC/734 (Corrected), September 19, 2008, www.iaea.org/Publications/Documents/Infcircs/2008/infcirc734c.pdf; Ian Anthony and Sibylle Bauer, "Controls on Security-Related International Transfers," *SIPRI Yearbook 2009: Armaments, Disarmament and International Security* (Oxford: Oxford University Press, 2009), pp. 459–481.
37. Sibylle Bauer, "Developments in the Nuclear Suppliers Group," *SIPRI Yearbook 2012: Armaments, Disarmament and International Security* (Oxford: Oxford University Press, 2012), pp. 376–386.
38. Siddharth Varadarajan, "NSG Ends India's 'Clean Waiver'," *The Hindu*, June 24, 2011, www.thehindu.com/news/national/nsg-ends-indias-clean-waiver/article2132457.ece; Siddharth Varadarajan, "Challenges Ahead for India's Nuclear Diplomacy," *The Hindu*, November 1, 2011, www.thehindu.com/opinion/columns/siddharth-varadarajan/challenges-ahead-for-indias-nuclear-diplomacy/article2586304.ece.
39. The White House, "Joint Statement by President Obama and Prime Minister Singh of India," November 8, 2010, www.whitehouse.gov/the-press-office/2010/11/08/joint-statement-president-obama-and-prime-minister-singh-india.
40. Daniel Horner, "NSG Revises Rules on Sensitive Exports," *Arms Control Today*, Vol. 41, No. 6 (July/August 2011), pp. 29–30, www.armscontrol.org/act/2011_%2007-08/Nuclear_Suppliers_Group_NSG_Revises_Rules_Sensitive_Exports.
41. Daniel Horner, "NSG Revises List, Continues India Debate," *Arms Control Today*, Vol. 43, No. 6 (July/August 2013, pp. 36–37, www.armscontrol.org/act/2013_0708/NSG-Revises-List-Continues-India-Debate; Daniel Painter, "The Nuclear Suppliers Group at the Crossroads," *The Diplomat*, June 10, 2013, http://thediplomat.com/2013/06/the-nuclear-suppliers-group-at-the-crossroads/.
42. Painter, "Nuclear Suppliers Group at the Crossroads."
43. "Turkey Not against India's Membership in NSG, Turkish FM Says," *Hürriyet Daily News* (Ankara), July 24, 2013, www.hurriyetdailynews.com/turkey-not-against-indias-membership-in-nsg-turkish-fm-says.aspx?pageID=238&nID=51356&NewsCatID=338.

44. Ministry of Foreign Affairs of Pakistan, Strategic Export Control Division, "Pakistan's Engagement with Multilateral Export Control Regimes," February 20, 2013, www.mofa.gov.pk/secdiv/pr-details.php?prID=1431; Shaiq Hussain, "Pakistan Eyeing MTCR Membership, Recognition as Nuclear Power," *Pakistan Today,* February 20, 2013, www.pakistantoday.com.pk/2013/02/20/national/pakistan-eyeing-mtcr-membership-recognition-as-nuclear-power/.

45. Mark Hibbs, "The Breach," *Foreign Policy*, June 4, 2010, www.foreignpolicy.com/articles/2010/06/04/the_breach.

46. Geoff Dyer, Farhan Bokhari, and James Lamont, "China to Build Reactors in Pakistan," *Financial Times*, April 28, 2010, www.ft.com/intl/cms/s/0/cf731b28-52d2-11df-a192-00144feab49a.html #axzz2xVIRMFZm.

47. Sanjeev Miglani, "China Pursues Pakistan Nuclear Deal; Dilemma in West," *Reuters*, December 15, 2010, www.reuters.com/article/2010/12/15/china-paksitan-nuclear-idAFL3E6NF08Q20101215; Hibbs, *Future of the Nuclear Suppliers Group*, pp. 2, 16.

48. Hibbs, *Future of the Nuclear Suppliers Group*, p. 15; Oliver Meier, "Germany Opposes United States on China-Pakistan Nuclear Deal," *Arms Control Now*, Arms Control Association blog, June 21, 2011, http://armscontrolnow.org/2011/06/21/germany-opposes-united-states-on-china-pakistan-nuclear-deal/.

49. Mark Hibbs, "Power Loop: China Provides Nuclear Reactors to Pakistan," *Jane's Intelligence Review*, December 30, 2013, pp. 50–53, http://carnegieendowment.org/email/DC_Comms/img/JIR1401%20F3%20ChinaPak.pdf.

50. Kim Kyu-won, "Successfully Launched Rocket was Retrieved by South Korea and Shows Advancement in NK Capabilities," *Hankyoreh Online*, January 22, 2013, reproduced in Foreign Broadcast Information Service (FBIS).

12

THE COMPREHENSIVE TEST BAN TREATY

Ola Dahlman

The ambition of prohibiting nuclear testing has been with us for more than half a century and the test ban treaty since 1996. The process towards entry into force of the treaty was interrupted when the US Senate rejected the treaty in 1999. This chapter will identify and discuss some of the key issues that are likely to be addressed if and when the treaty is being considered again. Can we maintain confidence in our nuclear-weapon systems without nuclear testing? How can we verify that other states refrain from testing? How would the entry into force of the treaty affect our efforts on nonproliferation and disarmament? Before dealing with those issues I will present a short background on nuclear testing, the test ban negotiations and the treaty.

Nuclear weapon testing

During a period spanning more than five decades, 2,052 nuclear test explosions were carried out, the vast majority related to nuclear weapons. The United States and the former Soviet Union conducted most of them and a summary of the historical testing is presented in Table 12.1. The US and Soviet testing were most intense in the 1960s, when more than one test a week was conducted. In October 1961, the Soviet Union conducted the most powerful explosion ever, having an estimated yield of close to 60Mt or some 4,000 times the yield of the Hiroshima bomb. In 1962, the two countries conducted 175 tests, one every second day. This was at the height of the Cold War and a period of intense development and build-up of nuclear weapons in the two countries. This was also a time when nuclear testing was a public concern. These earlier explosions were carried out in the atmosphere, in all some 517 tests. In 1963, the testing by United Kingdom, the United States, and the Soviet Union went underground, following the signing of the Partial Test Ban Treaty (PTBT). The US and Soviet testing ended following unilateral moratoria in 1990 and 1992 respectively. China and France concluded their testing once the Comprehensive Test Ban Treaty (CTBT) was negotiated in 1996. In May 1998, India announced three tests involving five nuclear devices. In the same month Pakistan announced that it conducted two tests involving six nuclear devices; doubt has been expressed on the number of devices detonated.[1] North Korea has announced three tests in 2006, 2009, and 2013, all observed to be low yield explosions. Israel, assumed to possess nuclear weapons, is not believed to have conducted any test explosions.

Table 12.1 Summary of nuclear testing

State	First test	First thermonuclear test	Number of tests	Number of devices tested
United States	1945	1952	1030	1125
Soviet Union	1949	1955	715	969
United Kingdom	1952	1957	45	45
France	1960	1968	210	210
China	1964	1967	45	45
India	1974		3	6
Pakistan	1998		2	6
North Korea	2006		3	3
Total			2052	2407

Source: Adapted from Ola Dahlman, Svein Mykkeltveit, and Hein Haak, *Nuclear Test Ban: Converting Political Visions to Reality* (Dordrecht, Netherlands: Springer, 2009).

Negotiations

Calls for the cessation of nuclear testing can be traced back more than half a century to the beginning of the nuclear age. Over the years a number of attempts to negotiate an end to nuclear testing failed, usually due to disagreement on verification provisions. However in 1963, the United States, the United Kingdom, and the Soviet Union agreed on the Treaty Banning Nuclear Weapon Tests in the Atmosphere, Outer Space and Under Water, known as the Partial Test Ban Treaty. By excluding underground testing from the ban, the PTBT eliminated the need for agreement on verification provisions. In 1974 the United States and the Soviet Union signed the Threshold Test Ban Treaty (TTBT), prohibiting nuclear weapon tests having a yield exceeding a limit of 150 kilotons TNT or about ten times the yield of the Hiroshima bomb. In 1976 the Peaceful Nuclear Explosion Treaty was signed, extending the 150 kilotons limit to explosions for peaceful purposes. Following lengthy arguments on how to estimate explosion yields, from seismological observations and the conduct of joint verification experiments, verification arrangements were agreed upon and the two treaties were ratified in 1990.[2]

The CTBT was long on the agenda of the Conference on Disarmament in Geneva, and a number of initiatives were taken with no success. In 1976 the Group of Scientific Experts was established to consider how seismological observations could facilitate the monitoring of a CTBT. The Group sustained its work for twenty years and provided a template of a verification system to the political CTBT negotiations that took place from 1994–1996.[3] A comprehensive account of the negotiations is given in *The Final Test*.[4] The United Nations General Assembly adopted the CTBT and it was open to signature on 24 September 1996. As of April 2014, 183 states had signed and 162 had ratified the treaty.[5]

Key provisions of the CTBT

The CTBT prohibits all nuclear test explosions of any yield, by all states and in all environments.[6] It is thus a comprehensive and nondiscriminatory treaty. The treaty provides for the establishment of a Comprehensive Nuclear Test-Ban Treaty Organization (CTBTO) in Vienna to implement its provisions and to support states in verifying compliance with the treaty.

The verification provisions of the CTBT are more far-reaching than those of other treaties. It provides for an International Monitoring System (IMS) comprising 337 stations and laboratories situated in 89 countries around the world. The IMS includes 50 primary and 120 auxiliary seismological stations, 80 stations to collect radionuclide particles, 40 of which shall also be capable of detecting noble gases upon entry into force of the treaty, and 16 radionuclide laboratories that analyze samples of filters from the stations. In addition, 60 infrasound and 11 hydroacoustic stations are to be employed. The data from the IMS stations are transmitted online to an International Data Center (IDC) within the CTBTO in Vienna. The IDC receives, processes, and analyzes the data in an agreed and standardized way and provides the results and data to states parties. In addition to information from the IMS a state can use any technical means of verification available to it.

The treaty also contains provisions for on-site inspections (OSI). A state can request an on-site inspection "to clarify whether a nuclear weapon test explosion or any other nuclear explosion has been carried out." Such a request has to be approved by 30 affirmative votes among the 51 members of the CTBTO Executive Council. An inspection can cover an area of up to 1,000 square kilometers and continue for up to 70 days. The inspection team can use a number of well-specified tools.

In order to enter into force, the CTBT requires the ratification of 44 countries listed in Annex 2 of the treaty. The list include those states which participated in the negotiations in the Conference on Disarmament in 1996 and possessed nuclear power or research reactors at the time of the negotiations. Eight states are still required to ratify before the treaty will enter into force: China, Egypt, Iran, Israel, and the United States have signed but not ratified, the Democratic People's Republic of Korea (DPRK), India, and Pakistan have not signed. A conference on Facilitating the Entry into Force of the CTBT, usually referred to as the Article XIV conference, is held bi-annually among the states that have signed the treaty. The conference in September 2013 at the United Nations in New York urged "all remaining States, especially those whose signatures and ratifications are necessary for the entry into force of the Treaty, to take individual initiatives to sign and ratify the Treaty without delay in order to achieve its earliest entry into force."[7]

Verification

Verification of compliance with the CTBT rests with the states parties. It is a political process based on a broad range of verification tools that have improved greatly over the last decade. The CTBT identifies three steps in the verification procedure: to monitor for evidence of clandestine tests, to engage in a consultation and clarification process to resolve issues of concern, and to request and conduct OSIs for further clarification. Should a clandestine activity be identified, the actions to be taken should be addressed on a case by case basis.

To verify the treaty a state makes an overall assessment whether or not other states are in compliance with the provisions of the treaty. Such an assessment is based on the political situation, the relations among the countries concerned, the issue at hand, and the verification information and data available. The less trust and confidence there are among states, the greater the need for verification. In assessing its need to verify the CTBT, a state will make a political judgment on where its main concern is, and different States may well come to different conclusions. A country's political will and its technical ability to develop a nuclear explosive device are key elements in such an assessment. Given its political priorities and the constraints on spreading nuclear weapons imposed by the Treaty on the Nonproliferation of Nuclear Weapons (NPT), it is likely that a state sees the need to focus its verification efforts primarily on a very limited number of other states. Conditions may change over time which may compel a state to reassess its verification priorities.

The adequacy of verification is in the eyes of the beholder, as there is no objective way of making a generally applicable assessment of what constitutes "adequate" verification. States might well have different requirements depending on their security situation. Several attempts have been made to address the adequacy of a verification regime. During Senate ratification of the 1988 Intermediate-range Nuclear Forces Treaty (INF), Ambassador Paul Nitze defined effective verification as follows: "if the other side moves beyond the limits of the treaty in any militarily significant way, we would be able to detect such violations in time to respond effect-ively and thereby deny the other side the benefit of the violation."[8] This definition underlines the relation between verification and the overarching security situation. It recognizes that few, if any, verification systems are able to detect a minor violation of a treaty or an agreement; there is always a minimum capability. Verification measures should thus on the one hand inspire confidence that no clandestine activities will go undetected, and on the other hand deter such activities. Also judgments on the deterrence value of a certain verification regime are subject-ive and some states might be more difficult to deter than other.

It is surprising that states have judged the need for verification differently in different treaties. The CTBT verification provisions stand in contrast to those of other multilateral disar-mament treaties such as the Biological Weapons Convention (BWC).[9] The BWC, established to cope with one of the most serious threats to the world, has no verification provisions, but refers compliance issues to individual states and to the United Nations Security Council. It is clearly difficult to verify the existence or absence of biological material that can be used for weapons or terrorist purposes, and at the same time not interfere severely with civilian indus-trial activities. Nuclear explosions, the most powerful man-made events on earth, are, however, much easier to detect. So, the CTBT extensive verification measures are there because there is an observable target, but verification has been a key issue ever since the test-ban discussions started.

Comparing the CTBT and the NPT, one might wonder why the Technical Secretariat (TS) of the CTBTO is given a more limited mandate than that of the IAEA. The TS is responsible for the installation and operation of the IMS stations and the International Data Center (IDC). The IDC receives and analyzes IMS data, following agreed procedures, and reports data and results to states parties. The TS was not given the responsibility to make an assessment of the observed events for good reason – the seismic events alone exceed 100 per day and a fair number of those would not be easily classified as having a natural origin from the observed signals alone. If the task to clarify the origin of events was to be given to an international organ-ization that has to act with impartiality and treat all observed events in all countries in the same way, geophysical events around the globe would need to be investigated to an extent that would make the system break down. The assessment of observations must be made in a political context and this can be done only by states, unless an international organization is given a far-reaching political mandate. This responsibility makes it important for countries to acquire expertise regarding verification measures and not expect the TS to provide answers about compliance or possible noncompliance.

Monitoring

A state may develop a national monitoring strategy, reflecting its security concern and its engagement in nuclear-weapon issues. Some countries are likely to show a high ambition while others may do very little or nothing. For political and security reasons, a state is likely to focus its attention on one or a few states of particular concern. It is also likely to focus on tests underground, as tests in the atmosphere or under water are most unlikely. The last atmospheric test took place in 1980 and very few underwater explosions have ever taken place. Explosions in these two media would hardly go undetected by IMS and satellite observations, in particular given that a large amount of radioactivity will be released into the atmosphere. The following discussion will thus focus on the monitoring of underground explosions.

The IMS was created to give, as far as possible, equal coverage and monitoring capability around the globe. It should provide all state parties with reliable, authenticated information and data to facilitate their monitoring of the CTBT. The IMS is living up to that goal. As of April 2014, 282 of the 321 IMS stations and 14 of the 16 radionuclide laboratories specified in the treaty had been installed.[10] The IMS is thus almost fully operational, proving high quality data and monitoring capabilities that in many cases surpass what was expected. The IMS global networks of radionuclide, infrasound, and hydroacoustics stations are unique and few such stations exist outside the IMS. These networks provide data that no country can gain access to on its own.

Under the CTBT, data and information produced by the IMS will have a number of inherent advantages. The IMS consists of high quality stations that are built and certified to specifications agreed to by the PrepCom. This gives IMS data high credibility that is further increased as the stations are to be operated by the Technical Secretariat of the CTBTO in a fully transparent way, in cooperation with the states parties hosting the stations. Data are also authenticated to ensure that they are not manipulated when sent from stations to the TS. IMS data are also convenient for states to use, as all parties to the treaty will be able to get any observations from all IMS stations around the world. Such a common data base may also facilitate a dialogue among countries on any observed event.

The IMS seismological stations are among the most capable. This especially applies to the array stations, which hardly exist outside the IMS. The IMS network has, in the northern hemisphere, a 90 percent detection probability of around magnitude 3.5, corresponding to a fully coupled explosion in hard rock of 0.1–0.2 kt.[11] The corresponding threshold at 10 percent probability is around magnitude 3, giving a considerable deterrence at yields of around 0.05 kt. Corresponding capabilities in the southern hemisphere are about 0.5 magnitude unit higher, corresponding to a factor of three in yield.

Yet the IMS seismic network constitutes only a small part of the total number of seismological stations deployed worldwide. Those seismological stations outside the IMS network, taken together, can provide detection and location capabilities significantly beyond those of the IMS in many parts of the world. The use also of data from stations at regional and local distances can achieve detection capabilities down to magnitude 2, corresponding to explosion yields of 5–10 tons.[12] Regional variations in transmission properties of the earth and the availability of sensitive seismic stations might give different capabilities.

The location is a critical parameter for the further assessment of an event. It will determine in which country and geophysical structure an event occurs and it is a critical input to deciding on an inspection area, should an on-site inspection be requested. There are two kinds of uncertainties in locating events: a statistical uncertainty, depending on observational errors, the number of observing stations, and their distribution around the event; and a systematic bias caused by differences between the velocity model used in the computations and the actual seismic wave velocities.

Comparing locations of events observed by the IMS and reported by the PTS, with those of reference events having an uncertainty of less than 5 km, Bergman and Engdahl found a mean difference of 22 km.[13] Fifty percent of the PTS events differ from the reference events by

16.5 km or less, which means that half of the events have an uncertainty of the order of the maximum on-site inspection area of 1,000 square km, corresponding to a circular area with a radius of 18 km. Using also local stations and calibrated travel times can reduced the uncertainty to below 10 km.[14]

Improving the seismological capability is not only a question of acquiring high-quality data from an increased number of stations; it is also a question of improving on the data analysis. Dramatic developments in data mining and exploitation have created the tools needed for a new and integrated approach to analyzing seismological observations.[15] A new paradigm for data analysis can be established where observed waveform data from selected stations are analyzed together in an integrated process to detect and locate the events and to clarify if they are of natural origin. In such an integrated procedure new observations will be assessed in relation to earlier events in the region, with well-established source parameters. This technique can lower detection thresholds and substantially improve the location accuracy by reducing systematic bias and achieve high location accuracies needed as a basis for possible OSI requests. Such an integrated analysis will also be most valuable in establishing if an observed event is of natural origin or if it needs further clarification.

Seismic signals from an underground explosion can be reduced if a test is conducted in a large cavity.[16] Experience with such decoupling techniques is limited, however, to only two nuclear explosions of low yields in cavities generated by substantially larger nuclear explosions. During an explosion in a shaft or a bore hole, the high pressure and temperature create a cavity with glazed surface that helps contain the radioactive material, including the radioactive noble gases. In a decoupled explosion, the very purpose is to reduce the pressure on the wall and in a mined cavity no glazed surface will be formed. This will increase the likelihood that radionuclide gases might escape. Adding these uncertainties to the logistical difficulties of creating a suitable cavity without being detected, should make decoupling a less attractive scenario for a potential evader.

In a nuclear explosion, an enormous amount of xenon is created: some 15–20 percent of the atoms that fission create a radioactive xenon atom at some stage. It is expected that only a small fraction of the xenon generated will be released, and efforts can be made to reduce this amount and even prevent leakage by a carefully contained explosion environment; it is thus hard to predict the detection capability. Given the many uncertainties it is, however, hard for the tester to prevent or predict xenon leaks. The very nature of this unpredictability is thus an important deterrence feature.

The development in radionuclide xenon monitoring is most dramatic since the signing of the CTBT. By April 2014, xenon detection equipment had been installed at 30 out of the 40 radionuclide monitoring stations that were initially planned to make noble gas measurements in addition to collecting radioactive particles.[17] Adding noble gas capability to the remaining stations of the radionuclide network will be considered at the first annual session of the conference of the states parties.

The IMS xenon network provides monitoring and deterrence capability down to low yields. The sensitivity of the xenon network, as of any other system, is limited by the operational performance of the individual stations, the extent of the network, and the background noise. There is a potential to increase the capability of the individual stations by making them more robust to reduce downtime, and to increase the sensitivity by replacing existing sensors with new and more sensitive ones. The xenon background is essentially generated by a few medical isotope production facilities. To limit or stop these releases at the facilities is feasible and would significantly increase the ability to detect weak xenon releases, and discussions with these industries have been initiated.

The possibility for states to use satellite observations to monitor the CTBT, as part of their national technical means, has increased significantly since the treaty was negotiated. This applies both to optical and radar systems. The optical systems have today a spatial resolution of one meter or even better; for radar systems the resolution is about 10 meters. Radar systems have night and all weather capability and also the ability to detect small deformations of the earth's surface at the cm scale. The number of observational satellites has increased and this gives good coverage with repeated observations of a scene within one or two days. The most dramatic development is that data from all those open systems are readily available at low cost. Computer software is also available to analyze the large amounts of data involved and to identify changes over time in a selected area. Satellite observations have developed into a valuable tool for states to use when monitoring limited areas of interest or to analyze a particular event.

The capabilities of the CTBT monitoring system were tested during three underground nuclear explosions conducted and announced by the DPRK on October 9, 2006, May 25, 2009, and February 12, 2013. All three explosions were detected at a fairly large number of seismological stations, the one in 2013 at more than 100, and located to within a few kilometers of each other. The entrance to the test tunnel can be observed on satellite photos.[18] The relative yields of the explosions, which can be estimated with less uncertainty than the absolute yields, were 1, 5 and 15 for the 2006, 2009 and the 2013 explosion respectively. These numbers may also be a good first estimate of the yields in kt for the three explosions. Radionuclide xenon observations were reported from the 2006 and 2013 explosions but not from the one in 2009, illustrating that radionuclide releases are unpredictable.[19]

Because a country is most likely interested in monitoring only a limited number of other countries and specific areas, it can then embark on what may be called precision monitoring.[20] The interest of monitoring DPRK after its first test is a good example. The monitoring state would then focus all effort and monitoring assets at its disposal on such limited areas and achieve greatly enhanced capabilities in those areas. Data provided by the IMS are one element; data from selected scientific stations, mainly seismological, are another. In addition, a country can use satellite observations and information obtained by open sources and national technical means. Precision monitoring would advance the confidence in the monitoring by significantly improving the detection and location capabilities and the ability to identify the nature of observed events.

The seismological dimension of precision monitoring will be based on data from carefully selected stations and on improved data analysis technique. Data will be selected from stations that have demonstrated a good capability to observe events in the selected area and provide a good azimuthal coverage of the area. These could be IMS stations, both primary and auxiliary, and also stations that have been established and operated for scientific purposes, some of them most likely at close distance from the area or region of interest. To embark on precision monitoring, a state would need to establish its own analysis capability, and the dramatic development in data mining would be particularly suitable to apply to monitoring of limited areas.

On-site inspections

The on-site inspection regime provides countries a powerful tool to detect and deter violations of the CTBT. The regime has strong political, technical, and operational elements and provides for intrusive inspection of an area of 1,000 square kilometers in another state party. The provisions of an OSI are spelled out in great detail in the treaty. It is worth noting that a state can use whatever means at its disposal to monitor the CTBT, but an OSI can only be initiated within the frame of the treaty provisions, and when approved by the Executive Council (EC) of the CTBTO.

To gain sufficient support for an affirmative vote, a country requesting an OSI to clarify whether a nuclear-weapon test explosion has been carried out must present credible evidence to the EC of the CTBTO in support of its request. The EC is required to approve a request for an OSI by at least 30 out of 51 votes. The EC is composed of a specified number of states parties from six geographical regions. The members are selected within each group, taking into account their technical engagement and contributions to the annual budget. This means that in practice the five nuclear weapon states will always be members of the EC. Concern has sometimes been expressed that it might be difficult to obtain the 30 votes needed to go ahead with an OSI, as it is difficult to foresee how discussion and decision-making in the EC may develop. It might be useful for states to make some joint effort to consider how the processes in the EC may develop.

For an OSI to be successful, it is essential that the triggering event is located with high accuracy and thus provide a good basis for selecting an inspection area that covers the site of the event. The more precisely the triggering event is located, the greater the probability that the inspection will be successful. An event location with a small uncertainty matched with high resolution satellite photos will provide a good basis to define not only an inspection area but also to establish an initial inspection plan. Given all the inspection tools and the substantial inspection time, of up to 70 days, it is highly unlikely that all the evidence of a testing operation can be concealed if the inspection team can focus on a small area that contains the explosion.[21] The fact that a clandestine test is likely to be detected during an OSI should serve as a strong deterrent.

A number of procedures and techniques can be applied during an OSI to search not only for traces of an explosion, but also of the testing operation. The techniques include, among others, visual inspections from over-flights and observations on the ground; on-site measurements of possible seismic "aftershocks" associated with the cavity region, observation of xenon and other nuclear products, and a number of geophysical measurements. Once a likely explosion site has been located, drilling can be conducted after EC approval, to confirm the existence of an explosion cavity and to take radionuclide samples from it.

The PrepCom, PTS, and states have conducted a lot of work to prepare for an OSI, including drafting an operational manual for the conduct of an OSI and a list of equipment to be used during an OSI. These two documents shall be adopted by the first Conference of the States Parties. A month-long exercise was carried out in Kazakhstan in 2008,[22] which showed that the logistics concept has to be further developed, drawing inter alias on the wealth of experience available on mobile laboratories for other applications. A systemic approach to an OSI, where the different technologies are applied in an optimal way, taking into account conditions on the ground, should be further developed to support the progress of an inspection. Preparations for a new integrated exercise to be conducted in 2014 are in progress.[23]

The CTBT and the safety, security, and reliability of nuclear weapons

The five recognized nuclear-weapon states have for more than two decades refrained from nuclear testing; are their nuclear weapons still safe, secure and reliable? This is an issue that has been discussed publicly for a long time in the United States, and much less in the other nuclear-weapon states. In its report the US Academy Committee notes that

> The Nuclear Weapon States have been able to maintain their nuclear-weapon programs under a nuclear-explosion test moratorium and are likely to be able to make nuclear weapons modifications that fall within the design range of their test experience without resorting to nuclear explosion testing.[24]

Three states, France, the United Kingdom, and Russia, ratified the treaty more than ten years ago, a clear demonstration of the confidence they have in their stockpiles.

The United States has for more than ten years operated a science-based stockpile steward-ship program (SSP), with a yearly budget of around $7 billion, to ensure its confidence in the active nuclear weapon stockpile.[25] This program has a number of components including: a surveillance program to carefully examine the individual components of deployed warheads; an experimental research program to improve the understanding of the explosion process for the different warheads; and a number of unique research facilities established to study the behavior of material during conditions similar to those in a nuclear explosion. Such data are important input to the advanced simulation and computing programs, where explosions are simulated in 3-dimensions and in great detail. The dramatic increase in computer capabilities has greatly facilitated the development of such programs, and some of the worlds most power-ful computers are also found at nuclear weapon research institutions. Tom D'Agostino, then administrator of the National Nuclear Security Administration (NNSA), described the success of the SSP:

> The SSP over the past decade has provided improved scientific and analytic tools, including advanced supercomputer simulation and sophisticated experimental capa-bilities, which were not available to the previous generation of designers/engineers. … We know more about the complex issues of nuclear weapons performance today than we ever did during the period of nuclear testing.[26]

The stewardship program also contains life-extension programs to maintain existing warheads in operational conditions for a prolonged period of time.

In a statement on the Nuclear Posture Review (NPR) the directors of the three US nuclear weapon laboratories stated that

> We believe that the approach outlined in the NPR, which excludes further nuclear testing and includes the full range of life extension options (refurbishment of existing warheads, reuse of nuclear components from different warheads and replacement of nuclear components based on previously tested designs), provides the necessary tech-nical flexibility to manage the nuclear stockpile into the future with an acceptable level of risk.[27]

Less is publicly known about similar programs in the other nuclear-weapon states, but they are most likely to have similar activities. The United Kingdom and France have, on a smaller scale, programs similar to the US Stewardship program.[28] Within the frame of a long term agreement on Defense and Security the two countries have established a joint program "to collaborate in the technology associated with nuclear stockpile stewardship in support of our respective inde-pendent nuclear deterrent capabilities."[29] The joint program "will assist both countries in maintaining the safety and reliability of their respective nuclear stockpiles and will improve expertise in countering nuclear terrorism."[30]

Russian President Dmitry Medvedev noted that "Under the global ban on nuclear tests, we can only use computer-assisted simulations to ensure the reliability of Russia's nuclear deter-rent."[31] The Russian nuclear program also includes an upgrade of experimental testing facilities.[32]

Former Chinese president Hu Jintao has emphasized that China's modernization program is designed to ensure that the "nuclear deterrent" is "safe, reliable, and effective" under "any" circumstance. Investment in modernization will be limited at very low level, and will be conducted under the CTBT regime.[33] China's official web page states that

> China has strictly abided by its commitment to a moratorium on nuclear testing and has actively participated in the work of the Preparatory Commission of the Comprehensive Nuclear Test Ban Treaty Organization, and is steadily preparing for the national implementation of the Treaty.[34]

The CTBT and nonproliferation

The CTBT has been linked to the NPT since the latter was negotiated in 1968.[35] The NPT is considered the cornerstone of the international nonproliferation regime. In article VI of NPT the nuclear-weapon states are obliged to "pursue negotiations in good faith on effective measures relating to cessation of the nuclear arms race at an early date and to nuclear disarmament, and on a treaty on general and complete disarmament under strict and effective international control." The CTBT was included in the "13 Steps" to implement article VI of the NPT that were encompassed in the final document of the 2000 Review Conference. The first step was the "urgency of signatures and ratifications, without delay and without conditions," to achieve the early entry into force of the CTBT.[36]

What is the reality of this linkage? In what ways is the CTBT contributing to nuclear disarmament and nonproliferation? The treaty and the process towards it increased the mutual confidence among the states, in particular between the nuclear weapon states. The fact that some countries block the entry into force of the treaty might have deteriorated this confidence. The US NPR notes that entry into force of the Comprehensive Nuclear Test Ban Treaty, and negotiation of a verifiable Fissile Material Cutoff Treaty are means to strengthening our ability to mobilize broad international support for the measures needed to reinforce the nonproliferation regime

The CTBT makes it more difficult for new states to acquire nuclear weapons and it limits the technical developments of new generations of nuclear weapons. The extensive verification arrangements demonstrate that it is possible to agree on and implement far reaching monitoring on a global scale and intrusive on-site inspection arrangements. The implementation of the extensive global monitoring system, that is now operational, has engaged states in a long-term cooperation. The verification provision and the way they were developed, in close cooperation with the scientific community, could be a good example for further agreements.

Entry into force?

The treaty has still not entered into force 16 years after it was open for signature. As noted above, before the CTBT can enter into force, 44 countries specified in an annex to the treaty must ratify, but eight have not yet done so. Why has the process towards entry into force stalled, and what can be done to get it moving again? The process was no doubt derailed in Washington when the US Senate on October 13, 1999 rejected the treaty. It is interesting to note that Russia ratified the treaty in June 2000, despite the US rejection.

The treaty is still in limbo. What are the prospects of entry into force? As discussed above, states should be more confident to join the treaty today than they might have been a decade and a half ago. Verification has developed most significantly and given states the possibility to monitor areas of concern down to levels that may be a 100 times lower than those expected when the treaty was opened for signature. States will benefit from an operational CTBTO international monitoring system, including stations to detect noble gases. In addition, states can use an increasing amount of additional observations from satellites and from a multitude of stations operated for other purposes. The readiness to conduct an on-site inspection has significantly improved. With those tools, states should be able to meet most far-reaching verification concerns.

The five recognized nuclear-weapon states have all been maintaining their nuclear weapons without testing for more than one and a half decades. They have all found their way to maintain their nuclear weapons safe, secure, and reliable. There has been no discussion anywhere of the need to go back to nuclear testing. On the contrary, in the United States – a country where this discussion has been public – responsible authorities have affirmed confidence in the US nuclear stockpile on a yearly basis.

Nuclear testing belongs to history, so why are we not able to bring the treaty into force? To maintain the credibility of international treaties is of key importance to the international community and to relations among states. The firm international reaction to the use of chemical weapons in Syria, and the swift agreement to destroy those weapons, is a good example of the desire to preserve the credibility of the Chemical Weapon Convention and the 1925 Geneva Protocol.[37] To maintain the credibility of the CTBT, that a large number of states negotiated and have ratified and some more have signed, is equally essential and a responsibility for all stated involved in the process. We risk deteriorating the credibility of the CTBT and the international treaty regime.

What is the likelihood that the treaty will enter into force any time soon? Nobody has that crystal ball. The treaty was derailed in Washington; it is likely that it has to be put back on the international agenda in Washington. President Obama has on many occasions declared that ratifying the CTBT is high on his nuclear disarmament agenda.[38] The Nuclear Posture Review report also states that "the United States will not conduct nuclear testing and will pursue ratification and entry into force of the Comprehensive Nuclear Test Ban Treaty."[39] The fate of the treaty, however, lies in the hands of the US Senate. At the time of writing, the US Congress is deeply involved in a self-defeating activity of inflicting severe damage to itself and the US society over financial issues. This illustrates that politics often is very local, far from logical, and unpredictable. So what may happen with the treaty in Washington is anyone's guess.

Another and more encouraging event is happening these very days: a first meeting in Geneva between high representatives from the new Iranian government and the five nuclear-weapon states and Germany on Iran's nuclear program. Even if nothing specific is publicly known at this time, the initial reports suggest constructive meetings and proposals in a good atmosphere. Ratifying the CTBT might be one constructive step that Iran could take to build confidence and to demonstrate that it has no nuclear-weapon ambitions. This may influence the attitude of Egypt and Israel, whose ratifications are also needed. Unlikely as it may sound, could the process towards entry into force of the CTBT restart in Tehran?

Notes

1. See Praful Bidwai and Achin Vanaik, *New Nukes: India, Pakistan and Global Disarmament* (New York: Olive Branch Press, 2000).
2. Lynn R. Sykes and Göran Ekström, "Comparison of Seismic and Hydrodynamic Yield Determinations for the Soviet Joint Verification Experiment of 1988," *Proceedings of the National Academy of Science USA*, Vol. 86, No. 10 (May 1989), pp. 3456–3460, www.pnas.org/content/86/10/3456.full.pdf+html.

3. Ola Dahlman, Svein Mykkeltveit, and Hein Haak, *Nuclear Test Ban: Converting Political Visions to Reality* (Dordrecht, Netherlands: Springer, 2009).

4. Jaap Ramaker, Jenifer Mackby, Peter D. Marshall, and Robert Geil, *The Final Test: A History of the Comprehensive Nuclear Test Ban Treaty Negotiations* (Vienna: The Provisional Technical Secretariat of the Preparatory Commission for the Comprehensive Nuclear Test-Ban Treaty Organization, 2003).

5. Comprehensive Nuclear Test-Ban Treaty Organization, Preparatory Commission, "Status of Signature and Ratification," CTBTO, www.ctbto.org/the-treaty/status-of-signature-and-ratification (accessed, April 14, 2014).

6. Comprehensive Nuclear Test-Ban Treaty Organization, Preparatory Commission, "Comprehensive Nuclear Test-Ban Treaty," CTBTO, www.ctbto.org/the-treaty/.

7. Comprehensive Nuclear Test-Ban Treaty Organization, Preparatory Commission, "Final Declaration and Measures to Promote the Entry into Force of the Comprehensive Nuclear-Test-Ban Treaty," report from the Conference on Facilitating the Entry into Force of the Comprehensive Nuclear-Test-Ban Treaty, New York, September 2013, www.ctbto.org/fileadmin/user_upload/Art_14_2013/Statements/Final_Declaration.pdf.

8. Paul H. Nitze, "The INF Treaty," statement before US Congress, Senate Committee on Foreign Relations, Senate Hearing 100-522, part 1, 100th Congress, 2nd Session, 1988, p. 289, http://babel.hathitrust.org/cgi/pt?id=mdp.39015014752847;view=1up;seq=295.

9. United Nations Office for Disarmament Affairs, "Convention on the Prohibition of the Development, Production and Stockpiling of Bacteriological (Biological) and Toxin Weapons and Their Destruction," signed April, 10, 1972, www.un.org/disarmament/WMD/Bio/.

10. Comprehensive Nuclear Test-Ban Treaty Organization, Preparatory Commission, "International Monitoring System," 2013, www.ctbto.org/map/#ims.

11. National Research Council of the National Academies, *The Comprehensive Nuclear Test Ban Treaty: Technical issues for the United States* (Washington, DC: The National Academies Press, 2012).

12. Ibid.; Committee on Technical Issues Related to Ratification of the Comprehensive Nuclear Test Ban Treaty for the National Academy of Sciences, *Technical Issues Related to the Comprehensive Nuclear Test Ban Treaty* (Washington, DC: National Academy of Sciences, 2002), www.nap.edu/openbook.php?isbn=0309085063; Tormod Kvaerna, Frode Ringdahl, Johannes Schweitzer, and Lyla Taylor, "Optimized Seismic Threshold Monitoring Part 1: Regional Processing," *Pure and Applied Geophysics,* Vol. 159, No. 5 (March 2002), pp. 969–987.

13. Eric A. Bergman and E. Robert Engdahl, "Analysis of the Location Capability of the International Monitoring System," poster presented at the ISS09 Conference, International Scientific Studies Project, Seismo-03/I section, Vienna, Austria, June 10–12, 2009, www.ctbto.org/fileadmin/user_upload/ISS_2009/Poster/SEISMO-03I%20%28US%29%20-%20Eric_Bergman%20and%20ER_Engdahl%20%28location%29.pdf.

14. Ola Dahlman, Jenifer Mackby, Svein Mykkeltveit, and Hein Haak, *Detect and Deter: Can States Verify the Nuclear Test Ban?* (Dordrecht, Netherlands: Springer, 2011).

15. Heidi Kuzma and Sheila Vaidya, "Data Mining," *Science for Security*, report from the International Scientific Studies Conference, Vienna, Austria, June 10–12, 2009, pp. 47–53, www.ctbto.org/fileadmin/user_upload/pdf/ISS_Publication/Data_Mining_47-52.pdf.

16. J.L. Stevens, J.R. Murphy, N. Rimer, "Seismic Source Characteristics of Cavity Decoupled Explosions in Salt and Tuff," *Bulletin of the Seismological Society of America*, Vol. 81, No. 4 (August 1991), pp. 1272–1291.

17. CTBTO, "International Monitoring System."

18. David Albright and Paul Brannan. "North Korean Site After Nuclear Test," ISIS Imagery Brief, The Institute for Science and International Security, October 17, 2006, http://isis-online.org/uploads/isis-reports/documents/dprktestbrief17october2006.pdf.

19. A number of publications contain further information on the tests. See CBTBO, Preparatory Commission, "Detection of Radioactive Gases Consistent with North Korean Test Underlines Strength of CTBTO Monitoring System," *CTBTO Spectrum*, No. 20 (July 2013), p. 26, www.ctbto.org/fileadmin/user_upload/pdf/Spectrum/2013/Spectrum20_p26.pdf; Paul Richards, "Seismic Detective Work: CTBTO Monitoring System 'Very Effective' in Detecting North Korea's Third Nuclear Test." *CTBTO Spectrum*, No. 20 (July, 2013), pp. 22–25; A. Ringbom, K. Elmgren, K. Lindh, J. Peterson, T. Bowyer, J Hayes, J. McIntyre, M. Panisko, and R. Williams, "Measurements of Radioxenon in Ground Level Air in South Korea Following the Claimed Nuclear Test in North Korea on October 9, 2006," poster presented at ISS09 Conference, Vienna, Austria, June 10–12 2009,

www.ctbto.org/fileadmin/user_upload/ISS_2009/Poster/RN-26D%20%28Sweden%29%20-%20Anders_Ringbom%20etal.pdf; Jonathan Medalia, "North Korea's 2009 Nuclear Test: Containment, Monitoring Implications," Congressional Research Service, November 24, 2010, www.fas.org/sgp/crs/nuke/R41160.pdf; Jack Murphy, Ben Kohl, Jeff Stevens, Joe Bennett, and H.G. Israelsson, "Exploitation of the IMS and Other Data for a Comprehensive, Advanced Analysis of the North Korean Nuclear Tests," poster, CTBTO website, www.ctbto.org/fileadmin/user_upload/SandT_2011/posters/T2P21%20B_Kohl%20Exploitation%20of%20the%20IMS%20and%20other%20data%20for%20a%20comprehensive,%20advanced%20analysis%20of%20the%20North%20Korean%20nuclear%20tests.pdf.

20. Dahlman *et al.*, *Detect and Deter*.
21. National Research Council of the National Academies, *The Comprehensive Nuclear Test Ban Treaty*.
22. CTBTO Preparatory Commission, "Report on the Conduct of the 2008 Integrated Field Exercise," CTBT/PTS/INF.1021, August 4, 2009.
23. CTBTO Preparatory Commission, "Concept for the Preparation and Conduct of the Next Integrated Field Exercise," CTBT/PTS/INF 1105, January 27, 2011.
24. National Academy of Sciences, *Technical Issues*.
25. Jonathan Medalia, "Comprehensive Nuclear-Test-Ban Treaty: Background and Current Developments," Congressional Research Service, June 10, 2013, www.fas.org/sgp/crs/nuke/RL33548.pdf; United States Department of Defense, *Nuclear Weapons Stockpile Stewardship and Management Plan (for Fiscal Year 2014),* http://nnsa.energy.gov/ourmission/managingthestockpile/ssmp; United States Department of Energy and National Nuclear Security Administration, "Nuclear Test Readiness, Warheads, Nuclear Security, Workforce and Engineering" (August 1, 2013); National Research Council of the National Academies, *The Comprehensive Nuclear Test Ban Treaty*; United States Department of Defense, "The Nuclear Posture Review Report," Washington, DC, April 2010, www.defense.gov/npr/docs/2010%20nuclear%20posture%20review%20report.pdf.
26. Thomas P. D'Agostino, Testimony on "US Strategic Posture" before the House Armed Services Subcommittee, US House of Representatives, February 27, 2008, http://nnsa.energy.gov/mediaroom/congressionaltestimony/02.27.08.
27. Tom Hunter, Michael Anastasio, and Georde Miller, "Tri-Lab Director's Joint Statement on the Nuclear Posture Review," Sandia National Laboratories Press Release, April 9, 2010, https://share.sandia.gov/news/resources/news_releases/tri-lab-directors'-statement-on-the-nuclear-posture-review/#.U0v7utyXSZ8.
28. Peter Burt, "UK-France Nuclear Co-operation: The 'Teutates' Project," presentation at Non-Proliferation Treaty PrepCom Meeting, April 23, 2013, http://nuclearinfo.org/sites/default/files/01%20NIS%20NPT%20presentation%20on%20Teutates%20project%20230413_0.pdf.
29. Government of United Kingdom. Office of the Prime Minister, "UK–France Summit 2010 Declaration on Defence and Security Co-operation," Press Release, November 2, 2010, www.gov.uk/government/news/uk-france-summit-2010-declaration-on-defence-and-security-co-operation.
30. Burt, "UK-France Nuclear Co-operation."
31. *Global Security Newswire,* "Russia to Use Supercomputers to Test Viability of Nuclear Arsenal," July 23, 2009, http://gsn.nti.org/gsn/nw_20090723_5131.php.
32. "Sarov and Snezhinsk Raised the Bar: The Prime Minister Signed an Addendum to the Long-Term Program of Development of the Nuclear Weapons Complex," *Perspective* (Russia), October 6, 2010, www.rg.ru/2010/06/10/atom.html.
33. Hui Zhang, "China's Nuclear Weapons Modernization: Intentions, Drivers, and Trends," Presentation, Institute for Nuclear Materials Management, 53rd Annual Meeting, Orlando, July 15, 2012, http://belfercenter.ksg.harvard.edu/files/ChinaNuclearModernization-hzhang.pdf.
34. Government of the People's Republic of China, "China's National Defense in 2010," March 2011, http://english.gov.cn/official/2011-03/31/content_1835499.htm.
35. United Nations Office for Disarmament Affairs, "Treaty on Non-Proliferation of Nuclear Weapons (NPT)," New York, July 1, 1968, www.un.org/disarmament/WMD/Nuclear/NPTtext.shtml.
36. United Nations Office for Disarmament Affairs, "Final Report of the 2000 Review Conference," report from the 2000 Review Conference of the Parties to the Treaty on the Non-Proliferation of Nuclear Weapons, New York, April 24–May 19, 2000, Part I, p. 14, www.un.org/disarmament/WMD/Nuclear/2000-NPT/2000NPTDocs.shtml.
37. For the texts of these documents, see Organization for the Prohibition of Chemical Weapons, "Convention on the Prohibition of the Development, Production, Stockpiling and Use of Chemical

Weapons and on their Destruction (Chemical Weapons Convention)," August 31, 1994, www.opcw.org/chemical-weapons-convention/; and United Nations, "Protocol for the Prohibition of the Use in War of Asphyxiating, Poisonous or Other Gases, and of Bacteriological Methods of Warfare," Geneva, June 17, 1925, www.un.org/disarmament/WMD/Bio/pdf/Status_Protocol.pdf.

38. Barack Obama, "Remarks by President Barack Obama, Hradcany Square, Prague, Czech Republic," The White House, Office of the Press Secretary, April 5, 2009, www.whitehouse.gov/the_press_office/Remarks-By-President-Barack-Obama-In-Prague-As-Delivered.

39. United States Department of Defense, "Nuclear Posture Review."

13

A NEW PATH FORWARD FOR THE CTBT

C. Paul Robinson

The Nuclear Testing Talks (NTT) between the United States and the Soviet Union in Geneva, Switzerland, stretched over three years, from late 1987 through 1990, and involved a re-negotiation of the verification provisions for the threshold test limitation treaties – the "Threshold Test Ban Treaty" (or TTBT) and the "Peaceful Nuclear Explosions Treaty" (PNET), originally negotiated in the mid-1970s.[1] Within that limited scope, the first task for negotiators was to plan and agree on details to cooperate in carrying out a Joint Verification Experiment (JVE), allowing teams from each side to perform direct on-site measurements of the yield of a nuclear test at a test site within the other's territory. Then, a month later, the roles were reversed, with a test detonated by the other side at their test site, with yield measurements undertaken by both sides. The delegations, plus key participants in these nuclear tests, next worked together in Geneva to exchange the JVE data and assess the overall performance of the measurements proposed for use in verifying the yields of subsequent nuclear tests. Finally, the rules for inspectors and equipment in traveling and operating in the other's territory, with rights, prohibitions, and obligations for their security were carefully enumerated.

When agreement was reached on which yield measurements could be used, detailed treaty language was negotiated for new Verification Protocols, to replace the existing ones. These included full descriptions of the rights to verify, with procedures to be employed to ensure effective verification of the two previously negotiated treaties.

The NTT process provided valuable perspectives on how to achieve better agreements. The delegations had begun with strong suspicions of each other's motives and intentions – perhaps a conditioned response from being on opposite sides in the Cold War. These tensions lessened considerably as a result of the cooperative work products that were produced. The primary purpose was unaltered – to achieve agreements that could build long-term confidence and better relations between the United States and the Soviet Union, rather than continuing to cause bitter debates over compliance. Indeed, the negotiations were able to complete new Verification Protocols, which along with their treaties, were ratified unanimously by the US Senate (on September 25, 1990) and by the Duma of the Russian Federation (on October 9, 1990). After completing an initial data exchange of test state boundaries and yields of past tests, the two Treaties and their Protocols entered into force on December 11, 1990, and *remain in force* between the member states of the Commonwealth of Independent States and the United States.

Both sides' primary task was to find ways to effectively verify the yields of nuclear explosions, which the original protocols had failed to achieve, through agreements that fulfilled the key requirements for all lasting treaties: fairness, reciprocity, operability, and verifiability.

The Comprehensive Test Ban Treaty (CTBT) negotiations were very different. Only after the rush to complete the CTBT was over, did it become apparent that there were significant flaws and shortcomings within the CTBT agreement, just as had occurred for the original threshold treaties – after they were first "finalized" in the mid-1970s. In the CTBT, it now seems clear that effective verification cannot be achieved by only relying on the International Monitoring System (IMS) – because of *evasion means* that can be used by those carrying out tests or explosions to disguise the yields measured by IMS sensors and thereby, not only prevent accurate yield measurement, but to hide completely the fact that nuclear tests were even being carried out. Such evasion scenarios may already be in use to hide nuclear explosions, and for very low – but still militarily useful – nuclear tests. These means of evasion operate to reduce the seismic waves generated by the blasts, and do so sufficiently to hide such explosions below the level of international detectability. Once such means for evasion are widely recognized and understood, it may be possible to overcome their use; although exactly how they may be overcome is not yet clear. It is likely to involve: much more intrusive routine accesses to test sites; sensors based on new phenomenology; "close-in" rather than remote sensors; and may even require automatic granting of permissions for on-site inspections. While overcoming these evasions means may prove to be quite challenging, it is vital that such evasion scenarios be addressed and corrected if any low yield threshold treaty or complete ban is ever to be ratified or enter into force.

If the lessons learned in the NTT effort could now be put to use to achieve the modifications needed in the current CTBT, it could very likely be the key to ending the current stalemate. This chapter explores how those lessons may be applied to the current CTBT gridlock in order to reveal the CTBT's problems and the actions that might be used to correct those problems. If this is done, it may be possible to return to the original path for developing new and verifiable test limitation agreements.

The past is prologue on testing treaties

There are many significant parallels between the conditions that originally existed in the late 1980s for the threshold treaties – which after being completed sat without ratification for fifteen or more years – and the current problems that plague the CTBT, now having remained unratified after nearly twenty years The threshold treaties became more and more controversial as both sides openly expressed their growing dissatisfactions with the treaties and their protocols – by sending a *demarche* to the other after subsequent high yield tests, accusing them of exceeding the 150 kiloton test yield limit. Similarly, for the CTBT today, there are suspicions and reports of nuclear tests continuing to be covertly detonated by some nations.[2] These have occurred against a growing backdrop of much larger yield nuclear explosions and tests being overtly conducted by some new nuclear weapon states (India, Pakistan, North Korea), who boastfully announced their successes. Thus, while the list of CTBT signatories has grown large, with many nations abiding by its terms, it can be said that a complete ban on tests or explosions is far from being realized, if not having already become irrelevant.[3]

In late 1987, in ministerial meetings between George Schultz for the United States and Eduard Shevardnadze for the Soviet Union, it was decided that an end must be brought to the continuing confusions over compliance with the threshold treaties. They agreed to embark on a new course (confirmed in a Joint Statement at the Washington Summit), that included: a commitment by the sides to cooperate in the designm and conduct of a joint verification experiment to cooperatively demonstrate improved verification measures (on nuclear tests to be undertaken at each other's test sites); and a commitment to begin full-scale negotiations whose purpose would be to agree on effective verification measures, making it possible to achieve ratification of the two threshold treaties. Their statement also confirmed a renewed focus on the longer-term future, in that, "these verification measures will, to the extent appropriate, be used in further nuclear test limitation agreements which may subsequently be reached."[4] The context for this addition was to "lock in" a formal commitment by both sides to a "step-by-step" approach in negotiating "further intermediate limitations on nuclear testing limiting leading to the ultimate objective of the complete cessation of nuclear testing as part of an effective disarmament process."[5] And, from that point, the sides remained committed to find a path to further limit nuclear testing. Each expressed beliefs that the path between a workable and effectively-verified limit of 150 kilotons and a "total cessation of nuclear testing" would likely involve a multi-step process of gradual reductions in the maximum yield, assuring at each step that effective verification could be achieved – by building on both "on-site measurements" and "on-site inspections" developed in the JVE and enshrined in new TTBT/PNET protocols.

For the CTBT treaty, many parallels with that history are unmistakable. Ever since its negotiation began in January of 1994 and through today, it has been controversial, and is now accompanied by widespread suspicion that violations of the CTBT treaty provisions continue to take place, using means to covertly conceal nuclear tests or explosions through decoupling its seismic signals – leaving its existing verification means (i.e., the IMS) incapable of either proving, or disproving such. The primary impetus to renegotiate the CTBT is thus clear: without changes in verification, it will remain impossible to verify that the basic obligation of its (current or future) signatories "not to carry out any nuclear weapon test explosion or any other nuclear explosion" is being met.[6]

The need for effective verification

It has been argued that just as strong fences make good neighbors, strong verification makes good treaties. A more general, and quite elegant, policy discussion on why strong verification is so crucially important for treaties was developed during the early- and mid-1990s by Ambassador Paul Nitze, who then served as the Senior Arms Control Advisor to presidents Ronald Reagan and George H.W. Bush. During those years Nitze worked within the State Department and lent his wisdom to the major arms issues of the times. He analyzed and advised on many treaty negotiation issues, but one of his seminal contributions was in pointing out the singular importance of having "effective verification" in order for arms control agreements to be successful.[7]

Ambassador Nitze even went so far as to charge that "poorly verified agreements are in reality far worse than having no agreements at all," especially when the agreements end up causing more damage to relationships – by tearing down rather than building up – trust between the parties.[8] The clarity of his truth became very real for the US NTT negotiating team when, in the fall of 1987, it took on the unenviable task in Geneva to begin negotiations with a newly-formed Soviet delegation, to try to achieve new agreements to replace the prior verification efforts – agreed in the original TTBT and PNET treaties – with more effective measures. The team was also challenged to break the stalemate that had prevented further testing agreements from being considered.

When the NTT work to ratify the threshold treaties was finished in October of 1990, I was asked as Ambassador and Chief Negotiator for NTT to provide for James Baker, the Secretary of State, ideas for a potential "Next Step (or Steps)," in order to continue a "step-by-step approach to limitations on nuclear testing." The United States made clear its belief at that time that nuclear weapons would continue to play a critical role in the US national strategy, and that some levels of testing would likely continue to be of importance in maintaining effectiveness, safety, security, and reliability of nuclear weapons. Yet the United States agreed that it would be prepared to consider other steps in the process of nuclear test limitations. I had imagined that there would likely be a minimum of at least two, and possibly three, steps in successive agreements to lower the yield thresholds from hundreds of kilotons levels to the range of tens of tons. In light of the knowledge of decoupling possibilities, I expected it would likely be necessary to create new technical monitoring capabilities in order to accurately measure these low levels. Wider experience in the reliability and anti-spoofing capabilities of proposed technologies would also be needed to ensure that such significantly lowered yield levels could indeed be effectively verified.

To assess the global picture over the prospects for the CTBT itself (or future limitations on nuclear testing) a comparison with the 1980s situation for TTBT is useful. Although recently there has not been a pattern to *demarche* others for violations, as was the case for the TTBT, yet there are widespread public reports that low yield nuclear tests appear to be being carried out by both Russia and (perhaps by) China, that would be violations of the CTBT.[9] Most of these tests appear to be below the threshold of seismic detectability, but without any knowledge of whether means were used to covertly hide these tests from being detected through the use of cavities surrounding the explosion. And, in the period since the CTBT was opened up for signatures and ratifications (on September 24, 1996), there have continued to be flurries of nuclear tests by other nations (India, Pakistan, North Korea) – and perhaps by other nations attempting to acquire nuclear weapons, who may have carried out tests, but for which confirmatory evidence is unavailable.

These events reveal another of the most fundamental problems in the current CTBT: it never states what would be considered a violation of the terms of the treaty, or as some have charged that the CTBT fails to define what it purports to prohibit, leaving it up to each side to make their own private choice as to what they are willing to accept as allowed versus prohibited.[10] The CTBT similarly fails to define what constitutes a nuclear test or to specify what tests would be allowed.[11] These omissions make it impossible to even know how to write a *demarche* charging noncompliance. These deficiencies will need to be corrected if ratification of the existing CTBT is to be achieved. Short of that, it is likely the present chaos over banning nuclear tests will continue, along with growing asymmetries in the nuclear test behaviors of large and small nations. Thus, to develop proposals for overcoming today's situation for the CTBT, a good beginning would be to revise the existing text, which itself was already frequently changed during the Clinton presidency's final term, even by the UN General Assembly in the end game, after ad referendum agreement by the negotiators. There is some basis for hope, if a similar process and plan previously used to revise the TTBT and PNET Protocols were undertaken for the CTBT. The major hurdle to that occurring will be to gain the political will to face up to the CTBT's fundamental shortcomings and to fix them.

Decoupling and disguising nuclear test yields

There are real possibilities to frustrate yield measurements of explosions. This history is very likely not known to many, but it addresses the core reason why the current CTBT verification measures for verifying a zero yield CTBT are ineffective. There exists a well-developed and proven technology that is capable of disguising the yield of low yield nuclear explosions by decoupling them from the surrounding soils – either by detonating them within cavities or within porous soils (of specific properties). In many cases such geometries can hide low yield tests completely.[12]

During the NTT negotiations in Geneva in 1989, when the US and USSR delegations were intent on achieving new protocols that would provide for direct on-site measurements of the yields of nuclear tests, a key question naturally arose: How can one be sure that a side provided notification to the verifying party of all upcoming tests, especially if they had intentions to exceed the maximum yield of 150 kilotons in some tests? The answer depended on how effectively the seismic energy of nuclear tests can be decoupled to reduce the apparent explosive yield, especially if the other side were not notified in advance, and thus not present to make on-site measurements of yield. At that time the United States already knew a lot about decoupling phenomena – initially from an explosion that had been carried out within a cavity produced by an earlier test, and from later detonations carried out within salt cavities (created by solution mining within salt deposits that lie within the US states of New Mexico and Mississippi). In those cases, it appeared that the yield estimates as determined from seismic waves could be muffled, i.e., reduced by factors of about thirty-five times lower, and in one notable case reduced by a factor of seventy times the apparent yield of the explosion. The United States has published openly in the scientific literature the information obtained on the decoupling achieved within all of these past experiments, and also developed and published theoretical models, some suggesting that practically-infinite decoupling might be achieved at lower yield levels for some cavities.[13]

What was a surprise to the United States was the extent of comparable past Soviet Union work on this topic, obtained in their own quite extensive experiments, along with models to project future results. Although little of this Soviet work was published in the open literature, the United States judged their experimental efforts and theoretical analyses to be quite sound. Each side made extensive presentations in Geneva about their past work on the effects of decoupling, with discussions to clarify understandings. Of course, the mutual understandings reached became critical in order to agree upon trigger levels for advance notifications of future planned tests. However, the long-existing practice to consider all information passed during negotiations to be held as classified between the negotiating partners, makes the extensive Soviet database on decoupling still mostly unavailable today. But it became crystal clear that techniques to hide or disguise actual explosion yields through decoupling techniques would present a fundamental problem, should any future agreements impose maximum test yields below a kiloton or less. Of course, the size and volume of cavities that could make sub-kiloton explosions appear to be much lower nuclear yields when measured off site (or even reduced below the level of detectability) would be much smaller in size than the large cavities needed to partially disguise 150 kiloton tests – making it much less risky that such cavity constructions might be discovered remotely. As the purpose in the 1980s Nuclear Testing Talks was to provide effective verification for a 150 kiloton explosion limit, it was recognized that for much lower threshold limits (expected to be tabled later in the step-by-step process) the use of decoupling in cavities sized to reduce yields of much less than a kiloton, was going to not only prove difficult, but might likely be impossible to verify. Thus, it seemed clear that some new scheme was going to have to be developed, and that perhaps it might be necessary to find entirely different technologies in order to even detect or to measure these lower explosion yields. When the yield for the current CTBT was set to be a zero yield, it guaranteed that the treaty could not be verified using the IMS system of distant sensors, or with any detection means we are aware of today.

Problems with the CTBT

Despite the attempts to build on the prior successes of the joint venture experiment and the newly ratified threshold treaties, the history of these prior efforts was never introduced into the CTBT negotiations or even for further discussion, or to be pursued in a subgroup as the bilateral US/Russia negotiations moved to become a multilateral forum for taking the next step in nuclear test limitations. The new negotiations were initiated in January 1994 within an Ad Hoc Committee on a Nuclear Test Ban within the Conference on Disarmament (CD), in Geneva. Admittedly, the international turmoil that ensued during those very years did handicap progress and divert attention – coming after the unexpected fall of the Berlin Wall, and immediately on the heels of the sudden and unforeseen break-up of the Soviet Union. And doubtless, the Soviet Union's disintegration into multiple nations dominated the attention of most senior policymakers on all sides during those years. At that time, issues such as helping to establish new governments and providing aid to the new nations seemed more urgent than the tasks of fixing arms control agreements. The growing realization (beginning in 1991) of an apparent end to the Cold War also reduced the urgency to press for resolving nuclear testing issues. Even against that backdrop, few would have predicted that the multiple steps envisioned in gradually reducing yield limitations would have been combined into one single step, i.e., to move instantly from 150 kilotons to "zero". That action made their verification task virtually impossible to meet, and it remains so today.

For the US side, I believe the changes that occurred as a result of the 1992 presidential elections also had major effects on the course of testing negotiations and are best described as *a sea change*. Following two successive Republican Party administrations, that had just carried through on a joint pledge with the Soviet Union to make the TTBT and PNET treaties effectively verifiable, the reins of government were turned over to a new Democratic administration under William J. Clinton, which embraced very different views on nuclear testing. It presaged a large shift to the left in US political views with major differences in the approaches taken to arms control. Instead of continuing step-by-step reductions of test yields, the prior agreements were brushed aside in favor of pursuing an immediate ban on testing. The new administration was committed to multi-lateral negotiations within the Conference on Disarmament to seek a "comprehensive test ban." Surprisingly, most, if not all of the negotiators within the ad hoc committee of the CD – particularly the P5 nations, including the United States – still believed they were there to develop a successor treaty to the TTBT.

In his final testimony to the US Senate Foreign Relations Committee prior to the CTBT ratification vote in October of 1999, Ambassador Stephen Ledogar – the lead US CTBT negotiator – described in detail the initial aims, candidly disclosing that, from the commencement of CTBT negotiations in January 1994 up to August 1995, the P5 states all had focused on a lowered threshold as the basis for the CTB treaty. In Ledogar's own words, he specifically stated, until the final year of the negotiations, the United States pushed for a "very low threshold of nuclear yield, while the other four argued that they needed a much higher threshold in order to gain any useful data" (from their nuclear tests). Ledogar also stated there: "In some cases the thresholds they pushed for were politically impossible to square with a notion of a comprehensive test ban. Russia for example insisted that if there was going to be any threshold among the five it would have to allow for so-called experiments with nuclear yields of *up to ten tons* of TNT equivalent."[14]

Yet, it is hard to reconcile all of those comments against the fact that, from the outset of the CTBT negotiation on January 25, 1994, all of the P5 members in the test-ban negotiations believed their negotiating goal was a much lowered threshold below the 150 kiloton limit of the original (US/Soviet) test limitation treaties. Only in mid-August of 1995, as the United States announced a sudden decision to revise its previous position from focusing on a defined threshold, did the approach change to an undertaking not to carry out any nuclear weapon test explosion or any other nuclear explosion. (This formulation was likely chosen to avoid specifying a new threshold yield.) On August 11, 1995 President Clinton himself issued the statement, which read: "I'm announcing today my decision to seek a zero-yield CTBT."[15]

The new negotiating position, which the United States immediately put forward in the Geneva Conference on Disarmament, took the others by surprise, as Ledogar later testified: "The Russians, who were miffed at being taken by surprise, climbed down from their original position slowly and painfully. It took until April 1996 before they signed onto the sweeping categoric prohibition that is found in the final text."[16] Yet, by then the window had mostly expired for the CD negotiators to complete their work in order to meet the deadline the 1995 NPT Review Conference had put forward to complete "negotiations on a universal and internationally and effectively verifiable Comprehensive Nuclear Test-Ban Treaty no later than 1996" as its quid pro quo for winning indefinite extension of the Nonproliferation Treaty.[17] Although a CTB treaty was achieved before the end of 1996 and opened for signing on September 24, 1996, the text that was adopted contained many problems. And today, major suspicions have been advanced that the treaty is already being violated. The combination of these difficulties makes it very unlikely that it can gather either universal ratification or entry-into-force (particularly with certain hard-line nations, e.g., India, Pakistan, North Korea, and Iran), along with thirty-nine other nations sitting squarely in control of the prospects for its ratification, as was provided for in Annex 2 to the CTB.[18]

Amending the CTBT?

The participants selected to negotiate the CTBT in the mid-1990s delegated much of the monitoring and verification issues to a longstanding subgroup – the Group of Scientific Experts (GSE), formed from precursor groups in 1976. For twenty years prior to 1996, it focused on sensors within a global network of international seismic stations to detect and measure yields, along with smaller monitoring nets of detectors based on other technologies to identify nuclear explosive events. These emerged and expanded to become the IMS, as specified within the CTBT agreement. But it appears that none of the details uncovered in the NTT regarding decoupling possibilities were ever introduced or discussed within the Geneva CD negotiation that produced the CTBT. There certainly are no provisions to either prevent or deal with these problems within the CTBT text itself. Thus, it allows for test yields of 10 tons (one-hundredth of a kiloton of TNT equivalent) to be hidden – the very level which the Russian side had asked be set as the "allowed threshold yield." Note that the decoupling factor for such explosions could effectively reduce the seismic signals emanating from these low yield nuclear explosions to as small as, or smaller than, common high explosive detonations for mining, road construction, or military uses. Since cavities sized to decouple these very small yield explosions are sufficiently capable in hiding such explosions – at appreciable distances from the test point, it would never even be known that a nuclear explosion had taken place.

Neither the US side, nor the Russians, nor any other party raised this objection to cavity or similar decoupling in the CD. It is proper to ask: Why was not proper attention drawn to the effective impossibility of ever verifying explosions in the 10 tons range? The participants in the 1990s CTBT negotiation certainly did go beyond the limits of their verification tools when they committed to making a zero-yield agreement that can be so readily evaded. Whatever the reasons, it seems that this important evasion scenario, which undermines CTBT verification, went unnoticed. This major mistake must be addressed now. In enshrining only the IMS within the CTBT Protocol, the existing treaty falls short of either identifying or measuring the yield of such low-level explosions if they are conducted in an evasive way (through use of cavities, etc.). There are also no ways to distinguish such low yield nuclear yield explosions from conventional high-explosive events.[19]

Only within the US National Research Council's (NRC's) report on the CTBT – released on March 30, 2012 – has this issue been specifically addressed. The NRC's focus was on: "How a nation might be able to carry out evasive nuclear explosion testing that could not be detected by the international monitoring system or any open networks." The NRC committee estimated that such evasive tests "are credible only for device yields below a few kilotons worldwide and at most a few hundred tons at well-monitored locations."[20] The range of yields assessed includes not only much larger yields, up to "a few kilotons" – but much lower yields, including the 10 ton level – which can be completely hidden. It thus excludes the 10 ton level that was so adamantly promoted by the Russian side as the appropriate threshold for the CTBT.[21] Such a yield is much lower (by 20–40 times) the maximum estimated yield level that this most recent NRC report concludes to be undetectable by the CTBT's IMS. Further, all explosions within that entire yield range could provide significant military utility – by generating critical data at partial yields on the inherent reliability and operability of new nuclear designs or specific weapons.

In the end, the 1994–96 negotiations of a Comprehensive Test Ban produced a document that is far from adequate to verify a "zero yield treaty." Just as finding ways to verify the TTBT and PNET agreements was initially very difficult, it was apparent that fixing them would require new thinking, new actions, and new negotiations. We may well have reached a similar point with respect to the intractable verification problems of the current CTBT. We might be able to use some of the same approaches that were successful two decades earlier to fix the threshold treaties, but in any judgment it is of vital importance to vigorously pursue correction of this major failure in CTBT verification with very high priority.

We are thus at a major crossroads, and either the current, un-ratified CTBT ought to be abandoned completely, or at a minimum be suspended to renegotiate key provisions to fix its major shortcomings. These include solving the problem of the current agreement's inability to verify if any nuclear explosions are taking place at yields in the range between a few kilotons and zero yield, which is a huge technical challenge.

The best approach now may well be to make an initial agreement as soon as possible to limit nuclear testing to a very low, but specified, yield level, as was the original goal of the CTBT negotiations at their outset in 1994, but at a sufficient level to assure that it completely closes the loophole that now allows undetected testing by signatories, should they choose to violate the CTBT prohibitions. Ratifying such a new testing agreement at a yield limit that all can agree is effectively verified, would then restart the original step-by-step process to once again allow it to move forward in seeking lower test yield limits. Agreement on such a new lowered threshold limit could provide a level playing field while steps to other (carefully specified) yield limits are subsequently pursued. Taking into account the effects of the known decoupling possibilities will be difficult, but including them now is essential. Only if the present difficulties are overcome can we begin to build the necessary confidence between all signatories that the world community would once again be embarking on the quest to achieve universally enforceable limits on nuclear testing, with full reciprocity for all nations. To remain in the position we now find ourselves, with an unratified, and unratifiable, CTB treaty – in which each nation is free to choose its own "allowed," but "undetectable," nuclear test yield levels, with little fear of being caught in violation – must not be allowed to continue.

Addressing other problems and "Next Steps"

Along with the fundamental problems of the CTBT – neither ensuring effective verifiability, nor guaranteeing universal reciprocity among the parties to the treaty – there are of course other serious problems that need to be fixed within the CTBT text itself.

In the now over fifty-year history of global attempts to control nuclear testing practices, past efforts were rife with opinions being "dressed up" as facts. This occurs within the current CTBT text itself.

In the Preamble to the current CTBT, it is stated that:

> Recognizing that the cessation of all nuclear weapon test explosions and all other nuclear explosions, by constraining the development and qualitative improvement of nuclear weapons and ending the development of advanced new types of nuclear weapons, constitutes an effective measure of nuclear disarmament and nonproliferation in all its aspects. … Further recognizing that an end to all such nuclear explosions will thus constitute a meaningful step in the realization of a systematic process to achieve nuclear disarmament.[22]

These passages were no doubt thought to be "inspirational," but unfortunately they are not *factual*, as there are few technically valid truths in these *opinions*. The fact is that it has long been proven possible to develop nuclear weapons that were never tested prior to their use. This is true not only for the first US nuclear weapon called the "Little Boy" device, which produced approximately 15 kilotons of yield over Hiroshima. It had never previously been "tested" to prove that it would produce a nuclear yield. Other nations have also taken a similar path, by choosing to put into their defense arsenals some nuclear-weapon devices that have not been tested. All of these devices were considered single-stage devices, yet over time, particularly in one foreign nation who pursued these, without nuclear testing, it was nevertheless possible to increase the yields of such untested single-stage devices upward to several hundreds of kilotons. Taking advantage of current state of the art, all of these devices could still be built at a very high level of reliability with their certification and proof of successful operation being determined only through high-explosive tests that produce no nuclear yield.

Additionally, while the opinion of the CTBT negotiators may have been that ending nuclear testing could stop proliferation, the fact is that now – more than twenty years since the US and the other major powers ended nuclear testing – there has been little success in reducing the continued proliferation of nuclear weapon states. Nor has anyone been able to relate any "causal relationship" between the testing of nuclear weapons by some states and decisions by proliferators to acquire their own nuclear weapons arsenal. Today some nations continue to pursue nuclear-weapon capabilities, while many of the existing nuclear-capable nations are still monotonically increasing the numbers of nuclear weapons in their arsenals. The US and Russian success in greatly reducing the numbers of nuclear weapons in their arsenals is a notable exception.

The Congressional Commission on the Strategic Posture of the United States, in their 2009 report to the Congress, supports this point. In summary, about half of the Commission agreed with a position to oppose CTBT Ratification and stated their belief that "passage of the treaty would confer no substantive benefits for the country's nuclear posture and would pose security risks."[23]

The most fundamental difficulty in dealing with evasion possibilities still revolves around the potential that cavities or porous soils can be used to disguise actual yield magnitudes or even completely hide that a nuclear explosion ever took place. This problem immediately suggests that new consideration be given to measures for enhancing test site transparency. Perhaps granting routine permissions in advance for on-site inspections at test sites, or even agreements to place instruments permanently within test sites, should be considered. As well, it is time to consider whether permanent local presences, and an "Open Skies" approach to on-site monitoring, might be considered.

Another step to move beyond where we find ourselves today – caught up in the intractable verification difficulties of a zero-yield standard – would be to develop and exchange ideas on new technical means for yield verification at much lower limits, by conducting new "Joint Verification Experiments" in the near future. These could be initially planned by the P5 nations, bringing in participation of other CTBT state parties as soon as promising ideas emerged. By working cooperatively together in resolving the current challenges, we just might over time succeed in resolving the daunting decoupling issues that now challenge effective verification of testing treaties at low yield levels, and we can work together to solve wider arms control and security issues.

Notes

1. See US Department of State, "Treaty Between the United States of America and The Union of Soviet Socialist Republics on the Limitation of Underground Nuclear Weapons Tests (and Protocol Thereto) (TTBT)," July 3, 1974, www.state.gov/t/isn/5204.htm; US Department of State, "Treaty Between the United States of America and the Union of Soviet Socialist Republics on Underground Nuclear Explosions for Peaceful Purposes (and Protocol Thereto)," December 11, 1990, www.state.gov/www/global/arms/treaties/pne1.html.
2. See, for example, Elaine M. Grossman, "Strategic Posture Panel Reveals Split Over Nuclear Test Pact Ratification," *Global Security Newswire*, May 7, 2009, www.nti.org/gsn/article/strategic-posture-panel-reveals-split-over-nuclear-test-pact-ratification; Lars-Erik De Geera, "Radionuclide Evidence for Low-Yield Nuclear Testing in North Korea," *Science & Global Security*, Vol. 20, No. 1 (2012), pp. 1–29.
3. For the current list of signatories see Comprehensive Nuclear Test-Ban Treaty Organization, Preparatory Commission, "Status of Signature and Ratification," CBTBO, www.ctbto.org/the-treaty/status-of-signature-and-ratification/.
4. Ronald Reagan, "Joint Statement on the Soviet-United States Summit Meeting," December 10, 1987, www.presidency.ucsb.edu/ws/?pid=33803.
5. Ibid.
6. Comprehensive Nuclear Test-Ban Treaty Organization, Preparatory Commission, "CTBT Treaty Text," www.ctbto.org/the-treaty/treaty-text/.
7. Nitze defined "effective verification" in the following way: "if the other side moves beyond the limits of the treaty in any militarily significant way, we would be able to detect such violation in time to respond effectively and thereby deny the other side the benefit of the violation." See Paul H. Nitze, "The START Treaty", Executive Report 102-53, statement before the Senate Committee on Foreign Relations, September 18, 1992, Washington, DC, p. 27.
8. Paul H. Nitze, "The INF Treaty," statement before US Congress, Senate Committee on Foreign Relations, Senate Hearing 100-522, part 1, 100th Congress, Second Session, 1988, part 1, p. 289, http://babel.hathitrust.org/cgi/pt?id=mdp.39015014752847;view=1up;seq=295.
9. See, for example, William J. Broad and Patrick E. Tyler, "Dispute Over Russian Testing Divides US Nuclear Experts," *New York Times*, March 4, 2001, www.nytimes.com/2001/03/04/world/dispute-over-russian-testing-divides-us-nuclear-experts.html; "Interview with Colonel-General Vladimir Nikolayevich Verkhovtsev, Chief of RF Defense Ministry 12th Main Directorate, by Vitaliy Denisov, Krasnaya Zvezda," Moscow Krasnaya Zvezda, September 4, 2009. Translated by Open Source Center Doc. ID: CEP20090905351001; Bill Sweetman, "Russia Develops Multiple Nuclear Systems," *Aviation Week*, November 11, 2013, http://aviationweek.com/awin/russia-develops-multiple-nuclear-systems.
10. Federation of American Scientists, "Article I: Basic Obligations," *Article-by-Article Analysis of the Comprehensive Test Ban Treaty*, May 18, 2011, www.fas.org/nuke/control/ctbt/text/artbyart/index.html.
11. Ibid.

12. Jon Kyl and Richard Perle, "Our Decaying Nuclear Deterrent," *Wall Street Journal*, June 30, 2009, http://online.wsj.com/news/articles/SB124623202363966157; Jon Kyl, "Why We Need to Test Nuclear Weapons," *Wall Street Journal*, October 20, 2009, http://online.wsj.com/news/articles/SB10001424052748704500604574483224117732120. A Congressionally-mandated study in 2009 led by William J. Perry and James R. Schlesinger was also unable to agree on whether the CTBT was in the interest of the United States, largely owing to concerns over verification. See William J. Perry and James R. Schlesinger, *et al., America's Strategic Posture: The Final Report of the Congressional Commission on the Strategic Posture of the United States* (Washington, DC: United States Institute of Peace Press, 2009).

13. L.A. Glenn and P. Goldstein, "Seismic Decoupling with Chemical and Nuclear Explosions in Salt," *Journal of Geophysical Research*, Vol. 99, No. B6 (June 1994), pp. 11723–11730, http://onlinelibrary.wiley.com/doi/10.1029/94JB00497/abstract; and Lynn R. Sykes, "Dealing with Decoupled Nuclear Explosions under a Comprehensive Test Ban Treaty," in *Monitoring a Comprehensive Test Ban Treaty*, edited by Eystein S. Husebye and Anton M. Dainty (Boston, MA: Springer, NATO ASI Series, Vol. 303, 1996), pp. 247–393.

14. Ambassador Stephen J. Ledogar. "Statement by Ambassador Stephen J. Ledogar (Ret.), Chief US Negotiator of the CTBUT Prepared for the Senate Foreign Relations Committee Hearing on the CTBT," October 7, 1999, www.fas.org/nuke/control/ctbt/text/100799ledogar%20.htm, emphasis added.

15. William J. Clinton, written statement by the President read by Robert Bell, in "Press Briefing by Special Assistant to the President for Defense Policy Robert Bell, August 11, 1995," The American Presidency Project, www.presidency.ucsb.edu/ws/?pid=59461.

16. Ledogar. "Statement by Ambassador Stephen J. Ledogar."

17. United Nations Office for Disarmament Affairs, "Decision 2: Principles and Objectives for Nuclear Non-Proliferation and Disarmament." NPT/CONF.1995/32, 1995 Review and Extension Conference of the Parties to the Treaty on the Non-Proliferation of Nuclear Weapons, New York, April 17–May 12, 1995, p. 2, www.un.org/disarmament/WMD/Nuclear/1995-NPT/pdf/NPT_CONF199501.pdf.

18. Comprehensive Nuclear Test-Ban Treaty Organization, Preparatory Commission, "Comprehensive Nuclear-Test-Ban-Treaty," CBTBO, Annex 2, pp. 92–93, www.ctbto.org/fileadmin/content/treaty/treaty_text.pdf.

19. This latter feature would appear to have been known by the CTBT drafters as evidenced by the request in Part III: Confidence Building Measures "to voluntarily disclose any purely chemical explosions of 300 tons or above," but it provides no real value to treaty compliance. See CTBTO, "CTBT Treaty Text," Part III: Confidence-Building Measures.

20. National Research Council of the National Academies. *The Comprehensive Nuclear Test Ban Treaty: Technical Issues for the United States* (Washington, DC: The National Academies Press, 2012), p. 112.

21. Ledogar, "Statement by Ambassador Stephen J. Ledogar."

22. CTBTO, "CTBT Treaty Text," Preamble, paras. 5–6.

23. Perry and Schlesinger, *et al., America's Strategic Posture*, pp. 83–84.

14

POLICY AND TECHNICAL ISSUES FACING A FISSILE MATERIAL (CUTOFF) TREATY

Zia Mian and Frank N. von Hippel

The largest obstacle to creating nuclear weapons, starting with the ones that destroyed Hiroshima and Nagasaki, has been to make sufficient quantities of fissile materials – highly enriched uranium (HEU) and plutonium – to sustain an explosive fission chain reaction.[1] Recognition of this fact has, for more than fifty years, underpinned both the support for and the opposition to adoption of an international treaty banning at a minimum the production of more fissile materials for nuclear weapons, commonly referred to as a fissile material cutoff treaty (FMCT).

The United States first proposed an FMCT during the Eisenhower administration in the mid-1950s, suggesting at the United Nations the need "to establish effective international control of future production of fissionable materials and to exchange firm commitments to use all future production exclusively for non-weapons purposes."[2] The Soviet Union rejected the proposal. The idea of an FMCT reemerged in the early 1980s, when the Soviet Union proposed at the United Nations a "cessation of production of fissionable materials for manufacturing nuclear weapons" as an early step in freezing the arms race and towards nuclear disarmament.[3] The United States rejected the offer.

With the end of the Cold War, and the United States and Soviet Union dramatically downsizing their nuclear arsenals, the two countries finally both decided to support an FMCT in the hopes of constraining nuclear buildups by other countries. In December 1993, the United Nations General Assembly adopted by consensus a resolution calling for negotiation of a "non-discriminatory, multilateral and internationally and effectively verifiable treaty banning the production of fissile material for nuclear weapons or other nuclear explosive devices."[4] The resolution declared that the General Assembly was "convinced" that a treaty meeting these criteria "would be a significant contribution to nuclear non-proliferation in all its aspects."[5] The United Nations Conference on Disarmament (CD) in Geneva was charged with conducting the negotiations. In 1995 the CD agreed to a negotiating mandate for FMCT talks, now known as the Shannon mandate after its author Canadian Ambassador Gerald Shannon.[6]

Negotiations on an FMCT have failed to start for two decades, however, despite the passage of repeated resolutions in support of negotiations by the General Assembly, by the 1995 Nuclear Nonproliferation Treaty (NPT) Review and Extension Conference and by subsequent NPT Review Conferences. Negotiations have been blocked by the CD's requirement for consensus on an annual agenda to proceed. This requirement has allowed individual countries

– Pakistan in recent years – to block the start of talks. In 2013, in an effort to at least allow preparatory work to proceed, the General Assembly voted to establish a Group of Government Experts on the FMCT to consider issues and make recommendations in 2015 "on possible elements which could contribute to such a treaty."[7]

This chapter lays out the international community's interests in establishing an FMCT. It then discusses the issues that confront its negotiation, focusing in particular on the possible scope of a treaty and challenges to its verifiability. Finally, it looks at the prospects for the successful negotiation of a treaty.

In the remainder of this chapter, we describe the proposed treaty as a Fissile Material (Cutoff) Treaty or FM(C)T to reflect the desire by many countries that it go beyond a simple cutoff and capture under international safeguards as much as possible of the pre-existing stocks of fissile materials not currently in nuclear weapons to preclude the possibility of their future use in nuclear weapons.

Benefits of an FM(C)T

A fissile material cutoff treaty would strengthen the nonproliferation regime, reduce the risk of nuclear terrorism, and help lay a basis for nuclear disarmament in a number of ways. The balance of these achievements and the extent to which they may be realized will depend on the specifics of an eventual treaty. The general benefits are summarized briefly below.

Strengthening the nonproliferation regime

An FM(C)T would contribute to strengthening collective trust and confidence that the nuclear-weapon states that are parties to the Nonproliferation Treaty are keeping their side of the bargain underlying the treaty. In Article 6 of the NPT, the weapon states committed "to pursue negotiations in good faith on effective measures relating to cessation of the nuclear arms race at an early date and to nuclear disarmament."[8] The final document of the 1995 NPT Review and Extension Conference, which served as the basis for the indefinite extension of the NPT, included an agreement by China, France, Russia, the United Kingdom, and United States (the NPT nuclear-weapon states) to "[t]he immediate commencement and early conclusion of negotiations on a non-discriminatory and universally applicable convention banning the production of fissile material for nuclear weapons or other nuclear explosive devices."[9]

This decision was reiterated as one of the thirteen steps toward nuclear disarmament agreed at the 2000 NPT Review Conference, and as part of the "Action Plan on Disarmament" agreed at the 2010 NPT Review Conference.[10]

Capping stockpiles

By the mid-1990s, four of the five NPT nuclear-weapon states, France, Russia, the United Kingdom, and United States had, in fact, declared that they had ended their production of fissile material for weapons. China communicated informally in the same time frame that it had suspended its production of HEU and plutonium for weapons. (See Table 14.1.) But China has been unwilling to renounce the option of restarting production – apparently motivated by concerns that a buildup of US ballistic missile defenses and long-range conventional strike weapons could threaten its nuclear deterrent.[11] An FM(C)T would turn this production moratorium into a legally binding irreversible ban for the NPT weapon states as well as nonnuclear-weapon states.

The other four nuclear-armed states, the Democratic People's Republic of Korea (North Korea), Israel, India, and Pakistan, are not parties to the NPT and are believed to be still producing fissile materials in their weapons programs (see Table 14.1.) Indeed, in South Asia, Pakistan and India both appear to be increasing their rates of production by building new fissile material production facilities.[12] For the NPT nuclear-weapon states and for nonnuclear-weapon states, therefore, a major incentive to pursue an FM(C)T is to cap the nuclear arms buildup in South Asia.

Expanding safeguards to Weapon States

The NPT requires mandatory International Atomic Energy Agency (IAEA) safeguards in nonnuclear-weapons states but requires no international monitoring of even civilian fissile materials in nuclear-weapon states. The NPT weapon states have made voluntary offers of facilities and fissile materials that are available for IAEA safeguards.[13] The United Kingdom and the United States have offered all their civilian nuclear facilities, while France, Russia, and China have made more limited offers. But the IAEA has actually applied safeguards at only a few facilities because it has very limited resources and sees the safeguarding of facilities in the weapon states as a low priority – at least in the absence of an FM(C)T. Some facilities in the non-NPT weapon states have facility-specific IAEA safeguards in place as a result of the condition of supply of these facilities.

An FM(C)T would help reduce this discriminatory aspect of the NPT by extending mandatory safeguards to at least enrichment and reprocessing plants in nuclear-weapon state parties to the treaty and to any new fissile materials that those plants produced. A broader Fissile Material Treaty that also obliged weapon states to not use for weapons pre-existing stocks of fissile materials in civilian nuclear fuel cycles or declared excess for military purposes would place those materials under international safeguards as well.

Reducing the risk of nuclear terrorism

After the end of the Cold War, it was learned that accounting for fissile materials had been very loose in some weapon states. This increased the possibilities for the undetected diversion of

Table 14.1 HEU and Plutonium production history in the nuclear-weapon States

Country	Highly enriched uranium		Plutonium for weapons	
	Production start	Production end	Production start	Production end
United States	1944	1992	1944	1988
Russia	1949	1987/88	1948	1997
United Kingdom	1953	1963	1951	1995
France	1967	1996	1956	1992
China	1964	1987/89 (moratorium)	1966	1991 (moratorium)
Israel	?	?	1963/64	Continuing
India	1992	Continuing	1960	Continuing
Pakistan	1983	Continuing	1998	Continuing
North Korea	?	?	1986	Continuing

Source: International Panel on Fissile Materials, *Global Fissile Material Report 2010: Balancing the Books: Production and Stocks.* Princeton University Press, 2010, http://fissilematerials.org/library/gfmr10.pdf (except for North Korea).

some of these materials for use by would-be nuclear terrorists. An FM(C)T would require that nuclear-weapon states meet internationally agreed standards for the control and accounting of at least fissile materials that the treaty made subject to international monitoring.

Laying the basis for nuclear disarmament

An FM(C)T would begin to extend into all the nuclear-weapon states institutions and practices necessary for the eventual achievement of a nuclear-weapon-free world in which all nuclear-weapon states place all their fissile material stocks and production facilities under strict international safeguards.

More immediately, the global stock of fissile materials available for nuclear weapons would be further reduced if a fissile material treaty required weapon states to explicitly declare excess for weapons use all civilian fissile material and committed them to transfer fissile materials excess to their weapons requirements to civilian use or disposal under international safeguards.

Scope of a fissile material (cutoff) treaty

An early vision of the basic goals or scope of an FM(C)T was laid out in 1957 in United Nations General Assembly Resolution 1148, which called for a "disarmament agreement" that would include:

a)   "the cessation of the production of fissionable materials for weapons purposes,"
b)   "the complete devotion of future production of fissionable materials to non-weapons purposes under effective international control," and,
c)   "the reduction of stocks of nuclear weapons through a program of transfer, on an equitable and reciprocal basis and under international supervision, of stocks of fissionable materials from weapons uses to non-weapons uses."[14]

This resolution was in part a United States effort to lock in a situation in which, at the time, the United States had larger stockpiles of HEU and plutonium than the Soviet Union.[15] The resolution had broader support, however, because other countries saw in an FM(C)T an opportunity to restrain and rollback the superpower arms race.

Reporting on the 1994–1995 discussions at the CD on the mandate for an ad hoc committee to negotiate an FM(C)T, Ambassador Shannon noted that:

> many delegations expressed concerns about a variety of issues relating to fissile material, including the appropriate scope of the Convention. Some delegations expressed the view that this mandate would permit consideration in the Committee only of the future production of fissile material. Other delegations were of the view that the mandate would permit consideration not only of future but also of past production. Still others were of the view that consideration should not only relate to production of fissile material (past or future) but also to other issues, such as the management of such material. It has been agreed by delegations that the mandate for the establishment of the Ad Hoc Committee does not preclude any delegation from raising for consideration in the Ad Hoc Committee any of the above noted issues.[16]

During the Cold War, the NPT nuclear-weapon states, especially the United States and Soviet Union, built very large nuclear arsenals. The number of US warheads peaked at about 30,000 in the mid-1960s, and the Soviet/Russian arsenal reached 40,000 in the 1980s. Since the end of the Cold War, the United States, Russia, France, and the United Kingdom have all cut back their nuclear arsenals. (See Table 14.2.) In the case of the United States and Russia, reductions have amounted to tens of thousands of weapons. The United Kingdom and France have reduced proportionately by hundreds of weapons each.

These nuclear arsenal reductions have freed up huge quantities of excess fissile material. Indeed, Russia has sold to the United States for power reactor fuel 500 metric tons of weapon-grade uranium (≥90 percent U-235), after down-blending it to an enrichment of about 5 percent U-235. This is often described as being the equivalent of the amount of HEU in 20,000 nuclear warheads.[17] The last of the 500 tons of blended-down Russian weapons HEU was shipped in November 2013. The United States has committed to down-blend about 200 tons of less than weapon-grade HEU and has allocated 152 tons of excess weapon-grade uranium to a reserve for future use as naval reactor fuel.[18]

Russia and the United States also have each declared 34 tons of plutonium from weapons to be excess for weapon use. France has declared no fissile material excess despite the reduction of its nuclear arsenal to half its Cold War peak.[19] The United Kingdom declared 0.9 tons of weapon-grade plutonium excess in 1998 but, in 2013, announced that fissile material from dismantled warheads will be returned to its military stockpile and will not be placed under IAEA safeguards.[20] Globally, roughly half of the material from weapons reductions has been declared as excess to military requirements. In addition, there are huge stockpiles of civilian plutonium that are a legacy of failed efforts in the industrialized states to commercialize plutonium breeder reactors. (See Table 14.3.)

Under the 1998 agreement on Plutonium Management Guidelines, all five NPT nuclear-weapon states committed to declare annually and publicly to the IAEA the quantities of plutonium in their civilian nuclear fuel cycles.[21] Although there is no explicit obligation in the guidelines that this plutonium will not be used for nuclear weapons, this level of transparency does imply an intention not to do so.

Pre-existing stocks under an FM(C)T

The NPT weapon states have agreed among themselves only to support a treaty that would ban future production of fissile materials for nuclear weapons. As in 1957, however, other states are concerned about how a treaty will deal with the very large stockpiles of weapon-usable

Table 14.2 Declared and estimated nuclear warhead stockpiles

Country	Nuclear warheads (current)	Nuclear warheads (historic peak)
United States	~ 7,700 (including retired)	31,255 (declared)
Russia	~ 10,000 (including retired)	~ 40,000 (high uncertainty)
United Kingdom	fewer than 225 (declared)	~ 520
France	fewer than 300 (declared)	~ 540
China	~ 240	~ 240
Israel	100–200	(unknown)
India	80–100	80–100
Pakistan	100–120	100–120
North Korea	Fewer than 10	Fewer than 10

Source: Adapted from Hans M. Kristensen and Robert S. Norris, "Global Nuclear Weapons Inventories, 1945–2013," *Bulletin of the Atomic Scientists*, Vol. 69, No. 5 (September/October 2013), pp. 75–81.

Table 14.3 Estimated and Declared (D) fissile material stockpiles of the nuclear-weapon states

Country	Highly Enriched Uranium		Separated Plutonium	
	Military	*Civilian*	*Military*	*Civilian*
United States	512 tons (D)	83 tons (D)	38.3 tons (D)	49.3 (D)
Russia	646 tons	20 tons	88	89.5 tons (D)
United Kingdom	19.8 tons (D)	1.4 tons (D)	3.2 tons (D)	91.2 tons (D)
France	26 tons	4.7 tons (D)	6.0 tons	57.5 tons (D)
China	16 tons	–	1.8 tons	0.01 (D)
Israel	0.3 tons	–	0.84 tons	–
India	2.4 tons	–	0.5 tons	5 tons
Pakistan	3.0 tons	–	0.15 tons	–
North Korea	?	–	0.03 tons	–

Note: Fissile material declared excess for military purposes is counted as civilian even though it is not under international safeguards, as is India's five tons of unsafeguarded plutonium intended for use as fast-breeder reactor fuel.

Source: International Panel on Fissile Materials, *Global Fissile Material Report 2013: Increasing Transparency of Nuclear Warhead and Fissile Material Stocks as a Step toward Disarmament*, Princeton University, October 2013, www.fissilematerials.org/library/gfmr13.pdf.

material that have already accumulated worldwide – estimated at about 1,400 metric tons of highly-enriched uranium and 500 tons of separated plutonium as of the end of 2012.[22] Almost all of this material is in the nuclear-weapon states and is still sufficient to increase many-fold the approximately 10,000 operational nuclear warheads in the global nuclear-weapon stockpile today.[23]

Assuming an average of 4 kg of plutonium and 25 kg of HEU per warhead, as suggested by the historical quantities produced by the Soviet Union and the United States, they each would require only 20 tons of plutonium and 125 tons of HEU for arsenals of 5,000 warheads. Even adding in 100 and 50 tons of HEU, respectively, to fuel US and Russian nuclear-powered ships and submarines for the next fifty years, the two countries could declare much more fissile material excess for military purposes. Russia could reduce its military stocks by about 400 tons of HEU and 60 tons of separated plutonium, and the United States by about 200 tons of HEU and 20 tons of plutonium. France and the United Kingdom also have more weapons materials than they need since each of them has downsized its nuclear-warhead stockpile by about a factor of two since the end of the Cold War.[24] The combined stocks of separated civilian but weapon-usable plutonium owned by United Kingdom, France, and Russia amount to about 200 tons. Altogether, the weapons states could declare over 600 tons of HEU and 250 tons of separated plutonium excess for military purposes and place these materials under IAEA safeguards.

For most of the past two decades, Pakistan has been the most vocal state in insisting that an FM(C)T address existing stockpiles as well as future production. Pakistan points specifically to a stockpile of about 5 tons of separated non-weapon-grade but weapon-useable plutonium accumulated by India for its breeder-reactor program.[25] Pakistan is not alone, however, in wanting to broaden the cutoff treaty proposal into a fissile material treaty that would include reductions of existing stocks of fissile material available for nuclear-weapons use. Many nonnuclear-weapon states see this as a means for the treaty to make nuclear disarmament more irreversible.[26]

As far back as 1996, at their Nuclear Safety and Security Summit in Moscow, four of the weapon states (France, Russia, the United Kingdom, and the United States) declared their intention to do exactly this: "We pledge our support for efforts to ensure that all sensitive nuclear material (separated plutonium and highly enriched uranium) designated as not intended for use for meeting defence requirements is safely stored, protected and placed under I.A.E.A. safeguards (in the Nuclear-Weapon States, under the relevant voluntary offer I.A.E.A.-safeguards agreements) as soon as it is practicable to do so."[27]

At the 2000 NPT Review Conference, all five of the NPT weapon states, including China, agreed to a final conference document that included a call for

> all nuclear-weapon States to place, as soon as practicable, fissile material designated by each of them as no longer required for military purposes under IAEA or other relevant international verification and arrangements for the disposition of such material for peaceful purposes, to ensure that such material remains permanently outside military programmes."[28]

Verification has not been totally absent from the HEU-disposal programs thus far. The United States verified that the blend-down of the 500 tons of excess weapon-grade HEU that Russia sold to the United States during 1993–2013 came from metal stated to be shredded nuclear-weapon components, and the IAEA monitored the blend-down of about 50 tons of excess US HEU.[29] Also, in their bilateral agreement to each eliminate 34 tons of weapon-grade plutonium, Russia and the United States committed that the IAEA will be allowed to verify the disposal process.[30] Nevertheless, the five NPT weapon states argue today against broadening a FM(C)T to cover pre-existing fissile materials on the ground that it would make negotiation of an FM(C)T impossible.

Production for civilian and naval-reactor fuel

It is generally agreed that an FM(C)T will permit production of fissile materials for civilian and naval-reactor fuel. This is despite the fact that neither use is necessary. The economic benefits of civilian plutonium separation and recycle in fuel are negative today. The value of plutonium-containing fuel is only a small fraction of the cost of separating the plutonium,[31] and there are no significant environmental benefits from recycling plutonium in the reactors that produced it.[32]

Also, the danger that reprocessing will destabilize the nonproliferation regime is very significant. Currently, Japan is the only nonnuclear-weapon state that separates plutonium, but South Korea is demanding the same "right."[33] In the past, Argentina, Brazil, South Korea, and Taiwan all pursued nominally civilian reprocessing programs that were later revealed to be covers for the development of nuclear-weapon capabilities. China, France, India, Japan, and Russia all separate plutonium from spent power-reactor fuel for recycle or use in breeder reactor development programs, however, so it currently appears to be politically infeasible to ban plutonium separation for civilian purposes in an FM(C)T.

Similarly, the United States, United Kingdom, Russia, and India all use HEU for naval propulsion reactor fuel. Here again, the example of the weapon states could destabilize the nonproliferation regime. Brazil is the first nonnuclear-weapon state to launch a program to develop nuclear submarines. It is planning to initially use low-enriched uranium (LEU) fuel but has left its options open with regard to the possible use of HEU in the future.

Large stockpiles of HEU for naval reactor use also could make nuclear reductions more difficult in the future. The United States is the only weapon state that has publicly declared a stockpile of HEU for future use in naval-reactor fuel but the huge size of this stockpile makes the problem apparent: 152 metric tons of weapon-grade uranium is enough, by the conventional metric of 25 kg per warhead, for 6,000 nuclear weapons.

France uses LEU for its naval reactors and China is believed to as well. In January 2014, the US Navy acknowledged the possible feasibility of switching to LEU fuel. The United Kingdom depends on the United States for naval nuclear technology. There is no indication that the Russian and Indian navies are interested in switching to LEU fuel.[34] Until the US Government becomes actively engaged in promoting LEU fuel for naval reactors, an agreement to ban HEU production or use for naval reactor fuel at some time in the future seems politically infeasible. As will be seen below, this creates a verification problem for the FM(C)T.

Challenges to the verification of an FM(C)T

Much of the verification of an FM(C)T in weapon states could be carried out using the same procedures that have been developed to verify that nonnuclear-weapon states are living up to their commitments under the NPT not to divert fissile material to weapons purposes. Originally, these techniques focused on assuring nondiversion of declared fissile materials from facilities offered for IAEA inspection. Since the discovery by the IAEA of Iraq's clandestine enrichment program in 1991, however, there has been increasing concern about the possibility of undeclared nuclear activities. This led to the development of the Additional Protocol to the safeguards agreements of nonnuclear-weapon states, which requires states that have ratified it to declare to the IAEA nuclear-related activities, such as the production of gas centrifuges, as well as activities in which nuclear material is actually being processed. The Additional Protocol also provides the IAEA with some limited inspection options if it has grounds to believe that a country's declaration is not complete.

Still, the challenge of detecting clandestine fissile material production activities has not been definitively dealt with and would be an issue in verifying an FM(C)T just as it is today for verifying the NPT in nonnuclear-weapon states. We therefore offer here a brief overview.

Detection of clandestine plutonium production

Plutonium production and separation have signatures that may be detected at a distance. The production of one gram of weapon-grade plutonium in a reactor requires the fission of about one gram of U-235, which also releases about one megawatt-day of heat. Disposal of this heat can be detected by infrared sensors.[35]

The separation of plutonium from irradiated uranium in a reprocessing plant can be detected from the radioactive gases that are released when spent fuel is chopped up and dissolved. The radioisotope that has been the focus of such detection efforts is the 11-year half-life radioisotope krypton-85.[36]

Detection of clandestine HEU enrichment

Gaseous diffusion uranium enrichment plants (GDPs) were huge and energy intensive and therefore easy to detect from space. The gas centrifuge enrichment plants (GCPs) that have replaced them are much more difficult to detect. A GCP that could produce enough HEU for a few weapons a year would be relatively small and its energy usage per square meter would be comparable to that of buildings housing light industry or offices.[37]

Also, the UF_6 gas in GCP centrifuges is below atmospheric pressure and leakage is therefore mostly inward. A small amount of gas does escape when tanks of UF_6 feed and product are attached and detached from the piping, however. The resulting deposits on surfaces are invaluable for on-site inspections, see below.

The tunneling and security arrangements associated with Iran's underground Fordow enrichment plant are clearly identifiable with even commercial satellite imaging. (See Figure 14.1.) Determination that this facility is a centrifuge enrichment plant most probably was the result of "human intelligence," i.e., reports from individuals with access to the site.

New verification challenges in the nuclear-weapon States

Beyond the common challenge to the NPT and the FM(C)T of potential clandestine production activities, an FM(C)T would pose new verification challenges involving on-site inspections in the weapon states. Below we discuss the four most important challenges that we have identified:

1. Reprocessing plants not designed for safeguards;
2. Enrichment plants that previously produced HEU;
3. HEU in naval fuel cycles; and
4. Military nuclear facilities.

Reprocessing plants not designed for safeguards

When a nonnuclear-weapon state decides to build a reprocessing plant, it must share the design information with the IAEA and allow the IAEA to verify the design during construction to

Figure 14.1 Iran's Fordow enrichment plant, May 10, 2013

assure, for example, that there is no undeclared piping that could be used to divert significant quantities of plutonium-bearing solution from the monitored process. But some of the weapon states have already operating reprocessing plants where such "design information verification" would be impossible.[38] It also would be impossible for the IAEA to install its own independent devices to measure plutonium concentrations and tank volumes in some process areas, because radiation levels are too high to allow access for the necessary installation work. This would apply to reprocessing plants in China, India, Israel, North Korea, Pakistan, Russia, and the United States.

IAEA verification of nondiversion of plutonium therefore would depend heavily on a mass balance between the plutonium in spent fuel entering the reprocessing plant and measurements of the plutonium product exiting in pure oxide form and the residual in the radioactive waste. This mass balance would be done in connection with an annual cleanout of the reprocessing plant.[39]

Even in new reprocessing plants, measurement accuracy is a problem, however. For Japan's Rokkasho Reprocessing Plant, the annual amount of plutonium separated at its design throughput of 800 metric tons per year would be about 8 tons per year. The measurement uncertainty of about 1 percent would correspond to about 80 kg per year, enough for ten Nagasaki or twenty modern implosion weapons. Having to start with an estimate of the amount of plutonium in the incoming spent fuel would exacerbate the situation since, currently, the uncertainty of these estimates is on the order of 5 percent.

Enrichment plants that previously produced HEU

Given the huge amount of excess HEU in the United States and Russia, there is no foreseeable need for either country to produce more HEU for either naval or research reactor fuel. However, Russia announced in 2012 that it has resumed the production of HEU of unspecified enrichment at one of its enrichment plants for possible use as fuel in nuclear-powered icebreaker ships and in fast reactors, both of which are civilian applications.[40] The United Kingdom depends upon the United States for its naval reactor HEU supply. France uses LEU fuel for its naval propulsion reactors, and China is believed to as well. India, however, reportedly is producing HEU to use as fuel for its growing nuclear submarine fleet.

The IAEA's most sensitive technique for the detection of undeclared HEU production in a facility is to take swipes of micron-sized dust particles from interior surfaces of the plant. The collected uranium particles are then subjected to secondary ion mass spectroscopy (SIMS) to determine their enrichment. Figure 14.2 depicts images with a SIMS of a 0.15 x 0.15 mm area of a planchette with uranium particles on its surface. U-235 ions are selected on the left and U-238 ions on the right. The pixels in the images become brighter the more ions they collect. Particles that are much brighter in the left image are HEU and those much brighter on the right are natural or low-enriched uranium. (See Figure 14.2.)

In a nonnuclear-weapon state, detection of HEU in such particles would be evidence of clandestine HEU production. The complication in the weapon states is that, in the past, some of the enrichment plants were used to produce HEU. There is also the problem that in some cases shut-down GDPs that produced HEU are adjacent to and have cross-contaminated operating GCPs that produce LEU.

The challenge therefore is to age-date the older HEU particles or to precisely measure isotopic ratios to determine the technology that produced the HEU.[41] Age-dating should be facilitated by the fact that the NPT weapon states mostly ended their production of HEU over two decades ago. The more-recently HEU-producing enrichment plants in India, Israel, North

**Sample SIMS images
(0.15 x 0.15mm μ-sized particles)**

Can HEU particles be dated?

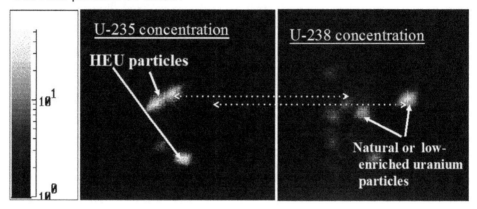

Figure 14.2 Mass spectrometer image of uranium particles

Source: Image provided by the International Atomic Energy Agency.

Korea, and Pakistan are relatively small and therefore could probably be safeguarded adequately without the use of uranium particle analysis.

HEU in naval fuel cycles

For the foreseeable future, it should not be necessary for any country other than India to produce HEU for naval fuel. For India – and the United States and Russia if IAEA monitoring is extended to pre-existing stocks of HEU for civil and nonproscribed military uses – the challenge would be to verify that HEU was not diverted from the naval fuel cycle to weapons. This challenge would be exacerbated by the fact that some countries – certainly the United States – consider the designs of their naval reactors and fuel to be sensitive information that cannot be exposed to IAEA inspectors.

A complete solution will only be possible through cooperative negotiations. In this context, it is relevant that the IAEA and Brazil, the first nonnuclear-weapon state to embark on a program to develop a nuclear-powered submarine, are engaged in discussions of how the IAEA can monitor the use of enriched uranium in Brazil's naval-reactor fuel cycle. Brazil currently plans on using LEU fuel but the IAEA monitors LEU in nonnuclear-weapon states to protect against the possibility that it might be used as feed for a small clandestine enrichment plant. The results of the IAEA's negotiations with Brazil will provide an important precedent for verification of nondiversion of HEU from weapon-state naval fuel cycles under an FM(C)T.[42]

If fuel designs are considered sensitive, it will be necessary to treat at least part of a naval fuel fabrication facility as a black box. The amount of HEU entering the fuel fabrication facility could be measured. The challenge would be to measure the amount of U-235 in the fabricated fuel – perhaps while it was concealed in a container. If the fuel were "thin," as measured by fast-neutron mean-free paths, this might be done by active interrogation with neutrons with energies less than the fission threshold of U-238, to measure U-235 fissions per incident neutron. Also, the fuel fabrication facility could be designed so that HEU could only enter or leave through monitored portals with the inspectors allowed to check for HEU within when there was no fabricated fuel present. The idea would be to ensure that no HEU left except inside a container that could be assayed. Such "containment and surveillance" is used in plutonium handling facilities to make up for material measurement uncertainties but it is doubtful that it would be considered adequate as a stand-alone arrangement without material measurements.

After fuel fabrication, the issue would become one of assuring that the fuel was loaded into a submarine or ship reactor and that no HEU remained in the container. This would require the inspectors to be present when the fuel was loaded and arrangements to assure that the fuel was actually being introduced into the reactor while not revealing its design.[43]

Finally, the reactor or reactor compartment would have to be sealed in a way that could be checked periodically to assure that it had not been opened until it was time for refueling, at which time inspectors would again observe the process to assure that all the spent fuel was transferred to a cask that could be sealed and subsequently monitored. Of course, after it was irradiated, concerns about diversion of HEU fuel would be somewhat reduced by the fact that the fuel would have to be reprocessed to recover its remaining HEU.

Military nuclear facilities

Under the FM(C)T, the IAEA would need the right to inspect any facility that it thought might house an undeclared enrichment or reprocessing facility. In the case of a reprocessing facility, the inspection would not have to be intrusive. The detection of fission products in the environment at concentrations significantly above the regional background could provide the basis for a compelling case that reprocessing was actually going on in a facility.

In the case of a nonnuclear-weapon state, the IAEA is willing to negotiate "managed access" at sensitive facilities to protect the host's sensitive military or business information while assuring that there are no undeclared nuclear activities. There are no sensitive facilities with nuclear activities in them in nonnuclear-weapon states – except potentially now in Brazil with its naval propulsion program.

Determining nonintrusively whether uranium enrichment was going on in a facility might require some on-site measurements. In the case of weapon states, however, the IAEA would likely not be allowed to make measurements that would reveal information relating to the military nuclear activities at the site.

The nuclear-weapon states that are parties to the Chemical Weapons Convention (all but Israel and North Korea) have already committed themselves to allow inspections anywhere – with managed access if necessary. This includes at chemical plants that consider their processes sensitive proprietary information. To enable verification in such facilities, the Organisation for the Prohibition of Chemical Weapons has developed a gas-chromatograph mass spectrometer that is blinded to all information except for the unique signatures of chemical weapon-related materials. The electronic measurements made by the instrument are compared to a library that contains only the characteristic signatures of chemical-weapon-related species, precursors, and degradation products. Beyond the positive or negative results of these comparisons, the instrument has no memory to store the measurements that it has made.

The characteristic signature of a centrifuge enrichment plant would be degradation products of UF_6, typically UF_2O_2. The spectral analysis program of a laser induced breakdown spectrometer could be designed to give a positive signal only if it detected the atomic spectra of uranium and fluorine at the same spot. An instrument for this purpose appears to have been developed at the US Los Alamos National Laboratory. In Figure 14.3 below, laser induced breakdown spectrometry (LIBS) uses a laser to create plasma from a small amount of surface material. A spectrograph analyzes the light emitted from the plasma to identify the elements that it contains. The Mars rover, *Curiosity*, contains such an instrument. The figure on the right shows a LIBS instrument developed by Los Alamos National Laboratory for IAEA safeguards applications. (See Figure 14.3.)

Prospects for an FM(C)T

Breaking the logjam of negotiations at the United Nations Conference on Disarmament will require decisions by key states to give priority to this goal. In the short term, the most obvious policy shift will be required from Pakistan. It will have to drop its objections to allowing the start of FM(C)T negotiations at the CD. Blocking talks on an FM(C)T enables Pakistan to continue to build up its fissile material stockpile and to highlight to the international community its concerns about a fissile material gap with India and the consequences of India's current military buildup, especially India's search for missile defenses, and the consequences of the 2005 US-India nuclear deal. Holding up an FM(C)T also allows Pakistan's nuclear establishment to keep open the prospect of a nuclear deal of its own.[44]

As of 2014, Pakistan has been able to block progress on an FM(C)T at the CD for over a decade because the United States and other leading states have been unwilling to give priority to an FM(C)T relative to more pressing issues such as the war in Afghanistan since 2001 for which Pakistan's cooperation has been required. When that war winds down it may be possible to give the FM(C)T more priority, especially for the United States. States wishing to begin work on an FM(C)T might also assure Pakistan that they will join an effort to find ways for

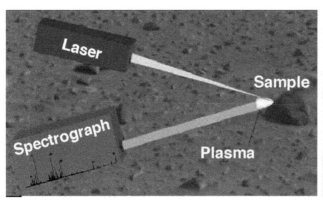

Figure 14.3 Laser-induced spectral analysis

Source: The image on the left is taken from US National Aeronautics and Space Administration, "Schematic of Laser-Induced Breakdown Spectroscopy," NASA mission website, www.nasa.gov/mission_pages/msl/multimedia/pia15103_prt.htm. The image on the right is reproduced from J.E. Barefield II, S.M. Clegg, Loan A. Le, and Leon Lopez, "Development of Laser Induced Breakdown Spectroscopy Instrumentation for Safeguards Applications," paper presented at Preparing for Future Verification Challenges: Symposium on International Safeguards, International Atomic Energy Agency, Vienna, November 1–5, 2010, www.iaea.org/safeguards/Symposium/2010/Documents/PapersRepository/134.pdf.

the treaty to cover at least some fissile material stockpiles in an effective way. One focus could be a willingness to address Pakistan's concerns about India's stockpile of unsafeguarded separated power reactor plutonium.[45]

Pakistan is not the only hold-out to progress on an FM(C)T. Israel's current prime minister, Benjamin Netanyahu, has made clear that, while it will not join Pakistan in blocking nego-tiations, Israel does not currently have any intention to sign an FM(C)T.[46] Israel sees the FM(C)T in the context of its larger security diplomacy with its neighbors and insists that a peace settlement with its Middle East neighbors must come before it accepts any treaty limitations on its nuclear program. Depending on how they progress, recent developments in the region such as Syria's accession in 2013 to the Chemical Weapons Convention, the prospect of a negotiated resolution of the crisis over Iran's nuclear program, and growing support, including in Israel, for a Middle East zone free of nuclear and all other weapons of mass destruction, could lead to increased pressure for a change in Israel's policy.[47]

China, like Israel, has reservations about joining an FM(C)T and thereby permanently capping its nuclear arsenal until other security issues are dealt with first. In the case of China, these issues are related to the potential of US long-range conventional precision strike weapons and ballistic-missile-defenses becoming a threat to the survivability of China's nuclear weapons and to the likelihood that these weapons would reach their intended targets.

For any FM(C)T treaty to be a meaningful contribution to the larger and longer term goal of verifiable nuclear disarmament will require a willingness by weapon states to open parts of their military programs to managed access by international inspectors. A key challenge will be military naval fuel cycles – some of which contain large amounts of HEU. Establishing a verification approach for naval fuel will require cooperative work in advance of an FM(C)T by nuclear-weapon states, nonnuclear-weapon states, and the IAEA. An alternative approach with additional security benefits would be a parallel agreement to design future nuclear propulsion reactors to be fueled by LEU.[48]

To verify an FM(C)T, the extra safeguards costs could double the IAEA's current safeguards budget for its activities in nonnuclear-weapon states – on the order of $250 million in 2013.[49] However, this is less than 1 percent of the current annual cost of US nuclear forces alone.[50] One option would be for all IAEA member states to pay for the extra safeguards effort. Not all members of the IAEA would initially be parties to the FM(C)T, however. A second option could be for all states parties to the FM(C)T to pay the additional safeguards costs. Under a third option, the nuclear-weapon states would pay for the extra safeguards costs. Regardless, since disarmament and nonproliferation are common interests, the international community should not have too much trouble finding a way to fund the verification of a treaty once it is agreed.

Notes

1. Key parts of this essay are based on a longer discussion of these issues in *Global Fissile Material Report 2008* by the International Panel on Fissile Materials (IPFM) and its companion volume reviewing the perspectives of some key states towards an FM(C)T. *Global Fissile Material Report 2008: Scope and Verification of a Fissile Material (Cutoff) Treaty* (Princeton, NJ: Princeton University Press, 2008). The companion volume is International Panel on Fissile Materials, *Country Perspectives on the Challenges to a Fissile Material (Cutoff) Treaty* (Princeton, NJ: Princeton University Press, 2008).

2. United Nations, "United States Memorandum Submitted to the First Committee of the General Assembly," United Nations document A/C.l/783, 12 January 1957. For a history of early United States discussions on an FMCT and related primary documents, see William Burr, "'We can't go on the way we are': US Proposals for a Fissile Material Production Cutoff and Disarmament Diplomacy during the 1950s and 60s," National Security Archive, June 16, 2010, www2.gwu.edu/~nsarchiv/nukevault/ebb321.

3. United Nations, "Statement by Andrei A. Gromyko, Minister of Foreign Affairs of the USSR," Plenary Meeting of the Second Special Session of the United Nations General Assembly Devoted to Disarmament, June 12, 1982; for a transcript see provisional verbatim record United Nations General Assembly twelfth special session, A/S-12/PV.12, June 18, 1982.

4. United Nations General Assembly Resolution A/RES/48/75L, 16 December 1993.

5. Ibid.

6. United Nations Conference on Disarmament, "Report of Ambassador Gerald E. Shannon of Canada on Consultations on the most Appropriate Arrangement to Negotiate a Treaty Banning the Production of Fissile Material for Nuclear Weapons or Other Nuclear Explosive Devices," CD/1299, March 24, 1995, available at www.fas.org/programs/ssp/nukes/armscontrol/shannon.html.

7. United Nations General Assembly Resolution A/RES/67/53, 4 January 2013, www.un.org/en/ga/search/view_doc.asp?symbol=A/RES/67/53. It calls for the Secretary General to seek the views of member states on an FMCT and for the creation of a United Nations Group of Governmental Experts (GGE) from twenty-five states (based upon equitable geographic representation) to meet in 2014 and 2015 and report in 2015 to the General Assembly and to the Conference on Disarmament.

8. For the text of the Nuclear Nonproliferation Treaty, see United Nations Office for Disarmament Affairs, "Treaty on the Non-Proliferation of Nuclear Weapons (NPT)," July 1, 1968, www.un.org/disarmament/WMD/Nuclear/NPTtext.shtml.

9. The initial duration of the NPT was set at twenty-five years, after which "a conference shall be convened to decide whether the Treaty shall continue in force indefinitely, or shall be extended for an additional fixed period or periods." Final Document, NPT Review and Extension Conference 1995, NPT/CONF.1995/32 (PARTI). See United Nations Office for Disarmament Affairs, "Decision 2: Principles and Objectives for Nuclear Non-Proliferation and Disarmament," NPT/CONF.1995/32, 1995 Review and Extension Conference of the Parties to the Treaty on the Non-Proliferation of Nuclear Weapons, New York, April 17–May 12, 1995, www.un.org/disarmament/WMD/Nuclear/1995-NPT/pdf/NPT_CONF199501.pdf.

10. For the final documents of the 2000 and 2010 NPT Review Conferences, see United Nations Office of Disarmament Affairs, www.un.org/disarmament/WMD/Nuclear/NPT_Review_Conferences.shtml.

11. Li Bin, "China," in *Country Perspectives on the Challenges to a Fissile Material (Cutoff) Treaty,* International Panel on Fissile Materials, Princeton University, 2008, pp. 7–13, http://fissilematerials.org/library/gfmr08cv.pdf.

12. Pakistan is building additional plutonium production reactors while India is expanding its uranium enrichment plant, building a second enrichment plant, and constructing new reprocessing plants.

13. International Panel on Fissile Materials, *Global Fissile Material Report 2007*, Princeton University, 2007, http://fissilematerials.org/library/gfmr07.pdf.

14. United Nations General Assembly "Resolution 1148 (XII)," November 14, 1957, www.un.org/en/ga/search/view_doc.asp?symbol=A/RES/1148(XII)&Lang=E&Area=RESOLUTION.

15. International Panel on Fissile Materials, *Global Fissile Material Report 2010: Balancing the Books: Production and Stocks*, Princeton University, 2010, http://fissilematerials.org/library/gfmr10.pdf. See also, e.g., US Arms Control and Disarmament Agency, "A Cutoff of Production of Fissionable Materials for Weapons Use with Demonstrated Destruction of Nuclear Weapons and Transfer of Fissionable Material Therefrom to Non-Weapons Uses," October 18, 1965, www2.gwu.edu/~nsarchiv/nukevault/ebb321/21.PDF.

16. United Nations Conference on Disarmament, "Report of Ambassador Gerald E. Shannon."

17. United States Enrichment Corporation, "Megatons to megawatts," www.usec.com/russian-contracts/megatons-megawatts.

18. International Panel on Fissile Materials, *Global Fissile Material Report 2010*.

19. Ibid.

20. For details of the United Kingdom's statement see "UK Nuclear Warhead Dismantlement Program," IPFM blog, August 26, 2013, fissilematerials.org/blog/2013/08/uk_nuclear_warhead_disman.html. For primary sources see Rob Edwards, "Three of Britain's nuclear warheads are being dismantled every year," August 11, 2013, www.robedwards.com/2013/08/three-of-britains-nuclear-warheads-are-being-dismantled-every-year.html.

21. International Atomic Energy Agency, "Communication Received from Certain Member States Concerning their Policies Regarding the Management of Plutonium," INFCIRC/549, March 16, 1998, www.iaea.org/Publications/Documents/Infcircs/1998/infcirc549.pdf.

22. International Panel on Fissile Materials, *Global Fissile Material Report 2013: Increasing Transparency of Nuclear Warhead and Fissile Material Stocks as a Step toward Disarmament*, Princeton University, October 2013, http://fissilematerials.org/library/gfmr13.pdf.
23. Hans M. Kristensen and Robert S. Norris, "Global Nuclear Weapons Inventories, 1945–2013," *Bulletin of the Atomic Scientists*, Vol. 69, No. 5 (September/October 2013), pp. 75–81.
24. The United Kingdom presumably is keeping its excess weapons HEU for future naval fuel use. France has shifted to using fuel enriched to the level that it produces for its nuclear power plants.
25. Zia Mian and A.H. Nayyar, "Playing the Nuclear Game: Pakistan and the Fissile Material Cutoff Treaty," *Arms Control Today*, Vol. 40, No. 3 (April 2010), pp. 17–24, www.armscontrol.org/act/2010_04/Mian.
26. In 2013, at the Conference for Disarmament, Iran, Ireland, South Africa, and Switzerland argued that an FMCT should include stockpile reductions if it was to make a contribution to disarmament. See Reaching Critical Will, "Stockpiles or No Stockpiles," *CD Report*, March 12, 2013, http://reaching criticalwill.org/disarmament-fora/cd/2013/reports/7501-stockpiles-or-no-stockpiles. Previously at the Conference on Disarmament, Brazil, Japan, and New Zealand also raised the need for including stocks in an FM(C)T.
27. "Moscow [G8] Nuclear Safety and Security Summit Declaration," April 20, 1996, www.g7.utoronto.ca/summit/1996moscow/declaration.html.
28. United Nations Office of Disarmament Affairs, "Review Conference of the Parties to the Treaty on the Nonproliferation of Nuclear Weapons," final document, 2000, www.un.org/disarmament/WMD/Nuclear/NPT_Review_Conferences.shtml.
29. International Atomic Energy Agency, "Management of High-Enriched Uranium for Peaceful Purposes: Status and Trends," IAEA-TECDOC-1452, June 2005, pp. 16, 18, www-pub.iaea.org/mtcd/publications/pdf/te_1452_web.pdf.
30. United States Department of State, "Agreement Between the Government of the United States of America and the Government of the Russian Federation Concerning the Management and Disposition of Plutonium Designated as No Longer Required for Defense Purposes and Related Cooperation as amended by the 2010 Protocol," April 13, 2010, www.state.gov/documents/organization/18557.pdf.
31. See e.g. Matthew Bunn, Steve Fetter, John Holdren and Bob van der Zwaan, "The Economics of Reprocessing vs. Direct Disposal of Spent Nuclear Fuel," *Nuclear Technology*, Vol. 150 (June 2005), p. 209; and Frank von Hippel, "The Costs and Benefits of Reprocessing," in *Nuclear Power's Global Expansion: Weighing Its Costs and Risks*, edited by Henry Sokolski (Carlisle, PA: Strategic Studies Institute, 2010).
32. Mycle Schneider and Yves Marignac, *Spent Nuclear Fuel Reprocessing in France*, International Panel on Fissile Materials, Princeton University, April 2008, http://fissilematerials.org/library/rr04.pdf.
33. Frank von Hippel, "South Korean Reprocessing: An Unnecessary Threat to the Nonproliferation Regime," *Arms Control Today*, Vol. 40, No. 3 (March 2010), pp. 22–29, www.armscontrol.org/act/2010_03/VonHippel.
34. US Department of Energy, "Report on Low Enriched Uranium for Naval Reactor Cores," Report to Congress, Office of Naval Reactors, January 2014.
35. Barbara G. Levi, David H. Albright, and Frank von Hippel, "Stopping the Production of Fissile Materials for Weapons," *Scientific American*, Vol. 253, No. 3 (September 1985), pp. 40–47; Hui Zhang and Frank N. von Hippel, "Using Commercial Imaging Satellites to Detect the Operation of Plutonium-Production Reactors and Gaseous-Diffusion Plants," *Science & Global Security*, Vol. 8, No. 3 (September 2000), pp. 219–271.
36. R. Scott Kemp, "A Performance Estimate for the Detection of Undeclared Nuclear-fuel Reprocessing by Atmospheric ^{85}Kr," *Journal of Environmental Radioactivity*, Vol. 99, No. 8 (August 2008), pp.1341–1348.
37. The building housing Iran's Natanz Pilot Enrichment Plant, with over 1,000 centrifuges, has an area of only about 2,000 m^2. Urenco centrifuges consume only about 5 Watts per SWU per year, www.urenco.com/page/20/Centrifuge-cascades.aspx. To produce 4,000 SWUs per year, sufficient to produce enough HEU for a weapon, would therefore require about 20 kWt.
38. For a list of reprocessing plants, see International Panel on Fissile Materials, *Global Fissile Material Report 2013*. The military reprocessing plants in Israel and North Korea would most likely shut down under an FM(C)T. The civilian reprocessing plants in France and the United Kingdom have been subject to Euratom safeguards.

39. Shirley Johnson, "Safeguards at Reprocessing Plants under a Fissile Material (Cutoff) Treaty," IPFM Research Report #6, International Panel on Fissile Materials, Princeton University, February 2009 , http://fissilematerials.org/library/rr06.pdf.

40. Pavel Podvig, "Russia is Set to Produce New Highly-enriched Uranium," International Panel on Fissile Materials blog, June 1, 2012 fissilematerials.org/blog/2012/06/russia_to_resume_producti. html.

41. A. Glaser and S. Burger, "Verification of a Fissile Material Cutoff Treaty: The Case of Enrichment Facilities and the Role of Ultra-trace Level Isotope Ratio Analysis," *Journal of Radioanalytical and Nuclear Chemistry*, Vol. 280, No.1 (April 2009), pp. 85–90. http://link.springer.com/article/10.1007%2Fs10967-008-7423-0.

42. At this stage, Brazil is using conventional pressurized water reactor fuel for its submarine reactor and does not treat the reactor or fuel design as sensitive.

43. Sébastien Philippe, "Safeguarding the Military Naval Nuclear Fuel Cycle," *Journal of Nuclear Materials Management*, Vol. 42, No. 3 (Spring 2014), pp. 40–52.

44. In late 2011, Zamir Akram, Pakistan's Ambassador to the CD, said Pakistan was willing to allow the start of talks if Pakistan received the same exemption from existing nuclear trade rules that had been granted to India in 2009 by the Nuclear Suppliers Group, the organization of nuclear technology and material exporters. Tom Collina and Daniel Horner, "The South Asian Nuclear Balance: An interview with Pakistani Ambassador to the CD, Zamir Akram," *Arms Control Today*, Vol. 41, No. 10 (December 2011), pp. 8–13, www.armscontrol.org/act/2011_12/Interview_With_Pakistani_Ambassador_to_the_CD_Zamir_Akram.

45. International Panel on Fissile Materials, *Global Fissile Material Report 2013*.

46. Avner Cohen and Marvin Miller, "Israel," in *Banning the Production of Fissile Materials for Nuclear Weapons: Country Perspectives on the Challenges to a Fissile Material (Cutoff) Treaty*, International Panel on Fissile Materials, Princeton University, September 2008, pp. 27–33, http://fissilematerials.org/library/FMCT-Perspectives.pdf.

47. Frank von Hippel, Seyed Hossein Mousavian, Emad Kiyaei, Harold Feiveson, and Zia Mian, "Fissile Material Controls in the Middle East: Steps toward a Middle East Zone Free of Nuclear Weapons and all other Weapons of Mass Destruction," International Panel on Fissile Materials, Princeton, October 2013, http://fissilematerials.org/library/rr11.pdf.

48. Chunyan Ma and Frank von Hippel, "Ending the Production of Highly Enriched Uranium for Naval Reactors," *Nonproliferation Review*, Vol., No. 1 (Spring 2001), pp. 86–101, http://cns.miis.edu/npr/pdfs/81mahip.pdf.

49. Including management and administrative overhead. The IAEA's total budget appropriations for 2013 were €344 million of which: €131 million was for "nuclear verification" (mostly safeguards) including development; €108 for other activities relating to nuclear power and radioisotopes; €97 million for policy, management and administration; and €8 million for capital improvements, International Atomic Energy Agency, *Regular Budget Appropriations for 2013*, GC(56)/RES/5, September 2012, www.iaea.org/About/Policy/GC/GC56/GC56Resolutions/English/gc56res-5_en.pdf.

50. Russell Rumbaugh and Nathan Cohn, "Resolving Ambiguity: Costing Nuclear Weapons", Stimson Center, Washington, DC, June 2012, Table 4, www.stimson.org/images/uploads/research-pdfs/RESOLVING_FP_4_no_crop_marks.pdf.

Deterrence, Counterproliferation, and the Use of Force

15

DETERRENCE, DEFENSE, AND PREVENTIVE WAR

Michael Rühle

How do deterrence, defense, and preventive war relate to nuclear proliferation? Can they be effective and legitimate instruments to prevent proliferation, or are they just means to cope with proliferation's consequences? Can they be treated as distinct tools or are they rather parts of a broader continuum of responses, with the lines between them blurred?

Answering these questions poses considerable challenges. The most obvious challenge is the ideologically charged nature of the debate about the relationship between nuclear proliferation and the use of force. Whenever issues are at stake that may affect the survival of mankind, analysis tends to become advocacy. Rather than providing dispassionate assessments and analyses, many scholars offer prescriptions: their research is intended to make the case for or against a certain course of action against a proliferator, or to warn of the potential consequences of a government's defense policy. In short, the debate tends to become polemical. The debate about how to deal with Iran's nuclear activities is a case in point.[1]

This leads to the second challenge for a coherent analysis of the respective roles of deterrence, defense, and preventive war: The lack of solid empirical evidence to bolster or buttress an argument. Despite decades of research, the number of actual cases that can be studied remains too small to draw persuasive conclusions. The impressive volume of academic studies on deterrence, nonproliferation, and preventive war notwithstanding, the fact remains that this entire field is essentially based on more or less plausible assumptions rather than on hard, irrefutable facts. Consequently, and much to the chagrin of scholars and commentators, policy-makers who need to decide on these matters will ultimately do so by relying on what they consider to be "commonsense" based on past experience rather than the (often contradictory) findings of academic research.

Another challenge is the multi-faceted nature of the subjects in question. Nuclear deterrence, for example, threatens the attacker with reprisals that could in some circumstances amount to the defender committing suicide – a massive credibility dilemma that cannot be fully resolved analytically. At the same time, however, nuclear deterrence is closely tied to other important dimensions of security policy, such as the need to reassure one's own population as well as allies, or the desire to shape other countries' perceptions of one's own power and resolve. Hence, rather than rendering concepts such as deterrence irrelevant, as some analysts have concluded, such paradoxes only bring home the fact that the management of international security requires more than academic rigor. Even concepts that might be found analytically wanting can fundamentally shape international security.[2]

These challenges are profound. However, it would be wrong to conclude that the lack of empirical evidence means that all views and opinions are of equal weight and merit. Even if the absence of rain cannot be explained with complete certainty, the complexity of the weather still remains a more plausible explanation for a drought than the sun dance of a voodoo priest. If anything, examining issues that cannot be "proven" requires an even greater amount of intellectual discipline. This is all the more true when it comes to questions as important as the future of the global nuclear order. What follows, therefore, is a "mainstream" analysis that seeks to stay close to the actual policies of nations and to avoid the prescriptive excesses of parts of the strategic community.[3]

The proliferation challenge

There are currently five nuclear-weapon states recognized by the Treaty on the Nonproliferation of Nuclear Weapons (NPT) – the United States, United Kingdom, France, Russia, and China – and four nuclear powers – India, Pakistan, Israel, and North Korea – outside the NPT framework. The fact that most countries of this latter group achieved their nuclear status a long time ago, and that several would-be nuclear weapon nations either reconsidered (South Africa) or were prevented from realizing their nuclear ambitions (Iraq, Libya, Syria), has made nuclear proliferation proceed rather slowly overall. The number of countries that have given up their nuclear programs is much higher than the number of those who carried them through. However, it is impossible to prove whether proliferation's slow pace is due to global nonproliferation efforts, the growing acceptance of political and moral norms, technological and financial obstacles, or simply the fact that most nations had no strategic interest in going nuclear in the first place.[4]

It is equally impossible to produce a unified theory of nuclear acquisition. The motives for countries to go nuclear are too diverse to allow for a single explanation. Among the likely causes for pursuing nuclear weapons are regional security concerns (Israel in the 1960s), fears of abandonment (South Korea in the 1970s; Taiwan in the 1970s and 1980s); balance-of-power considerations (China and India in the 1960s and 1970s; Brazil and Argentina in the 1970s; India and Pakistan since the 1970s); bargaining leverage (North Korea since the 1990s); regional hegemonic ambitions (Iraq in the 1980s; Iran today), and a craving for more prestige and respect (Libya in the 1980s), all of them intersecting with domestic factors, such as bureaucratic politics. What unites all these cases, however, is that the NPT did not appear to have been a major limiting factor, even for members of the treaty. While the NPT and its complementing regime of inspections and export controls help to ensure that developing a military nuclear program remains time-consuming, expensive, and difficult to hide over the long term, it has not prevented determined governments from pursuing nuclear ambitions.

The *sui generis* character of each proliferation case also makes predictions about future trends next to impossible.[5] If the debate about the prospects for a world with more nuclear-armed states has nevertheless intensified, it is because of several fundamental changes that have occurred since the end of the Cold War. These changes are so profound as to constitute a "second nuclear age," which may invalidate many assumptions that used to dominate the first nuclear age.[6] Among these changes are the diffusion of technology as a result of globalization, the increasing commercialization of proliferation (including through semi-private networks), the undiminished interest in civilian nuclear energy, cooperation between proliferators, and the migration of nuclear experts from established nuclear-weapon states to nuclear-aspirant countries. As a result, proliferation has become more difficult to track, as much of it is proceeding outside the classical inter-state nonproliferation regime.[7]

The terrorist attacks on the United States on September 11, 2001, have brought additional factors into play. One is nuclear terrorism. While it had long been a subtext of the nonproliferation debate, it was "9/11" that turned it into a major issue, first as an argument for military action against states that might supply terrorist groups with nuclear weapons (e.g., Iraq),[8] and later as a central argument for the reduction and eventual abolition of nuclear weapons.[9] Another factor is the possible emergence of a fundamentalist nuclear-weapon state, for example if a radical religious movement should come to power and thus inherit the entire infrastructure of a national nuclear arsenal. Finally, some of the pessimism that pertains with respect to an approaching "nuclear tipping point" may also be traced to the decline of Western norm-setting power. As countries in other parts of the world, notably Asia, are gaining in power and self-confidence, they may not feel obliged to play by rules and norms that were almost exclusively a Western creation.

Despite these worrying developments there is nothing inherently deterministic about the future proliferation landscape. Technological progress notwithstanding, the political and financial costs of a nuclear-weapon program remain too high for most nations to make it appear desirable. It is also far from certain that the emergence of some new nuclear aspirants would lead to a nuclear domino effect. Past forecasts of "proliferation cascades" turned out to be mistaken because some states chose to deal with a new nuclear-armed neighbor by means other than responding in kind, for example by entering into an alliance with another nuclear power. However, while a new proliferation wave is not inevitable, the factors that constitute the second nuclear age appear too powerful to allow one to assume that the proliferation landscape will remain unchanged. Consequently, assumptions about deterrence, defense, and preventive war will have to be continuously revisited and, if necessary, adapted.

Deterrence

The concept of deterrence is based on the assumption that one party can dissuade another from undertaking certain undesirable acts, such as launching an attack, either by threatening unacceptable consequences (deterrence by punishment) or the thwarting of the opponent's war aims (deterrence by denial). Since rational human beings tend to fear loss more than they value gain,[10] a deterrence system based on the destructive capabilities of nuclear weapons is believed to act not only as a powerful war prevention tool but also as a means to induce restraint in the behavior of nuclear-armed adversaries. While it is widely accepted that nuclear deterrence will only "work" against major threats, and is largely ineffective against smaller, non-existential challenges, the concept has become a key element of the security policies of all nuclear-weapon states. Simply put, nuclear deterrence today is both a theory and a strategy. It has shaped the international political order since the advent of nuclear weapons in 1945, and will continue to do so.[11]

Most of the theory and practice of nuclear deterrence evolved in the specific circumstances of the Cold War US-Soviet bilateral relationship. This evolution included a highly sophisticated Western strategic discourse that sought to identify (and overcome) the multiple dilemmas inherent in a security policy based on weapons of mass destruction. The Cold War also witnessed a degree of "nuclear learning"[12] by the political and military decision-makers on both sides, leading them to refrain from certain provocative actions, enhance their communication during crises, and introduce technical and procedural safeguards against the unauthorized or accidental use of nuclear weapons. Other specific achievements of the Cold War were the numerous bi- and multilateral arms control agreements, such as the Partial Test Ban Treaty, the Nuclear Nonproliferation Treaty, and strategic nuclear arms limitation and reduction agreements. In sum, nuclear deterrence during the first nuclear age had become increasingly regulated by rules and norms. Even the advent of (a few) additional nuclear-weapon states did not fundamentally alter the basic assumptions about this concept of deterrence.

Deterrence in a proliferated World

While the end of the Cold War between 1989 and 1991 has removed the only known specific political and military context in which nuclear weapons contributed to mutual deterrence and political restraint, this did not necessarily mean that nuclear anarchy would have to follow. The end of the Cold War has not led to an accelerated pace of proliferation, nor have there been any new nuclear crises on a par with, for example, the Cuban missile crisis. It is entirely possible that the new nuclear-weapon states that may emerge in the coming decades will seek to emulate the behavior of the superpowers during the Cold War, including by introducing technical safeguards and adopting certain elements of transparency or other forms of confidence-building and crisis management mechanisms.[13] In other words, while a multi-stakeholder system will be more difficult to manage by definition, a few more nuclear-weapon states need not necessarily change the fundamentals of deterrence as a major instrument for safeguarding one's national security and for restraining inter-state relations. Consequently, in the debate over how to respond to Iran's nuclear ambitions, just as in the preceding debate over Iraq, deterrence – in the sense of containment – has often been advocated as the best solution, especially when compared to the costs of military action.[14]

However, it is far from certain whether all current and future nuclear-weapon states will "learn" the same lessons – and at the same pace. As one observer has noted, the second nuclear age started in Asia, a continent that features a combination of regional rivalries, assertive nationalism, and nuclear arms that hardly compares with the Cold War experience of the United States and its NATO allies.[15] The Middle East offers an equally challenging combination of factors, with religious fundamentalism adding yet another layer of risk. In the Cold War, the assumption that states possess an instinct of national self-preservation that will induce nuclear restraint was highly plausible, even if several crises revealed that not all political and military leaders acted in line with the assumption of "rationality" that is the *sine qua non* for a stable deterrence regime.[16] However, once a nuclear-weapon state is in the grip of religious or ideological fanatics, the "rational actor" model may no longer apply. One must instead contemplate the possibility that the glorification of martyrdom may not just be an expression of religious dogma or purely rhetoric for domestic consumption, but actually guide the leadership's behavior in a crisis. Communicating specific deterrence messages to such a government would not yield the desired results, as such a state would be "beyond" deterrence. Put differently, with one or several nuclear-weapon states of this kind, a stable multi-stakeholder deterrence system would be impossible to maintain. In sum, whether deterrence remains an effective instrument to cope with nuclear proliferation largely depends on the nature of the new nuclear-weapons states.

Extended deterrence

While deterrence is a means of safeguarding national security in a world with more nuclear powers, extended deterrence, i.e., the extension of nuclear protection to allies, can be both a means of protection and an instrument of nonproliferation. As with central deterrence, extended deterrence suffers from paradoxes, such as attributing to the nuclear weapons of one state a special role in upholding the nonnuclear-weapon status of others. Moreover, the credibility dilemmas of extended deterrence are even greater than those of national deterrence, as the system implies the security guarantor's willingness to risk suicide to protect others.[17] As a result, researchers have sought to demonstrate that extended deterrence is largely a politically convenient fiction. Some have even argued that the very concept should be disbanded, as it would prevent the United States from ever seriously contemplating the elimination of nuclear weapons from its arsenal.[18]

It appears unlikely that such criticism will have a major impact on US policy, however. Available evidence suggests a causal relationship between credible US extended deterrence and nonproliferation that is simply too strong to be dismissed. Today, more than thirty nations rely on extended US deterrence, including the members of NATO, South Korea, Japan, and Australia. In addition, several other states without formal defense agreements, like Taiwan, are also believed to be beneficiaries of the US "nuclear umbrella". US protection satisfies the security interests of allies and thus reduces temptations to develop nuclear weapons of their own.[19]

Developments in Asia and the Middle East demonstrate that the significance of extended deterrence remains unchanged. Japan is one prominent example. The country's growing nervousness about China's military rise and the threat posed by North Korea has provoked a debate about a national nuclear option that would have been unthinkable only a few years ago, even if a near-term reversal of Japan's anti-nuclear stance remains highly unlikely. While Japan has never actively sought nuclear weapons, most experts agree that Taiwan and South Korea tried to lay the groundwork for a national nuclear option to hedge against a worsening regional security situation. It was only after the United States intervened politically in the 1970s that these programs were terminated. All this suggests that, irrespective of its credibility dilemmas, US extended deterrence dampens nuclear ambitions in the Asia-Pacific region, sparing it a nuclear arms race.[20]

Developments in the Middle East and the Gulf reveal a similar pattern. Since the uncovering of Iran's illicit nuclear activities in 2002, Saudi Arabia has publicly declared that it would go nuclear should Iran do the same, and many other countries in the region have announced the launch of civilian nuclear programs. Many experts believe that these decisions are part of a strategy to hedge against the regional dominance of a nuclear-armed Iran.[21] Hence, should Iran become a nuclear power and act irresponsibly, neighboring countries could convert their civilian nuclear capabilities into military ones. Accordingly, as with the Asia-Pacific region, the extension of US security commitments to countries in the Middle East and the Gulf has been suggested as the quickest and politically most convenient way to contain potential proliferation pressures in the region.[22]

Even in Europe, where proliferation pressures are marginal, the interest in a tangible American nuclear security commitment remains unchanged. NATO's 2010 Strategic Concept, which states that NATO will remain a nuclear Alliance for as long as nuclear weapons exist, and the decision to continue the deployment of some US nuclear weapons in Europe, demonstrate that extended deterrence remains part and parcel of the European security order.[23] All this suggests that if countries perceive major threats to their security, their stance vis-à-vis nuclear weapons is shaped by their own immediate political constellations rather than by universal nonproliferation norms. Through its extended deterrence commitments the US signals that even a deterioration of the strategic environment of its allies will not fundamentally compromise their national security. Unlike a national deterrent, which only comes into play once proliferation has occurred, extended deterrence thus remains an important nonproliferation tool.

Defense

The specter of a world in which deterrence by threat of punishment may no longer be sufficient inevitably raises the question of alternatives to this type of deterrence. The most radical solution, the complete elimination of nuclear weapons, is not within the scope of this study and will take decades to be realized, if at all.[24] Hence, the logical alternatives to deterrence by punishment are deterrence by denial (i.e., by defense) and – taking the concept of defense to its extreme – the preventive use of force.

The most visible sign that defense is receiving more attention is the increased acceptance of missile defense, particularly in the United States and among its allies. With the binary US-Soviet relationship no longer being the reference point, missile defense has lost much of its erstwhile stigma of being "destabilizing".[25] Moreover, as the arsenals of prospective new nuclear nations will be small, missile defense offers much more plausible damage limitation options than in the context of the massive nuclear exchange scenarios contemplated during the Cold War. The development of missile defenses has also been spurred by the proliferation of conventional missile technology, which makes the rationale for defense even more solid. Like air defenses, missile defenses are thus likely to become an integral part of the force postures of many countries. Since missile defenses will not replace but only augment deterrence based on nuclear forces, charges that a combination of missile defenses and offensive nuclear forces could indicate an intention to launch a first strike can never be fully dismissed. However, such arguments will not be convincing enough to discredit the move towards missile defenses. The major limiting factors will be technical and financial.

A new nuclear armed state could use its nuclear weapons to attack another state, but a far more likely "use" of its newly acquired nuclear arsenal would be that of a counter-deterrent, i.e., the attempt to dissuade others from interfering with that state's political and military designs. Such a counter-deterrent would allow this new nuclear state to wage war against its neighbors with conventional forces without having to fear a nuclear response. In such a context, the defender would have to rely on traditional conventional defense capabilities, as nuclear weapons might only come into play if one of the nuclear-capable protagonists was about to suffer a massive conventional defeat.

Conventional forces would also play a key role should a nuclear armed great power like the United States decide to intervene in order to protect its allies in the region and thwart the regional challenger's geopolitical aims. As the US nuclear arsenal would deter the attacker from employing its own nuclear weapons, conventional US military capabilities would play the crucial role of restoring the status quo. However, since the possibility of nuclear use would always be present, the political and military risks of such a conventional military intervention would be considerable.[26] It is this fact that explains both the desire of certain revisionist leaders (e.g., Saddam Hussein) to acquire nuclear weapons, and the interest of status quo powers, such as the United States, to prevent it.[27] It also explains why the United States, despite its formidable nuclear arsenal, will seek to maintain superior conventional forces.

Yet another dimension of defense in a world with more nuclear powers will be the military enforcement of certain rules against proliferators. This pertains to the military enforcement of economic or other sanctions against a particular state, based on UN Security Council Resolutions. However, it also includes specific frameworks, such as the Proliferation Security Initiative (PSI), which seeks to interdict naval vessels with suspicious cargo. Predictably, some commentators have criticized the PSI for its allegedly dubious legal basis and lack of transparency.[28] However, the growing number of participating countries demonstrates that the logic of interdiction is increasingly accepted as a necessary and legitimate supplement of a broader nonproliferation policy – all the more so because the interdiction of one shipment of centrifuges headed for Libya may have been a major factor in Colonel Gadhafi's decision to forgo a nuclear option. In sum, the notion of defense in a world with more nuclear states comprises not only a range of different weapons categories but also new rules to deal with certain proliferators.

Preventive war

Waging a preventive war is commonly regarded as the means of last resort in order to avoid being attacked. In the context of the many uncertainties of a multi-nuclear world with a larger number of nuclear armed states, preventive military action could be considered a legitimate option. However, examining the pros and cons of preventive war faces a particular obstacle: much of the research on this subject remains under the shadow of the 2003 US-led invasion of Iraq. The controversy surrounding the Iraq decision – a decision that sparked *realpolitik* concerns about a breakdown of the global order as well as emotional outrage at the war's alleged illegality – still reverberates. This has become evident in the debate over military action against Iran, a debate that is rich with Iraq analogies, despite its different legal, political, and military context. Thus, it is fair to state that the discrediting of the main rationales for the Iraq war – the mistaken belief that Saddam had a WMD arsenal – has almost become a general verdict against preventive action against any potential or real proliferators. This verdict makes any attempt at an unbiased analysis of the conditions for preventive war appear like an ex-post-facto rehabilitation of an unjustified war. Despite the heavy burden of the Iraq debate, however, the issue whether nuclear-weapon proliferation changes the legal basis of self-defense remains as important as the question whether the preventive use of force is militarily sound.

Art. 51 of the UN Charter provides an exception to the general prohibition on the use of force in Article 2(4) of the Charter. Absent Security Council authorization, therefore, self-defense is the only legally justified use of force under international law. However, international law also recognizes the use of force in anticipatory self-defense, i.e. when a threat is imminent. Taking military action against troops massing at one's border ("preemption") would thus be considered legal, whereas destroying the nuclear facilities of another state ("prevention") would not. While the UN has characterized proliferation as a threat to international peace and security, there is no consensus as to whether this justifies military action against a state that is trying to acquire nuclear weapons or that is suspected of having already acquired them. Some observers argue that the notion of self-defense takes on an entirely different meaning in the nuclear age, as taking action only once a threat was "imminent" in traditional terms could be too late. Consequently, the definition of what constitutes an imminent threat had to be broadened to also include those activities that lead to the development of nuclear weapons, even if this actual threat would materialize only in the mid to long term.[29] By contrast, others maintain that any attempt to relax the strict conditions on the use of force will destabilize the rule-based international system.[30]

While this debate is unlikely to be resolved, the willingness of governments to use force in many different circumstances shows that state practice is not always guided by the UN Charter framework.[31] Attacks against nuclear facilities have repeatedly happened in the past, suggesting that irrespective of the legal evaluation of such actions, decision-makers were willing to authorize them if they concluded that such attacks were the best available option. Moreover, such strikes were most effective when they hit a still nascent nuclear program, i.e., when the danger was far from "imminent" and the action taken was thus legally most problematic.[32] Hence, while attempts to better align international law on the use of force with the reality of the emerging nuclear security landscape will continue, legal considerations will probably not be decisive when a government contemplates using preventive force against a proliferator.[33]

Views also differ as to the ultimate effectiveness of preventive strikes, with a debate that has become too ideologically charged to offer clear-cut conclusions.[34] Leaving aside the challenge of obtaining reliable intelligence,[35] much depends on the yardstick that one applies: retarding a state's nuclear program by several years through a military strike could be considered a success, as it might buy time for political change, but the negative international ramifications and the attacked state's possible responses – direct or asymmetric – must also be taken into account.[36] In other words, the decision to use force preventively will probably be based on a cost-benefit analysis that will differ for each individual case and that may have little to do with the rather categorical views to be found in the literature on this subject. Finally, the fact that other controversial means to slow down a country's nuclear program, such as cyber attacks against nuclear facilities or assassinations of scientists, have also been applied, suggests that the preventive use of force – in very different manifestations – will continue to be an option in dealing with proliferation. The unsatisfactory outcome of the Iraq war, however, will make another fully-fledged invasion of a suspected proliferator a most unlikely occurrence.

Deterrence, defense, and preventive war: The broader context

The current debate on military responses to proliferation is burdened by the same deficits that haunt the entire field of deterrence and nonproliferation research: a small database that often invites contradictory conclusions; a US-centric focus; and a desire to promote normative aims that diminishes the value of many analyses. Above all, the debate is still dominated by the political repercussions of the Iraq war and the discussion on how to deal with Iran. Despite these complicating factors, in recent years the rules and mechanisms for dealing with proliferation have evolved to incorporate a military dimension. Some elements of this emerging regime can already be discerned.

First, despite its well-documented weaknesses, the Nonproliferation Treaty will remain the central framework for identifying unwelcome behavior and initiating appropriate responses. Even if initiatives to adapt the treaty – for example, by reinterpreting the relationship between its various obligations or by making withdrawal more difficult – have not yet met with international consensus, the treaty's inspection regime provides a degree of transparency that is widely regarded as indispensable.[37]

Second, dealing with proliferators will follow individual rather than "universal" approaches. This has already been demonstrated in the case of Libya's voluntary disarmament, the handling of the North Korean nuclear dossier through the "Six Party Talks," the Iraq war, the sanctions regime against Iran, but also by the US-India nuclear cooperation agreement. Each case was handled differently, with a variable set of "carrots" and "sticks" – and outcomes likewise varied.

Third, the UN Security Council is becoming the focal point of nonproliferation. Despite the widespread image of the NPT as an objective set of rules transcending national interests, the treaty is, in essence, a mechanism administered by the United Nations Security Council, which ultimately decides how the treaty should be interpreted and if and how violators should be punished. Hence, building a consensus among the UN Security Council's members remains the foremost challenge of any effective nonproliferation approach.[38]

Fourth, the nonproliferation regime will increasingly evolve by way of UN Security Council resolutions, with the US-inspired UNSCR 1540 of April 2004 as a point of departure. This resolution builds on the nonbinding declaration of 1992, which characterized nuclear proliferation as a threat to international peace and security. UNSCR 1540 enables the Security Council to take Chapter VII measures against a proliferator, even if that state is not a signatory of the NPT. It thus adds the dimension of enforcement to the nonproliferation regime that had been missing in the NPT.

Fifth, coercive measures, such as the interdiction of maritime smuggling in the framework of the Proliferation Security Initiative, or the enforcement of economic sanctions against proliferators, are increasingly accepted as useful instruments for increasing the effectiveness of the nonproliferation regime. Such measures address both the nuclear aspirants and their suppliers, thus promising a more comprehensive deterrent effect.

Sixth, nuclear deterrence remains the most obvious approach to deal with proliferation's consequences. However, it will be increasingly augmented by ballistic missile defenses as well as by nonnuclear offensive capabilities. This will allow nuclear-weapon states to reduce the salience of nuclear weapons in their national defense strategies, which in itself constitutes an important nonproliferation signal.

Seventh, the relevance of nuclear security assurances will grow. In some cases, promising a state protection ("positive" security assurances), or promising not to attack it ("negative" security assurances), may be the preferred way to stifle regional proliferation dynamics.[39] For example, if US allies feel threatened by the emergence of a nuclear-armed challenger, US "extended deterrence" might well be the politically most convenient and militarily non-provocative way to keep these countries from pursuing their own national nuclear options.

Finally, the preemptive or even preventive resort to force will remain a legitimate – if controversial – means to deal with cases that offer no other effective solution. This could take the form of physical or cyber attacks on a state's nuclear facilities or other measures all the way to an invasion. However, due to its high political, military, financial, and human costs the last option will constitute a rare exception.

The indispensable nation

The fact that the United States is at the core of most of these emerging trends, either politically, conceptually, or militarily, highlights the crucial role that this country continues to play in shaping the global nuclear order. Whether the issue is preventing proliferation through extended deterrence, prodding the UN Security Council to adopt tougher sanctions against proliferators, or establishing new legal guidelines through innovative rules and mechanisms such as UNSCR 1540 and the Proliferation Security Initiative, the US remains the lynchpin of global nonproliferation efforts. The Iraq war may have damaged the political and moral credibility of the United States, but it has not changed the centrality of the US role in rallying the international community around new nonproliferation approaches.

Even if the United States may not always be comfortable with this role, it will have little choice but to continue playing it. The nuclear age and US globalism have emerged in parallel. Accordingly, current assumptions on proliferation rest, either consciously or subconsciously, on a nonproliferation universe that is still US-dominated. What will happen once the emergence of peer competitors undercuts the leadership that the US has been exerting since the beginning of the nuclear age? As this analysis has shown, the nuclear abstinence of many states in pivotal geopolitical regions is conditioned on a predictable international system – a system that is still being upheld largely by the United States. Thus, if the United States were to reduce or even end its role as a nuclear guarantor, the largest wave of proliferation since the dawn of the nuclear era could well be the result.

Notes

1. See, for example, James M. Lindsay and Ray Takeyh, "After Iran Gets the Bomb: Containment and Its Complications," *Foreign Affairs*, Vol. 89, No. 2 (March/April 2010), pp. 33–49; Kenneth N. Waltz, "Why Iran Should Get the Bomb: Nuclear Balancing Would Mean Stability," *Foreign Affairs*, Vol. 91, No. 4 (July/August 2012), pp. 1–5; and Robert Jervis, "Getting to Yes with Iran: The Challenges of Coercive Diplomacy," *Foreign Affairs*, Vol. 92. No. 1 (January/February 2013), pp. 105–115.

2. As Lawrence Freedman aptly noted, deterrence has worked better in practice than in theory, "Framing Strategic Deterrence," *Royal United States Institute Journal*, Vol. 10, No. 4 (August 2009), pp. 46–50.

3. For a sober analysis of some of the analytical weaknesses of the contemporary nuclear debate see Lawrence Freedman, "Disarmament and other Nuclear Norms," *Washington Quarterly*, Vol. 36, No. 2 (Spring 2013), pp. 93–108.

4. See, inter alia, Alexander H. Montgomery and Scott D. Sagan, "The Perils of Predicting Proliferation," *Journal of Conflict Resolution* Vol. 53, No. 2 (April 2009), pp. 302–328.

5. See William Potter with Gaukhar Mukhatzhanova, (eds), *Forecasting Nuclear Proliferation in the 21st Century* (Palo Alto, CA: Stanford University Press, 2010), 2 Volumes.

6. See Paul Bracken, "The Structure of the Second Nuclear Age," *Orbis*, Vol. 47, No. 3 (Summer 2003), pp. 399–413.

7. See Michael Rühle, "Enlightenment in the Second Nuclear Age," *International Affairs*, Vol. 83, No. 3 (April 2007), pp. 511–522; US Department of Defense, "Task Force Report: Assessment of Nuclear Monitoring and Verification Technologies," Defense Science Board, Washington, DC, January 2014, www.acq.osd.mil/dsb/reports/NuclearMonitoringAndVerificationTechnologies.pdf.

8. "The gravest danger our Nation faces lies at the crossroads of radicalism and technology," Foreword by President George W. Bush, The National Security Strategy of the United States of America, September 2002.

9. Barack Obama, "Remarks by President Barack Obama, Hradcany Square, Prague, Czech Republic." The White House, Office of the Press Secretary. April 5, 2009, www.whitehouse.gov/the_press_office/Remarks-By-President-Barack-Obama-In-Prague-As-Delivered.

10. See Daniel Kahneman and Amos Tversky, "Choices, Values, and Frames," *American Psychologist*, Vol. 39, No. 4 (April 1984), pp. 341–350.

11. It is moot to speculate whether deterrence "worked" in the superpower relationship of the Cold War, as it would be based on counterfactual assumptions. The argument that the history of the Cold War would have been largely the same even without the existence of nuclear weapons cannot be empirically refuted, yet it appears far more plausible to assume a causality between the existence of nuclear weapons and the absence of great power war.

12. Joseph S. Nye, Jr., "Nuclear Learning and US-Soviet Security Regimes," *International Organization*, Vol. 41, No. 3 (Summer 1987), pp. 371–402.

13. See Michael Quinlan, "India-Pakistan Deterrence Revisited," *Survival*, Vol. 47, No. 3 (Autumn 2005), pp. 103–116.

14. See Richard K. Betts, "The Lost Logic of Deterrence," *Foreign Affairs*, Vol. 92, No. 2 (March/April 2013), pp. 87–99.

15. See Paul Bracken, *Fire in the East: The Rise of Asian Military Power and the Second Nuclear Age* (New York: Harper Collins, 2009).

16. See the numerous examples in Keith B. Payne, *The Fallacies of Cold War Deterrence and a New Direction* (Lexington, KY: The University Press of Kentucky, 2001), esp. pp. 50–52.

17. Former British Defense Secretary Denis Healey once quipped that it took "only five per cent credibility of American retaliation to deter the Russians, but ninety-five per cent credibility to reassure the Europeans." Denis Healey, *The Time of my Life* (London: Michael Joseph, 1989), p. 243.

18. See Barry M. Blechman, "Extended Deterrence: Cutting Edge of the Debate on Nuclear Policy," Policy Forum Online 09-066A, August 13th, 2009, www.nautilus.org/publications/essays/napsnet/forum/2009-2010/09066Blechman.html/.

19. See David S. Yost, "US Extended Deterrence in NATO and North-East Asia," in *Perspectives on Extended Deterrence*, Research and Documents, Fondation pour la Recherche Stratégique (Paris), No 3 (2010), pp. 15–36, www.frstrategie.org/barreFRS/publications/rd/2010/RD_201003.pdf; Andrew O'Neil, "Extended Nuclear Deterrence in East Asia: Redundant or Resurgent?" *International Affairs*, Vol. 87, No. 6 (November 2011), pp. 1439–1457.

20. For a discussion of nuclear and nonnuclear elements of US extended deterrence, see Brad Roberts, "Extended Deterrence and Strategic Stability in Northeast Asia," NIDS Visiting Scholar Paper Series, No.1, August 9, 2013, www.nids.go.jp/english/publication/visiting/pdf/01.pdf.

21. See Christopher Clary and Mara E. Karlin, "The Pak-Saudi Nuke, and How to Stop It," *American Interest*, Vol. 7, No. 6 (July–August 2012), pp. 24–30.

22. James A. Russell, "Extended Deterrence, Security Guarantees, and Nuclear Weapons: US Strategic and Policy Conundrums in the Gulf," *Strategic Insights*, Vol. 8, No. 5 (December 2009), pp. 17–26.

23. For an extensive treatment of European attitudes see David S. Yost, "Assurance and US Extended Deterrence in NATO," *International Affairs* Vol. 85, No. 4 (2009), pp. 755–780.
24. See the range of views assembled in George Perkovich and James M. Acton, *Abolishing Nuclear Weapons: A Debate* (Washington, DC: Carnegie Endowment, 2009).
25. By defending against Iraqi missiles launched against Israel during the 1991 Gulf War, US missile defenses helped to keep Israel out of the war, thus preventing the US-led coalition, which included several Arab states, from breaking apart.
26. For a discussion of such scenarios see Barry R. Posen, "US Security Policy in a Nuclear-Armed World or: What if Iraq had had Nuclear Weapons," *Security Studies*, Vol. 6. No. 3 (Spring 1997), pp. 1–31.
27. See Kevin M. Woods, David D. Palkki, and Mark E. Stout (eds), *The Saddam Tapes: The Inner Workings of a Tyrant's Regime, 1978–2001* (Cambridge, MA: Cambridge University Press, 2011), esp. p. 223.
28. For a comprehensive overview see Aaron Dunne, "The Proliferation Security Initiative: Legal Considerations and Operational Realities" SIPRI Policy Paper No. 36 (May 2013), http://books.sipri.org/files/PP/SIPRIPP36.pdf.
29. See David Sloss, "Forcible Arms Control: Preemptive Attacks on Nuclear Facilities," *Chicago Journal of International Law*, Vol. 39, No. 54 (January 2003), pp. 39–57; Guy B. Roberts, "The Counter-proliferation Self-help Paradigm: A Legal Regime for Enforcing the Norm Prohibiting the Proliferation of Weapons of Mass Destruction," *Denver Journal of International Law & Policy*, Vol. 27, No. 3 (June 1999), pp. 483–529.
30. See Mary Ellen O'Connell, "The Myth of Preemptive Self-Defense," The American Society of International Law, Task Force On Terrorism Paper Series, Washington, DC, August 2002, http://cdm266901.cdmhost.com/cdm/ref/collection/p266901coll4/id/2944.
31. See Anthony Clark Arend, "International Law and the Preemptive Use of Military Force," *Washington Quarterly*, Vol. 26, No. 2 (Spring 2003), pp. 89–103; for example, NATO's 1999 intervention in Kosovo, which was not legitimized by a mandate of the UN Security Council, was defended as upholding basic principles of the UN Charter which the divided Security Council had failed to protect.
32. See Sarah E. Kreps & Matthew Fuhrmann, "Attacking the Atom: Does Bombing Nuclear Facilities Affect Proliferation? Targeting Nuclear Programs in War and Peace: A Quantitative Empirical Analysis, 1941–2000," *Journal of Conflict Resolution*, Vol. 54, No. 6 (December 2010), pp. 831–859. For other historical examples see Lyle J. Goldstein, *Preventive Attack and Weapons of Mass Destruction: A Comparative Historical Analysis* (Palo Alto, CA: Stanford University Press, 2006).
33. Even in the controversial 2003 Iraq war, which many observers regarded as an illegal preventive war against a suspected proliferator, legal issues ultimately did not figure too prominently, all the less so as the intervention was not justified as a preventive war but as a Chapter VII enforcement action, with legal authority derived from several United Nations Security Council resolutions demanding that Iraq permit inspections.
34. See Edward N. Luttwak, "In a Single Night," *Wall Street Journal*, February 8, 2006, http://online.wsj.com/news/articles/SB113937026599968085. For an argument that Israel's 1981 attack on the Osiraq plutonium reactor even accelerated Saddam Hussein's nuclear program see Dan Reiter, "Preventive Attacks Against Nuclear Programs and the 'Success' at Osiraq," *The Nonproliferation Review*, Vol. 12, No 2 (July 2005), pp. 355–371.
35. For a frank insider account on US intelligence failures see Christina Shelton, "The Roots of Analytic Failures in the US Intelligence Community," *International Journal of Intelligence and Counterintelligence*, Vol. 24, No. 4 (September 2011), pp. 637–655.
36. For a sober Israeli analysis on Iran's retaliatory options see Amos Yadlin and Avner Golov, "If Attacked, How Would Iran Respond?" *INSS Strategic Assessment*, Vol. 16, No. 3 (October 2013), pp. 7–21, www.inss.org.il/index.aspx?id=4538&articleid=5965.
37. For an excellent discussion of the NPT see Steven E. Miller, with responses from Wael Al-Assad, Jayantha Dhanapala, C. Raja Mohan, and Ta Minh Tuan, *Nuclear Collisions: Discord, Reform & the Nuclear Nonproliferation Regime* (Cambridge, MA: American Academy of Arts and Sciences, 2012).
38. Whether the UNSC will rise to the challenge is another matter. For a critical analysis, see Pierre Goldschmidt, "Measures Needed to Strengthen the Nuclear Non-Proliferation Regime," in *NATO and the Future of the Nuclear Non-Proliferation Treaty*, Joseph F. Pilat and David S. Yost (eds), Occasional Paper no. 21 (Rome: NATO Defense College, May 2007), www.ndc.nato.int/download/publications/op_21.pdf.
39. A comprehensive overview is provided by Jeffrey W. Knopf, (ed.), *Security Assurances and Nuclear Nonproliferation* (Palo Alto, CA: Stanford University Press, 2012).

16

COUNTERPROLIFERATION AND THE USE OF FORCE

Robert S. Litwak

Nonproliferation policies encompass a broad continuum from cooperative to coercive. That President John F. Kennedy's frightening prediction of a world of thirty or more nuclear-weapon states has thankfully not come to pass is testimony to the fact that the vast majority of countries in the international system do not view the acquisition of nuclear weapons as vital to their national security. An essential condition of nuclear restraint has been the strategic calculations of the vast majority of states that their national security does not require the possession of nuclear weapons. This has been reinforced by the international norm against proliferation codified in the Nuclear Nonproliferation Treaty (NPT).

The United States may have a general interest in preventing proliferation and supporting the international nuclear nonproliferation regime, but it does not regard all would-be proliferators as specific threats to American security. The perception of threat derives from the interaction of capabilities with intentions, not just the former in isolation. US administrations distinguish between new and de facto nuclear proliferators – such as Israel, India, and Pakistan – that challenge an important international norm but do not directly threaten the United States, and those countries do pose such a security threat. Thus, the cases in which the United States would actually contemplate the use of force involve a sub-set of countries that are pursuing the acquisition of WMD capabilities and that have hostile intentions. Those states constitute hostile proliferators. In the post-9/11 period, an additional concern has been the nexus of proliferation and terrorism – that is, the nightmare scenario that a hostile state with WMD capabilities would transfer them to an undeterrable terrorist group, such as Al Qaeda. This chapter examines the conditions United States would use, or threaten the use of force, against a hostile state of proliferation concern.[1]

The rise of counterproliferation

US counterproliferation policies date to the early 1990s, when the Defense Department moved to operationalize the lessons of the Gulf War, during which US forces had been threatened by, and in turn, targeted Iraqi unconventional capabilities. In a 1993 address to the National Academy of the Sciences, US Secretary of Defense Les Aspin highlighted the new threats of the post-Cold War era, raising the specter of "a handful of nuclear devices in the hands of rogue states or even terrorists."[2] The Clinton administration's "Defense Counterproliferation

Initiative" (DCI) generated confusion and controversy over the analytical and policy distinction between "counterproliferation" and "nonproliferation." Confusion stemmed from an initial lack of clarity about whether the DCI was being advanced as a component of traditional nonproliferation policy or as an alternative to it.

The National Security Council (NSC) issued a memorandum of "Agreed Definitions" in February 1994 to increase programmatic coherence. It characterized counterproliferation as

> the activities of the Department of Defense across the full range of US efforts to combat proliferation, including diplomacy, arms control, export controls, and intelligence collection and analysis, with particular responsibility for assuring that US forces can be protected should they confront an adversary armed with weapons of mass destruction or missiles."[3]

Both this NSC memorandum and a subsequent interagency report underscored that the counterproliferation initiative was firmly embedded within a comprehensive nonproliferation policy.[4] But despite this affirmation that military capabilities were part of the continuum of nonproliferation instruments, questions about counterproliferation persisted because it was widely interpreted overseas as auguring possible unilateral and preemptive American military strikes against suspected targets producing or housing WMD in the Third World.[5]

The launching of the DCI coincided with the unfolding nuclear crisis with North Korea in 1993–94. During that period, several hard-line critics of the Clinton administration's handling of the crisis advocated military strikes against the North's nuclear facilities as the preferred alternative to diplomacy with this "rogue state." Thus, the North Korean crisis raised the specter of preemptive unilateral military action, while it reinforced the perception that counterproliferation was being advanced as an alternative to nonmilitary instruments of nonproliferation. Department of Defense officials attempted to assuage this concern through public assurance that counterproliferation was not synonymous with preemption. But they also acknowledged that military preemption might be undertaken if alternative nonproliferation instruments failed and if intelligence indicated an imminent threat against US or allied troops in the field.[6]

In the decade after the Cold War and Desert Storm, the use of force as an instrument of nonproliferation policy became an issue of contention between the United States and both its key NATO allies and other UN Security Council members. Russia, China, and France opposed the use of force to compel Iraqi compliance with the Security Council's disarmament resolutions, but had no credible alternative approach. Within NATO, European members eschewed the term counterproliferation, believing that it connoted preemptive military action and could therefore seriously undermine multilateral nonproliferation efforts.[7]

In the post-9/11 era, the George W. Bush administration directly linked the proliferation and terrorism issues in a speech three months after the attacks, declaring that "[r]ogue states are clearly the most likely sources of chemical and biological and nuclear weapons for terrorists."[8] In his January 2002 State of the Union address, the president referred obliquely to the necessity of preemptive military action in the post-9/11 era. He identified Iraq, Iran, and North Korea as an "axis of evil" and stated that his administration "will not stand by, as peril draws closer and closer. The United States of America will not permit the world's most dangerous regimes to threaten us with the world's most destructive weapons."[9] In a speech at West Point in June 2002, President Bush explicitly made the case for "preemptive action," citing the mass-casualty consequences of a WMD attack on American soil and the unique political character of the rogue regimes and terrorist groups whose threat defied traditional deterrence and containment strategies. "Deterrence," he argued, "means nothing against shadowy terrorist networks with no nations or citizens to defend. Containment is not possible when unbalanced dictators with weapons of mass destruction can deliver those weapons on missiles or secretly provide them to terrorist allies."[10]

This argumentation was central to the Bush administration's decision to launch a preventive war to topple the Saddam Hussein regime. The war was launched without the legitimizing imprimatur of the UN Security Council, though the Bush administration claimed that it was undertaking the military action to bring the Iraqi regime into compliance with the UN resolutions mandating Iraq's WMD disarmament. After the fall of Baghdad, the US hope to legitimize the Iraq war ex post facto was dashed by the failure to find stocks of chemical and biological weapons, which even the intelligence services of countries opposed to the US military intervention had believed existed. Since, as we now know, Iraq had been essentially disarmed of its WMD capabilities during the 1990s, the mystery is why Saddam Hussein simply did not come clean and permit intrusive inspections that would have undercut the United States's primary rationale in the UN Security Council deliberations for military action. The Duelfer report, detailing the comprehensive findings of the Iraq Survey Group, indicated that Saddam Hussein viewed the perpetuation of ambiguity about the status of his WMD programs as having strategic value. Saddam Hussein maintained that ambiguity not only with the outside world but with his regime's own senior officials (who were left guessing whether his claims of a "secret weapon" were true). The Iraqi leader believed that such ambiguity could deter a US attack in 2003, just as he was convinced that his chemical weapons arsenal had deterred a US march on Baghdad at the end of the 1991 Gulf War. Ironically, the ambiguity about Iraq's WMD capabilities that Saddam Hussein cultivated to retain "a strategic deterrent" (in the words of the Duelfer report) became the basis for the US military action that toppled his regime, as explicitly stated in the 2006 *National Security Strategy:* "It was [Saddam Hussein's] refusal to remove the ambiguity that he created that forced the United States and its allies to act."[11]

President Barack Obama inherited twin nuclear challenges with North Korea and Iran. President Obama described the two countries as "outliers" – states that flout international norms by defying their obligations under the Nuclear Nonproliferation Treaty. Senior White House aides confirmed that use of the term, which was made in an April 2010 interview with the *New York Times* about the administration's Nuclear Posture Review, was a calculated departure from the Bush-era moniker of "rogue state."[12] The shift in nomenclature from "rogue" to "outlier" was intended to convey that a pathway was open for these states to rejoin the "community of nations" if they came into compliance with international norms.

Historical cases

Under what conditions would the United States consider the use of force, either preventively or preemptively, to prevent a state of concern from acquiring nuclear capabilities? A comparative analysis of cases in which military force was either used or seriously contemplated can generate policy-relevant generalizations about the criteria and conditions governing the use of force as a nonproliferation policy instrument. There are strikingly few such historical cases. In the early 1960s, for example, the United States seriously considered, and ultimately rejected, a preventive strike on China's nuclear-weapon facilities.[13] This chapter will consider four cases: Israel's June 1981 bombing of Iraq's Osiraq nuclear reactor; the 1991 Gulf War against Iraq, and the subsequent enforcement of UN Security Council disarmament resolutions; the 1993–94 North Korean nuclear crisis; and the Israeli strike on a nuclear facility in Syria in 2007.

Each brief case summary will address a common set of questions under three categories.[14] The first category is the *character of the proliferation threat* precipitating the decision to use force or not: Is the threat imminent? Is the assessment based on sound intelligence? The second category relates to the *politico-military context*: Is the mission militarily feasible? Have nonmilitary alternatives been exhausted? Is the nonproliferation issue linked to another issue or embedded in a broader policy context? And does the proposed action have multilateral support or will it be undertaken unilaterally? The third category is the assessed *consequences* of the use or nonuse of force: Will the target state retaliate, directly or indirectly, against the United States or its allies? Could the action trigger a broader conflict – a so-called "catalytic" war? Could the attack have unacceptable collateral damage – either to the environment or in civilian casualties?[15]

Israeli raid on Iraq's Osiraq nuclear reactor, June 1981

On June 7, 1981, a squadron of Israeli F-15s and F-16s surreptitiously traversed Jordanian and Saudi Arabian air space to bomb Iraq's French-made Osiris-type reactor near Baghdad. Since the 1970s, Israel had closely monitored Iraq's concerted efforts to obtain nuclear technology. Under a 1974 bilateral nuclear cooperation agreement with France, Iraq had proposed the purchase of a 500 MW gas-graphite reactor, which would have produced large quantities of plutonium, ideal for a nuclear-weapon program. The French balked at this request and offered a 70 MW research reactor as an alternative.[16] Iraq's approach to nuclear commerce with France left little doubt that the Baghdad regime's primary interest was in acquiring fissile material rather than producing energy.

Israeli prime minister Menachem Begin viewed the prospect of a nuclear-armed Iraq under Saddam Hussein as an existential threat to Israel. Labor Party leader Shimon Peres reportedly cautioned Begin against military action, arguing that Israel would be diplomatically isolated and that the intelligence was inadequate. In early spring 1981, Mossad, Israel's intelligence service, predicted that the Iraqi reactor could go into operation as early as July. For Begin, a window of opportunity for action existed before the nuclear fuel (the bulk of which had not yet arrived from France) was loaded into the reactor. In tandem with this intelligence estimate, a key influence on Begin's decision making was Israel's scheduled parliamentary elections at the end of June. Begin feared that if Labor defeated his Likud Party, Peres would attempt to address the Iraqi nuclear threat diplomatically through the French and would never authorize a preventive strike on Osiraq.[17]

In the wake of the Israeli air strike on the Osiraq facility, international reaction was sharply critical. Rejecting Israel's claim of anticipatory self-defense, the UN Security Council condemned the attack as "a clear violation of the Charter of the United Nations and the norms of international conduct."[18] Not until a decade later, after inspectors from the United Nations Special Commission on Iraq (UNSCOM) discovered the magnitude of Saddam Hussein's covert nuclear-weapon program, was the Israeli assessment of Iraqi intentions validated. Though a tactical success, the efficacy of the 1981 air strike is still debated. Proponents declare that the blow to the Iraqi program bought time – not an inconsequential goal in nonproliferation policy. Skeptics counter that the Israeli raid was a strategic failure that failed to deter Iraq from acquiring nuclear weapons – and may indeed have provided further motivation. The stark reality is that Saddam exponentially expanded Iraq's nuclear program after 1981 – from 400 scientists and $400 million to 7,000 specialists and a $10 billion budget.[19]

The Gulf War and Operation Desert Fox

As part of Operation Desert Storm in January–February 1991, US and allied aircraft targeted Iraq's unconventional weapons and missiles to prevent their use against other countries in the region (most notably Israel) and to protect coalition forces. These missions were not conducted to roll back proliferation per se, but were rather an extension of war. Their legal basis derived from the pertinent UN Security Council resolutions authorizing the use of force to reverse Iraqi aggression in Kuwait. During the air war, coalition aircraft flew approximately 970 strikes against nuclear, biological, and chemical weapons sites. An additional 1,500 missions were aimed at suppressing Iraq's Scud missile force.[20]

UNSCOM's startling post-war revelations about the magnitude of Iraqi WMD capabilities that survived Desert Storm, as well as the assessment provided by the Department of Defense's own *Gulf War Air Power Survey*, highlighted the limited effectiveness of the US air campaign. These findings underscored both the critical importance of extensive intelligence for targeting unconventional weapons, and the ability of a determined proliferator to make such capabilities less vulnerable to attack through deception and mobility. For example, UNSCOM inspectors revealed the existence of twenty-one nuclear-related facilities in Iraq, whereas the pre-war target list included only two such sites. The *Survey* analysts concluded that the air campaign no more than "inconvenienced" Iraq's nuclear-weapon program, and that the actual destruction of *any* mobile Scud missiles by fixed-wing coalition aircraft could not be confirmed.[21]

During the post-Gulf War period, the United States and Britain employed instruments of coercive nonproliferation – economic sanctions and the threatened use of force – to try to compel Iraq's compliance with UN Security Council Resolution 687. Diminished international support for economic sanctions and the opposition of UN Security Council members Russia, China, and France to the use of force to assure compliance with UNSCR 687 emboldened Saddam Hussein to defy UNSCOM and engage in brinkmanship. Saddam Hussein linked his own fate to the survivability of Iraq's WMD capabilities by placing them under the control of his presidential guard, the Special Security Organization (SSO), headed by his son, Qusay. Thus, any US military strike on Iraq's WMD capabilities would be, in effect, an attack on Saddam Hussein personally. Indeed, UNSCOM officials believe that SSO units shuttled Iraq's WMD assets around Saddam Hussein's network of presidential palaces to defeat the UN's inspection regime.[22] A senior UNSCOM official referred to this tactic as Iraq's "philosophy of concealment through mobility."[23]

In 1998, a series of crises over Iraqi noncompliance and noncooperation with UNSCOM led to four days of sustained air attacks by the United States and Britain. The air campaign, code-named Operation Desert Fox, relied heavily on cruise missiles and was the most extensive use of force against Iraq since the end of the Gulf War in 1991. During the four-day air campaign, Secretary of State Madeleine Albright, Secretary of Defense William Cohen and National Security Advisor Sandy Berger declared that the US commitment to use force against Iraq was open-ended. But to what purpose? At the outset of Operation Desert Fox, Secretary Cohen stated that the goal was to degrade Iraq's WMD capabilities and "not to destabilize the regime."[24] The Clinton administration was caught politically between domestic critics, who wanted a more ambitious air campaign aimed at undermining Saddam Hussein, and UN Security Council members, who were reflexively opposed to the use of force and sought only Iraq's compliance with UNSCR 687.

By the end of Operation Desert Fox, US and British forces had flown more than 300 combat sorties and fired more than 400 cruise missiles at Iraqi targets. In early January 1999, General Henry H. Shelton, chairman of the Joint Chiefs of Staff, reported to Congress that the raids had inflicted more damage than originally estimated. The raids destroyed or severely damaged twelve missile production sites and eleven command and control facilities. But, in a striking admission, US and British planners acknowledged that they did not target chemical and biological weapons facilities out of fear that such attacks might release deadly toxins into the atmosphere and produce unacceptable civilian casualties.[25]

North Korea's nuclear program, 1993–94

Former secretary of defense William Perry has called the 1993–94 North Korean nuclear crisis the most dangerous episode of the post-Cold War era.[26] In US contingency planning during that crisis, the Clinton administration examined the option of military strikes on the North's advanced nuclear facilities. The Democratic People's Republic of Korea (DPRK) possessed an operational 5MW(e) graphite-moderated reactor and a reprocessing facility for spent nuclear fuel at Yongbyon, and had begun construction of two additional 50MW(e) and 200MW(e) nuclear reactors. The CIA estimated that the DPRK could have extracted as much as 12 kilograms of plutonium, enough for one or two weapons, from fuel rods in the Yongbyon reactor.[27] A January 1993 request from the International Atomic Energy Agency (IAEA) for a "special inspection" of suspect sites, which the DPRK was obliged to grant as an NPT signatory, was the immediate precipitant of the crisis. The Kim Il-sung regime rejected the request and threatened to withdraw from the Nonproliferation Treaty in March 1993, a move that prompted calls on Capitol Hill and in the press for a tough American counteraction, including the consideration of military options.

The row over International Atomic Energy Agency (IAEA) inspections took a significant escalatory turn in April 1994 when the DPRK announced its intention to shut down the Yongbyon reactor to remove spent fuel containing sufficient plutonium for an additional four or five bombs. In June 1994, the IAEA referred the matter to the UN Security Council and the United States moved to strengthen its defenses in South Korea in anticipation of a diplomatic campaign to impose economic sanctions on the North. The Kim Il-sung regime responded with defiance, declaring that sanctions would be tantamount to a declaration of war. The Clinton administration adopted the sanctions strategy after considering – and rejecting – the alternative of military preemption.

The significant possibility that a preemptive attack on the Yongbyon nuclear facilities would have a "catalytic" effect and trigger a general war on the Korean peninsula effectively removed the military option from consideration. In addition to the danger of inadvertent escalation, incomplete intelligence gave US policy-makers no assurance that air strikes would hit all the pertinent targets at Yongbyon, or that this military action would eliminate the North Korean nuclear threat if some illicit reprocessing of spent fuel to extract plutonium had occurred during earlier reactor shutdowns. In mid-June, as the Clinton administration prepared to push for UN Security Council sanctions and dispatch an additional 50,000 US forces to reinforce South Korea, the crisis was defused during former President Jimmy Carter's controversial trip to Pyongyang. That high-level diplomatic intervention yielded the immediate result of Kim Il-sung's pledge to "freeze" activity at the Yongbyon site. The Carter mission broke the impasse and led to intensive bilateral negotiations that culminated in the US-DPRK Agreed Framework of October 1994.

Israel's raid on Syria's Nuclear Reactor, 2007

In spring 2007, the United States was informed by a "foreign intelligence partner," presumably Israel, that Syria was constructing a nuclear reactor evidently modeled on the North Korean

facility at Yongbyon, capable of producing weapons-grade plutonium. To Bush, the report indicated that "we had just caught Syria red-handed trying to develop a nuclear weapons capability
with North Korean help."[28] In response, the Bush administration considered either bombing
the facility or reporting Syria's action to the IAEA. When Bush asked the US intelligence
community for its assessment, CIA director Michael Hayden reported the agency had "high
confidence" that the facility was a nuclear reactor, but that they had only "low confidence" of
a weapons program because of the absence of a facility to separate plutonium from the reactor
fuel rods. Bush rejected an Israeli request to bomb the facility, telling Prime Minister Ehud
Olmert, "I cannot justify an attack on a sovereign nation unless my intelligence programs stand
up and say it's a weapons program." The United States, he told Olmert, would therefore opt for
"the diplomatic option backed by the threat of force."[29] Another factor reportedly underlying
the decision was concern that a US attack on Syria could trigger an escalation in Syrian
meddling in Iraq, which the United States was desperately attempting to stabilize in the face
of a determined Sunni insurgency. Israel bombed the Syrian nuclear facility on September 6,
2007. That it was bombed during the construction phase before the nuclear core was loaded
reduced the risk of collateral damage to the environment.

Conditions and constraints

A comparative analysis of the cases presented above permits the identification of key criteria
and conditions governing the preemptive or preventive use of force as an instrument of nonproliferation policy. Although general propositions can be developed on the basis of historical
experience, any specific decision by policy makers should be context-dependent and contingent on an accurate assessment of the target state.

Character of the threat

The threshold issue for the use of force is a judgment about a regime's intentions, whether
hostile or not toward the United States. Although hostile intent is a necessary condition, it
alone is not sufficient to precipitate action. It is the conjunction of hostile intent and the capability to act upon it that would prompt US decision makers to consider the use of force. Sound
intelligence must indicate that the threat is imminent – either that WMD will be used or, much
more controversially, that an important technological threshold will be crossed.

Politico-military context

Once a state is deemed a hostile proliferator, several key considerations then affect decision
making about the use of force. In addition to sound strategic intelligence about a hostile proliferator's motivations and intentions, effective tactical intelligence is necessary to determine
whether or not a military option is even feasible. The challenge of obtaining this information
and then translating it into military action was highlighted by the Gulf War experience and the
post-conflict revelations by UNSCOM about the magnitude of Iraqi WMD capabilities and
the number of missiles that had escaped detection and destruction. In the 2003 Iraq war, the
strategic surprise was precisely the opposite: the absence of WMD stocks. In the 1994 North
Korean crisis, incomplete intelligence gave Clinton administration officials no assurance that all
pertinent nuclear-related targets could be destroyed through air strikes.

Beyond these intelligence requirements, the feasibility of military action also depends on the
political context. Because international norms insist that force be the instrument of last resort,

nonmilitary options should be exhausted before considering military instruments. Convincing others, most notably the UN Security Council, that all nonmilitary alternatives have been exhausted will be essential if the United States is to have any chance of gaining multilateral support for the use of force.

Consequences

A third set of criteria and conditions governing the use of force focuses on the consequences of its employment. In considering the use of force against a hostile proliferator, a primary concern must be the potential capability of the target state to retaliate. A policy maker could not discount the possibility that a hostile proliferator might lash out with any surviving unconventional capability against a US ally or American forces in the regional theater. Some of the defensive measures supported through the Defense Department's counterproliferation program could mitigate the consequences of retaliation, but the significant possibility of WMD retaliation would still be a major constraint on bringing force to bear against a hostile proliferator.

A senior US official who participated in the negotiation of the US-DPRK Agreed Framework argues that the North Koreans did not distinguish between a narrow US counterproliferation option on the North's nuclear facilities and general war. On the American side, the fear of inadvertent escalation and catalytic war – the possibility that a counterproliferation strike on the North's nuclear infrastructure would provoke all-out war on the Korean peninsula – was a key policy determinant.[30] This overriding concern, which was highlighted by the South Koreans in expressing their staunch opposition to military action, prompted the Clinton administration to pursue alternative nonmilitary approaches – initially, economic sanctions in the UN; later, bilateral negotiations leading to the Agreed Framework.

An additional factor tempering the resort to force has been the desire to limit collateral damage, both to the environment and to the civilian population. To avoid an environmental catastrophe the Israelis struck the Osiraq reactor before its fuel of highly enriched uranium had been loaded into the core and the facility was operational. Likewise, during Operation Desert Fox, the United States and Britain abstained from striking chemical and biological sites for fear of releasing dangerous toxins into the atmosphere.

US counterproliferation capabilities are unlikely to deter would-be proliferators from acquiring weapons of mass destruction. Those states' national security and domestic political motivations are deep-seated and powerful, and counterproliferation capabilities do not alter them.[31] Particularly in light of the cases discussed above, the likely impact of US counterproliferation policy will be to drive those states' programs further underground. The history of Saddam Hussein's WMD programs in the 1980s is stunning testimony to the ability of a determined proliferator to develop a massive, covert program. If counterproliferation capabilities and the threat of preventive military action will not forestall WMD acquisition, will they deter actual use by a hostile proliferator? Such capabilities could cut both ways. On the one hand, defensive measures, such as the acquisition by US forces of protective chem-bio suits, could convince a target state that it has nothing to gain militarily from WMD use. On the other hand, a target state might resort to WMD use if it believed that its ruling regime was on the verge of being overthrown. During the Gulf War, Iraq forward-deployed chemical munitions, and the question of whether Saddam Hussein pre-delegated authority to commanders to use unconventional weapons under certain conditions remains unresolved. An Iraqi official subsequently asserted that Baghdad would have used its WMD capabilities only in retaliation for the use of such weapons by coalition forces. But given the primacy of regime security to Saddam Hussein, the continuation of the war into Iraq – the so-called "march on Baghdad" – could very plausibly have precipitated Iraqi WMD use against the US-led coalition.[32] Indeed, Saddam Hussein evidently believed that his stockpile of unconventional weapons deterred the United States from expanding its war aims beyond the liberation of Kuwait and marching on Baghdad to change the Iraqi regime.

Prominent among the strategic surprises of the 2003 Iraq war was Saddam Hussein's nonuse of WMD against invading US and British forces in the one scenario – regime change – in which experts broadly agreed the Iraqi dictator would employ them. Indeed, US forces involved in the ground offensive to topple the Saddam Hussein regime widely employed their protective chem-bio suits. In light of Iraq's expected use of unconventional weapons, did the United States conduct counterproliferation strikes against Iraq's suspect WMD sites? Although no counterpart to the Department of Defense's 1993 *Gulf War Air Power Survey* has yet been published for the 2003 conflict, the existing public record is suggestive. According to the scant public information available on this question, US military planners reportedly eschewed air strikes on possible Iraqi WMD sites for fear of spewing chemical or biological toxins into the environment.[33] Instead, the war featured the use of American, British, and Australian Special Forces, who seized or blew up Iraqi command posts to prevent the transmission of orders to employ chemical and biological weapons. This cautionary experience is consistent with the general pattern of restraint evidenced in the non-wartime cases (discussed above) in which the use of force was considered to stem proliferation, and highlights the major constraints on counterproliferation missions such as those raised as options to deal with the North Korean and Iranian nuclear programs.

Implications

Past experience, including the most recent episode in Iraq, offers policy makers relevant insights into the conditions governing the use of force to forestall proliferation.

Preemption should be a rare necessity

The cases in which the United States would consider the use of force involve a small group of proliferators with a conjunction of capabilities and hostile intent. Under what conditions, short of war, would policy makers still resort to the use of force? One such condition would be if conflict with a WMD-armed adversary was judged to be imminent, or if a WMD-armed adversary directly threatened the United States or its allies. In that eventuality, the preemptive use of force would be considered the initiation of a war that was inevitable. Another contingency that would precipitate US military action goes to the heart of the administration's post-9/11 concept linking the dangers of terrorism and proliferation: the transfer of WMD capabilities by a hostile proliferator to a nonstate terrorist group. During the debate over military action against Iraq, US officials raised the specter that Saddam Hussein's Iraq might provide WMD capabilities to Al Qaeda. Similar concern has been expressed with respect to North Korea, which has threatened on one occasion to export nuclear materials. While the plausibility of a WMD transfer scenario is much debated, the United States can help deter such a transfer by making explicit that conclusive evidence of any such move by a hostile proliferator would trigger an overwhelming American military response, with the objective of regime change.

Force may be as problematic as its nonmilitary alternatives

Proponents of preemption often cite the June 1981 Israeli raid on Iraq's Osiraq nuclear facility as a model. But the Osiraq case, far from being a paradigm, was a rare instance in which all the conditions for success were present – specific and highly accurate intelligence, and the negligible risk of collateral damage and retaliation. More often in history, the utility of force has been affected by major constraints – the possibility of triggering a general war (North Korea, 1994), uncertain and disputed intelligence (Iraq, 2003), and the threat of unacceptable collateral damage to the population and environment (Iraq, 1998). In short, force is not a silver bullet. In considering the use of force, policy makers must balance the known costs of military action against the unknown costs of proliferation.

Successful nonmilitary prevention strategies will forestall the need for military preemption

The instances in which force has been considered or used for nonproliferation purposes have been *preventive* rather than *preemptive*. In none was actual WMD use imminent (apart from the 1991 Gulf War episode when Saddam Hussein reportedly authorized commanders to use unconventional weapons if coalition forces marched on Baghdad). Prevention strategies employ the full array of nonproliferation tools, including multilateral treaties, export controls, and economic coercion.

The vast majority of work done in the nonproliferation area falls under the rubric of *deterrence by denial*. This covers a wide range of activities: export controls to limit access to technology; physical security at sensitive sites to lockdown fissile material to prevent illicit diversion, an objective pioneered through the US Cooperative Threat Reduction program, which the Obama administration has proposed expanding to regions beyond its original focus on the former Soviet Union; and the interdiction of contraband cargoes through the Proliferation Security Initiative (PSI), a multinational effort launched by the Bush administration in May 2003, to prevent the trafficking of WMD technologies.

Future challenges

The Obama administration assumed office with no good options to deal with the North Korean and Iranian nuclear challenges. None is without risk. A complete nuclear rollback is possible in neither. What level of risk are US policy makers prepared to run? Though North Korea has the more advanced nuclear program, it is an impoverished, insular state whose besieged regime is simply seeking to survive. By contrast, Iran, with its oil wealth and radical activism, remains the more dynamic threat.

The US characterization of Iran's decision making as being "guided by a cost-benefit approach" is an important threshold assumption for strategy development (indicating as it does) that the Islamic Republic is not an irrational, undeterrable state. Although Iran (as one would similarly argue of North Korea) is deterrable, deterrence can fail through miscalculation and misperception. Diplomatic efforts are aimed at capping Iran's nuclear program, particularly its uranium enrichment program. Any plausible diplomatic resolution of the Iranian nuclear crisis would allow Iran to retain a hedge for a weapon with perhaps a one-year breakout timeline. American officials say that all options remain on the table to prevent Iran from crossing the threshold of weaponization, but acknowledge that a US (or Israeli) military strike on Iran's nuclear sites would only delay the Iranian program by three years and could have "unintended consequences."[34] A decision to bomb Iran's nuclear infrastructure carries a significant risk of military escalation, civilian casualties, and environmental damage, as well as bolstering the Iranian regime through a rally-round-the-flag effect after a US attack.

US declaratory policy has been strengthened to deter either the deliberate transfer or the accidental "leakage" of a nuclear weapon by a state to another state of concern or terrorist group. After North Korea's nuclear test in October 2006, President Bush declared that "the transfer of nuclear weapons or material by North Korea to states or nonstate entities would be considered a grave threat to the United States."[35] Pyongyang crossed the red line of *state-to-state transfer* with its covert provision of a prototype nuclear reactor to Syria. Shortly after Israel bombed that facility in September 2007 while it was under construction, the arrival of a North Korean cargo ship in a Syrian port prompted Secretary of Defense Robert Gates to warn against DPRK nuclear exports: "If such an activity were taking place, it would be a matter of great concern because the president has put down a very strong marker with the North Koreans about further proliferation efforts, and obviously any effort by the Syrians to pursue weapons of mass destruction would be a concern."[36] A key issue is whether the United States should maintain its current stance of calculated ambiguity. Or, to deter a nuclear transfer from a state to a terrorist group, such as Al Qaeda, should it explicitly threaten a regime-changing response?

Interdiction through the PSI will remain an important tool in preventing transfers of WMD technology and missile delivery systems to states of concern and nonstate actors. In late December 2010, for example, a North Korean ship suspected of carrying nuclear or ballistic missile technology bound for Burma was intercepted and, though not forcibly boarded, eventually turned back.[37] China argues that such interdiction activities constitute a violation of state sovereignty and has refused to join PSI. Accordingly, in April 2004, Beijing blocked the inclusion of PSI into UN Security Council Resolution 1540, which requires all states to implement measures to prevent terrorist groups from acquiring WMD and related technologies. For the foreseeable future, sovereignty concerns are likely to frustrate efforts to realize President Obama's call in his April 2009 Prague speech to transform PSI into a "durable international institution." While the use or threatened use of force against hostile proliferators garners much attention, nonmilitary instruments encompassed under the rubric of deterrence by denial will remain the mainstays of US nonproliferation policy.

Notes

1. This chapter draws heavily on the author's analysis in: *Outlier States: American Strategies to Change, Contain, or Engage Regimes* (Baltimore, MD and Washington, DC: Johns Hopkins University Press and Wilson Center Press, 2012), chapter 4; and *Regime Change: US Strategy through the Prism of 9/11* (Baltimore, MD and Washington, DC: Johns Hopkins University Press and Wilson Center Press, 2007), chapter 2.
2. Les Aspin, "The Defense Department's New Nuclear Counterproliferation Initiative," address to the National Academy of Sciences, Washington, DC, December 7, 1993.
3. The White House, "National Security Council Memorandum: Agreed Definitions," US National Security Council, February 18, 1994.
4. United States Department of Defense, Office of the Deputy Secretary, "Report on Activities and Programs for Countering Proliferation," Counterproliferation Program Review Committee, May 1995, www.dod.mil/pubs/foi/International_security_affairs/other/766.pdf.
5. See Mitchell Reiss and Harold Müller, (eds), *International Perspectives on Counterproliferaton*, Working Paper, no. 99 (Washington, DC: Woodrow Wilson Center, Division of International Studies, January 1995).
6. Thomas W. Lippman, "If Nonproliferation Fails, Pentagon Wants 'Counterproliferation' in Place," *Washington Post*, May 15, 1994, p. A11.
7. Jeffrey A. Larsen, "NATO Counterproliferation Policy: A Case Study in Alliance Politics," Air Force Academy Institute for National Security Studies, Occasional Paper #17 (November 1997), p. 3, www.fas.org/irp/threat/ocp17.htm.

8. White House, Office of the Press Secretary, "President Speaks on War Effort to Citadel Cadets," December 11, 2001, www.whitehouse.gov/news/releases/2001/12/20011211-6.html.
9. White House, Office of the Press Secretary, "President Delivers the State of the Union Address," January 29, 2002, www.whitehouse.gov/news/releases/2002/01/print/20020129-11.html.
10. White House, Office of the Press Secretary, "President Bush Delivers Graduation Speech at West Point," June 1, 2002, www.whitehouse.gov/news/releases/2002/06/20020601-3.html.
11. The White House, Office of the Press Secretary, *The National Security Strategy of the United States of America*, March 16, 2006, http://nssarchive.us/NSSR/2006.pdf [hereinafter, *National Security Strategy 2006*], p. 24.
12. David E. Sanger and Thom Shanker, "Obama's Nuclear Strategy Intended as a Message," *New York Times*, April 6, 2010, www.nytimes.com/2010/04/07/world/07arms.html
13. See William Burr and Jeffrey T. Richelson, "Whether to 'Strangle the Baby in the Cradle': The United States and the Chinese Nuclear Program, 1960–64," *International Security*, Vol. 25, No. 3 (Winter 2000/01), pp. 54–99, http://belfercenter.ksg.harvard.edu/files/burr_and_richelson_winter_00_01.pdf.
14. Alexander George, "Case Studies: The Method of 'Structured, Focused Comparison'," in *Diplomacy: New Approaches in History, Theory and Policy*, edited by Paul Gordon Lauren (New York: Free Press, 1979), pp. 43–68.
15. See Philip Zelikow, "Offensive Military Options," in *New Nuclear Nations: Consequences for U.S. Policy*, edited by Robert D. Blackwill and Albert Carnesale (New York: Council on Foreign Relations Press, 1993), pp. 162–163; Michèle A. Flournoy, "Implications for US Military Strategy," in *New Nuclear Nations: Consequences for U.S. Policy*, edited by Robert D. Blackwill and Albert Carnesale (New York: Council on Foreign Relations Press, 1993), pp. 148–152; and Barry R. Schneider, *Future War and Counterproliferation: US Military Responses to NBC Proliferation Threats* (Westport, CT: Praeger, 1999), pp. 157–162.
16. Shai Feldman, "The Bombing of Osiraq – Revisited," *International Security*, Vol. 7, No. 2 (Fall 1982), pp. 115–116.
17. Angus Deming, Ron Moreau, and David C. Marin, "Two Minutes over Baghdad," *Newsweek*, Vol. 97, No. 25 (June 22, 1981), p. 22.
18. Feldman, "The Bombing of Osiraq – Revisited," p. 136. The United States accepted this UN Security Council language after threatening to veto punitive economic and political sanctions against Israel advocated by Iraq.
19. Dan Reiter, "Preventive Attacks Against Nuclear Programs and the 'Success' at Osirak," *The Nonproliferation Review*, Vol. 12, No. 2 (July 2005), p. 362.
20. Thamas A. Keaney and Eliot Cohen, *Revolution in Warfare? Air Power in the Persian Gulf* (Annapolis, MD: Naval Institute Press, 1995), pp. 70–71. This volume is a revised and expanded version of the *Gulf War Air Power Survey Summary Report* (Washington, DC: GPO, 1993).
21. Keaney and Cohen, *Revolution in Warfare?*, p. 72.
22. Amatzia Baram, *Building Toward Crisis: Saddam Hussein's Strategy for Survival* (Washington, DC: Washington Institute for Near East Policy, 1998), pp. 80–82.
23. Robert S. Litwak, *Rogue States and US Foreign Policy: Containment after the Cold War* (Washington, DC: Woodrow Wilson Center Press and Johns Hopkins University Press, 2000), p. 147.
24. Bradley Graham and Dana Priest, "US Details Strategy, Damage," *Washington Post*, December 18, 1998, p. A1.
25. Warren P. Stobel, "Sticking it to Saddam," *US News & World Report*, January 11, 1999, p. 38. The following exchange with a reporter is from Secretary of Defense William Cohen, "Transcript of News Briefing by Secretary of Defense William Cohen," December 19, 1998, www.defenselink.mil/transcripts/1998/t12191998_t1219fox.html:

    "Q: [Are you not going after those] facilities that are dual use capable because of the concern that we have for the amount of damage to innocent civilians?

    Secretary Cohen: I indicated yesterday that we did not target those facilities that are dual use capable because of the concern that we have for amount of damage to innocent civilians.

    Q: Mr. Secretary, if you target them at night, why would they have anybody there?

    Secretary Cohen: People don't have to be in the facility in order to do damage to the area itself. We took that into account. We were not going to engage in acts which could result in many, many deaths to innocent people."

26. See Litwak, *Rogue States and US Foreign Policy*, chapter 6, for an overview, as well as the following works that trace the United States' nuclear diplomacy with North Korea leading to the conclusion of the Agreed Framework in October 1994: Mitchell Reiss, "North Korea: Living with Uncertainty," in *Bridled Ambition: Why Countries Constrain Their Nuclear Capabilities* (Washington, DC: Woodrow Wilson Center Press/Johns Hopkins University Press, 1995), pp. 231–319; Michael Mazarr, *North Korea and the Bomb: A Case Study in Nonproliferation* (New York: St. Martin's Press, 1995); Leon V. Sigal, *Disarming Strangers: Nuclear Diplomacy with North Korea* (Princeton, NJ: Princeton University Press, 1998); and Don Oberdorfer, *The Two Koreas: A Contemporary History* (Reading, MA: Addison Wesley, 1997), chapters 11–14.

27. David Albright, "How Much Plutonium Does North Korea Have?" *Bulletin of the Atomic Scientists*, Vol. 50, No. 5 (September/October 1994), pp.46–53.

28. George W. Bush, *Decision Points* (New York: Crown, 2010), p. 421.

29 . Ibid., p. 422.

30. See, for example, Robert Gallucci, "Interview: Robert Gallucci," interview conducted for *Kim's Nuclear Gamble*, Frontline, Public Broadcasting Service, March 5, 2003, www.pbs.org/wgbh/pages/frontline/shows/kim/interviews/gallucci.html.

31. For analyses of the motivations to acquire or give up nuclear weapons see Scott D. Sagan, "Rethinking the Causes of Nuclear Proliferation: Three Bomb Models in Search of a Bomb" in *The Coming Crisis: Nuclear Proliferation, US Interests, and World Order*, edited by Victor A. Utgoff (Cambridge, MA: MIT Press, 2000), pp. 17–50; and Mitchell Reiss, *Bridled Ambition*.

32. Amatzia Baram, "An Analysis of Iraqi WMD Strategy," *Nonproliferation Review*, Vol. 8, No. 2 (Summer 2001), pp. 34–35. Timothy V. McCarthy and Jonathan B. Tucker, "Saddam's Toxic Arsenal: Chemical and Biological Weapons in the Gulf Wars," in *Planning the Unthinkable: How New Powers Will Use Nuclear, Biological, and Chemical Weapons*, edited by Peter R. Lavoy, Scott D. Sagan, and James J. Wirtz (Ithaca, NY: Cornell University Press, 2000), p. 73.

33. David E. Sanger and Thom Shanker, "Allies Say They Took Iraqi Posts Early to Prevent Use of Chemical and Biological Arms," *New York Times*, March 23, 2003, p. B5, www.nytimes.com/2003/03/23/world/nation-war-weapons-allies-say-they-took-iraqi-posts-early-prevent-use-chemical.html.

34. "US Defence Chief Panetta Warns against Iran Strike," *BBC News*, November 10, 2011, www.bbc.co.uk/news/world-middle-east-15688042.

35. George W. Bush, "Bush's Statement on North Korea," *New York Times*, October 9, 2006, www.nytimes.com/2006/10/09/world/asia/09cnd-bushtext.html.

36. Mark Mazzetti and Helene Cooper, "Israeli Nuclear Suspicions Linked to Raid in Syria," *New York Times*, September 18, 2007, www.nytimes.com/2007/09/18/world/asia/18korea.html.

37. David E. Sanger, "US Said to Turn Back North Korea Missile Shipment," *New York Times*, January 12, 2011, www.nytimes.com/2011/06/13/world/asia/13missile.html.

17

SECURITY ASSURANCES AND NUCLEAR NONPROLIFERATION

Wyn Q. Bowen and Luca Lentini

Security assurances have long been a feature of international efforts to prevent the horizontal spread of nuclear-weapon capabilities to additional countries of control. Jeffrey Knopf describes *assurances* as promises given through "declarations or signals meant to convey a commitment to take or refrain from taking certain actions in the future."[1] Specifically, he defines them as "attempts by one state or set of states to convince another state or set of states that the senders either will not cause or will not allow the recipients' security to be harmed."[2] In the nuclear context, then, security assurances entail commitments made by one or more states to take, or to refrain from, particular actions with the aim of influencing the strategic calculus of another state, or states, in order to keep them off the nuclear-weapon path.

Three approaches have featured most prominently in the field of nuclear nonproliferation. Negative security assurances (NSAs) and positive security assurances (PSAs) have been provided to nonnuclear-weapon states (NNWSs) by nuclear-weapon states (NWSs) in the context of the Nuclear Nonproliferation Treaty (NPT) and regional nuclear weapon free zones (NWFZs). PSAs have also been provided in the form of bilateral security guarantees such as those provided by the United States to Japan and South Korea, or multilateral security commitments made in the context of military alliances such as the North Atlantic Treaty Organization (NATO).

This chapter provides an overview of PSAs and NSAs in the context of the NPT and NWFZs. Attention is given to the rationale underlying NPT-related security assurances, how these have evolved since the late 1960s and issues of contention between the NWSs and NNWSs. The chapter then considers formalized security guarantees. By way of illustration, the case of the formal treaty-based security guarantee between the United States and South Korea is considered. The chapter does not seek to provide exhaustive coverage of the history of security assurances in the area of nuclear nonproliferation. Rather, it seeks to provide an overview of some of the issues that have characterized the formulation and implementation of security assurances in practice.

Security assurances, the NPT and NWFZs

NWSs have provided security assurances in varying forms to NNWSs in the context of the NPT and NWFZs for over four and a half decades. NSAs involve a commitment by NWSs not to use, or to threaten to use, nuclear weapons against NNWSs. PSAs entail a commitment to provide assistance in the event NNWSs are the subject of nuclear threats or attack. Regardless of their exact form, security assurances in this context "have been intended to reduce recipients' concerns about being threatened by nuclear weapons, thereby making them feel less need to acquire a nuclear arsenal of their own."[3]

NPT negotiations

The desire for security assurances arose as a key issue for nonaligned states during the negotiation of the NPT in the 1960s, primarily because they were not part of formal security alliances such as NATO and the Warsaw Pact. As Jean du Preez notes, the nonaligned states, "sensing that their security interests could be addressed in such a treaty, successfully backed UN General Assembly Resolution 2153," which requested the Eighteen Nation Committee on Disarmament, "to consider urgently the proposal that the nuclear-weapon powers should give an assurance that they will not use, or threaten to use, nuclear weapons against non-nuclear weapon States without nuclear weapons on their territories."[4]

The nonaligned states lobbied hard during the NPT negotiations for a formalized NSA.[5] However, the NWS depository governments – the Soviet Union, the United Kingdom, and the United States – could not reach agreement on including a NSA in the actual text of the NPT. They opted instead to follow a UN Security Council route for addressing the thorny question of security assurances.[6] The inability to reach a consensus was directly influenced by the fact that China and France, the two other NWSs recognized under the NPT, were not going to sign the NPT.[7] The fact that nonnuclear NATO countries benefitted directly from extended nuclear deterrence in the face of "perceived conventional superiority of Warsaw Pact forces" also influenced the consideration of formalized NSAs.[8]

While assurances of any sort did not feature in the NPT text, in June 1968, the three depository states did partially respond to demands from the nonaligned states by negotiating the passage of United Nations Security Council Resolution 255 (UNSCR 255). On June 19, 1968, UNSCR 255 highlighted the concern of some states that had recently signed up to the NPT as NNWSs that, "appropriate measures be undertaken to safeguard their security." Specifically on security assurances, UNSCR 255 welcomed "the intention expressed by certain States that they will provide or support immediate assistance, in accordance with the Charter, to any non-nuclear-weapon State Party to the Treaty on the Non-Proliferation of Nuclear Weapons that is a victim of an act or an object of a threat of aggression in which nuclear weapons are used."[9]

The text of the positive security assurance in UNSCR 255 did not define what was meant by "immediate assistance" and, in this respect, left great scope for debate over what it might entail in the event nuclear weapons or nuclear threats were targeted against a NNWS party. As John Simpson argues, UNSCR 255 offered the NNWS "a rather weak assurance of assistance if the latter were subject to nuclear attack."[10] Indeed, for the majority of nonaligned states, UNSCR 255 "appeared to merely reiterate existing NWS commitments under the UN Charter,"[11] adding little therefore to their sense of security.

Regional NWFZs

The failure to secure a formal NSA in the NPT drove the nonaligned states to continue lobbying for the negotiation of formalized negative assurances. As Knopf notes, "existing security assurances" have all subsequently "arisen from commitments made outside the treaty itself."[12]

Notable in this respect have been the various NWFZs that have been negotiated for specific regions, all of which include NSAs.

Predating the NPT, of course, the Treaty of Tlatelolco (Latin America and the Caribbean) opened for signature in 1967 and included the first formalized NSA.[13] Indeed, this treaty "served as a template for incorporating similar negative security assurances in later NWFZs."[14] Subsequent regional NWFZs included the Treaty of Rarotonga (South Pacific), the Treaty of Pelindaba (Africa), the Treaty of Bangkok (South East Asia), and the Central Asian NWFZ.[15] Under Tlatelolco and Rarotonga, for example, NSAs have been provided by the NWSs to NNWSs signatories of these treaties. However, there have been sticking points for some of the NWSs on negative assurances in the context of the Pelindaba and Bangkok Treaties. For instance, with the Bangkok Treaty there have been concerns on the part of the NWS related to "the possible passage of nuclear-armed naval vessels through international waters covered by the zone."[16]

Under pressure from the nonaligned states the NWSs individually provided negative assurances within the framework of the UN General Assembly Special Sessions on Disarmament in 1978 and 1982, although all involved significant conditionality, other than those provided by China.[17] In 1978, as the *NPT Briefing Book* highlights, "China's statement was an unconditional one; the French one was limited to states in NWFZs; that of the USSR covered all states that renounced the production and acquisition of nuclear weapons and did not have them on their territories. The UK and the US made a commitment not to attack or threaten to attack a NNWS with nuclear weapons, but excluded from it NNWS allied with a nuclear-weapon state." In 1982, France later "provided NNWS with a broadly similar commitment to the UK and US."[18]

Post-Cold War denuclearization and NPT extension

There was little movement on security assurances in the context of the NPT from the early 1980s to the end of the Cold War. The next significant development occurred some two years after China and France had signed and ratified the NPT in 1992. In December 1994, security assurances were provided to Belarus, Kazakhstan, and Ukraine by Russia, the United Kingdom, and the United States, and to Ukraine by France, and later to Kazakhstan by China in February 1995. These assurances were provided in the context of the three countries having transferred to Russia the strategic nuclear weapons they had inherited from the Soviet Union and their decisions to sign the NPT as NNWSs.[19] The assurances made to the three former Soviet Republics corresponded with those subsequently made a few months later under UNSCR 984 in April 1995.[20]

The assurances in April 1995 were made in the context of incentivizing the nonaligned states to agree to the indefinite extension of the NPT on its 25th anniversary. A series of national statements were made by the NWS related to security assurances and which were recognized by UNSCR 984.[21] This new resolution marked a further development upon UNSCR 255 of 1968 because it incorporated negative as well as positive assurances.[22]

For its part, China reiterated a commitment to its unconditional NSA.[23] Specifically, Beijing stated it would not be "the first to use nuclear weapons against non-nuclear weapon States or nuclear-weapons-free zones at any time or under any circumstances" against NNWSs of the NPT or NNWSs that have entered into any comparable internationally recognized commitment not to manufacture or acquire nuclear explosive devices.[24] While France, Russia, the United Kingdom, and the United States brought their assurances "broadly into line with each other," unconditional assurances proved to be a step too far for Paris, London, and Washington.[25]

While they reaffirmed a commitment not to use or threaten to use nuclear weapons against NPT NNWSs, this was qualified "by excluding cases of invasion or any other attack on their respective countries, territories, armed forced or other troops, or against their allies or a state toward which they have security commitments, carried out or sustained by such state in alliance or association with a NWS." The United Kingdom and the United States also stated that their assurances did not apply if a NNWS was "in material breach of its NPT nonproliferation obligations." Moreover, the NATO states and Russia retained "the option of first use of nuclear weapons."[26]

The lack of a unified P5 statement on security assurances, and the continued absence of a legal instrument codifying NSAs and PSAs, was clearly highly disappointing for the Nonaligned Movement. Nevertheless, the progress that had been made in this and other areas did ultimately prove sufficient to avoid a block on indefinitely extending the treaty at the 1995 Review and Extension Conference.[27] Jean du Preez summarizes well the situation that confronted the nonaligned states in 1995: "if the NPT were allowed to expire, any security assurances would also expire. Faced with such a prospect, the NNWS supported the treaty's indefinite extension."[28] Their disappointment in, and dissatisfaction with, UNSCR 984 was subsequently reflected in a joint statement issued by the Group of 21. The statement noted that 984 had not accounted for "any of the formal objections by NNWS on the 'restrictive, restrained, uncertain, conditional and discriminatory character of the guarantees already provided'."[29]

The concerns of the nonaligned states were further exacerbated by developments in the United States during the late 1990s and early 2000s. Through Presidential Directive 60 in December 1997, the Clinton administration "appeared to preserve the option of US retaliation with nuclear weapons against an attack involving chemical or biological weapons [CBW]." Moreover, in November 1998, then-US Secretary of Defense Cohen described the ambiguity surrounding the context for nuclear-weapon use by NATO as contributing to deterrence by increasing the uncertainty on the part of any state that might use chemical or biological weapons. As Simpson notes, "a clear contradiction had emerged between the negative security assurances given in 1995 by the three NATO NWS and that organization's declaratory policy of retaining an option for first-use of nuclear weapons in CBW scenarios."[30] Following the terrorist attacks of September 11, 2001, the Bush administration's Nuclear Posture Review of December 2001 reconfirmed the readiness of Washington "to consider a nuclear response to a CBW attack", and it "also hinted at a new willingness to use nuclear weapons preemptively," for bunker busting purposes.[31]

It was not until the Obama administration took office that significant movement in the other direction occurred. Immediately prior to the 2010 NPT Review Conference, the administration's NPR stated that it was bolstering "its long-standing 'negative security assurance' by declaring that the United States will not use or threaten to use nuclear weapons against non-nuclear weapons states that are party to the Nuclear Non-Proliferation Treaty ... and in compliance with their nuclear non-proliferation obligations."[32] However, there was one caveat involving the potential modification of this policy if "warranted by the evolution and proliferation of the biological weapons threat."[33] As Simpson notes, the Obama administration's NPR "could be interpreted as offering unconditional security assurances to all states except the eight declared nuclear weapon states, Israel and Iran."[34]

While the question of security assurances has become less significant for the nonaligned states since 2000 with the rise of the disarmament agenda,[35] existing NSAs in the context of the NPT continue to be perceived as insufficient from the perspective of the Nonaligned Movement for a number of reasons: security assurances continue not to be bound up in a formal legal instrument; there are differences in the assurances provided across the five NWS;[36] and the various qualifications to security assurances are perceived to be unsatisfactory.[37]

Security guarantees

Security assurances have also been provided in the form of bilateral security guarantees – such as those provided by the United States to South Korea and to Japan, for example – or multilateral security guarantees in the context of military alliances such as NATO and the Warsaw Pact. The central role that such guarantees have played in international politics since the 1950s in restraining nuclear proliferation was highlighted by a UK Foreign and Commonwealth Office paper in 2009. It noted that, "including states which come under a 'nuclear umbrella,' such as NATO allies, well over half of the world's population is covered by a nuclear deterrent. The impression that only a small minority benefit from nuclear weapons is misleading."[38]

Security umbrellas and extended deterrence

Formal bilateral or alliance-based security guarantees have traditionally involved a commitment on the part of a NWS to provide a security umbrella to nonnuclear allies. As Knopf notes, "security guarantees generally imply extending a nuclear deterrent umbrella over an ally with the goal of convincing the ally that it does not need a nuclear deterrent of its own."[39] On the part of the security provider, or providers, the aim of PSAs in these contexts is to assure recipients that their security will be provided for.

The deployment of nuclear weapons on or in proximity to the territory of allied NNWSs has been one approach to bolstering the credibility of extended deterrent threats.[40] For example, the United States began deploying "tactical" nuclear weapons on the territory of European NATO allies in the mid-1950s starting in the United Kingdom and with the aim of strengthening the credibility of America's extended deterrence commitment to the alliance. As Kristensen notes, "within 10 years, deployments spread to Germany, Italy, France, Turkey, the Netherlands, Greece, and Belgium."[41] Today US tactical nuclear weapons remain deployed in several European NATO states. However, the ongoing debate over the contribution of these systems to alliance security remains a hot topic. Some argue that their continued deployment is paramount to the credibility of the US security guarantee to NATO Europe in terms of assuring allies and deterring potential adversaries.[42] Others have called into question the rationale for continuing with the presence of these systems given the push for a nuclear-weapon-free world, as epitomized in President Barack Obama's 2009 Prague speech.[43]

Credibility

At the heart of the challenge of maintaining an effective security guarantee that keeps a NNWS off the nuclear-weapon path will be the confidence of the beneficiary in the guarantee itself, and specifically in the threat being made on their behalf to deter aggression. Central to this confidence is the perception of the credibility of that threat.[44]

Daryl Press defines the credibility of a threat as "the perceived likelihood that the threat will be carried out if the conditions that are supposed to trigger it are met. A highly credible threat is one that people believe will be carried out; a threat has little credibility if people believe it is a bluff."[45]

Central to the success of security guarantees in preventing proliferation, then, is the requirement for recipients to perceive the security provider as maintaining a credible extended deterrence policy, doctrine, and posture. Indeed, it is widely accepted that the credibility of deterrence, extended or otherwise, depends on two variables including "the will and resolution to defend the interests in question," and the maintenance of the "capabilities for doing so that it regards – and persuades the opponent to regard – as appropriate and usable for the defence of those interests."[46] With extended deterrence, of course, it is not just the opponent, or potential opponent, that must be persuaded of the credibility of the deterrent threat, but also the ally on behalf of whom the threat is being made. The credibility of security guarantees is directly related therefore to the prevention of nuclear proliferation. To illustrate the challenge of maintaining a credible PSA in this context, the cases of South Korea and the US security commitment during the Cold War are examined.

The US security guarantee and South Korea in the Cold War

The US-Republic of Korea Mutual Defense Treaty was signed in October 1953 shortly after the end of the Korean War. Since then the treaty has provided the foundation for the American security guarantee to South Korea. As Kongdan Oh notes, this has been pivotal to deterring another North Korean attack and it has also "augmented South Korea's military forces and provided a nuclear umbrella, thus enabling the South Koreans to pursue economic progress with relatively low military budgets."[47] Nevertheless, the US-South Korea security relationship has not been without its significant ups and downs over the years. In particular, there have been points at which Seoul has seriously questioned the credibility of the US security guarantee, prompting the pursuit of a national nuclear-weapon capability.

Perhaps most significantly, a decision was taken in the early 1970s by South Korea to initiate a nuclear-weapon program. Prior to this decision, while Seoul had not been free of concerns about Washington's resolve to defend the country, the stationing of US forces and later tactical nuclear weapons on South Korean territory had provided sufficient assurance to head off a similar move.[48]

The decision on nuclear weapons can be traced to the US promulgation of the "Nixon Doctrine" in 1969, which sought to make America's allies in Asia more self-reliant for their own security. In the context of this doctrine, Washington unilaterally and without consultation announced that it would withdraw 20,000 American military personnel from South Korea by the middle of the 1970s. The decision came as a shock to the government of President Park Chung Hee who lobbied against it. It should be noted that, at the time, Seoul perceived a deteriorating security balance with North Korea because of its neighbor's expanding conventional military capabilities.[49] The north had also become increasingly belligerent and provocative, including the capture of a South Korean naval ship in June 1970.[50]

In combination, these factors served to cement a shift that was taking place in South Korean policy towards self-reliance for defense and security. President Park also believed that "building a sufficient conventional deterrent would be expensive and time-consuming."[51] So it was within this context of a rising sense of the North Korean threat, and questions over the reliability of the United States as a security provider, that Park secretly decided that South Korea needed to examine the development of a national nuclear-weapon capability. This effort included the development of a long-term plan for developing nuclear weapons and the pursuit of relevant materials and technology from abroad including, for example, plutonium reprocessing.[52]

This initial pursuit of nuclear weapons appeared to end in 1975, when Washington applied pressure on Seoul to stop the program. This pressure included a threat to stop cooperating on peaceful applications of nuclear energy and to reconsider the bilateral political and security relationship,[53] including the withdrawal of American forces and "ending military and financial assistance."[54]

South Korea responded by signing the NPT as a NNWS in 1975 "before it had produced any fissile material,"[55] and by "temporarily suspending some parts" of the nuclear-weapon program, although covert work did continue for some time beyond 1975.[56] Indeed, senior officials continued to make it clear that Seoul could potentially develop nuclear weapons if Washington reneged on its security commitments. For example, in 1977 the South Korean Foreign Minister stated, "we have signed the Non-Proliferation Treaty and thus our basic position is that we do not intend to develop nuclear weapons by ourselves. But if it is necessary for national security interests and people's safety, it is possible for Korea as a sovereign state to make its own judgement on the matter."[57] The situation was not helped by the Carter administration's announcement in 1977 of a further withdrawal of US military personnel. However, the cancellation of that decision in 1978 and the assassination of President Park in 1979 appear to have put an end to the discussion of a nuclear-weapon option in South Korea at that time. As Richard Bush notes, from then on confidence subsequently increased in the US security guarantee "in fits and starts while South Korea became increasingly relaxed about the threat from the weakening North."[58]

The South Korean case highlights two key challenges regarding the role of security guarantees in preventing proliferation. The first involves the inherent challenges associated with formulating, and then maintaining, *credible* security assurances given that domestic, regional, and international environments constantly evolve, as do decision makers' perceptions of political and strategic reality. Second, and related to the first, it is clear that formalized PSAs in the form of guarantees need to be managed over time if they are to remain effective as tools to keep NNWSs off the nuclear-weapon path.

Conclusion

An overview of the role of different types of security assurances in the context of preventing nuclear proliferation has highlighted various issues of contention between NWSs and NNWSs, and illustrated the challenges of developing credible assurances whether negative or positive in nature. It is clear that there is an inherent tension between NSAs in the NPT context and security guarantees. While both are designed to prevent further nuclear proliferation by reducing the insecurities of states, the former seek to do this by ensuring NNWSs are not subjected to nuclear threats and use, while the latter depend on nuclear threats being made by NWSs on behalf of NNWSs. As Knopf contends, "arguments that positive security guarantees require maintaining robust nuclear capabilities could make negative assurances appear insincere."[59]

Notes

1. Jeffrey Knopf, (ed.), *Security Assurances and Nuclear Nonproliferation* (Palo Alto, CA: Stanford University Press, 2012), p. 3.
2. Ibid.
3. Ibid., p. ix.
4. Jean du Preez, "The Demise of Nuclear Negative Security Assurances," Article VI Forum, Ottawa, Canada, September 28, 2006, p. 5, http://cns.miis.edu/programs/ionp/pdfs/visions_of_fission.pdf.
5. For coverage of this debate, see George Bunn, "The Legal Status of US Negative Security Assurances to Non-Nuclear Weapon States," *The Nonproliferation Review*, Vol. 4, No. 3 (Spring-Summer 1997), pp. 1–17, http://cns.miis.edu/npr/pdfs/bunn43.pdf.
6. Du Preez, "The Demise of Nuclear Negative Security Assurances," p. 5.
7. John Simpson, "The Role of Security Assurances in the Nuclear Nonproliferation Regime," in *Security Assurances and Nuclear Nonproliferation*, Jeffrey Knopf (ed.) (Palo Alto, CA: Stanford University Press, 2012), p. 62.
8. Simpson, "The Role of Security Assurances," pp. 58, 61.

9. The resolution was adopted by ten votes with five abstentions including one NWS, France, which had not signed the NPT at this stage. The fifth NWS, the People's Republic of China, did not become a member of the Security Council until 1971 after taking over the Republic of China's (Taiwan's) membership. See United Nations Security Council, "Questions Relating to Measures to Safeguard Non-Nuclear-Weapon States Parties to the Treaty on the Non-Proliferation of Nuclear Weapons," UNSCR 255 (1968), June 19, 1968, www.un.org/en/ga/search/view_doc.asp?symbol=S/RES/255(1968).

10. Simpson, "The Role of Security Assurances," p. 58.

11. Ibid., p. 62.

12. Knopf, *Security Assurances and Nuclear Nonproliferation*, pp. 16–17.

13. Treaty for the Prohibition of Nuclear Weapons in Latin America and the Caribbean (Treaty of Tlatelolco), Art. I, http://opanal.org/opanal/Tlatelolco/Tlatelolco-i.htm.

14. Simpson, "The Role of Security Assurances," p. 63.

15. For a brief overview of the status of NWFZs annex protocols ratified by NWSs, see Arms Control Association, "Nuclear-Weapon-Free Zones (NWFZ) At a Glance," September 2012, www.armscontrol.org/factsheets/nwfz.

16. Du Preez, "The Demise of Nuclear Negative Security Assurances," p. 6.

17. Simpson, "The Role of Security Assurances," pp. 59, 63.

18. John Simpson and Matthew Harries, *NPT Briefing Book, 2014 Edition* (London and Monterey, CA: King's College London and Center for Nonproliferation Studies, 2014), Part 1, p. 9, www.kcl.ac.uk/sspp/departments/warstudies/research/groups/csss/pubs/NPT-Briefing-Book-2014/NPT-Briefing-Book-2014.pdf.

19. Simpson and Harries, *NPT Briefing Book*, p. 9.

20. Simpson, "The Role of Security Assurances," p. 66.

21. Ibid.

22. Simpson and Harries, *NPT Briefing Book*, p. 9.

23. Ibid.

24. Du Preez, "The Demise of Nuclear Negative Security Assurances," pp. 6–7.

25. Simpson and Harries, *NPT Briefing Book*, p. 9.

26. Du Preez, "The Demise of Nuclear Negative Security Assurances," pp. 6–7.

27. Simpson, "The Role of Security Assurances," p. 67.

28. Du Preez, "The Demise of Nuclear Negative Security Assurances," p. 9.

29. Ibid., pp. 6–7.

30. Simpson, "The Role of Security Assurances," p. 69.

31. Ibid., p. 71.

32. US Department of Defense, "Nuclear Posture Review Report," Washington, DC, April 2010, p. 15, www.defense.gov/npr/docs/2010%20Nuclear%20Posture%20Review%20Report.pdf.

33. Ibid., p. 16.

34. Simpson, "The Role of Security Assurances," p. 74.

35. Ibid., p. 70.

36. Ibid., p. 64.

37. Knopf, *Security Assurances and Nuclear Nonproliferation*, pp. 16–17.

38. Foreign and Commonwealth Office, "Lifting the Nuclear Shadow: Creating the Conditions for Abolishing Nuclear Weapons," Government of the United Kingdom, February 5, 2009, p. 5, http://carnegieendowment.org/files/nuclear-paper.pdf.

39. Knopf, *Security Assurances and Nuclear Nonproliferation*," p. 17.

40. Simpson, "The Role of Security Assurances," p. 60.

41. Hans M. Kristensen, "US Nuclear Weapons in Europe. A Review of Post-Cold War Policy, Force Levels, and War Planning," National Resources Defense Council, February 2005, p. 24, www.nrdc.org/nuclear/euro/euro.pdf.

42. See, for example, Michaela Dodge, "US Nuclear Weapons in Europe: Critical for Transatlantic Security," Backgrounder No. 2875, Heritage Foundation, February 18, 2014, www.heritage.org/research/reports/2014/02/us-nuclear-weapons-in-europe-critical-for-transatlantic-security.

43. See, for example, Paul Ingram and Oliver Meier, (eds), "Reducing the Role of Tactical Nuclear Weapons in Europe: Perspectives and Proposals on the NATO Policy Debate," report by the Arms Control Association and British American Security Information Council, May 2011, www.armscontrol.org/system/files/Tactical_Nuclear_Report_May_11.pdf.

44. Knopf, *Security Assurances and Nuclear Nonproliferation*, p. 12.
45. Daryl G. Press, *Calculating Credibility: How Leaders Assess Military Threats* (Ithaca, NY: Cornell University Press, 2005), p. 10.
46. Gordon A. Craig and Alexander L. George, *Force and Statecraft: Diplomatic Problems of Our Time* (Oxford: Oxford University Press, 1983), p. 172.
47. Kongdan Oh, " US-ROK: The Forgotten Alliance," Brookings East Asia Commentary, No. 22, Brookings Institution, October 2008, www.brookings.edu/research/opinions/2008/10/south-korea-oh.
48. Richard C. Bush, "The US Policy of Extended Deterrence in East Asia: History, Current Views, and Implications," Brookings Arms Control Series, No. 5, Brookings Institution, February 2011, p. 3, www.brookings.edu/~/media/research/files/papers/2011/2/arms%20control%20bush/02_arms_control_bush.pdf.
49. The National Institute for Defence Studies, "Chapter 3: The Korean Peninsula: Emerging Prospects for Change," in *East Asian Strategic Review 2004* (Tokyo: *The Japan Times*, July 2004), p. 58, www.nids.go.jp/english/publication/east-asian/pdf/2004/east-asian_e2004_03.pdf.
50. Bush, "US Policy of Extended Deterrence in East Asia," p. 3.
51. Ibid.
52. See for example, Young-sun Ha, "Nuclearization of Small States and World Order: the Case of Korea," *Asian Survey*, Vol. 18, No. 11 (November 1978), pp. 1134–1151; Jonathan D. Pollack and Mitchell B. Reiss, "South Korea: The Tyranny of Geography and the Vexations of History," in *The Nuclear Tipping Point: Why States Reconsider Their Nuclear Choices*, Edited by Kurt M. Campbell, Robert J. Einhorn, Mitchell B. Reiss, and Vartan Gregorian (Washington, DC, Brookings Institution Press, 2004), p. 262; Michael J. Stiler, " US Nuclear Nonproliferation Policy in the North East Asia Region During the Cold War: the South Korea Case," *East Asia: An International Quarterly*, Vol.16, No. 3/4 (Autumn 1998), pp. 41–79.
53. Pollack and Reiss, "South Korea," p. 263.
54. Bush, "US Policy of Extended Deterrence in East Asia," p. 3.
55. Nuclear Threat Initiative, "South Korea: Overview," March 2014, www.nti.org/country-profiles/south-korea.
56. Bush, "US Policy of Extended Deterrence in East Asia," p. 3.
57. Ha, "Nuclearization of Small States and World Order," p. 1142.
58. Bush, "US Policy of Extended Deterrence in East Asia," p. 3.
59. Knopf, *Security Assurances and Nuclear Nonproliferation*, p. 12.

18

NUCLEAR FORENSICS

Klaus Mayer and Alexander Glaser

Whenever nuclear material is found out of regulatory control, questions on the origin of the material, on its intended use, and on hazards associated with the material need to be answered. Analytical and interpretational methodologies have been developed in order to exploit measurable material properties for gaining information on the history of the nuclear material. This area of research is referred to as nuclear forensic science or, in short, nuclear forensics. This chapter reviews the origins, types, and state-of-the-art of nuclear forensics; discusses the potential roles of nuclear forensics in supporting nuclear security; and examines what nuclear forensics can realistically achieve. It also charts a path forward, pointing at potential applications of nuclear forensic methodologies in other areas.

Background and definitions

Nuclear forensics has only recently emerged as a multidisciplinary area of research, combining methods of traditional forensics, radiochemistry, analytical chemistry, material science, isotope geochemistry, and nuclear physics. Nuclear forensics can "assist in the identification of the materials, as well as how, when, and where the materials were made, and their intended lawful use."[1] The capabilities of modern nuclear forensics are truly remarkable. Perhaps for this reason, nuclear forensics is often perceived as a scientific toolset that can easily and immediately answer every possible question an investigating authority might have about suspect nuclear material or about a related nuclear security event. In general, however, the process of nuclear forensic analysis is more complex. To appreciate this complexity, two fundamental distinctions have to be made: predetonation forensics versus postdetonation forensics and, most importantly, nuclear forensics versus attribution.

Predetonation versus postdetonation forensics

Postdetonation forensics was developed to detect and evaluate nuclear-weapon tests of adversaries during the Cold War period. In fact, the basic concepts underlying the method were already used by the United States to confirm the first Soviet test of a nuclear weapon, "First Lightning" or "Joe-1," in August 1949 using radiological methods on samples collected with airborne filters.[2] In contrast, predetonation nuclear forensics only gained significant attention since the early 1990s when interceptions of smuggled nuclear materials from the former Soviet Union were made in Europe, raising concerns about the possible existence of a black market for such material.

Analysis of the postdetonation debris of a nuclear device can be used to determine many predetonation characteristics. Specifically, when performed by experts from nuclear-weapon states, the analysis can reveal type, design, and level of sophistication of a weapon or device, which could also provide evidence about the origin of the material and the device. Technical challenges arise from the fact that the nuclear material was subject to extreme conditions and has subsequently been dispersed. In consequence, many of the macroscopic parameters describing nuclear material are lost. In this sense, postdetonation forensics relies on fewer signatures than predetonation forensics. In the hypothetical scenario of an explosion of a nuclear device, postdetonation forensics would generally involve a combination of unclassified and classified techniques and proceeds at a very different timescale than predetonation forensics.[3]

Nuclear forensics versus attribution

The boundaries between nuclear forensics and attribution are blurry. Strictly speaking, nuclear forensics consists exclusively in measurements made directly on the nuclear material or on other associated material. The interpretation of the measurement data allows describing the material (e.g., "the uranium in the sample contains 0.7 percent uranium-235"). Combining the description obtained from different parameters may then lead to nuclear forensic findings (e.g., "the impurity pattern in the uranium is consistent with natural uranium mined from sandstone deposits"). In contrast, an attribution process, in which the origin or route of intercepted nuclear material is reconstructed and perhaps even the group or individuals involved in an incident identified, combines the nuclear forensic findings with law enforcement and intelligence data. Hence, attribution requires interagency cooperation and an exchange of information between different communities. As highlighted below, attribution is a much more difficult and controversial process than the nuclear forensic analysis that it follows.

The technical basis and state of the art of nuclear forensic science

Fundamentally, nuclear forensic analysis seeks to determine parameters that describe physical, chemical, elemental, and isotopic properties of nuclear or other radioactive material of unknown origin. Predetonation nuclear forensics has significantly matured since its inception in the early 1990s and, today, a range of methods and analytical techniques are applied for measuring an increasing number of parameters that have been identified as being characteristic of the material.[4] As nuclear material may appear in quite a variety of chemical and physical forms throughout the nuclear fuel cycle, significant research and development efforts are required to identify useful signatures. Such development work in the laboratory, though being tedious and consuming time and resources, will result in methods and protocols that can be applied to seized material and provide useful clues. These methods include gamma spectrometry, alpha spectrometry, mass spectrometry, titration, chromatography, scanning electron microscopy, X-ray diffraction analysis, infrared spectroscopy, and Raman spectroscopy. The parameters to be measured may comprise the isotopic composition of the nuclear material, chemical form (e.g., oxide or metal), molecular structure, chemical impurities, isotopic composition of trace elements, physical form, and morphology. The development of an analytical plan, which prioritizes the parameters to be measured and the selection of the most suitable analytical methods, is the responsibility of the nuclear forensic laboratory undertaking the analysis. Such an analytical plan is established based on initial clues on the material, on circumstantial information, and on the insights the investigation authority wants to gain. Ultimately, the measured parameters form the basis of nuclear forensic findings.

Individual parameters or a combination of several parameters may be characteristic for the material and are referred to as "signatures." Two general types can be distinguished. Signatures that can be interpreted without additional information are called "predictive signatures." For example, the concentration of specific decay products in a sample determines the age of the material, i.e., the time that has elapsed since production or the last time material was purified. In contrast to that, "comparative signatures" require external data to understand the history of an unknown nuclear material. Comparative signatures are analogues to human fingerprints that have to be matched against a person or database, i.e., without a reference, they do not provide much information. In the case of nuclear forensics, the impurity pattern in natural uranium is an example of such a signature, as the comparison against literature values or databases enables matching a sample against a specific type of geological environment (uranium ore). Ideally, the original production facility and perhaps also the material's pathway until control was lost can be established with some or even high confidence.

Although material parameters such as the isotopic composition or chemical impurities can be measured with high precision and accuracy, the conclusions about the material history are often associated with significant uncertainties and do not always allow an unambiguous source attribution. The challenges associated with the confidence in conclusions arise from several factors, which are summarized below.

Analytical techniques

Confidence in the measurement results is generally achieved by using established and validated methods, by applying strict quality control, and by governing the entire process through a quality assurance program. The analytical techniques typically used in nuclear forensic investigations are well established and have served also for other applications. With the concept of "International Target Values," the IAEA defined uncertainty components that are considered to be reasonably and realistically achievable in routine measurements of nuclear material for safeguards purposes. The latest issue was published by the IAEA in 2010.[5] The uncertainty values listed in this document may serve as guidance also for measurements performed in the context of nuclear forensic investigations. The specific questions that may arise during a nuclear forensic analysis may, however, lead to the need for applying the technique in a way that is not covered by the method's initial validation. In other words, nuclear security incidents require a rapid and effective response, especially in the postdetonation scenario, and may trigger the necessity for employing methods that are not fully validated due to exigent circumstances of the incident.

Qualified experts

To carry out a nuclear forensic analysis, trained analysts with specific skills and experience in working with nuclear material are required. Moreover, subject matter experts need to be involved in interpreting the data and establishing the nuclear forensic findings. Throughout the entire nuclear forensic investigation (i.e., from sample taking to the data interpretation) the involvement of appropriately qualified and experienced experts is key to credible and defensible conclusions. Maintaining the "nuclear workforce" (e.g., through educational programs) and transferring tacit knowledge from one generation to the next (e.g., through vocational training of young professionals) are essential for sustaining nuclear forensic expertise.

Interpretational techniques

Interpretational techniques may be based on different approaches. Comparative evaluation for identifying the origin of unknown nuclear material can be performed using the exclusion principle, i.e., step-by-step reduction of the number of candidate facilities for the origin of an unknown nuclear material using an iterative process, which serves at the same time as analytical guidance.[6] Statistical methodologies have been adapted, which allow drawing conclusions from similarities between an unknown sample and a group of known materials based on multiple forensic parameters.[7] Simple one-to-one matching of unknown against known (as performed in fingerprint comparisons or in forensic DNA analysis) is rather unusual in the area of nuclear forensics.

Comparison data

Characterizing and archiving the parameters of material of known history is essential for understanding comparative signatures. Establishing comprehensive and systematic compilations of such data is still in its early stages. However, an understanding of relevant parameters has been developed based on the most characteristic signatures that have been identified.

Evidence management

Strict rules may have to be followed when the samples are linked to a criminal act, and the nuclear forensic findings are expected to support the prosecution. Close coordination between law enforcement and nuclear forensic investigators needs to assure compliance with procedural and legal requirements for entering nuclear forensic derived conclusions in a court of law.

Nuclear forensic investigations were conducted in a number of incidents and proved to provide useful information on the history of the seized material. This information either provided investigative leads or was directly used by the competent authority in the processing of the incident. The insights provided by (predetonation) nuclear forensic investigations in real incidents of illicit trafficking are important.

The emergence of illicit trafficking

Although there is evidence for earlier cases of illicit trafficking of nuclear material,[8] the issue emerged as a more persistent phenomenon in the early 1990s, shortly after the dissolution of the Soviet Union. The investigations of these early cases of nuclear smuggling often involved the analysis of the seized nuclear material. In many cases, the material could be traced back to an application and to a country of origin. Although the methodologies for nuclear forensic analysis as we know them today were still in their infancy, the conclusions often appeared simple and straightforward. As the phenomenon of illicit trafficking persisted, nuclear forensics developed from an *ad-hoc* application of material characterization techniques to a full scientific discipline aiming at understanding correlations between measureable parameters and the process history of the material.

Incidents of illicit trafficking are collected in the IAEA's Incident and Trafficking Database (ITDB), which was established in 1995. As of the end of 2013, the database included 2,477 incidents. Only officially confirmed incidents are included in the database, however. In the order of fifteen incidents per year involve nuclear material. Most of these seizures involve gram quantities of material, and only in a few cases, kilogram amounts of low-enriched, natural, or depleted uranium were seized. The IAEA stopped reporting individual events in 2007. More recent incidents are taken from other sources, but have been publicly reported and confirmed.[9]

Overall, in about sixty cases, the effort of conducting a comprehensive nuclear forensic investigation was undertaken. While in the 1990s most of the seizures could be linked to intentional movement of nuclear material across borders and classified as "nuclear smuggling," at present most of the cases refer to contaminated scrap metal. Moreover, we observe a change on geographical focus of the phenomenon. During the first decade of illicit trafficking, most of the incidents were reported from central European states, while more recent trafficking cases were mainly discovered in southeastern European countries, i.e., the Black Sea region. Since the beginning of the 1990s, only a relatively small number of incidents involving highly enriched uranium or plutonium have been reported (see Figure 18.1). Two illustrative cases are discussed below.

1994 Munich plutonium

In August 1994, a person arriving at Munich Airport on a Lufthansa flight from Moscow was arrested based on a tip-off from intelligence. In his suitcase, he carried nuclear material, which was later identified as a mixture of 363 grams of plutonium and 122 grams of uranium. Apart from that, 210 grams of enriched lithium metal (89.4 percent Li-6) were discovered in his luggage. The analysis of the material revealed that the plutonium was low burnup (87 percent Pu-239), hence close to weapon-grade material. Microscopic investigations revealed different morphologies of the plutonium particles, indicating different production processes. A comparative evaluation against reference samples from a German MOX fuel fabrication plant clearly showed a much finer grain size distribution for the seized material, indicating a different production process. Age-dating of the plutonium (both on the bulk material and on individual particles) suggested a production date for the material of the end of 1979 with an uncertainty of about a half year. The isotopic composition of the plutonium proved to be consistent with plutonium produced in Russian RBMK reactors. The belief that the material was of Russian

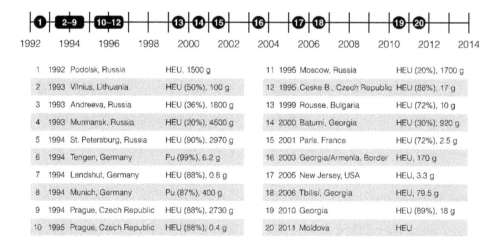

Figure 18.1 Incidents involving HEU and plutonium confirmed in the IAEA Incident and Trafficking Database (ITDB), 1993–2007

origin was reinforced by findings that clearly excluded western-type light-water reactors as the origin of the plutonium. Russian experts later performed their own analysis of the intercepted material, but the results were never published. Overall, despite a remarkably detailed and successful forensic analysis, the background of the case was complex, involving actors in Germany, Russia, and Spain, and was never fully resolved. The controversial role of the German foreign intelligence service (the Bundesnachrichtendienst, or BND) in the incident became the center of a two-year government investigation.[10]

1999 Bulgarian HEU

In May 1999, a person traveling by car and attempting to cross the Turkish-Bulgarian border was found to be carrying 10 grams of HEU (72 percent U-235) in a lead container concealed in the trunk of the car. The material had an unusually high U-236 content of 13 percent, and a nine-month forensic analysis found that the material was reprocessed uranium from high-burn-up fuel and originally had a U-235 content of 90 percent. The investigation was "the most thorough and far-reaching analysis of illicit nuclear material ever conducted."[11] Nonetheless, the attribution of the Bulgarian HEU remained incomplete. "Despite the comprehensive forensic investigation and wealth of data, neither the original source of the HEU nor the point at which legitimate control was lost has yet been unambiguously identified."[12]

These two prominent examples illustrate how difficult a comprehensive reconstruction of a case (including identification of the masterminds behind it) can be, even if the forensic analysis is considered successful. Over the years, the expectations on the reliability of nuclear forensic investigations and on the comprehensiveness of conclusions have only grown. While these expectations are often unrealistic, a thorough examination of intercepted material always results in useful hints on the history of the material and provides investigative leads.

Data interpretation in nuclear forensic investigations relies on the ability to establish a linkage between measurable parameters (signatures) and processes to which the material was exposed. To this end, the availability of reference information (on material of known process history) plays an important role. Compilations of such reference information – or data bases – and the accessibility thereof, however, are facing challenges due to sensitivities of the data.

While nuclear forensic science continues to be developed and further perfected, we also have to realize that the threat has evolved. In the early 1990s, the main concern focused on the proliferation risks associated with nuclear material that had been removed from regulatory control. In the early 2000s, in particular following the events of 9/11, the threat of nuclear terrorism added another dimension to the efforts spent in measures of prevention and preparedness. In parallel, the expectations related to the role of nuclear forensics evolved as well with a view on the support it could provide to law enforcement by providing investigative clues and through the deterrent character associated with the public messages on its capabilities.

What can be the role of nuclear forensics today?

The capabilities of modern nuclear forensics in a variety of contexts are remarkable. While postdetonation forensics were routinely applied during the times of atmospheric testing, and predetonation forensics attracted much attention following the end of the Cold War, this still leaves the questions of what the key roles of nuclear forensics can or should be today and how priorities for future research and development should be set. The different dimensions of these questions are explored below.

Nuclear forensics for national and international security

Shortly after the 9/11 attacks, concerns about the possibility of radiological and nuclear terrorism began to move to the center of the security debate – especially in the United States.[13] Most alarming in this context was and still is the possibility – even if considered remote – that a terrorist organization could set off a nuclear device in a metropolitan area. Many consider such a scenario credible given the availability of highly enriched uranium (HEU) in significant quantities at dozens of civilian sites,[14] often with poor security,[15] and the interest of some groups in carrying out such an attack.[16] The use of HEU in an improvised nuclear device based on the gun-type method is not considered a major technical challenge.

The possibility of state-sponsored nuclear terrorism later also became a growing concern. This was partly a consequence of the exposure of the A.Q. Khan network, which had connections to Libya, North Korea, and Iran.[17]

Combined, these new concerns became a focal point of US domestic and foreign policy. In response, in November 2002, the US Department of Homeland Security was created. It would consolidate a number of agencies and later also establish the Domestic Nuclear Detection Office (DNDO), which is now in charge of a "managed and coordinated response to radiological and nuclear threats, as well as integration of federal nuclear forensics programs."[18] In October 2006, the National Technical Nuclear Forensics Center (NTNFC) was established within DNDO to "ensure a ready, robust, and enduring nuclear forensics capability, to advance capabilities to conduct forensics on nuclear and other radioactive materials."[19]

A number of security initiatives were also launched on the multilateral or international level. In 2003, the United States, together with a number of partner countries, launched the Proliferation Security Initiative (PSI), mainly focused on interdiction of shipments related to weapons of mass destruction.[20] This initiative was backed up in April 2004 by UN Security Resolution 1540, which imposes binding obligations on all states to adopt legislation to prevent, inter alia, the proliferation of nuclear weapons and, specifically, the illicit trafficking of equipment and materials.[21] Related to these latter efforts, the US government launched the "Container Security Initiative" and the "Megaports Initiative" to enhance radiation detection capabilities for nuclear and radioactive materials in containerized cargo in major ports worldwide (now part of the "Second Line of Defense Program"). Since 2004, the United States has significantly ramped up the efforts to clean out civilian highly enriched uranium worldwide, consolidated under the Global Threat Reduction Initiative (GTRI).[22] Finally, at the broadest level, the Global Initiative to Combat Nuclear Terrorism (GICNT), initiated in 2006, became a partnership of eighty-five countries and four international organizations aimed at strengthening "global capacity to prevent, detect, and respond to nuclear terrorism by conducting multilateral activities that strengthen the plans, policies, procedures, and interoperability of partner nations."[23]

Overall, since the events of 9/11, there have been unprecedented US domestic and international efforts to prevent the theft and curb the trafficking of radiological and nuclear materials.

Ultimately, nuclear forensics play a central role for most of these efforts, because it would be the critical tool to enable attribution were the preparations for a terrorist attack discovered or such an attack to occur and remain unclaimed.

Recognizing this importance, especially in the United States, a parallel debate about the status of nuclear forensics began. It was triggered by concerns that US capabilities are inadequate or eroding. An influential report by the American Association for the Advancement of Science together with the American Physical Society in 2008,[24] and a later report by the

National Academies (2010),[25] examined the status of US nuclear forensic capabilities and developed recommendations to maintain a robust program.[26] Both reports emphasized, inter alia, the importance of international cooperation, including database development and the need for a larger forensic workforce, and recommended the accelerated development and deployment of state-of-the-art forensic techniques.

Attribution became a central theme in this discussion with a particular focus on the deterrent effect that would come with a robust attribution capability. The rationale behind this argument is that, unlike states, terrorist groups cannot be deterred to carry out an attack. Instead, credible attribution would need to identify the state sponsor, who provided fissile material for an "indirect" attack. This thinking is perhaps best summarized by Graham Allison in 2006 about then-North Korean leader, Kim Jong-il:

> Kim must be convinced that American nuclear forensics will be able to identify the molecular fingerprint of nuclear material from his Yongbyon reactor. He must feel in his gut the threat that if a nuclear weapon of North Korean origin explodes on American soil or that of a US ally, the United States will retaliate precisely as if North Korea had attacked the United States with a nuclear-armed missile: with an overwhelming response that guarantees this will never happen again.[27]

Some analysts continue to argue that a robust forensic and attribution capability can provide strong deterrence against illicit use of nuclear weapon materials.[28] The argument is based on the correct premise that production of fissile material is beyond the capabilities of nonstate groups. If such a group were therefore to acquire fissile material for a terrorist attack, it would ultimately be the responsibility of the country that had lost the control over the material.

There are several problems with the concept of deterrence through attribution capability, however. First, a thorough forensic analysis would likely require several months and be overtaken by events – especially following a hypothetical postdetonation situation. Second, if a state would indeed "plan" to use nuclear material for an unattributed attack or plan to transfer this material to a nonstate actor with explicit or tacit approval for use in a terrorist attack, it would make every effort to use material that is not in a forensic database. Similarly, those countries that are actively supporting the establishment and maintenance of nuclear forensic databases today are also the least likely to later provide nuclear material to third parties for illicit purposes. Finally, even if the origin of a material could be identified with high confidence, how would intent versus negligence be established? After all, given the sheer quantities of fissile material in the US and Russian stockpiles (e.g., more than 90 percent of the global HEU stockpile),[29] it is also quite possible that orphan nuclear material could ultimately be traced back to one of those sources. In brief: What kind of forensic evidence "justifies" what kind of response? However, even an incomplete attribution capability can be of significant value, of course, because it might help *exclude* certain origins for some recovered material and therefore help reduce uncertainty in an unfolding crisis.

In the United States, the establishment of strong attribution capabilities has been formalized with the Nuclear Forensics and Attribution Act, enacted in February 2010. The act asks the president to "pursue bilateral and multilateral international agreements to establish an international framework for determining the source of any confiscated nuclear or radiological material or weapon, as well as the source of any detonated weapon and the nuclear or radiological material used in such a weapon" and to "develop expedited protocols for the data exchange and dissemination of sensitive information needed to publicly identify the source of a nuclear detonation."[30]

A variation on the deterrence-through-attribution argument – one that is perhaps more practical – is the idea of leveraging strong attribution capabilities to encourage states to pursue and enforce the highest security standards for their nuclear materials. In particular, analysts have argued for a "global campaign leading to unambiguous physical protection standards." Pre-detonation nuclear forensics and attribution would be the critical tool to support and enforce such an effort.[31] These ideas have been an important theme of the Nuclear Security Summits held in 2010, 2012, and 2014.

Nuclear forensic methodologies for IAEA safeguards

Nuclear forensic science was first developed in a nuclear security context. The analytical methodologies that were developed and established, however, are being transferred to modern IAEA safeguards.

Nuclear forensic methods were first introduced as an ad-hoc tool used by the IAEA in May 1992 during its first inspections in North Korea. Shortly after North Korea's safeguards agreement with the agency entered into force, and following North Korea's submission of its "initial report" (as required by INFCIRC/153),[32] a high-level IAEA delegation visited the Yongbyon nuclear site, which had raised suspicions ever since a 5-MWe graphite reactor and a reprocessing plant were under construction there. During this visit, IAEA staff took swipe samples in the radiochemical facility, which would later reveal substantive inconsistencies in North Korea's initial report. For example, forensics analysis of more than 800 plutonium particles picked up in glove boxes indicated different isotopic signatures and different production dates (1989, 1990, and 1991), whereas North Korea only declared a single reprocessing campaign carried out in 1990.[33]

With the implementation of the Additional Protocol (INFCIRC/540) in the late 1990s, environmental swipe sampling techniques have become a routine safeguards tool.[34] The technique can be used, for example, to support conclusions about the absence of HEU production in a declared enrichment facility. Similarly, for bulk sample analysis, the measurement of impurities in nuclear materials, for example in uranium samples, allows safeguards authorities to verify the consistency of information. In combination with pattern recognition techniques, the analysis of chemical impurities enables one to check whether a sample does indeed originate from a particular facility or process stream. These safeguards applications are being supported by comprehensive investigations on the stability of impurity patterns throughout a chemical process as experienced, for example, from uranium mining to conversion. High-accuracy measurements of the isotopic composition of natural uranium samples have also proven to help distinguish between batches of different geographic origin.[35] Overall, modern nuclear forensic techniques have become an indispensable tool for IAEA safeguards.

Nuclear forensics for arms control and verification

Following the end of the Cold War, the United States and Russia agreed on a number of bilateral agreements related to the elimination, management, or disposition of excess fissile materials. Most importantly, this included the 1993 HEU blend-down agreement, under which Russia eliminated 500 metric tons of weapon-grade highly enriched uranium between 1993 and 2013, and the 2000 plutonium management and disposition agreement (PMDA), under which both sides have agreed to dispose of 34 metric tons of weapons plutonium. Both agreements have provisions based on isotopic measurements to ensure that weapon-grade material is being processed.[36] Besides these bilateral precedents, verification of nuclear arms control agreements has so far not systematically used nuclear forensic or other measurement techniques on nuclear materials. Future arms control treaties, however, could envision a more central role for nuclear forensics to support treaty verification. The most important examples and opportunities are briefly discussed below.

Comprehensive Test Ban Treaty (CTBT)

Verification of the CTBT would be based on an extensive International Monitoring System (IMS) using a variety of sensors to detect nuclear explosions in the atmosphere, underwater, and underground. In most circumstances, e.g., in the case of an underground explosion, attribution of a detected nuclear explosion would not be difficult or controversial. In some other scenarios, however, attribution could be challenging, especially of course if the country conducting the test sought to evade detection or attribution by carrying out the test in a remote location or in international waters. The most striking historic example remains the "mysterious flash" in the South Atlantic, which was detected by a dedicated satellite in September 1979 ("Vela Event 747"). No country claimed credit and no country was unambiguously identified as having conducted the test, but the most plausible explanation for the event remains a clandestine Israeli weapons test.[37] In the aftermath of the event, efforts were made to collect airborne radioactive debris in the region, but direct forensic evidence remained elusive.

Today, the CTBT monitoring system, which includes eighty state-of-the-art radionuclide stations worldwide, would have a much better chance of picking up unique signatures that would help characterize such an event. More importantly, postdetonation forensics could then be used to solve the "inverse problem" and determine features of the exploded device. Combined, these findings could provide critical evidence in attributing a clandestine nuclear-weapon test and confirming a possible violation of the CTBT.

Fissile Material Cutoff Treaty (FMCT)

The idea of banning the production of fissile materials for weapons purposes goes back to the late 1950s, but only with the end of the Cold War did NPT weapon states begin to seriously consider an FMCT. Efforts to start negotiations on an FMCT have been underway at the Conference on Disarmament since 1996. The overall scope of a possible FMCT has been a contested issue, in particular, if and how existing stocks of fissile materials in weapon states would be captured under such a treaty. Similarly, details of the verification regime would have to be agreed upon during the negotiations, even though many tools and approaches of the IAEA safeguards system could be directly applied. In fact, the NPT already constitutes a cutoff treaty for nonweapon states. Yet, an FMCT would also pose some new verification challenges, and nuclear forensics could help resolve some of them. By definition, nuclear-weapon states have military stocks of fissile materials and, while new production of fissile material for weapon purposes would be banned under the treaty, former military production facilities may continue to operate after conversion to civilian use. Situations may then arise, where the production date of a material sample needs to be determined to help confirm treaty compliance.

Enrichment plants are particularly relevant because historic HEU production can be expected to be reflected in particles collected in swipe samples, which are now used on a routine basis in safeguarded plants. The age of a macroscopic (microgram) uranium sample can easily be determined with nuclear forensic methods based on trace quantities of specific decay products in the sample.[38] Most importantly, the trace isotope uranium-234 decays to thorium-230 with a half-life of 246,000 years. A forensic analysis can then determine the fractional thorium-230 content in uranium to estimate the production date, i.e., the time elapsed since the last chemical separation of the parent nuclide from its daughter nuclide. The challenge arises in the case of microscopic (micron-sized) particles containing only few picograms of uranium. Such particles are typical for swipe samples taken at nuclear facilities. Here, the number of thorium-230 atoms could be as low as 100,000 in a particle that is 20–40 years old. Advanced ultra-sensitive mass-spectrometry begins to achieve such extreme, and previously unimaginable, detection goals.[39] The fact that many weapon states stopped production of weapons materials decades ago works in favor of the method. The potential contributions of nuclear forensics for FMCT verification can therefore only increase over time.

Verified fissile material declarations for nuclear disarmament

This is the most unconventional, but potentially also the most important application of nuclear forensics in the area of arms control verification. Existing nuclear arms control agreements between the United States and Russia place limits on the number of *deployed* strategic nuclear weapons. Verification of these agreements, such as New START, take advantage of the fact that deployed weapons are associated with unique and easily accountable delivery platforms, i.e., missile silos, submarines, and strategic bombers, to which agreed numbers of warheads are attributed. The next round of nuclear arms control agreements, however, may place limits on the *total* number of nuclear weapons and warheads in the arsenals. Such agreements would require fundamentally new verification approaches.[40]

One particular unprecedented challenge will be to gain confidence in the *completeness* of a declaration made by a country about the total size of its warhead stockpile, i.e., to ensure that an undeclared (secret) arsenal of nuclear weapons does not exist outside the verification regime. This is sometimes referred to as the "baseline problem."

One strategy – perhaps the only strategy – to systematically address this challenge is to focus on fissile material production and use instead. Weapon states have generally re-manufactured nuclear warheads on a regular basis. As a consequence, every kilogram of fissile material may have been in a number of warhead components since it was originally produced. In other words, most warheads produced since the beginning of the nuclear era no longer exist, and it may be extremely difficult or impossible to independently verify *ex post facto* that they have indeed been dismantled. If, however, confidence in the completeness of a state's fissile material declaration could be gained, then this could indirectly also serve to confirm the completeness of a nuclear warhead declaration. Confidence in the completeness would increase over time as the nuclear arsenals are drawn down and fissile materials are recovered from warheads, declared excess, and placed under international monitoring.

The United States and the United Kingdom have already made declarations about their respective inventories of military plutonium and highly enriched uranium. The US declarations are particularly valuable: they provide substantial detail on acquisition and use, include production data by year and site, and also list basic isotopic information of different material stocks. Confidence in the completeness of a fissile material declaration could be gained with a process dubbed "nuclear archaeology," which essentially relies on nuclear forensic analysis. The fundamental idea is to collect forensic evidence at former production facilities that can help establish total fissile material production at the site. The best-established example of nuclear archaeology was first proposed in the early 1990s and relies on measurements of the buildup of transmutation products in the graphite of graphite-moderated plutonium production reactors.[41] This so-called Graphite Isotope-Ratio Method (GIRM) estimates the cumulative neutron flow through the graphite and thereby the cumulative plutonium production in the reactor.

Equivalent methods might be used with other types of reactors, especially with heavy-water-moderated reactors that have been used for military plutonium production,[42] and possibly also for uranium enrichment plants.[43] In the best case, uncertainties in the lifetime production estimate of a particular facility can be in the order of a few percent,[44] but this would still translate into large absolute amounts of fissile material in terms of weapon-equivalents, especially in the cases of the United States and Russia. Combined with some other forensic evidence, however, estimates can be expected to be significantly more accurate. Overall, nuclear archaeology benefits from the fact that large amounts of source material and several production steps in different types of facilities are required for every kilogram of fissile material made.[45]

So far, the potential of nuclear archaeology to reconstruct fissile material production histories has only been demonstrated in a number of exercises; in one case, however, the method could have helped resolve the North Korean nuclear crisis. As part of the Six Party Talks,[46] in June 2008, North Korea reported its plutonium stockpile and use. In the same month, the United States submitted a discussion paper proposing elements of the verification activities to confirm the completeness of North Korea's declaration. The paper proposed to "conduct forensic measurements of nuclear materials and equipment" and, in the case of the Yongbyon graphite-moderated reactor, to "collect, and remove from the Party physical samples of the graphite moderator after the core has been de-fueled."[47] In October 2008, North Korea agreed on a number of verification measures, including access to all nuclear sites, and the use of scientific procedures to confirm the correctness and completeness of the declaration – but the process fell apart before the stage of sampling for nuclear forensics was reached. Given that North Korea had only produced in the order of 30–50 kilograms of plutonium by 2008, a nuclear archaeological analysis with a 5 percent error would have been equivalent to a maximum uncertainty of 2.5 kilograms of plutonium; in other words, at the time, the forensic analysis could have effectively excluded the existence of an undeclared nuclear device in the North Korean nuclear arsenal.

Overall, nuclear forensics, combined with other forensic evidence (including original production records), could therefore provide the critical tools to verify the completeness of fissile material declarations. Analysts have also emphasized that the sooner a nuclear archaeological analysis can be undertaken, the smaller the uncertainties in the estimate of lifetime fissile material production for a given facility.[48]

In principle, nuclear forensic techniques used for nuclear archaeology would not directly involve the fissile stocks themselves, which helps avoid security concerns that nuclear-weapon states may otherwise have. It should be noted, however, that direct measurements on fissile materials could considerably enhance confidence in nuclear archaeology, but would require countries to declassify isotopic information. Revealing such properties to international inspectors would be considered unacceptable by some nuclear-weapon states today. Once countries are willing to declare their fissile-material stockpiles, however, the security impact of the additional information made available during the verification of those declarations would be relatively minor.

Where do we stand? Where do we go from here?

Increasing the confidence in nuclear forensic conclusions and broadening the range of applications of nuclear forensic methodologies relies on accurate and sensitive analytical methods and on the availability of reference data for (comparative) evaluation of the observations. As distinguished from "predictive signatures," which do not require comparison data, and "comparative signatures," most of the signatures used in nuclear forensic investigations are of comparative nature, which necessitate the availability of empirically established data on material of known process history. The latter signatures provide more robust conclusions and allow establishing the history of unknown material with higher confidence. To some extent, reference information can be obtained from open source information and from the scientific literature. Yet, in order to enable drawing defensible conclusions, the availability of reference information (e.g., through appropriate databases) is essential. Such compilations could be realized through nuclear forensic databases or sample archives, sometimes referred to as "nuclear forensic libraries."

Ideally, one should strive for a comprehensive international database, in which data on all the signatures of all nuclear material is stored. In case of a nuclear security incident, the relevant reference data enabling a rapid and unambiguous identification of unknown material would be readily available. Such an approach, however, has proven too difficult to implement, and, in hindsight, unrealistic because data on nuclear material is associated with sensitivities, which can be due to commercial or national security issues. These sensitivities appear prohibitive for establishing an international database. In consequence, efforts were made to support the development of national nuclear forensics libraries, allowing states to keep control of the data and ensure the protection of sensitive information. The shortcomings of this approach are obviously the distribution of data (in national databases) and the delay involved when asking for queries in the databases of other states. Such a distributed approach obviously calls for an international directory, i.e., an overview of where national nuclear forensic libraries are available and of how queries can be requested.

The Nuclear Security Summits in 2010 and 2012 emphasized the importance of nuclear forensics and developed a number of related recommendations. Specifically, the Work Plan of 2010 listed a number of political commitments, including the following: "Participating States will explore ways to work together to develop national capacities for nuclear forensics, such as the creation of national libraries and an international directory of points of contact, to facilitate and encourage cooperation between States in combating illicit nuclear trafficking."[49] The concept of national nuclear forensic libraries appears to gain acceptance and mechanisms have to be explored and implemented enabling queries and allowing information sharing.

Regional databases appear a viable compromise between national and international databases. For example, the database available at the Institute for Transuranium Elements of the European Commission covers data on (fresh) fuel for power reactors and includes information provided by some western European and Russian fuel manufacturers.[50] Data protection is ensured by strict confidentiality agreements and is supported by a complete physical isolation of the database from any network. Irrespective of whether nuclear forensic libraries are strictly national, regional, or international, their maintenance, and the continuous update and vetting of the data, are essential.

Many of these considerations refer to predetonation nuclear forensics. We have to recognize that nuclear weapon states have significant experience in postdetonation nuclear forensics. Nonweapon states and nonmilitary laboratories within weapon states have only very limited experience in this area, which builds on the analysis of the limited amounts of openly available material such as trinitite.[51] This is unlikely to change in the future.

A more general challenge for nuclear forensics is the sustainability of technical capabilities. The challenge is actually twofold. First of all, the global nuclear workforce is aging, and there is a significant risk that tacit knowledge is not transferred to the next generation of scientists. Secondly, nuclear forensic investigations occur at low frequency. For maintaining the skills, nuclear forensic capabilities should be established at laboratories, where the analysis of nuclear material is performed on a routine basis. Typically, this would be for other non-security purposes, such as environmental or quality control, and ensures the availability of appropriate infrastructure and measurement equipment, of validated analytical techniques, and of suitably qualified experts. However, there are also many new potential security-related applications on the horizon. Nuclear forensic approaches to support arms control verification appear particularly promising. For the verification of the NPT, nuclear safeguards methodologies are already being complemented with investigative techniques transferred from the nuclear forensics area. In addition to maintaining capabilities for the current missions of nuclear forensics, it is therefore critically important to further develop and demonstrate relevant nuclear forensic techniques now so that they will be available when new challenges and opportunities arise.

Notes

1. International Atomic Energy Agency, "Nuclear Forensics Support, Reference Manual," *IAEA Nuclear Security Series* No. 2, Technical Guidance, Vienna, 2006, www-pub.iaea.org/MTCD/publications/PDF/Pub1241_web.pdf.
2. Michael Gordin, *Red Cloud at Dawn: Truman, Stalin, and the End of the Atomic Monopoly* (New York: Farrar, Straus, and Giroux, 2009). See in particular Figure 6.
3. Jay Davis, "Nuclear Forensics: A Capability We Hope Never to Use," APS Workshop on Nuclear Weapons Issues in the 21st Century, George Washington University, November 3, 2013, http://elliott.gwu.edu/sites/elliott.gwu.edu/files/downloads/events/4.8%20Davis%20slides.ppt.
4. Kenton J. Moody, Ian D. Hutcheon, and Patrick M. Grant, *Nuclear Forensics Analysis* (Boca Raton, FL: Taylor & Francis, 2005); Klaus Mayer, Maria Wallenius, and Zsolt Varga, "Nuclear Forensic Science: Correlating Measurable Material Parameters to the History of Nuclear Material," *Chemical Reviews*, Vol. 113, No. 2 (February 2013), pp. 884–900.
5. International Atomic Energy Agency, "International Target Values 2010 for Measurement Uncertainties in Safeguarding Nuclear Materials," STR-368, Department of Safeguards, Vienna, Austria, November 2010, www.iaea.org/safeguards/documents/International_Target_Values_2010.pdf.
6. K. Mayer, M. Wallenius, and A. Schubert. "Data Interpretation in Nuclear Forensics," IAEA Nuclear Security Symposium, IAEA-CN-166/13, Vienna, March 30–April 3, 2009, www-pub.iaea.org/mtcd/meetings/PDFplus/2009/cn166/CN166_Presentations/Session%209/013%20Mayer.pdf.
7. Martin Robel, Michael J. Kristo, and Martin A. Heller, "Nuclear Forensic Inferences: Using Iterative Multidimensional Statistics," 50th INMM Annual Meeting, Tucson, Arizona, July 12–July 16, 2009, https://e-reports-ext.llnl.gov/pdf/374432.pdf.
8. Victor Gilinsky and Roger J. Mattson, "Did Israel Steal Bomb-grade Uranium from the United States?" *Bulletin of the Atomic Scientists,* April 17, 2014, thebulletin.org/did-israel-steal-bomb-grade-uranium-united-states7056; Victor Gilinsky and Roger J. Mattson, "Revisiting the NUMEC Affair," *Bulletin of the Atomic Scientists,* Vol. 66, No. 2 (March 2010), pp. 61–75.
9. See in particular, Lyudmila Zaitseva and Friedrich Steinhäusler, "Nuclear Trafficking Issues in the Black Sea Region," EU Non-Proliferation Consortium, Non-Proliferation Papers, No. 39, April 2014, www.nonproliferation.eu/documents/nonproliferationpapers/lyudmilazaitsevafriedrichsteinhausler53451ed0bbecb.pdf.
10. "Die Hand im Feuer," *Der Spiegel*, 17/1995, pp. 28–37, www.spiegel.de/spiegel/print/d-9180723.html; "Lizenz zum Lügen," *Der Spiegel,* 51/1995, pp. 30–33, www.spiegel.de/spiegel/print/d-9248654.html; Eric Gujer, *Kampf an neuen Fronten* (Frankfurt am Main: Campus Verlag, 2006).
11. Moody, Hutcheon, and Grant, *Nuclear Forensics Analysis*, p. 354.
12. Ibid., p. 371.
13. It is generally assumed that the use of a Radiological Dispersal Device (RDD) or "Dirty Bomb" would not cause a large number of short-term or long-term casualties, but the economic and psychological impact of such an event could be significant. The security of radioactive sources therefore became a highly visible policy issue. See Charles D. Ferguson, Tahseen Kazi, and Judith Perera, "Commercial Radioactive Sources: Surveying the Risks," Occasional Paper No. 11, Center for Nonproliferation Studies, Monterey Institute of International Studies, Monterey, CA, January 2003, http://cns.miis.edu/opapers/op11/op11.pdf.

14. Francesco Calogero, "Nuclear Terrorism," Nobel Peace Prize Centennial Symposium, Oslo, Norway, December 6–8, 2001, www.pugwash.org/september11/sept11-calogero.htm; Alexander Glaser and Frank von Hippel, "Thwarting Nuclear Terrorism," *Scientific American*, Vol. 294, No. 2 (February 2006), pp. 56–63; Graham Allison, *Nuclear Terrorism: The Ultimate Preventable Catastrophe* (New York: Times Books, 2004).

15. In one widely reported example, ten students traveled to twenty-five research reactors at US college campuses as part of an ABC News investigation published in October 2005. In many cases, the students easily gained access to sites. See "Radioactive Road Trip," *ABC News*, October 13, 2005, http://abcnews.go.com/US/video?id=1879256, and http://abcnews.go.com/Primetime/story?id=1855888.

16. Matthew Bunn, "The Risk of Nuclear Terrorism and Next Steps to Reduce the Danger," Testimony for the Committee on Homeland Security and Governmental Affairs, US Senate, Washington, DC, April 2, 2008, http://belfercenter.ksg.harvard.edu/files/bunn-nuclear-terror-risk-test-08.pdf.

17. Gordon Corera, *Shopping for Bombs, Nuclear Proliferation, Global Insecurity, and the Rise and Fall of the A.Q. Khan Network* (Oxford: Oxford University Press, 2006); International Institute for Strategic Studies, *Nuclear Black Markets: Pakistan, A.Q. Khan and the Rise of Proliferation Networks: A Net Assessment* (London: International Institute for Strategic Studies, May 2007); William Langwiesche, *The Atomic Bazaar: The Rise of the Nuclear Poor* (New York: Farrar, Straus and Giroux, 2007).

18. US Department of Homeland Security, "About the Domestic Nuclear Detection Office," www.dhs.gov/about-domestic-nuclear-detection-office.

19. US Department of Homeland Security, "National Technical Nuclear Forensics Center," www.dhs.gov/national-technical-nuclear-forensics-center.

20. United States White House, Office of the Press Secretary, "Proliferation Security Initiative: Statement of Interdiction Principles," Fact Sheet, Washington, DC, September 4, 2003, www.state.gov/t/isn/c27726.htm.

21. United Nations Security Council, "Resolution 1540 (2004)," S/RES/1540 (2004), 495th meeting, April 28, 2004, http://daccess-dds-ny.un.org/doc/UNDOC/GEN/N04/328/43/PDF/N0432843.pdf.

22. International Atomic Energy Agency, "IAEA Welcomes US New Global Threat Reduction Initiative," IAEA Press Release, May 27, 2004, www.iaea.org/newscenter/news/2004/gtri_initiative.html.

23. US Department of State, "The Global Initiative To Combat Nuclear Terrorism," Office of Weapons of Mass Destruction and Terrorism. N.D., www.state.gov/t/isn/c18406.htm.

24. Michael M. May, Reza Abedin-Zadeh, Donald A. Barr, Albert Carnesale, Philip E. Coyle, Jay Davis, Bill Dorland, Bill Dunlop, Steve Fetter, Alexander Glaser, Ian D. Hutcheon, Francis Slakey, and Benn Tannenbaum, "Nuclear Forensics: Role, State of the Art, Program Needs," Report by the Joint Working Group of the American Physical Society Panel on Public Affairs and the American Association for the Advancement of Science, Center for Science, Technology and Security Policy, Washington, DC, February 2008, http://iis-db.stanford.edu/pubs/22126/APS_AAAS_2008.pdf.

25. National Research Council. *Nuclear Forensics: A Capability at Risk (Abbreviated Version)* (Washington, DC: The National Academies Press, 2010).

26. The 2010 National Academies report remains classified and only an abbreviated version is publicly available.

27. Graham Allison, "Deterring Kim Jong Il," *Washington Post,* October 27, 2006, www.washingtonpost.com/wp-dyn/content/article/2006/10/26/AR2006102601254.html.

28. Debra K. Decker, "Before the First Bomb Goes Off: Developing Nuclear Attribution Standards and Policies," Discussion Paper 2011-03, Belfer Center for Science and International Affairs, Harvard Kennedy School, April 2011, http://belfercenter.ksg.harvard.edu/files/Decker_DP_2011_FINAL.pdf.

29. International Panel on Fissile Materials, *Global Fissile Material Report 2013: Increasing Transparency of Nuclear Warhead and Fissile Material Stocks as a Step toward Disarmament*, Princeton University, October 2013, http://fissilematerials.org/library/gfmr13.pdf.

30. United States Congress, *Nuclear Forensics and Attribution Act,* H.R. 730, H.R. 730 (111th): Nuclear Forensics and Attribution Act, 111th Congress, 2009–2010, August 25, 2010, www.govtrack.us/congress/bills/111/hr730/text.

31. Daniel H. Chivers, Bethany F. Lyles Goldblum, Brett H. Isselhardt, and Jonathan S. Snider, "Before the Day After: Using Pre-Detonation Nuclear Forensics to Improve Fissile Material Security," *Arms*

Control Today, Vol. 38, No. 6 (July/August 2008), pp. 22–23, 25–28, www.armscontrol.org/act/2008_07-08/NuclearForensics. The authors argue: "If such [fissile] material should escape a state's control, the state should be forced to establish truly effective physical protection measures or face international condemnation and corrective action. Weapons-usable fissile material found outside of state control would present clear evidence that robust physical protection measures are not in place."

32. International Atomic Energy Agency, "The Structure and Content of Agreements Between the Agency and States Required in Connection with the Treaty on the Non-Proliferation of Nuclear Weapons," INFCIRC/153, (Corrected), June 1972, Paragraph 62, www.iaea.org/Publications/Documents/Infcircs/Others/infcirc153.pdf.

33. For an extensive discussion, see David Albright and Kevin O'Neill, (eds), *Solving the North Korean Nuclear Puzzle* (Washington, DC: Institute for Science and International Security, 2000).

34. For the text of INFCIRC/540, see International Atomic Energy Agency, "Model Protocol Additional to the Agreement(s) Between State(s) and the International Atomic Energy Agency for the Application of Safeguards," INFCIRC/540 (Corrected), September 1997, www.iaea.org/Publications/Documents/Infcircs/1997/infcirc540c.pdf.

35. Both methodologies (impurities and uranium isotopic signatures) were successfully applied when Saddam Hussein's clandestine nuclear-weapon program was uncovered in the early 1990s, and the origin of the uranium needed to be identified.

36. In the case of the plutonium disposition agreement, for example, an upper bound for the Pu-240/Pu-239 ratio is used as a criterion to provide confidence in the weapon-origin of the material. The language in the plutonium disposition agreement reads: "The monitoring Party shall be allowed to confirm, using an agreed method, that the Pu-240/Pu-239 ratio of the conversion product is no greater than 0.10. Confirmation of this ratio shall occur using agreed methods based on measurement of the isotopic composition of the conversion product upon its receipt at a fuel fabrication facility." See The Government of the United States of America and the Government of the Russian Federation, "Agreement between the Government of the United States of America and the Government of the Russian Federation Concerning the Management and Disposition of Plutonium Designated as No Longer Required for Defense Purposes and Related Cooperation, as Amended by 2010 Protocol," signed on April 13, 2010, www.fissilematerials.org/library/PMDA2010.pdf. For a discussion of the provisions used for the HEU blend-down agreement, see Ann Parker, "A Transparent Success: 'Megatons to Megawatts' Program," *Science & Technology Review*, Lawrence Livermore National Laboratory, April/May 2013, pp. 16–19.

37. Leonard Weiss, "Israel's 1979 Nuclear Test and the US Cover-up," *Middle East Policy Journal*, Vol. 18, No. 4 (Winter 2011), pp. 83–95; Jeffrey Richelson, *Spying on the Bomb: American Nuclear Intelligence from Nazi Germany to Iran and North Korea* (New York: Norton, 2006); see especially The National Security Archive, "The Vela Incident: Nuclear Test or Meteoroid?" National Security Archive Electronic Briefing Book, No. 190, May 5, 2006, www2.gwu.edu/~nsarchiv/NSAEBB/NSAEBB190.

38. M. Wallenius, A. Morgenstern, C. Apostolidis, and K. Mayer, "Determination of the Age of Highly Enriched Uranium," *Analytical and Bioanalytical Chemistry*, Vol. 374, No. 3 (October 2002), pp. 379–384; Zsolt Varga, Maria Wallenius, and Klaus Mayer, "Age Determination of Uranium Samples by Inductively Coupled Plasma Mass Spectrometry Using Direct Measurement and Spectral Deconvolution," *Journal of Analytical Atomic Spectrometry*, Vol. 25, No. 12 (December 2010), pp. 1958–1962; F. E. Stanley, "A Beginner's Guide to Uranium Chronometry in Nuclear Forensics and Safeguards," *Journal of Analytical Atomic Spectrometry*, Vol. 27, No. 11 (November 2012), pp. 1821–1830. Age-dating of plutonium samples is "trivial" compared to uranium samples due to the shorter half-life of the plutonium isotopes, in particular the short-lived plutonium-241, which has a relative high concentration in typical samples and decays into americium-241 with a half-life of only 14 years.

39. A. Glaser and S. Burger, "Verification of a Fissile Material Cutoff Treaty: The Case of Enrichment Facilities and the Role of Ultra-trace Level Isotope Ratio Analysis," *Journal of Radioanalytical and Nuclear Chemistry*, Vol. 280, No. 1 (April 2009), pp. 85–90, http://link.springer.com/article/10.1007%2Fs10967-008-7423-0.

40. International Panel on Fissile Materials, *Global Fissile Material Report 2009: A Path to Nuclear Disarmament*, Princeton University, October 2009, www.fissilematerials.org/library/gfmr09.pdf; Corey Hinderstein (ed.), *Cultivating Confidence: Verification, Monitoring, and Enforcement for a World Free of Nuclear Weapons* (Washington, DC: Nuclear Threat Initiative, 2010).

41. Steve Fetter, "Nuclear Archaeology: Verifying Declarations of Fissile Material Production," *Science and Global Security*, Vol. 3, Nos. 3–4 (1993), pp. 237–259.

42. Alex Gasner and Alexander Glaser, "Nuclear Archaeology for Heavy-Water-Moderated Plutonium Production Reactors," *Science & Global Security,* Vol. 19, No. 3 (2011), pp. 223–233, http://scienceandglobalsecurity.org/archive/sgs19gasner.pdf.
43. Sébastien Philippe and Alexander Glaser, "Nuclear Archaeology for Gaseous Diffusion Enrichment Plants," *Science & Global Security,* Vol. 22, No. 1 (2014), pp. 27–49.
44. Thomas W. Wood, Bruce D. Reid, Christopher M. Toomey, Kannan Krishnaswami, Kimberly A. Burns, Larry O. Casazza, Don S. Daly, and Leesa L. Duckworth, "The Future of Nuclear Archaeology: Reducing Legacy Risks of Weapons Fissile Material," *Science & Global Security,* Vol. 22, No. 1 (2014), pp. 4–26.
45. About 100,000 kg of natural uranium are needed to make 450 kg of weapon-grade uranium or 70 kg of weapon-grade plutonium. See International Panel on Fissile Materials, *Global Fissile Material Report 2009,* Figure 4.7.
46. Xiaodon Liang, "The Six-Party Talks at a Glance," Factsheet, Arms Control Association, May 2012, www.armscontrol.org/factsheets/6partytalks.
47. International Panel on Fissile Materials, *Global Fissile Material Report 2009,* Appendix 4A, pp. 63–66. The original discussion paper is also available at www.ipfmlibrary.org/gov08.pdf.
48. Wood, *et al.,* "Future of Nuclear Archaeology."
49. The White House, Office of the Press Secretary, "Work Plan of the Washington Nuclear Security Summit," April 13, 2010, www.whitehouse.gov/the-press-office/work-plan-washington-nuclear-security-summit.
50. J. Dolgov, Y. K. Bibilashvili, N. A. Chorokhov, A. Schubert, G. Janssen, K. Mayer, and L. Koch, "Installation of a Database for Identification of Nuclear Material of Unknown Origin," Proceedings of the 21st ESARDA Symposium, Sevilla, 1999, https://esarda.jrc.ec.europa.eu/index.php?option=com_jifile&filename=ZTNlNzRmMWI4YjkzZTIzNGRlZmI4MzI2MjU0NTJlYTA=.
51. J. Davis, "Post Detonation Nuclear Forensics," in *Nuclear Weapons Issues in the 21st Century,* edited by Pierce S. Corden, David Hafemeister and Peter Zimmerman, AIP Conference Proceedings, Vol. 1596 (AIP Publishing, 2014), pp. 206–209; Jeremy J. Bellucci and Antonio Simonetti, "Nuclear Forensics: Searching for Nuclear Device Debris in Trinitite-Hosted Inclusions," *Journal of Radioanalytical and Nuclear Chemistry,* Vol. 293, No. 1 (July 2012), pp. 313–319, http://link.springer.com/article/10.1007%2Fs10967-012-1654-9.

19

INTERDICTION AND LAW ENFORCEMENT TO COUNTER NUCLEAR PROLIFERATION

Susan J. Koch

The role of interdiction and law enforcement in countering nuclear proliferation has grown substantially over the past decade, yet much more remains to be done. A few interdiction and law enforcement instruments are targeted specifically at nuclear proliferation, but most focus more broadly on weapons of mass destruction (WMD) – nuclear, chemical, and biological– and missile delivery systems.

Interdiction

Proliferation security initiative

The primary catalyst for the emergence of interdiction as an important counterproliferation tool was the Proliferation Security Initiative (PSI), proposed by President George Bush at a speech in Krakow, Poland on May 31, 2003. The proposal grew out of a striking interdiction failure. On December 9, 2002, the United States and Spanish navies cooperated to board forcibly a North Korean vessel, the *So San*. The *So San*'s manifest claimed that it was carrying cement; that was true up to a point, but hidden under the cement was a cargo of SCUD missiles, warheads, and fuel. Just two days later, the United States released the ship and allowed it to continue to Yemen. The Yemeni Government had vigorously complained to Vice President Cheney and Secretary of State Powell about the seizure, and the United States quickly acceded.

The international legal authority to board the ship forcibly appears solid; the *So San* flew no flag, making it a stateless vessel subject to the international law against piracy, and its manifest was false. Legal scholars disagree about whether there was a comparable basis for the United States to hold the ship and its cargo.[1] Publicly, the White House claimed that it had no legal basis to hold the ship and its cargo,[2] but it seems most likely that the Bush Administration chose to release the *So San* for political reasons. The legal arguments for retaining the vessel, although debatable, were sufficiently strong that any consideration within the administration would certainly have continued for more than one or two days. On the other hand, the political arguments for acceding to Yemeni demands were powerful and urgent. In late 2002, the Bush administration placed its highest international priority on building and sustaining international (and especially regional) government support for the "global war on terrorism" and the coming war with Iraq.[3] Yemen was an important actual and potential partner in both efforts.

In announcing the release of the *So San* and its cargo, White House Press Secretary Fleischer foreshadowed the later creation of PSI, in terms suggesting that the Bush Administration would try to change the international legal framework regarding missile proliferation:

> There are many agreements around the world in international treaty law which have been agreed to, focused on nuclear proliferation, on biological proliferation, on chemical weapons proliferation. One thing that does come out of this that the United States thinks needs to be looked at by the world is that there are less stringent agreements on the international treaty level dealing with proliferation of missiles.[4]

When President Bush proposed the PSI some months later, he may have reinforced expectations that the Initiative would create new legal authorities to interdict proliferation shipments. He also made clear that the Initiative would be directed against WMD as well as missile proliferation:

> When weapons of mass destruction or their components are in transit, we must have the means and authority to seize them. So today I announce a new effort to fight proliferation called the Proliferation Security Initiative. The United States and a number of our close allies, including Poland, have begun working on new agreements to search planes and ships carrying suspect cargo and to seize illegal weapons or missile technologies.[5]

The United States invited ten close allies to join in implementing the Krakow proposal.[6] The resultant "Core Group" acted quickly, issuing the Statement of Interdiction Principles, basically the "constitution" of PSI, on September 4, 2003. Contrary to any expectations that may have been generated by the White House and the president, the Statement of Interdiction Principles did not expand the legal basis for interdiction or other measures to counter WMD proliferation. Instead, the statement is strictly a political, rather than legal, document, and stresses that the principles are designed

> to establish a more coordinated and effective basis through which to impede and stop shipments of WMD, delivery systems, and related materials flowing to and from states and nonstate actors of proliferation concern, consistent with national legal authorities and relevant international law and frameworks, including the UN Security Council.[7]

The Statement of Interdiction Principles does include a commitment by participants to "[r]eview and work to strengthen their relevant national legal authorities where necessary to accomplish these objectives, and work to strengthen when necessary relevant international law and frameworks in appropriate ways to support these commitments."[8] However, its main focus is on immediate action using existing authorities; in many cases, cooperation among participants is urged, especially where one may have interdiction authority and another may not.

From its beginnings, PSI was targeted against all WMD and delivery system proliferators, rather than against any specific states or actors of concern.[9] This has proved important on a few fronts. First, the history of WMD in Iraq and of Syria's nuclear program demonstrates the difficulty of identifying WMD proliferation threats, especially over the long term. Second, the absence of named targets undoubtedly reduced – even if it hardly eliminated – the controversy surrounding PSI, and contributed to its expansion.

The one criterion for PSI participation is adherence to the Statement of Interdiction Principles. Numbers grew rapidly, from the original eleven to over fifty in just one month, and to 102 by November 2012. Still, distribution is uneven. All European states except Monaco participate, but other regions are underrepresented. Sub-Saharan Africa, with just three PSI partners, is the most dramatic. Major states with important roles in international trade and/or WMD- and missile-related industries that have not adhered to PSI include Brazil, China, Egypt, India, Indonesia, Malaysia, South Africa, and Pakistan.[10]

The PSI founding states prided themselves on creating "an activity, not an organization."[11] The Statement of Interdiction Principles does not provide for any structure – no central secretariat, formally organized groups or even schedule of meetings. That, combined with the simple criterion for adherence, differing political commitments and varying counterproliferation capabilities, has led to wide divergence in participants' PSI involvement. The Core Group lasted for less than a year; as many new PSI adherents sought to join, the concept became unworkable. Since the end of the Core Group, there have been only four political-level meetings, in 2004, 2006, 2008, and 2013, all open to all adherents and marking anniversaries of the Krakow speech. In addition to the five-year gap between the 2008 and 2013 sessions, there was a marked decline in attendance, from 97 percent of PSI adherents in 2008 to just 71 percent in 2013.

The only regular PSI meetings since early 2004 have been of the Operational Experts Group (OEG). It has twenty-one members: the original eleven states plus Argentina, Canada, Denmark, Greece, New Zealand, Norway, Republic of Korea, Russia, Singapore, and Turkey. Criteria for membership included political or economic significance, commitment to PSI, and regional diversity. Most, except Russia and Argentina, have remained very active in PSI.

The OEG's basic role is to help translate the PSI principles into action, through planning and conducting exercises; identifying required and available counterproliferation capabilities and action, and sharing lessons learned from PSI successes and failures. Until 2009, the OEG met 3–5 times a year, supplemented with a few additional regional meetings and workshops. In early 2009, the OEG decided to meet less often in full session and more often in regional meetings, in order to involve more PSI adherents in its work. The first part of that approach – fewer plenary OEG meetings – has been realized. The second part – more regional meetings – by and large has not been. There has been an average of about one each per year.

PSI has witnessed a comparable decline in exercises. There have been about fifty announced PSI exercises, including live and table-top exercises, with mostly maritime, but also some ground, air, and port interdictions scenarios. Four exercises were held in just the first three months of the initiative, nine in 2004, but many fewer in subsequent years, reaching a low point in 2011, when there were none.[12]

OEG partners in June 2011 adopted the Critical Capabilities and Practices (CCP) initiative, designed to help partners build interdiction capabilities, but requiring less investment in time or money than exercises. CCP focuses on four interdiction-related areas: legal frameworks; identification and inspection; seizure and disposal; and rapid decision-making.[13] There is no public record of CCP activities or progress.

PSI participants also sought to use the tenth anniversary meeting in Warsaw in May 2013 to revitalize the Initiative. Following a pattern set by the first Nuclear Security Summit in April 2010, the Warsaw meeting produced both joint statements and individual national commitments. According to the Chairman's Summary:

> The four Joint Statements, taken together, represent the affirming countries' common view of future work for the Initiative.

- The first Joint Statement, on "Ensuring a Robust Initiative," underlines a need to conduct more regular and robust PSI events, including exercise rotations.
- The second Joint Statement, on "Enhancing Critical Interdiction Capabilities and Practices," encourages working together to share capacity building tools and resources among all PSI endorsing states.
- The third, statement on "Strengthening Authorities for Action," invites countries to continue working, both individually and cooperatively, to strengthen national and international authorities, including through adoption of new frameworks.
- The fourth and final Joint Statement, on "Expanding Strategic Communications," encourages outreach by PSI endorsing States to prospective partner states and the communication of PSI's principles and goals to the public and private sector.

Participating states committed to take concrete actions in support of their PSI commitments. These declarations of action ranged from conducting PSI exercise rotations to examining new national laws, including export control and international frameworks.[14]

All governments attending the tenth anniversary meeting endorsed the first and third Joint Statements. All but Russia endorsed the second and fourth.[15] The reasons for Russia's positions on the different statements have not been made public.

It is difficult to measure PSI's practical impact on WMD and missile proliferation. First, very little public information is available about actual interdictions. Governments often have a range of motives – domestic, international, political, military, intelligence, and/or economic – not to divulge interdictions or their role in them. Second, it is not always a straightforward task to identify an interdiction. For example, in May 2011, the *M/V Light* left North Korea for Burma with a suspect proliferation cargo. The US Navy began shadowing the vessel, and interdiction was virtually guaranteed. For unknown (and inexplicable) reasons, the North Koreans had used a ship flying the flag of Belize, which had concluded a ship-boarding agreement with the United States.[16] Eventually, to avoid being boarded, the ship returned to North Korea, without reaching Burma.[17] Some observers conclude that the *M/V Light* was not interdicted because it was not forcibly halted or boarded. Others argue the contrary, because the proliferation cargo was kept from its intended customer.

A similar, but even murkier, question is whether the stopping of proliferation shipments at their source qualifies as an interdiction. For example, one of the most common means of countering proliferation by air is to deny over-flight rights. If that denial means the plane never leaves the ground, has it been interdicted? Many would say no; others would stress that it achieves the basic aim of interdiction, as stated in the PSI Statement of Interdiction Principles: "to impede and stop shipments of WMD, delivery systems, and related materials."

Finally, in the few clear, public cases of interdiction, observers disagree about the role of PSI specifically. Many adherents cooperated on interdictions long before the creation of PSI and probably would have continued to do so without it. Has PSI facilitated interdictions over the past ten years, or would they have happened in any case? For example, in Fall 2003, the United States and United Kingdom tracked nuclear enrichment centrifuge components shipped on a German-registered vessel, from an A.Q. Khan facility in Malaysia bound for Libya. The German and Italian Governments immediately agreed to a US and UK request that the ship divert to an Italian port and be searched and seized there. The interdiction not only prevented nuclear proliferation to Libya, but also resulted in the end of the A.Q. Khan network and in Libya's decision to abandon its WMD and longer-range missile programs. Some observers credit the *BBC China* interdiction as a major PSI success; others argue that the four states involved would have done the same without the Initiative.[18]

Financial action task force

The Financial Action Task Force (FATF) is not usually associated with counterproliferation, let alone interdiction. However, it can play an important part in denying financing for, and thus effectively blocking, WMD and missile proliferation. The FATF was established in 1989 to combat money laundering, aiming in large part to counter drug trafficking. The thirty-six FATF members represent the world's financial leaders.[19] Most other states belong to one or more of the regional groups that are FATF Associated Members.

After its creation, FATF quickly developed recommended standards for banks and other financial institutions. Those are not legally binding, but have great political and economic force, especially given the importance of reputation in the financial sector. A central part of FATF work is to monitor, and to publicize, countries' implementation of the standards. Three times a year, FATF issues public documents that name "high-risk and noncooperative jurisdictions" in three categories: those with major "deficiencies and to which counter-measures apply;" those that have not made sufficient progress; and those working to improve compliance. As of October 2013, only Iran and North Korea were in the first category; eleven states were in the second; and twenty in the third.[20]

Just one month after 9/11, FATF explicitly expanded its mission and its standards to include terrorist financing. In 2008, a FATF Working Group issued a first report on possible further expansion, to counter WMD proliferation. A more detailed 2010 report offered twenty-three policy options to that end. However, the new FATF standards adopted in February 2012 included only one dedicated to proliferation finance; it simply requires states to comply with relevant United Nations Security Council resolutions.[21] While the outcome was disappointing to many, it is important to recall that many, if not most, FATF standards apply to any form of illicit international finance, including WMD proliferation.

Global initiative to combat nuclear terrorism

One counterproliferation instrument with an exclusively nuclear focus is the Global Initiative to Combat Nuclear Terrorism (GICNT). Jointly founded and chaired by the United States and Russia, the Initiative was patterned after PSI, with a Statement of Principles which is the only criterion for participation, absence of direct changes to national and international legal authorities, and a minimal structure with no set schedule of meetings.

Three of the GICNT Principles are particularly relevant to interdiction and law enforcement:

3. Improve the ability to detect nuclear and other radioactive materials and substances in order to prevent illicit trafficking; …
4. Improve capabilities of participants to search for, confiscate, and establish safe control over unlawfully held nuclear or other radioactive materials and substances or devices using them; …
6. Ensure adequate respective national legal and regulatory frameworks sufficient to provide for the implementation of appropriate criminal and, if applicable, civil liability for terrorists and those who facilitate acts of nuclear terrorism.[22]

At eighty-five partners, GICNT is smaller than PSI, but more diverse politically. Important states that adhere to GICNT but not PSI include China, India, Malaysia, and Pakistan. Three factors may be at work here: Russia's co-chairmanship; a greater international consensus against nuclear terrorism than against WMD proliferation; and the absence of a strong GICNT focus on interdiction, which remains controversial to some.

GICNT was slow to begin a sustained program of exercises, workshops and other capacity-building efforts. In 2010, it activated the Implementation and Assessment Group (IAG) and created two Working Groups on nuclear detection and nuclear forensics; both subjects have major potential roles in nuclear proliferation interdiction and law enforcement. As of December 2013, GICNT partners had held a total of forty-four capacity-building workshops and exercises. Fourteen of those directly concerned interdiction or law enforcement.[23]

Legal bases for counterproliferation interdiction and law enforcement

Criminalizing proliferation: National and International action

There has been some progress over the past decade in criminalizing WMD proliferation and in strengthening the legal bases and international political legitimacy of interdiction as a counterproliferation tool. Several states have improved their national laws against proliferation. Two important examples are Singapore (shortly after adhering to PSI), and Malaysia (in a national commitment at the first Nuclear Security Summit in April 2010).

Passed in April 2004, UN Security Council Resolution (UNSCR) 1540 represented a major advance in the international legal framework against WMD proliferation. Initially somewhat controversial, it has become steadily more accepted by the international community. That may best be seen in the periodic renewals of the Security Council Committee charged with overseeing its implementation. The 1540 Committee was originally established for two years, renewed for two years in 2006, for three years in 2008, and then for an almost unprecedented ten years in 2011.

Adopted under Chapter VII of the Charter, UNSCR 1540 is the first UN resolution to designate WMD and missile proliferation in general (rather than by a specific country) as a threat to international peace and security. The major obligations it places on member states are: to criminalize WMD and missile proliferation and support by nonstate actors; to enact and enforce effective controls on trade, transport, and finance of WMD, missiles, and related materials; and to provide effective physical security on WMD, missiles, and related materials.[24]

Member states have been slow to meet those obligations, as well as to fulfill voluntary provisions such as providing timely implementation reports and assisting other states to meet their requirements. UNSCR 1977, the 2011 resolution extending the 1540 Committee, also recommended new steps to improve 1540 implementation.[25]

The United States hoped that UNSCR 1540 would endorse PSI. Although it does not do so, it encourages international cooperation against WMD trafficking. It, *inter alia*:

> 10. … *calls upon* all States, in accordance with national legal authorities and legislation and consistent with international law, to take cooperative action to prevent illicit trafficking in nuclear, chemical or biological weapons, their means of delivery, and related materials.[26]

Subsequent international action has bolstered legal authorities for WMD interdiction, but those remain circumscribed. In some ways, the new legal instruments developed since the creation of PSI and passage of UNSCR 1540 are more important for their demonstration of the enhanced international political legitimacy of WMD interdiction than they are for their specific impact on legal authorities.

The first important new treaty concerned with interdicting and criminalizing proliferation is the 2005 Protocol to the amended Convention for the Suppression of Unlawful Acts Against the Safety of Maritime Navigation (SUA). The 2005 SUA Protocol makes it unlawful knowingly to ship by sea WMD, materials, equipment, or technology. States Parties must make violations "punishable by appropriate penalties which take into account the grave nature of those offences." Shipments of nuclear material and equipment are allowed if permitted under the NPT and IAEA safeguards. The Protocol provides procedures for boarding a ship reasonably suspected of violating, or about to be violating, the convention, but flag state consent is required.[27]

Despite the SUA Protocol's common goals with PSI, its States Parties include few of PSI's 102 adherents. The amended SUA and its Protocol entered into force in July 2010, when twelve states had ratified. As of December 2013, that number had grown to just twenty-four, and did not include the United States or most of its major allies.[28] Notably, only two of the original eleven PSI adherents have ratified the Protocol. The US Senate provided advice and consent to ratification over five years ago, in September 2008, but the implementing legislation required before presidential ratification has been stymied in the Senate.

The 2010 Convention on the Suppression of Unlawful Acts Relating to International Civil Aviation (known as the Beijing Convention) applies many of the WMD provisions of the 2005 SUA Protocol to air transport. The Convention makes it an offense knowingly to transport by air WMD, material, equipment, or technology unless permitted under the NPT and IAEA safeguards, and requires States Parties to make the offense "punishable by severe penalties."[29] The Convention will enter into force when twenty-two states have ratified; as of November 2013, only eight had done so.[30] The United States is not among them, nor is any US ally other than the Czech Republic. Although the United States was an original signatory, it had not submitted the Beijing Convention to the Senate for advice and consent to ratification as of December 2013. One of the US national commitments at the PSI tenth anniversary meeting was to ratify the Beijing Convention and the 2005 SUA Protocol.[31] Further, in the meeting's Joint Statement on Strengthening Authorities for Action, all the attending government undertook "to consider accession" to both agreements.[32] There has been little public progress on either commitment.

Counterproliferation: Iran and North Korea

The international community has been more willing to adopt strict counterproliferation measures against the Iranian and North Korean nuclear programs than against a more generalized, perhaps viewed as hypothetical, proliferation threat. The most powerful trade and financial sanctions have been national ones. Those have severely struck the Iranian economy. They have been less effective against North Korea, given the autarchic, despotic nature of the regime.

Although less sweeping than national sanctions, the UNSCRs on Iran and North Korea have imposed progressively broader and stricter prohibitions on nuclear-related trade and financial transactions with those countries. The UNSCRs on North Korea ban nuclear-related financial and economic transactions with that country, and discourage virtually all non-humanitarian economic dealings with it. They also include progressively stronger interdiction provisions. UNSCR 1718 (2006), adopted after North Korea's first nuclear test, called vaguely for interdiction cooperation against the DPRK:

> In order to ensure compliance with the requirements of this paragraph, and thereby preventing illicit trafficking in nuclear, chemical or biological weapons, their means of delivery and related materials, all Member States are called upon to take, in

accordance with their national authorities and legislation, and consistent with international law, cooperative action including through inspection of cargo to and from the DPRK, as necessary.[33]

UNSCR 1874 (2009), passed after North Korea's second nuclear test, called more clearly, and in detail, for interdiction of ships suspected of carrying cargoes in violation of the various resolutions on North Korea. However, flag state consent remained required, and the basic interdiction provision was not obligatory. Still, all states were required to seize and dispose of prohibited items.[34]

UNSCR 2094 (2013), adopted after North Korea's third nuclear-weapon test, made the maritime interdiction provisions obligatory, although flag state consent is still needed. UNSCR 2094 also adds a voluntary provision on air interdiction, the first of its kind in international decisions against WMD proliferation. This resolution, *inter alia*:

18. Calls upon States to deny permissions to any aircraft to take off from, land in or overfly their territory, if they have information that provides reasonable grounds to believe that the aircraft contains items the supply, sale, transfer or export of which is prohibited by [UNSCRs] …[35]

UNSCR 1929 (2010) basically replicated for Iran the voluntary maritime interdiction provisions of UNSCR 1874. Further, UNSCR 1929 dramatically broadened financial sanctions against Iran. Where there is reasonable ground for suspicion that financial activities could assist Iran's nuclear program or otherwise violate UN sanctions, each member state is urged to: prevent the provision of financial services involving its territory or entities under its jurisdiction; ban the creation of new Iranian (or joint) banking establishments on its territory; and ban the establishment of new accounts or offices in Iran by financial establishments under its jurisdiction. Further, each member state must require those under its jurisdiction to "exercise vigilance" in doing business with Iranian entities.[36]

Securing flag consent

One constant constraint on maritime interdiction is the requirement for flag consent. From the very beginning of PSI, the United States sought to loosen that restriction by concluding bilateral ship-boarding agreements, especially with leading ship-registry states.

The United States signed the first such agreement in February 2004 with Liberia, home of the world's second largest ship-registry. Panama, the largest ship-registry state, followed shortly thereafter, in May 2004. As of December 2013, the United States had concluded ship-boarding agreements with nine other major flag states: Antigua and Barbuda, Bahamas, Belize, Croatia, Cyprus, Malta, Marshall Islands, Mongolia, and St Vincent and the Grenadines.[37] Although the agreements are not identical, they all streamline the process of flag state consent. For example, the 2005 agreement with Belize provides that the flag state must respond to a boarding request within two hours; if it does not do so and cannot be contacted, the requesting government is deemed to be authorized to board and search the vessel.[38]

The most recent US bilateral ship-boarding agreements were signed in 2010. It is unclear why more have not been concluded in the subsequent years. Several other states provide flags of convenience. Boarding agreements with close, highly counterproliferation-capable allies like Germany, the Netherlands, and the United Kingdom probably are unnecessary. However, several others would be useful. Following are leading flag registry states with which the United

States has not concluded ship-boarding agreements: Aruba, Barbados, Bermuda, Burma, Cambodia, Canary Islands, Cayman Islands, Cook Islands, Germany, Gibraltar, Honduras, Lebanon, Liberia, Luxembourg, Mauritius, Netherlands Antilles, Sri Lanka, Tuvalu, and Vanuatu.

Conclusion

The record of interdiction and law enforcement in countering nuclear proliferation over the last decade is mixed. The list of achievements is impressive. Innovative, flexible tools against proliferation have emerged, such as PSI, the Global Initiative, UNSCR 1540, and the US bilateral ship-boarding agreements. The steadily growing, and now widespread, acceptance of interdiction is demonstrated by the growth in PSI participation, the strengthening of UNSCR interdiction provisions over time, and the conclusion of the 2005 SUA Protocol and the 2010 Beijing Convention. Furthermore, strong national and international sanctions against the Iranian and North Korea nuclear programs are in place.

Unfortunately, the list of shortcomings is also substantial. Active PSI participation is confined to a relatively few states, while the pace and intensity of capacity-building efforts have declined. Adherence to the 2005 SUA Protocol and the Beijing Convention is extremely limited, years after their passage; even the United States and its closest allies, whose commitment to counterproliferation should not be in doubt, are not parties. The effort by many FATF members to adopt numerous new standards against WMD proliferation mostly failed. More than nine years after adoption of UNSCR 1540, national compliance with its obligations is incomplete at best. For example, Malaysia should have been more aware than most of the need for strong national legislation against proliferation, given that it was home to the A.Q. Khan centrifuge plant. Yet Malaysia did not strengthen its laws against nuclear proliferation until almost seven years after the unraveling of the Khan network, and six years after passage of UNSCR 1540.

Finally, sanctions adopted in recent years may have devastated the Iranian economy, but have done little to date to slow its nuclear program. North Korea's program also continues apace. Legitimate firms have generally complied with the sanctions and we know of no contemporary counterpart to the A.Q. Khan network. Nevertheless, many companies and governments worldwide apparently are willing to defy national and international strictures against proliferation. Closely related, while the United States has a generally good record of prosecuting proliferators, that is not true of many states, including many close allies. Even the leading members of the A.Q. Khan network received minimal criminal sentences at most.[39]

The reasons for those shortcomings are unclear. Some political opposition to active counterproliferation continues, but that factor appears much weaker now than it was a decade ago. The major cause may be the inability of the international community or even of concerned individual governments to act decisively in the absence of an imminent threat. Even the chemical and biological weapons attacks of the past decades have not been enough to engender a sense of acute danger. Thus, FATF enacted its standards against terrorist finance just one month after 9/11, but has done little on WMD proliferation. The United States Congress quickly passed anti-terrorism legislation, but for over five years has delayed action on the SUA Protocol implementing legislation. It is difficult not to be concerned that a nuclear or massive chemical or biological proliferation catastrophe may be required for more consistent, decisive international action.

Notes

1. See for example, Craig H. Allen, *Maritime Counterproliferation Operations and the Rule of Law,* Praeger Security International Reports (Westport, CT: Praeger, 2007), p. 151; David B. Rivkin, Jr. and Lee A. Casey, "From *The Bermuda* to *The So San,*" *National Review Online*, January 2, 2003, www.national review.com/articles/205372/i-bermuda-so-san-i/david-b-rivkin-jr.

2. "There is no provision under international law prohibiting Yemen from accepting delivery of missiles from North Korea. While there is authority to stop and search, in this instance there is no clear authority to seize the shipment of Scud missiles from North Korea to Yemen. And therefore, the merchant vessel is being released." Ari Fleischer, Press Briefing, Office of the Press Secretary, The White House, December 11, 2002, http://georgewbush-whitehouse.archives.gov/news/releases/2002/12/20021211-5.html.

3. The invasion of Iraq occurred just slightly over three months later, on March 20, 2003.

4. Fleischer, Press Briefing.

5. George W. Bush, "Remarks by the President to the People of Poland," Wawel Royal Castle, Krakow, Poland, May 31, 2003, http://georgewbush-whitehouse.archives.gov/news/releases/2003/05/20030531-3.html.

6. These allies included Australia, France, Germany, Italy, Japan, the Netherlands, Poland, Portugal, Spain, and the United Kingdom.

7. Proliferation Security Initiative, "Proliferation Security Initiative: Statement of Interdiction Principles," available at www.psi-online.info/Vertretung/psi/en/07-statement/Interdiction-Principles.html.

8. Ibid.

9. "Participants agreed that the Initiative aimed to impede and stop trafficking of WMD, their delivery systems and related materials by any state or nonstate actor engaged in or supporting WMD proliferation programmes, at any time and in any place." US Department of State, "Proliferation Security Initiative: Chairman's Conclusions at the Fourth Meeting," October 10, 2003, http://2001-2009.state.gov/t/isn/rls/other/25373.htm.

10. US Department of State, "Proliferation Security Initiative: Participants," November 20, 2012, www.state.gov/t/isn/c27732.htm.

11. US Department of State, "Proliferation Security Initiative: Chairman's Conclusions at the Fourth Meeting."

12. See US Department of State, "Proliferation Security Initiative: Calendar of Events," available at www.state.gov/t/isn/c27700.htm.

13. See US Department of State, "PSI-Endorsing States Undertake Effort to Build Critical Capabilities and Practices (CCP) for Interdicting WMD," Fact Sheet, Bureau of International Security and Nonproliferation, June 10, 2011, www.state.gov/t/isn/166732.htm.

14. US Department of State, "Proliferation Security Initiative Tenth Anniversary High Level Political Meeting: Chairman's Summary," May 28, 2013, www.state.gov/t/isn/c10390.htm.

15. Ibid. The four Joint Statements and lists of supporting states are elaborated in this document.

16. See below for more discussion of ship-boarding agreements.

17. See David E. Sanger, "US Said to Turn Back North Korea Missile Shipment," *New York Times,* June 12, 2011, www.nytimes.com/2011/06/13/world/asia/13missile.html.

18. For examples of those two views, see Robert G. Joseph, *Countering WMD: The Libyan Experience* (Fairfax, VA: National Institute Press, 2009), p. 41, and Wade Boese, "Key US Interdiction Initiative Claim Misrepresented," *Arms Control Today*, Vol. 35, No. 5 (July–August 2005), pp. 26–27, www.armscontrol.org/print/1848.

19. The FATF members are: Argentina, Australia, Austria, Belgium, Brazil, Canada, China, Denmark, European Commission, Finland, France, Germany, Greece, Gulf Cooperation Council, Hong Kong, Iceland, India, Ireland, Italy, Japan, Republic of Korea, Luxembourg, Mexico, The Netherlands, New Zealand, Norway, Portugal, Russia, Singapore, South Africa, Spain, Sweden, Switzerland, Turkey, United Kingdom, and United States.

20. The second category included: Algeria, Ecuador, Ethiopia, Indonesia, Kenya, Myanmar, Pakistan, Syria, Tanzania, Turkey, and Yemen. The third category included: Afghanistan, Albania, Angola, Antigua and Barbuda, Argentina, Bangladesh, Cambodia, Cuba, Iraq, Kuwait, Kyrgyzstan, Laos, Mongolia, Namibia, Nepal, Nicaragua, Sudan, Tajikistan, Vietnam and Zimbabwe. See Financial Action Task Force, "High-risk and Non-cooperative Jurisdictions," February 2014, available at www.fatf-gafi.org/topics/high-riskandnon-cooperativejurisdictions/

21. "Countries should implement targeted financial sanctions to comply with United Nations Security Council resolutions relating to the prevention, suppression and disruption of proliferation of weapons of mass destruction and its financing. These resolutions require countries to freeze without delay the funds or other assets of, and to ensure that no funds and other assets are made available, directly or indirectly, to or for the benefit of, any person or entity designated by, or under the authority of, the United Nations Security Council under Chapter VII of the United Nations." Financial Action Task Force, "International Standards on Combating Money Laundering and the Financing of Terrorism and Proliferation: The FATF Recommendations," February 2012, p. 13, www.fatf-gafi.org/media/fatf/documents/recommendations/pdfs/FATF_Recommendations.pdf.
22. GICNT, "Statement of Principles," http://gicnt.org/download/sop/Statement_of_Principles.pdf.
23. GICNT, "Global Initiative to Combat Nuclear Terrorism: Multilateral Workshops and Exercises," www.gicnt.org/download/iag/Running_List_of_All_GICNT_Events_-_December_2013.pdf.
24. United Nations Security Council, "Resolution 1540 (2004)," S/RES/1540 (2004), 495th meeting, April 28, 2004, http://daccess-dds-ny.un.org/doc/UNDOC/GEN/N04/328/43/PDF/N0432843.pdf.
25. United Nations Security Council, "Resolution 1977 (2011)," S/RES/1977(2011), April 20, 2011, www.securitycouncilreport.org/atf/cf/%7B65BFCF9B-6D27-4E9C-8CD3-CF6E4FF96FF9%7D/CT%201540%20S%20RES%201977.pdf.
26. United Nations Security Council, "Resolution 1540."
27. International Maritime Organization, "Adoption of the Final Act and Any Instruments, Recommendations and Resolutions Resulting from the Work of the Conference: Protocol of 2005 to the Convention for the Suppression of Unlawful Acts against the Safety of Maritime Navigation," International Conference on the Revision of the SUA Treaties, LEG/CONF.15/21, November 1, 2005, www.state.gov/t/isn/trty/81727.htm.
28. The following states had adhered to the SUA Protocol as of December 2, 2013: Algeria, Austria, Bulgaria, Cote d'Ivoire, Dominican Republic, Estonia, Fiji, Greece, Jamaica, Latvia, Liechtenstein, Marshall Islands, Mauritania, Nauru, Netherlands, Norway, Palau, Panama, Saint Lucia, Saint Vincent and Grenadines, Saudi Arabia, Spain, Switzerland, and Vanuatu. International Maritime Organization, "Status of Conventions as at 28 February 2014," www.imo.org/About/Conventions/StatusOfConventions/Documents/status-x.xls.
29. International Civil Aviation Organization, "Convention on the Suppression of Unlawful Acts Relating to International Civil Aviation," September 10, 2010, www.icao.int/secretariat/legal/Docs/beijing_convention_multi.pdf.
30. Thirty states had signed the Beijing Convention as of November 2013. The eight which had ratified are: Angola, Cuba, Czech Republic, Dominican Republic, Guyana, Mali, Myanmar, and Saint Lucia. International Civil Aviation Organization, "Composite Table (Status of Treaties and Status of States vis-à-vis Treaties)," www.icao.int/secretariat/legal/LEB%20Treaty%20Collection%20Documents/composite_table.pdf.
31. US Department of State, "Proliferation Security Initiative 10th Anniversary High-Level Political Meeting Outcomes," Media Note, May 28, 2013, www.state.gov/r/pa/prs/ps/2013/05/210010.htm.
32. US Department of State, "Proliferation Security Initiative 10th Anniversary: Joint Statement on Strengthening Authorities for Action," May 28, 2013, www.state.gov/t/isn/jtstmts/211499.htm.
33. United Nations Security Council, "Resolution 1718 (2006)," S/RES/1718 (2006), October 14, 2006, www.un.org/sc/committees/1718/.
34. United Nations Security Council, "Resolution 1874 (2009)," S/RES/1874 (2009), June 12, 2009, www.un.org/en/ga/search/view_doc.asp?symbol=S/RES/1874(2009).
35. United Nations Security Council, "Resolution 2094 (2013)," S/RES/2094 (2013), March 7, 2013, p. 4, www.un.org/en/ga/search/view_doc.asp?symbol=S/RES/2094(2013).
36. United Nations Security Council, "Resolution 1929 (2010)," S/RES/1929 (2010), June 9, 2010, www.un.org/en/ga/search/view_doc.asp?symbol=S/RES/1929(2010).
37. US Department of State, "Ship Boarding Agreements," www.state.gov/t/isn/c277333.htm.
38. US Department of State, "Agreement Between the Government of the United States of America and the Government of Belize Concerning Cooperation to Suppress the Proliferation of Weapons of Mass Destruction, Their Delivery Systems, and Related Materials by Sea," January 20, 2009, http://2001-2009.state.gov/t/isn/trty/50809.htm.
39. For a detailed discussion, see David Albright, *Peddling Peril: How the Secret Nuclear Trade Arms America's Enemies* (New York: Free Press, 2010).

20

ECONOMIC SANCTIONS IN FURTHERANCE OF NONPROLIFERATION GOALS

Dianne E. Rennack

At the beginning of 2014, the United States continues to designate four foreign governments as state sponsors of acts of international terrorism, and identifies more than sixty countries as violators of basic international human rights standards relating to religious freedom, trafficking in persons, or illicit narcotics trade.[1] It limits or altogether denies US foreign aid, trade, or economic transactions to more than forty countries for stated purposes of domestic and regional stability, world peace, human rights, counter-terrorism, anti-crime, anti-communism and defense of democracy, transparency and anti-kleptocracy, or to meet international obligations, including those relating to the abduction of children or trade in conflict minerals.

In addition, the United States closely watches and generally forbids transactions with, and freezes the US-based assets of, nearly 600 pages of individuals and entities identified as "Specially Designated Nationals." A range of Executive Orders and legislation guiding US national security and foreign policy targets these nonstate individuals and entities in the Western Balkans, Belarus, Burma, Cote d'Ivoire, Cuba, the Democratic Republic of the Congo, Iran, Iraq, Lebanon, Liberia, Libya, North Korea, Russia, Somalia, Sudan, Syria, and Zimbabwe. Individuals and nonstate entities identified as foreign narcotics kingpins, narcotics traffickers, terrorists, foreign terrorist organizations, sanctions evaders engaged in Iran, Syria, or terrorism, members of transnational criminal organizations, and proliferators of weapons of mass destruction (WMD) are also subject to economic restrictions.

Of these various targets, and various motives, none has more fully engaged both the US Congress and the president – sometimes in concert but often at odds – than the goal of countering WMD proliferation and the means that should be employed to deter it.

The use of economic sanctions to stem WMD proliferation acquired a new dimension in the 1990s. While earlier legislation required the cutoff of foreign aid to countries engaged in specified nuclear proliferation activities and mentioned other sanctions as a possible mechanism for bringing governments into compliance with goals of treaties and international agreements,[2] it was not until 1990 that Congress enacted explicit guidelines for trade sanctions related to missile proliferation. In that year, a requirement for the president to impose sanctions against US or foreign persons engaged in trade of items or technology listed in the Missile Technology Control Regime Annex (MTCR) was added to the Arms Export Control Act and to the Export Administration Act of 1979. Subsequently, Congress legislated economic sanctions against countries that contribute to the proliferation of chemical, biological, and nuclear weapons, and the means to deliver them, in a broad array of laws.

The use of economic sanctions in furtherance of foreign policy or national security policy fell into disfavor in the mid- to late-1990s, in part in reaction to reports of the substantial toll paid by civilian populations when sanctions were cast broadly or wielded as a blunt force, concurrent failure to enforce multilateral sanctions requirements, as well as reports of suspected continued proliferation in Iraq.[3] At the same time, however, concerns about nuclear-weapon proliferation shifted into high gear, fueled by a series of developments:

- Nuclear-weapon tests conducted by India and Pakistan (1998), and later by North Korea (2006, 2009, and 2013);
- North Korea's formal withdrawal from the Nuclear Nonproliferation Treaty (2003);
- multiple missile tests by North Korea;
- reports of Iraq having weapons of mass destruction, possibly chemical and biological (leading, fatefully, to war in 2003);
- Iran's noncompliance with international agreements (which the International Atomic Energy Agency, or IAEA, began reporting in 2005); and
- the 2004 discovery that a leading nuclear scientist in Pakistan – A.Q. Khan – had been selling nuclear materials, technology, and knowledge, to the highest bidder, including North Korea, Iraq, Iran, and Libya, for more than a decade.

In the same time period, late 1990s-late 2000s, the United States shifted its focus away from unilateral punitive measures and towards counterproliferation and multilateral cooperation in adopting new trade standards and export controls,[4] including physically interdicting shipments of controlled materials.[5]

Defining economic sanctions

Generally, "economic sanctions" might be defined as "coercive economic measures taken against one or more countries to force a change in policies, or at least to demonstrate a country's opinion about the other's policies."[6] Among Washington policy makers, the most-often quoted study on the effectiveness of sanctions defines the term as: "the deliberate, government-inspired withdrawal, or threat of withdrawal, of customary trade or financial relations."[7] Economic sanctions typically include measures such as trade embargoes; restrictions on particular exports or imports; denial of foreign assistance,[8] loans, and investments; or control of foreign assets and economic transactions that involve US citizens or businesses. These definitions would exclude diplomatic demarches, reductions in embassy staff or closing of embassies, denying visas, mobilizing armed forces or going to war – tools clearly intended to change another's behavior. Also excluded here are the carrots, for example granting preferential trade status, supporting projects in the international banks, or offering military aid to incentivize some behavior. These, and other punishments and incentives, have their place in a greater foreign policy toolkit.

What do sanctions affect?

Responsibility to implement and administer any presidential decision or congressional requirement to impose economic sanctions is farmed throughout the interagency, but primarily to the:

- **Department of the Treasury**: to freeze assets, block transactions related to specific exports, deny Export-Import Bank funding, deny support in the international financial institutions, or block access to the US banking system;
- **Department of Commerce**: to control exports in order to comply with obligations as a party to treaties and international agreements (Missile Technology Control Regime, Chemical Weapons Convention, Nuclear Suppliers Group, to name a few), to control exports in order to meet foreign policy and national security requirements stated in the Export Administration Act of 1979 (50 USC. app. 2401 *et seq.*);
- **Department of State**: to curtail government-to-government arms and foreign aid transactions in order to comply with obligations as a party to treaties and international agreements, meet general US eligibility standards stated in the Arms Export Control Act, annual foreign operations appropriations general provisions, and other legislation-defined requirements; and
- **Department of Defense**: to curtail military-to-military relations, and arms sales and transfers.

The following US laws illustrate some of the requirements to curtail economic engagement to achieve nonproliferation goals:

- **Arms sales, leases, transfers, and exports**: Nearly all relevant laws invoke this, from the president determining basic eligibility (sec. 3, Arms Export Control Act (AECA); 22 USC. 2753), the pursuit of world peace and the security and foreign policy of the United States (sec. 38, AECA; 22 USC. 2778), the Secretary of State finding that such transactions "willfully aid or abet the international proliferation of nuclear explosive devices" and related behavior (sec. 40, AECA; 22 USC. 2780);
- **US government procurement contracts**: The President, and Departments of Commerce and State identify those who trade in equipment or technology identified under the Missile Technology Control Regime (MTCR) (secs. 72, 72, AECA; 22 USC. 2797a, 2797b) (secs. 11A, 11B, Export Administration Act of 1979 (EAA); 50 USC. app. 2410a, 2410b), or those who engage in trade related to chemical and biological weapons development (sec. 81, AECA; 22 USC. 2798) (sec. 11C, EAA; 50 USC. app. 2410c), or those who engage in trade related to unsafeguarded nuclear materials (sec. 821, Nuclear Proliferation Prevention Act of 1994; 22 USC. 6301);
- **Export licenses**: Department of Commerce invokes any of the above authorities, and more broadly its foreign policy and national security authorities in the Export Administration Act of 1979 (secs. 5 and 6, EAA; 50 USC. app. 2404, 2405);
- **Foreign aid**: The President is required to cut off foreign aid, and the other transactions listed above, to any nonnuclear-weapon state that delivers or receives nuclear enrichment equipment, materials, or technology, detonates a nuclear explosive device, or assists another state in such pursuits – these authorities have been applied to Pakistan, India, Libya, and North Korea (secs. 101 and 102, AECA; 22 USC. 2799a, 2799a-1). Similarly he is required to cut off most foreign aid, and all the above engagements, in any instance where he determines a foreign country has used or made substantial preparation to use chemical or biological weapons (sec. 307, Chemical and Biological Weapons Control and Warfare Elimination Act of 1991; 22 USC. 5605);
- **Support in the international financial institutions, Export-Import Bank financing, US private bank transactions**: To meet the obligations as a state party to the Chemical Weapons Convention, the Secretary of the Treasury, designated by the President, is required to curtail all manner of financial transactions and support, including freezing

assets, of any person bound by the Convention who fails to comply with a ban on chemical weapons – their use, development, production, or stockpiling (sec. 103, Chemical Weapons Convention Implementation Act of 1998; 22 USC. 6713); or those who engage in trade related to unsafeguarded nuclear materials (sec. 824, Nuclear Proliferation Prevention Act of 1994; 22 USC. 6303).

Who has the primary authority to impose economic sanctions?

The President

The President has broad statutory authority to impose sanctions, first by declaring a national emergency exists, and second by declaring that the crisis constitutes an "unusual and extraordinary threat, which has its source in whole or substantial part outside the United States, to the national security, foreign policy, or economy of the United States ...."[9] In times of a foreign threat, the President can "investigate, regulate, or prohibit" any transaction, acquisition, holding, use, transfer, transportation, importation, exportation, interest, or payment that is subject to US jurisdiction and involves a targeted person or entity. The President has used this authority in the absence of, or in advance of, or to stave off, legislative requirements defined by Congress to curtail relations. The procedure is straightforward: The President (1) declares a national emergency exists, (2) issues an Executive Order to state the target and terms of economic restrictions, and (3) annually extends the emergency conditions. Generally, the Department of the Treasury is responsible for implementing and administering these restrictions.

The President may terminate the national emergency at any time, and he may also change the terms of the sanctions regime as he sees fit. Congress may agree to a joint resolution to terminate the national emergency, but this certainly would require a veto-proof plurality if the President disagrees.

National emergency authorities are only one approach to economic sanctions, however, drawing on only one bailiwick of one department – Treasury – in the Executive Branch. The President also has at his disposal a vast range of diplomatic tools that, depending on the bilateral relationship, and with careful timing, can have surprising economic effect. Denying a visa, putting an individual or entity on a watchlist, canceling a meeting or showing favor to an adversary can chill a proliferator's activities.

The Congress

In other instances, Congress might take the lead, either by conferring new presidential authority to impose sanctions, or by requiring sanctions to be imposed unless the President determines and certifies that certain conditions have been met. Some sanctions are mandatory and are triggered automatically when certain conditions exist. Congress, for example, has required the imposition of economic sanctions when a nonnuclear-weapon state detonates a nuclear device or engages in trade in nuclear materials and knowledge.[10] Even as aid is restored to such a state, Congress has required the President or Secretary of State to certify that nonproliferation conditions have been restored before that aid can be disbursed. In the case of Pakistan, for example, Congress required, in enacting the Enhanced Partnership With Pakistan Act of 2009, that before security assistance was made available the Secretary of State certify that the Government of Pakistan is continuing to cooperate with the United States to dismantle nuclear supplier networks, as well as committing its resources to resolving regional terrorism, extremism, stability, money laundering, and rule-of-law matters.[11]

Table 20.1 Executive Orders issued pursuant to IEEPA authorities in furtherance of nonproliferation
objectives

Executive order	Purpose
12938, as amended (November 14, 1994; 59 F.R. 59099)	Proliferation of weapons of mass destruction
12947, as amended (January 23, 1995; 60 F.R. 5079)	Prohibiting transactions with terrorists who threaten to disrupt the Middle East peace process (relating to those who commit "grave acts of violence")
12957, as amended (March 15, 1995; 60 F.R. 14615)	Prohibiting certain transactions with respect to the development of Iranian petroleum resources
12959, as amended (May 6, 1995; 60 F.R. 24757)	Prohibiting certain transactions with respect to the development of Iranian petroleum resources
13059, as amended (August 19, 1997; 62 F.R. 44531)	Prohibiting certain transactions with respect to Iran
13159 (June 21, 2000; 65 F.R. 39279)	Blocking property of the Government of the Russian Federation relating to the disposition of highly enriched uranium extracted from nuclear weapons
13222, as amended (August 17, 2001; 66 F.R. 44025)	Continuation of export control regulations (with the expiration of the Export Administration Act of 1979)
13338, as amended (May 11, 2004; 69 F.R. 26751)	Blocking property of certain persons and prohibiting export of certain goods to Syria (relating to pursuit of weapons of mass destruction, terrorism, occupation of Lebanon, and stability in Iraq)
13382 (June 28, 2005; 70 F.R. 38567)	Blocking property of weapons of mass destruction proliferators and their supporters
13466 (June 26, 2008; 73 F.R. 36787) 73 F.R. 36787)	Continuing certain restrictions with respect to North Korea and North Korean Nationals (imposed on the same day the designation as a state sponsor of acts of international terrorism and Trading With the Enemy Act restrictions were lifted)
13551 (August 30, 2010; 75 F.R. 53837)	Blocking property of certain persons with respect to North Korea
13553 (September 28, 2010; 75 F.R. 60587)	Blocking property of certain persons with respect to serious human rights abuses by the Government of Iran and taking certain other actions (in part implements the requirements of the Comprehensive Iran Sanctions, Accountability, and Divestment Act of 2010)
13570 (April 18, 2011; 76 F.R. 22291)	Prohibiting certain transactions with respect to North Korea
13573 (May 18, 2011; 76 F.R. 29143)	Blocking property of senior officials of the Government of Syria
13574 (May 23, 2011; 76 F.R. 30505)	Authorizing the implementation of certain sanctions set forth in the Iran Sanctions Act of 1996, as amended
13582 (August 17, 2011; 76 F.R. 52209)	Blocking property of the Government of Syria and prohibiting certain transactions with respect to Syria
13590 (November 20, 2011; 76 F.R. 72609)	Authorizing the imposition of certain sanctions with respect to the provision of goods, services, technology, or support for Iran's energy and petrochemical sectors

Table 20.1 Continued.

Executive order	Purpose
13599 (February 5, 2012; 77 F.R. 6659)	Blocking property of the Government of Iran and Iranian financial institutions
13608 (May 1, 2012; 77 F.R. 26409)	Prohibiting certain transactions with and suspending entry into the United States of foreign sanctions evaders with respect to Iran and Syria
13617 (June 25, 2012; 77 F.R. 38459)	Blocking property of the Government of the Russian Federation relating to the disposition of highly enriched uranium extracted from nuclear weapons
13622, as amended (July 30, 2012; 77 F.R. 45897)	Authorizing additional sanctions with respect to Iran
13628 (October 9, 2012; 77 F.R. 62139)	Authorizing the implementation of certain sanctions set forth in the Iran Threat Reduction and Syria Human Rights Act of 2012 and additional sanctions with respect to Iran
13645 (June 3, 2013; 78 F.R. 33945)	Authorizing the implementation of certain sanctions set forth in the Iran Freedom and Counter-Proliferation Act of 2012 and additional sanctions with respect to Iran

Note: 50 U.S.C. 1701 note, The President also uses the authority in IEEPA to issue executive orders to implement United Nations Security Council Resolutions, some of which are the result of proliferation concerns, currently including multilateral sanctions applied against Iran and North Korea.

Source: The National Archives prints Executive Orders in the *Federal Register* and maintains a data base of Orders and subsequent amendments at www.archives.gov/federal-register/executive-orders/disposition.html.

Some behavior that would trigger the imposition of sanctions requires the President or Secretary of State to determine and certify that a violation of a standard has occurred. In most instances, the administration has considerable flexibility in making such determinations and also has the authority to waive sanctions if national interests are better met in doing so.

Today's evolving US-Iran relationship showcases the capacity Congress holds to influence and shape the United States' national security and foreign policy position. Beginning with enactment of the Iran-Iraq Arms Non-proliferation Act of 1992,[12] Congress declared:

It shall be the policy of the United States to oppose, and urgently to seek the agreement of other nations also to oppose, any transfer to Iran or Iraq of any goods or technology, including dual-use goods or technology, wherever that transfer could materially contribute to either country's acquiring chemical, biological, nuclear, or destabilizing numbers and types of advanced conventional weapons.

In that Act, Congress imposed mandatory economic sanctions, to prohibit: foreign military sales; export licenses for US Munitions List (USML) commercial arms sales, Commerce Control List items, and nuclear equipment, materials, or technology; US government procurement contracts for any person found to have transferred goods or technology so as to contribute knowingly and materially to Iran's weapons pursuits; and foreign aid, support in the international financial institutions, weapons codevelopment and coproduction agreements, other exchange agreements, and USML exports to any foreign government implicated in Iran's weapons plans.

From that point forward, Congress has unequivocally defined and shaped the United States' use of economic sanctions as the primary means to curb Iran's nuclear program. Following on its 1992 legislation, Congress required the President to block nearly every manner of trade and transaction with Iran, setting the highest standard for waiving restrictions on such engagement, in the Iran Sanctions Act of 1996; the Iran, North Korea, and Syria Nonproliferation Act; the Iran Nuclear Proliferation Prevention Act of 2002; the Iran Freedom Support Act; the Comprehensive Iran Sanctions, Accountability, and Divestment Act of 2010; the National Defense Authorization Acts for Fiscal Year 2012; the Iran Threat Reduction and Syria Human Rights Act of 2012; and the Iran Freedom and Counter-proliferation Act of 2012.[13]

Congress continues to press the President, and Secretary of State, in the wake of the United States entering into an interim nuclear agreement with Iran (and Russia, China, the EU3+3 – Britain, France and Germany – and the International Atomic Energy Agency in late November 2013.[14] To comply with the interim agreement, the United States and EU are expected to suspend sanctions related to insurance and transportation services, exports of petrochemicals, gold, precious metals, automotive sector goods exports, and servicing of Iran's civil aircraft. Not all in Congress embrace this strategy, however. Before the agreement was reached, the House had adopted and forwarded to the Senate a measure to further ratchet up restrictions on Iran's oil sales.[15] Many Members of Congress, from both sides of the aisle, are on record in support of forging ahead with new prohibitions, and credit the robust Congress-driven sanctions regime as the primary force that brought the government of Iran to negotiate. The President and Secretary of State are equally vociferous in their concerns that new legislative requirements – even with a proposed six-month delayed trigger – will derail any current agreement or future talks.[16]

And, of course, not all of Congress' activities result in legislation. It is also responsible for budgeting, advising on treaties, approving nominations, and overseeing Executive Branch decisions that form foreign policy and national security. The Senate Committee on Foreign Relations of the 110th Congress (2007–2008), for example, held no fewer than eighteen full-committee hearings on Iraq – US troop deployment, prosecution of the war, and the failure to find weapons of mass destruction.[17] The scrutiny helped keep US decision making relating to Iraq front and center in the 2008 Presidential election.

Do sanctions work?

In the late 1990s, most in Congress decidedly declared, through hearings, task forces, and legislative proposals, that sanctions were ineffective. They were in large measure moved to this assessment when India and Pakistan each tested nuclear explosive devices in May 1998, despite the sanctions certain to be imposed by the international community. The US government (and international community) responded with broad economic sanctions, only to discover that the economic prohibitions would take a devastating toll on US wheat growers set to compete in winter wheat auctions. Congress quickly moved to amend the law, with the President's support and signature, to allow Department of Agriculture subsidization of US commercial wheat sales to Pakistan. The result was lifting, in a matter of weeks, sanctions that had been imposed for what some argued was one of the most serious and dangerous of offenses, nuclear proliferation.[18] Others, however, contended that the longer-term consequences of denying Pakistan US agricultural commodities would have destabilized all of South Asia, and perhaps resulted in Pakistan failing as a state. It should be noted that Pakistan was, at the time of its nuclear tests, already under a number of other sanctions for reasons of its military government having taken power by overthrowing a democratically elected government, its external debt arrearage, and its shaky record in supporting US anti-terrorism efforts.

Selling wheat to Pakistan, in turn, invigorated a larger discussion on the use of food and medicine in foreign policy that resulted in the President directing the Secretary of the Treasury to issue new regulations to allow food and medicine transactions to Libya, Iran, Sudan (all terrorist states), and Yugoslavia (still under sanctions imposed during the breakup of the federated Yugoslavia and subsequent war).[19] That, in turn, led to the enactment of the Trade Sanctions Reform Act[20] to remove food and medicine from sanctions regimes, unless the recipient government was a state sponsor of acts of international terrorism.

The Peterson Institute for International Economics, in its seminal study on economic sanctions in which the researchers sought to quantify and rank various factors that go into using sanctions as a foreign policy, national security, or trade tool, concluded that economic sanctions are "at least partially effective" only about one third of the time. Sanctions imposed with "modest and limited goals" succeeded half the time. It makes the following succinct recommendations (in *italics*, below) to "maximize the opportunities for success."[21]

- *Don't bite off more than you can chew.* More modest goals are more attainable. But if one imposes sanctions to change a regime, impair another's military intentions, or bring about major changes, the likelihood of success greatly diminishes. And if aiming for great change, building a multinational force, and wielding a legitimate threat of force to back up the economic threat, improve the odds (but not by much).
- *Friends are more likely to comply than adversaries.* Friends and trading partners with a common history, though not subject to economic sanctions frequently, make better targets – they have more invested in the relationship and thus more to lose.
- *Beware autocratic regimes.* The statistics are poor when the government committing the objectionable behavior is autocratic or worse. If one seeks to change an autocratic regime toward democracy, for example, barely 20 percent of the cases where the targeted government is autocratic showed any measurable success.
- *Slam the hammer, don't turn the screw.* If one's intention is to make a statement, or act with some symbolic purpose, a light and incremental touch might be a reasonable option. But if the intent is to change objectionable behavior, striking swiftly and with authority is the ticket. The longer sanctions are imposed, the less likely they will achieve their stated goal (it's difficult to sustain multilateral regimes, and unilateral sanctions invite work-arounds). And have carrots – incentives – at the ready when it's time to negotiate or provide relief.
- *More is not necessarily merrier.* Does a multilateral sanctions regime show strength in numbers, or must those who implement it dilute their initial statement of intent and threat to build a coalition? A commitment to work in the United Nations Security Council to employ multilateral smart sanctions regimes emerged from the 1990s debate, but recent efforts in the United Nations to address catastrophe in Libya, Egypt, and Syria may make this entire discussion, at least in the near-term, obsolete.
- *Choose the right tool for the job.* How do sanctions fit into the continuum of policy options? Is a limited use of military force required to make the primary economic tool effective? In many instances, the United States and its multilateral partners have concocted two-track regimes, with one track conventional economic prohibitions and the second track covert action, limited military force, humanitarian aid, or civilian-targeted economic incentives. The right tool is affected by understanding the entire landscape: punishing proliferation or rewarding standing down from proliferation must take into account other sanctionable activities for both the sanctioner and sanctioned state to stay engaged.
- *Don't be a cheapskate or a spendthrift.* Costs incurred by one's domestic economy can be shocking. Seemingly straight-forward sanctions imposed on Sudan, for example, in the

course of its North-South civil war and violence in the Darfur region resulted in the loss of the United States' source of high-quality gum arabic – an ingredient required by a number of small businesses. The loud roar from producers of emulsified products gave new meaning to "unintended consequences," and Congress quickly legislated an exemption for Sudan's only significant export product, which undermined the sanctions.

• *Look before you leap.* Pushed by a political imperative to "do something," too often policy makers don't plan, don't assess their alliances, over-estimate their influence, under-estimate the costs, see where they're going and understand how and what it will take to get there.

Notes

1. The opinions and views expressed herein are those of the author and do not represent the views of the Congressional Research Service.
2. The International Atomic Energy Act of 1954 and the Nuclear Nonproliferation Act of 1978 sought to increase international participation in and adherence with the International Atomic Energy Agency (IAEA) and Nuclear Nonproliferation Treaty (NPT), respectively, and to that end, authorized the president to enter into international discussions, including the imposition of sanctions against those who abrogate or violate these international agreements.
3. A wealth of literature addresses the decade. For an overview, consider David Cortright and George A. Lopez, *The Sanctions Decade: Assessing UN Strategies in the 1990s* (Boulder, CO: Lynne Rienner Publishers, Inc., 2000), and Thomas G. Weiss, David Cortright, George A. Lopez, *et al.*, *Political Gain and Civilian Pain: Humanitarian Impacts of Economic Sanctions* (Lanham, MD: Rowman & Littlefield Publishers, Inc., 1997). For the earliest reporting on the humanitarian impact of post-1991 conflict Iraq sanctions that led to the corruption-riddled UN oil-for-food program, start with Marti Ahtisaari, "Report to the Secretary-General on Humanitarian Need in Kuwait and Iraq in the Immediate Post-Crisis Environment," UN Security Council, New York, March 20, 1991. www.un.org/Depts/oip/background/reports/s22366.pdf.
4. Ian F. Fergusson and Paul K. Kerr, "The US Export Control System and the President's Reform Initiative," Federation of American Scientists, CRS Report R41916, January 13, 2014, www.fas.org/sgp/crs/natsec/R41916.pdf.
5. Mary Beth D. Nikitin, "Proliferation Security Initiative (PSI)," Federation of American Scientists, CRS Report RL34327, June 15, 2012, www.fas.org/sgp/crs/nuke/RL34327.pdf.
6. Barry E. Carter, *International Economic Sanctions: Improving the Haphazard US Legal Regime* (Cambridge: Cambridge University Press, 1988), p. 4.
7. Gary Clyde Hufbauer, Jeffrey J. Schott, and Kimberly Ann Elliott, *Economic Sanctions Reconsidered* (3rd Edition) (Washington, DC: Peterson Institute for International Economics, 2007), p. 3.
8. Some contend that the denial of foreign aid should not be included in any sanctions discussion. Their position is that such aid is not an entitlement; no country should expect its availability. For this position, and an otherwise rollicking roast from one side of the sanctions debate, see Jesse Helms, "What Sanctions Epidemic?: US Business' Curious Crusade," *Foreign Affairs*, Vol. 78, No. 1 (January/February 1999), p. 2. The denial of foreign assistance is included in this discussion, however, because it fits the definition and has proven to be both a powerful tool in the US kit and a point of contention between the Executive and Legislative branches.
9. Declaration of national emergency during peacetime is mandated in title II of the National Emergencies Act (P.L. 94-412; 50 USC. 1621 et seq.). The President is authorized to impose sanctions when a national emergency exists under terms of the International Emergencies Economic Powers Act (P.L. 95-223; 50 USC. 1701 et seq.). In times of war, he may bypass the national emergency finding and jump straight to economic warfare, pursuant to sec. 5(b) of the Trading With the Enemy Act (P.L. 65-91; 50 USC. app. 5(b)).
10. Sections 101 and 102, Arms Export Control Act (P.L. 90-629; 22 USC. 2799aa, 2799aa-1); sec. 2(b)(4), Export-Import Bank Act of 1945 (P.L. 79-172; 12 USC. 635(b)(4)).
11. Enhanced Partnership with Pakistan Act of 2009 (P.L. 111-73; 22 USC. 8401 *et seq.*).
12. Title XVI of the National Defense Authorization Act for Fiscal Year 1993 (P.L. 102-484; 50 USC. 1701 note). Quote is from sec. 1602(a).
13. P.L. 104-172 (50 USC. 1701 note); P.L. 106-178 (50 USC. 1701 note); subtitle D of title XIII of P.L.

107-228 (Foreign Relations Authorization Act for Fiscal 2003; 22 USC. 2027); P.L. 109-293 (50 USC. 1701 note); P.L. 111-195; 22 USC. 8501 *et seq.*); sec. 1245 of P.L. 112-81; 22 USC. 8513a);P.L. 112-158 (22 USC. 8701 *et seq.*); and title XII, subtitle D of P.L. 112-239 (National Defense Authorization Act for Fiscal Year 2013; 22 USC. 8801 *et seq.*), respectively. For a concise summary of restrictions, requirements to impose, and authorities to waive, see Dianne E. Rennack, "Iran: US Economic Sanctions and the Authority to Lift Restrictions," Congressional Research Service, CRS Report R4331, February 14, 2014, www.fas.org/sgp/crs/mideast/R43311.pdf.

14. Marcus George, "Interim Nuclear Agreement Between Iran and Six Powers," *Reuters*, November 24, 2013, www.reuters.com/article/2013/11/24/us-iran-nuclear-agreement-text-idUSBRE9AN0BQ 20131124.

15. In the 113th Congress, 1st Session: the Nuclear Iran Prevention Act of 2013 (H.R. 850), passed the House on July 31, 2013, by a vote of 400–20. In the Senate, the Iran Nuclear Compliance Act of 2013 (S. 1765), introduced by Senator Bob Corker (ranking Minority on the Committee on Foreign Relations) on November 21, 2013, and referred the Committee on Banking, Housing and Urban Affairs, and the Nuclear Weapon Free Iran Act of 2013 (S. 1881), introduced by Senator Robert Menendez (chairperson, Committee on Foreign Relations) on December 19, 2013, and placed on the Senate Legislative Calendar under General Orders, give a glimpse of Congress' intentions if the negotiations fail or fall short of a cessation of Iran's nuclear program.

16. US Congress, House Committee on Foreign Affairs, "The Iran Nuclear Deal: Does It Further US National Security?" 113th Congress, 1st Session, December 10, 2013; US Congress, Senate Committee on Banking, Housing, and Urban Affairs, "P5 + 1 Interim Nuclear Agreement With Iran," 113th Congress, 1st Session, December 12, 2013.

17. US Congress, Senate Committee on Foreign Relations, "Legislative Activities Report," S. Rept. 111-12, committee print, 111th Congress, 1st Session, March 31, 2009 (Washington: GPO, 2009).

18. Both India and Pakistan were subject to curtailment of most foreign aid, defense sales, export licenses, military financing, credit guarantees, and support in both international and domestic banks, under terms of sec. 102(b)(2), AECA (22 USC. 2799aa-1) and sec. 2(b)(4), Export-Import Bank Act of 1945 (12 USC. 635(b)(4)).

19. Humanitarian Exemptions from Sanctions, Statement by the Press Secretary, the White House, April 28, 1999; Economic Sanctions, Press Briefing by Stuart E. Eizenstat, Under Secretary of State for Economic, business, and Agricultural Affairs, and Richard Newcomb, Director of the Office of Foreign Assets Control, Treasury Department; and Secretary Eizenstat's testimony before the Senate Committee on Agriculture, Nutrition, and Forestry, May 11, 1999; Department of the Treasury, Office of Foreign Assets Control, 31 CFR Parts 538, 550, and 560, 64 FR 41784, August 2, 1999 (effective date July 27, 1999). Regarding Yugoslavia: Executive Order 13088, as amended by Executive Order 13121 of April 30, 1999, 64 F.R. 24021.

20. Trade Sanctions Reform and Export Enhancement Act of 2000 (title IX, P.L. 106-387; 114 Stat. 1549A-67 *et seq.*). Around that time, Congress held several hearings on sanctions reform, and the 106th Congress considered more than 100 bills proposing reform. See, in particular: US Congress, House Committee on International Relations, "Economic Sanctions and US Policy Interests," 105th Congress, 2nd Session, June 3, 1998; US Congress, Senate, "Proceedings of the Senate Task Force on Economic Sanctions," 105th Congress, 2nd Session, September 1998, S. Doc. 105-26 (Washington: GPO, 1998); and US Congress, Senate Committee on Foreign Relations, "Hearings on Sanctions Reform," 106th Congress, 1st Session, May 11, July 1, July 21, 1999 (Washington: GPO, 1999).

21. The italicized bullet points are quoted from the concluding chapter of the PIIE study. The narrative that follows is the author's interpretation of the bullet point. Gary Clyde Hufbauer, Jeffrey J. Schott, Kimberly Ann Elliott, and Barbara Oegg, *Economic Sanctions Reconsidered* (Washington, DC: Peterson Institute for International Economics, November 2007), pp. 155–178.

Arms Reduction and Disarmament

21

BILATERAL AND MULTILATERAL NUCLEAR ARMS REDUCTIONS (START/GLOBAL DISARMAMENT)

Steven Pifer

Bilateral negotiations between the United States and Soviet Union, and after 1991 Russia, to regulate nuclear arms levels by treaty date back to the late 1960s. Early efforts at arms control focused on limiting the number of strategic delivery vehicles – first, strategic ballistic missile launchers and then strategic bombers – through the Strategic Arms Limitation Talks (SALT) process. Both countries later deployed multiple independently-targetable reentry vehicles on strategic missiles and air-launched cruise missiles on strategic bombers to dramatically increase their warhead levels, even with a limited number of strategic delivery vehicles. Warhead levels peaked in the late 1980s, when each side maintained some 8,000–10,000 strategic nuclear weapons on more than 2,000 delivery systems.

The first treaty to produce actual reductions in nuclear-weapon systems – the 1987 Intermediate Nuclear Forces (INF) Treaty – banned all US and Soviet land-based missiles with ranges between 500 and 5,500 kilometers, resulting in the elimination of some 2,692 ground-launched ballistic and cruise missiles. The Strategic Arms Reduction Treaty (START) followed four years later and mandated reductions in the numbers of US and Russian warheads as well as strategic delivery vehicles. The 2002 Moscow Treaty and the 2010 New Strategic Arms Reduction Treaty (New START) continued this trend, requiring that the US and Russia reduce their respective numbers of deployed strategic warheads to levels not seen since the early 1960s, as well as cuts in strategic delivery vehicles.

As of summer 2014, the United States and Russia faced several questions regarding their approach to nuclear arms control. Will they agree to further reduce their strategic force levels? How will they handle nonstrategic (tactical) nuclear weapons and nondeployed (reserve) strategic warheads, which, to date, have not been constrained? And how will they confront the multitude of other issues that have been linked to and may stall further negotiations on nuclear arms cuts?

One such issue is the need to broaden participation in the nuclear arms control process which, to date, has been almost exclusively a US-Soviet/Russia issue. Nuclear arms reductions cannot forever remain a bilateral question. Other countries will at some point need to engage, starting perhaps with the other three permanent members of the UN Security Council – Britain, China, and France.

This chapter examines the history of nuclear arms control from the 1960s to the present, current issues and future prospects, including the multilateralization of the nuclear arms reduction process.

Arms control motivations

Various reasons have motivated Washington and Moscow to explore limits on and reductions in their nuclear forces. A driving factor in American strategic thinking, which the Soviets (and later the Russians) seemed to embrace, is the concept of strategic stability.

Strategic stability consists of two components. The first is crisis stability, that is, achieving a balance of strategic forces that minimizes the incentives for one side to strike first with nuclear weapons, even in a situation of intense crisis. Crisis stability is strengthened if the opposing sides have survivable strategic systems that would allow each to carry out a punishing retaliatory strike, even if struck first.

Different weapons systems can have different effects on crisis stability. Arms control efforts have usually treated bombers more leniently than long-range ballistic missiles, as the latter were seen as more destabilizing due to their short flight times, which make them more suitable for a surprise, first strike.

Intercontinental ballistic missiles (ICBMs) with multiple independently-targetable reentry vehicles (MIRVs) have been seen as especially destabilizing because of their ability to threaten multiple targets on the other side. MIRVed ICBMs also present vulnerable and inviting targets in their silos: destroying a MIRVed ICBM in its silo can destroy up to ten warheads.

The second aspect of strategic stability is arms race stability, a situation in which neither side has an incentive to build large numbers of new weapons. Ballistic missiles with MIRVs threatened arms race stability – as well as crisis stability – by enabling each side to add many warheads at relatively low cost as they modernized their ballistic missile forces. A factor contributing to greater arms race stability was the recognition in Washington and Moscow that the other side would do everything necessary to maintain an essential equivalence of strategic nuclear forces. Both sides saw less utility in expending resources to augment their strategic arsenals.

A desire for predictability has provided a major impetus for pursuing limits on nuclear arms. Having top end limits on strategic force levels allows each side to plan its force structure with a fairly good idea of what the other side would have. A related reason has been transparency, which has increased as arms control agreements have incorporated more intrusive verification measures.

Other reasons for pursuing arms control have included avoidance of arms races, cost containment, and an interest in improving broader political relations. Cost was very much a factor for the Johnson administration in the 1960s, when it first explored the possibility of Strategic Arms Limitation Treaty talks with the Soviet Union. Johnson and his advisors concluded that an arms race would only drain resources without affecting the overall balance or enhancing US security.

At several points, arms negotiations between Washington and Moscow have helped spur an improvement in the broader political relationship between the two countries. The SALT process was a key element of the Nixon administration's policy of détente with the Soviet Union, and progress on arms control during the second Reagan term helped prompt a broader warming of US-Soviet relations.

Governments have also responded to nongovernmental pressure for nuclear arms control. For example, the 1963 Limited Test Ban Treaty, which required that all nuclear tests be conducted underground, resulted in large part from growing concern in America and elsewhere over the nuclear fall-out produced by above ground testing of nuclear weapons. Anti-nuclear movements in the United States and Europe began over six decades ago, and became especially large in the early 1980s. Their political influence called into question NATO's ability to field new nuclear missile systems.

An active nongovernmental community continues to work for reductions in, or even elimination of all, nuclear weapons. The "Ban the Bomb" movement has always had an idealistic strain, but it has had a realist strain as well. In 2007, four senior statesmen – Republicans George Shultz and Henry Kissinger and Democrats Bill Perry and Sam Nunn – made the realist case for moving to a world without nuclear arms in the first of several op-ed articles in the *Wall Street Journal*. They stressed the growing danger, as the number of nuclear-weapon states increased, that nuclear weapons might actually be used. The Global Zero organization has united statesmen, academics, and activists from around the world to make similar arguments.

US-Soviet arms control arrangements

The SALT process

The United States and Soviet Union began to explore the possibility of nuclear arms control in the mid-1960s. Moscow at first rebuffed US proposals to freeze strategic offensive and defensive forces, as a freeze would have locked the Soviet Union into a substantial numerical disadvantage. As the Soviets increased their production of ICBMs and submarine-launched ballistic missiles (SLBMs) to match US force levels, they became more open to negotiation.

US officials were also interested in addressing anti-ballistic missile systems, which were under development by both countries. They worried that unconstrained missile defenses could make nuclear arms control very difficult, because defenses could create incentives for the sides to increase, rather than limit or reduce, their strategic offensive forces.

The SALT I talks began in November 1969 and concluded in May 1972 with the signing of two agreements by President Richard Nixon and General Secretary Leonid Brezhnev.[1] The SALT I Interim Offensive Arms Agreement froze the number of each side's ICBM launchers (silos) at the number deployed as of July 1, 1972 and the number of SLBM launchers (tubes on ballistic missile submarines) at the number either deployed or under construction as of May 26, 1972.

The agreement did not restrict strategic or heavy bombers, an area in which the United States held a significant numerical advantage, and also left air defenses unconstrained. The agreement did not limit the number of warheads on ICBMs or SLBMs. The United States accepted the Soviet advantage in the number of ballistic missiles in part because its lead in MIRV technology allowed it to begin deploying Minuteman III ICBMs and Poseidon SLBMs with multiple warheads.

The second agreement resulting from the SALT I negotiation was the anti-ballistic missile (ABM) treaty, a treaty of unlimited duration which banned the countries from developing nationwide ABM defenses. It limited each side to two ABM deployment sites, one at its national capital and one at an ICBM field. Under the agreement, the number of ABM interceptor launchers at each site was capped at 100. The treaty also constrained the numbers and

Table 21.1 Operational US and Soviet strategic forces, 1974

	United States	Soviet Union
ICBM Launchers	1,054	1,575
SLBM Launchers	656	660
Intercontinental Bombers	496	140

Source: Thomas W. Wolfe, *The SALT Experience* (Cambridge, MA: Ballinger Publishing Co., 1979), p. 97.

---

locations of radars that could track ballistic missile warheads. In 1974, the countries agreed in a protocol to limit themselves to one ABM deployment site only with no more than 100 ABM interceptor launchers.

The Interim Offensive Arms Agreement and ABM Treaty focused their limits on launchers instead of missiles and missile interceptors due to limitations on monitoring technology. With early national technical means of verification, such as reconnaissance satellites, the sides could monitor numbers of launchers with confidence but not numbers of missiles.

The ABM Treaty was instrumental in strengthening strategic stability and enshrining a mutual deterrence relationship, sometimes referred to as mutual assured destruction or MAD, between the United States and Soviet Union. The ABM Treaty's tight limits on strategic defense ensured that each country could have confidence in its ability to inflict a punishing retaliatory strike on the other.

Negotiations on a follow-on agreement to the Interim Offensive Arms Agreement began in late 1972. During a meeting in Vladivostok in November 1974, President Gerald Ford and Brezhnev agreed that SALT II should limit each side to no more than 2,400 strategic delivery vehicles – ICBM launchers, SLBM launchers, and heavy bombers. Negotiations dragged out, however, and the sides did not come to agreement until 1979, when President Jimmy Carter and Brezhnev signed the SALT II Treaty.[2] The treaty constrained the United States and Soviet Union each to no more than 2,250 strategic nuclear delivery vehicles – ICBM launchers, SLBM launchers and heavy bombers. It also included nested sublimits to constrain MIRVed ICBM and SLBM launchers, and heavy bombers equipped to carry cruise missiles (1,320), MIRVed ICBM and SLBM launchers (1,200) and MIRVed ICBM launchers (820). The limits on MIRVed launchers, particularly MIRVed ICBM launchers, reflected US concern about the destabilizing nature of MIRVed ICBMs, particularly the Soviet SS-18, a large ICBM that could carry up to ten warheads.

SALT II limited strategic nuclear delivery vehicles but did not constrain the number of warheads. Over the course of the next ten years, both the United States and Soviet Union significantly increased their warhead numbers as they deployed MIRVed ballistic missiles and air-launched cruise missiles (ALCMs) on heavy bombers. Concern grew in some quarters in the United States that Soviet deployment of large, heavy ICBMs armed with MIRVs, especially the ten-warhead SS-18, might give Moscow the ability to attack and destroy US ICBMs in their silos.

Ultimately, SALT II fell victim to deterioration in the broader US-Soviet relationship. The discovery of a Soviet combat unit in Cuba and the December 1979 Soviet invasion of Afghanistan caused a dramatic plunge in relations. Carter put the treaty's ratification on hold.

Table 21.2 US and Soviet strategic offensive launchers, 1979

	United States	Soviet Union
ICBM launchers	1,054	1,398
MIRVed ICBM launchers	550	608
SLBM launchers	656	950
MIRVed SLBM launchers	496	144
Heavy bombers	573	156
Heavy bombers equipped to carry ALCMs	3	0

Source: US Department of State, "US and Soviet statement of data on the numbers of strategic offensive forces as of the date of signature of the treaty," June 18, 1979, www.state.gov/t/isn/5195.htm.

INF and START

When Ronald Reagan became president in 1981, he was skeptical of the process of arms control, which he felt had contributed to the Soviets' achieving an advantage in strategic nuclear forces. In his second term, however, Reagan began a serious dialogue with Soviet General Secretary Mikhail Gorbachev on nuclear arms. Those dealings produced two landmark agreements: a treaty banning all US and Soviet intermediate-range missiles, and the framework for the first treaty to require significant cuts in strategic forces.

The Soviets had long held an advantage in intermediate-range nuclear forces missiles, both globally and in Europe. After the Soviets began to deploy the new MIRVed SS-20 INF missile, which carried three warheads, NATO decided in 1979 to respond by deploying US Pershing II ballistic missiles and ground-launched cruise missiles (GLCMs) in Europe. At the same time, NATO offered a negotiating track to constrain INF systems.

The first period of INF negotiations ran from 1981 until the end of 1983 and made no real progress. US negotiators offered the "zero-zero" proposal, under which the United States would forgo the planned Pershing II and GLCM deployments in return for the Soviet Union eliminating all of its INF missiles. The Soviets countered with proposals that would have maintained their superiority in that class of weapons. The first US INF missiles arrived in Europe at the end of 1983, and Soviet negotiators broke off the talks.

Washington and Moscow agreed to resume the negotiations in 1985. Over the next two years, the sides narrowed differences as the Soviets moved to adopt "zero-zero." Reagan and Gorbachev signed the INF Treaty in December 1987.[3] The agreement banned all US and Soviet land-based ballistic and cruise missiles with ranges between 500 and 5,500 kilometers, resulting in the elimination by June 1991 of 1,846 Soviet missiles and 846 US missiles.[4]

The INF Treaty dramatically reduced the number of nuclear weapons in Europe and Asia. It created favorable conditions for the conclusion, in 1990, of the Conventional Armed Forces in Europe Treaty, and for parallel unilateral steps in 1991–92 by Washington and Moscow – known as the Presidential Nuclear Initiatives – to lower the number of tactical nuclear weapons.

The United States and Soviet Union conducted the START talks in parallel with the negotiations on INF missiles. By December 1987, negotiators had reached agreement on the main terms of what would become the START I Treaty. It took several additional years, however, to settle the finer details of the agreement.

In July 1991, President George H.W. Bush and Gorbachev signed START I. It required real reductions in US and Soviet strategic nuclear forces, limiting each side to no more than 1,600 strategic nuclear delivery vehicles, which could carry no more than 6,000 warheads. The treaty had several sublimits, permitting each side no more than 4,900 warheads on ICBM and SLBM launchers and no more than 1,540 warheads on heavy ICBM launchers. The latter limit effectively required that the Soviet military reduce by half its force of MIRVed SS-18 ICBMs. The treaty also required that each side deploy no more than 1,100 warheads on mobile ICBM launchers (the Soviets at the time were deploying ICBMs mounted on heavy truck transports and on special railcars).

START I did not count warheads directly, but used attribution rules. For example, the treaty attributed ten warheads to each SS-18 launcher, while US Minuteman III ICBM launchers were counted as three warheads. The treaty's terms gave preferential treatment to bombers, imposing less stringent limits on them.

START I meant significant reductions for both sides. As shown in the initial data exchange conducted in 1990, each had more than 10,000 attributed warheads on more than 2,200 strategic nuclear delivery vehicles in its arsenal. The treaty thus meant more than a 40 percent reduction in attributed warheads and at least a 25 percent cut in the number of strategic nuclear delivery vehicles.

Both the INF and START I treaties had intrusive verification measures that went well beyond anything considered during the SALT process. The treaties required that the sides regularly exchange large volumes of data and provided for on-site inspections to allow the other side to confirm declared data and observe eliminations of treaty-limited equipment, as well as for other purposes.

START I was signed just five months before the collapse of the Soviet Union. While all of the missile reductions required by the INF Treaty had been implemented by the time of the Soviet Union's demise in December 1991, START I had not yet entered into force. Following the Soviet Union's break-up, former Soviet strategic forces were located in Russia, Ukraine, Kazakhstan, and Belarus. In May 1992, the US-brokered Lisbon Protocol committed those four countries to carrying out Soviet treaty obligations and mandated that Ukraine, Kazakhstan, and Belarus eliminate all strategic weapons on their territory, leaving Russia as the sole nuclear-weapon state of the four. The START I Treaty finally entered into force in December 1994.

Just before leaving office, Bush and Russian President Boris Yeltsin signed the START II Treaty, which entailed even deeper reductions. It required that each side reduce its attributed warheads to no more than 3,000–3,500 and banned all heavy ICBMs and MIRVed ICBMs. The latter provisions were seen as particularly important for strategic stability, given the ability of MIRVed ICBMs to strike multiple targets. START II's ban on heavy and MIRVed ICBMs addressed the principal worry of US strategic planners for almost two decades: the MIRVed ICBM threat to the Minuteman force.

START II, however, became entangled in other questions, including NATO enlargement, NATO military action against Serbia, and growing US interest in missile defense. The treaty never entered into force. President Bill Clinton in 1997 agreed with Yeltsin on the basic parameters of a START III agreement, including a limit on each side of no more than 2,000–2,500 warheads, but the sides never concluded a full treaty.

The End of the ABM Treaty and SORT

President George W. Bush took office in January 2001 determined to accelerate US missile defense efforts and with little interest in arms control. The ABM Treaty, concluded in 1972, had

Table 21.3 US and Soviet strategic offensive forces, 1990

	United States	Soviet Union
Deployed ICBM launchers	1,000	1,398
Warheads attributed to ICBM launchers	2,450	6,612
Deployed SLBM launchers	672	940
Warheads attributed to SLBM launchers	5,760	2,804
Deployed heavy bombers	574	162
Warheads attributed to heavy bombers	2,353	855
Total launchers and bombers	2,246	2,500
Total warheads attributed to launchers and bombers	10,563	10,271

Source: Federation of American scientists, data from "Memorandum of understanding on the establishment of the data base relating to the treaty between the United States of America and the Union of Soviet Socialist Republics on the reduction and limitation of strategic offensive arms," November 1, 1978, www.fas.org/nuke/control/salt2/text/salt2-4.htm.

withstood several challenges over the intervening three decades. In the 1980s, the US government had concerns regarding Soviet compliance with the treaty.

In 1983, Reagan announced the Strategic Defense Initiative, popularly referred to as Star Wars, with the goal of creating a shield that could defeat even a large-scale ballistic missile attack against the United States. The Reagan administration poured billions of dollars into researching different technologies but, by the time of the George H.W. Bush administration in 1989, most experts had concluded that the United States lacked the technology and the resources to build the kind of missile defense that Reagan had initially envisaged. The Bush administration scaled back its ambitions to the goal of defeating a relatively small number of ICBM warheads.

Towards the end of the 1990s, concern grew in the Senate about the prospect of states such as Iran and North Korea acquiring ICBMs. This prompted greater interest in defending US territory against a limited ballistic missile attack. The Clinton administration developed plans for a national missile defense system. US officials sought to negotiate an amendment to the ABM Treaty to allow broader deployments, but their Russian counterparts showed no interest.

The Bush administration wanted to move quickly on missile defense and, in December 2001, gave the required six months notification of its intent to withdraw from the treaty, which it did in June 2002. Russian President Vladimir Putin expressed regret at the US decision but did not raise major objections. From June 2002 onwards, the United States was free to develop and deploy missile defenses without restraint. Within two years, the US military had begun the deployment in Alaska and California of what would ultimately number thirty ground-based interceptors designed to engage rudimentary ICBMs.

The Bush administration concluded its nuclear posture review in fall 2001 and announced that it would maintain 1,700–2,200 operationally deployed strategic warheads, regardless of what other countries might deploy. Bush originally suggested to Putin that the Russians make their own statement regarding their strategic force plans, but the Russian president pressed hard for a legally-binding treaty. With Russian strategic missiles aging and being retired, Russian strategic warhead numbers had begun to fall dramatically. Moscow sought to lock the United States into lower numbers as well.

Bush assented, and in May 2002 the two presidents signed the Strategic Offensive Reductions Treaty (SORT), which limited the United States and Russia to no more than 1,700–2,200 strategic warheads each. The treaty, less than two pages in length, lacked agreed definitions, counting rules, or verification measures. The START I Treaty, which would remain in force until the end of 2009, provided verification measures, but they were not well-suited to monitoring SORT's warhead limit.

Following signature of SORT, the Bush administration showed little interest in further arms control until the end of its second term. With START I's expiration looming in 2009, US and Russian officials discussed what might follow it. The Russians objected to Washington's offer to negotiate limits only on strategic warheads, not strategic nuclear delivery vehicles, and the Bush administration left office with no agreement on START I's follow-on.

New START

President Barack Obama took office in January 2009, committed to further reductions in nuclear arms and believing that arms control might help improve the broader US-Russian relationship. In April 2009, Obama gave a speech in Prague in which he embraced the goal of world without nuclear weapons. In the speech, Obama also cautioned that much had to happen to make such a world possible and stated that, as long as nuclear weapons existed, the United States would maintain a reliable nuclear deterrent.

Table 21.4 US and Russian strategic offensive forces, July 2009

	United States	Soviet Union
Deployed ICBM launchers	550	465
Warheads attributed to ICBM launchers	1,600	2,001
Deployed SLBM launchers	432	268
Warheads attributed to SLBM launchers	3,264	1,288
Deployed heavy bombers	206	76
Warheads attributed to heavy bombers	1,052	608
Total launchers and bombers	1,188	796
Total warheads attributed to launchers and bombers	5,916	3,897

Note: The START I counting rules significantly overstated the total number of US and Russian strategic forces. For example, a number of ICBM silos and SLBM tubes were empty but had not been eliminated according to START I rules. They thus were counted as if they contained strategic missiles with their attributed warheads.

Source: US Department of State, "START aggregate numbers of strategic offensive arms (as of July 1, 2009, as compiled from individual data submissions of the Parties)," Fact Sheet, October 1, 2009, www.state.gov/t/avc/rls/130149.htm.

In Obama's first meeting with Russian President Dmitri Medvedev in April 2009, the two agreed to launch a negotiation aimed at producing a successor to START I, which was due to expire that December. US and Russian negotiators needed until early 2010 to complete the New START Treaty, which Obama and Medvedev signed in April.

New START has three numerical limits. By the time the limits take full effect in February 2018, the United States and Russia each can have no more than 700 strategic delivery vehicles, that is, deployed ICBMs, SLBMs and nuclear-capable heavy bombers. A deployed ICBM or SLBM is a missile emplaced in an ICBM silo, mounted on a mobile ICBM launcher or stored in an SLBM missile tube. (With New START, the term "strategic delivery vehicle" replaced the term "strategic nuclear delivery vehicle" used previously. Strategic delivery vehicles refer to ICBMs and SLBMs rather than their launchers; "nuclear" was dropped because, as noted below, New START leaves open a possibility to equip ICBMs and SLBMs with conventional warheads.)

Each side is further limited to no more than 1,550 deployed strategic warheads, with each warhead on a deployed ICBM and SLBM counting toward the 1,550 limit and each deployed nuclear-capable heavy bomber counted as one warhead toward the 1,550 limit.

Finally, each side may have no more than 800 deployed and nondeployed ICBM and SLBM launchers and nuclear-capable heavy bombers. A nondeployed launcher would be an ICBM silo, mobile ICBM launcher or SLBM missile tube that did not contain a missile.

New START also contains extensive verification measures, including data exchanges, exhibitions, notifications, and on-site verification. For example, each side can carry out up to ten "Type One" inspections per year of deployed missiles and bombers. When inspecting an ICBM base or ballistic missile submarine port, the inspecting team is given a list of each deployed ICBM or SLBM at the site and the number of warheads on each missile. The inspection team then has the right to choose one of the missiles for inspection to confirm the number of installed warheads matches the number on the list. "Type Two" inspections allow the sides to inspect nondeployed systems.

New START will reduce US and Russian strategic force levels to their lowest levels since the early 1960s. In implementing the treaty, the US military has decided to "download" all of its MIRVed Minuteman III ICBMs so that they will carry only a single warhead. That will produce a more stabilizing force structure, as in a crisis single-warhead ICBMs would pose a considerably less attractive target than ICBMs equipped with multiple warheads. (Russia appears to be moving toward greater reliance on mobile ICBMs to reduce their vulnerability.)

Implementation of New START proceeded smoothly during its first three years. In March 2014, the sides' semi-annual data update showed that they were moving toward the treaty's limits, with Russia already having met two of them:

Looking Forward

Obama made clear when he signed the New START Treaty that he did not see it as the end point for nuclear arms reductions. In April 2010, he called for a further round of negotiations with Russia, which he said should include nonstrategic (tactical) nuclear weapons and nondeployed (reserve) strategic weapons. Were the Russians to take him up on this proposal, Washington and Moscow would for the first time be negotiating on their entire nuclear arsenals.

In June 2013, Obama used a speech in Berlin to propose that New START's limit of 1,550 deployed strategic warheads be reduced by one-third, which would bring that limit down to 1,000–1,100 deployed strategic warheads. Administration officials privately indicated that Washington would be prepared to make commensurate reductions in the limits of 700 deployed strategic missiles and bombers and 800 deployed and nondeployed strategic missile launchers and bombers. Obama also called for "bold" reductions in tactical nuclear weapons, though he did not offer a specific proposal.

Moscow has shown no interest in further nuclear reductions and explains that by citing its concerns about a number of other questions. Foremost among these are the US plan for missile defense in Europe. The Russians have cited other concerns, including Prompt Global Strike, the US effort to develop a rapid means of striking targets at long distances with conventional warheads; conventional force imbalances in Europe; outer space weaponry; and the need to take into account third-country nuclear forces. Above and beyond these specific issues, the overall deterioration in US-Russia relations over Ukraine complicates the prospects for future nuclear arms reduction negotiations.

Further Reductions of Strategic Weapons

Were Russia to agree to discuss further nuclear reductions, one question would be how the sides might reduce their strategic offensive forces below levels enumerated in the New START Treaty. If the sides could come to agreement on numbers, it might be relatively simple to record those numbers in a protocol to New START.

Table 21.5 New START numbers, March 2014

New START limit	United States	Russia
Deployed strategic delivery vehicles (700)	778	498
Deployed/nondeployed missile launchers and heavy bombers (800)	952	906
Deployed strategic warheads (1,550)	1,585	1,512

Source: US Department of State, "New START Treaty Aggregate Numbers of Strategic Offensive Arms," Fact Sheet, Bureau of Arms Control, Verification, and Compliance, April 1, 2014, www.state.gov/documents/organization/224449.pdf.

The sides would have to decide how far to reduce the limits. Obama's Berlin speech suggests that he is prepared to cut the deployed strategic warhead limit to 1,000–1,100. Russian officials have not indicated any preferred levels below the limit of 1,550 deployed strategic warheads, nor have they indicated a position with regard to levels below 700 deployed strategic delivery vehicles and 800 deployed and nondeployed missile launchers and heavy bombers. Some nongovernmental analysts in the past have suggested that Russia might be prepared to go as low as 1,000 deployed strategic warheads in a bilateral negotiation, but that reductions below that level would require a substantive agreement on missile defense and some commitment by third-country nuclear-weapon states.

Another issue the sides would need to consider in a new negotiation is whether to adjust the bomber weapon counting rule. New START counts each deployed nuclear-capable heavy bomber as a single deployed warhead, regardless of how many weapons the aircraft might be capable of carrying.

This discount rule is consistent with the tendency in past arms control negotiations to treat bomber weapons more leniently than ballistic missile warheads. However, as the overall limit on deployed strategic weapons is reduced, the number of "uncounted" bomber weapons could grow as a percentage of total deployed weapons.

One possible way to deal with bomber weapons would be to keep the discount principle but count each deployed heavy bomber as two or three weapons within the limit on deployed strategic warheads. An alternate approach would be to count all nuclear air-launched cruise missiles, short-range attack missiles and bombs located at airbases where deployed heavy bombers are located. This would do away with uncounted weapons and, in effect, treat ballistic missile warheads and bomber weapons equally.

Another issue that might be addressed in a negotiation for a successor to New START would be the issue of nondeployed strategic weapons, which are currently unlimited by New START. The US military maintains a large number of nondeployed strategic weapons to hedge against geopolitical surprise or a technical problem in a class of warheads.

Russian officials and analysts have expressed concern about the large number of nondeployed US ballistic missile warheads, particularly since those weapons could be "uploaded" on to US ICBMs and SLBMs, most of which have been downloaded so that they carry fewer than their maximum warhead capacity. In April 2010, Obama offered to include these weapons in a follow-on negotiation (along with nonstrategic nuclear weapons).

One way to limit nondeployed strategic warheads would be to negotiate a numerical limit to cover those weapons. That would most likely require verification measures to provide access to warhead storage areas. Neither side has to date indicated what level it might propose for such a limit.

Nonstrategic nuclear weapons

In April 2010, Obama proposed including nonstrategic nuclear weapons in further US-Russia negotiations, and NATO leaders at their May 2012 summit in Chicago indicated their readiness to reduce the Alliance's nonstrategic nuclear weapons if Russia took reciprocal actions. Russian officials thus far have shown little interest in negotiating on such weapons, an area in which Russia is believed to hold a significant numerical advantage. Moscow has called for the withdrawal of all nuclear weapons to national territory as a prerequisite for any broader negotiation on nonstrategic nuclear weapons. That would include removal of the roughly 200 US B61 nuclear bombs currently believed to be deployed on the territory of five NATO states.[5] Although US officials have privately said that such a withdrawal might result from a new arms control agreement, they and NATO officials rule out withdrawal as a precondition.

If the United States and Russia agreed to a negotiation on nonstrategic nuclear weapons, reaching accord on a numerical limit on such weapons could prove difficult, given the Russian numerical advantage. Some have suggested that the United States might offer to reduce its numerical advantage in nondeployed strategic warheads in return for Russian concessions on nonstrategic nuclear arms.

While New START limits both deployed strategic warheads and deployed strategic delivery vehicles, a negotiation on nonstrategic nuclear weapons might result in a numerical limit on the nuclear weapons (warheads) only, not their delivery vehicles. That is because those delivery vehicles, such as dual-capable tactical aircraft, have primarily conventional missions, using conventional weapons. Both the US and Russian militaries would likely oppose limits in a nuclear arms agreement that would significantly constrain their conventional force capabilities.

Given Russian reluctance to consider limits on nonstrategic nuclear weapons, NATO has considered the idea of transparency and confidence-building measures as a means to ease such weapons into an arms control dialogue. Over the past three years, a number of confidence-building measures have been floated. These include: transparency proposals regarding the numbers, types, and locations of nonstrategic nuclear weapons; an agreement to keep nonstrategic nuclear weapons "demated" or separated from their delivery vehicles (which may well be the current practice for most if not all US and Russia nonstrategic nuclear weapons); US and Russian commitments not to increase the number of their nonstrategic nuclear weapons (neither side is believed to have a need to increase the number of its weapons); and proposals to relocate weapons, for example, away from the NATO-Russian border, or to consolidate them at a fewer number of storage areas.

Since the 2012 summit, NATO officials have considered possible transparency and confidence-building measures, a process that has taken longer than many nongovernmental analysts had expected. The Alliance's arms control body in December 2013 reportedly could agree on just two possible transparency and confidence-building measures out of an original set of more than a dozen proposals.[6]

Big treaty or separate tracks?

If the United States and Russia agreed to negotiate a further reduction in their nuclear arsenals and include nondeployed strategic warheads as well as nonstrategic nuclear weapons, they could pursue several different courses.

One approach would be a "big treaty" which would constrain all US and Russian nuclear weapons – strategic and nonstrategic, deployed and nondeployed. (Those nuclear weapons that have been retired and are awaiting dismantlement might be constrained separately.) The advantage of such an approach is that it offers a mechanism to offset the area of US numerical advantage (nondeployed strategic warheads) and the area of Russian numerical advantage (nonstrategic nuclear warheads).

For example, a treaty might specify a limit for each side of no more than 2,000 total nuclear weapons, which would still leave the United States and Russia each with more than six times as many nuclear weapons as the nearest third country. Within that 2,000 limit, there might be a sublimit of 1,000 deployed strategic warheads constraining the weapons of greatest concern (most of these weapons sit atop ICBMs and SLBMs that can be launched in a matter of minutes). Assuming that each side maintained 1,000 deployed strategic warheads, the 2,000 limit would allow each 1,000 additional warheads – nondeployed strategic warheads and nonstrategic – to fit within the overall ceiling. Each side would have the freedom to choose its mix of nondeployed strategic warheads and nonstrategic weapons, but the result would be that the US numerical advantage in nondeployed strategic warheads would be reduced along with the Russian numerical advantage in nonstrategic nuclear weapons.

Using a single aggregate limit to force the sides to offset their areas of respective numerical advantage reportedly had considerable appeal to US officials in 2011 as a possible next step after New START. The idea appeared, however, to lose appeal in Washington in 2013. US officials privately expressed concern that it would not be possible to conclude a big treaty during the remaining years of the Obama administration. Those officials thus suggested taking different approaches to different types of nuclear weapons.

As noted above, encapsulating lower numbers for the three limits in the New START Treaty could be done in a straightforward manner. The sides could simply agree to a protocol to the treaty that would change the numbers, e.g., lower the 1,550 limit on deployed strategic warheads to 1,000.

The sides might address nonstrategic nuclear weapons and nondeployed strategic weapons in a parallel track (or tracks). There is value in maintaining some connection between these two classes of weapons, in order to take advantage of the possibility to offset areas of US and Russian numerical advantage.

Given that the sides have not negotiated limits on these kinds of weapons previously, this negotiating track would likely require more time than concluding a protocol to change the numerical limits in New START. The sides would have to deal with the more challenging verification issues associated with direct limits on nonstrategic and nondeployed strategic nuclear weapons. The sides might want to begin with transparency and confidence-building measures as a first step. It would be desirable, but difficult, to agree at the outset that the ultimate objective would be legally-binding limits covering nonstrategic and nondeployed strategic nuclear weapons.

Of course, entering into any discussion along these lines would presuppose Russia's readiness to negotiate further reductions in nuclear arms. That may require addressing the associated concerns that the Russians have raised.

Issues related to further nuclear reductions

Missile defense

Russian officials argue that the issue of missile defense must be addressed before they would consider further nuclear reductions. They assert that unconstrained US missile defenses could grow to a point where they could threaten Russian strategic ballistic missiles.

Moscow has focused its concern over the past three years on US plans for missile defense in Europe. In September 2009, the Obama administration announced the European phased adaptive approach to missile defense, which involves deploying increasingly advanced SM-3 missile interceptors near and in Europe to defend primarily against existing and future Iranian ballistic missiles.

The first phase began in 2011, with the deployment of a US warship equipped with Standard SM-3 Block IA interceptors in the eastern Mediterranean Sea, which offers protection for Turkey against existing Iranian medium-range ballistic missiles. The SM-3 is armed with a kinetic kill vehicle that uses an infrared seeker to, in effect, crash the kinetic kill vehicle into the target ballistic missile warhead. In Phase 2, scheduled for 2015, SM-3 Block IB interceptors will be deployed in Romania with a more advanced seeker on the interceptor's kill vehicle. That will be followed by the deployment in Phase 3 of SM-3 Block IIA interceptors in Poland in 2018; the SM-3 Block IIA will have a higher velocity and be more capable of engaging intermediate-range ballistic missiles. Phase 4 envisaged the deployment of still faster SM-3 Block IIB interceptors in Europe, but the Pentagon cancelled that phase in March 2013 due to cost and technology concerns.

The cancellation of Phase 4, which was supposed to give the SM-3 capabilities to engage ICBMs, did not seem to mollify Russian concerns. US officials pointed out, however, that the SM-3 Block IB and Block IIA lack the velocity needed to engage ICBMs. While those interceptors could engage intermediate-range ballistic missiles, Russia – like the United States – is banned from having such missiles by the INF Treaty. Moscow nevertheless continues to express concern about US missile defense plans.

In November 2010, NATO leaders and Russian President Dmitry Medvedev agreed to explore the possibility of a cooperative NATO-Russia missile defense for Europe. In exchanges between the US Department of Defense and Russian Ministry of Defense in early 2011, the sides discussed what a cooperative missile defense might look like. Their views reportedly converged on a number of key issues: NATO and Russia would each retain control over a decision to launch its own interceptors; transparency regarding missile defense capabilities would be useful; the sides should conduct joint missile defense exercises, building on previous US-Russian and NATO-Russian exercise experience; a jointly manned "data fusion center" would combine early warning and tracking information from NATO and Russian radars and other sensors and provide the enhanced product to both sides on a near real-time basis; and a jointly manned "planning and operations center" would discuss issues such as possible threats, ballistic missile attack scenarios and ways to coordinate intercepts of hostile missiles.

These discussions, which were mirrored by exchanges in several unofficial "Track II" exchanges, did not progress further. Russia began to insist on a legally binding guarantee that US missile defenses not be directed against Russian strategic missiles. Russian officials said that the agreement should include "objective criteria," by which they meant limits on the number, velocity and location of missile interceptors.

US officials declined to negotiate such a treaty, in part because of the virtual certainty that the Senate would not give consent to a treaty that set limits on missile defenses. They have told Russian officials, however, that the United States would be prepared to offer a written political assurance that US missile defenses are not targeted against Russian ballistic missiles.

In order to allay Russian concerns, US officials have offered other transparency measures. In late 2011, US Missile Defense Agency head LTG Patrick O'Reilly said that he would be ready to organize visits by Russian technical experts, bringing their own equipment, to observe US missile defense tests. In spring 2013, US officials proposed an executive agreement under which each side would provide the other information about its planned missile defenses over the next ten years, the idea being that Russia would receive a clear and annually updated projection of US missile defense capabilities and plans. That would allow Moscow sufficient time to react if it believed that those plans would undermine its strategic ballistic missile force.

At some point, if strategic offensive force levels continue to decline while missile defenses capable of engaging ICBMs and SLBMs grow, a legally binding treaty constraining missile defenses may make sense (in parallel with legally binding treaty constraints on strategic offensive forces). But it is difficult to see the requirement for such a treaty now. Under current plans, when the New START Treaty limits take full effect in 2018, the United States will deploy no more than forty-four ground-based interceptors capable of engaging strategic ballistic missiles. At that point, Russia will be allowed some 1,500 deployed strategic warheads on its ICBMs and SLBMs. Given such a large difference between offense and defense, a politically-binding assurance, accompanied by transparency measures and a cooperative NATO-Russia missile defense arrangement for Europe should address any real Russian concerns. Washington and Moscow, however, remain stalemated over the issue.

Prompt global strike

Russian officials have expressed growing concern over US plans to develop conventional weapons capable of rapidly hitting targets at long distances, a system called Prompt Global Strike (PGS). Some Russian analysts fear that the US military could use conventional PGS weapons to strike Russian strategic forces, leadership targets or key communication nodes.

Indeed, the US military believes that, with increasingly accurate PGS systems, certain targets may now be struck effectively with long-range conventional weapons. The George W. Bush administration considered arming two Trident D-5 SLBMs on each Ohio-class SSBN with conventional warheads. Congress did not fund that, but the concept got the Russians' attention. In early New START negotiations, Russian negotiators sought to ban the deployment of conventional warheads on ICBMs and SLBMs. In the end, the sides agreed that any deployed conventional warheads on strategic ballistic missiles would count toward the limit of 1,550 deployed strategic warheads.

Following conclusion of the New START Treaty, the Defense Department indicated that it would not pursue the option to arm ICBMs and SLBMs with conventional warheads. Instead it devoted greater attention to developing hypersonic glide vehicles. They would be launched by a ballistic missile and accelerated to hypersonic speed, but they would not fly a ballistic path to their target. They instead would "glide" along the upper reaches of the atmosphere. As such, they would not appear to be accountable under the New START Treaty. (Russia and China are working on hypersonic glide vehicles as well.)

Some analysts have challenged the need for PGS systems, questioning whether there is a serious mission requirement for such weapons. They also cite problems such as warhead ambiguity − it would not be clear to a state that detected a launch whether the warhead was conventional or nuclear − and destination ambiguity − the system's maneuverability might lead an observing state to conclude incorrectly that it was the intended target.[7]

Whether and how arms control deals with conventional PGS will depend on which systems are actually deployed. Department of Defense officials have indicated that, were the United States to deploy hypersonic glide vehicles, they would constitute a "niche" capability − that is, they would number no more than a few dozen. One possible outcome, if the numbers were indeed small, would be to count vehicles and their warheads under the New START limits (this would become less attractive if/as the New START limits were reduced, as each deployed conventional warhead would "cost" a deployed nuclear warhead).

Multilateral arms reductions

There have been a number of multilateral agreements regarding nuclear-weapon issues, including the 1963 Limited Test Ban Treaty, 1968 Nonproliferation Treaty, and 1996 Comprehensive Test Ban Treaty. There have to date, however, been no formal multilateral negotiations regarding nuclear arms reductions, with the exception of negotiations in early 1992 to "multilateralize" the START I Treaty, so that Russia, Belarus, Kazakhstan, and Ukraine could take on the Soviet obligations after the Soviet Union's collapse in 1991.

Arms reductions negotiations thus far have been bilateral, first between the United States and Soviet Union, and later between the United States and Russia. That reflects in large measure the fact that US and Soviet/Russian nuclear forces are so much larger than those of any third country. (See Table 21.6 for global nuclear-weapon stockpiles.)

The Soviets tried in the past to bring British and French nuclear forces into bilateral negotiations with the United States. For example, during the 1981–83 INF negotiations, Soviet negotiators suggested that British and French nuclear forces partially offset Soviet INF missile systems. They claimed that a NATO-Soviet balance existed. US officials, however, steadfastly refused to include or take account of third-country nuclear forces.

The New START Treaty opens the possibility of expanding the bilateral US-Russian negotiations to a multilateral format. The preamble notes that the treaty sets the goal of a "step-by-step process of reducing and limiting nuclear arms … with a view to expanding this process in the future, including to a multilateral approach." That said, the United States is prepared to reduce below New START levels in a bilateral format. Russian officials, on the other hand, seem to suggest that now is the time to address multilateral reductions.

The continuing disparity in size between the US and Russian nuclear arsenals, on the one hand, and the arsenals of other nuclear-weapon states, on the other, complicates negotiations. It is likely that neither Washington nor Moscow is prepared in the near term to accept equal limitations with third countries. Convincing third countries to accept an agreement with unequal limitations will prove a stiff challenge.

Another complicating factor is that, thus far, the United States and Russia have agreed to limit only deployed strategic forces. While Britain and France have SLBMs, and China has a small number of ICBMs and may be nearing an operational SLBM capability, many third-country nuclear weapons are for use on delivery systems that would not be defined as "strategic" under the terms of the New START Treaty. Indeed, one argument for broadening US-Russian negotiations to include all nuclear weapons – strategic and nonstrategic, deployed and nondeployed – is that it would put Washington and Moscow in a stronger position to engage third countries on limiting and reducing their nuclear weapons.

Of the seven other states known or thought to possess nuclear weapons – Britain, France, China, India, Pakistan, Israel, and North Korea – a multilateral approach would likely start with the first three. France, China, and Britain are believed to have the third, fourth, and fifth largest nuclear arsenals. All three, along with the United States and Russia, are permanent UN Security Council members and nuclear-weapons states as recognized by the Nonproliferation Treaty (NPT).

Table 21.6 Global nuclear-weapon stockpiles

United States	4,650
Russia	4,480
France	300
China	250
Great Britain	225
Pakistan	100–120
India	90–110
Israel	80
North Korea	?

Note: US and Russian totals do not include weapons that have been retired and are in the dismantlement queue. North Korea is believed to have produced sufficient plutonium for 8–12 bombs but has not yet shown that it can operationalize weapons.

Source: Adapted from Hans M. Kristensen and Robert S. Norris, "Global Nuclear Weapons Inventories, 1945–2013," *Bulletin of Atomic Scientists*, Vol. 69, No. 5 (September/October 2013), pp. 75–81.

Of the three countries, Britain has indicated a readiness to participate in a multilateral nuclear arms control negotiation at the appropriate time. The British have reduced their nuclear arsenal by more than 50 percent since its peak in the latter 1970s, eliminating tactical and strategic bomber weapons and now maintaining operational nuclear warheads only for their SLBM force. The British currently maintain a stockpile of some 225 warheads and plan in the next decade to cut their stockpile to about 180 warheads, of which 120 would be operational.[8]

France, which has been much more reticent about taking part in nuclear arms control negotiations, has a stockpile of no more than 300 warheads, according to a statement by President Nicholas Sarkozy in 2008, down from 540 weapons in the early 1990s. French weapons are predominately for SLBMs, though the French military maintains a small number of air-delivered weapons.[9]

China has also taken an unforthcoming position regarding participation in nuclear arms control negotiations. The Chinese military is modernizing its nuclear forces but appears to be increasing its nuclear arsenal at only a modest pace. It is believed to have a stockpile of about 250 weapons. China has the most diverse mix of the three countries, placing nuclear weapons on land-based missiles (including ICBMs that can reach the United States), bombers, and SLBMs.[10]

If drawing third countries into a negotiation on reductions and limitations will be difficult, as appears to be the case, the United States and Russia might consider whether there are steps that could gradually move in that direction. The five permanent UN Security Council members (the P-5) have since 2009 conducted a dialogue on how they might move forward with regard to their disarmament commitments under the NPT and 2010 NPT review conference's action plan.

Specifically, the P-5 has discussed steps to strengthen the NPT regime and how to advance the objective of a treaty to end the production of fissile materials for use in nuclear weapons. They have also addressed transparency regarding their nuclear-weapon programs, mutual confidence-building steps, verification issues and experiences, and a possible standard reporting form for steps that they take with regard to reducing nuclear weapons. The Chinese have led a P-5 working group tasked with developing a glossary that defines key nuclear and nuclear-weapon terms in order to facilitate mutual understanding.

These constitute baby steps toward multilateralizing the nuclear reduction process. It would be useful if the P-5 dialogue produced agreement on some transparency measures, such as an agreement under which each of the P-5 states would report publicly – or to each other – the total number of nuclear weapons in its arsenal, along with information about the types of weapons and their delivery systems. While they might draw on the data exchanges required by the New START Treaty for ideas, it is unrealistic to expect an agreement would entail such a detailed level of data as New START. China, for example, uses mobility, tunnels, and other measures to hide the location of its long-range nuclear-weapon systems. Beijing would likely fear that disclosure of locations – which New START requires for ICBM launchers – would make them vulnerable to attack. But agreement on some basic data exchange, which could contribute to mutual confidence, might prove more possible.

A more dramatic step, but one that would still fall short of including Britain, China, and France in a multilateral negotiation, would be for Washington and Moscow to ask those countries to make unilateral political statements to the effect that they would not increase the total number of their nuclear weapons so long as the United States and Russia continue to reduce their nuclear arsenals. That would help to avert concerns in Washington and Moscow that one country – China is usually mentioned in this regard – might build up its nuclear forces as the two superpowers reduced theirs.

Agreements to limit and reduce nuclear weapons have come a long way since the first exploratory discussions between US and Soviet officials in the 1960s. Whereas SALT limited strategic offensive forces in ways that still permitted a build-up of warheads, the START agreements have mandated reductions, both of warheads and delivery systems. Whether and how soon the United States and Russia can move beyond New START to further reduce their deployed strategic nuclear forces and bring other nuclear weapons into the negotiation is unknown as of early 2014. Likewise, finding a proper means of broadening the bilateral process to include other nuclear-weapon states, starting with Britain, France and China, also remains a question to be resolved.

Notes

1. For an account of the SALT I negotiating process, see Coit D. Blacker and Gloria Duffy (eds), *International Arms Control: Issues and Agreements* (Palo Alto, CA: Stanford University Press, 1984), pp. 219–254. For a more detailed history, see John Newhouse, *Cold Dawn: The History of SALT* (New York: Holt, Rinehart and Winston, 1973).
2. For a fuller discussion of the SALT II negotiations, see Strobe Talbott, *Endgame: The Inside Story of SALT II* (New York: Harper Colophon Books, 1979).
3. For a full account of the INF negotiations, see Maynard W. Glitman, *The Last Battle of the Cold War: An Inside Account of Negotiating the Intermediate Range Nuclear Forces Treaty* (New York: Palgrave MacMillan 2006).
4. Federation of American Scientists, "Intermediate-Range Nuclear Forces," December 1987, www.fas.org/nuke/control/inf/intro.htm.
5. Hans M. Kristensen and Robert S. Norris, "US Nuclear Forces, 2014," *Bulletin of the Atomic Scientists*, Vol. 70, No. 1 (January/February 2014), p. 92.
6. Oliver Meier and Simon Lunn, "Trapped: NATO, Russia and the Problem of Tactical Nuclear Weapons," *Arms Control Today*, Vol. 44, No. 1 (January/February 2014), pp. 18–24.
7. For a fuller discussion of the issues posed by Prompt Global Strike systems, see James M. Acton, *Silver Bullet? Asking the Right Questions about Conventional Prompt Global Strike* (Washington, DC: Carnegie Endowment for International Peace, 2013).
8. Kristensen and Norris, "Global Nuclear Weapons Inventories, p. 79
9. Ibid.
10. Ibid., pp. 79–80.

22

NUCLEAR WEAPON-FREE ZONES

Susan Burk

For nearly seven decades, governments have pursued initiatives to reduce the dangers posed by the spread of nuclear weapons while preserving countries' access to the economic and social benefits of the peaceful atom. The most well-known of these initiatives is the 1968 Treaty on the Nonproliferation of Nuclear Weapons (NPT). Open to all states, the NPT reflected a basic bargain with a balance of obligations: states without nuclear weapons pledged not to acquire them, states with nuclear weapons pledged to pursue negotiations toward nuclear disarmament, and all states would have access to the peaceful benefits of nuclear energy. Nonnuclear-weapon states (NNWS) agreed to accept International Atomic Energy Agency (IAEA) safeguards on their nuclear activities, and all states committed to apply safeguards to nuclear exports to NNWS. The NPT did not ban nuclear testing, nor did it provide the NNWSs with the legally binding negative security assurances they sought from the NPT nuclear-weapon states (NWS).[1] The drafters of the NPT, however, acknowledged the interest of groups of states to pursue regional nonproliferation initiatives by including a provision in the NPT that nothing in that treaty affected the rights of groups of states to conclude nuclear weapon-free zones (NWFZ).

Like the NPT, NWFZ treaties served both nonproliferation and nuclear disarmament goals by limiting the areas where nuclear weapons could be produced, tested, deployed, or used.[2] They also were an opportunity, as it turned out, to improve upon certain aspects of the NPT.

Pre-NPT NWFZs

Even before the NPT, groups of states recognized the value of regional nonproliferation arrangements to insulate their territories and citizens from the nuclear threat represented by the Cold War. The earliest proposal for a NWFZ in a populated area was offered by Polish Foreign Minister Adam Rapacki in a speech at the UN General Assembly in October 1957. Seeking to establish a denuclearized zone in Central Europe, the Rapacki Plan called for Poland, Czechoslovakia, the German Democratic Republic, and the German Federal Republic to "undertake not to produce, stockpile, import for their own use, or allow the deployment in their territories of any types of nuclear weapons, and also not to install, or allow to be installed, in their territories equipment or installations for delivering nuclear weapons...."[3] The Plan called on France, the United States, Great Britain, and the Soviet Union to commit not to deploy or use nuclear weapons against the zone.[4] The proposal ran counter to NATO strategy at the time, and failed to gain the support of the United States and its Western allies who also questioned its enforceability. Similar initiatives in the 1950s and 1960s to establish NWFZs in Sweden, Finland and Romania foundered for the same reason. Nevertheless, the Rapacki Plan opened the door to other proposals and influenced the development of guidelines for NWFZs.

The first tentative step toward a nuclear-weapon-free area was taken in 1959 with the conclusion of the Antarctic Treaty banning nuclear weapons, nuclear tests and disposal of nuclear waste from this unoccupied continent.

The 1962 Cuban Missile Crisis galvanized support for establishing a NWFZ in Latin America. When, in 1962, Brazil submitted a draft resolution to UN General Assembly calling for such a zone, Cuba conditioned its support on the inclusion of Puerto Rico and the Panama Canal Zone in a NWFZ, and on the elimination of foreign military bases, in particular Guantanamo Naval Base.[5] The following year, a Mexican initiative to make Latin America a NWFZ received strong support in the UN General Assembly.

The Treaty of Tlatelolco, establishing the first NWFZ in a populated area, was opened for signature on February 14, 1967. It prohibits the testing, use, manufacture, production, or acquisition by any means, as well as the receipt, storage, installation, deployment, and any form of possession of any nuclear weapons, directly or indirectly, by the parties to the treaty. Nuclear explosions for peaceful purposes were explicitly permitted under a set of guidelines to guarantee transparency and to minimize damage to the surrounding area.[6] Tlatelolco established a multifaceted control system to verify compliance with the treaty's nonproliferation commitments that includes bilateral or multilateral IAEA safeguards, semi-annual reporting by the parties, and special inspections if violations are suspected. The treaty also established the Agency for the Prohibition of Nuclear Weapons in Latin America (OPANAL), as well as a five-member Council to oversee the control system and to support compliance and implementation of the treaty.

Two Additional Protocols to Tlatelolco apply the treaty's denuclearization provisions to territories in the zone under the responsibility of extra-territorial states, and provide negative security assurances to treaty parties. Both Protocols are in force for all eligible states, including the five NPT NWS (United States, United Kingdom, France, Russia, and China – the P5).

The successful negotiation of the Treaty of Tlatelolco became a model and inspiration for other NWFZs. And its Additional Protocols established the approach all subsequent NWFZs would pursue to link the NWS, in particular, to the zone. As interest in establishing NWFZs grew, international consideration of principles and guidelines for NWFZs intensified.

Emerging principles and guidelines for NWFZs

In 1975, an Ad Hoc Group of Governmental Experts under the auspices of the Geneva-based Conference of the Committee on Disarmament (now the Conference on Disarmament) undertook a comprehensive study of NWFZs, transmitting it to the United Nations in August of that year.[7] The study reflected an exhaustive analysis of, and range of views on, the NWFZ concept including on issues of scope, definitions, obligations of parties, responsibilities of extra-territorial states, and verification and compliance. Drawing on the Experts Study, the UN General Assembly adopted a definition of a NWFZ as any treaty-based zone established by a group of states that provides for the total absence of nuclear weapons in the zone, and for an international system of verification and control to ensure compliance.[8] In contrast to the obligations assumed by NNWS under the NPT, parties to NWFZs could not permit the deployment of nuclear weapons on their territories.

The UN definition also recognized the critical role of the NWS in realizing the objectives of NWFZs, specifically calling on the NWS to refrain from contributing in any way to a violation of the treaty or convention, to refrain from using or threatening to use nuclear weapons against the states included in the zone, and to accept these obligations in a legally binding instrument.[9] Under this approach, NWFZs, like the NPT, could reflect a balance of obligations between the NNWS Parties and the NWS.

The Final Document of the 1978 UN Special Session on Disarmament further encouraged the establishment of NWFZs, "on the basis of agreements or arrangements freely arrived among the states of the zone concerned," and reflecting the unique characteristics of each region.[10] In 1985, the United States signaled its support in principle for NWFZs that satisfied seven criteria including that there be adequate verification of compliance with the zone's provisions, and that the zone not interfere with a regional state's right to grant or deny transit privileges, nor impose restrictions on freedom of navigation on the high seas or international airspace.[11]

During the 1990s, the United Nations Disarmament Commission (UNDC) produced a set of agreed principles and guidelines for NWFZs that enjoy broad support today.[12] The UNDC report emphasized that the initiative for the zone should originate within the region concerned and that all regional states should participate in the negotiations on and the establishment of such a zone. The UNDC guidelines also called for consultations with the NWS during the negotiations of each treaty and its relevant protocol(s), and affirmed that any NWFZ should be in conformity with the principles and rules of international law, including the United Nations Convention on the Law of the Sea.

NWFZs gain ground

As membership in the global NPT regime grew, so, too, did frustration with the pace of super-power nuclear arms control and disarmament efforts. Nuclear-weapon-free zones offered a way for the NNWS to support nonproliferation and disarmament on their own terms. Consultations with the NWS would prove important, however, for securing their support as potential Protocol Parties, especially to obtain the legally binding negative security assurances that set NWFZ agreements apart from other nonproliferation measures.

South Pacific nuclear weapon-free zone: Treaty of Rarotonga

The South Pacific region, remote and thinly populated, had been an attractive location for nuclear testing including by the United States and the United Kingdom in the 1940s and 1950s. The conclusion of the Limited Test Ban Treaty (LTBT)[13] ended US and UK testing in the region, but France's decision to establish a nuclear test site in French Polynesia in 1963, together with growing concerns about the adverse impact of nuclear waste dumping on critical marine resources, energized South Pacific states to consider political options to protect the region. The South Pacific Forum endorsed a New Zealand proposal in 1975 to establish a NWFZ in the South Pacific. An Australian effort in 1983 to resurrect the initiative resulted in a meeting of the Forum the following year endorsing principles for such a zone and setting up a Working Group to develop a treaty text. The Working Group used the Treaty of Tlatelolco, Antarctic Treaty, Seabed Treaty, the LTBT, and the NPT as guides for its work.[14] The Treaty of Rarotonga (Cook Islands) was signed in August 1985, one short year after negotiations began. It entered into force in December 1986.

The Rarotonga Treaty prohibits the manufacture, acquisition, possession, or control of any nuclear explosive devices by its Parties anywhere inside or outside the Zone, and requires the Parties to prevent the testing or stationing of nuclear explosive devices within the zone. The treaty defines "nuclear explosive device" to preclude so-called "peaceful" nuclear explosives, acknowledging the international consensus that had emerged since the negotiation of the Tlatelolco Treaty and NPT that such PNEs were technically indistinguishable from nuclear explosives for military purposes. The treaty prohibits the dumping of radioactive wastes and other radioactive matter at sea anywhere in the zone, and the stationing of any nuclear explosive devices in the territories of the parties, and Parties remain free to decide whether to allow transit, port visits, and overflight of foreign ships and aircraft in the zone.

The treaty established a control system to verify Parties' compliance that includes NPT-type IAEA safeguards, information exchange and reporting, and a Consultative Committee that may be convened to consider any matter, including amendments or complaints. The Consultative Committee is empowered to call for a special inspection, as necessary.[15] A significant new feature was Rarotonga's provision to require comprehensive, NPT-type safeguards as a condition of nuclear supply to any NNWS, and that any nuclear export to a NWS be safeguarded.

Rarotonga has three Protocols to cover territories in the zone under the control of extra-territorial states; to provide negative security assurances for treaty parties, and to ban nuclear testing anywhere in the zone. All states eligible to adhere to the Protocols have signed and ratified them, except the United States. The United States has signed the three Protocols and submitted the ratification package to the US Senate on May 2, 2011.

African nuclear weapon-free zone: Treaty of Pelindaba

Concern about the spread of nuclear weapons and the consequences to inhabitants of French nuclear testing in the Sahara led the UN General Assembly to adopt a resolution in 1961 calling for Africa to be considered a denuclearized zone.[16] It was not until 1991, however, after South Africa had dismantled its small nuclear arsenal and acceded to the NPT as a NNWS, that the Organization of African Unity (OAU) established a Joint Group of Experts to draft a treaty to establish Africa as a NWFZ. A treaty text was completed and approved by African Heads of State in June 1995. The Treaty of Pelindaba was opened for signature on April 11, 1996 in Cairo where forty-seven of the fifty-three eligible African states signed. The treaty entered into force on July 15, 2009.

Like Tlatelolco and Rarotonga, Pelindaba Treaty Parties forswear the manufacture, stockpiling or other acquisition, possession or control over any nuclear explosive device by any means anywhere. But unlike those earlier NWFZ treaties, Pelindaba also prohibits research on any nuclear explosive devices, closing off a potential loophole but introducing a verification challenge. In recognition of South Africa's nuclear past, the treaty obligates its Parties to declare any capability to manufacture nuclear explosive devices, to dismantle and destroy any devices manufactured prior to the treaty coming into force, and to allow the IAEA and a Commission established by the treaty to verify the destruction and dismantling of devices and facilities. Like Rarotonga, the Pelindaba Treaty prohibits the dumping of radioactive wastes. It promotes nuclear science and technology for peaceful purposes, and encourages the Parties to make use of the IAEA's technical assistance program and to strengthen intra-regional cooperation to that end.

Pelindaba Parties undertake to conclude a comprehensive safeguards agreement with the IAEA to verify the nondiversion of nuclear material from peaceful use to use for nuclear explosives. Like Rarotonga, the treaty also requires that comprehensive safeguards be a condition of supply of any nuclear material to a NNWS. The treaty establishes the African Commission on Nuclear Energy (AFCONE) with responsibilities for ensuring compliance with the treaty by serving as a clearing house for national reports on matters pertaining to the treaty, and as a forum to consider complaints one Party may bring about the compliance of another. The Commission also is charged with promoting regional and international cooperation on the peaceful uses of nuclear energy in Africa.

In a departure from Tlatelolco and Rarotonga, African negotiators included provisions in the Pelindaba Treaty requiring the parties to maintain the highest standards of security and physical protection for nuclear materials, and prohibiting the parties from any action aimed at armed attacks against nuclear installations within the zone.[17] The Treaty of Pelindaba has three Protocols. Protocol I provides the important negative security assurance, while Protocol II prohibits nuclear testing in the zone. Protocol III covers territories in the zone under the control of extraterritorial states. Because they are the only countries still possessing territories in the region, only France and Spain are eligible to join Protocol III; France has done so. The five NWS signed Protocols I and II. All but the United States have ratified those Protocols. The US ratification package for the Pelindaba Protocols was submitted to the US Senate on May 2, 2011, together with the ratification package for the Treaty of Rarotonga.

Southeast Asian nuclear-weapon-free zone: Treaty of Bangkok

The process culminating in the conclusion of the Treaty of Bangkok establishing an NWFZ in Southeast Asia began in 1971 with a declaration by the original five members of the Association of Southeast Asian Nations (ASEAN) – Indonesia, Malaysia, the Philippines, Singapore, and Thailand – on a Zone of Peace, Freedom and Neutrality (ZOPFAN). Concerns about the presence of foreign military bases in the region, as well as the assumed presence of nuclear weapons, both spurred regional interest in establishing an NWFZ, and conspired to prevent progress on it. The United States, which had its own military base in the Philippines, was concerned that a treaty would not prevent the Soviet Union from stationing nuclear weapons in Vietnam.[18]

The end of the Cold War and the closure of the US bases in the Philippines provided an opening for ASEAN states to revive consideration of an NWFZ Treaty for Southeast Asia. Territorial disputes in the South China Sea between ASEAN members and nuclear-armed China provided a further incentive.

In 1993, ASEAN Foreign Ministers decided to establish a NWFZ in the region. Aided by the models provided by Tlatelolco and Rarotonga, the Treaty of Bangkok was opened for signature on December 15, 1995, where it was signed by all eligible Southeast Asian states.

The treaty's basic undertakings are the same as other zones: Parties commit not to develop, manufacture or otherwise acquire, possess or have control over, station or transport and test nuclear weapons inside or outside the zone, or to allow any other State to take such actions. A prohibition on dumping at sea or discharge in the atmosphere of any radioactive material or wastes by treaty parties or any other state is included as a basic undertaking. Parties are to use nuclear energy exclusively for peaceful purposes and to adhere to rigorous nuclear safety guidelines and standards. Disposal of radioactive wastes must be in accordance with IAEA standards.

Unlike previous zones, however, and out of concern for the unique geographic character of the region and its fragile ecosystem, the treaty's zone of application is defined to include not only the territories of all states in the region, but also their respective continental shelves and Exclusive Economic Zones (EEZ).[19]

Parties are required to conclude a full-scope (i.e., NPT) safeguards agreement with the IAEA covering their own peaceful nuclear activities, and to require appropriate IAEA safeguards as a condition of any export of nuclear material or equipment used in the production of nuclear material (NPT safeguards for NNWS and applicable IAEA safeguards in the case of exports to NWS). In another departure from previous zones, however, the Bangkok Treaty encourages its Parties to accede to the Convention on Early Notification of a Nuclear Accident.

The Bangkok Treaty provides that each Party may decide for itself whether to allow visits of foreign ships and aircraft, as well as transit of its airspace and navigation through territorial seas and archipelagic waters "in a manner not governed by the rights of innocent passage, archipelagic sea lanes passage or transit passage."

To oversee implementation and compliance, the treaty establishes a Commission of representatives from all the Parties, and a subsidiary body, the Executive Committee, charged with overseeing verification of the treaty consistent with the treaty's Control System consisting of IAEA safeguards, reports, and information exchange, and fact-finding missions that can be requested by a State Party to clarify and resolve ambiguous situations and to address compliance concerns. Detailed procedures governing Fact Finding Missions are contained in an annex to the treaty.

The Bangkok Treaty has a single Protocol, open to the P5, that obligates its Parties to respect the treaty, not to contribute to any act which would constitute a violation of the treaty or Protocol, and not to use or threaten to use nuclear weapons against treaty parties.

Unresolved concerns about the zone's application to EEZs, together with perceived inconsistencies within the treaty about its impact on its parties' freedom to grant or deny transit, overflight, and port visits, prevented the United States and other P5 from supporting the Protocol at the conclusion of negotiations. The regional states moved forward anyway, opening the Bangkok Treaty for signature on December 15, 1995, and welcoming its entry into force on March 28, 1997. The announcement by US Secretary of State Hillary Clinton at the 2010 NPT Review Conference that the United States would submit the Protocols to the Pelindaba and Rarotonga Treaties to the Senate for advice and consent to ratification, and that the United States would consult with the Parties to the Bangkok and Central Asian NWFZ (CANWFZ) Treaties in an effort to resolve the impediments to moving forward on their Protocols, provided a jump start to diplomatic engagement with ASEAN after almost ten years.

In 2011, the P5 and the Bangkok Treaty Parties, all members of the ASEAN, embarked on a process of consultations aimed at resolving the concerns some P5 had with the Protocol. Although no details were provided, at the East Asia Summit in November 2011, ASEAN welcomed the successful conclusion of negotiations with the P5 and announced that the Protocol would be signed in July 2012. The signing ceremony was postponed, however, when ASEAN determined that it would need additional time to consider the reservations that several P5 states indicated they intended to present upon signing.

Central Asian Nuclear Weapon-Free Zone (CANWFZ): Treaty of Semipalatinsk[20]

The break-up of the Soviet Union, the decision of three former Soviet states – Ukraine, Belarus, and Kazakhstan – to join the NPT as nonnuclear weapon states, and a legacy of nuclear-related environmental damage, especially in the area of the Soviet nuclear test site in Kazakhstan, provided an opening and an incentive for proponents of an NWFZ in Central Asia. Mongolia led the charge, declaring itself a NWFZ in 1992 while calling for a regional zone.

Proposals to establish a CANWFZ were offered by Uzbekistan in 1993, and again in 1994 joined by Kyrgyzstan. Agreement among the five states of Central Asia (C5) emerged in 1997 when the Presidents of Kazakhstan, Kyrgyzstan, Tajikistan, Turkmenistan, and Uzbekistan jointly issued the Almaty Declaration[21] that called for the establishment of a CANWFZ in connection with a broader call for action to address the environmental crisis in the Aral Sea

Basin and acknowledgement of the environmental impact of prior nuclear-weapon activities in the region.

With regional consensus on a way forward achieved, experts from the C5, the P5, the UN and IAEA met in Bishkek, Kyrgyzstan, in July 1998 to consider draft basic elements of a CANWFZ Treaty. Regional experts continued to meet with support from the UN and IAEA, reaching agreement on the basic provisions of the treaty by 2005. The CANWFZ Treaty that emerged obligated its parties not to conduct research on, develop, manufacture, stockpile or otherwise acquire, possess or have control over any nuclear weapon or other nuclear explosive device, and not to allow the stationing, storage or use of any nuclear weapons or other nuclear explosive devices in their territories. The treaty further barred the disposal of radioactive wastes of other states in the territories of the Parties but defines such wastes to permit the possible import of low- and medium-level waste.[22] It called on the Parties to assist efforts toward the environmental rehabilitation of territories contaminated as a result of past nuclear weapons and explosives activities, and banned nuclear explosions for any purpose in accordance with the Comprehensive Nuclear Test Ban Treaty (CTBT). Transit and transport of foreign ships and aircraft through territories within the zone was left to the discretion of each State Party. The treaty raised the verification bar by requiring that the Parties conclude an IAEA Additional Protocol in addition to an NPT safeguards agreement, and to require the same as a condition of supply of exports of nuclear material and equipment to NNWS.

The treaty established a consultative mechanism to review compliance and any other matter related to implementation, and provided for the possibility of dispute settlement. A single Protocol open to the NWS provides the essential legally binding negative security assurances that link the nuclear nonproliferation undertakings of the treaty parties with the NWS commitment not to use or threaten use of nuclear weapons against them.

Throughout the negotiation, the C5 states, and those supporting them, recognized the value of regular consultations with the P5. Efforts to address concerns shared by the United States, United Kingdom, and France (P3) over the relationship between the C5 and Russia, specifically the impact of the 1992 CIS Collective Security Treaty (Tashkent Treaty) between Russia and four of the C5 were not successful. The P3 sought assurances that the Tashkent Treaty would not take precedence over the CANWFZ Treaty, i.e., by sanctioning the redeployment of Russian nuclear weapons in Central Asia. In an effort to satisfy what some might argue was an internal contradiction between the objective of the NWFZ and established criteria that a zone should not disturb existing security arrangements to the detriment of regional security, the negotiators developed a text reflecting studied ambiguity.

Although ambiguity was not enough to assuage the concerns of the P3 at that time, the five Central Asian states signed the CANWFZ Treaty on September 8, 2006, and it entered into force on March 21, 2009. Following the US statement at the 2010 NPT Review Conference, the United States launched a renewed effort among the P5 and between the P5 and the C5 to address the obstacles to Protocol signature after 2010. While no reportable progress has been made to clear the way for signature, efforts are being made by both sides to find a way forward that satisfies all concerns.

Other zone proposals

Proposals have been made to establish NWFZs in South Asia, Central Europe, and Northeast Asia, but conditions do not exist in any of these regions that make establishment of a NWFZ that would satisfy established criteria a near- or medium-term proposition. The Arctic also has emerged as a possible candidate for a future NWFZ as climate change and the shrinking polar ice cap presage opportunities for increased military maritime activity there.

The Middle East, however, has assumed particular prominence in the nuclear-free zone debate as a consequence of the 1995 decision to link NPT Parties' support for establishing a Middle East Weapons of Mass Destruction Free Zone (MEWMDFZ) to the decision to extend the NPT indefinitely. The first proposal to establish an NWFZ in the Middle East was put forward by Iran and Egypt in 1974, but was broadened to include all weapons of mass destruction in a statement by Egyptian President Mubarak in 1990. Although the goal of such a zone has been embraced, at least in principle, by all regional states, political and security conditions in the Middle East, including the upheaval created by the Arab Spring, and noncompliance by several NPT Parties in the region have complicated discussions on a way forward. Notably, a key debate in recent years has been whether establishment of a WMDFZ would contribute to peace in the Middle East or whether conditions of peace must exist before such a zone can be created. That these same competing views were reflected in the 1975 CD Experts Study on NWFZs[23] demonstrates the difficulty of moving beyond long-held positions where there is intra-regional insecurity, instability, and conflict.

Leveraging NWFZs best practices to strengthen the global regime

While NWFZs supplement and reinforce the global NPT regime, they do not suffer the same internal tensions as the NPT with its membership divided between nuclear "haves" and "have-nots." The regional parties to each NWFZ Treaty all assume identical undertakings as nonnuclear-weapon states and are subject to the same verification and enforcement provisions. Comprehensive IAEA safeguards agreements are a requirement common to each NWFZ, and existing NWFZ treaties reflects their Parties' efforts to strengthen regional enforcement by establishing consultative mechanisms, dispute settlement provisions, and information exchange procedures to deal with compliance questions that may arise. These additional compliance and enforcement mechanisms increase the Parties' accountability to their neighbors, and regional ties among NWFZ parties create incentives for self-enforcement. For any state to violate the terms of the NWFZ treaty would risk undermining the entire structure of regional security.

As described above, certain regions have used their NWFZ treaty to address other issues including physical security and safety of nuclear materials (Pelindaba), regional environmental considerations through anti-dumping provisions (Rarotonga, Bangkok), export controls by requiring comprehensive safeguards as a condition of supply (Pelindaba, Rarotonga, CANWFZ), and strengthened safeguards by requiring Parties' adherence to the Additional Protocol (CANWFZ).

The Parties to NWFZs have recognized the value of coordination among the various zones, holding three conferences of NWFZ Focal Points since 2005 to share experiences and consult on ways to institutionalize greater cooperation among the zones including through regular sharing of information and best practices.[24] These meetings might be described as a "show of force" by the now more than 100 countries covered by NWFZs. Just as existing NWFZs served as models for subsequent zones, the solidarity on display at NWFZ conferences aims to generate support for additional NWFZs, including those that are not likely to be agreed to in the foreseeable future, as well as pressure on the NWS to accede to the various treaty protocols and step up their nuclear disarmament efforts. Discussions among NWFZ parties on best practices that led to efforts to conform the basic undertakings of the various NWFZ treaties, for example by making the IAEA Additional Protocol a requirement in all the agreements, or by ensuring that peaceful nuclear activities conducted by NWFZ parties meet international standards of physical security and nuclear safety, would strengthen the regional treaties while providing important reinforcement to the global nonproliferation regime.

By reinforcing the global nuclear nonproliferation regime including with robust verification and enforcement mechanisms for each region, NWFZs also benefit the NWS whose support for the Protocols is necessary to achieve the "balance" between NNWS commitment to foreswear nuclear weapons with NWS commitment not to use or threaten to use such weapons that was not attainable in the NPT. States party to NWFZ treaties, all of whom currently are also NPT Parties in good standing, have a legitimate interest in receiving assurances they will not be the target of weapons they have pledged not to possess. International calls for a global, nondiscriminatory NSA convention are unlikely to produce such an agreement for the same reasons that NPT negotiators found it too difficult to incorporate NSAs in that treaty. Nuclear-weapon-free zone treaties, however, offer the NWS the case-by-case opportunity many say they support, in principle, to transform national policies not to use or threaten to use nuclear weapons against certain states to legally binding obligations.

The cooperation of the NWS has been deemed "necessary for the maximum effectiveness" of such NWFZs and their Protocols.[25] To date, however, the record of the NWS in bringing these NSA Protocols into force is decidedly mixed. Although all five NWS have done so for the Treaty of Tlatelolco, it is the exception. When there has been inadequate consultation with the NWS during the negotiation of a NWFZ treaty, differences of interpretation are inevitable and have prevented the entry into force of the Protocols. Efforts by NWFZ negotiators to consult with the NWS and address their concerns during treaty negotiations, however, have not automatically shortened the period between treaty conclusion and the signature and/or ratification of the Protocols by all the NWS. The reasons for this vary from state-to-state and treaty-to-treaty: the P5 is not a monolith. But without such cooperation, the hurdles for the NWFZ Protocols are much higher. Involving the NWS early on in the process of developing a NWFZ enables them to prepare the ground for eventual adherence to the associated NWFZ protocols.

Even with the obstacles to unanimous NWS support for the existing NWFZ protocols, the security bargain among the NWFZ Parties, based on mutual nonacquisition of nuclear weapons and reinforced compliance and enforcement mechanisms, provides substantial benefits not only for regional security and stability, but for the global nuclear nonproliferation regime, as well.

Notes

1. The author is especially grateful to Mr Dean Rust, Dr Barclay Ward, and Dr William Potter for their valuable insights during the writing of this chapter. It does not represent the views of the US Department of State or the US Government. The views expressed are the author's, who takes full responsibility for them and any errors of fact. Negative security assurances are assurances by NWS that they will not threaten to or use nuclear weapons against NNWS. The NNWS reportedly sought assurances that they would not be vulnerable to nuclear threats, but the varied security interests of different groups of states and concerns about future contingencies prevented NWS agreement on a common NSA. See US Arms Control and Disarmament Agency (ACDA), *Arms Control and Disarmament Agreements: Texts and Histories of Negotiations*, 6th edition (Washington, DC: ACDA, 1990).
2. Excellent summaries of the histories of individual NWFZs, and treaty texts, have been prepared by the James Martin Center for Nonproliferation Studies, "NWFZ Clearinghouse," Monterey Institute of International Studies, April 28, 2010, http://cns.miis.edu/nwfz_clearinghouse.
3. Centre Virtuel de la Connaissance sur l'Europe (CVCE), "The Rapacki Plan," February 14, 1958, www.cvce.eu/content/publication/2005/12/22/c7c21f77-83c4-4ffc-8cca-30255b300cb2/publishable_en.pdf.
4. Ibid.

5. ACDA, *Arms Control and Disarmament Agreements*. Cuba's first conditions were met with Additional Protocol I which obligated states to apply the denuclearization provisions of the treaty to territories within the geographic zone for which, de jure or de facto, they are responsible. The treaty did not force the closure of Guantanamo.

6. The NPT also permitted the use of nuclear explosives for peaceful purposes as there was interest in using such technology for civil purposes, e.g., excavation for canals.

7. United Nations, "UN Document A/10027/Add. 1, Comprehensive Study of the Question of Nuclear-Weapon-Free-Zones in All its Aspects," October 8, 1975, www.un.org/disarmament/HomePage/ODAPublications/DisarmamentStudySeries/PDF/A-10027-Add1.pdf.

8. United Nations Agency for the Prohibition of Nuclear Weapons in Latin America and the Caribbean, "Comprehensive Study of the Question of Nuclear-Weapon-Free Zones in all its Aspects," UN General Assembly Resolution 3472 (XXX), December 11, 1975. www.un.org/disarmament/WMD/Nuclear/NWFZ.shtml.

9. Ibid.

10. United Nations, "UN Document S-10/2, Final Document of SSOD-1: Resolutions and Decisions of the Tenth Special Session of the General Assembly," May 23–June 30, 1978, www.un.org/disarmament/HomePage/SSOD/A-S-10-4.pdf.

11. In the third NPT Review Conference, the United States listed seven criteria for NWFZs, including: (1) The initiative for the creation of the zone should come from the States in the region concerned; (2) All States whose participation is deemed important should participate; (3) The zone arrangement should provide for adequate verification of compliance with its provisions; (4) The establishment of the zone should not disturb existing security arrangements to the detriment of regional and international security or otherwise abridge the inherent right of individual or collective self-defense guaranteed in the Charter of the United Nations; (5) The zone arrangement should effectively prohibit its Parties from developing or otherwise possessing any nuclear device for whatever purpose; (6) The establishment of the zone should not affect the existing rights of its Parties under international law to grant or deny other states transit privileges within their respective land territory, internal waters, and airspace to nuclear powered and nuclear capable ships and aircraft of nonparty nations, including port calls and overflights; and (7) The zone arrangement should not seek to impose restrictions on the exercise of rights recognized under international law, particularly the high seas freedoms of navigation and overflight, the right of innocent passage of territorial and archipelagic seas, the right of transit passage of international straits and the right of archipelagic sea lanes passage of archipelagic waters. See US State Department, "United States Information Pertaining to the Treaty on the Non-Proliferation of Nuclear Weapons," Third Review Conference of the Parties to the Treaty on the Non-Proliferation of Nuclear Weapons, NPT/CONF/III/18, July 29, 1985, p. 4, www.un.org/disarmament/WMD/Nuclear/pdf/finaldocs/1985%20-%20Geneva%20-%20NPT%20Review%20Conference%20-%20Final%20Document%20Part%20II.pdf.

12. United Nations, "Official Records of the General Assembly, Fifty-fourth Session, Supplement No. 42(A/54/42)," 1999, www.opanal.org/Docs/Desarme/NWFZ/A54_42iAnnexI.pdf.

13. The 1963 Limited Test Ban Treaty prohibited nuclear-weapon tests or any other nuclear explosions in the atmosphere, outer space, or under water.

14. James Martin Center for Nonproliferation Studies, "Inventory of International Nonproliferation Organizations and Regimes," Monterey Institute of International Studies, May 10, 2013, http://cns.miis.edu/inventory/.

15. For the text of the Rarotonga Treaty, and especially the treaty's discussion of the Consultative Committee, see International Atomic Energy Agency, "South Pacific Nuclear Free Zone Treaty," INFCIRC/331, February 1986, Articles 10–11, Annexes 3–4, www.iaea.org/Publications/Documents/Infcircs/Others/inf331.shtml.

16. United Nations, United Nations General Assembly (UNGA), "Resolution 1652 (SVI)," 1063rd Plenary Meeting, November 24, 1961, http://daccess-dds-ny.un.org/doc/RESOLUTION/GEN/NR0/167/05/IMG/NR016705.pdf?OpenElement.

17. In its article-by-article analysis of the treaty submitted to the US Senate on May 2, 2011, the United States reported that the drafters of the treaty were concerned principally with the risk of cross-border radioactive contamination in the event a facility containing nuclear materials was attacked, but that this obligation pertained only to treaty parties, not to protocol parties.

18. International Law and Policy Institute (ILPI) "An Introduction to the Issue of Nuclear Weapons in Southeast Asia," Background Papers, Nuclear Weapons Project, June 2013, http://nwp.ilpi.org/?p=2024.

19. The inclusion of EEZs in the treaty's definition of the zone of application was an obstacle for several NWS when the obligations under the Protocol were tied to the zone as defined by the Treaty. Not only was there no agreement on the boundaries of individual states' EEZs in Southeast Asia, but NSAs are generally interpreted as assurances provided to states, not geographical areas.

20. Not all of the Central Asian states accept the designation of "Treaty of Semipalatinsk" as the title for the treaty. Exchange with Dr William Potter, Director, James Martin Center for Nonproliferation, Monterey Institute of International Studies. Dr Potter served as an expert advisor to the C5 during the CANWFZ negotiations.

21. United Nations, "Use of Mercenaries as a Means of Violating Human Rights and Impeding the Exercise of the Rights of Peoples to Self-determination," UNGA A/52/112, annex, March 18, 1997, www.un.org/en/ga/search/view_doc.asp?symbol=A/RES/52/112&Lang=E

22. Scott Parrish and William Potter, "Central Asian States Establish Nuclear-Weapon-Free Zone Despite US Opposition," Monterey Institute of International Studies, James Martin Center for Nonproliferation Studies, September 5, 2006, http://cns.miis.edu/stories/060905.htm.

23. United Nations, "UN Document, A/10027/Add.1, Comprehensive Study of the Question of Nuclear-Weapon-Free-Zones in All its Aspects," October 8, 1975, pp. 39–40, www.un.org/disarmament/HomePage/ODAPublications/DisarmamentStudySeries/PDF/A-10027-Add1.pdf.

24. Mexico hosted the first conference of NWFZ Parties April 26–28, 2005. Mongolia hosted a follow-up conference in Ulaanbaatar in 2009. Chile hosted the third NWFZ conference on April 30, 2010 in New York.

25. United Nations Office for Disarmament Affairs, "Decision 2: Principles and Objectives for Nuclear Non-Proliferation and Disarmament," NPT/CONF.1995/32, 1995 Review and Extension Conference of the Parties to the Treaty on the Non-Proliferation of Nuclear Weapons, New York, April 17–May 12, 1995, www.un.org/disarmament/WMD/Nuclear/1995-NPT/pdf/NPT_CONF 199501.pdf.

23

LATIN AMERICA'S ROAD TO A REGION FREE OF NUCLEAR WEAPONS

Rafael Mariano Grossi

In times when billions are still being invested in modernization of nuclear weapons, when some countries are striving for development of advanced nuclear technology and at least one does not shy away from testing nuclear devices, the need for a stable and reliable nonproliferation regime is stronger than ever.

The existing regime with the Nonproliferation Treaty (NPT) at its cornerstone has been in place for several decades now but many argue that it has come to its limits in dealing effectively with the increasing nuclear challenges and threats. The nuclear cases that have been absorbing most of the world's attention in the last decade, in particular Iran's continuous uranium enrichment despite the international community's strong calls for Iran to suspend it, and the nuclear tests performed by the Democratic People's Republic of Korea (DPRK), are weakening the credibility of the regime, exposing its inability to arrive at a constructive and permanent solution to effectively deal with these issues. And the chronic stalemate surrounding the issue of the disarmament is in no way improving this delicate situation, but rather highlighting and intensifying the division between developed and developing countries, or the "haves and have nots."

But as a "silver bullet" that would resolve all of these concerns has yet to be invented, one could look into and hopefully draw some useful lessons from the already existing successful regional recipes to deal with the nuclear nonproliferation issue, one of them being nuclear-weapon-free zones (NWFZ). Created to prevent the development and spread of nuclear weapons, they could be seen as a practical mechanism to address some of the regional security issues, strengthening the existing nonproliferation regime and, more idealistically, bringing forward the vision of a world free of nuclear weapons. Analyzing the existing NWFZ and learning from their experience might prove to be a useful signpost for some regions on their road to a long-lasting and more stable and secure situation.

Acknowledging the importance of other regional initiatives, Latin America and the Caribbean present a distinctive example in the history of nuclear-weapon-free zones not only because the region had the privilege to become the very first NWFZ in the world, but also because the Treaty of Tlatelolco, which was opened for signature in 1967, presented several features that made the establishment of the zone possible even under difficult political circumstances of that time and place, marked by long-standing mutual suspicions, and for many even tacit competition between the two most advanced nuclear countries on the continent, Argentina and Brazil.

Certainly it is not conceivable or even wise to try to apply mechanically the Latin American model in its totality to other regions. Every region is politically different and what turned out to be successful in Latin America might fail if applied as such somewhere else in the world. Nevertheless, it is still worthwhile to examine the path of the countries of the region towards mutual trust and confidence and establishment of the first NWFZ, and to see if this model could be used for regions such as the Middle East or the Asian Subcontinent where nuclear is still a dividing factor and an impending risk, and the need for sustainable and peaceful solutions is crucial to the global security.

Tlatelolco as the first NWFZ Treaty

The establishment of a nuclear-weapon-free zone in Latin America and the Caribbean prohibiting all nuclear weapons in the region was possible thanks to a great effort and mobilization of the countries concerned. Brazil, Mexico, Chile, Ecuador, and Bolivia were at the forefront, believing that confidence-building, mutual trust and cooperation were key to prevent further spread of nuclear weapons and their technology. And although the road to ratification of the Treaty of Tlatelolco by all thirty-three parties was a rather complex process, the outcome proved to be beneficial for all parties involved and a certain stepping stone in the international community's efforts to pursue a stable and long-lasting nonproliferation regime.

Interestingly, the time the treaty was being discussed was characterized by one of the biggest nuclear crises in the history of the Cold War, namely the Cuban missile crisis. The proposal to establish the Latin American NWFZ was first presented by Brazil at the UN General Assembly in 1962, only a month before the United States was considering military action in Cuba after the Soviet attempt to install there nuclear missiles. These events had undoubtedly affected the perceptions of the Latin American governments and, as a consequence, strengthened their efforts to draw up a plan prohibiting development and stationing of any nuclear weapons on the continent.[1]Reducing the political influence of the two superpowers, Unites States and the Soviet Union, over the region was an additional incentive. And as the goal was very noble, the proposal to declare the whole region as a NWFZ gained the support of the vast majority of the Latin American countries and the United Nations General Assembly.

The Treaty for the Prohibition of Nuclear Weapons in Latin America and the Caribbean and its Additional Protocols was opened for signature in Tlatelolco, Mexico, in February 1967, after a couple of years of very intensive negotiations. This step was welcomed by the UN General Assembly in its resolution 2286 as an "event of a historic significance in the efforts to prevent the proliferation of nuclear weapons and to promote international peace and security."[2] Twenty-one Latin American and Caribbean states signed the treaty at the outset, sending a strong message to the international community and affirming the Latin American conviction in favor of the proscription of nuclear weapons.[3]

Yet, arriving at the conclusion of the treaty was demanding and required fine diplomatic skills, creativity, and flexibility to prepare a document acceptable to all countries, including the more reluctant ones, like Argentina or later Brazil. At that time, Argentina had a very advanced civil nuclear program and although no decision regarding a possible development of nuclear weapons had been contemplated, some in the country feared that a NWFZ might obstruct Argentina's plans for further advancements in the nuclear field.

Simultaneously, when the military government took over in Brazil after the coup in 1964, the country turned from a great supporter of the initiative to a skeptical negotiating partner. Brazil's sudden change of heart overshadowed the negotiations and gave Argentina's own lukewarm position on the treaty additional leverage. Unsurprisingly, both countries proved to have similar demands concerning the treaty, rooted in their advancement in nuclear technology in comparison to their neighbors. Their apprehensions, and desire to preserve the right of decision in all aspects of nuclear policy, were the drivers behind their reluctance to support the treaty.[4] An evident example of the convergence of Brazil's and Argentina's positions was their interpretation of the treaty as allowing nuclear explosions for peaceful purposes, which contrasted sharply with the views of other Latin American countries. On the other hand, both opted for a full prohibition of transportation of nuclear devices through the zone by nuclear-weapon states whereas others believed that such should be decided individually by each interested party.[5] Eventually the standpoints of the two biggest nuclear players on the sub-continent remained crucial for the negotiations and shaped the provisions of the treaty, making it a unique and an adaptable one.

The treaty entered into force on April 25, 1969, one year earlier than the treaty on Nuclear Nonproliferation (NPT), which was being negotiated almost simultaneously. Eleven states of the region ratified it at the outset; others, like Argentina, Brazil, Chile, or Cuba, took more time to complete the process. Eventually, the treaty had been ratified by all concerned parties thirty-three years after it was first opened for signature, Cuba being the last one to do so in 2002.

Given the political situation in the region, and the apprehension towards the treaty expressed by some states, the provision for its entry into force as laid down in Article 28 that required all relevant countries to deposit their instruments of ratification, the ratification of the two additional protocols and the conclusion of bilateral safeguards agreements with the International Atomic Energy Agency (IAEA), could have been seen as demotivating. However, a very clever maneuver attributed to the Mexican Chief delegate, Ambassador Alfonso Garcia Robles, made it possible to waive the conditions laid down in Article 28, which was synonymous with the treaty entering into force immediately for those willing to do so.[6] Others, who for some reason believed the time for the treaty taking effect on their territory was not yet right, were allowed to delay its entry into force as long as they believed necessary.[7] Agreeing to this ingenious approach, the states of the region understood that although the objectives of the treaty were commonly shared, political conditions were not yet ripe and required the creation of an intermediate, transitional phase. That way states could choose the most acceptable moment for the treaty to enter into force but at the same time it obliged them not to take any actions contrary to its provisions and made it possible for them to stay closely connected through the Meeting of the Signatories, as stipulated in Article 6.[8]

Brazil is a very good example of how this approach worked in real life. The country ratified the treaty right in the beginning but did not waive the conditions of Article 28, which meant that it would enter into force for Brazil only after ratification by all other states of the region or if Brazil eventually decided to waive the conditions. Eventually Brazil agreed to the second option in 1994, after Argentina's ratification and immediate entry into force in the very same year. The creative solution to the ratification made the treaty acceptable, and most of all viable, for the region.

In order to ensure its proper management and implementation, the treaty established an intergovernmental administrative organ called the Agency for the Prohibition of Nuclear Weapons in Latin America and the Caribbean (OPANAL), which originally was supposed to be a verification authority safeguarding nuclear activities in the countries of the zone. But this aspect never really materialized as it was understood that OPANAL could not have the technical capabilities required to perform verification.[9] Therefore this verification role was handed over to the IAEA. And each party to the treaty was obliged to accept full scope IAEA safeguards, putting all their nuclear activities under the IAEA's control. In an effort to ensure Brazil's and Argentina's adherence to the treaty, in 1992 the IAEA was granted exclusive rights to perform so called "special inspections."[10] OPANAL's largely formalistic role became limited to monitoring the observance of the treaty's provisions and the control system by its parties. According to the rules, any violation of the treaty may be reported by the General Conference of OPANAL to the UN Security Council and the UN General Assembly as well as the Organization of American States (OAS) for their further action. Undoubtedly, moving the responsibility for verification from a regional and, at the time, inexperienced organization lacking the technical capacity to perform a controlling role, to an international body such as the IAEA, whose main activity has been safeguarding of nuclear material and installations worldwide, strengthened and at the same time made credible the verification system for the zone.

Brazil and Argentina nuclear cooperation

Obviously, the relationship between Argentina and Brazil, the two biggest and most advanced nuclear countries on the continent, has been a conditioning factor for the whole region. An apparent competitive factor in some of the areas of the bilateral relationship included the nuclear one. Without an improvement and rapprochement in their overall relations and a decisive move towards cooperation instead of competition, chances for a successful completion of the NWFZ project would have been minimal. Confidence building was therefore crucial but it was also a long process requiring plenty of goodwill and farsightedness of their leaders. It took several years and many bilateral agreements and declarations before the two countries were able to build a relationship that could be characterized by mutual trust.

Regarding its nuclear status, Argentina started its development as early as in the 1950s as a part of the IAEA's Atom for Peace Program. Its first commercial nuclear power reactor, the first in Latin America, was brought into operation in 1974. Argentina had good experience in all the main technologies, including the most sensitive ones like reprocessing, having operated a reprocessing lab-scale plant from 1969 to 1973. It also had a small and indigenously constructed uranium enrichment unit in Pilcaniyeu using gaseous diffusion technology. The existence of this facility was secret for many years and was announced to the world only in 1983 together with an explanation that it was meant to produce low-enriched uranium for the country's research reactor as well as for export. Brazil's first commercial nuclear power plant followed eight years after Argentina's, in 1982. Enrichment activities were launched at the Navy Experimental Center in Sao Paulo in 1987.

Yet, although at different stages of nuclear advancement and determined to develop individual independent nuclear programs, the first agreement referring to cooperation for the development and application of the peaceful uses of nuclear energy dates back to 1980.[11] Already then, both nations were aware that cooperation would be more beneficial than competition and started moving towards strengthening ties.

There were several factors that influenced that kind of cooperation, including their common and critical position towards the international nonproliferation regime manifested in strong reluctance to join the NPT and a strong belief on the right of every country to acquire advanced nuclear technology.[12] This suspicion on the perceived dangers inherent to the international nonproliferation regime brought them closer together.

However, the refusal to join NPT had its downsides. Combined with the enrichment attempts, it made the world suspicious that both countries' ultimate goal could have been the development of nuclear weapons. This perception was strengthened by the leading role that military played in the development of the respective nuclear programs especially in Brazil, and the inability to inspect the enrichment facilities as both countries remained outside the IAEA full-scope safeguards agreements. In a way, these actions were an expression of the nuclear independence that both wanted to preserve.[13]

Sitting in the same boat, they made a steady effort to improve cooperation not only in nuclear but also other fields, including economics and culture. In the years between 1980 and 1994, numerous declarations were signed that strengthened their collaboration in several fields and started a fully new era in their relations.

The return of civilian governments in Argentina in 1983 and Brazil in 1985 proved to be immensely helpful. The Iguacu Declaration on Nuclear Policy of 1985 established a Joint Working Group with the purpose of instituting a regular channel for dialogue and exchange of information to ensure that nuclear programs were only for peaceful purposes. Another significant initiative on the road of dialogue and cooperation was undertaken by Argentina's first president after the return to a democratic rule, Raul Alfonsin, in 1987. Alfonsin had his doubts about the real intentions of the previous military regime and wanted to exclude the possibility of a nuclear arms race in the region altogether. The announcement of Argentina's enrichment program on the eve of his assumption of the presidency in 1983 had left a deep impression on Alfonsin, who decided that democracy needed to assert itself over the established mind-set of those responsible for the nuclear program in the country. That prompted him to make a move against the preferences of the nuclear constituency in Argentina and invite Brazil's President Jose Sarney to visit Argentina's uranium enrichment facility in the Patagonian desert. This generous and surprising gesture made it almost impossible for his counterpart not to reciprocate and was followed by a visit of Argentina's president to the Brazilian enrichment site in Ipero. Although symbolic in nature, both invitations were very meaningful in providing transparency to nuclear activities.

This long confidence-building process eventually culminated in the presidential meeting of Argentina's Carlos Menem and Brazil's Fernando Collor de Mello[14] in Iguazu Falls in 1990, where they made very clear and concrete declarations. Of particular importance was the agreement to create a bilateral system of nuclear accounting and control, to adhere to the IAEA safeguards and the Treaty of Tlatelolco (after some amendments were introduced), and to renounce nuclear weapons. The Guadalajara Agreement that was signed right after this historic meeting sealed these commitments and eventually, by applying a mix of diplomacy and goodwill, the two major competitors became real partners whose cooperation was a significant step towards achieving the goal of the region free of nuclear weapons.

An independent Brazilian-Argentine Agency for Accounting and Control of Nuclear Materials (ABACC) was established in 1991 and entrusted with the administration of the Common System of Accounting and Control of Nuclear Materials (SCCC). The bilateral system was meant to monitor and verify the nuclear material being used in nuclear activities in both countries and ensure that it was not being diverted into any military purposes that the agreement prohibits. At the same time, the Argentine and Brazilian governments, the ABACC and the IAEA started negotiating the implementation of the IAEA safeguards in the two countries. These negotiations were concluded by signing a Quadripartite Agreement in 1991 dividing the verification responsibilities between the ABACC and the IAEA, a decision that undoubtedly satisfied the international community's demands for more control.[15]

The Argentina-Brazil agreement that came into force in 1994 paved the way for Argentina to ratify the Treaty of Tlatelolco, and for Brazil to waive the condition under Article 28 the very same year after amendments proposed by Brazil, Argentina, and Chile were agreed.[16] Eventually, both countries also joined the NPT as nonnuclear-weapon states, Argentina in 1994 and Brazil in 1998.

The question why the initial skepticism and reluctance towards the NPT changed can be explained on two levels: national and international. The first one had to do with the establishment of a binational system of nuclear material accounting. The second one could be drawn to the fact that the decision to change direction – at least in the sense of accepting long resisted norms like the NPT – was taken autonomously and was not imposed from outside. It was an independent move of two sovereign countries that decided to contribute to international peace and security by committing themselves to using nuclear technology only for peaceful purposes and preventing further spread of nuclear weapons.

Latin America NWFZ as a possible model for other regions

Trust and confidence are clear prerequisites for fruitful and sustainable cooperation and the experience of Latin America and the Caribbean shows that reaching that level is possible even under difficult political circumstances. It should encourage others to move towards a constructive dialogue and diplomacy, towards strengthening ties and collaboration despite political complexity. In some cases, such as the Middle East or the Asian Subcontinent, the Latin American experience could serve as a possible model for the establishment of a zone free of nuclear weapons, which would contribute decisively to regional and international peace and security.

But before one can even consider the possibility of going that far, several important steps towards improving the situation and relations in these regions could and need to be taken to create a proper environment for discussions that should eventually contribute to a gradual confidence building.

Taking Brazil and Argentina as an example, the two countries were the only ones on the continent well advanced in nuclear technology and keeping an ambiguous stance on the development of nuclear weapons. Still, they managed to gradually build trust through highly visible and reciprocal visits of the respective heads of state, which were followed by exchanges of a technical nature. This process was crucial towards their ratification of the Treaty of Tlatelolco, becoming part of the regional NWFZ, and also joining the NPT.

Looking at the Middle East, achieving this level of confidence seems to be more difficult. Israel's position on their possession of nuclear weapons, which is tantamount to a "neither confirm nor deny" policy, creates a challenge since it is seen by the Arab States as one of the obstacles for a conclusive dialogue. At the same time, repeated violations of treaty obligations by some states in the region, like Iraq, Libya, Iran, or Syria, do not contribute to an atmosphere of cooperation and trust either. Small steps are needed but the more complicated the situation, the more rewarding even a tiny success.

International initiatives

In the case of the Middle East, assistance from the international community plays a very important role. Up to now, several initiatives have been undertaken in this regard, the first one being the United Nations General Assembly (UNGA) Resolution in 1974. This resolution calling for the establishment of a NWFZ was originally proposed by Egypt and Iran and has been adopted annually by UNGA ever since, and as of 1980, even without a vote.[17] Other efforts include multiple resolutions by the UN Security Council, the NPT Review Conference,[18] and the IAEA General Conference.[19]

But it was only recently that despite all the differences of views and difficulties in convincing the interested parties to come to the table, some positive developments made it look like the time was ripe for discussions and moving the issue forward. The first one was the agreement between the United States, Russia, and the United Kingdom at the 2010 NPT Review Conference, to hold in 2012 a regional conference devoted to the subject. The second was the convening of the IAEA Forum on Experience of Possible Relevance to the Creation of a Nuclear Weapon Free Zone in the Middle East in 2011.

Starting with the latter, it should be pointed out that the decision to organize such a forum was taken by the IAEA General Conference already in 2000 but it took eleven years until the conditions and general atmosphere allowed for it to be eventually convened.[20] The principal idea of the Forum was to use the experience of the already existing zones and study the processes and conditions that led to their establishment in the context of the Middle East region. Clearly this was more of a theoretical exercise, but it helped to better visualize the various concepts and their possible relevance for a Middle East NWFZ (MENWFZ).

As Assistant Director General at the IAEA at that time, I helped Director General Yukiya Amano to coordinate together with the designated Chair, Ambassador Jan Petersen of Norway, the months-long consultation process leading to the IAEA Forum that helped to build up a consensus on the forum and a positive atmosphere around it. The discussions both before and during the two days of the forum showed that given the adequate political guarantees and clear parameters all parties have an interest in engaging in a dialogue. One common denominator was the recognition that obstacles such as lack of trust, difficult inter-state relations, and a complicated geopolitical situation were as true for other regions as they are for the Middle East, but that they can be overcome by good will and a commitment to a dialogue. This, as well as other suggestions made during the forum, such as building confidence among the interested parties and using every opportunity that arises on the international agenda to break the impasse, was underlined as crucial elements of the equation.[21] And although the IAEA forum might not have been a major breakthrough, its relevance to the process should be seen in the open approach and willingness of all involved to come to the table, listen and discuss, and thereby create an impetus for further deliberations.

The positive experience of the IAEA Forum undoubtedly created a momentum for the 2012 conference, as agreed at the NPT Review Conference. The preparatory process showed immediately that the political agreement to host a Conference would not translate automatically into such an event actually taking place. It took more than a year until the Finnish Undersecretary of State Jaakko Laajava was designated by the United Nations Secretary General as the facilitator and Finland as a host of the conference. 2012 was to be a breakthrough in the process. The disappointment was high when, despite the very concrete preparatory steps and intensive consultations held by the Finnish diplomat, the 2012 conference was cancelled or rather postponed without a clear date. The inability to conduct it as planned resulted in a loss of momentum for bringing the issue a step forward and again created mistrust and a feeling of powerlessness, especially as the reasons for the postponement did not seem to be very clear.[22]Without a new official date, the atmosphere is tense as shown by the NPT Preparatory Committee in Geneva in April 2013, when Egypt left the meeting in protest against postponement of the conference.

The failure to convene the announced 2012 conference so far has been an unfortunate setback for the Middle East NWFZ. The tensions that it created underscore the fact that the efforts to bring the process forward should not slow down and that all necessary steps need to be taken to enable the conference to happen. The current impasse can only be overcome by the active participation and close collaboration of the international community and directly involved parties.

Processes and substance

When discussing the possibility of a Middle East NWFZ, certain aspects of experience related to the Tlatelolco Treaty could be of interest. Possibly one of the most relevant provisions would be the procedure for the treaty's entry into force. Although several countries were not necessarily supportive of the NWFZ in the beginning, and it would take years before the Treaty of Tlatelolco entered into force for them, the mechanism suggested by Garcia Robles made it possible for the treaty to become active for several countries before all of them ratified it. At the same time, the mere fact of the treaty's entry into force for the vast majority of the countries created an undeniably strong pressure on Argentina and Brazil to eventually follow suit. This mechanism could also be explored when discussing a NWFZ in the Middle East. Considering the mistrust and lack of confidence in the region, such flexibility would allow countries to choose the most appropriate moment for ratification of a treaty and, what is most important, it would encourage discussions and allow for a confidence-building process to continue to create necessary conditions for further engagement.[23] In this connection, the establishment for the Middle East of an equivalent of OPANAL could prove to be a useful standing forum for nuclear related matters on a routine basis.[24]

The Latin American experience also means creation of a regional safeguards system in a form of the ABACC. Such regional verification organization bringing together scientists and practitioners from countries involved might be attractive in the Middle East, and in particular for Pakistan and India. The Quadripartite Agreement and ABACC have been seen as a temporary alternative to the Additional Protocol (AP) that both Brazil and Argentina have yet to conclude. As much as the official adherence to the AP would reassure the international community and nuclear industry possibly even more, it has been acknowledged that the guarantees put in place through ABACC and its system of routine inspections at nuclear facilities are satisfying. If adding the IAEA's final assessment of the reports on the outcome of the inspections on top of this structure, the created system provides for a high degree of confidence that no forbidden nuclear activities are actually taking place.[25] This has even been recognized recently by the Nuclear Suppliers Group (NSG) that accepted the Quadripartite Agreement as an "alternative to the Additional Protocol."[26]

From a national perspective, Argentina benefited greatly from submitting its nuclear program to safeguards and becoming a member of the NPT. Accepting all commitments under the treaty, Argentina became a member of the NSG and with this access was able to export its nuclear technology to developing and industrialized countries alike, a move that put its civilian nuclear program back on track after the stagnation of its domestic nuclear industry in the 1980s. This would not have been possible without Argentina's commitment to the nonproliferation regime. This economic and commercial calculation might also act as an incentive for India, Pakistan or Israel to seek solutions allowing them to become part of the international nonproliferation regime and fully and without exception enjoy its benefits, such as the access to the nuclear market that is currently nonexistent or, as in case of India, limited.

Admittedly, there are evident differences between the above mentioned regions and Latin America. In South America the situation was never as difficult and tense. Argentina and Brazil were never enemies but only competitors. They were suspicious of each other's activities but were not in a military conflict. They might have been considering, but never actually developed, nuclear weapons. They solved any controversies that could have ended up in a more serious confrontation, like the dispute over shared water resources in the Rio de la Plata area,[27] before they entered into serious negotiations and cooperation on nuclear issues.[28]

The relations between the Arab States and Israel, and between the two South Asian countries, are much more complex and tainted by decades of war and violence. First and foremost, there is an issue of possession of nuclear weapons. Nuclear weapons make up an integral part of the military doctrine in both India and Pakistan and Israel is widely believed to be the only country in the Middle East to possess such weapons, even if the Israeli government has never confirmed their actual existence. Giving them up or even only submitting themselves to international or regional control mechanisms would require a huge amount of trust and an enormous amount of goodwill on all sides.

Taking all of this into consideration, the prospect for a positive development in a form of a zone free of nuclear weapons might appear to be gloomy, and certainly the task before both regions is not an easy one. Establishing a nuclear-weapon-free zone will be a long process requiring plenty of patience and creative diplomacy. But the Latin American experience can give some useful advice on how to start and even on how to proceed. A gradual approach, taking regional aspects and peculiarities into consideration should be developed. This would be crucial for the creation of a stable, peaceful environment for discussions without any assignment of guilt. Further down the road, certain elements of transparency and confidence building like creating cooperative structures aimed at building confidence will be important stepping stones towards setting up joint mechanisms. It is here where other regional experiences and the involvement of experts having taken part in such initiatives could play a very useful role.

Conclusions

Nuclear-weapon-free zones definitely have a potential to contribute to the establishment of a world where nuclear weapons do not have a place. Latin America's valuable experience as the first such zone in the world has inspired and paved the way for the others. Currently five NWFZs in Latin American, Africa, Central Asia, Southeast Asia, and the South Pacific cover 133 countries, which is a remarkable achievement.

In the case of Latin America and the Caribbean, the developments were marked and heavily influenced by Brazil-Argentina relations and the gradual confidence building which eventually culminated in their access to the NPT and the creation of a safeguards system for verification of nondiversion of nuclear material. Being very important for the international nonproliferation regime, these commitments consolidated a stable regional framework upon which both countries could embark on far reaching economic and social integration processes.

Experience shows that it should not be impossible for the Middle East or the Asian Subcontinent to achieve the same level of trust and confidence as is currently enjoyed by countries in the Latin America and Caribbean region. Learning from the experience of the others and applying its most fitting parts to one's situation should be at the forefront. The international community plays a very important role in all of this. The United Nations, the IAEA, the Preparatory Commission for the Comprehensive Test Ban Treaty Organization, regional organizations, nuclear powers and other interested parties need to work together to show the way. Without their full support and active involvement in respective areas of expertise, success would be limited, if not impossible. And the stakes are high. An eventual renouncement of nuclear weapons by India, Pakistan, and Israel, establishing a zone free of nuclear weapons and joining the NPT as nonnuclear-weapon states would not only bring peace and security to the respective regions, as it did in Latin America, but would also be a hugely stabilizing factor for the whole world.

Notes

1. Monica Serrano, "Common Security in Latin America-Treaty of Tlatelolco," Research Paper, University of London 1992, pp. 19–25; John R. Redick, "Latin America's Emerging Nonproliferation Consensus," *Arms Control Today*, Vol. 24, No. 2 (March 1994), p. 3.
2. United Nations General Assembly, "Consolidation of the Regime Established by the Treaty for the Prohibition of Nuclear Weapons in Latin America and the Caribbean (Treaty of Tlatelolco)," Resolution No. 58/31, November 20, 2000, https://gafc-vote.un.org/UNODA/vote.nsf/91a5e1195dc97a630525656f005b8adf/e9a22d2025d8729385256dc20059fcc7?OpenDocument&ExpandSection=5.
3. John R. Redick, "Tlatelolco and Regional Nonproliferation Initiatives," Agency for the Prohibition of Nuclear Weapons in Latin America and the Caribbean (OPANAL), 1995, www.opanal.org/Articles/cancun/can-Redick.htm.
4. John R. Redick, "Nuclear Illusions: Argentina and Brazil," Occasional Paper No. 25, The Henry L. Stimson Center, December, 1995, pp.16–18, www.acamedia.info/politics/IRef/StimsonC/redick.pdf; Redick, "Tlatelolco and Regional Nonproliferation Initiatives."
5. Redick, "Nuclear Illusions," p. 17.
6. Ambassador Alfonso Garcia Robles was awarded a Nobel Peace Prize in 1982 for his contribution to disarmament and efforts in the establishment of the Latin America and the Caribbean NWFZ.
7. Paul D. Beamont and Thomas Rubinsky, "An Introduction to the Issue of Nuclear Weapons in Latin America and the Caribbean," Background Paper, No. 2, Nuclear Weapons Project, International Law and Policy Institute, December 2012, pp. 5–6.
8. Ibid.
9. Julio Carasales, "The Argentine-Brazilian Nuclear Rapprochement," *The Nonproliferation Review*, Vol. 2, No. 3 (Spring-Summer 1995), p. 43, http://cns.miis.edu/npr/pdfs/carasa23.pdf.
10. Jozef Goldblat, "Nuclear-Weapon-Free Zones: A History and Assessment," *The Nonproliferation Review*, Vol. 4, No. 3 (Spring-Summer 1997), p.21, http://cns.miis.edu/npr/pdfs/goldbl43.pdf.
11. In 1980, Brazil and Argentina signed the very first nuclear agreement that allowed them to cooperate in the field of peaceful uses of nuclear energy, including exchange of information and materials.
12. Redick, "Latin America's Emerging Nonproliferation Consensus," p. 5.
13. Clovis Brigagao and Marcelo F. Valle Fonrouge, "A Regional Model of Confidence Building for Nuclear Security in Argentina and Brazil," *The International Journal of Peace Studies*, Vol. 3, No. 2 (July 1998), www.gmu.edu/programs/icar/ijps/vol3_2/Brigagao.htm.
14. President Collor de Mello is well known for his opposition to nuclear explosions and much publicized decision to close down a nuclear test site at the Air Force base in Serra do Cachimbo in September 1990.
15. Redick, "Nuclear Illusions," p. 28.
16. For more information on the amendments see Redick, "Nuclear Illusions."
17. In 1980, Israel joined the consensus to adopt the resolution without a vote.
18. The 1995 NPT Review Conference adopted a resolution sponsored by the United States, Russia, and the United Kingdom calling for creation of a Weapons of Mass Destruction Free Zone.
19. IAEA General Conference Resolutions on the Application of IAEA safeguards in the Middle East call for the application of safeguards on all nuclear facilities in the region "as a necessary step for the establishment of the NWFZ."
20. International Atomic Energy Agency, "Application of IAEA Safeguards in the Middle East," General Conference Decision, GC(44)/DEC/12, September 22, 2000, www.iaea.org/About/Policy/GC/GC44/GC44Decisions/English/gc44dec-12_en.pdf.
21. Summary of the IAEA Forum on Experience of Possible Relevance to the Creation of a Nuclear Weapon Free Zone in the Middle East.
22. The United States said in a statement that the conditions in the Middle East and the lack of agreement between the participating states prevented the conference from convening. Russia's official reason for the postponement was the lack of agreement of all states in the region to participate in the conference.
23. Redick, "Tlatelolco and Regional Nonproliferation Initiatives."
24. Ibid.
25. David S. Jonas, John Carlson, and Richard S. Goorevich, "The NSG Decision on Sensitive Nuclear Transfers: ABACC and the Additional Protocol," *Arms Control Today*, Vol. 42, No. 9 (November 2012),

pp. 14–17, www.armscontrol.org/act/2012_11/The-NSG-Decision-on-Sensitive-Nuclear-Trans fers-ABACC-and-the-Additional-Protocol.

26. Government of Brazil, Ministry of Foreign Affairs, "Nuclear Suppliers Group (NSG)," Press Release, No. 237, June 24, 2011.

27. The dispute between Brazil and Argentina over Rio de la Plata was caused by Brazil's plans to build a hydropower plant in Itaipu that would have helped Brazil to solve its problems with energy supplies. Argentina was objecting to this project for various reasons, but one of them being the fear that such plant would compromise Argentina's projects for this area, such as the construction of another big hydropower project, the Corpus Dam. Eventually, the Tripartite Agreement signed in 1979 by Argentina, Brazil, and Paraguay solved the controversy.

28. Paulo S. Wrobel, "From Rivals to Friends: The Role of Public Declarations in Argentina-Brazil Rapprochement," in *Declaratory Diplomacy: Rhetorical Initiatives and Confidence Building*, edited by Michael Krepon, Jenny S. Drezin, and Michael Newbill (Washington, DC: Henry L. Stimson Center, April 1999), pp. 136–137.

24

THE WMD-FREE ZONE IN THE MIDDLE EAST

Where is it heading?

Mohamed I. Shaker

The establishment of a Weapons of Mass Destruction Free Zone (WMDFZ) in the Middle East has been a long-held goal. The following comments constitute a modest attempt to draw a preliminary framework of the main elements that can pave the way for a future zone. The time has come to think seriously about a real and vibrant zone and identify the challenges and the opportunities ahead. Principally, this chapter highlights this preliminary work as a means of providing confidence to all states and initiating a meaningful dialogue on regional security.

The long-standing interest in a Middle East WMDFZ

The proposal for the establishment of a zone free of nuclear weapons in the Middle East dates back to 1974 when the governments of Iran and Egypt called for such an arrangement at the UN General Assembly. As a result, the General Assembly adopted Resolution 3263, which stated that the General Assembly, after "having considered the question of the establishment of a nuclear-weapon-free zone in the region of the Middle East,"

1. *Commends* the idea of the establishment of a nuclear-weapon-free zone in the region of the Middle East;
2. *Considers that*, in order to advance the idea of a nuclear-weapon-free zone in the region of the Middle East, it is indispensable that all parties concerned in the area proclaim solemnly and immediately their intention to refrain on a reciprocal basis, from producing, testing, obtaining, acquiring or in any way possessing nuclear weapons;
3. *Calls upon* the parties concerned in the area to accede to the Treaty on the Non-Proliferation of Nuclear Weapons;
4. *Expresses the hope* that all States, in particular the nuclear-weapon States, will lend their full co-operation for the effective realization of the aims of the present resolution;
5. *Requests* the Secretary-General to ascertain the views of the parties concerned with respect to the implementation of the present resolution, in particular with regard to its paragraphs 2 and 3, and to report to the Security Council

at an early date and, subsequently, to the General Assembly at its thirtieth session;

6. *Decides* to include in the provisional agenda of its thirtieth session the item entitled "Establishment of a nuclear-weapon-free zone in the region of the Middle East."[1]

In 1991, on Egypt's recommendation, the zonal idea was reaffirmed and its scope was extended to include the other two categories of weapons of mass destruction, that is, chemical and biological weapons, stating that the General Assembly:

1. Urges all parties directly concerned to consider seriously taking the practical and urgent steps required for the implementation of the proposal to establish a nuclear-weapon-free zone in the region of the Middle East in accordance with the relevant resolutions of the General Assembly, and, as a means of promoting this objective, invites the countries concerned to adhere to the Treaty on the Non-Proliferation of Nuclear Weapons;

2. Calls upon all countries of the region that have not done so, pending the establishment of the zone, to agree to place all their nuclear activities under International Atomic Energy Agency safeguards;

3. Invites all countries of the region, pending the establishment of a nuclear-weapon-free zone in the region of the Middle East, to declare their support for establishing such a zone, consistent with paragraph 63 (d) of the Final Document of the Tenth Special Session of the General Assembly, and to deposit those declarations with the Security Council;

4. Also invites those countries, pending the establishment of the zone, not to develop, produce, test or otherwise acquire nuclear weapons or permit the stationing on their territories, or territories under their control, of nuclear weapons or nuclear explosive devices;

5. Invites the nuclear-weapon States and all other States to render their assistance in the establishment of the zone and at the same time to refrain from any action that runs counter to both the letter and the spirit of the present resolution;

6. Invites all parties to consider the appropriate means that may contribute towards the goal of general and complete disarmament and the establishment of a zone free of weapons of mass destruction in the region of the Middle East;

7. Requests the Secretary-General to conduct further consultations with the States of the region and other concerned States, on the basis of the study undertaken by him in accordance with paragraph 8 of resolution 43/65, as well as the views and suggestions submitted by Member States in accordance with paragraph 9 of resolution 45/52, taking into account the evolving situation in the region, to explore further the ways and means of establishing a nuclear-weapon-free zone in the Middle East;

8. Also requests the Secretary-General to submit to the General Assembly at its forty-seventh session a report on the implementation of the present resolution;

9. Decides to include in the provisional agenda of its forty-seventh session the item entitled "Establishment of a nuclear-weapon-free zone in the region of the Middle East."[2]

Neither the 1974 nor the 1991 initiatives detailed the main elements of such a zone, although the latter initiative provided for certain steps to be taken towards the establishment of the zone by the UN Security Council, the nuclear-weapon states as recognized by the Nonproliferation Treaty (NPT), and the nations of the Middle East.

In the same way, the Middle East Resolution which was adopted at the 1995 NPT Review and Extension Conference was not expected to deal with the main elements of the suggested zone. The resolution stated that the Review and Extension Conference:

1. Endorses the aims and objectives of the Middle East peace process and recognizes that efforts in this regard, as well as other efforts, contribute to, inter alia, a Middle East zone free of nuclear weapons as well as other weapons of mass destruction;

2. Notes with satisfaction that, in its report (NPT/CONF.1995/MC.III/1), Main Committee III of the Conference recommended that the Conference "call on those remaining States not parties to the Treaty to accede to it, thereby accepting an international legally binding commitment not to acquire nuclear weapons or nuclear explosive devices and to accept International Atomic Energy Agency safeguards on all their nuclear activities";

3. Notes with concern the continued existence in the Middle East of unsafeguarded nuclear facilities, and reaffirms in this connection the recommendation contained in section VI, paragraph 3, of the report of Main Committee III urging those non-parties to the Treaty on the Non-Proliferation of Nuclear Weapons that operate unsafeguarded nuclear facilities to accept full-scope International Atomic Energy Agency safeguards;

4. Reaffirms the importance of the early realization of universal adherence to the Treaty, and calls upon all States of the Middle East that have not yet done so, without exception, to accede to the Treaty as soon as possible and to place their nuclear facilities under full-scope International Atomic Energy Agency safeguards;

5. Calls upon all States in the Middle East to take practical steps in appropriate forums aimed at making progress towards, inter alia, the establishment of an effectively verifiable Middle East zone free of weapons of mass destruction, nuclear, chemical and biological, and their delivery systems, and to refrain from taking any measures that preclude the achievement of this objective;

6. Calls upon all States party to the Treaty on the Non-Proliferation of Nuclear Weapons, and in particular the nuclear-weapon States, to extend their cooperation and to exert their utmost efforts with a view to ensuring the early establishment by regional parties of a Middle East zone free of nuclear and all other weapons of mass destruction and their delivery systems.[3]

An ad-hoc technical committee established by the League of Arab States was tasked with drafting a treaty on the establishment of a WMD-free zone. Even though the committee made some progress, it was frozen in 2007 at the Riyadh Arab Summit as a result of the frustration caused by the lack of commitment by both regional and extra-regional stakeholders. The committee, when suspended, had yet to agree on and settle a number of key issues, such as verification mechanisms within the zone, as well as its geographical delimitation.

A dramatic turn of events took place at the 2010 NPT Review Conference. The Secretary General of the UN and the cosponsors of the 1995 Middle East Resolution – the United

States, United Kingdom, and Russia – in consultation with the states of the region, were expected to convene a conference in 2012, to be attended by all states of the Middle East, on the establishment of a Middle East free of nuclear weapons and all other weapons of mass destruction on the basis of arrangements freely arrived by the States of the region, and with the full support and engagement of the nuclear-weapon states.

The 2010 Review Conference considered that the 2012 Conference should take as its terms of reference the 1995 Middle East Resolution. In compliance with these provisions and other provisions of the final declaration of the NPT Review Conference of 2010, the Secretary General of the UN and the cosponsors of the 1995 Resolution and in consultation with the states of the region appointed Ambassador Jaakko Laajava from Finland as a facilitator. As a mandate, the facilitator was expected, inter alia, to support implementation of the 1995 Middle East Resolution by conducting consultation within the states of the region in that regard and undertaking preparations for the convening of the 2012 Conference.[4] The facilitator was also expected to assist in implementation of follow-on steps agreed by the participatory regional states at the 2012 Conference. The facilitator is expected to report to the 2015 NPT Review Conference and its Preparatory Committee meetings.

Unfortunately, the expected conference on the zone did not take place in 2012 and this was a source of great disappointment and dismay to the states of the region. It was not held in Helsinki as predicted, which was the choice for the conference venue. Unfortunately, the facilitator is expected to report finally to the 2015 Review Conference that his mission has failed, unless in the remaining period before the Conference a breakthrough can be achieved. It is difficult at present to predict the course of events to follow any negative reports by the facilitator, especially at the NPT 2015 Review Conference. The atmosphere at the Review Conference would probably be tense with unpredictable reactions. Finally, in order to rescue the NPT from further misgivings and disappointments, the remaining year before the 2015 Review Conference convenes will be crucial for the NPT regime itself. Would it be possible to accomplish in a year what we have not been able to accomplish in two years?

Modalities of a WMDFZ

This negative atmosphere should not prevent us however from thinking aloud of a preliminary framework for a WMD-free Zone in the Middle East which I must admit has not received yet enough attention. An attempt to draw up such a preliminary framework is therefore necessary. We shall try in what follows to deal with six components of a possible future zone encompassing nuclear, chemical, and biological weapons as well as their delivery systems. The six components deserve careful consideration as follows:

Parties to the zone

The first key issue that needs to be addressed is the geographical delimitation of the zone. It would not be out of the ordinary for a WMD-free zone to be initially established by a core group of Middle Eastern countries, such as Egypt and other Arab state members of the League of Arab States, Israel, and Iran. In this regard, the Treaty of Tlatelolco, which established the Latin American nuclear-weapon-free zone, provides an illuminating precedent since it allowed states to join the zone and be committed to it without awaiting the adherence of other states before the entry into force of the treaty.

However, without the presence of Israel and Iran, it would not be possible to reach such an arrangement in the Middle East. Hence, the establishment of the zone requires the participation of both countries in the negotiations over the establishment of the zone. In addition, there have been suggestions about the possibility of admitting Turkey to the zone, or at least, to accredit Turkey a special status as a neighboring state to the zone. Turkey is an active participant in Middle Eastern politics and carries great weight in current deliberations about the security of the region as a whole. The possible impediment to the adherence of Turkey to the zone or to be associated with it, in one way or another, would be its NATO membership and the presence of American tactical nuclear weapons and missiles defense systems on Turkish territory.

There has also been speculation to associate Pakistan and India with the zone. However, their role in the project might bode well for the provision of security assurances to the actual members, rather than being themselves parties to the zone. The question of neighboring states and their status with regard to the zone is a problematic one. It may take us to the so-called notion of greater Middle East that was left to rest a long time ago.

Weapons banned

All three categories of weapons of mass destruction must be included in the scope of a future zone. Nuclear, chemical, and biological weapons should also be broadly defined. Again, the Treaty of Tlatelolco does provide for a definition of nuclear weapons.[5] A WMD-free zone agreement could follow suit.

Some argue that radiological weapons should also be incorporated but this would complicate matters further for a variety of reasons, not least because there is no existing multilateral treaty on radiological weapons. However, it would be a new terrain to explore. As for the delivery systems associated with nuclear, chemical, and biological weapons, the agreement should include a ban on all sorts of delivery vehicles that can appear attractive for a WMD payload, including those operating in the terrestrial, naval, and atmospheric domains.

Main undertakings of the parties to a WMD-free zone

The parties to a WMD-free zone in the Middle East would be expected to reaffirm in the text of the treaty establishing the zone their commitment to continue to respect and honor their obligations therein. Most importantly, member states should adhere to the most important WMD-related treaties, such as the 1968 NPT for nuclear weapons, the 1993 Chemical Weapons Convention (CWC) for chemical weapons, and the 1972 Biological and Toxin Weapons Convention (BTWC) for biological and toxin weapons.[6] At the same time, members of a future WMD-free zone may also wish to be party to the major missile- and export-control related multilateral agreements, such as the Hague Code of Conduct against Ballistic Missile Proliferation, the Missile Technology Control Regime, the Wassenaar Arrangement, and the Nuclear Suppliers Group (NSG). They should also be active implementers of UN Security Council Resolution 1540 which deals with WMD terrorism, a rising topic of interest globally and especially pertinent for the Middle Eastern region.

Regarding those states that have not yet adhered to all or some of these WMD-related treaties and conventions, they would be expected to join them during a specified timeframe starting from the date of the opening for signature of the WMD-free zone treaty. The main provisions of the WMD-free zone treaty may simply refer to all treaties and conventions related to the subject matter of a WMD-free zone that need to be adhered to by all parties to the zone. A referral provision may turn out to be a practical procedure to follow. This should not exclude provisions that may be required in the special case of the Middle East zone, such as the establishment of a regional verification organization.

The need for a regional verification organization

In the nuclear field in particular, a regional organization could be similar to, and inspired by, the Euratom or the Brazilian-Argentine Agency for Accounting and Control of Nuclear Materials (ABACC), possibly ending up with a system benefiting from a mixture of the two.[7] This is an aspect that should receive special attention in the negotiations leading to a WMD-free zone. It should be recalled that the NPT verification and safeguards system is tailored to allow the International Atomic Energy Agency (IAEA) and its inspectors to verify Euratom inspections. The idea of mutual visits and inspections of nuclear facilities between Egypt and Israel was raised in talks between Amr Moussa, the then foreign Minister of Egypt, and Shimon Perez, now President of Israel. However, those talks led nowhere as Perez refused to open up Dimona. The newly established regional verification organization should work closely with the IAEA, the Organization for the Prohibition of Chemical Weapons (OPCW) and a future biological weapons setup. With regard to the 1992 BTWC, the establishment of the zone would be an excellent opportunity to introduce a verification system that has been absent since 1972, a serious loophole.

Security Assurances

The NPT nuclear-weapon states should be asked for negative security assurances, and possibly for positive security assurances. Whereas a negative security assurance is a guarantee by a state that possesses nuclear weapons that it will not use or threaten to use nuclear weapons against states that do not possess nuclear weapons, a positive security assurance is a guarantee by a nuclear-weapon state that it will come to the aid of a nonnuclear-weapon state if it is attacked by another state with nuclear weapons. Nuclear-weapon states should also be willing to abide by any agreement banning the deployment of nuclear weapons in the region. A fitting example of good security assurances is provided by 1995 UN Security Council Resolution 984. The resolution says that nonnuclear-weapon states party to the NPT would receive assurances that "the Security Council will act immediately in accordance with the relevant provisions of the UN Charter" to protect nonnuclear-weapon states against attacks or threats of aggression in which nuclear weapons are used. Both positive and negative security assurances should be extended to cover the use and threat of use of chemical and biological weapons.

Pakistan and India may be able to offer negative security assurances similar to those provided by the NPT's five nuclear-weapon states with respect to existing nuclear-weapon-free zones around the world. This issue may arise in negotiating the zone because it leads to the following serious question: would the parties to a WMD-free Zone in the Middle East seek such assurances and guarantees from Pakistan and India, or would they consider such a step a recognition by the parties to the zone of the nuclear weapon status of both countries to the detriment of the NPT?

Peaceful Nuclear Cooperation

The establishment of a zone may, for example, open up opportunities for intensive cooperation in the area of peaceful uses of nuclear energy. A possible outcome could be the establishment of a regional nuclear fuel cycle, thus taking stock of the one of the 2005 IAEA expert group reports on multilateral approaches to the nuclear fuel cycle. As such, the expected multifaceted advantages are numerous, not least the beneficial spillover effects on mutual confidence and trust.

The Iran dimension and a regional fuel cycle

On November 23, 2013, Iran and the 5+1 negotiator group (the United States, Russia, China, France, the United Kingdom, and Germany) signed an agreement in Geneva as a potential first step towards addressing certain elements of Iran's suspected nuclear-weapon ambitions.[8] This so-called Interim Agreement also revived a latent hope among some to launch a nuclear cooperation between Iran and its Arab neighbors in the field of peaceful uses of nuclear energy including the regionalization of Iran's sensitive technologies. If this were to happen it would be the ideal diplomatic as well as technical breakthrough for solving the Iranian nuclear program. In this case, Iranians and Arabs would be stakeholders of this regional setup that would allow all of the parties to check on each other and benefit from regional cooperation.

If these initial steps proved successful, the next steps could possibly involve Arab powers joining the Iranian and 5+1 group in the second phase of the protracted negotiations with Iran. Suggesting this would be similar to the experience in the Pacific in the negotiations with North Korea. However these stages play out, the countries of the region – especially Arab powers that are on the verge of investing in nuclear power – could make an important contribution to peace in the region. The present negotiations are too important to allow sidestepping Arab participation in the ongoing talks.

Regionalization of the nuclear fuel cycle in its ideal or optimal form may indicate to some extent self-reliance and probably a division of labor or expertise, among its participants. It is quite possible, and even desirable, that no one participant in the cycle would have all the essential elements of the cycle. Its operation would greatly depend on the cooperation and coordination between its members and not in isolation from other states or similar groups.

With regard to enrichment, a consensus almost exists: All sensitive nuclear technologies should preferably be internationalized or regionalized. The advantages of regionalization include:

- Regionalization would be a gradual build-up. It will proceed in phases.
- Every individual state would have a say in one way or another.
- Economies of scale in the operation and the running of such an enterprise.
- The existence of effective regional control as well as international control by the IAEA. Regional effective control would be the basis and the prelude to international control by the IAEA. With both levels of control, we would minimize risks and guarantee international responsibility. We should learn from the Euratom experience, and maybe ABACC, as unique arrangements, involving Argentina, Brazil, and the IAEA, and under the umbrella of the Agency for the Prohibition of Nuclear Weapons in Latin America and the Caribbean (OPANAL).[9]
- Strengthening non-proliferation norms, each party to the cycle will be checking on the others.
- Bridging the gap between the developed and the less developed countries in nuclear technology.
- Regionalization in the Middle East may facilitate the establishment of a WMD-Free Zone in the Middle East. One must admit that the WMD-Free Zone itself may lead to a regional nuclear fuel cycle.

The internationalization or the regionalization of the sensitive technologies in Iran may be the way out of the present crisis. It may not only be the ideal diplomatic solution we are all seeking, but also a technical, economic, and political solution as well, a so-called multifaceted solution.

What does this solution mean? It means that Arab neighbors of Iran, whether individually or as members of an Arab nuclear fuel cycle in the making, would be sharing with Iran in the ownership and the management of its sensitive technologies without necessarily having access to the technologies themselves, which will remain the private domain of Iran. Moreover, each party to such an agreement would be checking on the others, thereby strengthening non-proliferation norms.

Arabs and Iranians will certainly have to agree on such an arrangement, and the world at large as well. This would be an ideal way to bring the two civilizations closer to each other, Arabs and Persians, Shiaa and Sunni Muslims, which would open avenues of cooperation as well as overcoming and settling problems that have kept them far apart on many crucial issues in the region. This reconciliation would engender stability and security in one of the most strategic areas of the world.

It might be said by hardline supporters of sanctions on Iran that what we are suggesting is virtually rewarding a violator that should not escape punishment. What is hoped to be accomplished is to bring Iran to the fold as a positive and peaceful contributing member to its milieu and immediate sphere, which would engender a new era in the region and the world at large. A possible significant result of such an accommodation is Iran's opening to the world and more important, the rebirth of a new Iran.

What about Israel in such a new step? Israel will have to adhere to the Non-Proliferation Treaty (NPT) and accept full scope IAEA safeguards as it is the only country in the Middle East that has not yet adhered to the NPT. Israel should also demonstrate good will in joining other countries of the region in Helsinki, to negotiate together a WMD-free Zone in the Middle East. Israel will also have to honor its commitment to the "Two-State" solution in Palestine. If Israel were to do so, it will be accepted in the region. This would engender a new era in the whole region, stable and secure.

It would not be easy to convince the Iranians and their Arab neighbors to promote the regionalization of the nuclear fuel cycle in the Middle East region. If the idea were to trigger the interest of all potential parties, it would take a long time to negotiate the suggested scheme of the fuel cycle. The negotiations would definitely entail the involvement and commitment of the 5+1 and the IAEA to achieve such a goal. Therefore, I suggest involving the Arab neighbors of Iran in the next phase of the negotiations with Iran. Their presence this time could also open other venues of cooperation.

Conclusions

Despite these clear technical elements relating to the establishment of the zone, there are obviously nontechnical, that is political, obstacles that remain. However, precisely through the process of discussion upon these technicalities, political will and greater understanding of each side's considerations can be created. It is thus that I advocate an immediate commencement on such a project. The League of Arab States technical committee should be reformed and resume its work actively in close cooperation with all participants in the Helsinki Conference process, including Iranians and Israelis, with a task completion as a clear target.

This is something that the Facilitator of the Middle East Action Plan can recommend to be accomplished leading to the 2015 NPT Review Conference, although pursuing it through the NPT does not come without its own problems, especially if real progress towards the zone lagged behind.

Notes

1. United Nations General Assembly, "Establishment of a Nuclear-weapon-free Zone in the Region of the Middle East," General Assembly Resolution 3263, 2309 plenary meeting, December 9, 1974, www.securitycouncilreport.org/atf/cf/%7B65BFCF9B-6D27-4E9C-8CD3-CF6E4FF96FF9%7D/Disarm%20ARES3263%20%28XXIX%29.pdf.

2. United Nations General Assembly, "Establishment of a nuclear-weapon-free zone in the region of the Middle East," A/RES/46/30, 65th plenary meeting, December 6, 1991, www.un.org/documents/ga/res/46/a46r030.htm.

3. United Nations, "1995 Review and Extension Conference of the Parties to the Treaty on the Non-Proliferation of Nuclear Weapons," NPT/CONF.1995/32 (Part I), New York, 1995, www.un.org/disarmament/WMD/Nuclear/pdf/finaldocs/1995%20-%20NY%20-%20NPT%20Review%20Conference%20-%20Final%20Document%20Part%20I.pdf.

4. United Nations, "2010 Review Conference of the Parties to the Treaty on the Non-Proliferation of Nuclear Weapons," NPT/CONF.2010/50 (Vol. I), New York, 2010, www.un.org/ga/search/view_doc.asp?symbol=NPT/CONF.2010/50(VOL.I).

5. For the text of the Treaty of Tlatelolco, see United Nations Office for Disarmament Affairs, "Treaty for the Prohibition of Nuclear Weapons in Latin America," UN Document A/6663, February 14, 1967, http://disarmament.un.org/treaties/t/tlatelolco/text.

6. For the texts of the Biological Weapons Convention and Chemical Weapons Convention, see United Nations Office for Disarmament Affairs, "Convention on the Prohibition of the Development, Production and Stockpiling of Bacteriological (Biological) and Toxin Weapons and on their Destruction," March 26, 1975, www.un.org/disarmament/WMD/Bio/pdf/Text_of_the_Convention.pdf; and Organization for the Prohibition of Chemical Weapons, "Convention on the Prohibition of the Development, Production, Stockpiling and Use of Chemical Weapons and on their Destruction, July 29, 2005, rev.," www.opcw.org/index.php?eID=dam_frontend_push&docID=6357.

7. See Nuclear Threat Initiative, "Brazilian-Argentine Agency for Accounting and Control of Nuclear Materials (ABACC)," N.D., www.nti.org/treaties-and-regimes/brazilian-argentine-agency-accounting-and-control-nuclear-materials-abacc.

8. For the text of the agreement, released by the United States White House, Office of the Press Secretary, "Fact Sheet: First Step Understandings Regarding the Islamic Republic of Iran's Nuclear Program," November 23, 2013, www.whitehouse.gov/the-press-office/2013/11/23/fact-sheet-first-step-understandings-regarding-islamic-republic-iran-s-n.

9. For the OPANAL homepage, see Agency for the Prohibition of Nuclear Weapons in Latin America and the Caribbean, www.opanal.org/index-i.html.

25

RENUNCIATION

Restraint and rollback

Benoît Pelopidas

There are a multitude of terms describing the set of decisions leading to the final outcome of a given actor not possessing nuclear weapons: restraint and rollback are only two of them, along with forbearance and reversal. This chapter reviews the problems with the current conceptualizations and proposes another analytically and politically relevant concept, i.e., renunciation. (The debate on the desirability and feasibility of global nuclear disarmament is beyond the scope of this chapter.) Then, this chapter reviews the latest evidence and interpretations regarding the cases of Belarus, Ukraine, Kazakhstan, South Africa, and Sweden, with the debates around the interpretation of the Libyan case as a guiding principle. The concluding section outlines avenues for future research, proposals for innovation in terms of level of analysis or epistemology, and future policy initiatives.

Seizing frequent and purposeful nonnuclear strategies in the nuclear age

The concepts of restraint or rollback in the nuclear-weapon related literature suffer from a double problem: a nonnuclear strategy – be it national or global – appears as a default option, the absence of something rather than a deliberate and purposive national and international security strategy and, in terms of policy, it leads to an over-emphasis on future and foreign nuclear threats at the expense of current threats posed by existing weapons on the territory of the analysts.[1]

These concepts reveal the hegemony of "proliferation" as the core policy problem to be solved and a supposed core driver of the historical dynamic of the nuclear age.[2] In spite of widespread recognition that the pace of proliferation has been slower than expected, the field remains focused on the proliferation puzzle: it only shifts from its demand to its supply side and sometimes tries to combine them.[3] Even many fervent advocates of denuclearization paradoxically endorse the proliferation framework, from the Swedish disarmament advocate Alva Myrdal in the 1970s to former Cold Warriors who are now advocating global nuclear disarmament as a measure to prevent further proliferation to terrorist groups with which nuclear deterrence is not expected to work.[4] Even a group of international historians who are precisely trying to "problematize" generalizations about nuclear history ended up calling themselves the Nuclear Proliferation International History Project.[5] This is true even if important studies have considered nuclear hedging as a possible goal in itself.[6] The recent extension of the proliferation paradigm to nonstate actors, and the redefinition of nuclear-weapon statehood by the International Atomic Energy Agency (IAEA) and Western intelligence services as possessing a significant quantity of fissile material rather than having actually detonated a nuclear weapon, illustrates this focus on the proliferation puzzle, both as an understanding of the dynamic of global nuclear history and the policy problem to be solved.[7]

This framework constitutes a biased understanding of the historical record: it neglects the facts that, according to our current knowledge, no new nuclear-weapon program has started since 1985, with the possible exception of Syria; that successful proliferation has been more rare than reversal and that only a very limited number of states had an interest in developing those weapons in the first place; and that many decisions about nuclear-weapon acquisition were rarely thought about in terms of proliferation.[8]

Moreover, cases commonly labeled as failed nuclear proliferation have recently been rein-terpreted in light of declassified documents as not seriously attempting to acquire nuclear weapons in the first place. For instance, the most recent scholarship on Brazil and Argentina questions the extent of their effort towards the acquisition of nuclear weapons. As for Brazil, Mathias Spektor reinterprets the three core claims on which the suspicion of proliferation lies. According to him, the Brazilian quest for uranium enrichment technology, construction of unsafeguarded nuclear facilities, the missile program under military control in the 1980s, and the repeated affirmation of Brazil's right to undertake peaceful nuclear explosions at least until 1990 should be reinterpreted as part of a broader project of domestic economic modernization and affirmation of its international autonomy. Indeed, Spektor argues that the proponents of nuclear-weapon development were rare and quite isolated.[9] Additionally, at least one clear instance in which a Brazilian government rejected a proposal to build nuclear weapons has been identified. In 1984, the Minister of the Air Force Délio Jardim de Mattos proposed detonating a nuclear device the next year to celebrate the end of the dictatorship; President Figueiredo turned the proposal down, following the advice of the Brazilian National Security Council.[10] Similarly, new evidence suggests that Argentina's interest in developing nuclear weapons may have been exaggerated by earlier analyses. Declassified documents now suggest that the purpose of Argentina's starting to build a secret enrichment facility in 1978 was not to build weapons, but rather to fuel nuclear-powered submarines or research reactors.[11]

Finally, most forecasting studies looking for cases of proliferation end up rejecting the prospects of a cascade and identifying only a few additional possible cases of proliferation in the coming decades.[12]

This focus on proliferation has significant implications for the framing, timing, and pacing of conceivable policy solutions to the problem.[13] It creates a selection bias towards the cases which have developed an interest in nuclear-weapon technology at any point in nuclear history, even when this set of cases is quite limited. More broadly, it has massive consequences on what is considered possible or not based on what is perceived to have been possible in the past.[14] This bias is strengthened by a three-tiered problem that has to do with the increasing use of statistical analysis in the field.

First, even if the universe of cases was broadened beyond the countries which at some point in time have had an interest in developing nuclear-weapon related technology (i.e., forty cases in the most pessimistic scenario), the question remains whether the use of statistical methods can be justified. The main reasons for skepticism have to do with the limited number of cases and the limited confidence one can have in the available data due to nuclear secrecy and language barriers, among other obstacles. The issue of the size of the universe remains even if you increase it by creating a data point for every case per year.[15]

Second, and consequently, the limited confidence one can have in the available data is under-estimated and compensated by the authority granted by numbers as conveyers of objective knowledge so that a dangerous sense of overconfidence in the findings is likely to appear.[16] Even if the experts generating those findings do not have a direct policy impact, this problem remains due to the impact they might have on the general public's perception of the issue, and the ability of those numbers to provide an alibi for a policy which would turn out to be much less evidence-based than it is claimed to be.[17] This legitimizing-delegitimizing effect also works retro-spectively. For example, the framing of nuclear history as proliferation history assumes that nonproliferation as a set of policies was a success overall and that, had things been done differ-ently, there might have been many more nuclear-armed states; similarly, the focus on proliferation legitimizes the practices of arms control, nuclear deterrence, and the pursuit of strategic stability.[18]

Third, this leads to a properly political problem: while most statistical analysis claims to be probabilistic and not deterministic, it has to become deterministic when it makes case-specific policy recommendations for the future. In other words, it has to assume that the patterns iden-tified in the segment of the past considered relevant by the analyst will repeat themselves in some form which can be predicted. This implies hidden political and value judgments about the link between the past and the future, and denies the political ability to introduce something radically new in the world.[19] Most of the existing research rejects the idea of a "silver bullet" that would be a necessary and sufficient condition for a given entity not to end up in posses-sion of a nuclear-weapon system as part of its arsenal.[20] As a consequence, the South African and the Libyan reversals were not anticipated, were considered as surprises, and were suspected of being either temporary or hiding something else.[21] At the end of the day, restraint or roll-back as concepts make sense within the "proliferation paradigm" which defines both an implicit understanding of the course of global history and the key policy problem that needs to be solved. As a result, not acquiring nuclear weapons is reduced to or retrospectively labeled as incomplete or failed proliferation, as if it were lacking a strategic rationale of its own.

It is true that the notion of disarmament is also massively problematic because of its ambi-guity and political implications. Disarmament can characterize the end state of a given actor not possessing nuclear weapons or it can designate a process, for which the starting point, pacing, and end result remain open for discussion. The consequence of this ambiguity of disar-mament is that you can use it in the same way 'proliferation' is commonly used, i.e., to narrow down the scope of future possibilities. In order to claim that disarmament is rare or never happened, all you have to do is to adopt a stringent enough definition for the concept that no historical case would fit.

As a consequence, one way of seizing rollback and restraint as policy-relevant and mean-ingful analytical concepts would be to lay out nonnuclear strategies or alternative paths to a nonnuclear understanding of security and collective identity.[22] This follows quite naturally if the field of nuclear studies comes back to its *raison d'être*: the reason for studying nuclear-weapon related issues in isolation from others is an implicit assumption about the specific nature of a nuclear explosion and its consequences. If the field decides to adhere to the exceptional effects of nuclear-weapons use to delineate its analytical concepts, then the limitations of the approach in terms of proliferation become obvious because it excludes the risks of existing weapons and focuses on those reasons that do not yet exist.

Experiences and drivers of renunciation: Three points of consensus

Another concept encompasses all strategies leading an actor to end up without nuclear weapons, i.e., renunciation of nuclear weapons. It includes the absence of interest in nuclear-weapon development in the entire existence of the actor (usually neglected by the scholarship due to the selection bias noted above), the existence of an interest and several stages of development which does not lead to a fully formed nuclear arsenal (usually labeled as "exploration," then "pursuit" and then "restraint" or "failure"), and finally the development of a nuclear arsenal which is then dismantled (usually labeled as "rollback"). One can maintain an analytical distinction between the different stages of development of the program and still engage with the issue of nuclear latency in a nonteleological way, but only this overarching notion of renunciation is consistent with the usual understanding of the uniqueness of the nuclear risk and the most frequent strategy of lack of interest in nuclear-weapon acquisition.[23]

All paradigms in international relations have developed insights on nuclear-weapon related choices, and there are three points of consensus here.[24] First, security, nuclear weapons and nuclear-weapon decision-making have been decoupled. In other words, seeking security cannot be identified with seeking nuclear weapons and this latter behavior is not only justified by security concerns. Almost twenty years ago, Scott Sagan already noted that: "an all too common intellectual strategy in the literature is to observe a nuclear weapons decision and then work backwards, attempting to find the national security threat that 'must' have caused the decision."[25]

Second, nuclear-weapon related decisions are better understood in connection to identity conceptions. This is the case across epistemologies, theoretical positions and case studies. Interestingly, studies of countries which ended up keeping nuclear weapons emphasize this notion very strongly too.[26]

The third point of consensus in this body of literature is that the domestic level of analysis is decisive but requires a broader understanding of the normative social environment, which cannot be limited to the domestic sphere.[27] For example, Itty Abraham recognized that the domestic battle about a nuclear-weapon program is fought within state boundaries even if he has brilliantly shown that there is no such thing as a strictly indigenous nuclear-weapon program.[28] This increasing consideration of the international social environment crosses the epistemological divide between positivism and post-positivism.[29] Constructivists embracing a positivist epistemology have been at the forefront of the analysis of this change in terms of the emergence and diffusion of a norm or set of norms against nuclear-weapon acquisition which will have an impact on domestic decisions in that respect.[30] This idea is now widely accepted, even by scholars broadly inspired by the realist tradition.[31] This focus on norms which have an impact on the domestic level of decision-making led to an emphasis on new actors as normative entrepreneurs: not only leaders, but also grassroots movements, and small states.[32]

Beyond those three points of consensus, all the canonical variables of every international relations theory appear in the analysis. While structural realism cannot really account for renunciation as a purposive and deliberate strategy and suffers from underdetermination in its specification of the variables at play, the core principles of the realist logic survive through the consideration that security assurances should be a key driver of renunciation.[33] Similarly, great power politics enters the discussion of renunciation through sanctions as a tool for nonproliferation.[34] Structural logics also appear in the scholarship at the regional level as sources of conflict creating additional obstacles to renunciation or as sources of economic pressure adding incentives to specific "domestic models of political survival."[35] The neoliberal institutionalist and constructivist literature is having an ongoing debate about the role of the Nonproliferation Treaty as an important driver for renunciation, either via utility calculations that allow for cooperation due to the shadow of the future, or via a logic of appropriateness that allows for norms of accepted behavior to shape nuclear-weapon related decisions.[36] At the level of political regimes, most recent research suggests that dictators in "personalist dictatorships," defined by weak institutional constraints facing the leader, are more likely to start a nuclear-weapon program or not to adopt a sustained policy of renunciation. But this argument does not speak to the likelihood of achieving the nuclear ambitions of this regime.[37] Similarly, at the individual level of analysis, the national identity conception of the leader seems to be a necessary condition for the initiation of a nuclear-weapon program but not its likelihood for reaching completion.[38]

While the different traditions in international relations theory keep arguing about the most important drivers of nuclear-weapon acquisition or renunciation, the possibility of getting to know them and the best ways of doing so, three points of consensus have emerged: processes of nuclear-weapon acquisition and renunciation should not be reduced to a security-seeking behavior; they are better understood when connected to identity conceptions; and those factors are working primarily in the domestic realm, which in turn is colored by a transnational social environment.

The revealing Libyan puzzle: New documentary evidence on global nuclear history

The Libyan case is of particular relevance to policy makers and scholars alike. For policy makers, it is the only post-Cold War case of renunciation of nuclear weapons after a long-term pursuit which did not involve the use of force; for scholars, it challenges a number of implicit assumptions about the country, the logic of nuclear history, and nuclear-weapon acquisition. In this section, the Libyan case is used to frame the evidence that has been uncovered about other cases: Sweden, Switzerland, South Africa, Ukraine, Belarus, and Kazakhstan.

First, the Libyan experience suggests that a dictator who actively pursued nuclear weapons can change course and give up on such an ambition – it is a unique case of reversal in which the man who made the decision to start a nuclear-weapon program also decided to end it after more than three decades. It is unanimously recognized that Colonel Gaddafi made both decisions to start the nuclear-weapon program, soon after he took power in 1969, and to give up the program, which was publicly announced in 2003. This goes against the pathological implication of the proliferation metaphor, i.e., even dictatorial regimes can recover from the nuclear temptation, which does not mean that some elements in the regime do not hope to pursue nuclear weapons again at a later point in the future. Similarly, it now appears that the Iraqi regime, which had pursued nuclear weapons intensely in the 1980s, had given up on its ambitions after 1991.[39] In a way, the cases of Ukraine, Belarus, and Kazakhstan confirm this finding. In the first half of the 1990s, the three post-Soviet republics were under the rule of leaders elected in a competitive authoritarian system in transition. The collapse of the Soviet Union gave birth to those republics with a significant portion of the former Soviet arsenal on their soil. Even if the issues of retargeting and command and control of the warheads remained, the pathological connotation of the proliferation metaphor would have expected those leaders to keep the weapons.[40] On the contrary, they cooperatively agreed to sign the Lisbon protocol of the START I Treaty and give them back to Russia.[41] Of course, this does not mean that we should replace a teleology of proliferation with the opposite one. From 1990 onwards, the Libyan case suggests that hedging and ambiguity can be a strategy, since it pursued negotiations towards renunciation while keeping contact with the Khan network.[42]

Second, the Libyan case shows that neither an external shock to the regime nor a revolution is required for renunciation to occur, even when the program has been running for decades. This is all the more important as the South African case suggests that dramatic change in the regime was needed for renunciation to happen, with the father of the program, head of the National Party, and head of government Pieter Botha's heart attack opening the way for the election of Frederick de Klerk who is commonly associated with the decisions to dismantle the weapon program and to begin the transition to democracy.[43] The debate on the impact of the invasion of Iraq on Libyan renunciation is not about the utility of force.[44] Those who deny any role to coercion in this case insist that the decision was made before the invasion took place, while their opponents emphasize Libya's dual strategy until the end and insist that the terrorist attacks on the United States of September 11, 2001, and the war in Iraq, created "a sense of urgency" to make a final decision about the nuclear-weapon program.[45] As a matter of fact, force had been used against Gaddafi, with the underlying goal of regime change. In April 1986, Operation El Dorado Canyon targeted him, but he continued his efforts after that.[46] Scholars on both sides of this debate agree that providing confidence-building measures that there would be no regime change were decisive.[47] So, it is not clear whether the use of force and regime change in neighboring countries possibly played a role. Even if it did, however, the process of renunciation could only succeed once Gaddafi was convinced that regime change was not an option any longer.

Third, if Libya gave up its nuclear ambitions after receiving a guarantee of regime survival, it did not receive anything close to a positive nuclear security guarantee.[48] The same could be said of South Africa, Ukraine, and all the states which have never developed any nuclear-weapon ambitions.[49] The nuclear component of the security guarantee is neither a necessary nor a sufficient condition for renunciation across cases. In other words, there is a way out of the nuclear straitjacket between an independent nuclear-weapon system and/or an extended nuclear deterrence agreement. The most recent research by Thomas Jonter based on the archives of Swedish nuclear decision-making suggests that, contrary to the narrative from the former Foreign Minister Carl Bildt, the expectations of a specifically nuclear security guarantee did not play a significant role in the Swedish decision to give up its nuclear-weapon program at the end of the 1960s.[50] If the probabilistic effects of a nuclear security guarantee on the likelihood of pursuing or acquiring nuclear weapons remain debated in the quantitative literature, it is clear that "positive and negative security assurances can potentially work at cross purposes. Stronger commitments to protect or assist a country in case of aggression run counter to the very purpose of negative security assurances."[51]

Fourth, the Libyan renunciation cannot be reduced to a shortage of resources or some sort of capacity determinism, i.e., if you do not go for the bomb, it is not because you cannot.[52] It is now unanimously recognized that Libya did not have enough fissile material to build a weapon and did not have delivery vehicles or maintain a program to build them.[53] However, this limited set of resources cannot explain the timing of the Libyan renunciation. As a matter of fact, difficulties in terms of procurement of nuclear technology had existed since the early stages of the program in the 1960s, and since 1992, the UN Security Council and the European Union had withdrawn or relaxed sanctions which had targeted Libya for two decades. Consequently, the constraint on the regime in terms of access to resources was not at its highest when Gaddafi gave up the nuclear-weapon program.[54] Such a capacity determinism often assumes that with the spread of the technology, building nuclear weapons is becoming easier and easier, faster and faster. The most recent research suggests that the opposite is true: nuclear-weapon programs increasingly tend to fail and take longer and longer.[55] Interestingly, in many cases, external help, often categorized as a result of interconnectedness and a sign of the ease with which the technology spreads, can actually hamper a nuclear-weapon program.[56] Such a capacity determinism is often implicitly or explicitly based on the principle that specific domestic players, mostly scientific and military actors, would benefit from a nuclear-weapon program and, as a consequence, will lobby for it. However, those players seem to have been much less predictable. The Swedish military turned its back against the weapon program it originally supported and the French army was originally opposed to the *force de frappe*. In Argentina, Admiral Carlos Castro Madero played an important role in favor of renunciation by postponing the discussions of the security implications of the nuclear plans adopted in 1979 in the interministerial commission in charge of it.[57]

Implications for policy of the existing (lack of) knowledge and ways forward

When it comes to restrain and rollback, there are no certainties or silver bullets. The following makes two observations about this absence and outlines avenues for future research.

First, this absence is not complete. To echo Bernard Brodie regarding renunciation of nuclear weapons, it seems that the "twin facts" are that most countries made the decision not to pursue those capabilities and, even among those who tried, more gave up than successfully completed a nuclear-weapon acquisition program. Those are crucial findings once one recognizes that the core goal of global nuclear-weapon policy making is to avoid the use of one of those weapons in anger. In terms of policy, one of the key lessons is that restraint and reversal have frequently surprised analysts tempted by worst-case assumptions and thinking about the nuclear problem in isolation. Policy makers should expect further surprises rather than hope to become able to anticipate them perfectly, but should not see them only as proliferation surprises.

Second, this absence of regularity in the findings is good news for those who want to promote nonproliferation and disarmament. It shows a potential for change that does not necessarily require force and cannot be reduced to deterministic understandings of the history of the nuclear age. This absence of regularity suggests that domestic actors expected to have vested interests in supporting nuclear-weapon programs do not always do so or can change their mind, and that the pronuclear-weapon camp can lose the political battle.

In line with the findings from the most recent scholarship, two urgent tasks in the field consist in better understanding the framing of the universe of possibilities in nuclear-weapon policy and developing our historical knowledge through the opening of archives over time.

Developing a better understanding of possible nuclear-weapon policies requires researchers to focus more on the role of experts in nuclear-weapon policy. They frame possibilities in two contradictory ways. On the one hand, they broaden the scope of the possibilities by bringing new policy ideas through which renunciation can actually be implemented, provided that they get access to the relevant policy makers, who are listening and have the necessary political will to lead the policy to implementation.[58] On the other hand, experts and epistemic communities limit the scope of policy innovation and possibilities for renunciation by framing it as unlikely or even impossible within the framework of the proliferation paradigm.[59] A renewed empirical and theoretical engagement with transnational epistemic communities discussing nuclear-weapon issues is needed to better grasp the two contradictory ways in which they frame these issues.[60] More specifically, redefining policy impact beyond policy-making elites and recognizing that dismissing a policy idea as impossible or impractical is an important act of authority would be valuable steps. Giving a voice to representatives of sustained and purposive renunciation would also allow for a fuller understanding of global nuclear history as a history of possible worlds. Primary candidates would be in countries that are excluded from the nuclear conversation precisely because they were never interested in or suspected of pursuing nuclear weapons, and as a consequence were outside the scope of the proliferation puzzle.

Theoretical refinement needs to involve the voices of proponents of renunciation in constituencies assumed to be pronuclear, like the military and the scientists, whether or not their concerns and critiques won the battle of ideas.[61] Another way of calling into question the framing of possible nuclear futures is to investigate closely the categories experts use as a supposed transhistorical grammar of the nuclear age. Historicizing those categories, contextualizing them, and tracing the evolution of their meaning over time would change our appreciation of their validity across time and, in turn, their authority which largely derives from their longevity.

This leads to a second proposal about developing our historical knowledge on unexplored cases. The use of primary documents is essential in this endeavor given the endemic secrecy in the nuclear arena, the tendency of social scientists to generalize, and the risk of echo leading to a confirmation bias within the relatively small community of nuclear experts. The latter problem is particularly likely to happen when analysts rely on oral history interviews and their interlocutors are aware of the scholarship on their country. They then authenticate it by repeating it to the researcher.[62]

Making primary documents publicly available and training nuclear researchers in foreign languages would also limit the problem of expert authority by broadening the community of potential interpreters and by preserving a space for revisionism and critique. The latest interpretation of landmark cases suggests that analysts should refocus the effort towards the identification of pathways towards a nonnuclear national security strategy rather than identifying patterns which so far have not been found across cases. By doing so, they would gain policy-relevance as it has been clearly shown that a misguided understanding of the historical record leads to misconceived nuclear policies.[63] In that respect, two hasty retrospective interpretations damaging the appeal of a strategy of renunciation of nuclear weapons are the idea that Gaddafi's end and the Russian incursion in Crimea in 2014 could have been avoided had the countries kept their nuclear weapons or programs. Engaging with them while avoiding the pitfall of epistemic arrogance is urgent.

Notes

1. The best treatment of the "othering" of the nuclear problem remains Hugh Gusterson, "Nuclear Weapons and the Other in the Western Imagination," *Cultural Anthropology*, Vol. 14, No. 1 (February 1999), pp. 111–143.
2. Some analysts have convincingly argued that this persistent focus in turn reveals a persistence of assumptions inspired by the realist tradition, which seems to be the default framework for policy analysis of nuclear weapons related choices, even of small and neutral states. See Halit M. Tagma, "Realism at the Limits: Post Cold War Realism and Nuclear Rollback," *Contemporary Security Policy*, Vol. 31, No.1 (April 2010), pp. 165–188; Ursula Jasper, "Ambivalent Neutral: Rereading Switzerland's Nuclear History," *Nonproliferation Review*, Vol. 19, No. 2 (June 2012), p. 267.
3. Jacques E.C. Hymans, *The Psychology of Nuclear Proliferation: Identity, Emotions and Foreign Policy* (Cambridge: Cambridge University Press, 2006); Maria Rost Rublee, *Nonproliferation Norms: Why States Choose Nuclear Restraint* (Athens, GA: University of Georgia Press, 2009); Etel Solingen, *Nuclear Logics: Contrasting Paths in East Asia and the Middle East* (Princeton, NJ: Princeton University Press, 2007); Jacques E.C. Hymans, "The Study of Nuclear Proliferation and Nonproliferation: Toward a New Consensus?" in *Forecasting Nuclear Proliferation in the 21st Century*, edited by William Potter and Gaukhar Mukhatzhanova (Palo Alto, CA: Stanford University Press, 2010), pp. 35–36; Sara Z. Kutchesfahani, *Politics and the Bomb: The Role of Experts in the Creation of Cooperative Non-Proliferation Agreements* (London: Routledge, 2013).
4. In the 1990s, even American critiques of "nuclearism" as an ideology regarded proliferation as "the most dangerous weapons situation of all" and subscribed to capacity determinism which leads to describe biological and chemical weapons as "the poor man's bomb." See Robert J. Lifton and Richard Falk, *Indefensible Weapons: The Political and Psychological Case against Nuclearism* (New York: Basic Books, 1991), pp. xi–xii; George P. Shultz, William J. Perry, Sam Nunn, and Henry A. Kissinger, "Steps in Reducing Nuclear Risks: The Pace of Nonproliferation Work Today Doesn't Match the Urgency of the Threat," *The Wall Street Journal*, March 2013, http://online.wsj.com/news/articles/SB100014241278873243

38604578325912939001772; George P. Shultz, William J. Perry, Sam Nunn, and Henry A. Kissinger, "Deterrence in the Age of Nuclear Proliferation," *The Wall Street Journal*, March 2011, http://online. wsj.com/news/articles/SB10001424052748703300904576178760530169414.

5. In general, the academic subfield is called "proliferation" or "nonproliferation studies," not disarmament studies or nuclear-weapon policy. See Hymans, "Study of Nuclear Proliferation," p. 35.

6. Ariel E. Levite, "Never Say Never Again: Nuclear Reversal Revisited," *International Security*, Vol. 27, No. 3 (Winter 2002/03), pp. 59–88.

7. Jacques E.C. Hymans, "When Does a State Become a 'Nuclear Weapons State?': An Exercise in Measurement Validation," in *Forecasting Nuclear Proliferation in the 21st Century*, edited by William Potter and Gaukhar Mukhatzhanova (Palo Alto, CA: Stanford University Press, 2010), pp. 102–123.

8. Benoît Pelopidas, *Renoncer à l'arme nucléaire. La séduction de l'impossible?* [Giving up nuclear weapons. The seduction of the impossible?] (Paris: Sciences Po University Press, Forthcoming); Harald Müller and Andreas Schmidt, "The Little-Known Story of Deproliferation: Why States Give Up Nuclear Weapons Activities," in *Forecasting Nuclear Proliferation in the 21st Century*, edited by William Potter and Gaukhar Mukhatzhanova (Palo Alto, CA: Stanford University Press, 2010), pp. 124–158. On the latter aspect, see Pervez Hoodbhoy, "Introduction," in *Confronting the Bomb: Pakistani and Indian Scientists Speak Out*, edited by Pervez Hoodbhoy (Oxford: Oxford University Press, 2013), xxv. For the Soviet Union, see David Holloway, *Stalin and The Bomb* (New Haven, CT: Yale University Press, 1994). However, one needs to note the most recent discovery that Brazilian scientists tested an implosion device known as the "Bomba Marambaia" in 1953. See Carlo Patti, "The Origins of the Brazilian Nuclear Program 1951–1955," *Cold War History*, forthcoming.

9. Mathias Spektor, "Explaining Brazil's Nuclear Behavior," paper presented at the conference, "Uncovering the Sources of Nuclear Behavior: Historical Dimensions of Nuclear Proliferation," Zurich, Switzerland, June 18–20, 2010.

10. Michael Barletta, "The Military Nuclear Program in Brazil," CISAC Working Paper, Center for International Security and Cooperation, Stanford University, August 1997, p. 19, http://iis-db.stanford.edu/pubs/10340/barletta.pdf; Carlo Patti, "Brazil in Global Nuclear Order" (PhD dissertation in International Relations, Universitá degli Studi di Firenze, 2012), pp. 208–209.

11. Interpretations in that direction started with Julio Carasales in 1999 and Jacques Hymans in 2001 and 2006, and have subsequently continued. See Julio C. Carasales, "The So-Called Proliferator That Wasn't: The Story of Argentina's Nuclear Policy," *Nonproliferation Review*, Vol. 6, No. 4 (Fall 1999), pp. 51–64; Jacques E.C. Hymans, "Of Gauchos and Gringos: Why Argentina Never Wanted The Bomb, and Why America Thought It Did," *Security Studies*, Vol. 10, No. 3 (Spring 2001), pp. 153–185; Hymans, *Psychology of Nuclear Proliferation*. See also Diego Hurtado de Mendoza, "Periferia y fronteras tecnológicas: Energía nuclear y dictadura militar en la Argentina (1976–1983) [Technological Periphery and Frontiers: Nuclear Energy and the Military Dictatorship in Argentina (1976–1983)]," *Revista Iberoamericana de Ciencia Tecnología y Sociedad*, Vol. 5, No. 13 (September 2009), pp. 27–64.

12. William C. Potter and Gaukhar Mukhatzhanova, "Forecasting Proliferation: The Role of Theory, an Introduction," in *Forecasting Nuclear Proliferation in the 21st Century*, edited by William Potter and Gaukhar Mukhatzhanova (Palo Alto, CA: Stanford University Press, 2010), pp. 1–12; James J. Wirtz and Peter R. Lavoy, *Over the Horizon Proliferation Threats* (Palo Alto: Stanford University Press, 2012).

13. Campbell Craig and Jan Ruzicka, "The Nonproliferation Complex," *Ethics & International Affairs*, Vol. 27, No. 3 (Fall 2013), pp. 329–348; Anne I. Harrington de Santana, "The Strategy of Non-proliferation: Maintaining the Credibility of an Incredible Pledge to Disarm," *Millennium*, Vol. 40, No.1 (August 2011), pp. 3–19; David Mutimer, *The Weapon State: Proliferation and the Framing of Security* (Boulder, CO: Lynne Rienner, 2000); Benoît Pelopidas, "The Oracles of Proliferation: How Experts Maintain a Biased Historical Reading that Limits Policy Innovation," *Nonproliferation Review*, Vol. 18, No.1 (March 2011), pp. 297–314.

14. Benoît Pelopidas, "La Couleur du Cygne Sud-Africain: Le Rôle des Surprises dans L'Histoire Nucléaire et les Effets d'une Amnésie Partielle. [The color of the South African swan: The role of surprises in nuclear history and the effects of a partial amnesia]," *French Yearbook of International Relations*, Vol. 11 (July 2010), pp. 683–694; Moeed Yusuf, "Predicting Proliferation: The History of the Future of Nuclear Weapons," *Brookings Foreign Policy Paper Series*, No. 11 (January 2009), www.brookings.edu/research/papers/2009/01/nuclear-proliferation-yusuf.

15. Tanya Ogilvie-White, "Is There a Theory of Nuclear Proliferation?: An Analysis of the Contemporary Debate," *The Nonproliferation Review*, Vol. 4, No.1 (Fall 1996), p. 43, http://cns.miis.edu/npr/pdfs/ ogilvi41.pdf; Müller and Schmidt, "Little-Known Story of Deproliferation," pp. 124–158.

16. Theodore Porter, *Trust in Numbers: The Pursuit of Objectivity in Science and Public Life* (Princeton, NJ: Princeton University Press, 1995); Daniel Kahneman, *Thinking Fast and Slow* (New York: Penguin, 2011), part 3.

17. Benoît Pelopidas, *When Experts Back Policy Makers' Historical Memory and Biases: The Shared "Nuclear Proliferation Paradigm" in the US since the 1960s* (Unpublished manuscript).

18. Pelopidas, "Renoncer à L'Arme Nucléaire." Nicholas Miller presents a recent argument defending the "proliferation paradigm" via its component of "reactive proliferation," as well as the efficacy of US nonproliferation policy after the 1964 Chinese test. See Nicholas L. Miller, "Nuclear Dominoes: A Self-Defeating Prophecy?" *Security Studies*, Vol. 23, No. 1 (January–March 2014), pp. 33–73.

20. Hannah Arendt, *The Human Condition* (Chicago, IL: University of Chicago Press, 1958), pp. 175–247; Hannah Arendt, *Between Past and Future: Eight Exercises in Political Thought* (New York: Penguin Books, 1993), pp. 3–16.

20. For the original case against monocausality in nonproliferation research, see Scott D. Sagan, "Why do States Build Nuclear Weapons?: Three Models in Search of a Bomb," *International Security*, Vol. 21, No. 3 (Winter 1996/1997), pp. 54–86, http://iis-db.stanford.edu/pubs/20278/Why_Do_States_Build_Nuclear_Weapons.pdf. Regarding security guarantees, see Wirtz and Lavoy, "Over the Horizon." For an analysis of extended nuclear deterrence agreements, absence of capabilities, and an external shock as neither a necessary nor a sufficient condition for renunciation to nuclear weapons across cases, see Pelopidas, "The Oracles of Proliferation" and "Renoncer à L'Arme Nucléaire."

21. Ursula Jasper, *The Politics of Nuclear Non-Proliferation: A Pragmatist Framework for Analysis* (London: Routledge, 2013); Pelopidas, "Couleur du Cygne Sud-Africain," pp. 683–694.

22. Regina C. Karp, *Security without Nuclear Weapons?: Different Perspectives on Non-Nuclear Security* (Oxford: SIPRI, 1992); Mitchell B. Reiss, *Without the Bomb: The Politics of Nuclear Nonproliferation* (New York: Columbia University Press, 1988); Mitchell B. Reiss, *Bridled Ambitions: Why Countries Constrain their Nuclear Capabilities* (Washington, DC: Woodrow Wilson Center Press, 1995).

23. Scott D. Sagan, "Nuclear Latency and Nuclear Proliferation," in *Forecasting Nuclear Proliferation in the 21st Century*, edited by William Potter and Gaukhar Mukhatzhanova (Palo Alto, CA: Stanford University Press, 2010), pp. 80–101.

24. Hymans, "Study of Nuclear Proliferation," pp. 36–37.

25. Sagan, "Why do States Build Nuclear Weapons?" p. 63.

26. For the "oppositional nationalists" position, see Hymans, *Psychology of Nuclear Proliferation*. For the "enduring rivals" position, see T.V. Paul, *Power Versus Prudence: Why Nations Forgo Nuclear Weapons* (Montreal: Mc Gill-Queen's University Press, 2000). For the "inward-looking model of political survival," see Solingen, "Nuclear Logics." On the post-positivist side, see Jasper, "Politics of Nuclear Non-Proliferation," p. 188.

27. Hymans, "Study of Nuclear Proliferation," pp. 36–37.

28. Itty Abraham, *Making of the Indian Atomic Bomb: Science, Secrecy and the Postcolonial State* (London: Zed Books, 1998); Itty Abraham, "The Ambivalence of Nuclear Histories," *Osiris*, Vol. 21, No. 1 (2006), pp. 49–65, www.jstor.org/stable/10.1086/507135.

29. On the post-positivist side, see Abraham, "Making of the Indian Atomic Bomb;" Jasper, "Politics of Nuclear Non-Proliferation," pp. 1–2, 190–196.

30. Rublee, *Nonproliferation Norms*.

31. Francis J. Gavin, "Nuclear Proliferation and Non-Proliferation During the Cold War," in *Cambridge History of the Cold War. Vol. 2: Crises and Détente*, edited by Melvyn Leffler and Odd Arne Westad (Cambridge: Cambridge University Press, 2010), p. 415.

32. Hymans, *Psychology of Nuclear Proliferation*; Lawrence S. Wittner, *The Struggle against the Bomb* (Palo Alto, CA: Stanford University Press, 2003); Lawrence S. Witner, *Confronting the Bomb. A Short History of the World Nuclear Disarmament Movement* (Palo Alto, CA: Stanford University Press, 2009); Marianne Hanson, "Advocating the Elimination of Nuclear Weapons: The Role of Key Individual and Coalition States," in *Slaying the Nuclear Dragon. Disarmament Dynamics in the Twenty-First Century*, edited by Tanya Ogilvie-White and David Santoro (Athens, GA: University of Georgia Press, 2012). For a critique of their direct impact based on the NPT review conferences, see Claudia Kissling, *Civil Society and Nuclear Non-Proliferation: How do States Respond?* (Aldershot: Ashgate, 2013).

33. The best critiques along this line remain Tagma, "Realism at the Limits," pp. 165–188; and Solingen, "Nuclear Logics." See also, James J. Wirtz, "Conclusions," in *Security Assurances and Nuclear Nonproliferation*, edited by Jeffrey W. Knopf (Palo Alto, CA: Stanford University Press, 2012), pp. 275–291.

34. Etel Solingen, *Sanctions, Statecraft and Nuclear Proliferation* (Cambridge: Cambridge University Press, 2012).
35. Paul, "Power Versus Prudence;" Solingen, "Nuclear Logics."
36. William Potter, "The NPT and the Sources of Nuclear Restraint," *Deadalus*, Vol. 139, No. 1 (Winter 2010), pp. 68–81; Xinyuan Dai, *International Institutions and National Policies* (Cambridge: Cambridge University Press, 2007), pp. 69–99; Rublee, *Nonproliferation Norms*.
37. Christopher Way and Jessica Weeks, "Making it Personal: Regime Type and Nuclear Proliferation," forthcoming, *American Journal of Political Science*, online version published November 20, 2013, http://onlinelibrary.wiley.com/doi/10.1111/ajps.12080/pdf.
38. See Hymans, *Psychology of Nuclear Proliferation*. Hymans' book is based on four case studies: Argentina, Australia, India, and France. The author himself recognizes that the Indian case does not fit his theory; in the French case, the relevant leader Pierre Mendes-France barely falls in the conceptual category the author sees as a driver for proliferation; and his argument that Argentina ultimately did not have a nuclear-weapon program remains disputed. See also Jacques E.C. Hymans, *Achieving Nuclear Ambitions: Scientists, Politicians and Proliferation* (Cambridge: Cambridge University Press, 2012).
39. Malfrid Braut-Hegghammer, "Revisiting Osirak: Preventive Attacks and Nuclear Proliferation Risks," *International Security*, Vol. 36, No. 1 (Summer 2011), pp. 101–132.
40. Lucan A. Way, "Authoritarian State Building and the Sources of Regime Competitiveness in the Fourth Wave: The Cases of Belarus, Moldova, Russia and Ukraine," *World Politics*, Vol. 57, No. 2 (January 2005), pp. 231–261.
41. William Potter, "The Politics of Nuclear Renunciation: The Cases of Belarus, Kazakhstan and Ukraine," *Stimson Center Occasional Paper*, No. 22 (April 1995), http://cns.miis.edu/reports/pdfs/1995_potter_politics_of_nuclear_renunciation.pdf; Nikolai Sokov, "Ukraine: A Postnuclear Country," in *Forecasting Nuclear Proliferation in the 21st Century Vol. 2*, edited by William Potter and Gaukhar Mukhatzhanova (Palo Alto, CA: Stanford University Press, 2010), pp. 255–284; Stephen F. Burgess and Togzhan Kassenova, "The Rollback States: South Africa and Kazakhstan," in *Slaying the Nuclear Dragon. Disarmament Dynamics in the Twenty-First Century* edited by Tanya Ogilvie-White and David Santoro (Athens, GA: University of Georgia Press, 2012), pp. 85–117; Anuar Ayazbekov, "Kazakhstan's Nuclear Decision-Making 1991–1992," *Nonproliferation Review*, Vol. 21, No. 2 (June 2014), pp. 149–168.
42. Malfrid Braut-Hegghammer, "Libya's Nuclear Turnaround: Perspectives from Tripoli," *Middle East Journal*, Vol. 62, No. 1 (Winter 2008), p. 68; Peter Viggo Jakobsen, "Reinterpreting Libya's WMD Turnaround – Bridging the Carrot-Coercion Divide," *Journal of Strategic Studies*, Vol. 35, No. 4 (August 2012), p. 500; Jasper, "Politics of Nuclear Non-proliferation," p. 124. The jury is still out on whether this was a deliberate dual track or mismanagement. See Hymans, *Achieving Nuclear Ambitions*, pp. 239–243; Wyn Q. Bowen, "Intelligence, Interdiction, and Dissuasion: Lessons from the Campaign against Libyan Proliferation," in *Over the Horizon Proliferation Threats*, edited by James J. Wirtz and Peter R. Lavoy (Palo Alto, CA: Stanford University Press, 2012), p. 226.
43. Jean du Preez and Thomas Maettig, "From Pariah to Nuclear Poster Boy: How Plausible Is a Reversal?," in *Forecasting Nuclear Proliferation in the 21st Century Vol. 2*, edited by William Potter and Gaukhar Mukhatzhanov (Palo Alto, CA: Stanford University Press, 2010), pp. 302–336; Terence McNamee, "Afrikanerdom and Nuclear Weapons: A Cultural Perspective on Nuclear Proliferation and Rollback in South Africa," PhD diss., London School of Economics and Political Science, 2002; Helen H. Purkitt and Stephen F. Burgess, *South African's Weapons of Mass Destruction* (Bloomington, IN: Indiana University Press, 2005).
44. It is more a debate about whether or not the precedent of Iraq increased Ghadafi's existential fear. Contrast Jakobsen, "Reinterpreting Libya's WMD Turnaround," pp. 500–502, with Jasper, "Politics of Nuclear Non-Proliferation," p. 169.
45. Contrast Harald Müller, "The Exceptional End to the Extraordinary Libyan Quest," in *Nuclear Proliferation and International Security*, edited by Morton Bremer Maerli and Sverre Lodgaard (London: Routledge, 2007), pp. 73–95; Randall Newnham, "Carrots, Sticks, and Bombs: The End of Libya's WMD Program," *Mediterranean Quarterly*, Vol. 20, No. 3 (Summer 2009), p. 78, www.cimicweb.org/cmo/libya/Documents/Security/20.3.2009.%20newnham%20libya%20wmd.pdf; Bruce Jentleson and Christoper Whytlock, "Who Won Libya?: The Force-Diplomacy Debate and its Implications for Theory and Policy," *International Security*, Vol. 30, No. 3 (Winter 2005/2006), p.75; and Jasper, "Politics of Nuclear Non-proliferation," p. 194; with Jakobsen, "Reinterpreting Libya's WMD Turnaround," p. 502; and Braut-Hegghammer, "Libya's Nuclear Turnaround," p.71.

46. Jentleson and Whytlock, "Who Won Libya," p. 58.
47. Jakobsen, "Reinterpreting Libya's WMD Turnaround," p. 504; Jentleson and Whytlock, "Who Won Libya," p. 74.
48. Wyn Q. Bowen, "Libya, Nuclear Rollback, and the Role of Negative and Positive Security Assurances," in *Security Assurances and Nuclear Nonproliferation*, edited by Jeffrey W. Knopf (Palo Alto, CA: Stanford University Press, 2012), pp. 89–110.
49. Sokov, "Ukraine."
50. Thomas Jonter, "The United States and Swedish Plans to Build the Bomb, 1945–68," in *Security Assurances and Nuclear Nonproliferation*, edited by Jeffrey W. Knopf (Palo Alto, CA: Stanford University Press, 2012), pp. 219–245.
51. Bruno Tertrais, "Security Assurances and the Future of Proliferation," in *Over the Horizon Proliferation Threats*, edited by James J. Wirtz and Peter R. Lavoy (Palo Alto, CA: Stanford University Press, 2012), p. 258. For a summary of the debates in the quantitative literature on the causes of proliferation, see Scott D. Sagan, "The Causes of Nuclear Proliferation," *Annual Review of Political Science*, Vol. 14 (2011), p. 233, www.annualreviews.org/doi/pdf/10.1146/annurev-polisci-052209-131042.
52. Scott Kemp shows how widespread weapon-enabling gas centrifuges have been since the 1950s but this has not been enough to cause rampant proliferation. R. Scott Kemp, "The Nonproliferation Emperor Has No Clothes. The Gas Centrifuge, Supply-Side Controls, and the Future of Nuclear Proliferation," *International Security*, Vol. 38, No. 4 (Spring 2014), pp. 39–78.
53. Jasper, "Politics of Nuclear Non-Proliferation," p. 125.
54. Wyn Q. Bowen, *Libya and Nuclear Proliferation: Stepping Back from the Brink* (London: Routledge, 2006), p. 52.
55. Hymans, "Achieving Nuclear Ambitions."
56. Alexander H. Montgomery, "Stop Helping Me: When Nuclear Assistance Impedes Nuclear Programs," in *The Nuclear Renaissance and International Security*, edited by Adam Stulberg and Matt Fuhrmann (Palo Alto, CA: Stanford University Press, 2013). For a study of the Soviet help to the Chinese program, see Liu Yanqiong and Liu Jifeng, "Analysis of Soviet Technology Transfer in China's Development of Nuclear Weapons," *Comparative Technology Transfer and Society*, Vol. 7, No. 1 (April 2009), pp. 66–110.
57. Thomas Jonter, *Explaining Nuclear Forbearance: Sweden and the Plans to Acquire Nuclear Weapons, 1945–1968* (Palo Alto, CA: Stanford University Press, forthcoming); Pelopidas, "Renoncer à L'Arme Nucléaire;" Hymans, "Psychology of Nuclear Proliferation," p. 213.
58. For case studies of Argentina and Brazil as well as the cooperative threat reduction program along those lines, see Kutchesfahani, "Politics and the Bomb."
59. Pelopidas, "La Couleur du Cygne;" Pelopidas, "Renoncer à L'Arme Nucléaire."
60. Emanuel Adler, "The Emergence of Cooperation: National Epistemic Communities and the International Evolution of the Idea of Nuclear Arms Control," *International Organization*, Vol. 46, No. 1 (Winter 1992), pp. 101–145, www.jstor.org/stable/2706953?.
61. Hoodbhoy, "Confronting the Bomb." On scientists leaving nuclear-weapon programs, see Hymans, *Achieving Nuclear Ambitions*. For more information on the military side, see Jerome D. Frank and John C Rivard, "Antinuclear Admirals: An Interview Study," *Political Psychology*, Vol. 7, No. 1 (March 1986), pp. 23–52, www.jstor.org/stable/3791155.
62. Raymond L. Garthoff, "Evaluating and Using Historical Hearsay," *Diplomatic History*, Vol. 14, No. 2 (April 1990), p. 229, http://onlinelibrary.wiley.com/doi/10.1111/j.1467-7709.1990.tb00086.x/abstract.
63. Francis J. Gavin, *Nuclear Statecraft: History and Strategy in America's Atomic Age* (Cornell, NY: Cornell University Press, 2012); Pelopidas, "La Couleur du Cygne."

26

THE ROLE OF TECHNOLOGY IN MONITORING AND VERIFICATION

Amy F. Woolf

Monitoring and verification for arms control and nonproliferation is increasingly important. This chapter examines the role of technology in the monitoring and verification of arms control and nonproliferation obligations. It does not review the capabilities of specific technologies, or assess the value of the information provided by those technologies. Instead, it identifies the unilateral and cooperative mechanisms used to collect information needed to verify compliance and the role this information plays in the process of determining whether a nation's activities and facilities are consistent with its arms control or nonproliferation obligations.

The chapter begins with a general description of the verification process, identifying the objectives and components of a comprehensive verification regime. The monitoring process, or the collection of information about activities and facilities, is one of these components. It then reviews three cases where the United States or international community has sought to verify compliance with arms control or nonproliferation obligations to demonstrate how the interaction among different mechanisms can contribute to both the collection of relevant data and the assessment of compliance with arms control and nonproliferation obligations.

Characteristics of a comprehensive verification regime

Verification is the process that the international community or individual countries use to gain confidence that participants in an arms control or nonproliferation regime are complying with the obligations assumed in that regime. These obligations are often codified in legally binding international treaties, but they could also be outlined in less formal agreements among countries or between countries and international organizations. Although the goal is, generally, to verify *compliance* with the assumed obligations, most discussions focus on the ability to detect evidence of potential *violations*. The two goals are not necessarily inconsistent, as the ability to detect evidence of violations can not only deter participants from pursuing noncompliant activities, but also build confidence in the viability of the agreement.

Objectives of a verification regime

An effective verification regime should enable participants in an agreement to determine whether the forces, facilities, and activities of other countries are within the bounds established by the limits and obligations in the agreement. The regime should enable each country to gain confidence in the absence of activities that might undermine the core objectives of the agreement or threaten the security of other participants. No verification regime can provide perfect information or remove all doubts about the existence of possible violations. Nevertheless, the verification regime must be capable of detecting evidence of violations either before those activities create risks to the security of other participants or in time for the other participants to respond and offset the emerging threats to their security.

The ability to detect evidence of violations in a timely fashion can not only assure compliant participants of their ability to protect their own security, but can also discourage others from pursuing noncompliant activities. If the verification regime provides the means to monitor and evaluate activities at declared facilities, a country seeking to evade treaty limits would have to pursue these activities outside the monitored infrastructure. The cost and complexity of establishing covert operations, however, when combined with the consequences if the activity were detected, might be sufficient to discourage the country from pursuing the noncompliant activity.

The ability of the verification regime to provide the participants with evidence of violations in a timely fashion can also bolster their confidence in the viability of the treaty regime by demonstrating that the participants are willing to meet their obligations. If the treaty lacked adequate mechanisms to allow the participants to monitor and evaluate others' facilities and activities, doubts and uncertainties could undermine commitments to the regime. But, a verification regime that provides the participants with opportunities to cooperate in sharing information and the means to develop a better understanding of the other country's facilities and activities can build confidence in the agreement by demonstrating that the countries are committed to the process of implementing the agreement.

This last element of the verification process proved to be particularly valuable during the implementation of the Strategic Arms Reduction Treaty (START), signed by the United States and Soviet Union in July 1991.[1] When implementing the treaty, the United States and Russia demonstrated that they could work together to resolve compliance questions, while gaining a better understanding of the forces and activities of the other nation. The New START Treaty, which entered into force in February 2011, retained some and modified other components of START's verification regime, allowing it to continue the START Treaty's tradition of transparency and cooperation.

This last element is also evident in the safeguards process that the International Atomic Energy Agency (IAEA) uses to monitor compliance with the Nuclear Nonproliferation Treaty (NPT). The IAEA has little reason to suspect that most countries would seek to acquire nuclear weapons in the absence of the treaty or the safeguards process. Yet, by allowing the IAEA to monitor their facilities and track their materials, these countries underscore their commitment to pursue the peaceful uses of nuclear technology while remaining free of nuclear-weapon capabilities. Their cooperation and compliance demonstrate the value of the safeguards process for building confidence in the basic bargain of NPT.

Components of a verification regime

Many discussions of the verification process focus on the ability of participating countries and international organizations to monitor programs and activities. They tend to measure a regime's effectiveness according to the participants' ability to collect vast quantities of data about activities and facilities in other countries. This leads to the often unspoken conclusion that more information will not only add to the participants' understanding of others' activities, but also increase the probability that they will detect noncompliant activities.

However, a comprehensive, effective verification regime will contain far more than just rigorous monitoring mechanisms. These mechanisms, alone, cannot provide – at all times and in all cases – a complete understanding of the activities and intentions of parties to the treaty. Specifically, the parties to an agreement will not be able to assess whether other parties' activities and facilities are compliant unless the agreement itself clearly identifies permitted and prohibited activities and facilities and allows the participants to distinguish between the two. Ambiguity in the text of the agreement will inevitably lead to ambiguity and misunderstandings in judgments about compliance.

A well-crafted agreement that outlines the limits, restrictions, and obligations adopted by all the participants will help the participants both recognize compliant activities and anticipate potential paths to noncompliant activities. This information will allow them to focus their monitoring efforts in ways that will provide valuable information about activities at declared facilities and early indicators of efforts to pursue covert activities at undeclared facilities. The text of the agreement may also include collateral constraints to complicate efforts to evade the limits and increase confidence in the validity of data. For example, the text might restrict activities that could interfere with the collection of information, mandate that the participants provide access to suspect facilities, or mandate that the participants provide notifications when they alter or adjust permitted activities. Further, noncompliance with these procedural requirements can serve as an early indicator of potential noncompliance with the agreement's central limits.

In addition, the data collected by monitoring mechanisms cannot answer questions about the country's compliance with an agreement until it has been subject to further analysis and evaluation. The countries must determine whether the information is relevant and reliable, compare it to information from different sources to resolve ambiguities, and combine it with information from other sources to develop a broader picture of the other monitored country's activities. Even with extensive analysis, however, the participants may be left with a degree of ambiguity and uncertainty about the precise meaning of the information. As a result, conclusions about compliance will rest on both political and technical assessments about the purpose of ambiguous activities and potential risks to participants' security.

Monitoring in a verification regime

Monitoring mechanisms can be cooperative, with the country under scrutiny providing access, data, and information to the other participants in an agreement, or unilateral, with participants collecting data and information without agreed access to the monitored nation's facilities or activities. Moreover, nations can use technology to collect data and information, or they can use nontechnical and human interactions for this purpose.

Most unilateral monitoring mechanisms rely on the application of technology. These mechanisms can include satellites, radar installations, and other electronic surveillance capabilities – known as national technical means (NTM) of verification – that operate outside the territory of the monitored nation and can collect information on specific locations or wide swaths of territory. They could also include on-site, autonomous, tamper-proof systems that might record activity at declared facilities. Because these systems operate either continuously or without prior notification, they can provide information about activities at declared, permitted facilities and, possibly, information about the existence of undeclared, noncompliant facilities and activities, even if the monitored nation seeks to conceal that information.

Cooperative monitoring can include both technical and nontechnical mechanisms. For example, the participants in an agreement can cooperate by exchanging data on the current status and planned changes in their declared facilities, materials, and activities. They can then agree to allow inspectors to visit these facilities to determine the accuracy of the data provided in exchanges. During these visits the inspectors might use simple monitoring tools or sophisticated technologies to capture and record information. The participants might also allow the presence of manned inspection posts outside declared facilities to monitor materials and equipment as they enter or exit the facility. The participants might also agree to install sensors at specific locations to monitor activities within specific facilities. These tools may be either simple or sophisticated, depending on the type of information needed to achieve the goals of the monitoring process.

The interaction between unilateral and cooperative monitoring mechanisms can help detect noncompliant activities, deter violations, and build confidence in an agreement. For example, cooperative monitoring mechanisms may be vulnerable to interference, denial, and deceptive practices. Data can be inaccurate, inspectors may be blocked, and cooperation may be sporadic. However, the participants in an agreement may be able to detect evidence of denial and deception by comparing information collected through cooperative channels with that obtained by unilateral mechanisms. In addition, efforts to deny access to relevant data and information can, by themselves, constitute a violation of the agreement. Conversely, although unilateral monitoring systems may be better able to provide unfiltered information, shared data and on-site inspections can provide a degree of "ground truth" that allows the parties to add detail and expand their understanding of the monitored activities and facilities. Moreover, even if remote or autonomous systems can collect all the required data, a country's willingness to cooperate and open its facilities to inspections can signal its commitment to the successful implementation of the agreement.

While some agreements have relied on unilateral monitoring mechanisms and others have presumed extensive cooperation between the participants, no verification regime relies exclusively on one or the other method. Even when the United States and Soviet Union relied almost exclusively on NTM to monitor their early arms control treaties, the treaties presumed at least a minimum of cooperation because they prohibited activities that would interfere with the operation of those systems. At the other extreme, when the UN Special Commission on Iraq (UNSCOM) and the International Atomic Energy Agency (IAEA) monitored activities and facilities in Iraq in the 1990s, they expected Iraq to cooperate in providing data on its programs and access to its facilities. But they recognized the potential for (and actual use of) denial and deception by Iraq. As a result, they also had access to information collected autonomously, without Iraqi cooperation, both during and after the conflict.

Monitoring and intelligence

Many of the unilateral monitoring mechanisms used in arms control verification are the same as those used to gather intelligence outside the arms control process. For example, the United States and Russia would use their NTM to provide basic intelligence information about the other country's nuclear forces and activities even if they did not have to verify compliance with arms control agreements. But the information needed to verify compliance with a treaty may be more discrete and specific than the general information desired for intelligence purposes. In some cases, therefore, monitoring for verification may be easier than monitoring for intelligence, as the terms of the agreement would focus the collection efforts on those items and locations addressed by the limits in the agreement. In other cases, however, monitoring for verification can be more difficult, as analysts would have to sift through reams of unrelated information to find the data that is relevant to the treaty terms. At the same time, cooperative monitoring for verification, which, by its nature, focuses on collecting data needed to assess compliance, can provide added details and collateral information useful for intelligence purposes.

Although some overlap is inevitable, historically, the requirements of monitoring for verification have been viewed as distinct and separate from those of monitoring for intelligence. However, in a study published in January 2014, the Defense Science Board argued that, in the future, proliferation is likely to be a continuous process that would require "persistent surveillance" to monitor ongoing activities in countries of concern. The study argues that the goal should be to detect undesirable nuclear activity "as early in the planning and acquisition of a capability as possible," even if the activity, at that point, did not violate any international standards or agreements. According to the study, "this leads to the need for a paradigm shift in which the boundaries are blurred between monitoring for compliance and monitoring for proliferation."[2] With this broader perspective, all monitoring mechanisms would gather intelligence information even if the data were not directly related to the limits or requirements of a particular agreement.

Using technology in monitoring for verification

US-Soviet/Russian arms control

Unilateral vs. cooperative monitoring

The bilateral arms control agreements that the United States and Soviet Union signed during the 1970s relied primarily on unilateral monitoring mechanisms, although some provisions mandated cooperation to enhance the capabilities of the unilateral mechanisms. When they signed the 1972 Anti-Ballistic Missile Treaty and Interim Agreement on Offensive Arms, the two countries planned to use their own satellites and remote sensing equipment (NTM) to collect the information needed to verify compliance. At the same time, they agreed that they would not interfere with the other country's NTM or conceal their forces or activities in ways that would impede verification by NTM. In the second Strategic Arms Limitation Treaty (SALT II), signed in 1979, the United States and Soviet Union expanded their pledge not to interfere with the collection of information by banning the deliberate denial of telemetry (data generated during a missile flight test) about weapon characteristics when that denial would impede verification. They also agreed that some systems would have external features, evident to NTM, that distinguished them from similar systems.

In the arms control agreements signed in the late 1980s and early 1990s, the United States and Soviet Union (or Russia) continued to rely on NTM for the bulk of the information needed to monitor restricted forces and activities, but they also expanded the use of cooperative measures that would confirm and add details to the information collected by NTM. For example, in the 1987 Intermediate-Range Nuclear Forces Treaty (INF) the countries agreed to exchange detailed data on the systems limited by the treaty and to notify the other country when they planned to move or destroy these systems. They also established a continuous monitoring presence outside one missile assembly facility in each country so they could monitor all vehicles leaving the facility and confirm that they did not carry missiles banned by the treaty. Finally, they agreed to permit on-site inspections at facilities that had housed these systems so that they could confirm the information provided in the data exchanges and collected by NTM.

As with the INF Treaty, the 1991 Strategic Arms Reduction Treaty (START) included a mix of unilateral and cooperative monitoring mechanisms. START mandated that the parties exchange extensive data detailing the numbers and locations of affected weapons and mandated that they notify each other when they moved these systems or changed their status under the treaty. It also called for numerous types of displays and on-site inspections that allowed the countries to confirm the accuracy of data provided in the data exchange and to confirm the status of items limited by the treaty. These included inspections where the parties could count the number of warheads on deployed missiles to ensure that the number did not exceed the number attributed to that type of missile in the agreed data base. START also provided for continuous perimeter and portal monitoring at assembly facilities for mobile ICBMs to help the countries count the numbers of these systems entering the force.

START also expanded SALT II's agreement not to encrypt data generated during missile flight tests; the countries agreed that they would broadcast the data and exchange tapes to help with its interpretation. Taken together, these cooperative monitoring mechanisms allowed each side to draw a comprehensive picture of the other's forces by monitoring and tracking them throughout their service lives. The level of detail was designed not only to provide compre-hensive data, but also to minimize ambiguities and uncertainties that might arise during the treaty's implementation.

The 2010 New START Treaty contains a monitoring and verification regime that resem-bles the regime in START, in that its text contains detailed definitions of items limited by the treaty; provisions governing the use of NTM to gather data on each side's forces and activities; an extensive database that identifies the numbers, types, and locations of items limited by the treaty; provisions requiring notifications about items limited by the treaty; and inspections allowing the parties to confirm information shared during data exchanges. The provisions are not the same as those in the original START Treaty because the limits and restrictions in the treaties are not identical and the political relationship between the two countries is different than it was in 1991. Nevertheless, the cooperative monitoring measures in New START focus both on deterring and detecting potential violations and on maintaining transparency, cooper-ation, and openness between the two sides.

The role of technology

The capabilities of US and Soviet NTM shaped the limits and restrictions the countries adopted in their bilateral treaties. For example, the treaties signed in the 1970s imposed limits on the numbers of missile launchers, rather than the numbers of warheads on deployed missiles. The launchers were large enough for the countries to identify and count with satellites. Even when they agreed to limit warheads under the 1991 START Treaty, they counted the number of missile launchers and bombers, then calculated the number of warheads by multiplying the number of launchers by the number of warheads "attributed" to that type of launcher in the data provided by the country deploying the missile. The 2010 New START Treaty also contains a limit on warheads, but uses NTM and cooperative measures to count missile launchers and bombers. The countries declare the aggregate number of warheads deployed on the counted numbers of missiles and bombers, but the treaty provides no mechanism that allows them to count or confirm the warhead number.

Both START and New START permit the countries to inspect deployed missiles to count the number of warheads on that missile, but neither treaty uses the results of that inspection to calculate the number of warheads deployed across the force. Under START, these inspections were designed to confirm that the number of warheads deployed on a type of missile did not exceed the number listed in the data base for that type. The countries were allowed to view the missile and count reentry vehicles, using, if necessary, hand-held neuron detectors to confirm the absence of nuclear materials in reentry bodies that should not count as deployed warheads. This technology, however, was highly optimized to the goal at hand. It was designed to allow confirmation of the absence of a warhead, but was not sensitive enough to provide information about existing warheads.

The INF and START Treaties also allowed for the limited use of technology during inspections, as a part of the effort to confirm the accuracy of data on the characteristics of systems limited by the treaty. For example, under the INF Treaty, the United States installed scanning equipment outside the Votkinsk missile assembly facility so that it could measure the dimensions of missile motors leaving the facility. This would allow the United States to confirm that the motors were designed for the SS-25 missile, permitted but limited under START, and not the SS-20 missile banned by INF. However reports indicate that the inspectors often found visual inspections and simple technologies, like hand-held measuring devices, as effective as complex technologies to confirm the categories of data required under INF and START.

IAEA safeguards and the nuclear nonproliferation treaty

Unilateral vs. cooperative monitoring

One hundred and ninety nations are parties to the NPT. With the exception of the five nuclear-weapon states – each of which had tested a nuclear device before 1967[3] – all parties to the treaty have pledged that they will not acquire nuclear weapons or other nuclear explosive devices. Each has signed a safeguards agreement with the International Atomic Energy Agency. These agreements provide the IAEA with the legal authority to monitor activities inside each participating nation to ensure that the nation does not divert sensitive nuclear materials and technologies from civilian to military purposes and that it does not establish and operate covert, undeclared nuclear facilities. Further, by cooperating in the implementation of the safeguards agreements, the parties to the treaty have the opportunity to demonstrate their commitment to compliance with their nonproliferation obligations.[4]

The safeguards system that the IAEA uses to verify compliance with the NPT relies heavily on cooperative monitoring mechanisms, both to collect data about materials and activities at declared facilities and to draw a more comprehensive picture of nuclear-related activities in monitored countries. At the same time, over the past twenty years the IAEA has increased its reliance on unilateral monitoring mechanisms to identify possible undeclared activities and facilities that could merit the collection of additional data.

According to the IAEA, the objective of the safeguards system is to "detect any undeclared nuclear material or activities in the State as a whole; to detect any undeclared production or processing of nuclear material in declared facilities or locations outside facilities where nuclear material is customarily used; and to detect any diversion of declared nuclear material in declared facilities or locations outside those facilities."[5] The goal is to detect these activities in a "timely manner," before a noncompliant country has amassed the materials and know-how needed to produce nuclear weapons.[6] The safeguards process begins with data and declarations, provided by the monitored country to the IAEA, about the locations of facilities in its nuclear enterprise, about the operations at those facilities, and about the quantities of materials at those facilities. Within these facilities, the IAEA applies on-site inspections and technical monitoring tools to account for the materials in the facility, with the agreement and cooperation of the monitored country.

Prior to 1991 and the discovery of Iraq's illicit nuclear-weapon program, the safeguards system focused on the timely detection of efforts to divert significant quantities of nuclear material from declared, peaceful nuclear activities to the manufacture of nuclear weapons. After the discovery of Iraq's program, the international community and the IAEA recognized the need to strengthen the safeguards so that they could detect not only diversion and possible illicit activities at declared facilities but also the presence of covert activities or facilities across the territory of a monitored country. The objective was to develop a safeguards system that could verify not only the "correctness" of states' declarations of nuclear material, but their also their "completeness."[7]

To achieve this broader objective, the IAEA has sought the legal authority, through the Additional Protocol, to gain access to undeclared facilities that might be a part of a nuclear infrastructure.[8] It has also adopted a concept known as the "state-level approach" to safeguards, which allows it to "draw a picture of a state's complete nuclear fuel cycle" and its "entire nuclear program to obtain any clues that the state might be engaged in undeclared nuclear activities."[9] As a result, the safeguards system is changing from a "mechanistic approach emphasizing nuclear material accountancy at declared facilities to a flexible state-level approach drawing on accountancy, investigations, and the collection and analysis of information drawn from multiple sources to make judgments not only about declared activities, but also about the absence of undeclared activities."[10]

The emerging safeguards system still relies, to a considerable degree, on cooperative monitoring mechanisms. The countries must still provide the IAEA with extensive data and declarations about the locations of, and activities at, their declared facilities, and they must still account for the materials stored at or flowing through those facilities. At the same time, though, the IAEA has begun to employ data collected by unilateral monitoring mechanisms operated by commercial or national entities. This wider array of data allows the IAEA to construct a more complete picture of the country's declared nuclear activities and to implement safeguards in ways that would complicate efforts to conceal clandestine pursuits.

The role of technology

The IAEA uses monitoring technologies and measurement equipment to keep track of the quantities of nuclear materials at declared facilities. This has long been the core of the safeguards mission and is designed to allow the IAEA to determine whether nuclear materials have been diverted away from declared facilities. It is difficult for the IAEA to track this material precisely in facilities that process large quantities of materials in bulk, as discrepancies in the data may occur when materials are lodged in pipes or other equipment at the facility. As a result, the IAEA must determine whether the uncertainty arises only from measurement uncertainties or other acceptable technical reasons, or if it is possible that some diversion has occurred. Hence, technology alone cannot confirm the presence or absence of diverted materials; analysis of the data and an assessment of the result advise the conclusion.

The IAEA has also developed technologies that allow inspectors to evaluate nuclear materials found during on-site inspections.[11] For example, it employs technologies that allow for environmental sampling during on-site inspections with inspectors taking "swipes" from surfaces of equipment and buildings. According to the IAEA, this "is a powerful tool for detecting undeclared nuclear material at declared facilities or at undeclared locations."[12] In recent years the IAEA has also installed remote monitoring equipment at nuclear facilities that include cameras and other unmonitored surveillance equipment. The systems may allow the IAEA to reduce the number and frequency of on-site inspections in some countries, allowing it to save money and to direct its human resources to inspections in countries where there are greater concerns about compliance.

As was noted above, the IAEA has begun to rely on monitoring technologies that do not require the cooperation of the monitored country. The IAEA does not have its own satellite capabilities and cannot gather this type of data on its own, but it can investigate locations or activities identified in information it receives from other sources. For example, it has access to information from high-resolution, commercial satellite-based sensors, from international data bases, and from participating nations' intelligence capabilities. These capabilities improve its ability to monitor nuclear sites and facilities worldwide and to, possibly, detect covert facilities in monitored countries.

UNSCOM and IAEA implementation of Iraqi disarmament

Unilateral vs. cooperative monitoring

In April 1991, the United Nations Security Council approved Resolution 687, which called on Iraq to accept the destruction and removal, under international supervision, of all its chemical and biological weapons and stocks of agents and all its ballistic missiles with ranges greater than 150 kilometers. Iraq was also required to destroy, remove, and render harmless all its nuclear-weapon-related materials. The United Nations established a Special Commission on Iraq (UNSCOM) to implement the chemical, biological, and missile portions of the resolution, while the IAEA was responsible for identifying and destroying Iraq's nuclear capabilities. The IAEA would rely on both unilateral and cooperative monitoring mechanisms to achieve this objective.

Although Iraq was required to cooperate with the inspectors and provide unfettered access to its facilities, it impeded the process at almost every turn. For example, under Resolution 687 Iraq was required to provide a declaration on the full scope of its nuclear-weapon facilities and materials to the IAEA within fifteen days. This declaration was supposed to include the locations of all materials, facilities, and capabilities that it had acquired before the war and their status after the war (most had been destroyed). Iraq was also was supposed to provide IAEA inspectors with access to any sites where they suspected Iraq may have pursued nuclear-related activities or stored nuclear materials.

Iraq initially reported that it had no nuclear-weapon program. In July 1991, under international pressure, it released details of an extensive, secret nuclear development program, but it continued to deny that the program was for the development of weapons. It also interfered with the inspection process. It harassed and threatened inspection teams, interfered with helicopter flights, refused access to facilities, and removed and destroyed evidence. It detained inspectors and confiscated materials discovered during inspections and delayed inspections while it sanitized sites and removed incriminating equipment.

Although the absence of cooperation interfered with the IAEA's mission, the IAEA was still able to discover the scope of Iraq's nuclear-weapon program, in part, because it had access to intelligence collected by the United States and other nations, both before and after the war. According to some sources, the United States had begun to focus its intelligence assets on Iraq in the late 1980s, after it grew concerned about Iraq's possible acquisition of equipment that could contribute to a nuclear program. Further, the US intelligence community "intensified its efforts to determine the extent of Iraqi nuclear progress" after Iraq invaded Kuwait in August 1990 by increasing its acquisition of satellite imagery and its monitoring of Iraqi communications.[13] This intelligence helped guide the inspectors' decisions on where to go and which facilities to inspect.

The fact that Iraq provided data that was both incomplete and often inaccurate shows both the limits of cooperative monitoring and the way in which cooperation in monitoring can affect confidence in compliance. In the case of Iraq, the absence of cooperation undermined, significantly, confidence in Iraq's commitment to eliminate its nuclear, chemical, and biological weapons programs. Iraq's obstruction convinced many that Iraq was not only hiding details of what it had before the 1991 war, but was also hiding details about what it had hidden away and planned to reconstitute after the war. By demonstrating its lack of commitment to candor and cooperation, it may have contributed to the Bush Administration's assessments, in 2002 and 2003, that it had reconstituted its nuclear program. The lack of cooperation fed a lack of confidence that produced worst-case and, sometimes, unjustified assessments of Iraq's intentions.

The role of technology

The IAEA inspections in Iraq provide a clear example of how technology and nontechnical mechanisms can complement each other during the monitoring process. Without satellite data and information collected by remote sensing technologies, the inspectors would have had little guidance on where to look for Iraq's nuclear-weapon facilities. At the same time, they would have found it difficult to understand the scope of the program without the inspectors on the ground. As one US official noted, "through remote intelligence means, we could learn just enough to create real concerns and suspicions about Iraqi WMD activities. But without inspectors on the ground, we didn't know enough to resolve these concerns or to confirm these suspicions."[14]

Two anecdotes from the Iraqi inspections process highlight the role of technology and the synergy between unilateral and cooperative monitoring mechanisms. During the 1980s, the IAEA had conducted inspections at declared facilities in Iraq's Tuwaitha Nuclear Research Center. These inspections occurred in portions of only three of 100 buildings in the complex. The inspectors did not have access to other facilities in the complex, even though they were central to Iraq's clandestine nuclear capabilities. Moreover, the inspectors were unaware of the size or scope of the entire facility until they saw satellite images of the entire complex after the war.[15] This demonstrates the limits of on-site inspections in the absence of support from data collected by unilateral monitoring mechanisms.

But satellite imagery may also provide a limited picture of a country's activities. After the war, the IAEA inspectors discovered that Iraq had used calutrons – a Second World War-era technology – to enrich uranium at Tuwaitha. Satellite imagery detected the movement of "large disc-shaped objects" away from the facility, but analysts viewing the images did not know what the objects were.[16] Some suspected they might be calutrons, but others could not believe Iraq would employ such an old technology. It was only after an American scientist who had worked on the Manhattan project viewed the images that the IAEA could conclude that Iraq, indeed, had enriched uranium with these devices.

Conclusion

Technology plays in an important role in monitoring and verification for arms control and nonproliferation. Without comprehensive verification regimes, the countries that sign these agreements would not be able to gain and sustain confidence in compliance. Comprehensive verification regimes would not be able to provide this confidence without the data, information, and understanding gained through remote and on-site technologies. But technology is not the only factor in an effective verification regime. The ability to detect violations and recognize compliance also depends on clarity in the terms of the agreement, the evaluation and interpretation of sometimes ambiguous data, and judgments about the intent of treaty partners. Technology is a critical tool, but verification, is, at its core, a political process that also relies on human judgment.

Notes

1. After the demise of the Soviet Union in December 1991, Soviet nuclear weapons remained on the territories of Russia, Ukraine, Belarus, and Kazakhstan. The non-Russian republics returned the nuclear weapons on their territories to Russia, so, although they were technically parties to the treaty, Russia was responsible for most of the treaty implementation.

2. US Department of Defense, "Task Force Report: Assessment of Nuclear Monitoring and Verification Technologies," Defense Science Board, Washington, DC, January 2014, p. 33, www.acq.osd.mil/dsb/reports/NuclearMonitoringAndVerificationTechnologies.pdf.

3. The Nuclear Nonproliferation Treaty recognizes the United States, Russia, the United Kingdom, France, and China as nuclear-weapon states.

4. Trevor Findlay, *Unleashing the Nuclear Watchdog: Strengthening and Reform of the IAEA* (Ontario: Canadian Center for Treaty Compliance, 2012), p. 57, www.cigionline.org/sites/default/files/Unleashing_the_Nuclear_Watchdog.pdf.

5. International Atomic Energy Agency, "The Conceptualization and Development of Safeguards Implementation at the State Level," GOV/2013/38, Vienna. August 12, 2013. p. 5, http://arms-controllaw.files.wordpress.com/2012/06/state-level-safeguards-concept-report-august-2013.pdf.

6. "Timely detection" is measured against the amount of time it would take for a country to convert weapons-usable plutonium and uranium into components suitable for a nuclear explosive device. This time could be around a week for plutonium and a year for highly enriched uranium or thorium. The IAEA seeks to maintain a 90–95 percent chance of detecting this type of activity. See Findlay, *Unleashing the Nuclear Watchdog*, p. 70.

7. Findlay, *Unleashing the Nuclear Watchdog*, p. 62.

8. According to the IAEA, the Additional Protocol grants the IAEA complementary inspection authority to that provided in underlying safeguards agreements. Under the Protocol, the IAEA is granted expanded rights of access to information and sites to provide assurance about both declared and possible undeclared activities. See International Atomic Energy Agency, "Factsheets and FAQs: IAEA Safeguards Overview: Comprehensive Safeguards Agreements and Additional Protocols," www.iaea.org/Publications/Factsheets/English/sg_overview.html.

9. Mark Hibbs, "The Plan for IAEA Safeguards," Carnegie Endowment for International Peace, November 20, 2012, http://carnegieendowment.org/2012/11/20/plan-for-iaea-safeguards/ekyb.

10. Adam M. Scheinman, "Calling for Action: The Next Generation Safeguards Initiative," *The Nonproliferation Review*, Vol. 16, No. 2 (July 2009), p. 259.

11. James Tape and Joseph Pilat, "Nuclear Safeguards and the Security of Nuclear Materials," in *Nuclear Safeguards, Security, and Nonproliferation; Achieving Security with Technology and Policy*, edited by James E. Doyle (Waltham, MA: Butterworth-Heinemann, 2008), p. 23.

12. Findlay, *Unleashing the Nuclear Watchdog*, p. 100.

13. Jeffrey Richelson, *Spying on the Bomb: American Nuclear Intelligence from Nazi Germany to Iran and North Korea* (New York: W.W. and Norton & Co., 2007), p. 353.

14. Robert Einhorn, "Understanding the Lessons of Nuclear Inspections and Monitoring in Iraq: A Ten-Year Review," Institute for Science and International Security, June 14, 2001, http://isis-online.org/einhorn/.

15. Richelson, *Spying on the Bomb*, p. 448.

16. Ibid., p. 451.

PART III

Nuclear Energy and Security

Nuclear Energy and Proliferation Risks

27

THE FUTURE OF NUCLEAR POWER

Reducing risks

Jacques Bouchard

Today, 440 nuclear power reactors are generating 13 percent of the world's electricity. They are located in thirty countries and most of them were built in the 1970s and 1980s. In spite of a strong increase in the worldwide electricity consumption, around 3 percent per year during the last two decades, new construction of nuclear power plants has been practically stopped in the 1990s and restarted slowly in the first decade of the twenty-first century, mainly in Asia. The Fukushima accident, following the great earthquake and tsunami in eastern Japan, has led some countries to reconsider their nuclear programs but, after taking into account the lessons of this accident, the driving forces for developing this source of energy remain and many countries, already equipped with nuclear power plants or not, have plans to build new plants.

The risk of facilitating the proliferation of nuclear weapons is one of the main issues associated with the development of peaceful use of nuclear energy. The Atoms for Peace deal introduced by President Eisenhower offered the benefits of civilian use of nuclear power in exchange for a definite renunciation of the development of nuclear-weapon programs. It is the basis of the Nonproliferation Treaty (NPT) signed by all countries with only three exceptions (although a fourth country, North Korea, withdrew from the treaty). Nevertheless, a few countries have used a civilian program to hide weapon development while others started a weapon program without any civilian applications.

This illustrates the paradox in the relation between nuclear power and proliferation risks: Developing the use of nuclear power could lead to an increase of proliferation risks; stopping to use nuclear power could also increase the risks of proliferation.

In the first hypothesis, it is clear that still more regulations and controls will be needed to avoid a country developing civilian uses of nuclear energy and diverting part of its civilian facilities to contribute to a secret weapon program. This was already a necessity for nuclear reactors, in particular those which could the most easily have been used to produce weapon-grade plutonium. It will be still more necessary when sensitive nuclear fuel cycle facilities, mainly for enrichment or reprocessing, are implemented in more countries. Technically speaking, solutions exist for both a secure design and strict controls for such facilities. In addition to existing dispositions – the NPT, safeguards by the International Atomic Energy Agency (IAEA), and the Additional Protocol – new international agreements will be necessary to fix the conditions for, and the limits on, future power plants and fuel cycle facilities.

Stopping the civilian use of nuclear energy will not suppress the risks of proliferation. There is natural uranium everywhere and the development of an unsophisticated enrichment technology could be done very discreetly by a country willing to start a nuclear-weapon program. The required knowledge is no longer a problem and dual-use technology components can be acquired in spite of the limitations introduced, in particular, by the Nuclear Suppliers Group (NSG). Furthermore, the end of peaceful uses of nuclear energy will lead to the reduction, if not suppression, of international safeguards, which in turn will result in a lack of visibility and the ability to discover clandestine operations.

Two conclusions can be drawn: First, proliferation risks are not an argument in favor of the renunciation of the benefits of nuclear energy for satisfying human needs. And second, a wider use of this important energy resource will require international agreement on new regulations and safeguards.

After a brief review of the present situation for nuclear energy demand in the frame of the worldwide increase of peaceful energy needs, this chapter provides a description of the common mode between civilian and military applications of nuclear energy with the two paths, uranium or plutonium, for weapon development, and then a summary of progress already under development, or yet to be achieved, to be made in order to conciliate in the future a wider use of nuclear power with a strong proliferation resistance.

Understanding the current nuclear environment

Nuclear energy demand

Worldwide nuclear power development entered a new phase at the turn of the twenty-first century as a consequence of climate change concerns and of a strong increase in fossil fuel prices. By the middle of the first decade of the century, there were numerous projects of new building, in particular in the United States, China, and in more than fifty countries expressing their wish to become "newcomers" benefiting from nuclear power.[1] At the same time, the nuclear industry started the construction of new Generation III reactors (EPR and AP1000) in Finland, France, and China. At the end of the decade, more than thirty reactors were in construction in China; India was ready to start a program of large Generation III PWRs provided by industrial companies of Russia, United States, and France; and the United Arab Emirates had ordered four APR 1400 nuclear power plants from the Korea Electric Power Corporation (KEPCO).

This new interest in nuclear power, sometimes called a "renaissance," was moderated by three events: the world economic crisis of 2008; the fast development of the production of nonconventional fossil fuels, mainly in the United States; and the accident at the Fukushima Daiichi nuclear power plant following the great earthquake and tsunami in the eastern part of Japan. The economic crisis led to a temporary slowdown of all the new nuclear power projects around the world; the prospect offered by shale gas and other oil and gas resources created a new situation involving the competitiveness of various electricity generation sources, in particular in the United States; and the Fukushima accident reactivated old antinuclear trends and led to the reaffirmation of the previous decision to stop the use of nuclear energy in Germany while creating more uncertainties for the future in some other European countries, including Belgium and Switzerland.

In spite of these difficulties, the main driving forces in favor of the wider use of the nuclear energy resource remain:

- *Economics:* The construction of nuclear power plants requires a large investment but provides a continuous source of electricity without any risk of cost fluctuations. As an example,

France, with 75 percent of its electricity coming from nuclear energy, has the lowest electricity prices in Western Europe.

- *Climate change*: Nuclear power is a carbon-free source of energy. It is the only way to reduce significantly the CO_2 emissions from electricity generation. As an example, the greenhouse gas emission per capita is nearly 50 percent more in Germany than in France.
- *Safety*: Nuclear energy has the lowest rate of casualties among all the sources of base-load electricity. Chernobyl and Fukushima resulted in the contamination of important areas, but even if the comparison is not easy, other energy sources have also had large environmental consequences (coal mines, accidental releases of oil, pollution, gas leaks, etc.). In normal operations, nuclear power is quite clean.

Predictions of the future are never easy. Nevertheless significant trends are well identified:

- The world's population will continue to grow at least for a few decades to reach nine or ten billion before the middle of the century.
- In spite of strong efforts to reduce the energy consumption in industrialized countries, energy demand will continue to increase, mainly owing to the population growth and to improvements in the standards of living in developing countries.
- The huge consumption of fossil resource should be a concern for the next generations, even taking into account the additional part of nonconventional oil and gas. The prices will continue to increase, and the environmental consequences, in particular climate change risks, are also a concern.
- The various atmospheric pollutions created in a large part by burning coal are increasing with severe consequences in term of casualties, amounting to several million premature deaths per year as indicated in a recent communication from the World Health Organization.[2]
- Renewables – windmills or solar – were developed and implemented on a large scale by several countries. However, they have shown their limits and are no longer considered to be a solution for replacing fossils or nuclear in the base-load generation of electricity.

Many international agencies, including the Organisation for Economic Co-operation and Development (OECD), the International Energy Agency, the Nuclear Energy Agency, the IAEA, the World Energy Council, and the World Nuclear Agency, generate energy growth predictions. They offer a large range of figures, which illustrates the difficulty of predicting the future policies in many countries. Nevertheless, most of them show the trend of growing demand supported in particular by the large programs officially announced by several countries, including China, India, Russia, and South Korea, and by the growing interest of newcomers, notably Turkey, Vietnam, the United Arab Emirates, and Saudi Arabia.

To illustrate the future proliferation risks associated with the peaceful use of nuclear power, we could consider a medium growth scenario which gives an increase by a factor of four in nuclear energy production by the middle of the century, with an installed capacity of 1,400 GWe consisting mainly of Generation III light water reactors.

The common mode for civilian and military uses of nuclear energy

Evaluation of the proliferation risks related to the use of nuclear power for civilian applications, primarily from the perspective of electricity generation at the present time, requires identifying the common mode between nuclear power and nuclear weapons, either in knowledge, technologies, components, or materials. The development of nuclear weapons requires knowledge, materials, and technology.

Apart from basic knowledge, the physics necessary for the design of nuclear weapons is quite different from that which is applied to the design of nuclear power reactors. The computational codes in neutronics, thermal hydraulics, or mechanics used by the civilian nuclear industry are of no help in understanding the phenomena and, furthermore, in making any applications in the field of nuclear-weapon physics. As it is practically impossible to stop the spreading of knowledge – at best, it can be delayed for the most sensitive information – many academic laboratories are more competent in understanding elements of weapon physics than most of the engineers working on the design and optimization of nuclear reactors.

Most of the technology is also completely different for the development of nuclear weapons and of nuclear reactors. Except for the preparation of special materials, nothing is common, or even similar, between weapons and power programs. All the techniques needed to build a nuclear weapon can be derived from other kinds of industrial operations, but none from the nuclear reactor industry.

In fact, the only common mode between the civilian and military applications of nuclear energy is the use in both cases of special nuclear materials, i.e., uranium and plutonium. Historically, the processes used to obtain enriched uranium, whatever the level of enrichment, or pure plutonium of any isotopic composition were first developed for military applications before being used for, or replicated in, for civilian programs. This illustrates clearly where the risk of proliferation associated with the use of nuclear power for peaceful applications resides. Nevertheless, there is a paradox: While a growing demand for nuclear energy may be considered to increase the risks of proliferation if safeguards measures are not sufficient, a complete renunciation of the benefits of this important source of energy for the future of humankind will not suppress the risks, and may even increase them as nuclear use becomes more difficult to control. This paradox is mainly due to the possibility of developing nuclear weapons by using only enriched uranium.

Proliferation through the uranium path

One pathway to the development of nuclear weapons is the use of uranium highly enriched in the isotope 235. It requires natural uranium, enrichment technology, and metal processing. There is no need for nuclear reactors or reprocessing technology and, thus, the path could be followed in a country, or even in a world, where there is no longer any civilian uses of nuclear power. On the other hand, materials or technologies used for peaceful applications can be diverted, which can result in progress toward a military program with less effort and more rapidly.

Today, for most operating nuclear power plants, the fuel is low enriched uranium oxide that cannot be used directly for making weapons. Assuming the possibility of a discreet diversion of some of this fuel, the process to obtain weapon-grade material will be a little simpler than starting from natural uranium, but both require an enrichment plant.

The development of nuclear weapons normally requires uranium enriched above 90 percent of U-235. Slightly lower enrichments can be considered with some costs related to the weapon's performance. For many decades, specialists have argued that there is no risk involving uranium enriched below 20 percent. It is a very conservative threshold, but a cautious measure if one looks to avoiding any risks.

The use of highly enriched uranium for civilian applications has been limited to research reactors. It has been considered for high temperature reactors but without industrial development so far. In both cases, the 20 percent limit can be applied, provided that the design of the reactor core and of the fuel is modified accordingly. Conversion of existing research reactors is underway and the adoption of an international norm to limit the enrichment below 20 percent for civilian applications could and should be the right way to avoid the risk of direct diversion of this special nuclear material for military use.

The question of enrichment facilities is more complex. Practically all the technologies used in commercial plants are dual-use technologies, which means that they can produce either low or high enrichment depending on the way in which the process is organized. In the past, gaseous diffusion was the primary technology used to enrich uranium. Today centrifuge enrichment is used for most industrial applications. Laser technologies are under development and could be a solution in the future. All of these technologies can be applied to produce various levels of enrichment. Modifications in the process can be made in order to use a low enrichment facility to produce weapon-grade material. This is not a difficult issue technically.

If a country decides to start its own uranium enrichment program with facilities able to produce significant amounts – perhaps the equivalent of several kilograms per year of highly enriched uranium – claiming that the program is aimed to produce fuel for future nuclear power plants, there is clearly a risk of possible diversion to feed a weapon program.

The principal risk associated with the use of enriched uranium for peaceful applications is not so much the possibility of diversion of highly enriched uranium, the use of which can be avoided for civilian programs. It is the possible conversion of civilian enrichment plants to produce weapon-grade materials. The risk of diversion of existing stocks of highly enriched uranium in countries already equipped with nuclear weapons is another matter not related to the civilian use of nuclear power.

Many international discussions have been, and are still being, devoted to possible ways to limit the risk of clandestine operations in uranium enrichment facilities. For example, in 2005 a team of experts mandated by the Director General of the IAEA recommended that only multinationally owned and operated facilities be allowed. This issue has been discussed in the context of the ongoing negotiations on the Iranian facilities, and their successful conclusion, if it occurs, would be a major contribution.

Proliferation through the plutonium path

A second route to proliferation involves the use of plutonium with a content of even isotopes as low as possible. It is produced by the irradiation of natural or depleted uranium in a reactor. The definition of weapon-grade plutonium, that is, some limits on the content of even isotopes, is not easy to express. The limits will be very low for the realization of high-performance weapons, in particular to satisfy miniaturization criteria related to the capacity of long-range missiles. However, it has been demonstrated that with relatively high contents in Pu-240 or Pu-242, it is still possible to build a device without optimal weapon performance but capable of delivering some energy. Thus, contrary to the uranium case, there is not a threshold separating usable and nonusable plutonium for weapon applications or, rather, in terms of proliferation risks. Today, it is commonly considered that the proliferation risk of plutonium includes the possible development of nuclear weapons or improvised nuclear devices used by terrorists.

From a proliferation perspective, the main difficulty comes from the fact that plutonium is an unavoidable by-product of nuclear power generation using uranium fuel. Part of the plutonium is burned in the reactor, but most of it remains in the spent fuel which is unloaded from the reactor after a few years of irradiation and stored provisionally before being reprocessed, buried, or stored for longer times. In the normal operation of power plants, the isotopic quality of the plutonium in the unloaded spent fuel will be very poor, but it is always possible to proceed to short irradiations with premature unloading of the fuel to obtain better quality weapon-usable material. It is easier to take this step with some types of reactors. This situation will not be any different with a thorium fuel cycle, which produces U-233, another efficient material for building weapons.

The plutonium content of the spent fuel unloaded from light water reactors (LWRs), which are the most commonly used reactors today, is quite large – more than 100 kg per year for a 1,000 MWe plant. Currently, most of the spent fuels are stored, waiting for a later decision on reprocessing or fuel disposal, and the accumulation of plutonium in them is rather impressive. There is already about 1,500 tons of plutonium in spent fuel, with the total reaching 5,000 tons by the middle of the century. (See Table 27.1.)

Some countries reprocess the spent fuel as soon as possible and recycle their plutonium in light water reactors in mixed oxide (MOX) fuel, thus limiting the growth of their stockpiles of spent fuel. But, this can be done usefully only once. After the first recycle, most of the plutonium is still stored in MOX spent fuels.

In the end, there are only two options for the plutonium created during the operation of current nuclear power plants: either to bury it in a geological depository or to burn it in fast neutron reactors. The first option could be direct disposal of the spent fuel without any treatment other than conditioning it or disposal of separate plutonium coming from reprocessing the spent fuel. The second option limits the disposal of waste to fission products and some minor actinides, but it involves a progressive replacement of light water reactors by fast reactors. Accelerator-driven systems are specific designs of fast reactors with safer operation, at least in theory, but with higher cost and no production of energy. Their use can be envisaged for burning plutonium if there is a closing down of the use of nuclear energy for electric power generation.

From the proliferation point of view, the burying option is safer in the short term. It avoids separating the plutonium and keeps the spent fuel self-protected by its own radiological activity. But the plutonium is still there. In the longer term, it will progressively lose its self-protection and the depository will become a rich and dangerous plutonium mine. The reverse applies for the burning option, where the plutonium is destroyed, but which requires chemical or electrochemical treatment of the spent fuel and then the fabrication of the plutonium in new fuel for recycling in reactors. During these operations the radiological protection of the plutonium is reduced even if the way it is done today can obviously be improved.

The choice between the two options has been debated for a long time. Today, after a failed attempt to license a repository for spent fuels at Yucca Mountain, the United States is reconsidering its options for the future while extending the provisional duration of intermediate storage. Only Sweden has made a clear choice for the burying option and has well advanced in the process of building a repository for direct disposal of spent fuels with special condition-

Table 27.1 Spent fuel and plutonium accumulation

Year	2005	2025	2050
Nuclear capacity (GWe)	360	650	1400
LWR capacity (GWe)	320	550	1200
Stored spent fuels (Mtons)	0.2	0.5	1.0
Plutonium amount (tons)	1500	4000	8500

Hypotheses: – Scenario in the medium of various forecasts
– Recycling limited to a few countries
– Progressive replacement of LWRs by FRs after 2040

ing. Several other countries which operate a limited number of nuclear power plants are still considering this option, but have not yet succeeded in finding a suitable location for a repository that is acceptable to the local population.

The burning option is favored by France, United Kingdom, Japan, Russia, China, and India, and is still considered as a future option by many other countries. The reprocessing of spent fuel has been undertaken at the industrial scale and commercialized, along with the fabrication of MOX fuel currently used in nearly thirty power plants operated in Europe. As is required for the complete implementation of this option, the development of fast reactors is underway in most of these countries.

Whatever the future, in terms of practical choices between the burning or burying options, the plutonium path will continue to pose an important risk of proliferation that is directly related to the use of nuclear power for peaceful applications. With uranium resource availability (and cost) and waste management, it is the third criteria for defining a viable, long-term civilian nuclear energy policy.

Looking at future developments

The once-through route

Also called the open cycle option, the once-through route by implication considers as waste the spent fuel unloaded from light water reactors and requires disposing of it in a repository without any intention to recover it in the future. While specialists consider that this approach can be done safely in appropriate deep geological formations, public acceptance remains a big issue in most countries. As noted, proliferation risks are minimized in the short term but not completely absent as it is necessary to let the spent fuels cool down in interim storage for several decades. Interim storage, either wet or dry, should be safeguarded very strictly to avoid the risk of diversion of fuel elements. The amount of plutonium included in a regular LWR spent fuel element is nearly one kilogram. Thus, the diversion of a few elements and a small clandestine facility for reprocessing would be sufficient to allow the production of a dangerous nuclear device.

Furthermore, given the difficulties of opening a repository for spent fuels, several countries currently favor a "wait and see" policy consisting of long-term interim storage in order to keep open for the future the options of either burying the spent fuel or burning the plutonium in the spent fuel. This policy offers time to perform R&D aimed at improving both technologies, but can be criticized for transferring this burden to future generations. The proliferation risks involved reinforce the necessity of the strict safeguarding of storage facilities.

Disposing of spent fuel in a repository will lead, after a long period of cooling down, to a rich plutonium mine. However, while the public expresses actual fears about potential radiological consequences a hundred thousand years from now, nobody appears really concerned by the proliferation risks that would emerge in a few thousand years or less. At a minimum, it may be possible to suppress any indication of the repository's location, but the present trend is rather to keep it as visible as possible.

Another consequence of the once-through route is the continuous necessity for uranium enrichment in the long term. Besides the debate on the sustainability of nuclear energy with this option, this means that improved proliferation resistance of enrichment facilities and/or an international agreement on the possible implementation and management of these facilities will be needed.

The risks associated with reactor design

Several types of reactors have been and are still being considered for building nuclear power plants. The most commonly used today are light water reactors – either pressurized water reactors or boiling water reactors – a technology initially developed for naval reactors. In both cases, the fuel is low-enriched uranium well under the 20 percent threshold for proliferation risk. The loading/unloading of the fuel is a heavy operation requiring the opening of the main reactor vessel, which takes several days. The normal time of reactor operations between two reloadings is twelve to eighteen months. The plutonium generated in the fuel during this period of irradiation is not weapon-grade, even though there is no clear quality threshold for such a determination. This type of reactor is also quite easy to safeguard, as the fuel assemblies, in limited number, can be checked under water. Moreover, the complexity of the operation to extract an assembly from the reactor core creates a level of proliferation resistance. For all these reasons, LWRs are not considered as a proliferation risk, assuming they are submitted to international controls.

At the beginning of the nuclear era, graphite reactors (GRs) and heavy water reactors (HWRs) were developed using natural uranium for the fuel. They were used by countries developing nuclear weapons because both types allow the production of weapon-grade plutonium (assuming a sufficiently short time of irradiation of the fuel). Their design facilitates such short irradiation times with continuous loading/unloading of the fuel elements through open channels. Soon after their development, reactors for nuclear power plants were built using a similar design. In most cases, however, they were rapidly replaced by LWRs for economic and safety reasons. While graphite reactors are no longer in operation except in the United Kingdom and Russia, heavy water reactors were successfully industrialized by Canada and built in many countries, some of which wanted to avoid the need for enriched uranium. The proliferation risks associated with HWRs (and GRs) cannot be underestimated as long as they are fuelled with natural uranium and have a continuous loading/unloading capability. Should these reactors have a future, it will be necessary to fix some constraints on their fuel and their design, in order to allow their efficient safeguarding.

The concept of high temperature reactors (HTRs), based upon a very specific fuel composed of small enriched uranium particles enrobed in graphite with a silicon carbide coating, has not yet been commercialized despite a few efforts to do so in the past decades. From the point of view of proliferation risks, these reactors should be extremely proliferation-resistant, but the enrichment of the uranium used for the fuel should be limited to under the proliferation threshold – 20 percent – in order to avoid the use of highly enriched uranium in civilian applications. This limitation does not seem to be a problem for the development of HTRs, and is a critical principle for thinking about proliferation resistance.

Fast reactors (FRs) also have not yet been commercialized, even though some large scale prototypes have been built and operated, in particular in France and Russia. FRs represent a big challenge. They are the only way we know today to burn all of the plutonium in fuel, and to make efficient use of uranium (or thorium) resources. However, their technology, whatever the choice of coolant, is quite new as compared to light water boilers, making it more difficult to make these reactors economically competitive. With the current design of existing reactors, or new plant under construction in several countries, their proliferation risks are not negligible.

The first weakness is the fresh fuel, a mixed oxide of uranium and plutonium for which, in case of diversion, the recovery of the plutonium is not a technical challenge. The plutonium used for the fuel is either from LWR spent fuel or from the recycling of FR fuel itself, and is thus not weapon grade. However, it cannot be excluded as usable in a terrorist device. The fuel reloading is a complex operation requiring not only shutting down the reactor for several days, but also deploying heavy handling tools. This operation cannot be hidden if the reactor is under permanent safeguarding.

The development of FRs is not aimed at burning excess plutonium, but also to allow the full use of the uranium resources. The latter goal requires that the FRs be designed and operated in what is called the breeder version. To reach this goal, it is necessary to have breeder zones around the core containing only natural or depleted uranium in order to benefit from the neutrons coming out of the core to produce plutonium. This creates another issue for proliferation, as the plutonium generated in these breeder zones is, in current designs, mostly weapon grade. In normal operation, this plutonium from the breeder zones is mixed with plutonium from the core for recycling. Nevertheless, there is a risk of diversion which cannot be underestimated.

In the frame of the Generation IV International Forum, research is being conducted to develop FRs which can satisfy the criteria of economics, safety, and nonproliferation. It is the first time that proliferation risks have been taken as a design criterion from the beginning. Several possible solutions are under study involving both the reactor and its fuel cycle facilities.

The risks associated with enrichment facilities

As noted, enrichment facilities represent one of the weakest points from a proliferation risk perspective, as they are based upon dual-use technologies. They were developed first for military applications and progressively adapted to satisfy the needs of nuclear power programs. As the risk of a misuse of civilian facilities was rapidly identified, several attempts were made to develop specific technologies allowing only low-level enrichment or to make it quite difficult to modify a plant to produce highly enriched uranium.

None of these attempts were successful and the technologies currently in use (gaseous diffusion and gas centrifuge), or under development (laser technologies), are able to produce both levels of enrichment. With present knowledge, there is no technical way to design a facility producing low-enriched uranium that cannot be quite easily modified to provide at least limited amounts of highly enriched uranium. Therefore, avoiding proliferation risks should rely only on management and safeguards measures.

The proposal of multinational facilities – with several countries owning and operating civilian enrichment plants – is one possible way to limit proliferation risks. This approach is also consistent with the fact that to be profitable an industrial plant should have a production capacity sufficient to feed several tens of LWRs.

Safeguarding an enrichment plant efficiently, for example a plant using centrifuge technology, will require a permanent presence to monitor the balance of input and output and to allow detection of any change in the process that can lead to the production of weapon-grade enriched uranium.

As LWRs will be the main tools for an expansion of nuclear power generation in the next decades, it is urgent to reach an international agreement on new industrial enrichment facilities and the way they should be managed and safeguarded. Furthermore, the prospect of the clandestine development of "simpler" facilities aimed at producing highly enriched uranium in countries without nuclear power will remain a risk. It will therefore be necessary also to reach some international agreement on surveillance and detection.

The risks associated with fuel recycling facilities

For historical reasons, partly due to the fact that reprocessing technologies were first developed for military applications, the current route for recycling, either in LWRs or in FRs, implies a first step of chemical separation of uranium and plutonium from the spent fuel and the purification of the separated elements. This step is followed by a second step, fuel fabrication, including the adjusted mixing of uranium and plutonium according to the reactor specifications.

To reduce the proliferation risks associated with a possible diversion of the pure plutonium between the two steps, improvements could be made to co-locate reprocessing and fuel fabrication into a single facility, to reduce the purification phase, to mix uranium and plutonium at the end of the first step, and to have only a minimum capacity of storage of materials between the reprocessing output and the fabrication input. Without complete purification, the materials will remain self-protected by their own radiological activity and the fabrication of the fuel should be done in a remote facility.

A variant of this option, which is seriously being considered today in the framework of the Generation IV studies, consists of burning not only the plutonium but also the minor actinides, mainly americium and neptunium, which have long-lived isotopes responsible for most of the residual waste activity after a few thousand years. Besides its utility in the management of high-level waste, such an approach could also be of importance for protecting against proliferation risks. The main drawback of this option will be the necessity of remote operation for fuel fabrication, transport and handling of fresh fuel in the reactor.

In the 1980s, Argonne National Laboratory developed a concept of full recycling, the integral fast reactor (IFR), based upon the use of a metallic fuel and the technology of pyroprocessing. The merits of a metal alloy versus mixed oxide or other compounds are still being debated among specialists, along with the advantages or drawbacks of pyroprocessing compared to aqueous reprocessing. Unfortunately, after a large R&D effort, the IFR program was stopped in the United States. There is, however, still some work going on in other countries, in particular South Korea.

Conclusions

Whatever the technology choices for reactor design, fuel and reprocessing, the full actinide recycling in fast neutron reactors seems today the best option for a sustainable future of the civilian use of nuclear energy. It will satisfy the main criteria, i.e., complete use of natural uranium resources, an easier management of high-level waste, and a full protection against the proliferation risk. Large R&D programs are devoted to this option in several countries. Japan has recently decided to devote its FR prototype, MONJU, to this program. France is designing a new FR prototype, ASTRID, partly for the same objective, which is required by the 2006 Act on Waste Management. Russia, India, and China are also working on similar programs.

The actinide recycling strategy implies a progressive replacement of LWRs by FRs and decreasing use of uranium enrichment leading to a reduction, then a suppression, of the corresponding proliferation risks, at least in relation to the peaceful use of nuclear energy. There will always remain the risks of the clandestine use of enrichment independent of nuclear power programs.

Notes

1.   These countries include Algeria, Chile, Egypt, Ghana, Indonesia, Jordan, Kazakhstan, Libya, Morocco, Philippines, Poland, Saudi Arabia, Thailand, Tunisia, Turkey, UAE, Vietnam, and Yemen.
2.   World Health Organization, "Burden of Disease from Ambient Air Pollution for 2012: Summary of Results," March 2014, www.who.int/phe/health_topics/outdoorair/databases/AAP_BoD_results_March2014.pdf; World Health Organization, "Ambient (Outdoor) Air Quality and Health," Fact Sheet, No. 313, March 2014, www.who.int/mediacentre/factsheets/fs313/en.

28

NUCLEAR POWER
AND PROLIFERATION

Tatsujiro Suzuki

The relationship between nuclear proliferation and the civil nuclear power program has been and remains one of the central concerns associated with application of nuclear technologies for nonmilitary applications since the beginning of nuclear power development in the 1950s.

After almost sixty years of history, it was shown in several cases that nuclear-weapon programs were triggered or at least assisted by the existence of civilian nuclear power programs. On the other hand, global institutional schemes, such as the Nonproliferation Treaty (NPT) and safeguards activities by the International Atomic Energy Agency (IAEA), as well as bilateral agreements between states, have been effective in limiting proliferation far more than was originally expected.

Even after the tragic nuclear accident at the Fukushima Daiichi nuclear power plant in 2011, it is expected that demand for nuclear power programs will grow and, more importantly, demand for sensitive nuclear fuel cycle capability will also grow. In addition, since the 9/11 terrorist attack in the United States in 2001, concerns over nuclear terrorism have been growing so that nuclear security measures over weapon-usable materials need to be strengthened.

This chapter reviews the historic and generic relationships between civilian nuclear power programs and nuclear proliferation. The discussion then focuses on global nuclear power developments after the Fukushima accident. Third, the chapter discusses key issues associated with so-called "weapon-usable materials" and technologies which can produce such materials. Finally, the chapter discusses possible countermeasures to deal with these materials and sensitive technologies needed to produce them.

The inevitable link between civilian nuclear power and nuclear weapons

Since the beginning of the nuclear era in 1946, there was a concern over the potential risks of nuclear proliferation associated with the expansion of civilian application of nuclear energy technologies. The famous Acheson-Lilienthal Report published in 1946 stated:

> We have concluded unanimously *that there is no prospect of security against atomic warfare* in a system of international agreements to outlaw such weapons *controlled only by a system which relies on inspection and similar police-like methods. National rivalries in the development of atomic energy readily convertible to destructive purposes are the heart of the difficulty.*[1]

It reminded us of the inevitable link between civilian nuclear power programs and nuclear-weapon proliferation. In fact, "splitting the atom" is a common principle and technology for both civilian nuclear energy and nuclear weapons. Fissile materials, uranium and plutonium, are essential components of both nuclear weapons and of nuclear energy. About one kilogram of fissile material releases an energy equivalent to the explosion of about 18 thousand tons (18 kilotons) of chemical high explosives. This tremendous scale of power is the main characteristic that attracts both energy and military strategists. Unfortunately, this is the basic dilemma that nuclear technology is inherently a dual-use technology.

While there are other fissile materials, such as uranium 233, neptunium-237, and americium-241, this chapter focuses on the most common fissile materials, i.e., enriched uranium and plutonium.

Enriched uranium

In nature, uranium 235 makes up only 0.7 percent of natural uranium, and the rest is uranium 238. The first nuclear bomb dropped in Hiroshima used about 60kg of uranium enriched to about 80 percent in uranium 235. This level of enrichment is not commonly used for civilian nuclear power programs. Typical commercial nuclear fuel contains about 4 to 5 percent of enriched uranium. This is the main difference between civilian nuclear fuel and bomb materials. Uranium enriched higher than 20 percent is considered as directly usable for nuclear explosive and thus IAEA defines it as highly enriched uranium (HEU). To minimize their masses, however, actual weapons typically use uranium enriched to 90 percent uranium-235 or higher. Such uranium is sometimes defined as weapon-grade. In contrast, enriched uranium commonly used for civilian nuclear power is called low enriched uranium (LEU). A minimum of 20kg of 90 percent HEU (i.e., 18kg of uranium 235) is needed to produce a nuclear explosive and thus IAEA defines it as "significant quantity" (SQ) for HEU. Because uranium 235 and uranium 238 are chemically identical, the process of enriching uranium requires a sophisticated isotope separation technology. The most common enrichment technology currently used is gas centrifuge technology.

Plutonium

Plutonium is an artificial isotope produced in nuclear reactors by neutron absorption of uranium 238. The Nagasaki bomb used 6kg of plutonium and the IAEA defines a SQ as only 8kg. But the design of a plutonium bomb is more difficult than bombs using HEU. A so-called implosion-type bomb requires more sophisticated technology and thus it is believed that nuclear testing is necessary for verifying the design. The plutonium in typical power-reactor spent fuel (reactor-grade plutonium) contains 50–60 percent plutonium-239, and about 25 percent plutonium-240. In contrast, so-called weapon-grade plutonium contains about 90 percent or higher of plutonium 239. It was once believed that reactor-grade plutonium was not usable for nuclear weapons, as the large fraction of plutonium-240 in reactor-grade plutonium would reduce the explosive yield of a weapon to insignificance by predetonation. But with implosion designs, such predetonation would not reduce the yield below about 1,000 tons TNT equivalent which is still a devastating explosive power. There has been a debate over the usability of reactor-grade plutonium for nuclear weapons. In a 1997 report, the US Department of Energy concluded that "Virtually any combination of plutonium isotopes ... can be used to make a nuclear weapon ... reactor grade plutonium is weapons-usable whether by unsophisticated or by advanced nuclear weapon states."[2]

Plutonium can be separated from spent nuclear fuel by a chemical process called "reprocessing," and once it is separated, plutonium can be easily accessible and thus it is highly vulnerable to nuclear thefts. Reprocessing technology is relatively simpler than uranium enrichment and thus it is often used as a means for acquiring weapon–usable material. For civilian nuclear power programs, reprocessing is also considered valuable as recycling plutonium can save uranium resources by about 30 percent. In addition, fast breeder reactors (FBRs) using plutonium as their primary fuel, once commercialized, can be a self-sustaining energy resource. Therefore, nuclear fuel cycles and FBR are often seen as ultimate goals of civilian nuclear power programs. However, FBRs have not yet been commercialized and thus the commercial demand for plutonium is rather limited for the foreseeable future.

Prospects of nuclear power expansion after fukushima and its implications for nonproliferation

According to the latest statistics of the IAEA, as of May 7, 2014, 435 nuclear power plants (372.8 GWe) are operating and 72 units are under construction. Two units are in a long-term shutdown. The largest increase in nuclear capacity is expected to happen in the Far East, notably in China and the Republic of Korea (ROK).[3] (See Figure 28.1.) The IAEA also made projection numbers for the future expansion of nuclear power capacity every year based on published reports of future plans and the construction of new nuclear power plants. The projection made in 2013 shows significant growth in world capacity but its projection was lowered compared to the 2011 projection and reflects the large uncertainties. (See Table 28.1.) This is primarily due to the slowdown effects of the Fukushima Daiichi nuclear accident in 2011.

The 2013 projection shows 435 GWe (low) to 722 GWe (high) in 2030, compared with the 2011 projection of 501 GWe to 746 GWe. Similarly, the 2013 projection estimated 440 GWe (low) to 1,113 GWe (high) in 2050, compared with the 2011 projection of 560 GWe to 1,228 GWe. The higher estimate involves significant growth (about three times that of today), but the lower estimate is basically only a 20 percent increase over current capacity. As a result, the share of nuclear power is expected to decrease steadily in the next several decades. Even under the higher projection, its share in global power capacity will decline from current 7.6 percent to 5.6 percent in 2050.[4] Meanwhile, for the East Asian region, under the high projection estimate,

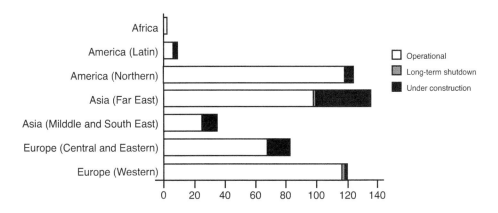

Figure 28.1 Status of nuclear power programs as of April 26, 2014

its share is expected to increase from current 5.0 percent to 8.0 percent in 2050, but the lower projection estimate also shows a significant decline from 5.0 percent to 3.7 percent.

In short, it is important to recognize that there is a significant uncertainty in the future expansion of nuclear power, and that even under the highest growth scenario, the share of nuclear power can go down steadily in the coming decades. This has significant implications for global energy and environmental policy.

From the standpoint of nuclear nonproliferation, we need to look at different perspectives. First, the number of countries that show an interest in introducing nuclear power is increasing. More importantly, although the capacity of growth itself may not be so significant, the political implications can be more noteworthy if new nuclear countries emerge in a politically unstable region such as the Middle East or South Asia. For example, India and Pakistan are not members of NPT but it is expected that their civilian nuclear power programs will grow in the coming decades. In the Middle East, although most countries except Israel are members of the NPT, Iran, the United Arab Emirates (UAE), Saudi Arabia, and Turkey are among those states who have expressed an interest in introducing civilian nuclear power programs. There are also plans of new nuclear programs in South East Asian countries such as Vietnam, Indonesia, and Thailand.

Second, in the response to demand from new nuclear power countries, competition among nuclear suppliers is increasing. The most notable example deals with India. Although India is not a member of the NPT, major supplier countries, including the United States, France, and Russia, have concluded bilateral agreements with India for the peaceful use of nuclear energy. This was a result of the decision in 2008 by the Nuclear Suppliers Group to treat India as an "exception." The decision to treat India as an exceptional case has raised international concern over potential negative impacts on the nuclear nonproliferation regime.[5]

Table 28.1 Future IAEA projections of global nuclear power capacity, 2013

	Actual in 2011	Estimates for 2030		Estimates for 2050	
		Estimated		Estimated	
		in 2011	in 2013	in 2011	in 2013
World Total					
Nucl. Capacity (GWe)					
Low estimate	368.8	501	435	560	440
High estimate		746	722	1228	1113
Share (%)					
Low estimate	7.1	5.2	4.5	2.7	2.2
High estimate		6.2	6.2	6.0	5.6
Far East					
Nucl. capacity (GWe)					
Low estimate	79.8	180	147	220	189
High estimate		255	268	450	412
Share (%)					
Low estimate	5.0	6.4	5.3	4.2	3.7
High estimate		7.5	8.1	8.6	8.0

Source: International Atomic Energy Agency, "Energy, electricity and nuclear power estimates for the period up to 2050," 2011 Edition, www-pub.iaea.org/MTCD/Publications/PDF/RDS1_31.pdf; International Atomic Energy Agency, "Energy, electricity and nuclear power estimates for the period up to 2050," 2013 Edition, www-pub.iaea.org/MTCD/publications/PDF/RDS-1-33_web.pdf.

Third, a new group of suppliers are also emerging. In 2009, the Republic of Korea and the UAE signed a $20.4 billion nuclear cooperation deal, with South Korea for the first time being a nuclear system supplier. This business deal shocked many traditional nuclear suppliers, including France and the United States. This deal has proven that advanced nuclear countries are not the only suppliers, and more nuclear suppliers may be emerging in the future global nuclear energy market. In fact, China has already agreed to supply power reactors to Pakistan.

Fourth, new states are also emerging as uranium fuel suppliers. In addition to traditional big uranium suppliers, such as Canada, Australia, and South Africa, new suppliers such as Mongolia and Kazakhstan are now entering the global market.

Given all the above changes, international nuclear business may face structural changes which may have significant nonproliferation implications. Among those, the United States is no longer dominant in the nuclear suppliers' market and its international influence may be reduced significantly in the long run. Higher levels of competition among nuclear suppliers may lead to relaxed regulations or conditions attached to nuclear exports. An absence of enforcing international regulation over nuclear safety and nuclear security may create "loop-holes" in global nuclear business transactions. It is imperative for the global community to increase its attention over nuclear business transactions in order to minimize the risks of nuclear proliferation and breaches of nuclear security.

Emerging risks: Weapon-usable material and its technologies

While structural changes in the global nuclear market are already alarming, more imminent and serious risks are emerging. These emerging risks arise from an increasing quantity of weapon-usable materials and the technologies and facilities to produce these materials.

HEU and uranium enrichment facilities

Owing primarily to nuclear disarmament efforts, global stockpiles of HEU have been shrinking, and the latest estimate is about 1,380 tons. (See Figure 28.2.) It should be noted that civilian HEU stockpiles are only a small fraction of the total global stockpile. It should also be noted that a large fraction of excess HEU stockpiles have been blended down to low-enriched uranium and have been sold on the global nuclear fuel market.[6]

HEU is used in many countries for civilian research reactors and there are about one hundred facilities using HEU worldwide. As of December 2012, thirty-three countries had at least 1kg of HEU. The global civilian HEU stockpile is now about 15 tons. Originally the United States, Russia, and the United Kingdom exported HEU for civilian purposes. Under the Global Threat Reduction Initiative, the United States has been accepting spent HEU from recipient countries. It should also be noted that all civilian HEU in nonnuclear-weapon states is under IAEA safeguards.

Enrichment facilities and technologies may pose significant proliferation risks in the coming decades, as they are essential components of civilian nuclear power programs. Currently, ten countries have enrichment facilities producing civilian nuclear fuel, but the number of such facilities and enrichment capacities is expanding in response to growing nuclear power programs.

Technically speaking, once an enrichment facility is constructed for civilian purposes (i.e., for producing low uranium enrichment), such facility could easily be converted to produce HEU. Table 28.2 shows how this can be done within a short period of time. A small enrichment plant (150 tSWU/year) for about 1GWe nuclear power reactor can produce 20 tons of

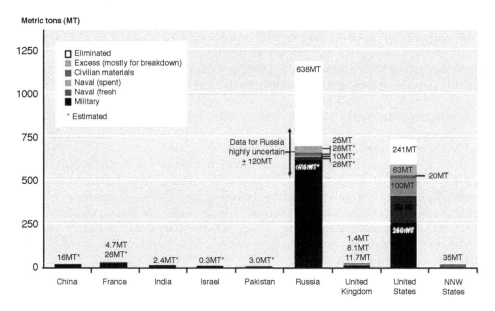

Figure 28.2 Enrichment facilities and possible conversion for HEU production

LEU (enriched to 4 percent U-235) in one year, with depleted uranium of about 0.2 percent (tails). If operation mode is changed to 0.31 percent, it can also produce 654kg of HEU (enriched to 93 percent U-235) in one year. Eventually, if 4 percent LEU is used as a feed material, it can produce 100kg of HEU (enriched to 93 percent U-235) within only eight days. This illustrates that a small civilian enrichment facility can be converted to produce HEU in a very short time. Such conversion can be easily detected if a facility is under IAEA safeguards. Therefore, it is very important that facilities be placed under IAEA safeguards. It is suspected that North Korea developed its own enrichment facility, which only came to light after it withdrew from the NPT. Accordingly, there are no IAEA safeguards currently in place on this facility.

It is also possible to build an undeclared (secret) enrichment facility once such technology is developed or transferred by other states. Iraqi secret enrichment facilities were later revealed by UN special inspections. Iran built its enrichment facility without declaring it to the IAEA, although it is now under IAEA safeguards.

Table 28.2 Enrichment facilities and possible conversion for HEU production

Feed	Time	Product	Depleted tails
150 metric tons natural uranium	1 year	20,000 kg LEU (4%)	0.2% U-235
150 metric tons natural uranium	1 year	654 kg HEU (93%) [26 bombs]	0.31%
150 metric tons natural uranium	40 days	100 kg HEU (93%) [4 bombs]	0.65%
20,000 kg 4% LEU	8 days	100 kg HEU (93%) [4 bombs]	3.55%

Source: International Panel on Fissile Material (IPFM), "Global Fissile Material Report 2006," www.fissilematerials.org/ipfm/site_down/ipfmreport06.pdf.

In short, in order to minimize proliferation risks, placing international safeguards on all enrichment facilities is critically important. In addition, efforts to prevent illicit transfers of enriched uranium and enrichment technology should be enhanced.

Plutonium and reprocessing

Unlike HEU, the global plutonium stockpile is steadily increasing, primarily due to increased civilian reprocessing activities. The current global plutonium stockpile is estimated to be about 495 tons as of the end of 2012. Unlike HEU, about half of this stockpile is for civilian use. (See Figure 28.3.) Since 1997, nine countries (Belgium, China, France, Germany, Japan, Russia, Switzerland, the United Kingdom, and the United States) have been declaring their plutonium inventories according to the IAEA Plutonium Management Guideline.[7] This has been useful for improving transparency of civilian plutonium stockpile and activities in each country.

The United Kingdom has the largest plutonium stockpile at about 94 tons, followed by France (58 tons), Russia (50 tons), and Japan (44 tons). All four of these countries currently have commercial reprocessing programs. The United Kingdom is now planning to close down its THORP reprocessing plant when its commercial contract is completed. France and Russia continue reprocessing operations and Japan is about to start its first commercial reprocessing plant in Rokkasho (800 tons/year). In addition, India and China are planning to build commercial reprocessing plants in the future.

Once plutonium is separated, it is relatively accessible and thus tighter protection and control is needed. Safeguarding large-scale reprocessing plants is also relatively difficult, but advanced accounting techniques combined with containment and surveillance measures have been developed to minimize the diversion risks of large reprocessing facilities. Still, the expansion of reprocessing activities that result in increasing stockpiles of separated plutonium is a major source of proliferation concern as well as nuclear security concerns. Efforts to minimize

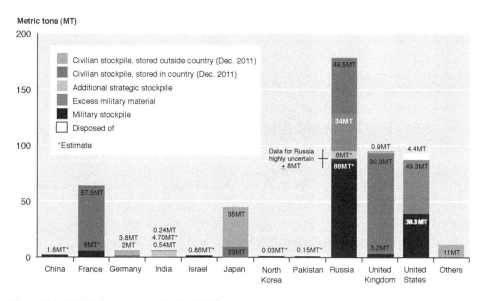

Figure 28.3 Global plutonium stockpile (2012)

the number of such facilities and to minimize stockpiles of separated plutonium should be enhanced. The joint communiqué at the Hague Nuclear Security Summit of 2014 states: "We encourage States to minimise their stocks of HEU and to keep their stockpile of separated plutonium to the minimum level, both as consistent with national requirements."[8] Therefore, reducing stockpiles of separated plutonium is now a common goal on the global agenda in order to minimize the risks to nuclear security as well as proliferation.

Unlike enrichment activities, reprocessing and the separation of plutonium are not essential parts of civilian nuclear activities. Spent fuel can be managed safely by long-term storage and by geological disposal without reprocessing. Reprocessing is often driven by a need for spent fuel management due to difficulties of finding possible sites to accept long-term storage of spent fuel. This is primarily a social-political issue and not a technical issue. Technical solutions for spent fuel storage and disposal do exist and this should not be the argument for reprocessing. Interim storage, especially dry cask storage, is the best solution for managing spent fuel without harming civilian nuclear power activities. Japan's reprocessing program is an important example in this context. The absence of a good spent fuel management strategy has become one of the primary reasons for the construction of a large scale reprocessing program at Rokkasho village in Aomori. It is advisable for Japan to consider alternative options in order to avoid unnecessary reprocessing.[9]

Latent capability

As noted above, once enrichment and reprocessing facilities and technology are acquired, a state is technically capable of producing enough weapon-usable material for a nuclear weapon within a short period of time, probably within months not years. Therefore, nuclear fuel cycle capabilities are often called a "latent capability" for nuclear weapons. Article IV of the NPT says that "Nothing in this Treaty shall be interpreted as affecting the inalienable right of all the Parties to the Treaty to develop research, production and use of nuclear energy for peaceful purposes without discrimination and in conformity with Articles I and II of this Treaty."[10] Therefore, it is often argued by NPT member states that they have a right to access peaceful uses of nuclear technology, including sensitive nuclear fuel cycle capability. This debate over latent capabilities and inalienable rights is and has been a fundamental dilemma of the global nuclear energy and nonproliferation regime. There is a need to explore new approaches to minimize the proliferation risks of latent capability while assuring inalienable rights of NPT nonnuclear-weapon states.

Responding to emerging risks: Institutional and technical options

What are possible measures to respond to emerging risks of expansion of civilian nuclear power programs, especially as stockpile of weapon-usable materials and latent capabilities for nuclear weapons spread worldwide? The following five both institutional and technical options need to be explored simultaneously.

Enhancing safeguards, security, and safety measures

First, international measures such as safeguards, security, and safety need to be enhanced further. For safeguards, the Additional Protocol (AP) has been already a major milestone for strengthening safeguards measures, especially responding to undeclared activities. As of March 12, 2014, 143 countries signed the AP and 122 countries had ratified it.[11] This is a tremendous achievement for the global nonproliferation regime. Universal compliance with the AP should be strongly promoted to minimize the risks of undeclared nuclear programs.

For nuclear security, one important international convention is the amended Convention on Physical Protection of Nuclear Materials. As of December 2013, among 149 parties, only forty-four countries ratified the amended Convention.[12] It is important for the international community to increase the number of parties to this important convention. The IAEA has published many important documents and reports on this subject, notably "Nuclear Security Recommendations on Physical Protection of Nuclear Material and Nuclear Facilities (INFCIRC/225/Revision 5)"[13] and "Objective and Essential Elements of a State's Nuclear Security Regime."[14]

One of the important lessons learned from the Fukushima Daiichi nuclear accident was the importance of synergistic effects between nuclear safety and security. For example, secure storage of spent fuel is now important for both nuclear safety and security. Sabotage at nuclear facilities can also cause both safety and security concerns. It would be advisable for all nuclear countries to increase their efforts to optimize measures to improve both safety and security.

Strengthening bilateral agreements and nuclear suppliers' guidelines

Limiting technology transfers of sensitive technologies and materials is also critical. One important, legally enforcing measure is bilateral agreements between nuclear suppliers and recipient countries. The best example of such an agreement is the one between the United States and the UAE, which was concluded in 2009 and is now considered the "gold standard" for bilateral agreements. In this agreement, the UAE pledged not to develop domestic enrichment and reprocessing activities.[15] Of course bilateral agreements cannot be universal because they depend on the conditions of both supplier and recipient countries, and thus this "gold standard" may not be universally applicable. Still, it can be a good model for other nuclear suppliers and recipient countries in future bilateral agreements on civilian nuclear power programs.

The Nuclear Suppliers Group (NSG), a 48-member voluntary group for export control of nuclear technologies, has long been an important club for establishing global norms in nuclear exports. The NSG amended its rules on sensitive enrichment and reprocessing technologies in 2009, which clarify conditions for, and restrictions on, the transfer of such technologies.[16]

Such efforts to limit transfer of sensitive technologies may be effective in slowing down proliferation but they cannot eliminate the domestic developments entirely. Still, international coordination to enhance such efforts needs to be strengthened.

Multilateral nuclear fuel cycle approaches

In November 2003, Mohamed ElBaradei, then Director General of IAEA, said at the United Nations General Assembly:

> In light of the increasing threat of proliferation, both by states and terrorists, one idea that may now be worth serious consideration is the advisability of limiting the processing of weapon-usable material in civilian nuclear programs, as well as the production of new material through reprocessing and enrichment, by agreeing to restrict these operations exclusively to facilities under multilateral control.[17]

Although putting nuclear materials under international control is not a new idea, his proposal received wide attention. Since then, many proposals have been made and some of them have been realized. For example, Russia established the International Uranium Enrichment Center in 2007. Any NPT member can join as a partner with limited ownership, and an enriched uranium reserve was established under the same scheme.[18] Another good example is the International Nuclear Fuel Bank originally proposed by the Nuclear Threat Initiative, a nonprofit organization in the United States. The IAEA approved this proposal and established the fuel bank owned and operated by the IAEA.[19]

The International Framework for Nuclear Energy Cooperation (IFNEC), originally proposed by the US government as a Global Nuclear Energy Partnership (GNEP), has been discussing the concept of Comprehensive Fuel Service (CFS) under the Reliable Nuclear Fuel Supply Working Group (RNFSWG).[20] The goal is to discuss conditions for assuring reliable fuel supply and services for the back-end of the fuel cycle, especially spent fuel and waste management, so that needs for domestic fuel cycle capabilities can be reduced through dependence on such reliable international fuel services.

These efforts are noteworthy, but it is not clear how these projects and schemes have discouraged domestic development of sensitive nuclear fuel cycle programs. It is often argued that multinational arrangements could discriminate between "have" and "have not" countries. The arrangements could be considered as a violation of Article IV of NPT. Universality and equal treatment of all parties under the NPT needs to be assured, while incentives to develop domestic nuclear fuel cycle capabilities can be reduced effectively. Efforts to explore multilateral approach will be and should be continued through sincere dialogue among interested parties.

Improving transparency and minimization of HEU and Pu stockpiles

Currently, there is no obligation for a country to declare its stockpiles of HEU and separated plutonium (Pu). The IAEA Plutonium Management Guideline (INFCIRC/549) is the only international agreement under which countries can voluntarily declare their own stockpile of plutonium (and are encouraged to do so for HEU as well). Improving transparency of both HEU and plutonium stockpiles would be beneficial for improved international confidence. More countries can and should declare their HEU and plutonium stockpiles for better transparency.

But that is obviously not good enough. Pursuing the reduction of such stockpiles should be the global common norm. It is noteworthy that the Global Threat Reduction Initiative initiated by the United States has achieved significant reduction of weapon-usable materials, especially HEU.[21] Most recently, the Japanese and US governments announced that Japan will return all HEU and weapon-grade plutonium (about 331kg) from its Fast Critical Assembly (FCA) to the United States at the Hague Nuclear Security Summit in March 2014.[22] Such efforts should be encouraged further.

Strengthening the nuclear industry's voluntary efforts

In addition to various governmental efforts, private industry can and should contribute to reducing the risks of nuclear proliferation associated with civil uses of nuclear technologies. There are two noteworthy examples.

One is the Nuclear Power Plant Exporters' Principles of Conducts.[23] This is a unique joint effort initiated by a US think tank, the Carnegie Endowment for International Peace, and leading global nuclear exporters such as AREVA, ATOMEA, Candu energy, GE, Hitachi, Mitsubishi Heavy Industry, Rosatom, and Westinghouse. The Principles, agreed in 2011, cover many areas such as safety and public confidence, including nuclear nonproliferation and safe-guards.[24] Although these Principles are not mandatory, the participants agreed to meet regularly to review the progress and current status.

The second example is the World Institute for Nuclear Security (WINS), which was established in 2008.[25] This is another initiative launched by a US think tank, the Nuclear Threat Initiative, to improve nuclear security activities in private industry. It is a voluntary association intended to share best practices among its members. WINS now has both corporate and individual members and has hosted many workshops and published various reports to help private industry members enhance nuclear security practices.

Those voluntary efforts can and should be enhanced through effective cooperation between private and public sectors as well as through international institutions.

Conclusion

It is widely recognized that there is an intrinsic link between nuclear proliferation and civilian nuclear programs. From the beginning, this fundamental dilemma has been the main policy issue for both nuclear energy experts and international security experts. Various international regimes have been established, and regulations and voluntary measures have also been introduced. Such efforts have made significant contributions to reduce the risks of nuclear proliferation and nuclear security associated with civilian nuclear programs.

After the Fukushima Daiichi nuclear accident in 2011, global nuclear power programs may face serious difficulties in expanding globally. Still, it is also expected that nuclear capacity will grow significantly and, in particular, that the countries using nuclear power will grow. This trend will increase the need to develop uranium enrichment and spent fuel management services. As a result, many countries may want to develop sensitive nuclear technologies, particularly uranium enrichment and reprocessing capabilities.

In addition, global concerns over nuclear security have increased significantly and increasing stockpiles of weapon-useable material have become a source of international security concerns.

Given those trends, it is vital for the international community to explore new and innovative approaches to minimize risks of nuclear proliferation and nuclear security associated with civilian nuclear programs.

Notes

1. United States Department of State, "Report of Committee on Atomic Energy by a Board of Consultants. [The Acheson-Lilienthal Report]," March 16, 1946, www.learnworld.com/ZNW/LWText.Acheson-Lilienthal.html (emphasis added by the author).
2. US Department of Energy, "Nonproliferation and Arms Control Assessment of Weapons-usable Fissile Material Storage and Excess Plutonium Disposition Alternatives," Washington, DC, January 1997, www.ipfmlibrary.org/doe97.pdf.
3. International Atomic Energy Agency, "Power Reactor Information System (PRIS)," May 7, 2014, www.iaea.org/pris.
4. International Atomic Energy Agency, "Energy, Electricity and Nuclear Power Estimates for the Period up to 2050," 2011 Edition, www-pub.iaea.org/MTCD/Publications/PDF/RDS1_31.pdf; International Atomic Energy Agency, "Energy, Electricity and Nuclear Power Estimates for the Period up to 2050," 2013 Edition www-pub.iaea.org/MTCD/publications/PDF/RDS-1-33_web.pdf.
5. Wade Boese, "NSG, Congress Approve Nuclear Trade with India," *Arms Control Today*, Vol. 38, No. 8 (October 2008), pp. 27–28, www.armscontrol.org/act/2008_10/NSGapprove.

6.   International Panel on Fissile Materials (IPFM), "Global Fissile Material Report 2013: Increasing Transparency of Nuclear Warhead and Fissile Material Stocks as a Step toward Disarmament." Princeton University, October 2013, http://fissilematerials.org/library/gfmr13.pdf.

7.   For the reports to the IAEA by these countries, see the INFCIRC/549 series, posted at the International Atomic Energy Agency, "Information Circulars: Documents, Numbers 501–550," IAEA website, www.iaea.org/Publications/Documents/Infcircs/Numbers/nr501-550.shtml.

8.   The Hague Nuclear Security Summit Joint Communiqué, March 24, 2014. www.nss2014.com/sites/default/files/documents/the_hague_nuclear_security_summit_communique_final.pdf.

9.   Masafumi Takubo and Frank N. von Hippel, "Ending Reprocessing in Japan: An Alternative Approach to Managing Japan's Spent Nuclear Fuel and Separated Plutonium," International Panel on Fissile Material, Research Report No. 12, Princeton, New Jersey, November 2013, http://fissile materials.org/library/rr12.pdf.

10. United Nations, "Treaty on the Nonproliferation of Nuclear Weapons," July 1, 1968, Article IV, available at www.un.org/en/conf/npt/2005/npttreaty.html.

11. International Atomic Energy Agency, "Conclusion of Additional Protocols: Status as of 12 March 2014," IAEA website, www.iaea.org/safeguards/documents/AP_status_list.pdf.

12. International Atomic Energy Agency, "Convention on the Physical Protection of Nuclear Material," Registration No. 1533, December 17, 2013, www.iaea.org/Publications/Documents/Conventions/cppnm_status.pdf.

13. International Atomic Energy Agency, "Nuclear Security Recommendations on Physical Protection of Nuclear Material and Nuclear Facilities," *IAEA Nuclear Security Series*, No. 13, Vienna, Austria, 2011, INFCIRC/225/Revision 5, www-pub.iaea.org/books/IAEABooks/8629/Nuclear-Security-Recommendations-on-Physical-Protection-of-Nuclear-Material-and-Nuclear-Facilities-INFCIRC-225-Revision-5.

14. International Atomic Energy Agency, "Objective and Essential Elements of a State's Nuclear Security Regime," *IAEA Nuclear Security Series*, No. 20, Vienna, Austria, 2013, www-pub.iaea.org/MTCD/Publications/PDF/Pub1590_web.pdf.

15. Aaron Stein, "US-UAE Nuclear Cooperation," Nuclear Threat Initiative website, August 13, 2009, www.nti.org/analysis/articles/us-uae-nuclear-cooperation.

16. Daniel Horner, "NSG Revises Rules on Sensitive Exports," *Arms Control Today*, Vol. 41, No. 6 (July/August 2011), pp. 29–30, www.armscontrol.org/act/2011_%2007-08/Nuclear_Suppliers_Group_NSG_Revises_Rules_Sensitive_Exports.

17. Jim Wurst, "ElBaradei Calls for International Control of Nuclear Material Production," *Global Security Newswire*, November 4, 2003, www.nti.org/gsn/article/elbaradei-calls-for-international-control-of-nuclear-material-production-319.

18. International Uranium Enrichment Center, homepage, http://eng.iuec.ru.

19. Angela Weaver, "IAEA Nuclear Fuel Bank: Where We Stand Today," Poniblogger's Blog, Center for Strategic and International Studies, July 11, 2013, https://csis.org/blog/iaea-nuclear-fuel-bank-where-we-stand-today.

20. The International Framework for Nuclear Energy Cooperation (IFNEC), "IFNEC Reliable Nuclear Fuel Services Working Group (RNFSWG) Summary," February 24, 2013, www.ifnec.org/Meetings/RNFSWGMeetings.aspx.

21. US Department of Energy, National Nuclear Security Administration, "Global Threat Reduction Initiative," http://nnsa.energy.gov/aboutus/ourprograms/dnn/gtri.

22. Government of Japan. Ministry of Foreign Affairs, "Joint Statement by the Leaders of Japan and the United States on Contributions to Global Minimization of Nuclear Material," The Hague Nuclear Security Summit, March 24–25, 2014, www.mofa.go.jp/dns/n_s_ne/page18e_000059.html.

23. Nuclear Power Plant Exporters' Principles of Conduct, "The Principles of Conduct," Brussels, Belgium, March 6, 2014, http://nuclearprinciples.org/the-principles.

24. Nuclear Power Plant Exporters' Principles of Conduct, "The Principles of Conduct: Non proliferation and Safeguards," Principle No. 5, http://nuclearprinciples.org/principle/nonproliferation-and-safeguards.

25. World Institute for Nuclear Security, organization homepage, www.wins.org/index.php?article_id=61.

29

ADVANCES IN PROLIFERATION RESISTANT TECHNOLOGIES AND PROCEDURES

Yusuke Kuno

When the peaceful uses of nuclear energy are promoted – with the understanding that some sensitive technologies such as reprocessing and enrichment could be misused and nuclear materials could be diverted for production of nuclear weapons –the question, how the issue of nuclear energy can expanded and deployed far more widely without contributing to nuclear-weapon programs, is frequently raised.

Proliferation resistance (PR) is the concept of reducing the probability of any misuse or diversion in the full life cycle of nuclear energy systems (NESs).

Proliferation resistance has been discussed for several decades, and seeks to establish impediments or barriers to the misuse of civil nuclear energy systems to produce fissile material for nuclear weapons. Both the International Project on Innovative Nuclear Reactors and Fuel Cycles (INPRO) and the Generation IV International Forum (GIF), which are two well-known international programs studying sustainable innovative nuclear energy systems, have commonly defined proliferation resistance as "that characteristic of a nuclear energy system that impedes the diversion or undeclared production of nuclear material or misuse of technology by States in order to acquire nuclear weapons or other nuclear explosive devices."[1]

Proliferation resistant measures are important to increase the difficulties faced by proliferators. National proliferation threats posed by the host state need to be carefully distinguished from the potential security threats posed by nonstate actors. The latter are treated separately as a part of physical protection rather than being considered under PR. Nevertheless, the measures taken for PR may also be able to reduce the risk of terrorists acquiring fissile material.

In this context, PR is an impediment to the misuse of civil nuclear energy systems to produce fissile material for nuclear weapons. It involves not only technical but also institutional characteristics. A profound study on the PR concept in relation to the peaceful use of nuclear energy was conducted by John Carlson, who argued that the principal barriers to nuclear proliferation consist of "institutional measures," such as the following:

- treaty-level peaceful use commitments – principally the Treaty on the Nonproliferation of Nuclear Weapons (NPT);
- verification of performance of these commitments – especially by IAEA safeguards; and
- national controls on the supply of nuclear materials, equipment and technology – including those coordinated through the Nuclear Suppliers Group.

Further institutional measures under consideration include the following:

- fuel supply assurance schemes and "fuel leasing," to obviate any need for additional states to develop the full fuel cycle; and
- multilateralizing proliferation-sensitive stages of the fuel cycle (i.e., enrichment and reprocessing).

"Technical measures" for proliferation resistance include the following:

- avoiding the production of weapons-grade material – and introducing technical barriers to producing such material;
- ensuring the nuclear material is difficult to access (e.g., through high radiation levels) – increasing the difficulties of diversion by states or theft/seizure by terrorists; and
- avoiding the separation of plutonium.[2]

PR is normally described by the general institutional measures as shown in the first three bullets, and the technical measures in the last three bullets, although Carlson touched upon the multilateralization of the nuclear fuel cycle, including fuel supply assurance schemes, as further institutional measures.

In a broader sense, PR can divided into three parts: institutional measures based on international regimes such as treaties/agreements on nonproliferation, additional institutional measures based on material/equipment/technology control on the supply side and on the reduction of incentives for weaponization through a demand side approach (e.g., multilateral use of nuclear technologies), and technical measures to reduce proliferation risk (e.g., use of unattractive materials and processes that make diversion difficult). (See Figure 29.1.)

This chapter focuses particularly on *advances in PR technologies* and on *advances in PR procedures* such as multilateral nuclear approaches (MNAs) which can provide additional institutional measures for proliferation resistance. Some remarkable progress has been observed in these areas in recent years. Section 2 discusses the advances in PR technologies that can be considered to prevent the diversion of nuclear materials from civilian nuclear fuel cycles to weapon programs. Section 3 then discusses procedures, particularly focusing on MNAs, as advanced and additional institutional PR measures. Two approaches for PR assessment procedures are also introduced in this section. Finally Section 4 provides some conclusions and discusses challenges to optimize PR measures for peaceful use of nuclear energy in the short and long terms.

Advances in proliferation resistance technologies

Classification of proliferation resistance technologies

The ultimate objective of PR is to reduce proliferation risks. In this context, technical or technological approaches have been studied to pursue effective PR. Technical terms for PR should be considered from the following three viewpoints: acquisition by material diversion and process misuse, processing to convert acquired material to weapon-use materials (e.g., metallic form), and utilization for weapon production.

In this regard, the focus is often on the nuclear fuel cycle. A representation of the nuclear fuel cycles for light-water reactors (LWR) and fast breeder reactors (FBR) is shown in Figure 29.2. It includes facilities for uranium mining, enrichment, fuel production, power generation, reprocessing, fuel production with recovered Pu, and waste management. The proliferation risk of power reactors, particularly, the universally employed commercial light–water reactors, have not been addressed. This is because only spent fuels can be acquired, which require further processing steps to recover the plutonium. In this context, there is a higher risk of nuclear proliferation with enrichment and reprocessing, where weapon-usable fissile materials can be handled directly.

Thereby, proliferation resistance for addressing the acquisition of material by diversion or misuse may consist of technologies that enable one to avoid the employment of enrichment and reprocessing.

Technologies that reduce the proliferation risk of an NES, making it difficult to divert nuclear materials and difficult to misuse nuclear facilities, are also regarded as PR technologies for these acquisition scenarios, as well as those involving processing. These technologies involve the use of complex chemical forms and physical features, e.g., debris, along with isotopic features reducing fissile material quality; and concentrations with high levels of plutonium 238, which lowers the attractiveness of nuclear material due to its high heat generation and may enhance PR against its utilization/weaponization. Other factors such as financial resources and time required for proliferation are usually employed to assess PR technological effectiveness.[3] However, these "other factors" are not discussed in this article. The following sub-sections discuss more specific technologies contributing to the individual PR measures.

Technologies to avoid enrichment and reprocessing/recycling

There are several power reactor technologies that make it possible to avoid enrichment, including heavy-water reactors, graphite-moderated reactors, and fast breeder reactors. These, however, can produce sensitive nuclear materials such as weapon-grade plutonium. These reac–

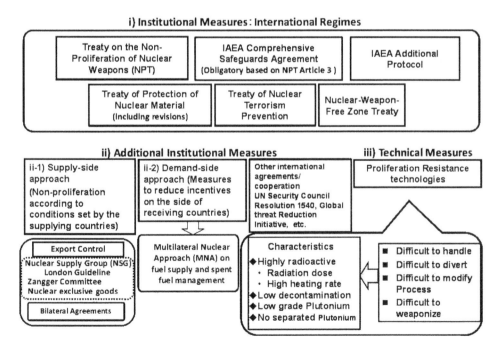

Figure 29.1 International efforts for nuclear nonproliferation: broader "proliferation resistance"

tors are also considered to have relatively higher proliferation risks than light-water reactors. The current Canadian deuterium uranium (CANDU) reactor, one example of a heavy-water reactor, has an online refueling function and does not need enriched uranium to achieve criticality due to its more efficient heavy water moderator. In this regard, simply avoiding uranium enrichment may not be able to help to reduce proliferation risks.

Reprocessing can be avoided through using "once-through" fuel cycles, where spent fuel is treated as waste, and is stored and eventually disposed of in a geologic repository, although the once-through cycle is regarded as an inefficient use of uranium resources. However, cost effectiveness is another key factor to be taken into account. Frank N. von Hippel discussed the higher cost of producing this recycled fuel as opposed to using fresh uranium reactor fuel, as well as the high proliferation risks of reprocessing.[4] The Nonproliferation Impact Assessment (NPIA) studied once-through alternatives that use uranium-based or uranium/thorium-based fuel in thermal-neutron reactors.[5] Further, NPIA dealt with heavy water reactors (HWRs) and high-temperature gas-cooled reactors (HTGRs). Once-through fuel cycle alternatives avoid the production of materials that can be used in a nuclear explosive device without significant further processing, and spent fuels keep high PR due to their high radiation. Therefore the alternatives are preferable on purely technical grounds. The options available for strengthening this approach include expanding the capacity of the current providers of international enrichment services at the front end, and pursuing international/regional fuel cycles at the back end.

The two different aspects of economic efficiency and energy resource efficiency should be differentiated between the short term and the long term. The reprocessing and once-through proliferation risks can also be separately discussed in the short and long terms. Carlson noted that the once-through cycle is not entirely free of proliferation concern because it produces large Pu concentrations in spent fuel repositories, which present a potential proliferation risk

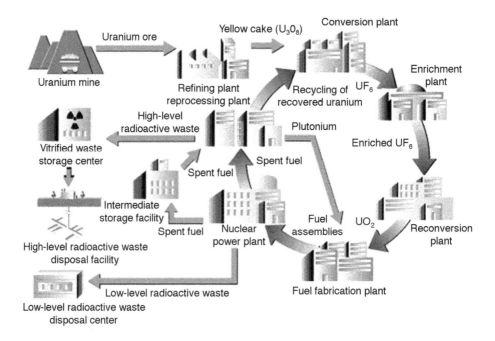

Figure 29.2 Typical nuclear fuel cycle

for later generations as "plutonium mines."[6] (See Figure 29.3.) As time goes on, the radiation levels will decrease, making the spent fuels more accessible.

The short-term proliferation risk of reprocessing can be prevented by the strict implementation of institutional measures and NPT-based safeguards. However, it is probable that no one can guarantee nonproliferation from plutonium mines over a long period of time, e.g., beyond thousands of years. Thus, the once-through method may not be the best solution for nuclear nonproliferation from a long-term perspective, although it is regarded as one of the most effective PR methods for spent fuel management in the short-term.

Technologies to reduce proliferation risks from diversion and misuse

The overall proliferation risks for NESs including the nuclear fuel cycle are discussed here. This item, therefore, may include safeguards-based technologies, or "safeguards-by-design" (SBD), to detect diversion/misuse; processes to make it difficult to divert nuclear materials and difficult to misuse nuclear facilities; and reactor technologies to reduce fissile nuclear materials.

Safeguards-based technologies for detecting diversion/misuse

Uranium enrichment technologies, which have been developed to large-scale maturity, have been used as a basis to produce weapon-grade material convenient for military explosives use. The details of the design information for enrichment plants are traditionally treated as state secrets, which make an external evaluation of the detailed technical capability problematic. The primary technical differences between low-enriched uranium (LEU) production and weapon-grade, highly enriched uranium (HEU) production are typically the number of stages in a cascade, geometric accommodations to prevent criticality in a higher enriched product, and enhanced light gas removal systems, rather than the individual isotopic separation units. Therefore, it seems reasonable to accept that SBD to accommodate International Atomic Energy Agency (IAEA) safeguards and other extrinsic measures are entirely dominant in a PR assessment of enrichment technology, rather than intrinsic features. The IAEA has described the SBD concept as an approach in which "international safeguards are fully integrated into the design process of a new nuclear facility from the initial planning through design, construction, operation, and decommissioning."[7] SBD has two main objectives: to avoid costly and time-consuming redesign work or retrofits of new nuclear fuel cycle facilities, and to make the implementation of international safeguards more effective and efficient at such facilities. SBD-guidance for gas centrifuge enrichment plants was issued by the US-DOE NSSA Next Generation Safeguards Initiative.[8] The verification methodology established by the IAEA, including Design Information Verification (DIV)/Design Information Questionnaire (DIQ), Physical Inventory Verification (PIV)/ Interim Inventory Verification (IIV) with Non-destructive Analysis (NDA)/Destructive Analysis (DA), the application of Containment and Surveillance (C/S), and environmental swipe sampling is described, followed by requirements and specifications such as safeguards equipment and the layout that designers should incorporate into their design.

Reprocessing technologies involve shielded facilities with remote handling capabilities.[9] Some aqueous/solvent extraction technologies named e.g., PUREX, COEX, UREX processes, dry processing (pyroprocessing) and other technologies such as precipitation and ion exchange method are well-known. It is said that there are particularly high proliferation risks in the processes to separate plutonium, and possibly certain minor actinides. The International Meeting on Next Generation Safeguards held on December, 2010 in Washington, DC, focused

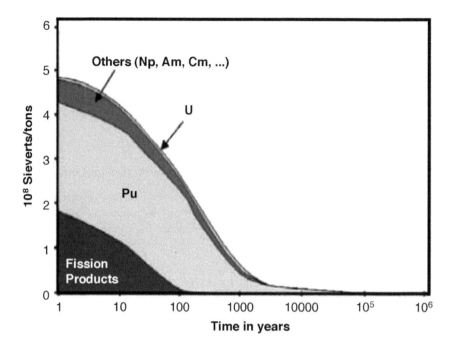

Figure 29.3 Long-term radio-toxicity of standard PWR spent fuel vs. time

on the SBD concept. The Working Group for Aqueous Reprocessing Facilities provided recommendations on SBD for facility owner/operators and designers.[10] Physical design and its verifiability, material accountancy measures, transparency of operations and operating procedures, accommodation and accessibility for inspectors, and plant administration and safeguards culture were all viewed as important. Emphasis was placed on the need to improve the formality of the design process in order to enhance the SBD between all concerned parties and to lead to a more efficient implementation of international safeguards. In addition, SBD recommendations must account for the possibility of nonstandardization because new reprocessing plants are likely to be unique and customized for their respective host country.

A specific SBD concept with state-of-the-art safeguards technologies to be introduced to a large scale commercial reprocessing facility, the Rokkasho Reprocessing Plant, has been discussed as a facility where some efficient technologies were adopted.[11] The incorporation of proliferation-resistant technologies into the design of facilities – SBD – can contribute to the effectiveness and efficiency of performing safeguards.

Fuel cycle technologies to make diversion/misuse difficult

A comparative assessment of nuclear nonproliferation for a wide range of nuclear fuel cycle alternatives was made in Nonproliferation Impact Assessment.[12] It covers the once-through cycle, full actinide recycling, and partial actinide recycling methods.

In the NPIA discussion of full actinide recycling, the spent fuel from light-water reactors is reprocessed, and transuranic elements are removed from the waste stream and recycled. The ability to minimize long-term waste hazards and treat spent fuel as a resource by consuming transuranics in fast neutron reactors may alter proliferation risks. This category involves fast reactor recycling alternatives and thermal/fast reactor recycling alternatives. Full actinide recycling alternatives produce materials with much higher intrinsic proliferation and security risks than a once-through fuel cycle. The key to that influence is the ability to dramatically reduce the long-term radiotoxicity hazards and proliferation risks, which could help overcome political and public acceptance obstacles.

As for partial actinide recycling methods, the materials from LWR spent fuel are recycled in thermal-neutron reactors. Some of the transuranic elements are removed from the waste stream and recycled, but a significant portion remains in the waste stream. The alternatives include burning reprocessed plutonium in LWR (e.g., LWR-uranium/plutonium mixed oxide [MOX]), deep burning reprocessed transuranic elements in HTGRs, and direct use of spent PWR fuel In CANDU (DUPIC) where LWR spent fuel is recycled/used in HWRs without separation of plutonium.[13] The partial recycling alternatives may offer some of the benefits, but also suffer from most of the drawbacks of the closed fuel cycle alternatives.

A chemical barrier can provide technical difficulty in chemically recovering and purifying the plutonium. The discussion of full and partial actinide recycling methods involved the assessment of the proliferation risks in some separation technologies called the COEX, UREX, and NUEX processes and the pyroprocess, in which some advances in the inherent technical difficulty of physically executing the proliferation steps for material acquisition/production are studied. For such studies, the complexity of the required modifications, the cost of modifications, the safety implications of modifications, the time required for modifications, and the facility throughput, along with other aspects, are considered. This preliminary assessment in NPIA suggests only a modest improvement in reducing the proliferation risk over existing PUREX technologies, and these modest improvements apply primarily to nonstate actors. Either of these alternatives can relax the issues on long-term proliferation risks.

Reactors to reduce fissile nuclear materials

The isotopic barrier pertains to fissile material quality. A higher composition of fissile isotopics increases the material's attractiveness. The isotopic composition of Pu-238 is also a key for the discussion on material attractiveness. The radiological hazard barrier reflects the difficulty of approaching and handling a material and could be interpreted as contributing to the technical difficulty of proliferation. Bathke *et al.* first published a figure-of-merit (FOM) formulation in 2008 and suggested that it could be used to evaluate the attractiveness of nuclear materials (for weapons).[14] The three-factor FOM formulation was based on the intrinsic properties (qualities) of the nuclear materials:

- bare spherical metal critical mass, as compared to that of 20 percent enriched uranium;
- heat generated by a critical mass, as compared to that produced in Pu with 80 percent Pu-238;
- radiation doses generated, as compared to that emitted by spent fuel (500 rem/h dose rate).

The spontaneous neutron emission rate was added later in a series of their studies to make the formulation fit more practical circumstances.

In this regard, reactor technologies producing a lower quality of plutonium, namely a lower isotopic composition of fissile material, should contribute to PR. Some typical technologies that represent effective proliferation resistance as well as the efficient use of nuclear energy resources are shown here.

Very high or high temperature reactors ((V)HTRs) with so-called TRISO (tri-structural-isotropic) type plutonium fuels graphite-moderated, demonstrate a typical deep burn performance and produce low grade plutonium, where, for example, >90 percent of the Pu-239 is burned with ~100 GWday/MT, and the burned fuel is chemically difficult to reprocess.[15]

For another example of the efficient burnup of excess plutonium from the spent fuels of nuclear reactors, plutonium rock-like oxide (ROX) fuel has been studied.[16] The ROX fuel, which is typically composed of PuO_2 UO_2 and ceramic material called YSZK, is expected to provide a high Pu transmutation capability, irradiation stability, chemical/geological stability and also chemical difficulty to reprocess, which is regarded as a disadvantage for full actinide recycling, however. The compositions of Pu-239 in several different materials/spent fuels can dramatically be reduced in LWR-MOX and particularly LWR-ROX cases (see Figure 29.4), where the total amount of plutonium finally remaining in the spent fuels for disposal is also reduced. A fast reactor, which may be used as a plutonium breeder for world energy security in the future, can also be applied for burning plutonium at present.[17]

The use of neptunium (Np)/americium (Am) with natural or depleted uranium in breeder blankets generates high Pu-239 enriched plutonium with a certain portion of Pu-238 isotope content. It may be regarded as proliferation resistant because the heat generation, which depends mostly on the Pu-238 concentration in the plutonium, makes weapon production difficult. Many studies have been conducted based on such an approach principle.[18] Although the produced material, which has a relatively high isotopic composition of Pu-238, can be effective for nonproliferation, the device, the fast breeder reactor itself, can easily produce weapon-grade plutonium if it is operated without Np/Am. Therefore it still has to rely on institutional measures such as safeguards.

Advances in proliferation resistance procedure

Technical barriers with some advanced technologies can help to reduce proliferation risks in a limited fashion. Institutional measures play essential roles for PR in helping to ensure the peaceful use of NES. This section discusses multilateral nuclear approaches (MNAs), as advanced institutional PR procedures beyond conventional institutional measures, including the NPT, IAEA safeguards, the Nuclear Suppliers Group, and bilateral agreements. Two typical approaches for PR assessment procedures that have recently been developed are also addressed in this section.

Multilateral nuclear approaches

MNAs have been highlighted since the beginning of the twenty-first century because they could cover at least some weakness in the intrinsic and the existing extrinsic PR measures. For example, the multilateral use of nuclear fuel cycle facilities can reduce the probability of the proliferation of sensitive nuclear technologies (SNTs) and prevent the diversion or misuse of nuclear materials and facilities through regional cooperation.

The growth of nuclear power with an insufficient supply of uranium fuel may lead states to attempt to acquire uranium enrichment technology based on their "inalienable" right, as stated in Article IV of the NPT, whereas, in a similar fashion, such power growth may increase their interest in plutonium recycling/recovery because of the accumulation of spent fuels due to concerns about energy security and waste management.

Comprehensive fuel services that include assured arrangements for the acceptance and disposition of spent fuel can offer potentially transformative means to discourage the spread of both enrichment and reprocessing capabilities.

MNAs, which can, in general, internationally provide services on the front-end and back-end of the fuel cycle to the states possessing nuclear power plants, can contribute to nuclear nonproliferation and PR for the nuclear fuel cycle.

Several proposals on MNAs have recently been studied and a few have already been implemented, in which there is no restraint on the peaceful use of nuclear energy as a consequence of issues that might involve the proliferation of SNTs having been taken into account.[19] Recent discussions, however, tend to focus on reliable fuel supply, namely the front-end of the nuclear fuel cycle, where the proliferation of uranium enrichment capacity can be deterred. At the same time, the multilateral capability to provide services to manage spent fuel (SF) properly may actually be more important.[20]

A brief overview of the historical transition of studies on MNAs is shown in Figure 29.5, where MNA proposals are categorized as "fuel supply assurance," "regional SF storage," "regional fuel cycle center," and "take back SF." Detailed reviews of those MNA proposals are made elsewhere.[21] In October 2003, the proposals made by the then-Director General of the IAEA, Mohamed ElBaradei, stated that reprocessing and enrichment operations must be restricted under multinational control; NES shall have nuclear nonproliferation resistance; and multinational approaches should be considered for the management and disposal of SFs and radioactive waste. However, it was anticipated that it would take a long time to overcome the issues with his idea of a multilateral system of SNTs and radioactive substances. Later, a group of experts to study MNAs was formed (ElBaradei Commission). The results of the study by the expert group at the IAEA were summarized in INFCIRC/640, which has an impact on the successive examination of the multinational approach framework. Table 29.1 lists some recent remarkable approaches proposed since 2003.[22]

As described in Table 29.1, as of December 2011, the IAEA nuclear fuel bank, the LEU reserve in Angarsk, Russia, and the United Kingdom's NFA proposal were approved by the IAEA Board of Governors, and the US AFS began its operation in 2012.

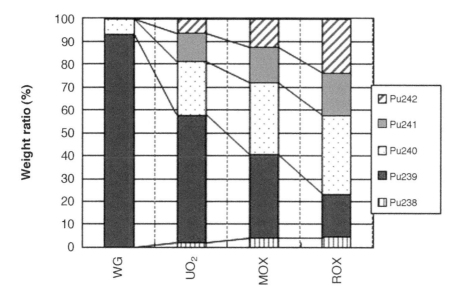

Figure 29.4 Comparison of Pu in different materials

Most of the previously proposed MNAs in the twentieth century were never implemented in any form. This was probably because nuclear proliferation was not recognized as a sufficiently serious issue and there was no strong economic motivation. Many proposals included unfair double standards, i.e., asymmetry between "haves" and "have nots," and were inconsistent with market mechanisms. In addition, the need for MNAs may not have matured or become critical at that time. However, the situation has been changing over the last few years since some of the above mentioned proposals have been approved by the IAEA Board of Governors.

The establishment of multilateral cooperative systems, which includes services for fresh fuel supply, spent fuel take-back/take-away, interim storage, reprocessing, and possibly repository disposal, may be able to contribute to the enhancement of nuclear nonproliferation (a potential to deter the proliferation of SNT's proliferation and an increase in transparency); economic rationality; promotion of confidence-building; and potential prevention of the occurrence of unfair business practices such as government-to-government transactions based on cradle-to-grave services enabled by the privileges of nuclear-weapon state status. This kind of internationally cooperative framework may become essential for the future sustainable utilization of nuclear energy and nuclear nonproliferation in particular, to avoid proliferation of SNTs.

Different concepts for INPRO/GIF proliferation resistance assessment methodologies

Two different approaches to PR assessment methodologies for NES have been developed by IAEA-INPRO and GIF. The original PR evaluation methodology developed in INPRO focuses on the subject of how to assess an innovative nuclear energy system (INS) embedded in an existing (or planned) nonproliferation regime.[23] It primarily guides the INPRO assessor to confirm that adequate PR has been achieved in the INS, but also gives some guidance to the developer of nuclear technology on how to improve PR. To fulfill the basic principle of proliferation resistance, INPRO established five user requirements: a state is to establish a sufficient legal framework, e.g., statutes, treaties, and agreements (User Requirement 1, [UR1]); a designer is to keep the attractiveness of nuclear material and technology low (UR2); make the diversion of NM difficult and detectable (UR3); incorporate multiple barriers (UR4); and optimize the costs of intrinsic and extrinsic proliferation resistance measures (UR5).

The development of a methodology for the identification and analysis of credible acquisition paths was discussed at a collaborative project called "Proliferation Resistance: Acquisition/Diversion Pathway Analysis" (PRADA), where it was concluded that the robustness of barriers is not a function of the number of barriers or of their individual characteristics, but is an integrated function of the whole, and is measured by determining whether the safeguards goals can be met.[24]

A follow-up project to PRADA, the INPRO Collaborative Project on "Proliferation Resistance and Safeguardability Assessment Tools" (PROSA) is being conducted to identify and define the interface of the proliferation resistance and safeguardability assessment tools of both methodologies at the different evaluation levels, and to examine the validity of the refined methodologies and their usefulness by evaluating a mutually beneficial reference case.[25] Updating INPRO-PR was also examined as part of the PROSA project. The discussion concluded that the IAEA's mandate under Article IV of the NPT (peaceful use) precludes the IAEA from taking a discriminatory position on whether or not a given member state should possess a given peaceful use technology (this is a matter of member state policies, sovereignty and bilateral trade relations). Rather, all nuclear energy technology used for peaceful purposes,

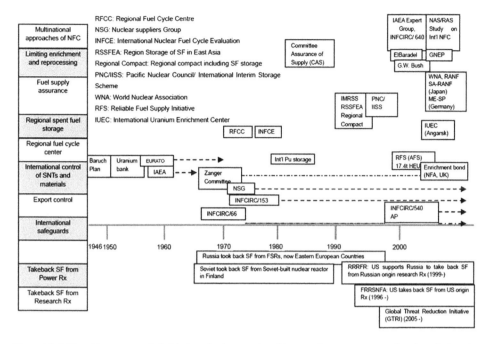

Figure 29.5 Transition proposals/initiatives for international/regional management of nuclear fuel cycles

in full compliance with treaty undertakings including NPT Articles I and II as verified by international safeguards (Article III), are an inalienable right guaranteed under NPT Article IV. Therefore the intrinsic features that accommodate the effective and efficient implementation of key extrinsic measures (e.g., safeguards and trade obligations) have considerably more effect on state-level proliferation resistance than the purely intrinsic features currently considered under UR2.

A GIF working group on Proliferation Resistance and Physical Protection (PR&PP) used a different approach to evaluate the PR of NES from INPRO, where the measures employed included the following four intrinsic, and two extrinsic measures: proliferation technical difficulty (TD), proliferation cost (PC), proliferation time (PT), fissile material type (MT), detection probability (DP), and detection resource efficiency (DE). The GIF approach considers an NES primarily from the standpoint of the designer of the system and identifies specific proliferation challenges, system responses, and outcomes.[26] A "pathway analysis" is performed to identify acquisition scenarios that a state could pursue to obtain nuclear weapons by taking advantage of its peaceful nuclear materials and facilities. The above-shown six proliferation resistance measures have been identified to compare pathways. Metrics that enable the evaluation of the GIF measures are also provided in the methodology. Analysts may use qualitative, semi-quantitative, or quantitative analyses to estimate these measures. The results are intended for three types of users: system designers, program policy makers, and external stakeholders. Program policy makers will likely be interested in high-level results that discriminate among choices, whereas system designers will be more interested in information that directly relates to design options that will improve the proliferation resistance of the NES. Here, the methodology is organized to allow evaluations to be performed at the earliest stages of system design.

Table 29.1 MNA proposals from 2003 to the present

Proposals/initiatives	Description and features of proposals
"Multilateral approaches to the Nuclear Fuel Cycle: an expert group's report on MNA submitted to the Director General of the International Atomic Energy Agency" (INFCIRC/640, so called "Pellaud Report")	Experts appointed by ElBaradei identified options for possible MNA of the front-end and back-end of the nuclear fuel cycle for strengthening nuclear nonproliferation, without disturbing market mechanisms. The study identified five suggested approaches to MNAs. The report presents seven labels as MNA assessment elements including the removal or banning of: proliferation; assurance of supply; siting-choice of host country; access to technology; multilateral involvement; special safeguards provision; and nonnuclear inducements.
Reserve of nuclear fuel (renamed as American Assured Fuel Supply [AFS])	The US Department of Energy (DOE)'s proposal of creating a LEU reserve down-blended from 17.4 metric tons of HEU dismantled from the US's excess nuclear weapons. The reserve assures reliable fuel supply for states that forgo enrichment and reprocessing.
Russia global nuclear power infrastructure (GNPI)	The Russian Federation proposal includes the creation of a system of international centers, providing uranium enrichment services, on a nondiscriminatory basis and under the control of the IAEA.
US Global Nuclear Energy Partnership (GNEP)	A US DOE proposal that includes the development of proliferation-resistant reprocessing technology, and advanced fast reactors, minimizing nuclear waste and establishing reliable fuel supply and SNF take-back services. A consortium of nations with advanced nuclear technologies would ensure that countries who agree to forgo their own investment in enrichment and reprocessing technologies will have reliable access to nuclear fuel.
Ensuring security of supply in the International Nuclear Fuel Cycle	The World Nuclear Association (WNA) proposal of a three-level mechanism to ensure enrichment services. The proposal originally had a precondition for nonsupplier states to forgo domestic development of sensitive technologies and facilities, but later it abandoned such a precondition.
Concept of Multilateral Mechanism for Reliable Access to Nuclear Fuel	The proposal by six enrichment services supplier States (the United States, United Kingdom, Russia, France, Germany, and Netherlands) for two levels of enrichment assurance for customer states that have chosen to obtain suppliers on the international market and not to pursue sensitive fuel cycle activities.
IAEA Fuel Bank	The Nuclear Threat Initiative's proposal to create an LEU stockpile owned and managed by the IAEA that could be made available should other supply arrangements be disrupted. "Having the right to receive LEU from the guaranteed supply mechanism shall not require giving up their right to establish or further develop a national fuel cycle or have any impact on it." The IAEA Board of Governors approved the establishment of the bank in 2010.
Enrichment Bonds ([renamed as Nuclear Fuel Assurance (NFA)])	The UK proposal, a bonding principle that would, in the event that the Agency determines that specified conditions have been met: guarantee that national enrichment providers would not be prevented from supplying enrichments services; and provide prior consent for export assurances. Nonsupplier states are not required to give up their rights to develop an indigenous fuel cycle by receiving alternate nuclear fuel.

Table 29.1 Continued.

Proposals/initiatives	Description and features of proposals
International Uranium Enrichment Center (IUEC) at Angarsk and its LEU Reserve	A Russian proposal to establish an International Uranium Enrichment Centre (IUEC), including a LEU reserve. The IUEC would operate as a commercial joint stock company. It would be a "black box" and the IUEC's participating states could not access Russian enrichment technologies. Nonsupplier states are not required to give up their rights to develop an indigenous fuel cycle by receiving nuclear fuel from the stockpile. The LEU reserve was established in December 2010.
Multilateral Enrichment Sanctuary Project (MESP)	A German proposal for an international enrichment center established by a group of interested states, with extraterritorial status, operating on a commercial basis as a new supplier in the market under IAEA control providing enrichment services. An enrichment plant would have to be constructed as a "black box" and would therefore only be accessed and maintained by the supplier.
Nuclear Fuel Cycle (EU-Non-paper)	The EU non-paper proposed criteria for assessment of MNAs for fuel supply reliability. These criteria included proliferation resistance; assurance of supply; consistency with equal rights and obligations of suppliers, companies, consumer states and the IAEA; and market neutrality.
Japan's initiative for Mutual Assured Dependence	Proposed an internationalization of the nuclear fuel cycle facilities. All enrichment and reprocessing plants would be internationalized and all of them, including the existing and new facilities without exception, shall take the form of ownership and control by multiple countries/companies. Such facilities are based on universality, transparency (verifiability), and economic viability.
Nuclear Islands: International leasing of Nuclear Fuel Cycle Sites	A proposal to enhance nuclear nonproliferation by centralization of sensitive facilities within restricted zones under long-term leasehold contracts and a newly established organization, the International Nuclear Fuel Cycle Association (INFCA). Countries and existing multilateral consortia would not be asked to give up their inalienable right under Article IV of the NPT, although all countries would voluntarily agree to exercise that right only pursuant to uniform, nondiscriminatory leasehold contracts and protocols with the INFCA and the IAEA that would ensure conformity with Articles I and II of the NPT.

The difference can be described as follows: the URs in INPRO are assessed in relation to how they contribute to strengthening the safeguardability of the NES, whereas all the PR measures/features of the GIF approach are assessed by considering both the declared and undeclared facilities and activities, to complete the proliferation pathway from the acquisition and processing of material to the fabrication of a nuclear explosive device as well as overt misuse following breakout.

In either case, the vulnerabilities of safeguards may limit their role as effective countermeasures to the risk of break-out. In this context, the incorporation of the technological part of PR for nuclear facilities is effective, although, as discussed, it may limitedly contribute to the nonproliferation.

Conclusion

In a broad sense, PR involves institutional measures such as the NPT, IAEA safeguards, bilateral agreements, export control and national regulations on nonproliferation; proliferation resistant technologies such as reactor technologies to reduce fissile nuclear materials, the introduction of "SBD" to improve the detection of diversion/misuse, and the employment of technical difficulty for misuse/diversion; and the application of MNAs to proliferation-sensitive stages of the fuel cycle, i.e., enrichment and reprocessing.

Among these, institutional measures with advanced safeguards technologies based on SBD, along with some technologies to make it difficult or less attractive to misuse/divert nuclear facilities/materials, would be effective for nuclear nonproliferation in the short-term. For long-term issues such as the disposal of fissile materials, SF, which employ reactor technologies and their related nuclear fuel cycle technologies to reduce the quantity and quality of fissile nuclear materials, can improve proliferation risks.

There are some technological challenges for SNTs, because little improvement in proliferation resistance technologies is expected even in advanced SNTs. Furthermore a substantial challenge for PR may be the method how to disseminate even highly proliferation-resistant technologies such as the above mentioned reactor technologies and advanced nuclear fuel cycle technologies to the world, because the potential proliferator may not intentionally employ such technologies.

In this context, the concept of MNAs may be more effective for both strengthening nuclear nonproliferation and promoting the peaceful use of nuclear energy. To realize these MNAs, strong initiatives and profound discussions supported by the international community may be essential.

Notes

1. George Pomeroy, Robert Bari, Edward Wonder, Michael Zentner, Eckhard Haas, and Thomas Killeen, "Approaches to Evaluation of Proliferation Resistance Fundamentals for Future Nuclear Energy Systems," 49th Annual Meeting: Institute of Nuclear Materials Management (IMNN), Nashville, TN, July 13–17, 2008, www.iaea.org/INPRO/CPs/PRADA/approaches.pdf.
2. John Carlson, "Introduction to the Concept of Proliferation Resistance," ICNND Research Paper, No.8, revised, June 3, 2009, http://a-pln.org/sites/default/files/apln-analysis-docs/Proliferation_Resistance.pdf.
3. See, for example, International Atomic Energy Agency, "Evaluation Methodology for Proliferation Resistance and Physical Protection of Generation IV Nuclear Energy Systems," Revision 6, Generation IV, GIF/PRPPWG/2011/003, September 30, 2011, www.gen-4.org/gif/upload/docs/application/pdf/2013-09/gif_prppem_rev6_final.pdf.
4. Frank von Hippel, "Reprocessing Nuclear Fuel a Dangerous Option," *The Cap Times*, September 18, 2009, http://host.madison.com/news/opinion/column/guest/frank-von-hippel-reprocessing-nuclear-fuel-a-dangerous-option/article_0bd69b4a-a3d2-11de-bfd5-001cc4c03286.html; Frank von Hippel, "Plutonium, Proliferation and Radioactive-Waste Politics in East Asia," Nonproliferation Policy Education Center, January 3, 2011, www.npolicy.org/article_file/von_Hippel_Paper.pdf.
5. United States Department of Energy, National Nuclear Security Administration, Office of Nonproliferation and International Security, "Nonproliferation Impact Assessment for the Global Nuclear Energy Partnership: Programmatic Alternatives (Draft)," December 2008, Executive Summary, http://nnsa.energy.gov/sites/default/files/nnsa/inlinefiles/GNEP_NPIA.pdf.
6. Carlson, "Introduction to the Concept of Proliferation Resistance."
7. International Atomic Energy Agency, "Facility Design and Plant Operation Features that Facilitate Implementation of IAEA Safeguards," SGCP-CCA, Report STR-360, February 2009, www.iaea.org/safeguards/documents/STR_360_external_version.pdf.
8. United States Department of Energy, National Nuclear Security Administration, Office of Nonproliferation and International Security, "Implementing Safeguards-by-Design at Gas Centrifuge Enrichment Plants," ORNL/TM-2012/364, September 2012, http://nnsa.energy.gov/sites/

default/files/nnsa/11-12-multiplefiles/2012-11-15%203%20NGSI%20SBD%20Guidance_GCEPs-final.pdf.

9. International Atomic Energy Agency, "Spent Fuel Reprocessing Options," IAEA-TECDOC-1587, August 2008, www-pub.iaea.org/MTCD/publications/PDF/te_1587_web.pdf.

10. Shirley Johnson, Mike Ehinger, Mark Schanfein, "Report on the NGS3 Working Group on Safeguards by Design for Aqueous Reprocessing Plants," PNNL-20226, February 2011, www.pnnl.gov/main/publications/external/technical_reports/PNNL-20226.pdf.

11. See, for example, P.C. Durst, R. Wallace, I. Therios, M.H. Ehinger, R. Bean, D.N. Kovacic, A. Dougan, K. Tolk, and B. Boyer, "Advanced Safeguards Approaches for New Reprocessing Facilities," Pacific Northwest National Laboratory, PNNL-16674, June 2007, www.pnl.gov/main/publications/external/technical_reports/pnnl-16674.pdf; Shirley Johnson and Michael Ehinger, "Designing and Operating for Safeguards: Lessons Learned From the Rokkasho Reprocessing Plant (RRP)," Pacific Northwest National Laboratory, PNNL-19626, August 2010, www.pnl.gov/main/publications/external/technical_reports/pnnl-19626.pdf.

12. NNSA, "Nonproliferation Impact Assessment for GNEP."

13. Brian Wang, "DUPIC Fuel Cycle: Direct Use of Pressurized Water Reactor Spent Fuel in CANDU," *Next Big Future*, April, 15, 2009, http://nextbigfuture.com/2009/04/dupic-fuel-cycle-direct-use-of.html.

14. Charles G. Bathke, Bartley B. Ebbinghaus, Brad W. Sleaford, Richard K. Wallace, Brian A. Collins, Kevin R. Hase, Martin Robel, Gordon D. Jarvinen, Keith S. Bradley, John R. Ireland, M.W. Johnson, Andrew W. Prichard, and Brian W. Smith, "The Attractiveness of Materials in Advanced Nuclear Fuel Cycles for Various Proliferation and Theft Scenarios," *Nuclear Technology*, Vol. 179, No. 1 (July 2012), pp. 5–30.

15. Minoru Goto, "Conceptual Design Study of High Temperature Gas-cooled Reactor for Plutonium Incineration," Presentation at IAEA Deep Burn Technical Meeting, Vienna, Austria, August 5–8 2013, www.iaea.org/NuclearPower/Downloadable/Meetings/2013/2013-08-05-08-07-TM-NPTD/6_pu_incineration.pdf.

16. Akie Nishihara *et al*. Atomic Energy Society of Japan, Hiroshima, September 2012.

17. E.g., Fast Breeders as Plutonium Burners, www.minatom.ru/News/Main/view?id=7441&idChannel=65 possible other site http://russianforces.org/blog/2005/03/fast_breeders_as_plutonium_bur.shtml.

18. See, for example, Günther Kessler, *Proliferation-proof Uranium/Plutonium Fuel Cycles* (Karlsruhe, Germany: KIT Scientific Publishing, November 24, 2011); Masaki Saito, V. Artisyuk, Y. Peryoga, and K. Nikitin, "Advanced Nuclear Energy Systems for Protected Plutonium Production," International Conference on Innovative Technologies for Nuclear Fuel Cycles and Nuclear Power, Vienna, June 23–26, 2003, www.nr.titech.ac.jp/coe21/coe/results.html (this site can be translated through Google).

19. Yusuke Kuno and J.S. Choi, *Nuclear Eye*, Vol. 55, No. 5 (2009), pp. 59–62; Tariq Rauf, "Realizing Nuclear Fuel Assurances: Third Time's the Charm," presentation at the Carnegie International Non-Proliferation Conference, Washington, DC, June 24, 2007, www.carnegieendowment.org/files/fuel_assurances_rauf.pdf.

20. Individual Countries' Proposals at IAEA INFCIRC/659(USA), INFCIRC/708(RUS), INFCIRC/707(UK), INFCIRC/704(GER), INFCIRC/683(JAP).

21. Satoru Tanaka, Yusuke Kuno, *et al*., "A Study on the Establishment of an International Nuclear Fuel Cycle System for Asia," March 2013, www.flanker.n.t.u-tokyo.ac.jp/modules/lab Downloads/; National Academy of Sciences and National Research Council, *Internationalization of the Nuclear Fuel Cycle: Goals, Strategies, and Challenges* (Washington, DC: The National Academies Press, 2009).

22. Tariq Rauf and Zoryana Vovchok, "Fuel for Thought," *IAEA Bulletin*, Vol. 49, No. 2 (March 2008), pp. 59–63, www.iaea.org/Publications/Magazines/Bulletin/Bull492/49204845963.pdf; Makiko Tazaki and Yusuke Kuno, "The Contribution of Multilateral Nuclear Approaches (MNAs) to the Sustainability of Nuclear Energy," *Sustainability*, Vol. 4, No. 8 (August 2012), pp. 1755–1775, www.mdpi.com/2071-1050/4/8/1755.

23. International Atomic Energy Agency, "Guidance for the Application of an Assessment Methodology for Innovative Nuclear Energy Systems: INPRO Manual – Safety of Nuclear Fuel Cycle Facilities," IAEA-TECDOC-1575 Rev. 1, November 2008, www.iaea.org/INPRO/publications/INPRO_Manual/TE_1575_CD/PDF/TE_1575_vol9_2008.pdf.

24. International Atomic Energy Agency, "INPRO Collaborative Project: Proliferation Resistance: Acquisition/Diversion Pathway Analysis (PRADA)," IAEA-TECDOC-1684, May 2012, www-pub.iaea.org/MTCD/publications/PDF/TE_1684_web.pdf.
25. International Atomic Energy Agency, "Collaborative Projects: Proliferation Resistance and Safeguardability Assessment Tools (PROSA)," June 2012, www.iaea.org/INPRO/CPs/PROSA; and private communication to IAEA PROSA Officers.
26. International Atomic Energy Agency, "Evaluation Methodology for Proliferation Resistance and Physical Protection of Generation IV Nuclear Energy Systems," Revision 6, Generation IV, GIF/PRPPWG/2011/003, September 30, 2011. See also Pomeroy *et al.*, "Proliferation Resistance of Nuclear Energy Systems."

30

MULTINATIONAL APPROACHES TO THE NUCLEAR FUEL CYCLE

John Carlson

Multinational approaches to the nuclear fuel cycle aim to obviate any legitimate need for states to have national programs based on proliferation-sensitive nuclear technologies – primarily uranium enrichment and reprocessing. In so doing, multinational approaches are intended to strengthen the nuclear nonproliferation regime and contribute to the confidence needed to progress nuclear disarmament.

The need for multinational approaches arises because the technologies used for producing nuclear fuel – uranium enrichment and reprocessing – are inherently dual-use. These technologies were developed originally to produce fissile material – highly enriched uranium and separated plutonium – for nuclear weapons.[1] Any state with enrichment and/or reprocessing capabilities has the potential to use these for military purposes.

Multinational approaches address security of supply and other justifications given for national enrichment and reprocessing programs, by providing alternatives to such programs. Current multinational concepts include assurances of nuclear fuel supply, nuclear fuel banks, and multinational control of proliferation-sensitive nuclear facilities.

What is meant by the term "multinational approaches?" Increasing vertical integration in the nuclear industry is leading to a number of transnational commercial operations, sometimes described as multinational. Such commercial arrangements can complement the objectives of multinational approaches by reducing the spread of national enrichment and reprocessing programs. These arrangements however continue to be based on facilities that are under national control. By contrast, multinational approaches refer to cooperative arrangements between two or more states – i.e., governments rather than companies – that will reduce the number of proliferation-sensitive programs under solely national control. Multinational approaches could involve a group of states, could be regionally-based, or could involve multilateral organizations such as the International Atomic Energy Agency (IAEA).

While multinational approaches are usually framed in the context of stopping the spread of sensitive nuclear capabilities, potentially they are also important for states that already have such capabilities, whether nonnuclear-weapon states or nuclear-armed states (i.e., the nuclear-weapon states recognized by the Nuclear Nonproliferation Treaty [NPT] and those outside the treaty).[2] Sensitive nuclear technologies are not only a proliferation issue (i.e., with respect to the spread of nuclear weapons), but also an issue for disarmament. As nuclear disarmament progresses, the potential for rapid break-out from disarmament commitments will be just as great a concern as the potential for break-out from nonproliferation commitments.

Civil nuclear programs and proliferation risk

Enrichment and reprocessing technologies, being dual-use, can be used for military as well as civil purposes. While the production of nuclear weapons requires activities such as weaponization and development of suitable delivery systems, production of fissile material remains the most substantial technical challenge for a would-be proliferator.[3]

The situation of a state that has established dual-use capabilities under a peaceful nuclear program is sometimes described as nuclear latency. Nuclear latency may be inadvertent: e.g., while such a state has the basic capability to produce fissile material for nuclear weapons, it may well have (at least in foreseeable circumstances) no intention of doing so. On the other hand, nuclear latency could also be deliberate – a state could establish enrichment or reprocessing capabilities with an eye to having a nuclear weapon option should its strategic circumstances change in the future. This situation could amount to nuclear hedging – i.e., where the state's intention is to establish the option of acquiring nuclear weapons within a relatively short time frame should it decide to do so. In the worst case, the state has already decided to become nuclear-armed.[4]

Some commentators refer to a state with enrichment or reprocessing capabilities as a virtual nuclear-weapon state. The common example given is Japan, sometimes described as being "just a screwdriver turn away" from nuclear weapons. This is simplistic, overlooking the other capabilities required, such as weaponization and delivery systems, as well as Japan's longstanding and strongly held commitment against nuclear weapons.[5] However, even a state as firmly committed to nonproliferation as Japan could change its position in the future – a concern reinforced by comments from some Japanese politicians about the need to ensure a nuclear weapon option.[6] Similar comments have been made by some politicians in the Republic of Korea, which is seeking enrichment and reprocessing capabilities.[7] While such comments do not represent today's mainstream political opinion, they illustrate the potential dangers of having enrichment and reprocessing capabilities in solely national hands.

If a number of states engaged in hedging, this could result in *virtual* arms races, with the risk of degenerating very quickly into real arms races, break-out from the NPT, and even nuclear war. It is difficult to tell what a state's intentions may be. Even inadvertent latency could be destabilizing, motivating additional states to seek equivalent capabilities. From a nonproliferation perspective, the fewer national enrichment and reprocessing programs the better, and vice versa – the more widespread these capabilities become, the greater the risk of proliferation.

Proliferation risk is changing

Proliferation risk has been manageable to date because the number of states with sensitive nuclear capabilities has been relatively limited, and those with safeguarded enrichment and reprocessing facilities have not sought to proliferate. Historically, proliferation programs have been based on undeclared or unsafeguarded facilities, leading to the common assumption that proliferation risk lies with clandestine rather than declared programs.

This situation is changing, however. Iran's efforts to legitimize what started as a clandestine enrichment program points to a new challenge, safeguarded proliferation – a program that is conducted under safeguards but may be intended to support break-out to nuclear-weapon production. The wider spread of centrifuge enrichment technology via the black market opens the possibility of new "civil" programs starting beyond the reach of international export controls. In the future, a further challenge is the spread of fast breeder reactors, involving greater use of reprocessing and plutonium fuels – this could present serious risks of nuclear terrorism as well as proliferation.

Today, as shown in Table 30.1, in addition to the nine nuclear-armed states, there are at least eight nonnuclear-weapon states that have demonstrated enrichment capability, and four that have demonstrated reprocessing capability, ten states in all (two have done both). Although in some cases the enrichment and/or reprocessing activity is no longer current, in principle these capabilities could be re-established.

The challenge to safeguards

As discussed in the next section, an essential nonproliferation measure is the commitment by nonnuclear-weapon states party to the Nuclear Nonproliferation Treaty to accept IAEA safeguards on all their nuclear material and activities. IAEA safeguards are designed to detect diversion of nuclear material from peaceful purposes. Diversion also encompasses having undeclared material/facilities, i.e., failure to place nuclear material and nuclear facilities under safeguards.

The specific risks to nonproliferation (and also disarmament) objectives presented by civil enrichment or reprocessing capabilities can be outlined as:

- *diversion* of product from declared facilities – i.e., attempted evasion of safeguards;
- operation of *clandestine* (undeclared) facilities – declared programs can provide cover and support for clandestine activities – e.g., through R&D, replication/manufacturing of equipment, and masking of environmental signatures;
- *rapid break-out* – i.e., renunciation of treaty commitments – using declared facilities, or a combination of declared facilities/materials and undeclared facilities.

A key objective of safeguards is to provide timely warning of diversion, to allow for international intervention before a proliferator has time to turn diverted nuclear material into nuclear weapons. Centrifuge enrichment technology presents a serious challenge to this objective – the relative ease of concealing centrifuge plants and the potential speed of break-out mean that adequate warning time cannot be guaranteed. Even if removal of enriched uranium from safeguards, or use of a safeguarded facility for high enrichment, is detected immediately, the time required for international deliberations – in the IAEA Board of Governors and the Security Council – could result in practical intervention not being possible within the necessary timeframe.[8]

Similar timeliness issues are raised where stocks of separated plutonium are held. The risks are exacerbated where high-fissile plutonium is involved, e.g., with fast breeder reactor blankets or spent fuel from large "research" reactors, such as Iran's Arak reactor. There is a real concern that if plutonium is diverted, and the state has made the necessary preparations in advance, the plutonium could be turned into nuclear weapons before effective intervention is possible.

Safeguards do not provide an effective counter to these emerging proliferation problems. Apart from the question whether safeguards can provide timely warning, there is also the problem that safeguards cannot determine a state's future intentions – and intentions can change over time.

This discussion indicates that enrichment and reprocessing programs present too high a risk to leave in national hands. It might be argued that to date the problem cases have been few, and have not involved commercial facilities. But there can be no doubt that the more these capabilities spread, the more likely they are to be misused. Further, the influences and pressures on states – both external and internal – will change over time. It cannot be assumed that every state apparently committed to nonproliferation today will remain so for all time.

Sensitive nuclear technology: National and international interests

The international interest in ensuring the peaceful use of nuclear energy was recognized at the very outset of the nuclear age. One of the first issues addressed by the newly established United Nations in 1946 was "the problems raised by the discovery of atomic energy." Proposals were advanced for placing nuclear programs under international control in order to prevent the spread of nuclear weapons (at that time held only by the United States).[9] Unfortunately the level of mistrust between the United States and the Soviet Union prevented agreement on this.

Following the first Soviet nuclear test in 1949, attention turned to preventing the proliferation of nuclear weapons to further states. The concept of cooperation under peaceful use guarantees was developed. In the 1953 Atoms for Peace initiative the US proposed the establishment of an international organization under the United Nations to operate a bank of nuclear material and to develop arrangements for this material to be allocated for peaceful uses.[10]

The Soviet Union, however, rejected any form of international custody of nuclear material. When the IAEA was established in 1957, its Statute reflected elements of the nuclear material bank concept, but this was wholly voluntary – member states could make nuclear materials available to the IAEA, the Agency would store any such materials, and it would supply these to member states on request.[11] In practice nuclear energy was starting to develop in other directions. A few states had the capability to develop indigenous nuclear programs – for most, national programs were enabled by bilateral supply agreements, under which reactors and fuel were supplied by the United States or the Soviet Union.

Nuclear nonproliferation treaty

The negotiation of the NPT commenced in the early 1960s. By 1968 when the text of the Treaty was agreed and opened for signature, the number of nuclear-weapon states had grown to five – in addition to the US and the Soviet Union, there were the United Kingdom (first test 1952), France (1960), and China (1964).

Table 30.1 States with demonstrated enrichment and/or reprocessing capability (past or current)

Nuclear-weapon states	Nuclear-armed states	Nonnuclear-weapon states	
Both enrichment and reprocessing capabilities		*Enrichment capability*	*Reprocessing capability*
United States	India	Argentina	*Belgium*
Russia	Pakistan	*Australia*	*Germany*
United Kingdom	North Korea	Brazil	*Italy*
France	Israel	Germany	Japan
China		Iran	
		Japan	
		Netherlands	
		South Africa	

Note: For the nonnuclear-weapon states shown in italics, the enrichment and/or reprocessing activity is no longer current.

The NPT reflected the concept of cooperation under peaceful use guarantees that had influenced the Atoms for Peace initiative. Nonnuclear-weapon state parties are prohibited from acquiring nuclear weapons, and are required to accept IAEA safeguards on all their nuclear material to verify compliance with this commitment. The parties undertake to cooperate in the peaceful uses of nuclear energy, and parties are described as having an *inalienable right* to research, production, and use nuclear energy for peaceful purposes, provided these activities are in conformity with the Treaty's nonproliferation and safeguards obligations.

When the NPT was negotiated, it was generally believed that proliferation risk would be limited because only the nuclear-weapon states and a small number of advanced industrialized states (e.g., Germany and Japan) would have enrichment and reprocessing capabilities. It was not anticipated that these capabilities would spread widely. It was also believed that IAEA safeguards would provide *timely warning* of any misuse of nuclear facilities.

Recent research has shown that during the NPT negotiations UK officials warned their US counterparts that centrifuge enrichment presented a serious risk to the NPT's objectives.[12] Unfortunately this warning was not heeded, and the draft NPT was not amended to reflect this risk. The United Kingdom's warning proved prescient, as there has been a gradual spread of proliferation capabilities, particularly centrifuge enrichment technology. This has been accelerated by black market activities, notably involving the Pakistan-based A.Q. Khan network.

It can now be seen that the problem of the spread of enrichment and reprocessing was not well anticipated in the language of the NPT. This makes it essential for the international community to focus on how the NPT should be applied in today's circumstances. It is important to recognize that the Treaty's reference to the "inalienable right" to use nuclear energy does not mean an unqualified right to develop specific technologies such as enrichment and reprocessing, especially where a state's interest in these may be nonpeaceful, e.g., establishing a nuclear weapon option.

Multinational approaches and national rights and interests

It is neither necessary nor cost effective for every state with nuclear power to have uranium enrichment and reprocessing programs. Because possession of such capabilities could increase international tensions – potentially leading to virtual arms races – and also because of the technical complexity and high costs, most states have not sought to establish these capabilities. The commercial market, with a limited number of enrichment and reprocessing service providers, has proven to be a reliable basis for nuclear fuel supply.

While energy independence may be cited as justification for a national fuel cycle, few states are in a position to achieve real independence. Apart from technological capabilities, not many have uranium resources sufficient to maintain a nuclear power program independent of external supply. For most states, international cooperation is likely to be a necessity, and for all states such cooperation will offer major advantages. Participation in international fuel cycle arrangements will lead to better outcomes than pursuing national independence.

Dispassionate consideration of a future framework for sensitive stages of the nuclear fuel cycle took a negative turn when in 2004 President George W. Bush suggested that states should voluntarily renounce enrichment and reprocessing, and proposed that the Nuclear Suppliers Group (NSG) limit supply of enrichment and reprocessing equipment and technology to those states that already possessed a "fully operational capability".[13] Many states, particularly in the Nonaligned Movement (NAM), saw this as an attempt to deny their rights and to preserve the technological advantage of existing nuclear suppliers. As a consequence, proposals for multilateral nuclear fuel cycle arrangements, even those as clearly beneficial as nuclear fuel banks, have been opposed.

At the 2010 NPT Review Conference, the NAM stated that it rejects "any attempts aimed at discouraging certain peaceful nuclear activities on the grounds of their alleged 'sensitivity' and emphasizes that any ideas or proposals pertaining to the nonproliferation of any peaceful nuclear technology are inconsistent with the objectives of the NPT."[14] This negative reaction, while shortsighted, is not surprising. Greater diplomatic effort is required to demonstrate that alternatives to national fuel cycle programs can offer security of supply on nondiscriminatory and equitable terms, with advantages through collaborative approaches (for example in spent fuel management), as well as the obvious advantage of reducing proliferation risk.

There is no contradiction between multinational approaches to the fuel cycle and sovereign rights. It is an exercise of a state's sovereignty to enter into an agreement – the basis of any international agreement is that states are prepared to act, or not act, in certain ways where they see this is in their national interest. If a state wants to be assured that its neighbors' nuclear programs are exclusively peaceful, and considers that the level of assurance will be stronger if proliferation-sensitive activities are circumscribed, it must accept the principle of reciprocity – the state must accept the same commitments that it expects of others.

The overwhelming international interest is to ensure an effective nonproliferation regime. It is also important to ensure stability in energy supply. These are vital national interests for every state – the international interest is not distinct and potentially inconsistent with the national interest, but in fact reflects an aggregation of the national interests of individual states.

There is a need to break through the political rhetoric, to get away from emotive and misleading arguments about rights and return the discussion to the real issue – reducing proliferation risk. In recent years several initiatives, outlined in the following section, have sought to avoid the political arguments about rights by instead creating conditions of supply such that states will have no legitimate reason to develop national enrichment and reprocessing programs.

Multinational approaches to the nuclear fuel cycle

As noted above, international operation of the nuclear fuel cycle was proposed unsuccessfully in the 1940s. The subject was looked at again by the International Nuclear Fuel Cycle Evaluation (INFCE) in the 1970s,[15] and by the IAEA's study of proposals for multilateral approaches in 2005.[16] Current multinational concepts include removing the need for national programs in proliferation-sensitive areas – e.g., through assurances of nuclear fuel supply and nuclear fuel banks – and placing sensitive nuclear facilities under multinational control.

The most practical alternative to national control of sensitive nuclear programs is some form of multinational control, of the kind referred to in the NSG Guidelines:

> If enrichment or reprocessing facilities, equipment or technology are to be transferred, suppliers should encourage recipients to accept, as an alternative to national plants, supplier involvement and/or other appropriate multinational participation in resulting facilities. Suppliers should also promote international (including IAEA) activities concerned with multinational regional fuel cycle centers.[17]

A key objective of the multinational approach is to establish technical and institutional barriers against a state attempting to misuse enrichment and reprocessing capabilities. The less control an individual state has over such capabilities, the harder it will be to misuse them. Of course no barrier can be totally effective – a state can always seize facilities regardless of who owns and operates them – but arrangements such as black box technology (discussed below) can be important in making misuse more difficult, providing more time for international intervention.

A historical example of a multilateral enrichment venture is Urenco, the enrichment consortium established by the United Kingdom, Germany, and the Netherlands. Urenco is a joint enterprise for developing centrifuge enrichment, established by the three governments under the 1971 Treaty of Almelo. Each state has an enrichment operation, and the Treaty sets out areas for joint collaboration, e.g., shared technology development, protection of technology, and peaceful use commitments. The level of multinational control with Urenco does not go as far as other models outlined here, and Urenco does not offer participation to enrichment customers, but there is a degree of joint oversight. Another historical example of a multinational enrichment venture is Eurodif, which is a commercial entity under French law.[18] There was a protracted legal dispute between France and Iran over Eurodif supply issues – Iran uses this dispute to claim that supply assurances cannot be relied on. Putting aside the rights and wrongs of this claim,[19] most current multinational concepts are based on government-to-government agreements, giving the participants rights enforceable in international, as distinct from domestic, law. In addition many multinational concepts involve the IAEA as guarantor, thus increasing the credibility of the assurances provided.

The contemporary example of a multinational enrichment venture is the International Uranium Enrichment Centre (IUEC) at Angarsk, Siberia, outlined below. Also there are now two nuclear fuel banks, one already operational (as part of the Angarsk IUEC), and one in the process of establishment (IAEA).

Assurances of supply

Proposals for assurance of supply were prompted by claims by certain states (e.g., Iran) that they needed independent nuclear fuel capabilities so they would not be vulnerable to denial of nuclear supply on political grounds.

International Framework for Nuclear Energy Cooperation (IFNEC)

Currently IFNEC is the most comprehensive and advanced proposal for supply assurances, in combination with other forms of international cooperation. IFNEC is the successor to the Global Nuclear Energy Partnership (GNEP), initiated by the United States in 2006. IFNEC now has a substantial international character, having grown to thirty-two participating states – including seventeen developing countries – and thirty-one observer states.[20]

IFNEC aims to establish international supply frameworks to enhance reliable, cost-effective fuel services and to identify other areas of global infrastructure that could be improved through international cooperation within the current market framework. The basic concept is that nuclear suppliers would provide comprehensive fuel service arrangements, including fuel leasing and spent fuel disposition options. A key feature of IFNEC is that participating states are not asked to renounce any rights. IFNEC has adopted a pragmatic approach – to set aside political arguments about national rights and instead focus on practical problems and solutions. The practical and economic benefits of international cooperation would obviate any legitimate reason for nuclear consumers to pursue national programs in proliferation-sensitive technologies.

Other fuel assurance proposals include the following:

World Nuclear Association (WNA) proposal (2006)

The WNA developed a "Three Tier" concept, based on (a) existing market mechanisms; (b) collective guarantees by existing uranium enrichment companies supported by commitments from governments and the IAEA; and (c) recourse if necessary to government stocks of enriched uranium product. To be eligible, states would need to be in full compliance with IAEA safeguards and to renounce the development, building, or operation of enrichment facilities.

Reliable access to nuclear fuel proposal (2006)

Also known as the "Six-Country" proposal, this modified version of the WNA proposal was made by the six governments offering commercial enrichment services on the global market: France, Germany, the Netherlands, Russia, the United Kingdom, and the United States. To be eligible, states need not forswear the development of enrichment capabilities, but must not currently have such facilities; must have a comprehensive safeguards agreement with an Additional Protocol in place with the IAEA, and have no outstanding safeguards issues. The third tier of assurance, enriched uranium stock, would be held by a supplier state, but control of these stocks could be transferred to the IAEA.

IAEA standby arrangements system (2006)

Japan proposed the establishment of an IAEA-administered database in which all states with the ability to supply front end services[21] would provide the IAEA with annual information on their supply capacities. In the event of a supply disruption, the IAEA would act as an intermediary to match the customer state with a new supplier. All states in compliance with IAEA safeguards would be eligible.

Nuclear fuel assurance proposal (2007)

Initially proposed by the United Kingdom, and subsequently supported by the Netherlands and Germany (the Urenco partners). The basis is an enrichment bond, established between a supplier state, recipient state, and the IAEA. The supplier would be precluded from denying exports of enriched uranium to a recipient state that met the requirements of international law and nonproliferation criteria. The IAEA would determine whether the conditions had been met, and the supplier state would be obliged to comply with the IAEA's decision.

Terms for reliable uranium service transactions through leasing (2007)

This concept envisions a trust, comprising private/public investment banks, private nonproliferation entities, and high net-worth individuals, negotiating supply contracts with suppliers. Essentially a mechanism to enable the existing market to function more efficiently, pooling of nuclear fuel purchases and attendant services would produce a competitive market for emerging nuclear energy states and other lessees while suppliers could more easily manage their supply decisions with a predictable demand.[22]

Fuel bank proposals

The concept of a fuel bank is an extension of the assurance of supply concept in which a quantity of enriched uranium is held by a state or the IAEA and disbursed to a state whose regular supply arrangements have been disrupted. The fuel bank may be either virtual (consisting of assured access by the bank administrator to a given quantity of enriched uranium) or involve the physical possession of uranium in the reserve. There are currently two such fuel banks – one in operation by Russia at the Angarsk International Uranium Enrichment Centre, and one initiated by the Nuclear Threat Initiative (NTI), being established in Kazakhstan under IAEA auspices.

US proposal on a reserve of nuclear fuel (2005)

The US announced it would down-blend 17 tons of high-enriched uranium deemed in excess of national security needs to use as a reserve of nuclear fuel "to support assurances of reliable nuclear fuel supply for states that forego enrichment and reprocessing". Though this low-enriched uranium (LEU) would serve to complement any IAEA reserve and support IAEA supply assurances, it would remain under US control and be subject to obligations attached to US-origin material.

Nuclear threat initiative fuel bank (2006)

In 2006 NTI provided the IAEA with $50 million for the establishment of an LEU reserve under IAEA control to ensure fuel supply to customer states on a nondiscriminatory, nonpolitical basis. Subsequently other states[23] have contributed a further $100 million. However, the proposal was blocked in the IAEA Board of Governors by developing states who saw the fuel bank as in some way impinging upon their right to develop uranium enrichment.

The proposal was finally approved by the Board in December 2010. Kazakhstan offered to host the fuel bank, and the IAEA and Kazakhstan are discussing the technical details. The IAEA fuel bank aims to have enough LEU to meet the fuel fabrication needs for two or three reloads of fuel for a 1,000 MW(e) light water reactor.[24]

Russian LEU reserve proposal (2009)

As part of its proposal to establish international nuclear fuel centers under the supervision of the IAEA, Russia announced a proposal for 120 tons of low-enriched uranium to be held at the International Uranium Enrichment Centre (IUEC) at Angarsk to ensure stable fuel supplies to power plants in case of disruption not related to technical or commercial considerations, including "insurmountable political difficulties." This reserve material would be accessible to any IAEA member state that honors its nonproliferation commitments, and supply from the fuel bank would be determined by the IAEA. The proposal was approved by the IAEA Board of Governors in November 2009.

Multinational control

Global nuclear power infrastructure (2006)

This Russian proposal involves a network of international nuclear fuel cycle service centers around the world, under IAEA control and providing those services on a nondiscriminatory basis. Russia has proposed four types of fuel cycle service centers within its borders – the IUEC at Angarsk, a reprocessing and spent fuel storage facility, a personnel training and certification facility, and a nuclear research and development facility.

International uranium enrichment centre (2007)

Russia established the IUEC with the mission "To ensure equal and assured access for all countries to the benefits of atomic energy."[25] The IUEC effectively multilateralizes an existing facility through enrichment contracts with the Angarsk Electrolysis Chemical Complex that are guaranteed by the Russian government. The IUEC provides guaranteed access to enrichment for participant states, which may join IUEC through an agreement with the Russian government, provided they meet established nonproliferation criteria. Current participants (as of December 3, 2014) are Kazakhstan, Armenia, and Ukraine, and several other states have indicated an interest in joining.

Other proposed multinational concepts

International Nuclear Fuel Agency (INFA) (1979)

A proposal by the Stockholm International Peace Research Institute (SIPRI). All national enrichment facilities would be brought under the authority of INFA. Laser enrichment and plasma separation would be stopped, centrifuges would be phased out, and gaseous diffusion/chemical-exchange technology would be employed in an effort to use only technology that presents serious obstacles to national misuse. Withdrawal from INFA would not be permitted, and INFA would be empowered to enact sanctions against violators.[26]

Multilateral Enrichment Sanctuary Project (MESP) (2007)

A German proposal for a new, multilateral enrichment facility (or facilities) to be built and operated by an international company (or companies) and administered by the IAEA on territory ceded to the Agency by a host nation. The IAEA would control all movements of nuclear materials in and out of the territory and would act as the regulatory authority for those facilities. Enrichment services would be guaranteed to all states satisfying criteria set by the IAEA, and would not be required to forego the development of indigenous enrichment facilities.

Multilateralization of the nuclear fuel cycle (2007)

An Austrian proposal, providing a road map towards full multilateralization of the fuel cycle. It has two tracks: (a) increasing transparency and confidence in the international fuel cycle by requiring states to report their nuclear activities to the IAEA, which would then publish a periodic review of the fuel cycle services market; and (b) establishment of a nuclear fuel bank, similar to the NTI project, to be administered by the IAEA, and the IAEA assuming the role of a virtual broker for all transactions involving nuclear materials. Existing fuel cycle facilities would be multilateralized in a similar manner to the Angarsk IUEC, and new facilities would be multilateralized from the outset. Once all facilities were fully multilateralized, a legally binding international agreement would prohibit the national pursuit of sensitive nuclear technologies, thus moving from incentive-based to restrictive multilateral fuel cycle arrangements.

Nuclear islands concept (2010)

A proposal for creation of an International Nuclear Fuel Cycle Association (INFCA) that would encompass all uranium enrichment activities within Internationally Secured Leased

Areas; later INFCA's jurisdiction would be extended to cover other sensitive fuel cycle activities. INFCA is intended to augment the IAEA and facilitate the IAEA's work. INFCA suppliers and customers would be required to do business only with other INFCA members.[27]

Black box technology

Under the *black box* approach, sensitive technology is not transferred, but is limited to the technology holder. Equipment is supplied as complete turnkey systems and facilities, without transfer of enabling design and manufacturing technology, under conditions that do not permit or enable replication of the facilities. The transferee has no access to classified aspects of the technology – manufacturing, installation, and maintenance are carried out by the technology holder.

The NSG Guidelines require, as far as practicable, that any supply of enrichment facilities and equipment should be on a black box basis.[28] This is the established practice of Urenco, which is supplying centrifuge installations to France and the US on a black box basis, and also of Tenex,[29] which has supplied centrifuge installations to China.

Though usually thought of as a technical proliferation barrier, black box arrangements can also be considered a subset of multinational control of facilities, because for black box arrangements to be effective the technology holder would have to maintain sufficient involvement in the facility to ensure there is no opportunity for the host state to access protected technology.

Conclusions

Multinational approaches are not an unrealistic aspiration – already there are practical precedents, such as Urenco and the Angarsk International Uranium Enrichment Centre. The Urenco and IUEC precedents have important characteristics that can be built upon in future models, for example: a treaty providing for mutual oversight of facility operations (Urenco); consumers having product supply guarantees and equity participation (IUEC); and supply of sensitive technology only on a black box basis (Urenco, also Russian practice).

While the priority must be ensuring there are no further wholly national programs in proliferation-sensitive stages of the fuel cycle – and this needs to include dissuading Iran from expanding its enrichment program – it is also necessary to address the future of existing programs. States being asked to accept restrictions on national nuclear programs are sure to argue that the new approaches should be nondiscriminatory and should apply also to the nuclear-armed states and others with sensitive nuclear programs. Accordingly, concepts are needed for the transitioning of all nationally controlled enrichment and reprocessing programs to an appropriate alternative model within a realistic timeframe.

Gaining support for multinationalization of proliferation-sensitive stages of the fuel cycle will be challenging. However, achieving a future free from the danger of nuclear war requires a change in current mindsets, from an emphasis on national fuel cycle programs to new approaches based on the common interests of nonproliferation, nuclear disarmament, energy security, and strengthened international cooperation.

Notes

1.   Highly enriched uranium (HEU) is uranium enriched to 20 percent or more in the isotope uranium-235. HEU for nuclear weapons is typically enriched to more than 90 percent U-235. Separated plutonium is plutonium extracted from irradiated fuel through reprocessing.

2. The term nuclear-weapon states (NWS) usually refers to the five NWS recognized by the NPT, i.e., US, Russia, UK, France, and China. In addition to these, four other states, outside the NPT, (a) have nuclear weapons (India and Pakistan), (b) are believed to have nuclear weapons (Israel), or (c) have conducted nuclear tests (DPRK).

3. Fissile material may also be acquired through legitimate transfer (e.g., reactor fuel) or illicit procurement (including theft or seizure), but independent production of fissile material has been the goal of all proliferation programs to date. "Weaponization" is a shorthand term for a range of activities including warhead design and associated modeling and calculations; high-explosive lenses and implosion testing; specialized high-energy electrical components; high-flux neutron generators; and design and testing of warhead re-entry vehicles.

4. On nuclear latency and nuclear hedging, see John Carlson, *Assessing and Minimizing Proliferation Risk*, in a forthcoming publication of the International Luxembourg Forum; and Ariel Levite, "Never Say Never Again: Nuclear Reversal Revisited," *International Security*, Vol. 27, No. 3 (Winter 2002/03), pp. 59–88.

5. Some commentators point to Japan's space program as providing ballistic missile capabilities.

6. See, for example, remarks of Japan's defense minister, Satoshi Morimoto, prior to his appointment, reported in the *Japan Times*, September 6, 2012, http://info.japantimes.co.jp/text/nn20120906 b4.html.

7. See, for example, a speech by Chung Mong-joon to the April 2013 Carnegie International Nuclear Policy Conference, reported in David E. Sanger, "In US, South Korean Makes Case for Nuclear Arms," *New York Times*, April 9, 2013, www.nytimes.com/2013/04/10/world/asia/in-us-south-korean-makes-case-for-nuclear-arms.html.

8. One problem here is that production of highly enriched uranium is not prohibited – if a state started to do this, vital time could be lost on legalistic arguments.

9. See e.g., the Baruch Plan, Presented to the United Nations Atomic Energy Commission, June 14, 1946, www.atomicarchive.com/Docs/Deterrence/BaruchPlan.shtml.

10. Dwight D. Eisenhower, "Draft of the Presidential Speech Before the General Assembly of the United Nations," November 28, 1953, www.eisenhower.archives.gov/research/online_documents/atoms_for_peace/ Atoms_for_Peace_Draft.pdf.

11. See International Atomic Energy Agency, "The Statute of the IAEA," October 23, 1956, Article IX and Article XI.C, www.iaea.org/About/statute.html IAEA Statute.

12. John Krige, "The Proliferation Risks of Gas Centrifuge Enrichment at the Dawn of the NPT," *The Nonproliferation Review*, Vol. 19, No. 2 (July 2012), pp. 219–227, www.tandfonline.com/doi/abs/10.1080/10736700.2012.690961#.UYswj7VBO4I.

13. George W. Bush, "President Announces New Measures to Counter the Threat of WMD," speech at the National Defense University, February 11, 2004, http://georgewbush-whitehouse.archives.gov/news/releases/2004/02/20040211-4.html.

14. Nonaligned Movement, "Working Paper Presented by the Group of Non-Aligned States Parties to the 2010 Review Conference of the Treaty on the Nonproliferation of Nuclear Weapons (NPT)," April 30, 2010, p. 8, http://isis-online.org/uploads/conferences/documents/NAM_Working_Paper_for_2010_NPT_RevCon_30April2010.pdf.

15. International Atomic Energy Agency, *Report of the International Nuclear Fuel Cycle Evaluation* (Vienna: IAEA, 1980).

16. International Atomic Energy Agency, "Multilateral Approaches to the Nuclear Fuel Cycle: Expert Group Report submitted to the Director General of the International Atomic Energy Agency," INFCIRC/640, February 22, 2005, www.iaea.org/Publications/Documents/Infcircs/2005/infcirc640.pdf.

17. International Atomic Energy Agency, "Communication Received from the Permanent Mission of the Netherlands regarding Certain Member States' Guidelines for the Export of Nuclear Material, Equipment and Technology," INFCIRC/254/Rev.10/Part 1, July 26, 2011, paragraph 7(b), www.iaea.org/Publications/Documents/Infcircs/ 2011/infcirc254r10p1.pdf.

18. In addition to France, the parties in Eurodif are Belgium, Italy, Spain, and Iran.

19. In fact the dispute arose initially because (in retrospect, fortuitously) Iran refused to take scheduled product deliveries.

20. IFNEC members as of December 2013 were: Argentina, Armenia, Australia, Bahrain, Bulgaria, Canada, China, Estonia, France, Germany, Ghana, Hungary, Italy, Japan, Jordan, Kazakhstan, Kenya, Republic of Korea, Kuwait, Lithuania, Morocco, Netherlands, Oman, Poland, Romania, Russia,

Senegal, Slovenia, Ukraine, the United Arab Emirates, the United Kingdom, and the United States. See the International Framework for Nuclear Energy Cooperation, "Membership," www.ifnec.org/About/Membership.aspx.
21. Uranium production, conversion, enrichment, and fuel fabrication.
22. Stephen Goldberg, James Glasgow, James Malone, "'TRUST,' An Innovative Nuclear Fuel Leasing Arrangement," Presentation to the World Nuclear Fuel Cycle Conference, Helsinki, Finland, April 18, 2007, www.wnfc.info/proceedings/2007/presentations/goldberg_glasgow_maloneppt.pdf. The authors cite the 1994 HEU Purchase Agreement between the United States and Russia, accomplished in a budget neutral fashion, as an excellent model.
23. The United States, the European Union, Kuwait, the United Arab Emirates, and Norway.
24. Roughly 50–90 tonnes of LEU in total.
25. International Uranium Enrichment Center, Mission Statement, http://eng.iuec.ru.
26. Allan Krass, Peter Boskma, Boelie Elzen, and Wim A. Smit, *Uranium Enrichment and Nuclear Weapon Proliferation* (London: Taylor & Francis, 1983), pp. 88–91.
27. Christopher E. Paine and Thomas B. Cochran, "Nuclear Islands: International Leasing of Nuclear Fuel Cycle Sites to Provide Enduring Assurance of Peaceful Use," *The Nonproliferation Review*, Vol. 17, No. 3 (November 2010), pp. 441–474, http://cns.miis.edu/npr/pdfs/npr_17-3_paine_cochran.pdf.
28. NSG Guidelines, INFCIRC/254/Rev.10/Part 1, paragraph 6(e).
29. Tenex is the abbreviation of Tekhsnabexport, the Russian enrichment operator.

Nuclear Security and Terrorism

31

REDUCING THE RISKS OF NUCLEAR THEFT AND TERRORISM

Matthew Bunn and Nickolas Roth

Despite the dramatic progress made in over two decades of international cooperation to improve nuclear security – including the four-year effort to secure all vulnerable nuclear material world-wide launched by US President Barack Obama in 2009 – the risk of nuclear terrorism remains unacceptably high, and some nuclear material remains dangerously vulnerable to nuclear theft.[1] Though the leaders at successive global summits on nuclear security have identified nuclear terrorism as one of the top threats to international security, this conclusion remains controversial. Policymakers in many countries doubt whether it is really plausible that terrorists could get nuclear material or make a nuclear bomb; that even if they did, it would probably be used on New York or Washington, making it primarily a US problem; and that in any case their own nuclear material is adequately secured. This complacency is the enemy of action.

This chapter assesses whether terrorists are actually seeking nuclear weapons; whether a terrorist organization could, if it had the needed nuclear materials, be capable of building a nuclear bomb; whether terrorist organizations could plausibly get the needed nuclear materials; and what the consequences of a terrorist nuclear attack might be. (A sidebar describes other types of nuclear and radiological terrorism.) The chapter then describes the substantial progress made in reducing the risk of nuclear theft in recent years and the gaps that still remain. Finally, the chapter offers suggestions for strengthening nuclear security for the long haul.

Do terrorists want nuclear weapons?

The danger of nuclear terrorism is driven by three key factors – terrorist intent to escalate to the nuclear level of violence; potential terrorist capability to do so; and the vulnerability of the weapons or materials needed to enable terrorists to carry out such an attack – the motive, means, and opportunity for a monstrous crime.[2]

The first question is terrorist intent. Most terrorist groups have always been focused on small-scale violence for local political purposes. For them, the nuclear level of violence is irrelevant and counterproductive.

But we now live in an age that includes a few groups intent on inflicting large-scale destruction to achieve more global objectives. In the 1990s, the Japanese terror cult Aum Shinrikyo first sought to buy nuclear weapons in Russia, then to make them themselves, before turning to biological weapons and the nerve gas they ultimately used in the Tokyo subways.[3]

Starting also in the 1990s, al Qaeda repeatedly sought nuclear materials and the expertise needed to make them into a nuclear bomb. Ultimately, al Qaeda put together a focused program reporting directly to Ayman al-Zawahiri (now head of the group), which progressed as far as carrying out crude but sensible conventional explosive tests for the nuclear program in the desert of Afghanistan.[4]

The killing of Osama bin Laden and the many other blows against al Qaeda have surely reduced the risk that al Qaeda could put together and carry through a nuclear bomb project. But by how much? The core organization of al Qaeda has proved resilient in the past. There is every reason to believe Al-Zawahiri remains eager to inflict destruction on a nuclear scale.[5] Indeed, despite the large number of al Qaeda leaders who have been killed or captured, nearly all of the key players in al Qaeda's nuclear program remain alive and at large – including Abdel Aziz al-Masri, an Egyptian explosives expert who was al Qaeda's "nuclear CEO."[6] No one knows what capabilities a secret cell of al Qaeda may have managed to retain or build. And regional affiliates and other groups in the broader violent Islamic extremist movement – particularly some of the deadly Pakistani terrorist groups – may someday develop the capability and intent to follow a similar path.

North Caucasus terrorist groups sought radiological weapons and threatened to sabotage nuclear reactors. There is significant, though less conclusive, evidence that they sought nuclear weapons as well – particularly confirmation from senior Russian officials that two teams were caught carrying out reconnaissance at Russian nuclear weapon storage sites, whose very locations are a state secret.[7]

More fundamentally, with at least two, and probably three, groups having gone down this path in the past twenty-five years, there is no reason to expect they will be the last. The danger of nuclear terrorism will remain as long as nuclear weapons, the materials needed to make them, and terrorist groups bent on large-scale destruction co-exist.

Could terrorists build a nuclear bomb?

Unfortunately, it does not take a Manhattan Project to make a nuclear bomb. Indeed, over 90 percent of the Manhattan Project effort was focused on making the nuclear materials, not on designing and building the weapons. Numerous studies by the United States and other governments have concluded that it is plausible that a sophisticated terrorist group could make a crude nuclear bomb if it got enough separated plutonium or highly enriched uranium (HEU).[8] A "gun-type" bomb, such as the weapon that obliterated Hiroshima, fundamentally involves slamming two pieces of HEU together at high speed. An "implosion-type" bomb, which is needed to get a substantial explosive yield from plutonium, requires using explosives to crush nuclear material to a higher density – a more complex task, but still plausible for terrorists, especially if they got knowledgeable help.

Long before the existence of the Internet and the vast amount of information it made available, and long before globalization and the remarkable resulting spread of technology, a study by the US Office of Technology Assessment summed up the situation:

> A small group of people, none of whom have ever had access to the classified literature, could possibly design and build a crude nuclear explosive device.... Only modest machine-shop facilities that could be contracted for without arousing suspicion would be required.[9]

Many analysts argue that, since states spend billions of dollars and assign hundreds or thousands of people to building nuclear weapons, it is totally implausible that terrorists could carry out this task. Unfortunately, this argument is wrong, for two reasons. First, by getting stolen nuclear material, terrorists would be bypassing making nuclear material, which is what states spend billions seeking to accomplish. Second, it is far easier to make a crude, unsafe, unreliable bomb of uncertain yield, which might be delivered in the back of a truck, than to make the kind of nuclear weapon a state would want in its arsenal – a safe, reliable weapon of known yield that can be delivered by missile or combat aircraft.

Could terrorists plausibly get nuclear material?

Unfortunately, the answer to this question is also "yes." There are approximately twenty well-documented cases of actual theft and smuggling of plutonium or HEU in the public record.[10] Many of these involved only gram quantities of material, but often the smugglers claimed these were only samples of much larger quantities they had available. In all but one of these cases, no one noticed that the material was missing until it was seized – suggesting that other thefts have likely gone undetected.

At least three lines of evidence confirm that important nuclear security weaknesses continue to exist. First, seizures of stolen HEU and separated plutonium continue to occur, including, mostly recently, HEU seizures in 2003, 2006, 2010, and 2011.[11] These seizures may result from material stolen long ago, but, at a minimum, they make clear that stocks of HEU and plutonium remain outside of regulatory control. Second, in cases where countries do realistic tests to probe whether security systems can protect against teams of clever adversaries determined to find a weak point, the adversaries sometimes succeed – even when their capabilities are within the set of threats the security system is designed to protect against. Third, in real nonnuclear thefts and terrorist attacks around the world, adversaries sometimes demonstrate capabilities and tactics well beyond what many nuclear security systems would likely be able to handle.[12]

Consequences, probabilities, and risks

The consequences of nuclear terrorism would be catastrophic. The heart of a major city could be reduced to a smoldering radioactive ruin, leaving tens to hundreds of thousands of people dead. The perpetrators or others might claim to have more weapons already hidden in other major cities and threaten to set them off if their demands were not met – potentially provoking uncontrolled evacuation of many urban centers. Devastating economic consequences would reverberate worldwide. Kofi Annan, while serving as Secretary-General of the United Nations, warned that the global economic effects of a nuclear terrorist attack in a major city would push "tens of millions of people into dire poverty," creating a "second death toll throughout the developing world."[13] Nuclear security is not a US problem but a global problem.

No one knows what the real probability of such an event might be. But the consequences are so extreme that even a small probability is enough to justify urgent action to reduce the risk. No one would operate a nuclear power plant upwind of a major city if the probability of a catastrophic release were one in a hundred each year – the risk would be agreed by all to be too high. Yet the world community may face a still higher risk of catastrophic disaster from the way that nuclear weapons and the materials needed to make them are managed in the world today.

Progress in strengthening nuclear security – and remaining gaps

Reducing the threat of nuclear terrorism requires a multi-layered defense that goes after both the materials that might be used in a terrorist nuclear attack and the actors that might use them.

Such a defense should include security measures to prevent nuclear weapons and weapons-usable nuclear materials from being stolen; measures to stop nuclear smuggling; efforts to counter the terrorist groups interested in nuclear and radiological attacks and resolve the underlying drivers of mass destruction terrorism; preparedness for emergency response; steps to prevent and deter state assistance with nuclear or radiological terrorism; and more.[14]

Keeping nuclear weapons and materials from being stolen, however, is by far the most effective step that can be taken to reduce the risk, for once the material is gone, it could be anywhere, and all the later lines of defense are variations on looking for needles in haystacks. The amount of plutonium needed for an implosion bomb is the size of a grapefruit; the HEU for a simpler gun-type bomb would fit in two two-liter bottles. While these materials are radioactive, they are not so radioactive as to make them difficult to carry or easy to detect. (The radiation from HEU metal in particular is so weak and easy to block that many of the radiation detectors in use at border crossings today would have little chance of detecting HEU metal with appropriate shielding.) Moreover, the huge length of key borders, the immense legitimate traffic across them, the deeply entrenched smuggling of many other types of contraband that takes place worldwide, and the corruption of some border officials, all conspire to make the smuggler's job easier and the defender's job more challenging. The rest of this chapter, therefore, will focus primarily on nuclear security.

How big is the nuclear security problem? While the numbers were once much larger, unclassified estimates suggest that today, nuclear weapons are stored at over 100 sites in fourteen countries (the nine states which possess nuclear weapons and five more countries in Europe where US nuclear weapons are stored). Weapons-usable nuclear material exists in hundreds of buildings in some thirty countries around the world.[15]

International cooperation and nuclear security

Ultimately, it is up to each state to ensure that any nuclear weapons or weapons-usable material it possesses are secure and accounted for. But given that weapons and materials can easily be smuggled across borders, every state has an interest in making sure other states provide effective nuclear security – and there are many ways international cooperation can strengthen nuclear security, through treaties, voluntary initiatives, international organizations, technical cooperation, and evolving norms.

For over two decades, the United States has been cooperating with the states of the former Soviet Union to strengthen security and accounting for nuclear weapons and weapons-usable nuclear materials. The most egregious weaknesses of the 1990s – gaping holes in fences, sites with no detector to set off an alarm if someone was carrying out plutonium or highly enriched uranium, staff going unpaid for months at a time – have been fixed.[16]

More recently, cooperation to improve nuclear security has become a global effort, as implied by the names of the Global Threat Reduction Initiative (a US-funded effort working on projects ranging from converting HEU-fueled reactors to improving security for radiological sources) or the Global Partnership Against the Spread of Weapons and Materials of Mass Destruction (a grouping of countries providing funding for projects to dismantle weapons and improve proliferation controls).

Today, the global nuclear security framework includes, among other elements:[17]

- International treaties, such as the 1980 Convention on the Physical Protection of Nuclear Materials and its 2005 amendment, and the 2005 International Convention on the Suppression of Acts of Nuclear Terrorism, and other legally binding instruments, ranging from nuclear supply agreements with requirements for nuclear security to UN Security Council Resolution 1540, which legally obligates all states to provide "appropriate effective" security and accounting for any stockpiles of nuclear weapons and weapons-usable materials they may have.

- A strengthened nuclear security effort at the International Atomic Energy Agency (IAEA), which leads the development of recommendations and guidance on nuclear security; offers peer review services when states request them; offers a wide range of training courses; organizes a variety of meetings and workshops; maintains databases, such as the Incident and Trafficking Database; and provides limited assistance to countries in implementing nuclear security.[18]
- Multilateral initiatives, such as the Global Partnership noted above, the Global Initiative to Combat Nuclear Terrorism, and others;
- Bilateral and multilateral technical cooperation, particularly US-funded cooperation both to improve nuclear security and to remove nuclear material from some sites entirely.

In his Prague speech in April 2009, President Obama called for a four-year effort to secure all vulnerable nuclear material worldwide, and announced that he would convene a global summit on nuclear security – which was held in Washington in 2010, and endorsed the four-year goal as part of a broad communiqué and "work plan" of measures to strengthen nuclear security around the world. At the time of writing, two subsequent summits have been held –in Seoul in 2012, and in The Hague in 2014 – with the fourth and probably last scheduled to take place in the United States in 2016. This process has elevated the discussion of nuclear security from an obscure topic for specialists to the level of presidents and prime ministers; has built increased international understanding of the threat and support for action; and has provided a forcing function, with leaders' desire to have something to announce resulting in a variety of pledges and commitments that otherwise might not have occurred, or might have taken many years. At the 2014 nuclear security summit, for example, a majority of participants pledged to implement IAEA nuclear security recommendations and accept periodic peer reviews of their nuclear security arrangements; Japan announced that it would eliminate some of the most dangerous material that exists in any nonnuclear-weapon state; and participants launched a new initiative to improve security for radiological sources.[19]

Nuclear security progress

Countries around the world have substantially improved their nuclear security measures over the past two decades. In a recent survey of nuclear experts in the majority of the countries where nuclear weapons or weapon-usable nuclear material exist, all of the participants reported that their countries had made their nuclear security measures either more stringent or much more stringent over the past fifteen years.[20] Countries have established requirements that operators protect against particular sets of potential adversary capabilities (known as the "design basis threat" or DBT) or strengthened their DBTs; consolidated nuclear weapons and materials to fewer locations, making it possible to achieve more security at lower cost; put in place modernized security and accounting equipment; strengthened regulations and inspection programs; and beefed up training and qualification of personnel.

In particular, during the four-year effort President Obama launched in 2009:[21]

- Thirteen countries eliminated all of the weapons-usable nuclear material on their soil;
- All of the sites in nonnuclear-weapon states where enough high-quality HEU for a

gun-type bomb existed at a single site were either eliminated or had significant security upgrades put in place;

- While cooperative nuclear security and accounting upgrades had been completed at most warhead bunkers and nuclear material buildings in Russia before the four-year effort began, significant additional improvements were completed during that time;
- Similarly, substantial further improvements reportedly occurred in Pakistan (though nuclear security work there remains shrouded in secrecy);
- The number of states that have ratified the 2005 amendment to the Convention on the Physical Protection of Nuclear Material (CPPNM) more than doubled and the number of states that had ratified International Convention for the Suppression of Acts of Nuclear Terrorism (ICSANT)increased by more than half (though as of mid-2014 the United States had still failed to ratify both agreements);
- The International Atomic Energy Agency's (IAEA) nuclear security effort was elevated from an office to a division; the IAEA physical protection recommendations were strengthened; and many more states began taking advantage of the IAEA's nuclear security peer review and nuclear security planning services;
- Several states established new nuclear security "centers of excellence," which will provide training and in some cases maintain equipment or provide advice and analysis to regulators.

Remaining vulnerabilities

Despite the many elements of nuclear security progress, serious vulnerabilities remain. Around the world, there are stocks of nuclear weapons or materials whose security systems are not sufficient to protect against the full range of plausible outsider and insider threats they may face. As incidents like the 2012 intrusion at the Y-12 nuclear facility –where three activists spent more than an hour in a heavily secured area before being detained – make clear, many nuclear facilities and transporters still grapple with serious problems of security culture.[22] It is fair to say that every country where nuclear weapons, weapons-usable nuclear materials, major nuclear facilities, or dangerous radiological sources exist has more to do to ensure that these items are sustainably secured and accounted for.

Nuclear security measures in most countries are shrouded in secrecy. No government or international organization has a complete understanding of the risks of theft posed by all the different sites and transport operations around the world. Based on the very partial information available in unclassified sources, it appears that some of the most substantial remaining risks are:[23]

- In Russia, which has the world's largest stockpiles of nuclear weapons and materials in the world's largest number of buildings and bunkers, and nuclear security measures that, while much improved, still have important weaknesses (particularly in protecting against insider theft);
- In Pakistan, which has a relatively small but rapidly growing nuclear stockpile, at a small number of locations, and a substantial nuclear security effort – but where that effort must protect against enormous threats from both insiders and outsiders;
- In India, which also has a relatively small but growing stockpile, a substantial terrorist threat (though not comparable to the threat in Pakistan), and which has declined most cooperation on nuclear security; and
- At HEU-fueled research reactors, which often have only minimal nuclear security measures in place.

More broadly, the global nuclear security framework remains weak. Remarkably, there are no global rules that specify how secure nuclear weapons or the material needed to make them should be; no agreed mechanisms to verify or build confidence that states really have put effective nuclear security measures in place; and, once the nuclear security summits come to an end, no obvious forum for continuing high-level dialogue on what the next steps in nuclear security should be.

Toward sustainable nuclear security

What, then, should be done to fill the remaining gaps? Unfortunately, policymakers still have only a limited understanding of what policy tools will be most effective in leading not only to installing effective nuclear security and accounting systems, but also to ensuring that they will be used effectively and sustained for the long haul. Nevertheless, a few steps are clearly called for.[24]

First, the United States and other interested governments should take steps to combat the complacency that still exists in many countries. Policymakers, nuclear managers, and nuclear staff around the world will not take the requisite actions unless they are convinced that nuclear terrorism is a real and urgent threat to their countries' security, worthy of a significant investment of their time and money, and that improvements on their part are necessary to reduce the risk. To make that case, the US government and other interested governments should:

- Develop a detailed report on what it knows about the threat of nuclear terrorism (at different levels of classification appropriate for different audiences) and distribute it to key officials in other countries;
- Undertake discussions among intelligence agencies (which are the group most governments rely on to tell them about threats to their security);
- Work with countries to get them to establish programs of realistic tests of nuclear security systems' ability to protect against intelligent adversaries looking for ways to overcome them (an approach that has often helped convince US policymakers that further action to improve US nuclear security were needed); and
- Establish and share detailed analyses of incidents and lessons learned (to the extent possible within the bounds of necessary secrecy), to highlight the reality of the threat and help nuclear security managers understand what steps are needed to address it.[25]

Second, countries need to take action to strengthen their requirements for nuclear security. Countries should establish and sustain a DBT that will protect nuclear weapons, weapons-usable material, and major nuclear facilities against the full spectrum of adversaries their intelligence agencies judge to be credible threats – including both outsiders and insiders. All nuclear weapons and weapons-usable nuclear material everywhere should at least be protected against a baseline threat that includes a well-placed insider; a modest group of well-trained and well-armed outsiders, capable of operating as more than one team; and both an insider and the outsiders working together.[26] Countries facing more substantial threats should provide still higher levels of protection. A broad range of possible adversary tactics should be included in these DBTs. A political commitment to such a baseline DBT could be a major deliverable for the 2016 nuclear security summit, significantly strengthening the global nuclear security framework.

States need to ensure that all of the national and international organizations who play major roles in providing effective nuclear security have the resources needed to do their jobs – including money, trained personnel, and units focused on the nuclear security mission. This includes not just the money needed to install effective nuclear security and accounting equipment, but the money, people, and organizations to operate, sustain, and improve it over time. And they should accept regular reviews of their nuclear security arrangements by independent teams. Review and advice from experts outside the group that designed and is implementing a nuclear security system can often be extremely helpful in finding areas for improvement.

Third, states need to do more to consolidate nuclear weapons and materials at fewer locations, as the only way to eliminate the risk of nuclear theft from a site completely is to ensure that there is no weapons-usable nuclear material left there to steal. Current programs to minimize civilian use of HEU are making progress and deserve strong support and robust funding. They should be accelerated and expanded with the goal of phasing out the civilian use of HEU and eliminating stocks of HEU at civilian sites. The US and other countries should undertake new efforts to consolidate civilian separated plutonium and limit the buildup of ever-larger stockpiles. At the same time, the US, Russia, and other interested countries should expand cooperative efforts to consolidate military stocks of nuclear weapons, separated plutonium, and HEU as well.[27]

Fourth, it is essential to build organizational cultures in which all staff members take security seriously and are continuously on the lookout for vulnerabilities that should be fixed – and in which the organization is focused on continuous improvement in nuclear security, not just on complying with regulations. States should require that each organization handling nuclear weapons and weapons-usable materials have a program in place to assess and improve its nuclear security culture. Such organizations should also have programs in place to share and implement best practices (such as through the World Institute for Nuclear Security, or WINS), and to provide the training needed for everyone from managers to guards to do their jobs effectively. States should ensure that nuclear operators have incentives to achieve excellent nuclear security performance, and operators should structure incentives to motivate key staff to take security seriously and invest their time and effort in finding and fixing vulnerabilities and suggesting improvements.[28]

Finally, the world needs a stronger global nuclear security framework, a structure that helps states cooperate to establish standards and goals for nuclear security; discuss and decide on next steps to improve nuclear security; confirm that states are fulfilling their responsibility to provide effective security; and track states' progress in fulfilling their nuclear security commitments. Such a strengthened framework could include several elements. The first step, of course, would be to get states to ratify and implement the existing conventions (implementing them even before ratifying them, if ratification is delayed), carry out the existing recommendations, and participate in the voluntary initiatives already in place. But more needs to be done as well.

Establishing effective rules about how secure nuclear weapons or materials should be – such as the baseline DBT described above – would be a very important step in strengthening the global nuclear security framework. Past experience suggests that negotiating treaties takes too long and results in too few specific requirements to be an effective pathway – but political commitments made by groups of like-minded states may work better. The states pledging to implement such a baseline DBT could call on others to join them and offer assistance to those who might like to make the commitment but need help to do so.

States should also take a broad range of steps to assure other states that their nuclear security is effective. Such steps could range from inviting international peer review of nuclear security systems to having the teams charged with testing nuclear security effectiveness train together.

The United States and other donor states should continue their technical cooperation with other countries. In particular, despite intense tensions over the Ukraine and the broader decline in the US-Russian relationship, the US and Russia should continue to cooperate on nuclear security, sharing ideas, best practices, and peer reviews to improve nuclear security in both countries and ensure that improved security and accounting measures are sustained, and working together to help third countries as well.

Continuing a global nuclear security dialogue beyond the end of the summits is also essential. The IAEA can potentially play an important part of this role, shifting its international meetings on nuclear security toward real working sessions designed to reach agreement on next steps.[29] But in the end, multiple forums are likely to be needed, including an expanded emphasis on nuclear security in the Global Initiative to Combat Nuclear Terrorism, an increased emphasis on announcing nuclear security deliverables at G8 or G20 summits as part of the Global Partnership, review meetings for the CPPNM, and potentially a new forum below the summit level.[30]

Conclusion: Nuclear security for the long haul

The steps suggested here would not be easy. Complacency, secrecy, sovereignty, politics, cost concerns, and bureaucracy will all pose formidable obstacles that must be overcome. But the very real successes already achieved make clear that progress is possible. After a nuclear terrorist attack, it will be very difficult to explain why practical steps to prevent it had not been taken. States around the world need to take action to build a global system that will provide effective nuclear security for as long as nuclear weapons and the materials needed to make them continue to exist.

Notes

1. This chapter draws on Matthew Bunn, Martin Malin, Nickolas Roth, and William H. Tobey, *Advancing Nuclear Security: Evaluating Progress and Setting New Goals* (Cambridge, MA: Project on Managing the Atom, Belfer Center for Science and International Affairs, Harvard Kennedy School, March 2014), http://belfercenter.ksg.harvard.edu/files/advancingnuclearsecurity.pdf (accessed April 28, 2014). A great deal of additional information and commentary is available at http://nuclearsecuritymatters.belfercenter.org.
2. See William H. Tobey and Pavel Zolotarev, "The Nuclear Terrorism Threat," Pattaya, Thailand, January 13, 2014, http://belfercenter.ksg.harvard.edu/files/nuclearterrorismthreatthailand2014.pdf (accessed March 8, 2014). For an earlier joint US-Russian account, see Matthew Bunn, Yuri Morozov, Rolf Mowatt-Larssen, Simon Saradzhyan, William H. Tobey, Viktor I. Yesin, and Pavel S. Zolotarev, *The US-Russia Joint Threat Assessment of Nuclear Terrorism* (Cambridge, MA: Belfer Center for Science and International Affairs, Harvard Kennedy School, and Institute for US and Canadian Studies, June 2011), http://belfercenter.ksg.harvard.edu/publication/21087/ (accessed March 11, 2014).
3. See, for example, Sara Daly, John Parachini, and William Rosenau, *Aum Shinrikyo, al Qaeda, and the Kinshasa Reactor: Implications of Three Case Studies for Combating Nuclear Terrorism* (Santa Monica, CA: RAND, 2005), www.rand.org/content/dam/rand/pubs/documented_briefings/2005/RAND_DB458.pdf (accessed June 5, 2014).
4. George Tenet, *At the Center of the Storm: My Years at the CIA* (New York: HarperCollins, 2007), p. 275.
5. Indeed, in 2003 al Qaeda asked a radical Saudi cleric, Nasir bin Hamd al-Fahd, for a religious ruling or *fatwa* authorizing the use of nuclear weapons against American civilians, which al-Fahd provided. (At the time, al-Fahd was the "constant companion" of a leader of an al Qaeda cell in Saudi Arabia that was negotiating to buy three of what it believed were nuclear weapons.) See Rolf Mowatt-Larssen, *Al Qaeda Weapons of Mass Destruction Threat: Hype or Reality?* (Cambridge, MA: Belfer Center for Science and International Affairs, Harvard Kennedy School, January 2010), http://belfercenter.ksg.harvard.edu/files/al-qaeda-wmd-threat.pdf (accessed May 1, 2014). Al-Zawahiri 's 2008 book, *Exoneration,* repeats all of the arguments raised in al-Fahd's *fatwa,* citing similar sources in ancient Islamic writings, and elaborating the arguments further in places. Rolf Mowatt-Larssen, "Al-Qaeda's

Religious Justification of Nuclear Terrorism," Belfer Center for Science and International Affairs, Harvard Kennedy School, November 12, 2010, http://belfercenter.ksg.harvard.edu/publication/20518/ (accessed May 1, 2014). For the text of al-Zawahiri 's book, see Ayman al-Zawahiri, *Exoneration: A Treatise Exonerating the Community of the Pen and the Sword from the Debilitating Accusation of Fatigue and Weakness*, March 2008, translated at the Federation of American Scientists, www.fas.org/irp/dni/osc/exoneration.pdf.

6. For a partial list, see Tobey and Zolotarev, "The Nuclear Terrorist Threat."

7. For more on North Caucasus groups, see Bunn *et al.*, *Joint Threat Assessment,* pp. 27–30.

8. Matthew Bunn and Anthony Wier, "Terrorist Nuclear Weapon Construction: How Difficult?" *Annals of the American Academy of Political and Social Science,* Vol. 607 (September 2006), pp. 133–149.

9. US Congress, Office of Technology Assessment, *Nuclear Proliferation and Safeguards* (Washington, DC: OTA, 1977), www.princeton.edu/~ota/disk3/1977/7705/7705.PDF (accessed May 1, 2014), p. 140.

10. For a discussion of cases through 2006, see International Institute for Strategic Studies, "Illicit Trafficking in Radioactive Materials," *Nuclear Black Markets: Pakistan, A.Q. Khan and the Rise of Proliferation Networks: A Net Assessment* (London: International Institute for Strategic Studies, 2007), pp. 119–138. More recent seizures of stolen HEU have occurred in 2010 and 2011. Beyond the cases of stolen material, in recent years there have been several seizures of scrap metal contaminated with surprisingly large amounts of HEU; it appears that one or more HEU-processing facilities in the former Soviet Union has been or is being dismantled without sufficient care for the resulting scrap. Interview with US laboratory nuclear smuggling expert, July 2013.

11. For discussions, see Center for Nonproliferation Studies, "Illicit Trafficking in Weapons-Useable Nuclear Material: Still More Questions Than Answers," December 11, 2011, www.nti.org/analysis/articles/illicit-trafficking-weapons-useable-nuclear-material-still-more-questions-answers/ (accessed March 8, 2014); US Congress, Senate Committee on Foreign Relations, *Enhancing Non-Proliferation Partnerships in the Black Sea Region: A Minority Staff Report* (Washington, DC: US Government Printing Office, 2011), http://wid.ap.org/documents/np-minority-report.pdf (accessed March 8, 2014); Nick Amies, "US Concerns Over Nuclear Smuggling Between Europe, North Africa," *Deutsche Welle*, May 10, 2011, www.dw.de/dw/article/0,,15434811,00.html (accessed March 11, 2014); and Desmond Butler, "Officials Say Crime Ring has Uranium," *Associated Press*, September 27, 2011, www.theguardian.com/world/feedarticle/9866962 (accessed March 8, 2014).

12. As just one example, consider the robbery of the cash depot in Västberga, Sweden in 2009, which involved thieves arriving and departing by helicopter; using a fake bomb at the police heliport and caltrops (spikes) spread on the road to delay police response; and the use of explosives and automatic weapons. This and other cases' substantial adversary capabilities are described in Bunn *et al.*, *Advancing Nuclear Security*.

13. Kofi Annan, "A Global Strategy for Fighting Terrorism: Keynote Address to the Closing Plenary," The International Summit on Democracy, Terrorism and Security (Madrid: Club de Madrid, 2005), www.un.org/News/Press/docs/2005/sgsm9757.doc.htm (accessed June 5, 2014).

14. See "Beyond Nuclear Security," in Matthew Bunn, *Securing the Bomb 2008* (Cambridge, MA: Project on Managing the Atom, Belfer Center for Science and International Affairs, Harvard Kennedy School of Government and Nuclear Threat Initiative, November 2008), pp. 70–87, www.nti.org/media/pdfs/Securing_The_Bomb_2008.pdf (accessed March 8, 2014). See also Michael Levi, *On Nuclear Terrorism* (Cambridge, MA: Harvard University Press, 2007).

15. Nuclear Threat Initiative and Economist Intelligence Unit, *NTI Nuclear Materials Security Index: Building a Framework for Assurance, Accountability, and Action*, January 2012, p. 3, www.nti.org/media/pdfs/NTI_Index_FINAL.pdf; International Panel on Fissile Materials, *Global Fissile Material Report 2013: Increasing Transparency of Nuclear Warhead and Fissile Material Stocks as a Step toward Disarmament*, Princeton University, 2013, http://fissilematerials.org/library/gfmr13.pdf. The NTI Nuclear Materials Security Index lists twenty-five remaining countries with a kilogram or more of HEU or separated plutonium; in addition, Jamaica, Ghana, Syria, and Nigeria have just under a kilogram of this material in the cores of Slowpoke or Miniature Neutron Source Reactors (MNSRs), and Indonesia reportedly has just over a kilogram of HEU in waste from past nuclear activities.

16. See discussion in Matthew Bunn, *Securing the Bomb 2010: Securing all Nuclear Materials in Four Years* (Cambridge, MA: Project on Managing the Atom, Belfer Center for Science and International Affairs, Harvard Kennedy School of Government and Nuclear Threat Initiative, April 2010), www.nti.org/media/pdfs/Securing_The_Bomb_2010.pdf (accessed April 30, 2014), pp. 31–40, and Bunn *et al.*, *Advancing Nuclear Security*, pp. 24–28.

17. See Bunn *et al.*, *Advancing Nuclear Security*, pp. 49–60.
18. It is important to understand, however, that IAEA safeguards are not intended to ensure that material is secure. Safeguards involve international inspectors checking – in some cases once a month, in others as little as once a year – that declared nuclear material is still present and in civilian use. But more than 99 percent of the time, the inspectors are not there, and there is no international force contributing to the security of the material.
19. See commentary and links at http://nuclearsecuritymatters.belfercenter.org.
20. Matthew Bunn and Eben Harrell, *Threat Perceptions and Drivers of Change in Nuclear Security Around the World: Results of a Survey* (Cambridge, MA: Project on Managing the Atom, Harvard University, March 2014), http://belfercenter.ksg.harvard.edu/files/surveypaperfulltext.pdf (May 1, 2014).
21. Bunn *et al.*, *Advancing Nuclear Security*, pp. 13–60.
22. For a detailed account of the incident, see US Department of Energy, Office of the Inspector General, *Inquiry into the Security Breach at the National Nuclear Security Administration's Y-12 National Security Complex*, DOE/IG-0868 (Washington, DC: DOE, August 2012), http://energy.gov/sites/prod/files/IG-0868_0.pdf (accessed March 8, 2014), p. 14.
23. Bunn *et al.*, *Advancing Nuclear Security*, pp. 14–29.
24. These recommendations draw on those in ibid., pp. 61–77.
25. Such distribution of information on incidents and lessons learned about how to prevent them is routine in nuclear safety, and in some other areas of security (such as civil aviation). For an example of such an approach applied to security, see Matthew Bunn and Scott D. Sagan, *A Worst Practices Guide to Insider Threats: Lessons from Past Mistakes* (Cambridge, MA: American Academy of Arts and Sciences, April 2014), www.amacad.org/content/publications/publication.aspx?d=1425 (accessed May 1, 2014).
26. Matthew Bunn and Evgeniy P. Maslin, "All Stocks of Weapons-Usable Nuclear Materials Worldwide Must be Protected Against Global Terrorist Threats," *Journal of Nuclear Materials Management*, Vol. 39, No. 2 (Winter 2011), pp. 21–27.
27. See Matthew Bunn and Eben Harrell, *Consolidation: Thwarting Nuclear Theft* (Cambridge, MA: Project on Managing the Atom, Harvard University, March 2012), www.nuclearsummit.org/files/Consolidation_Thwarting_Nuclear_Theft.pdf (accessed March 8, 2014).
28. Matthew Bunn, "Incentives for Nuclear Security," Proceedings of the 46th Annual Meeting of the Institute for Nuclear Materials Management, Phoenix, Arizona, July 10–14, 2005 (Northbrook, IL: INMM, 2005), http://belfercenter.ksg.harvard.edu/files/inmm-incentives2-05.pdf (accessed March 8, 2014).
29. Trevor Findlay, *Beyond Nuclear Summitry: The Role of the IAEA in Nuclear Security Diplomacy After 2016* (Cambridge, MA: Project on Managing the Atom, Belfer Center for Science and International Affairs, Harvard Kennedy School, March 2014), http://belfercenter.ksg.harvard.edu/files/beyondnuclearsummitryfullpaper.pdf (accessed May 1, 2014).
30. Bunn *et al.*, *Advancing Nuclear Security*, pp. 74–76.

32

INDUSTRY EFFORTS TO ADDRESS NUCLEAR SECURITY

Roger Howsley

The nuclear industry is highly experienced in managing risk and this is most commonly associated with its safety and operational performance. Some major accidents and incidents, including those at Three Mile Island, Chernobyl and most recently at Fukushima, have highlighted the potential and actual consequences of safety failures, and the industry has reacted to enhance their performance and capability. The situation in relation to nuclear security is somewhat different because there has not been a serious failure of security with widespread consequences, and this factor, and the responsibility of the state for security, has meant that security has not always had the same attention given to it by the industry as have safety and operations. This situation changed after the terrorist attacks in the United States in 2001, even though they were unrelated to nuclear facilities, and gave an enormous stimulus to nuclear security. Governments began to reassess the potential consequences of a successful terrorist threat, to develop more extensive international guidance through the International Atomic Energy Agency (IAEA), encouraged states to sign up to international conventions, and bolstered national regulation and regulators. The industry also began to seek more effective ways of collaborating, but came up against significant difficulties in discussing security and sharing best practices, which is common practice in the safety and operational field. The difficulties industry experienced were for a variety of reasons including:

- *State Responsibility for Security.* The IAEA and its member states make clear that the responsibility for nuclear security rests entirely with the state, and while undoubtedly true, this statement does not present the full picture or adequately portray how responsibilities within the state are subdivided and how the nuclear industry and its licensees contribute to the achievement of a secure nuclear environment. In fact, by definition, states are accountable for all aspects of national policy, be it finance, education or agriculture, so why does the "State being accountable for nuclear security" persist as almost the first statement that appears in any communiqué from the international community and the IAEA?

  There are probably two reasons. First, to indicate that there is no international organization or regional entity (such as the European Union) that has power over individual states to dictate their nuclear security arrangements. States are free to decide whether to sign conventions or related international instruments, and free to determine the nuclear security regime within their territory. Those states that sign conventions will be bound by their conditions but the defined nuclear security requirements are typically very general and open to considerable interpretation by individual states. In essence, the international nuclear security regime is voluntary and, unlike the parallel in civil aviation, is not mandated or overseen by any international body (in civil aviation the International Civil Aviation Organization performs this role).

Secondly, nuclear operators and other custodians of nuclear material depend on the state to assess the nature and significance of the security threats, to have in place the measures to help reduce the occurrence of terrorism and other threats within the state, and to have the necessary laws and law enforcement arrangements to manage and respond to threats. These are largely beyond the capability of the nuclear industry, just as they are for any sector, so the state must be accountable for ensuring that the security regime (including that for nuclear operations) is effective and to establish laws and regulations within which the industry must operate. Inevitably, this has had the effect of placing the focus for security at the level of the state, whereas nuclear safety is more frequently seen as the responsibility of the licensee.

- *Information Security and Secrecy*. Nuclear security information, quite rightly, is subject to national information classification rules, which means that it is restricted to accountable personnel with a "need to know." This has resulted in highly compartmentalized information and a culture of secrecy, making it very difficult to share information and develop networks of practitioners, at either the national or international level, to benchmark approaches and performance. Interestingly, when the World Association of Nuclear Operators (WANO) was being established after the Chernobyl accident in the mid-1980s, it too faced problems of confidentiality around operating information and performance, but eventually overcame them.

  The secrecy associated with nuclear security information in the civil sector is also a legacy of the Cold War and the extensive efforts taken by those governments to protect all nuclear-related information in the national interest of the state. It is highly questionable whether excessive secrecy provides any benefit to the development of effective security regimes in the civil nuclear sector, where security should be managed as part of an enterprise-wide, all-hazards approach to risk management.

- *Prescriptive Regulatory Approaches*. The combination of the "State being accountable" and nuclear security-related information being classified and restricted had the effect in many states of making the regulatory approach highly prescriptive, with the nuclear operator having to comply with detailed instructions and requirements laid down by the regulator or state authorities, usually referred to as the "Competent Authority." This term is itself unfortunate because its use implies that other entities are not competent or have no need to be competent, which is clearly not the case.

These obstacles to industry involvement in nuclear security arrangements still persist in some countries, but there has been a noticeable shift in attitudes and behaviors in recent years as nuclear security has come under closer scrutiny. In part this is because more nuclear regulators at a national level have been combined into a single regulatory entity and the differences in regulating safety and security have become all too apparent to them. Safety regulators have understood for many years that the "controlling mind" for safety must rest with the licensee and that the licensee must have flexibility to achieve regulatory objectives without constant interference and direction from regulatory staff. This is now being more widely understood for nuclear security and regulators are encouraging operators to take more ownership of their security programs and to improve their security culture.

There has also been a realization that nuclear security "best practices" can be shared by industry and other practitioners if appropriate care is taken to protect facility-specific information; peer review by industry organizations of the type carried out by WANO and the Institute for Nuclear Power Operations (INPO) for safety and operations is still some years away but the IAEA has expanded its nuclear security review services to those states that request it, and this has had benefits.

Another factor which has influenced thinking is that the costs of nuclear security to the industry have increased markedly in the last ten years and executive management are placing a higher priority on making sure that the investments are worthwhile and being managed effectively. This will increasingly have the effect of bringing security out of the "silo" and help integrate it into mainstream corporate thinking and risk assessment processes. It is also likely to drive professional development and certification requirements for those personnel with nuclear security accountabilities – this has been largely overlooked in the past because of the same combination of historic factors; prescriptive regulation, the discouragement of industry to share information, compartmentalized information and a focus on physical protection ("guns, guards and gates") as the primary security objective.

In conclusion, changes to the regulatory approach to emphasize industry's role, the sharing of best practices, and improved professional development and certification are some of the key factors that will have a major impact on the effectiveness of nuclear security implementation and industry's contribution to that objective. Each of these factors is now examined in more detail.

The evolution of better regulation

Regulated industries around the world – from aviation, maritime, and cyber security to financial markets and insurance – are beginning to recognize that more effective approaches to regulation are required.

A common feature of the new approaches to regulation is the involvement of industry during the development of regulations, to ensure that it both understands the objectives of the regulation and how best it can contribute to its development and implementation.

States might choose to discharge their responsibilities by designing and strictly enforcing "step-by-step" prescriptive regulations, essentially instructing licensees how they must implement every aspect of the security arrangements. However, the risks surrounding nuclear security are so complex and dynamic that it is impossible to generate enough rules to encompass every decision a licensee must make. This is why establishing an effective nuclear security program should involve teamwork and commitment – from both the licensees and the regulator.

An alternative to prescriptive regulations is one that is based on performance outcomes and risk assessment. The outcome-focused, risk-based approach uses a framework of measures, or indicators, that assess how well an operator meets the outcomes defined by the regulator. To provide such assurances, licensees are required to develop, analyze and report on key performance indicators (KPIs), which are a set of quantifiable measures used to gauge how well an organization is meeting its strategic and operational goals, including regulatory requirements.

Licensees send the reports that result from such analyses to their own management and the regulator. These reports greatly increase the quality of security performance data available to the regulator, which improves the capacity to detect threats and respond to risk. At the same time, the regulator continues to gather data independently using such measures as external tests, inspections, and audits.

In common with safety incident reporting, the reporting of certain serious lapses or events is also mandatory. This allows the regulator to detect whether a wider pattern of problems exists in the delivery of security, and to develop measures for addressing them. It also allows licensees who have discovered a lapse to propose appropriate rectification measures to the regulator. In contrast to the prescriptive rules-based approach in which the regulator typically sanctions licensees (even for honest mistakes), the outcome-focused approach encourages the regulator to work with licensees to solve problems, while maintaining the necessary independence. This leads to much better communication, more cordial relationships, and improved security. The ultimate goal of better regulation is to replace the tick-box culture with targeted inspections of high-risk facilities, and to promote a culture of continuous improvement leading to excellence in security management and the improvement of professional standards.

An outcome-focused approach to nuclear security regulation depends to a great extent on the knowledge and ability of both the regulator and the licensee (including the licensee's board, executive management, and staff). For this reason, it is essential to ensure that regulators and licensees have received the professional training they need to successfully carry out their full range of responsibilities and that both parties are "demonstrably competent."

In conclusion, the threat from terrorism will continue to evolve, and proactive thinking and engagement are necessary to stay ahead of the threat. A responsive security regulatory framework which learns lessons, involves licensees at the development stage, and requires professional training and the demonstrable competence of those personnel with security management and regulatory functions is believed to be the most effective approach for the future, and supports the IAEA's guidance on sustaining a nuclear security regime.

The sharing of best practices

The nuclear industry is a heterogeneous sector with a plethora of technologies, facility designs and ownership – from fully state-owned to fully private. Almost every discussion about nuclear security is preceded by caveats about the need for "facility specific" considerations to be taken into account, but experience from nuclear safety and operations has demonstrated that sharing best practices between organizations is a powerful way to generate and motivate change. This has been amply illustrated by INPO and WANO over the last thirty years, but their remit from the start has excluded nuclear security management for the reasons previously described.

Following the terrorist attacks in 2001, and the growing attention being given to nuclear security, there was increasing frustration amongst industry practitioners about the lack of a forum where security experiences could be discussed and shared by professionals without compromising "facility-specific" details. A visionary group within the Nuclear Threat Initiative (NTI) began to explore the possibility and appetite for establishing such an international forum and, with involvement from the IAEA, spent three years discussing options, opportunities, and barriers. By 2008, a strategy had been established and, coincident with the IAEA General Conference in the September of that year, the World Institute for Nuclear Security (WINS) was launched in Vienna, funded by foundation grants from NTI, the US Department of Energy, and the governments of Norway and Canada. At the opening ceremony, Mohamed ElBaradei, the then Director General of the IAEA, remarked: "I am confident that establishing a forum to help share and promote best practices will improve nuclear security, and contribute to and complement the efforts of the IAEA."[1] Predictably, there was considerable resistance in some states to the notion that security information could or should be shared, and that it was not possible to define best practices. WINS focused its early work on addressing both of these concerns, and recognized that while there was no universal definition of a best practice, there were common characteristics which make a practice the best. In relation to nuclear security, these included:

- Impact/Effectiveness: The practice has demonstrated impact, applicability, and benefits to nuclear security programs;
- Efficiency: The practice has demonstrated cost and resource efficiency, where the expense is appropriate to the benefits;
- Sustainability: The practice has demonstrated sustainable benefits and/or is sustainable within nuclear and related organizations; and
- Collaboration/Integration: The practice builds effective partnerships among various organizations and integrates nuclear security with other functions such as nuclear safety, emergency planning and design.

WINS organized its first workshops and much of its early research examining how to share best practices and how to document the results of the discussions. It drew heavily on experience from the stakeholder dialogue program that was conducted by British Nuclear Fuels in the period from 1999–2005, which involved facilitated working groups with a wide range of stakeholders, including those opposed to nuclear energy. One of the working groups had specifically addressed the issue of nuclear security and developed a methodology for discussing security issues in an unclassified way and identifying how security might be improved. Keys to the approach were:

- To use professional facilitators to guide the discussions;
- To agree to ground rules to avoid the disclosure of sensitive information;
- To stay focused on nuclear security management and not to stray into safeguards; nonproliferation, or the particular benefits of one technology or fuel cycle approach over another; and
- To avoid politics to the extent possible.

It soon became apparent that many of the issues being discussed at the WINS workshops had strong parallels with nuclear safety and operations, including the following:

- Effective and efficient security depended on commitment from the organizational leadership who had to understand and own the security program;
- Nuclear security was more effective if considered an enterprise-wide issue and integrated into the organizations' risk management portfolio, overseen by a broad group of functional and operational directors, rather than being the purview of the security department;
- Having a responsible attitude of "needing to share" important security information was more effective than the historical alternative of restricting information on the basis of "needing to know;"
- There were strong linkages between nuclear security, safety, emergency planning, and response, and these linkages needed to be recognized and strengthened; and
- Performance metrics were challenging because of the almost absent occurrence of security incidents, but leading and lagging indicators could be identified and used to good effect.

Over the following four years, WINS managed over fifty international workshops and round-table discussions and published thirty international best-practice guides on a wide variety of nuclear security management issues.[2] Further guides are planned and all are subject to regular revision to keep them current.

The process of creating each guide follows a core improvement cycle. First, a subject matter expert is commissioned to research and write a draft guide on a specific topic of importance to the industry (all of the guides are written from an operator's perspective). Frequently, workshops are held which bring nuclear security professionals together from around the world for additional suggestions, insights, and feedback. Once the final draft is complete, the guide is sent for peer review and then to a professional technical editor. Guides are then translated in up to ten additional languages depending on the perceived need and availability of funds.

Each of the guides includes an introduction ("Why You Should Read This Guide"); a body of text that presents both policy issues and practical, hands-on suggestions; and at least two appendices. Appendix A consists of self-assessment questions targeted at specific stakeholders, such as the board, the chief executive officer, and the security director. Appendix B consists of a maturity scale (five levels) that ranges from ineffective to world-class. Together, the appendices enable stakeholders to benchmark how well they and their organizations are doing in a particular area of security management and oversight, and to understand what needs to be done to move to the optimal level.

The five levels of nuclear security management maturity have proved effective and useful to WINS members because they set out, in simple to understand language, what a security program "feels like" at the different levels. For example, is security perceived as a regulatory overhead – expensive and intrusive, or as a strategic investment – owned by the Board of Directors? The language used for each of the five levels reflects the type of comments that might be made with operator management during conversations about the security program, and that is why it is easy to assess an operator's overall performance against best practices.

The success of the WINS guides can be measured by the feedback from its members that now total over 1,900 in almost 100 countries: in the most recent membership satisfaction survey:

- Over 90 percent of WINS members had modified their approach to nuclear security because of their interaction with WINS;
- Over 99 percent thought WINS a valuable forum; and
- Over 94 percent would recommend the workshops.

In total, WINS members have downloaded over 28,000 copies of the guides.

Professional development and certification

As WINS developed and gained experience from its members one common issue began to stand out as being particularly important. It seemed the norm for most accountants, engineers, and safety professionals employed in the industry to belong to chartered professional institutes that certified their competence on an on-going basis. Nuclear operators and safety professionals were generally required to undertake extensive competency training in order to become qualified nuclear plant operators. But the same did not seem to be at all common for security professionals and others with senior managerial or regulatory responsibilities relating to security (certified training for armed guards is common practice though).

WINS began to question whether it was reasonable for senior managers, responsible for multi-million dollar security programs, to have to rely on the training acquired in their police or military-related careers, as seemed so often to be the case. There is no doubt that former police and military professionals are highly trained and skilled in their respective area, but it would be difficult to argue that an expert in securing a nuclear facility would be able to step into the position of a police or brigade commander without extensive training; the reverse also seemed to be true. Decisions made by security managers could clearly have an impact on the public and its safety. There could be liability issues for the organizations in which they work – and it therefore seemed unreasonable to continue the practice of on-the-job training, slowly accumulating knowledge and experience over a period of years.

WINS believed that the time had come to enhance the professional standing of personnel with security management responsibilities, because it is both a challenging and highly responsible management discipline. The view that managing a complex nuclear security program is simply about managing guns, guards, and gates underestimates the managerial challenges and is overly simplistic. Nuclear security management is every bit as sophisticated, challenging and important as any other professional role, and it needs proper consideration and attention. As today's regional and global conflicts suggests, nuclear materials and associated facilities could be prime targets. The spectrum of known threats targeting nuclear facilities and licensees includes, but is not limited to, terrorism, extremism, cyber, insider, organized crime, and espionage. We need to recognize that the political and public anxiety over a successful attack, from any of these threats, on a nuclear facility or against materials that are in transit, demands that the people charged with managing the security programs be demonstrably competent and certified to discharge their very wide duties.

It had also been recognized that security management must be a corporate activity and implemented across the organization as a fundamental aspect of risk management and corporate reputation and responsibility. Guns, guards, and gates do very little to prevent cyber threats and the potential actions of insiders, both of which are of growing concern. The scientific community of engineers, scientists, and technicians employed in the nuclear industry has a key role to play in contributing to the security program, as well as needing to understand their security responsibilities. Leadership, teamwork, cross-functional awareness, proper communications, and trust are the underpinning qualities of organizations that have the best security culture. And having leaders and managers that really understand and are competent to manage security programs are fundamental requirements.

Research conducted by WINS indicated, based on conservative estimates, that there are likely to be about 200,000 personnel worldwide with accountabilities for the security of nuclear and other radioactive material, if the nuclear, medical, and industrial sectors, their regulators and associated response forces are included.[3] The research made assumptions about organizational structures and was only intended to be approximate to establish the scale of the issue. If one then assumes that the average annual staff turnover is 10 percent (also conservative), then the on-going demand for professional training at different levels in organizations is of the order of 20,000 people per annum.

Certified competence for nuclear security should not be limited to just those professionals working within the security department; security has to be seen as a strategic organizational issue, led by the board and its executive managers, and overseen by competent regulators. In addition to board members and executives with organizational oversight accountabilities, a proportion of senior management including operational and functional directors, the technical and engineering community, security management, regulators, and off-site responders need to be demonstrably competent.

Nuclear security education – current status

Important steps are being taken by the IAEA to develop and encourage academic institutes, principally universities, to offer Masters Degrees (two-years study) and Certificates (one-year study) in nuclear security, and to use a consistent syllabus, based on IAEA guidance documents. There are also nuclear security courses available to nuclear engineering students at some universities that contribute to broader undergraduate or post-graduate qualifications. The efforts by the academic community to develop a cadre of graduates with nuclear security knowledge is important and will play a key role in developing academically knowledgeable personnel over the years ahead. The worldwide total number of students enrolling on these courses is not publically available but is probably in the range of 50–100 per annum. The IAEA currently has no plans to accredit or certify either the academic organizations or the courses and we believe that this needs to change.

The IAEA is also active in developing an international network of so-called nuclear security support centers (NSSCs), otherwise known as centers of excellence, many of which have been opened in the last few years, coincident with the Nuclear Security Summit process. These centers have great potential for becoming national institutes to promote accredited training for their own personnel and for their governments to decide that certified training for nuclear security management will be introduced, perhaps, to begin with, on a voluntary basis.

Additionally, there are a significant number of nuclear security "awareness" courses being held around the world, funded by some IAEA member states and run by both the IAEA and contractors. These awareness courses, costing millions of dollars annually, are generally available to whoever is nominated to attend, irrespective of their nuclear security responsibilities, do not lead to any test of understanding or on-going competence, and are not certified. As a means of developing an international framework of competent nuclear security professionals, they are largely ineffective and are mostly not sustainable.

Professional development for security managers is not a new concept, nor is the certification of their competence. The International Civil Aviation Organization (ICAO) headquartered in Montreal, Canada, and the John Molson School of Business of Concordia University in Montreal, its academic partner, have worked together to establish and certify an Aviation Security Management program (AVSEC PMC) that has run successfully for more than twenty years, based on the ICAO's security standards.[4]

Ideally, there would be considerable merit in the IAEA partnering with national authorities, as well as their regulators and licensees, to develop a worldwide competency framework for nuclear security and an associated certification scheme, but this is likely to be either unachievable or would take years, just as it has in other, more traditional, professions. It may be more realistic for proactive states to demonstrate an expression of intent to introduce certified training and to encourage their regulators and licensees, with the support of specialist institutes, to develop and implement certification schemes based on IAEA and other relevant guidance, including best practices for nuclear security management of the kind developed by WINS and which have been designed with this purpose in mind.

The involvement of professional institutes in this process is essential, since regulators should not be accrediting themselves, and it would be unwise for regulators to be the accreditation agency of licensees, for obvious reasons. However, regulators are in a key position to drive forward the requirement for certification and to require managers and practitioners with accountability for nuclear security to be demonstrably competent. It is entirely possible for schemes to be introduced and for all relevant personnel to be subject to certification within a period of five years, and this should be the goal.

The WINS Academy

As a contribution to the field of professional development for nuclear security management, WINS has developed the "WINS Academy" which is being made available online during 2014, with the support of Pearson, the world's leading learning company. The academy is intended to promote best practices and professional development opportunities covering the following fields:

1   The nuclear security regulator who, on behalf of the state authorities, has prime responsibility for establishing effective regulations, for keeping them under revision and for ensuring that they are implemented by those that have custody of the nuclear materials (the operators);

2   The board of directors (in the private sector) and the government administrators (for government-run organizations) who are accountable for overseeing the risk management arrangements for the organization on behalf of the shareholders (private or government departments);

3   The executive management team that is responsible for operating the organization and for implementing the required security program to ensure that it is effective and efficient throughout the organization and in relevant parts of the supply chain and other external suppliers that could impact on the program;

4   The scientific, technical, and engineering community within the organization that has responsibilities to both comply with the security program and has a key role to contribute to the program;

5   The security management team that are subject matter experts and who provide a service to the organization to help ensure that the security program is informed by professional knowledge, and who may manage or oversee the security guard force and other security specialists;

6   The off-site armed response organizations, typically the local police, who would be the first external agency to respond to a serious security incident and who would need to be able to respond in a fast and effective manner to contain any situation that could not be managed by the operator,

7   Those managers accountable for the security of radioactive materials in nonnuclear sectors, such as those that use radioactive sources for medical or industrial purposes and where the theft or sabotage of the radioactive materials could have a significant safety, environmental, or reputational impact on the organization or the public; and

8   Communicating with civil society, which needs to provide democratic support for the use of nuclear and radioactive sources for industrial, medical and other uses within the state, and must have sufficient confidence that the regulatory and operational controls provide a sufficiently safe and secure environment to provide its support on an on-going basis.

The subject of professional development and the need for demonstrable competence for security management were explicitly recognized in the Nuclear Security Summits and associated events, including the Nuclear Industry Summit held in the Netherlands in March 2014. Thirty-five of the participating states at the Nuclear Security Summit subscribed to a Joint Statement that committed them to ensuring "that management and personnel with accountability for nuclear security are demonstrably competent."[5] This commitment was reflected in the Joint Statement from the Nuclear Industry Summit, in which the major nuclear organizations in the world also committed themselves to further enhancing nuclear security and "Ensuring that all personnel with accountabilities for security are demonstrably competent by establishing appropriate standards for selection, training, and certification of staff."[6]

Conclusions and future developments

In many countries, the management of nuclear security is maturing into a modern profession and is becoming more effective as a result. There is a realization that the responsible sharing of experience and best practice brings benefits, as does a closer working relationship between security and safety professionals who share many common challenges. The better regulators are working with industry to help establish performance-based security programs, and the better companies are managing security as a strategic issue rather than a regulatory burden. More attention is being paid to evolving threats such as cyber attacks and how these can be managed within the conventional security framework of physical protection.

A significant number of states and operators announced at the recent Nuclear Security Summits their intention to give professional development and competency requirements more attention than hitherto, with commitments to ensure that staff with accountability for nuclear security are "demonstrably competent." These commitments, if honored, will be a major step forward in improving the effectiveness of nuclear security implementation and regulation, and balance the extensive efforts to upgrade physical protection systems and associated technology. Progress will be able to be assessed at the next and probably final Nuclear Security Summit events in Washington, DC in 2016.

The time has also come for coordinated and sustained action to strengthen the global governance of nuclear security. Examples of successful global governance can be found in many other industries and provide us with model templates. Ways have to be found to improve communication and assurances over the effectiveness of security implementation. The introduction of peer review mechanisms across industry is seen by some as the logical way forward, to build on the success of INPO and WANO, but there remains reluctance by some states to allow this to happen for reasons of confidentiality. Ultimately we have to ask ourselves whether sharing information amongst professional practitioners, with the benefits that it brings, is a bigger risk than maintaining excessive secrecy and the potential it has for cloaking complacency, since complacency is probably the biggest challenge we face.

Notes

1. Mohamed ElBaradei, quoted in Nuclear Threat Initiative, "World Institute for Nuclear Security (WINS) is Launched in Vienna; New Organization Will Strengthen Security for Nuclear Materials," Press Release, Nuclear Threat Initiative, September 28, 2008, p. 2, www.nti.org/media/pdfs/release_WINS_092908.pdf?_=1316466791.
2. For more information, see the World Institute for Nuclear Security website, www.wins.org.
3. World Institute for Nuclear Security, "Global Needs Analysis for Nuclear Security Training," 2013, pp. 1–8, www.wins.org/files/wins_white_paper_global_needs_analysis_web.pdf.
4. International Civil Aviation Organization, "AVSEC Professional Management Course," N.D., www.icao.int/security/isd/avsecpmc/Pages/default.aspx.
5. Joint Statement, "Strengthening Nuclear Security Implementation," Nuclear Security Summit, The Hague, the Netherlands, March 24–25, 2014, p. 3, www.nss2014.com/sites/default/files/downloads/strengthening_nuclear_security_implementation.pdf.
6. "Joint Statement of the 2014 Nuclear Industry Summit," 3rd Nuclear Industry Summit, Amsterdam, the Netherlands, March 23–25, 2014, p. 3, www.nss2014.com/sites/default/files/documents/nis2014-jointstatement_final.pdf.

33

ILLICIT TRAFFICKING IN NUCLEAR MATERIALS

Assessing the past two decades

Lyudmila Zaitseva

The issue of illicit trafficking in nuclear material started to attract the attention of the world community in the early 1990s, coinciding with the collapse of the Soviet Union in December 1991. The political crisis and severe economic downturn in Russia and the other countries of the former Soviet Union (FSU), accompanied by run-away inflation, collapse of the standards of living, rise of unemployment and criminality, and underfunding of the nuclear sector, were the background to the sudden rise in nuclear crime. The inadequate security practices at the former Soviet nuclear facilities, which were designed to protect against intruders from the outside, rather than from the insider threat, as well as the problem of open and poorly protected borders with the FSU countries, aggravated the situation even further. Criminals could divert and move their illicit goods across national borders without much risk of being detected.

The first nuclear trafficking cases recorded in Russia, Germany, Czech Republic, and some other countries in Central Europe in the years following the collapse of the Soviet Union raised a lot of concerns about the security of the old Soviet stockpiles of nuclear weapons and fissile materials. Indeed, many nuclear facilities with significant amounts of fissile material – both in the military and civilian sector – had glaring security deficiencies making them vulnerable to theft and sabotage. Fearing the possibility of nuclear theft and transfer of the former Soviet weapon-usable material to state or nonstate actors, the United States and some other donor countries initiated steps to address these threats. In the 1990s, the first cooperative efforts to improve nuclear security began between the former Soviet nuclear scientists and their Western counterparts. Protection against both internal and external threats had to be provided at dozens of nuclear-weapon sites, research laboratories, uranium enrichment facilities, processing and storage sites, and naval fuel facilities, housing hundreds of metric tons of weapons-usable nuclear materials.

This chapter will explore nuclear material trafficking patterns observed since the collapse of the Soviet Union. It will discuss the global trends in illicit trafficking of all types of radioactive material, and concentrate on the incidents involving fissile nuclear material to assess their dynamics over the two decades. It will then describe the impact of the international cooperative efforts to prevent and deter thefts and combat illicit trafficking, and conclude by addressing the future challenges for illicit trafficking for other states, and potential additional steps that could be taken to address them.

Global trends in illicit trafficking

Criminal and other unauthorized activities involving nonfissile radioactive material, such as theft, loss, illegal disposal, and inadvertent shipment of ionizing radiation sources (e.g., caesium-137, strontium-90, iridium-192, cobalt-60, etc.) had been recorded in many countries well before the 1990s. These incidents were tackled from the point of public safety, rather than security. Only when the first thefts and smuggling incidents involving fissile nuclear material – especially the types suitable for making a nuclear explosive device, highly-enriched uranium (HEU) and plutonium-239 – were detected between 1992 and 1994, was the problem of nuclear trafficking recognized as a major security threat on a global scale. In 1995, the International Atomic Energy Agency (IAEA) responded to this threat by establishing its Incident and Trafficking Database (ITDB), which collects state-confirmed incidents of nuclear and other radioactive material out of regulatory control. As of 2013, the ITDB has recorded 2,331 such incidents in the period from 1993 to 2012, including 419 incidents of unauthorized possession and related criminal activities, 615 incidents of theft and loss, and 1,244 incidents of other unauthorized activities and events. (See Figure 33.1.) The remaining sixty-nine cases were not included into any of these categories due to the insufficient information to determine the category.

Figure 33.1 above shows a clear increase in the overall number of cases since the 1990s, from an average of about 50 per year to about 150 since 2000.[1] There are two main reasons behind this increase. First, the reporting practices by participating states have improved over the years with more and more states confirming more and more incidents. Better threat awareness in the wake of September 11, 2001 terror attacks in the United Sates, especially with regard to radioactive sources that could be used for making radiological dispersal devices (RDDs), and strengthened cooperation with the IAEA were the main causes for the improved reporting.

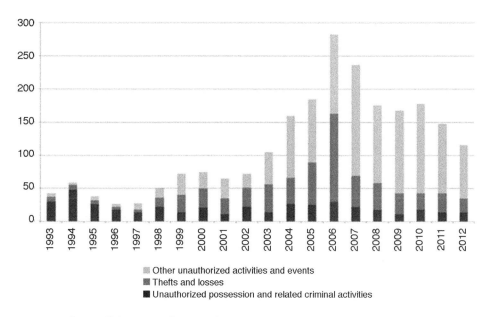

Figure 33.1 Illicit trafficking and other unauthorized activities involving nuclear and other radioactive materials confirmed by states to the IAEA Incident and Trafficking Database (ITDB) between 1993 and 2012

This expanded the geographical reach of the database from mainly the former Soviet republics and Central Europe to virtually the whole globe. Second, many countries have installed radiation detection equipment at their borders, ports, and other points of entry, as well as at scrap yards and smelting facilities inside their territories, to monitor the movement of radioactive material and detect abandoned radioactive sources. Besides, some countries carried out massive campaigns to locate and recover uncontrolled, or "orphaned," radioactive sources. The consequence of all these efforts was a growing number of detected and reported incidents. However, it is important to be aware of the nature of these incidents. As can be seen in Figure 33.1 above, losses and other unauthorized activities, such as unauthorized disposal, unauthorized movement or discovery of orphaned radioactive sources, account for most of the increase in the number of cases since the 1990s. These are the so called loss-of-control incidents, which primarily involve various types of material recovery, rather than cases with a clear criminal component, such as theft, sale attempts, and intentional smuggling. After reaching a peak of about fifty cases reported to the IAEA in 1994, incidents of a criminal nature have since stabilized, averaging between 20 and 25 per year.

It should be noted, however, that many more nuclear trafficking incidents were reported in open sources in the 1990s, than officially confirmed by states to the IAEA. For example, the Database on Nuclear Smuggling, Theft, and Orphan Radiation Sources (DSTO), run at the University of Salzburg, Austria, recorded 300 additional cases reported in open sources from January 1993 to December 1999, almost 100 percent more than was confirmed to the IAEA over the same period.[2] Besides, DSTO records seventy-seven incidents for the years 1991 and 1992, which remained outside the scope of the IAEA ITDB. Using the DSTO data, which combines open-source incidents with the state-confirmed reports collected by the IAEA, one can observe that the peak in nuclear trafficking activities in the 1990s was reached already in 1993 with about 100 cases. Remaining at about the same level in 1994, the incidents decreased by about a half in 1996 and 1997, only to sharply rise again and reach a new peak in 1999 with 142 cases. This rise, however, was already due mainly to the incidents of a different nature than those in the early 1990s, i.e., orphaned radiation sources rather than profit-motivated theft and smuggling of radioactive material. From then on, incidents without apparent criminal intent increased even further and now account for most of the incidents recorded annually since 2004. (See Figure 33.2.)

Nuclear material trafficking

DSTO has recorded 620 incidents involving nuclear material for the period 1991 to 2012. The number of incidents grew very quickly in the early 1990s, from 14 in 1991 and 36 in 1992 to 47 in 1993 and 63 in 1994. (See Figure 33.3.) Following a sudden drop in the mid-1990s, the occurrence stabilized at an average of about 25 cases per year. The peak values of 1993 and 1994 have not been reached since.

The proliferation significance – or the sensitivity – of the trafficked material has clearly deteriorated since the 1990s. If HEU, plutonium and LEU incidents recorded in the 1990s accounted for about 40 percent of all cases involving nuclear material, they have averaged only 14 percent of such incidents since 2000. Most of the nuclear material cases registered between 2000 and 2012 have involved the least sensitive material, i.e., natural uranium, depleted uranium, and thorium. Since 1991, about 73 percent of nuclear material incidents involved these low-grade materials, 20 percent involved LEU and the remaining 7 percent involved HEU and plutonium outside of radioactive sources. Of these incidents, 73 were thefts, 80 were loss-of-control incidents (i.e., losses and recoveries of material out of regulatory control), 55

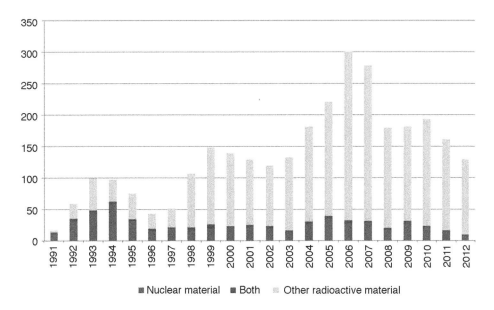

Figure 33.2 DSTO incidents, 1991–2012

were interdictions at borders, and the remaining 412 cases were seizures by law-enforcement authorities domestically. Almost a half (287) of all incidents involving nuclear material recorded in the DSTO accounts for profit-motivated cases, i.e., attempted sales (see Figure 33.4). The geographical spread of these incidents has expanded from mostly Russia, Central Europe, and Turkey in the early and mid-1990s to Kazakhstan, Georgia, and India in the late 1990s and to the African continent, Brazil, and China in more recent years. Since 1994, profit-motivated incidents have continuously declined; only three to ten such cases per year have been recorded since 2007.

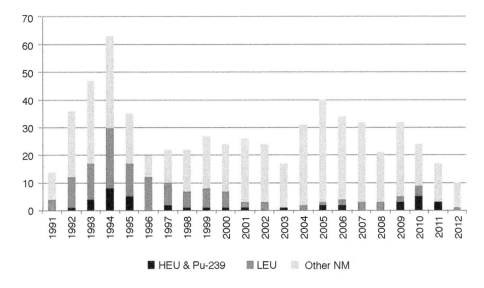

Figure 33.3 DSTO incidents involving various types of nuclear material, 1991–2012

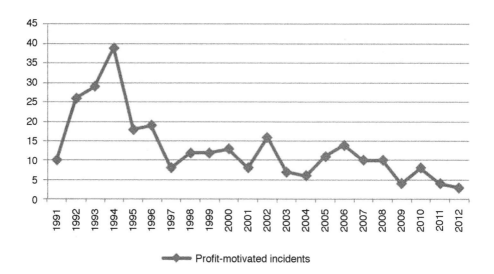

Figure 33.4 Profit-motivated incidents involving nuclear material worldwide as recorded in DSTO,
1991–2012

The parallel decline in the number of both, incidents involving HEU and LEU and profit-motivated cases, is a positive development, signifying success of the international efforts to secure nuclear material. This decline is largely due to the significant reduction of nuclear thefts from former Soviet facilities. For instance, trafficking incidents involving nuclear material in Russia have significantly declined since 1994. (See Figure 33.5.)

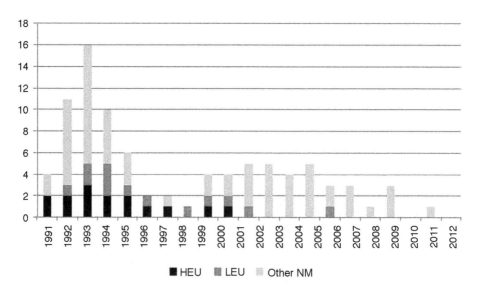

Figure 33.5 DSTO incidents involving nuclear material worldwide as recorded in Russia, 1992–2012

Uranium thefts from Russian nuclear facilities dropped from 29 in the 1990s to only four recorded since then.[3] The majority of the nuclear thefts in Russia were recorded in the early to mid-1990s. DSTO lists 21 such incidents in the period 1992 to 1995, although the actual number is likely higher. For example, according to a statement by a Ministry of Atomic Energy (Minatom) official in 1998, around 30 diversions of nuclear material were recorded at Minatom facilities in these four years. A year later, the Head of Minatom's Nuclear Material Control and Accounting Division, V. Yerastov, reported even more such diversions (52) over the same period.[4] No successful HEU thefts from Russian nuclear facilities have been confirmed since 1995. DSTO records a total of 90 nuclear material incidents recorded in Russia between 1992 and 2012, including 15 cases of HEU, 13 cases of LEU, and 62 cases of less sensitive types of nuclear material.

Weapons-usable nuclear materials

In its ITDB Database, the IAEA documents 15 confirmed incidents involving unauthorized possession of HEU and plutonium in the period 1993–2012.[5] DSTO records four additional highly credible cases involving kilogram amounts of the Russian HEU, which were discussed at length in open sources, but have not been officially confirmed by the Russian authorities to the IAEA. These 19 incidents involved a total of almost 20 kilogram (19,571 g), 98 percent of which was HEU (19,201 g) and the remaining 2 percent was plutonium-239 (370 g). (See Table 33.1.)

Most of this material – over 16 kilograms – was seized inside Russia. It was diverted by insiders from various Russian nuclear facilities, ranging from research labs (Luch Scientific Production Association) and fuel fabrication facilities (Elektrostal Machine-Building Plant) to submarine construction sites (Sevmorput Shipyard) and naval fuel storage depots (Andreeva Guba). Contrary to both HEU thefts from naval sites, all confirmed HEU thefts from the Russian civilian nuclear facilities went undetected. Like in many other diversions of uranium, the security and control systems at source facilities failed to register the disappearance of significant amounts of HEU and the management was unaware of the missing materials until they were intercepted by law enforcement services and traced back to the source. The HEU and plutonium confiscated from criminal rings in Germany and Czech Republic in 1994 and 1995 are believed to be of Russian origin.[6] HEU seized in the more recent incidents in Bulgaria, France, Georgia, and Moldova is also suspected to have originated in Russia, although this has not been confirmed by the Russian authorities.

The majority of HEU and plutonium incidents were recorded before the end of 1995. All known thefts of Russian HEU were committed in this period as well. The latest case was reported by the Russian Federal Security Service in 1998, when a group of conspiring employees at an undisclosed nuclear facility in Chelyabinsk region attempted a diversion of 18.5 kg of weapon-usable material, presumably HEU. The security officers thwarted the attempt and seized the material before it could leave the facility.[7] The lack of more recent diversions is a clear indication of the success of the national and international efforts to improve nuclear security in Russia and other FSU countries. The HEU seized in a few cases since the 1990s appears to be old material, which could have been stolen years ago, before the implementation of security upgrades. For example, an anonymous Minatom official interviewed about the seizure of 3.7 kg of 21 percent HEU in Elektrostal in 2000 pointed out that the material might have been stolen in the mid-1990s and the perpetrator had been searching for a potential buyer since then.[8] The forensic analysis of the HEU seized on the Bulgarian-Romanian border in 1999, which was carried out by the Lawrence Livermore National Laboratory in the United States,

Table 33.1 Highly-credible incidents involving unauthorized possession of HEU and Pu-239, 1992–2013

Date	Location	Source facility	Material	Amount (g)	IAEA confirmed
6 Oct 1992	Podolsk, Russia	Luch Scientific-Production Association	HEU (90%)	1500	No
29 Jul 1993	Andreeva Guba, Russia	Andreeva Guba Naval Fuel Depot	HEU (36%)	1800	No
28 Nov 1993	Polyarny, Russia	Sevmorput Shipyard	HEU (20%)	4500	No
March 1994	St. Petersburg, Russia	Elektrostal Machine-Building Plant	HEU (90%)	2972	Yes
10 May 1994	Tengen-Wiechs, Germany	Unconfirmed	Pu	6.2	Yes
13 Jun 1994	Landshut, Germany	Unconfirmed	HEU (87.7%)	0.795	Yes
25 Jul 1994	Munich, Germany	Unconfirmed	Pu	0.24	Yes
8 Aug 1994	Munich Airport, Germany	Unconfirmed	Pu	363.4	Yes
14 Dec 1994	Prague, Czech Republic	Unconfirmed	HEU (87.7%)	2730	Yes
Jun 1995	Moscow, Russia	Elektrostal Machine-Building Plant	HEU (21%)	1700	Yes
6 Jun 1995	Prague, Czech Republic	Unconfirmed	HEU (87.7%)	0.415	Yes
8 Jun 1995	Ceske Budejovice, Czech Republic	Unconfirmed	HEU (87.7%)	16.9	Yes
29 May 1999	Rousse, Bulgaria	Unconfirmed	HEU (72.65%)	10	Yes
2000	Elektrostal, Russia	Unconfirmed	HEU (21%)	3700	No
16 Jul 2001	Paris, France	Unconfirmed	HEU (72.57%)	0.5	Yes
26 Jun 2003	Sadahlo, Georgia	Unconfirmed	HEU (89%)	~170	Yes
1 Feb 2006	Tbilisi, Georgia	Unconfirmed	HEU (89%)	79.5	Yes
11 Mar 2010	Tbilisi, Georgia	Unconfirmed	HEU (89%)	18	Yes
27 Jun 2011	Chisinau, Moldova	Unconfirmed	HEU	4	Yes

Source: DSTO and IAEA ITDB Fact Sheet , 2007, www.iaea.org/newscenter/features/radsources/pdf/fact_figures 2007.pdf (accessed 28 January 2014).

established it was a reactor-irradiated material reprocessed in 1993.[9] The laboratory analysis of the almost identical sample of HEU intercepted in Paris in 2001 had estimated that the date of the latest chemical separation was November 1994, noting that the material was likely to have the same origin as the HEU interdicted in Bulgaria.[10] Investigators of the more recent HEU seizures in Georgia in 2003, 2006, and 2010 also believed the confiscated uranium – identical in its enrichment level in all three cases – had been stolen in the early to mid-1990s.[11] After conducting a detailed analysis, Russian experts estimated that the HEU seized in 2006 had been processed more than a decade previously, i.e., before 1996.[12] Based on the analysis of these recent cases, researchers suggested that the "HEU samples seized in Bulgaria and France can be traced to one, possibly two thefts," the latest of which occurred before 2000, and the HEU samples seized in Georgia could be attributed to one theft.[13]

As with any other type of smuggling, the interdiction of nuclear trafficking, both within the country of origin and at borders, is unlikely to be 100 percent successful. According to an assessment by the Russian Federal Security Service (FSB) made in mid-1990s, law enforcement and security officials in Russia could then intercept roughly 30 to 40 percent of diverted nuclear materials.[14] Therefore, despite the lack of new evidence of nuclear theft, it is quite plausible that more weapon-usable material was successfully diverted from nuclear facilities in Russia and other post-Soviet states, and possibly smuggled abroad in the early and mid-1990s, than has been recovered so far. All of the known diversions of weapon-usable material involved kilogram amounts, not grams. Thus, confiscation of several caches of gram amounts of HEU over the last 15 years point to the likely existence of additional, larger batches of stolen material, which have not yet been recovered. Each of the recent seizures was accompanied by allegations of more material available for sale. Considering that the three Georgian HEU cases appear to be interrelated, as suggested by the same enrichment level, material packaging pattern, and some of the same actors involved, such allegations may be credible. In addition to the similar enrichment level, the uranium seized in Rousse (1999) and Paris (2001) had almost identical packaging – cylindrical lead containers with glass ampoules inside, embedded in a yellow paraffin wax. Given that the description of the HEU container intercepted in Chisinau in 2011, also appears very similar, it is possible that the Moldovan HEU came from the same source and from the same sellers. Referring to anonymous US and UN officials, an AP report alleged that the seized sample had been traced to "specific Russian enrichment facilities and was matched later with at least one earlier seizure of uranium."[15]

There is no information of any thefts of uranium enriched to the levels similar to what has been seized either in Georgia (around 89.5 percent), or in Bulgaria and France (around 72 percent). In all three Georgian cases, Novosibirsk was mentioned as a likely origin of the HEU. Indeed, this Siberian city is home to the Novosibirsk Chemical Concentrate Plant, one of Russia's main facilities for producing both LEU and HEU. Although Russian authorities have not confirmed that the Georgian HEU originated in Novosibirsk, there has been an earlier report discussing a possible leak of enriched uranium from the Novosibirsk factory. According to a local newspaper, a significant amount of uranium of unspecified enrichment disappeared from the facility in the summer of 2002. The theft was apparently discovered during a routine inventory of the plant.[16] Earlier that year, Yuriy Vishnevskiy, the head of the Russian Nuclear Regulatory Agency Gosatomnadzor, made a statement about leakages of low-enriched and weapons-grade uranium from Russia's nuclear facilities over the past decade, in which the Novosibirsk plant was one of the two facilities he mentioned by name, the other one being the Elektrostal Machine-Building Plant. However, he did not say whether low or highly enriched uranium had been stolen or when the thefts had occurred.[17] Thus, the recent record in HEU trafficking is encouraging in so far that it has not shown any new evidence of nuclear theft from the former Soviet stockpiles.

Low-grade nuclear materials

Low-enriched uranium (LEU) is mostly used to fuel nuclear power plants. Although it is not suitable to make nuclear weapons in its existing form, in large amounts it could shorten the pathway to weapon-grade uranium for countries possessing enrichment capabilities. A total of 124 incidents involving thefts and seizures of LEU were recorded in DSTO between 1991 and 2012, 88 of them confirmed by states to the IAEA. Having reached a peak in 1994, they dropped towards the end of the 1990s to about a third of the peak value, and decreased even further from then on, with an average of about 2.5 cases per year since 2000. (See Figure 33.6.) Ten of these incidents were reported as thefts, all of them recorded between 1992 and 1995. In several cases, stolen LEU was recovered on a number of occasion and in different locations (and some even in different countries). Thus, one theft may have resulted in several seizures of different caches of the stolen LEU.

Most of the recorded LEU thefts occurred at nuclear fuel production and storage facilities, some of them involving over 100 kg of LEU. Thus, in December 1995, Kazakhstani special services detained two Kazakhstani citizens in the city of Ust-Kamenogorsk in possession of 4 kg of LEU they attempted to transport to buyers in Russia. In the course of the investigation, Kazakh officials discovered an additional 146 kg of LEU in the possession of the two men. The LEU was diverted from the Ulba Metallurgy Plant, which produced fuel pellets for nuclear power plants, by conspiring employees upon a request by a local metal trader. By the time the investigation was finished in March 1996, the network encompassed 18 individuals.[18] Since then, nine more seizures of LEU were recorded in Kazakhstan, the most recent one in 2010.

But the largest, and probably most spectacular, theft occurred in Lithuania in August 1992, when a 7-meter long nuclear fuel rod disappeared from the now decommissioned Ignalina nuclear power plant. The 280-kg assembly, containing over 100 kg of LEU (2 percent U-235), left the premises of Ignalina attached to the bottom of a duty bus. Although its disappearance was eventually noticed during the inventory checks in 1992, the management of the plant remained adamant about the theft speculations and maintained that they expected the assembly to be soon found or blamed the "loss" on an accounting error. They had to acknowledge the theft in December 1994, when Lithuanian police seized the first cache of the stolen LEU in a sting operation in the city of Kaunas. A former guard from Ignalina was reportedly arrested trying to sell the uranium, but managed to escape.[19] The subsequent investigation revealed that the theft had been implemented by the reactor operation personnel in collusion with the facility guards.[20] Lithuanian authorities confiscated parts of the missing LEU, weighing from 240 g

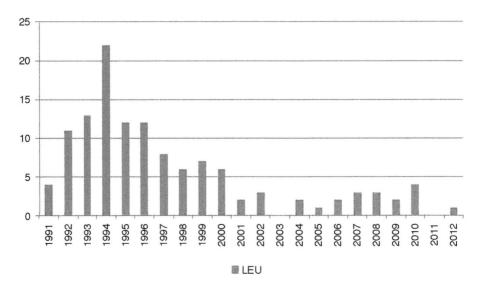

Figure 33.6 DSTO incidents involving LEU recorded worldwide, 1992–2012

to almost 60 kg, on eight more occasions between January 1995 and March 2002.[21] In 2002, the prosecutors believed that 15 kg were still to be recovered.[22]

Attempted sales or seizures of LEU from unauthorized possession have become very rare in recent years. Besides, similar to the situation with HEU seizures, LEU interdicted in some of the recent incidents appears to be "old" material, diverted in the 1990s. Thus, in April 2006, two residents of Elektrostal, Russia, were arrested in a sting operation, during which they intended to sell a sample of 22 kg of LEU they possessed. One of the suspects had bought the material in the mid-1990s and stored it for over ten years in the hope of selling it at a profit.[23] In September 2005, Ukrainian authorities recovered LEU they believed had been stolen from the damaged Chernobyl nuclear power plant ten years previously. During a routine search of the reactor's perimeter, the security personnel discovered a plastic bag with 14 pieces of nuclear fuel. A spokesman for the plant said that the uranium "was probably missing since 1995", when a group of people was arrested and convicted of stealing nuclear fuel from the destroyed reactor's central hall. The material was presumably hidden in the compound when additional security measures were introduced.[24]

Trafficking incidents involving natural uranium or "yellowcake" (uranium oxide concentrate) are typically of little concern due to the technological complexity and high costs associated with the enrichment process, which separates uranium isotopes in order to increase U-235 concentration. However, clandestine acquisition of such materials from other countries may be an attractive option for states with enrichment capabilities but insufficient uranium reserves. For example, in 1968 Israel acquired 200 tons of yellowcake from a Belgium stockpile in a complex clandestine operation involving a diversion at sea.[25] In 1987, when Pakistan needed uranium for its secret nuclear-weapon program, it reportedly engaged in covert uranium mining activities in the Darzab District of the neighboring Afghanistan.[26] Between September 2000 and February 2001, Libya received a covert shipment of 1.75 tonnes of uranium hexafluoride (UF_6), which was arranged through the Pakistan-based A.Q. Khan network.[27] In 2003, the claim, now thought to be false, that Iraq had sought to purchase natural uranium from Africa, was central to the Bush administration's justification of war against Iraq, on the grounds that Baghdad was trying to reconstitute its nuclear-weapon program. Thus, as long as some states have secret nuclear ambitions, countries with natural uranium reserves are potentially at risk of theft and diversion from their mining and reprocessing facilities. In 2012, uranium mining was carried out in 19 countries: Kazakhstan, Canada, Australia, Niger, Namibia, Russia, Uzbekistan, United States, China, Malawi, Ukraine, South Africa, India, Brazil, Czech Republic, Romania, Germany, Pakistan, and France.[28] At least eight of them are considered as politically unstable or involved in major counterterrorism activities.

DSTO records 160 thefts and seizures of natural uranium, some of them involving 100 kg or more. In the 1990s, such incidents were recorded mainly in Eurasia: Russia, Germany, Romania, Switzerland, Kazakhstan, India, and Tajikistan. The trend that has emerged since then indicates that the African continent is becoming increasingly vulnerable to trafficking in natural uranium, with the Democratic Republic of Congo (DRC), Tanzania, Namibia, Kenya, and South Africa reporting thefts and seizures. For example, two employees of the Rossing Uranium Mine in Namibia – the fifth largest uranium producer – stole 170 kg of natural uranium concentrate powder from the facility operated by Rio Tinto. In September 2009, they were arrested together with an accomplice, a member of the Namibian Defense Forces, in an attempt to sell the material. According to the management, this was the largest theft of uranium from the facility for many years, which may have involved Rossing security guards, since the thieves "were extremely familiar with the mine's internal security procedures." Commenting on the theft, the facility director claimed that a uranium black market was "emerging in South

Africa, and that groups in South Africa try to obtain uranium from the region for shipment to third countries."[29] Two years later, an even bigger theft was reported at another uranium mine in Namibia. In August 2011, Namibian authorities arrested five suspects in possession of four 50-liter barrels of natural uranium concentrate (sodium diuranite), stolen from Areva's Trekkopje mine. The barrels, which weighed 324 kg in total, were found at a house in Swakopmund.[30] DSTO has recorded a total of 24 natural uranium incidents in Africa since 2001 – two of them in the DRC, five in Namibia, five in Kenya, five in South Africa, and seven in Tanzania.

Impact of US-Russian and other cooperative efforts

Fearing the possibility of theft and diversion from the former Soviet stockpiles of weapon-usable nuclear materials and illegal transfer to state and nonstate actors, US and other international efforts to address these threats began soon after the disintegration of the Soviet Union. Protection against both internal and external threats had to be provided at dozens of nuclear weapons sites, research laboratories, uranium enrichment facilities, processing and storage sites, and naval fuel facilities, containing hundreds of metric tons of weapon-usable nuclear materials. The US Department of Defense addressed the security of Russia's nuclear weapons and nuclear stockpiles from their dismantlement through its Cooperative Threat Reduction (CTR) program, also known as the Nunn-Lugar Program. The CTR program has deactivated more than 7,500 nuclear warheads, safeguarded fissile materials, and redirected the work of former weapons scientists and engineers. The US Department of Energy (DOE) tackled the problem of nuclear security in Russia and other countries in Eurasia through two major nonproliferation programs: the first line of defense that improves the security of nuclear weapons and materials at their source, and the Second Line of Defense (SLD) that combats illicit trafficking of nuclear and other radioactive material by installing radiation detection equipment at borders, airports, and seaports.

The first line of defense provides assistance through its material protection, control, and accounting (MPC&A) program. The goal of this program is to improve and enhance the security of the Russian nuclear weapon sites and facilities housing fissile nuclear materials in Russia and other countries of concern. The scope of the MPC&A program includes 73 Russian nuclear warhead sites, 37 Russian nuclear material sites (11 Navy fuel storage sites, 7 Rosatom weapons sites, and 19 Rosatom civilian sites), and 13 nuclear material sites outside of Russia.[31] The MPC&A program has made considerable progress securing Russia's nuclear warhead and material facilities. Until the end of Fiscal Year 2012, comprehensive security upgrades have been completed for 218 of about 250 buildings housing HEU or plutonium in FSU countries. In FY 2013, it was planned to finish the upgrades at 11 additional buildings.[32] The budgetary request for FY 2014 decreased the funding for MPC&A activities, as the program shifted "to a sustainability phase with the Russian Federation and security costs are increasingly transitioned to the Russian side."[33]

The Second Line of Defense cooperates with foreign governments to strengthen their capability "to deter, detect, and interdict illicit trafficking in nuclear and other radioactive materials across international borders and through the global maritime shipping system."[34] It has two main components: the Core Program and the Megaports Initiative. The Core Program installs radiation detection equipment at foreign border crossings, airports, and seaports, primarily in Russia and former Soviet republics. In response to heightened concerns about radiological terrorism after the September 11, 2001 terrorist attacks, SLD has expanded its engagement beyond the FSU countries. To date, the SLD program has enhanced radiological detection capabilities in 24 countries, providing fixed radiation detection systems, handheld detectors, communications equipment, personnel training, and sustainability support under this program. Besides, SLD has provided vehicle-based mobile detection systems, which complement fixed detection equipment at border crossings. Such systems, with both gamma and neutron detection capabilities, are a powerful nuclear security tool for patrolling the "green" borders and interdicting domestic nuclear trafficking in intelligence-driven law enforcement operations. By the end of FY 2012, SLD deployed 34 mobile systems to 11 countries and installed radiation detection equipment at a cumulative total of 493 foreign points of entry.[35] This includes all of the 383 Russian border crossings.[36] The SLD target for FY 2013 was to equip a total of 513 sites. By FY 2018, the program is scheduled to provide radiation detection equipment to 622 sites and deploy 148 mobile detection systems in 44 countries.[37] The SLD Megaports Initiative, launched in 2003, cooperates with other countries to equip major international seaports with radiation detection systems. The program is operational in 35 countries and seeks to equip 100 seaports with radiation detection systems by 2015.[38] By the end of FY 2012, the initiative completed installations at 44 Megaports. One more port was scheduled for completion in 2013.[39]

The 1993 US-Russia HEU Purchase Agreement, commonly known as the Megatons to Megawatts Program, designed to downblend more than 500 metric tons of HEU from about 20,000 dismantled Russian nuclear warheads, has recently been completed. In December 2013, the last shipment of converted LEU arrived in the United States. Over the past 15 years, this fuel has been used in US power reactors, supplying nearly 10 percent of the nation's electricity.[40] Since its launch in 2004, the US Global Threat Reduction Initiative (GTRI), with the cooperation of its international partners, successfully removed or dispositioned over 5,110 kg of HEU and plutonium from research reactor facilities in more than 40 countries around the world, and eliminated HEU entirely from 26 countries and Taiwan.[41] Besides, in support of President Obama's four-year effort to secure the world's most vulnerable nuclear material within four years, the US DOE completed security upgrades at 32 sites in Russia (for a total of 218 sites), completed 24 bilateral physical protection assessments of foreign facilities holding US-supplied nuclear material, and provided physical protection training to nearly 2,500 foreign officials, and secured more than 10 metric tons of HEU and 3 metric tons of weapons-grade plutonium from Kazakhstan's BN-350 reactor, and transferred the material to long-term storage.[42]

There are several other US and international programs and initiatives on nuclear security and combating nuclear trafficking, including, but not limited to: the US Department of State Export Control and Related Border Security program (EXBS) and Nuclear Smuggling Outreach Initiative (NSOI); US Department of Defense International Counterproliferation Program (ICP); IAEA Nuclear Security Program; G-8 Global Partnership Against the Spread of Weapons and Materials of Mass Destruction (GP); Global Initiative to Combat Nuclear Terrorism (GICNT); and UN Security Council Resolution 1540. All these joint efforts have dedicated significant resources to nonproliferation and border security priorities and delivered assistance to dozens of countries. As a result, they have dramatically reduced the risk of nuclear theft and improved the interdiction capabilities in Russia and other recipient countries. No successful thefts of HEU or LEU have been recorded since the mid-1990s, the overall number of smuggling cases involving these materials has decreased, and hundreds of illicit trafficking incidents have been interdicted globally, including several involving HEU. For example, three Moldovan law enforcement officials, who participated in the latest HEU interdiction in June 2011, received US counterproliferation training in the United States a few weeks earlier.[43] Two of the Bulgarian customs officials, who made the seizure of an HEU sample in May 1999, had received ICP Program training.[44] This program alone has trained over 600 Georgian officials through more than 30 events held in Georgia since 1998. Although it has not been established with certainty, it is likely that some of the officials involved in the three HEU interdictions in the country since 2003 had received this training.[45]

Future challenges and the way forward

Although great progress has been achieved in securing nuclear material and combating illicit trafficking in Russia and other FSU and Eurasian countries, some risks still remain or may emerge in other regions, as uranium trafficking incidents in Africa, South America, and Australia have recently shown. In fact, the future will pose three major challenges to global nuclear security, potentially jeopardizing the results obtained until now.

First, the desire for nuclear power was not derailed by reactions to the Fukushima Daiichi nuclear accident. There is a foreseeable increase in international demand for nuclear material as a consequence of plans for a large number of nuclear power plants to be built in the next 30 years. This will also increase the amount of yellowcake and LEU produced and traded internationally, i.e., the risk for material diversion will increase as well. Should organized crime with its well developed worldwide logistical infrastructure for drugs, weapon, and people trafficking also engage in trafficking of nuclear material, the international community will face a formidable opponent. The still continuing War on Drugs, started by the United States in 1971, is a sober reminder of the difficulties in winning against organized crime. Illicit trafficking of uranium and LEU is only possible when the existing MPC&A approach is inadequate. This applies in particular to the front end of the nuclear fuel cycle, i.e., uranium (and potentially also thorium) mining and milling. In order to improve the situation in the future, a systematic approach is needed, relying on the cooperation between facility operators, intelligence, customs, and regulators.

Second, the application of combined gamma-neutron shielding in containment used for trafficking HEU is indicative of a professional approach based on the knowledge of nuclear physics. In view of the fact that relatively small volumes of weapon-usable uranium or plutonium are involved in trafficking, due to their high density, traffickers may hide even kilogram amounts using such shielding methods. Thus, the challenge of interdicting already stolen HEU or plutonium can only be met by increasing the use of neutron detectors at border crossings, seaports, and airports.

Third, deteriorating economies, as well as political instability, in some countries may bring about new threats to the security of nuclear material. Indeed, sabotage and theft at nuclear facilities cannot be excluded in conditions of chaos and anarchy. Besides, unemployment, impoverishment, and lack of prospects for the future contribute to growing criminality and may provide incentives for nuclear theft and trafficking even in countries without any or much of a previous record in this type of crime. Therefore, it is important that the internationally coordinated efforts to counter illicit trafficking are continued and enhanced on a global scale.

Notes

1. The peak recorded in 2006 was largely due to a change in the reporting practice of by just one state. Once this state reverted to its prior practice in 2007, the incidents declined again. International Atomic Energy Agency, IAEA Illicit Trafficking Database (ITDB), Fact Sheet, Vienna, Austria, 2008, www.iaea.org/newscenter/features/radsources/pdf/fact_figures2007.pdf (accessed January 20, 2014).
2. Lyudmila Zaitseva and Friedrich Steinhäusler, "Database on Nuclear Smuggling, Theft, and Orphan Radiation Sources (DSTO)," Division of Physics and Biophysics, University of Salzburg, Austria, January 2014.

3. DSTO.
4. V.M. Kuznetsov, "Osnovnyye problemy i sovremennoye sostoyaniye bezopasnosti predpriyatiy yadernogo toplivnogo tsikla Rossiyskoy Federatsii," [Main Problems and Current State of Security of Nuclear Cycle Facilities in the Russian Federation] AtomSafe, www.atomsafe.ru, Moscow, 2001.
5. IAEA, ITDB Fact Sheet, 2013.
6. William C. Potter and Elena Sokova, "Illicit Nuclear Trafficking in the NIS: WHAT'S NEW? What's True?" *The Nonproliferation Review*, Vol. 9, No. 2 (Summer 2002), pp. 112–120, http://cns.miis.edu/npr/pdfs/92potsok.pdf.
7. Kuznetsov, "Osnovnyye problemy i sovremennoye sostoyaniye bezopasnosti predpriyatiy yadernogo toplivnogo tsikla Rossiyskoy Federatsii."
8. Russian Federal Inspectorate for Nuclear and Radiation Safety (Gosatomnadzor), "Anomalii v uchete i kontrole yadernykh materialov" [Anomalies in Nuclear Materials Control and Accounting], 29 August 2000. See also Kuznetsov, "Osnovnyye problemy i sovremennoye sostoyaniye bezopasnosti predpriyatiy yadernogo toplivnogo tsikla Rossiyskoy Federatsii."
9. S. Niemeyer and I. Hutcheon, "Forensic Analysis of a Smuggled HEU Sample Interdicted in Bulgaria," IAEA-CN-98/2/09 IA, www.iaea.org/inis/collection/NCLCollectionStore/_Public/33/057/33057956.pdf (accessed January 30, 2014).
10. S. Baude, "HEU Seized in July 2001 in Paris: Analytical Investigations Performed on the Material," IAEA-CN-154/009, Proc. International Conference on Illicit Nuclear Trafficking: Collective Experience and the Way Forward, IAEA, Edinburgh, November 19–22, 2007, pp. 397–398.
11. Government of Georgia, Presentation by a Georgian official, Presentation at the International Conference on Illicit Trafficking Issues in the Black Sea Region, Chisinau, Moldova, November 7–8, 2013.
12. Lawrence Scott Sheets and William J. Broad, "Smuggler's Plot Highlights Fear Over Uranium," *New York Times*, January 25, 2007, www.nytimes.com/2007/01/25/world/europe/25nuke.html.
13. Center for Nonproliferation Studies, "Illicit Trafficking in Weapons-Usable Nuclear Material: Still More Questions than Answers," December 11, 2011, www.nti.org/analysis/articles/illicit-trafficking-weapons-useable-nuclear-material-still-more-questions-answers/ (accessed 30 January 2014).
14. Rensselaer W. Lee, *Smuggling Armageddon: The Nuclear Black Market in the Former Soviet Union and Europe* (New York: St Martin's Griffin, 1999), p. 2.
15. Desmond Butler, "Officials Say Crime Ring has Uranium," *Associated Press*, September 27, 2011, www.guardian.co.uk/world/feedarticle/9866962.
16. Andrey Kuznetsov, "Bomba dlya gubernatora" [A bomb for the governor], *Novaya Sibir*, December 20, 2002. In NIS Nuclear Trafficking Database.
17. "V RF zafiksirovany sluchai utechki yadernykh materialov s atomnykh oektov – Gosatomnadzor" [Leaks of nuclear materials from nuclear facilities have been registered in Russia according to Gosatomnadzor], Interfax, October 14, 2002. In NIS Nuclear Trafficking Database.
18. "Utechka Urana Mozhet Povlech Mezhdunarodnaya Skandala, A Utechka Informatsii - Mezhdunarodnuyu Pomoshch," *Delovaya Nedelya*, October 11, 1996. See also "Ukrast Uran? Net Nichego Proshche," *Kazakhstanskaya Pravda*, May 14, 1997, in NIS Nuclear Trafficking Database.
19. "Headline: Confiscated U May Be Part Of A Lost Fuel Assembly," *Nuclear News*, February 1995, p. 63, abstract cited on Nuclear Threat Initiative website, www.nti.org/analysis/articles/confiscated-u-may-be-part-lost-fuel-assembly/.
20. RIA Novosti, "Container with Uranium Found in Lithuania," Nuclear.Ru, March 18, 2002 (Source: RIA Novosti, March 16, 2002).
21. DSTO.
22. "Lithuanian Authorities Recover Part of Stolen Nuclear Container," *Associated Press*, April 5, 2002.
23. RIA Novosti, "Prokuratura peredala v sud delo o nezakonnom oborote yadernyh othodov [Prosecutor's Office Transferred a Nuclear Trafficking Case to Court]," June 2, 2006.
24. Aleksandar Vasovic, "Ukrainian Authorities Find Radioactive Material Believed Stolen from Chernobyl," *Associated Press*, September 28, 2005.
25. William Burr and Avner Cohen, "Israel's Secret Uranium Buy: How Argentina Fuelled Ben-Gurion's Nuclear Program," *Foreign Policy*, July 1, 2013, www.foreignpolicy.com/articles/2013/07/01/israels_secret_uranium_buy.
26. "Pakistan Secretly Transporting Uranium Ore from Afghanistan," BBC Summary of World Broadcasts, Part 1 The USSR; A. INTERNATIONAL AFFAIRS; 3. THE FAR EAST; SU/0213/A3/1, July 26, 1988.

27. International Institute for Strategic Studies, *Nuclear Black Markets: Pakistan, A.Q. Khan and the Rise of Proliferation Networks: A Net Assessment* (London: IISS, 2007).

28. World Nuclear Association, *World Uranium Mine Production*, July 2013, www.world-nuclear.org/info/Nuclear-Fuel-Cycle/Mining-of-Uranium/World-Uranium-Mining-Production/ (accessed January 31, 2014).

29. WikiLeaks, "Cable 09WINDHOEK348," August 30, 2011, http://wikileaks.org (accessed January 28, 2014).

30. Marshallino Beukes, "Uranium Theft Case Heads to Regional Court," *Namib Times*, September 6, 2013.

31. United States Department of Energy (US DOE), National Nuclear Security Administration (NNSA), "International Materials Protection and Cooperation," http://nnsa.energy.gov/aboutus/ourprograms/dnn/impc (accessed January 30, 2014).

32. US DOE, "FY 2014 Congressional Budget Request: National Nuclear Security Administration," DOE/CF-0084, Vol. 1, April 2013, p. DN-5, http://energy.gov/sites/prod/files/2013/04/f0/Volume1.pdf (accessed January 25, 2014).

33. Ibid., p. DN-15.

34. NNSA, "International Materials Protection and Cooperation."

35. US DOE, "FY 2014 Congressional Budget Request," pp. NN-7 and DN-108.

36. Douglas P. Guarino, "Nuclear Security Program Review Complete, But Questions Remain," *Global Security Newswire*, March 7, 2013, www.nti.org/gsn/article/nonproliferation-program-review-complete-questions-remain (accessed March 20, 2014).

37. US DOE, "FY 2014 Congressional Budget Request," pp. DN-82.

38. US DOE, NNSA, "Megaports Initiative," *Congressional Budget Request*, p. DN-82. http://nnsa.energy.gov/aboutus/ourprograms/nonproliferation/programoffices/internationalmaterialprotectionandcoointernat/-5 (accessed January 25, 2014). See also US Department of Energy, "FY 2014 Congressional Budget Request."

39. US DOE, "FY 2014 Congressional Budget Request," p. DN-109.

40. US DOE, NNSA, "Under US-Russia Partnership, Final Shipment of Fuel Converted From 20,000 Russian Nuclear Warheads Arrives in United States and Will Be Used for US Electricity," Press Release, December 11, 2013; http://nnsa.energy.gov/mediaroom/pressreleases/megatonstomegawatts (accessed January 30, 2014)

41. US DOE, NNSA, "GTRI: Removing Vulnerable Civilian Nuclear and Radiological Material, Fact Sheet," October 31, 2013; http://nnsa.energy.gov/mediaroom/factsheets/gtri-remove (accessed 30 January 2014).

42. US DOE, NNSA, "The Four Year Effort," YGG-13-0337, December 12, 2013, http://nnsa.energy.gov/sites/default/files/nnsa/12-13-inlinefiles/2013-12-12%204%20Year%20Effort.pdf (accessed January 30, 2014).

43. US Government Printing Office, *Enhancing Non-proliferation Partnerships in the Black Sea Region* (Washington, 2011); www.gpo.gov/fdsys/pkg/CPRT-112SPRT68115/html/CPRT-112SPRT68115.htm (accessed March 20, 2014).

44. Jennifer D.P. Moroney, Aidan Kirby Winn, Jeffrey Engstrom, Joe Hogler, Thomas-Durell Young, and Michelle Spencer, "Assessing the Effectiveness of the International Counterproliferation Program," RAND Corporation, 2001, www.rand.org/content/dam/rand/pubs/technical_reports/2011/RAND_TR981.pdf.

45. Ibid.

34

COOPERATIVE THREAT REDUCTION AND ITS LESSONS

Andrew C. Weber and Anya Erokhina

Following the collapse of the Soviet Union in 1991, the newly independent States were faced with the extraordinary challenge of securing approximately 30,000 nuclear weapons.[1] United States security officials were alarmed at the threat these weapons, in potentially unsecure sites, presented to national and global security. Senators Sam Nunn and Richard Lugar launched the US Department of Defense (DOD) Cooperative Threat Reduction (CTR) program to reduce these nuclear and other weapons of mass destruction (WMD) dangers. Although the Nunn-Lugar CTR program was created in response to a unique historical circumstance, the urgent threat of WMD proliferation and terrorism makes its lessons relevant today.

Recent reports of nuclear material trafficking, security incursions at nuclear sites, and increasing terrorist activity overall demonstrate that such threats are still present; the need to modernize and upgrade the security systems of nuclear arsenals and facilities remains.

To combat this challenge, US President Barack Obama outlined a new global nuclear security agenda, first in Prague April 2009 and again in a speech in Berlin in June 2013. His global nuclear security agenda includes ensuring effective security of all nuclear materials, consolidating or reducing the use of weapon-usable materials in civilian applications, and working cooperatively to advance nuclear security overall. The United States is working to implement this agenda in partnership with more than fifty international partners.

The CTR program's mission, project activities, evolution, and lessons learned – which emphasize cooperation and burden sharing – are particularly effective in implementing not only the global nuclear security agenda, but also in reducing chemical and biological threats globally.

This chapter briefly reviews the history of the CTR program, and highlights several lessons from more than twenty years of CTR nuclear, chemical, and biological related work around the world. It also explains why the CTR program remains an effective tool for enhancing global security, building partnerships, and reducing WMD threats.

History is made

The CTR program was unprecedented in its vision and success, and serves as a unique model for responding to emerging global WMD threats. However, the program's success was far from guaranteed when it began more than twenty years ago. Revolutionary thinking, patience, persistence, and shared national security goals were required to overcome decades of fierce Cold War competition. This competition was just starting to ebb when Senators Nunn and Lugar ushered the legislation for the CTR program onto the US Senate floor.

During the Cold War, the United States and the Soviet Union sought to ensure their national security by stockpiling massive nuclear-weapon arsenals. When the CTR program first came into law in November 1991, the United States and Russia possessed 98 percent of the world's nuclear weapons.[2] All of the information related to a country's nuclear-weapon program – from production to material composition to elimination – was protected at the highest levels of security classification. Nuclear weapons were viewed by many in the two governments as the ultimate guarantor of national survival. Despite this history, the United States and Russia shared the belief that nuclear security was something at which neither country could afford to fail. This joint recognition allowed the CTR program to become a vehicle for cooperation.

The idea for the program was spurred by Senator Nunn's meeting with then-Soviet President Gorbachev during an August 1991 trip to Moscow shortly after the failed Soviet coup d'état attempt.[3] Throughout the Cold War, the Senator had focused on nuclear security and the prevention of WMD proliferation. Influenced by this, one of his first questions to President Gorbachev was on the effectiveness of command and control of the Soviet nuclear forces during the coup. Apparently Gorbachev's answer was less than satisfying. Senator Nunn emerged from the discussion fearful that the security of the world's largest stockpile of nuclear weapons may be in jeopardy, and that it was a US responsibility to assist.

Senator Nunn soon found a bipartisan ally in Senator Richard Lugar, who was also deeply engaged in international security and nonproliferation issues and equally concerned with developments in the former Soviet Union. The two were faced with the daunting task of alerting their colleagues to the imminent dangers emerging from collapsed Soviet states, and convincing them that it was both within the United States' ability and interest to aid a long-time adversary.

After a Herculean effort to rally stakeholders across the political spectrum, congressional leaders and policymakers determined that Russia and its new nuclear-armed neighbors were unable to meet the terms of the 1991 Strategic Arms Reduction Treaty – a bilateral arms treaty reducing strategic nuclear weapons – eliminate chemical weapons, and adequately secure existing nuclear stockpiles. The paradigm for how the United States achieved national security vis-à-vis Russia had shifted from one of competition to partnership and cooperation.

After that August trip to Moscow, it took three more months for the US Senate to pass the Soviet Nuclear Threat Reduction Act of 1991. On December 12, 1991 President George H.W. Bush signed the legislation, which established what became known as the Nunn-Lugar CTR program.[4] The initial legislation allowed $400,000 of DOD funds to be reappropriated from other DOD programs to destroy nuclear weapons, chemical weapons, and other weapons; transport, store, disable, and safeguard weapons in connection with their destruction; and establish verifiable safeguards against the proliferation of such weapons.

Both the content and scope of the CTR program have evolved since that time to ensure the program's utility in addressing the full range of WMD threats. The initial legislation accounted for the fact that nuclear weapons were not the only threat emerging from the collapsed Soviet Union – more than thirty thousand tons of chemical weapons[5] and the legacy of an advanced offensive biological weapons program also posed threats to international security. Recognizing that the threat of WMD and terrorism is ever-changing and not isolated to only the former Soviet Union, the CTR program has since expanded its geographical scope. The program's annual budget in 2014 was over $500 million and it is authorized to reduce the threats of nuclear, chemical, and biological weapons and related materials and expertise in four geographic regions, covering close to thirty countries.[6]

Two decades of lessons learned

From its inception as a former Soviet Union program more than twenty years ago to its global reach today, the CTR program has accumulated valuable lessons that can be applied to future threat reduction efforts. Its projects in Eurasia have been the longest-standing engagements, and as a result are the most illustrative of the enduring relationships necessary for future threat reduction efforts.

This section offers four lessons that can be applied to future security-related global partnerships, particularly those that focus on topics sensitive to some countries: patience and transparency build trust; overcoming bureaucracy requires creativity; relationships open doors; and always be innovating. Project-specific examples that best illustrate each of these lessons, and the benefits they can bring, are presented. These case studies were chosen because they cover the entire lifecycle of a program – from the initial stages of a new initiative to the relationship building process, and finally the expansion into new partnerships. These lessons can serve as a guide to practitioners and scholars for improving today's programmatic efforts to address emerging WMD proliferation and terrorism challenges.

Patience and transparency build trust

Just as a country's nuclear weapons are kept under lock and key, so are the some of the organizations that operate them. In the Russian Ministry of Defense (MOD), the 12th Main Directorate – Glavnoye Upravleniye Ministerstvo Oborony or GUMO – is one such organization that had for years remained effectively invisible to the public.[7] Charged with nuclear-weapon security, the 12th GUMO oversees Russia's deployed nuclear stockpile – it controls nuclear-weapon movements, services nuclear warheads, and sets nuclear-weapon storage and transit security standards for the armed services. Patience and transparency on the part of the DOD CTR program negotiators and implementers were required not only to allow the 12th GUMO to gradually reveal itself in bilateral meetings, but also to build trust in an inherently suspicious environment. The unprecedented partnership between DOD CTR and one of the most important and sensitive organizations in the Russian MOD resulted in coveted access to warhead storage sites, thereby enabling vital threat reduction work.

When the CTR program was first beginning its engagement activities, the existence of the 12th GUMO was a Russian state secret and even the public mention of its name or of its staff was a Federal crime. While the 12th GUMO was one of the most appropriate and important CTR program partner organizations, its veiled existence within the Russian bureaucracy[8] initially made it a difficult and suspicious counterpart to engage.

CTR program representatives had to wait patiently for the 12th GUMO representatives sitting in the back row of the Russian delegation to reveal themselves during the numerous bilateral meetings, workshops, and technical discussions required to negotiate and implement strategic offensive nuclear delivery system elimination activities. Over a three-year period, the Directorate shifted from being the silent observer in meetings to a vocal participant by 1994. It took a year to agree on an initial project, and an additional seven years to gain access to weapon storage sites.

The cornerstone of CTR-12th GUMO engagement between 1995 and 2013 was the Automated Inventory and Control Management System (AICMS) project to develop software and procure hardware for the automated tracking and cataloging of nuclear weapons. Before the implementation of AICMS, the 12th GUMO tracked nuclear-weapon movements by hand in logbooks. Every warhead had its own dedicated logbook or "passport" that recorded all of its movements since arriving from the production line. For a country that at the time had over 18,000 nuclear warheads,[9] such an inventory system was susceptible to human error, fraud, and information security breaches. The goal of the AICMS project was to take all of that "passport" information, digitize it, and then continue to automate the remaining warhead locations and movements.

The concept seems simple enough. But how do you provide confidence to a highly suspicious Russian organization that its former adversary would *not* use the US-developed hardware and software to track critical warhead deployment movements? Despite the tense historical circumstances, the CTR program found solutions and workarounds to improve 12th GUMO confidence that US intentions in its nuclear security engagements were genuine.

As the first step in this project, the CTR program needed to build and deliver the hardware – items such as communication systems, computers, and fax machines – to various 12th GUMO sites. All of these were meant to be used on a daily basis, and from Russia's perspective this would provide a daily opportunity for potential US espionage. To allay these concerns, the CTR program paid Russian companies to build the equipment and also funded 12th GUMO representatives to travel to those production facilities so that they could observe the equipment production, packaging, and shipment.

In the early 1990s, the 12th GUMO did not have the required technical expertise to develop its own software, so the CTR program turned to trusted US commercial vendors and chose two well-known IT firms to develop AICMS. In order for the 12th GUMO to allow such a system to be installed at their sites, however, they needed to verify that the lines of code were free of loopholes, security shortcuts, or suspicious pieces. The CTR program brokered a deal between Russia and these IT companies that resulted in protecting the companies' proprietary information while strengthening the 12th GUMO's confidence.

The 12th GUMO chose several of its own technical experts, and the CTR program paid for their travel to the US company sites so that they could read the millions of lines of code themselves. The companies set their own rules for how this information could be viewed while still being protected. In the end, the Russian technical experts entered a "sensitive booth" without any pens, paper, or anything in their pockets – essentially bringing nothing except for the clothes on their backs – and stared at a computer screen with the lines of code until they were satisfied and could report positively back to the 12th GUMO leadership.

Once the hardware was delivered and the software installed, the 12th GUMO had another opportunity to test the integrity of AICMS during the training sessions on its operation and sustainment. The 12th GUMO and its technical experts were encouraged by the CTR program representatives to try and hack the system themselves by using x-rays, testing for emanation, and various other tactics. Not only did this help the 12th GUMO gain confidence that the US could not intercept the information signals that were being passed through AICMS, but it also built trust that the CTR program was not a vehicle for espionage. Most importantly, these tests helped develop the 12th GUMO's indigenous technical capability and demonstrated that AICMS provided effective, accurate, and secure nuclear warhead tracking and information.

The success and trust built through the AICMS project allowed for more advanced nuclear security projects to go forward, and for deeper engagement with the 12th GUMO. For example, the DOD CTR program received unprecedented access to warhead storage sites to ensure that physical security upgrades it had funded were being installed correctly. The 12th GUMO even installed a phone at one of its main sites to facilitate monthly teleconferences on CTR program implementation. Previously, there was no way to directly call the Directorate.

Instead of pushing projects or activities upon the 12th GUMO, the CTR program was able to ensure that a true partnership was formed by waiting patiently for the Directorate to engage at its own pace. The transparency measures developed within the AICMS project also built trust between the CTR program and the 12th GUMO that allowed for progress in other areas of nuclear security. The result of this long-term engagement strategy was an exceptional relationship with one of the most secretive nuclear security organizations in the world.

Overcoming bureaucracy requires creativity

At an early stage in its development, the DOD CTR program was able to demonstrate the value of taking the time to assess possible approaches to projects in a deliberate fashion, adjusting to yield better results, and allying with other departments to achieve efficiency. At a time when gaining momentum on the nuclear security project was critical, the CTR program was able to jumpstart the nuclear material, protection, control and accounting (MPC&A) program in Russia, and then seamlessly transfer it to another US government implementer.

Back in 1993, the MPC&A program was divided into two, parallel sub-programs – "government-to-government" and "lab–to–lab." The former was managed and funded entirely by the DOD CTR program, and the latter was managed and mostly funded by the Department of Energy (DOE). Both of these approaches aimed to improve all facets of Russia's nuclear material security system: physical protection such as guards, barricades, alarms; control measures such as storage, tamper-proof cameras, seals; and accounting such as inventory systems and measurements.[10] Together these elements helped comprise a robust security system that protected nuclear material from being stolen or diverted for nefarious purposes. Even though the two programs launched at the same time, it became clear that one of them was achieving progress at a much faster rate than the other.

The details and functions of the MPC&A government-to-government program were negotiated between the US and Russian bureaucracies at the ministerial level. As a result, a long, drawn-out process left tangible threat reduction objectives at the mercy of grander political maneuvering. Basic requirements for CTR program implementation, such as site access to Russian laboratories that housed fissile material, were initially denied. Without that access, the CTR implementers were unable to determine program requirements or present informed recommendations for Russia's equipment and training needs. Despite political agreement for site access, US experts were repeatedly denied permission to carry out site surveys at agreed facilities.[11] This prevented the provision of assistance and security upgrades.

Between 1993 and 1995, the "government-to-government" MPC&A program under DOD CTR had not made much progress. The bureaucratic approach to negotiations was not moving fast enough to be effective due to the cumbersome process of coordinating and receiving requisite approvals. Since the negotiators were government officials instead of practitioners, political motivations too often trumped a focus on the practical benefits of nuclear material security engagement.

In contrast, the lab-to-lab MPC&A program under DOE managed to bypass the politics and was able to target nuclear security practitioners directly at the labs in a truly collaborative way. It was a bottom-up approach that encouraged partnership between US and Russian scientists with minimal interference from government bureaucrats. At the start of 1994, the participating US and Russian laboratories created the Joint US-Russian Steering Committee and drew up work plans with contracts specifying concrete deliverables.[12] By June of that same year, this program produced tangible results at the first engagement site at Arzamas-16, and following this initial success, numerous[13] other Russian sites had lab-to-lab projects up and running.[14]

On a practical level, the lab-to-lab program was more flexible and efficient because it favored working level and technical discussions over onerous bureaucratic processes. Because the collaboration was between scientists, a results-focused approach was easier to attain due to shared scientific interests. Additionally, the desirability of the projects themselves motivated participation – after all, this was a unique opportunity for former enemies to enter otherwise closed sites to collaborate.

Beginning in 1996, the DOD CTR-funded government-to-government program joined with the lab-to-lab program and was placed under the management and funding of DOE. This resulted in a streamlined, single MPC&A program while also freeing up critical CTR funds to successfully implement other WMD threat reduction projects.[15]

Faced with the strain of delivering results quickly and gaining traction both at home and abroad, few programs have the time to pause and analyze the costs or benefits of their international engagement approaches. The MPC&A lesson serves as a reminder that self-assessment, course correction, and interagency cooperation help to develop successful programs. Breaking down stove-pipes and avoiding turf wars ensures a unified and successful US government strategy for international partner engagement.

Relationships open doors

There is no substitute for the importance of continually working to develop and strengthen relationships through cooperative efforts. One does not want to be exchanging business cards in a crisis – either with members of one's own government or potential international partners. Cooperative partnerships developed in peacetime can help to prevent WMD from ever being used, and at a minimum will help to establish the relationship foundations necessary for more effective crisis response. Examples such as Kazakhstan, and most recently Libya and Syria, demonstrate how relationships developed through the CTR program can be leveraged to secure and eliminate WMD globally.

At the 2012 Nuclear Security Summit in Seoul, Presidents Nazarbayev, Medvedev, and Obama announced completion of a seventeen-year long trilateral project at the Semipalatinsk Test Site. The three countries partnered to secure over a dozen nuclear weapons-worth of plutonium and to secure the site. This legacy material from underground Soviet multiple low- and no-yield nuclear experiments remained in a vast network of tunnels in Degelen Mountain. Following the collapse of the Soviet Union, scientists and military personnel abandoned the test site, leaving behind residual materials in the tunnels, holes, and containers that posed a proliferation threat. Although the tunnels had been sealed with rubble in the 1990s, unsecured, the material within those tunnels could be recovered relatively easily by enterprising arms traffickers, and then potentially sold, and used in a WMD terrorist attack.

The Degelen project started after former Director of the Los Alamos National Laboratory Dr Sigfried Hecker visited the site and observed large scale metal scavenging operations near and inside the test tunnels. At the time, scrap metal scavengers had free reign of the 300 square kilometer Degelen area of the test site. Alarmed by this possibility, the trilateral effort to secure this site was negotiated so that the DOD CTR program would fund the effort to secure the material; Russia would provide the scientists and critical information on its location; and Kazakhstan would assume responsibility for the field work and provide the necessary permits and authorizations.

The key to getting the project, or more accurately a long series of increasingly sensitive projects involving progressively greater quantities of fissile material, started was the trusting relationship Hecker had developed with leadership of the Russian nuclear-weapon design laboratories and the Kazakhstan National Nuclear Center. A number of DOD experts had also built solid relationships with Kazakhstani and Russian counterparts during years of field work to seal the test tunnels.

Indeed, it is unlikely the Degelen efforts could have been launched at all, had the right partners not already known and built trust with each other. One key champion of the effort was Vladimir Maximovich Kutsenko, a Senior Russian Atomic Energy Agency official during all of the Degelen projects. Kutsenko, who had served as Chief of Security for the Semipalatinsk Test Site before, during, and after the chaotic collapse of the Soviet Union, had deep knowledge of the situation. Another key leader throughout was Vladimir Shkolnik, who had presided over independent Kazakhstan's nuclear enterprise in various government leadership positions since independence. Experts from Los Alamos National Laboratory and the Defense Threat Reduction Agency, among others, were involved in the effort over many years. This continuity of personnel on all sides was an essential element of success.

Another key to this productive partnership was an agreement at the outset to keep the work confidential. This was intended primarily to limit public awareness that there was so much at-risk fissile material in the tunnels, but it also demonstrated among the partners that we could share very sensitive information without leaks. As a result, each year the Russian weapons designers provided more detailed information to us about the experiments and materials likely left behind. After one banquet in Kurchatov, Kazakhstan, a Russian official personally probed whether the United States would support removal of some of the most sensitive "special technical equipment" for shipment back to Russia. He was told that we would, thereby launching a project to remove, pack, and ship it from Kazakhstan via special railcars to a secure storage site in Russia.

This cooperation also resulted in Kazakhstan's enhanced capacity to secure sites and materials within its borders. With President Nazarbayev's direct intervention, Kazakhstan passed a law putting the entire Degelen area off limits to intruders. With the DOD provision of technical assistance to the security forces and wide area surveillance systems, the entire Degelen area is now under constant monitoring and is well secured.

Always be innovating

After decades of successful nuclear security work, cooperative engagements are ready to advance to an even higher level of technical capability and breadth, but this also requires more time, transparency, and trust. The breadth of WMD threats facing the international community is growing and changing. In response, the CTR program must continue its innovative legacy and develop creative, nimble approaches to arms control and nonproliferation challenges.

The longstanding biological engagement with Georgia provides a compelling example of how the CTR program responded to new threats after 9/11 by moving away from dismantlement and security efforts toward a new capacity-building approach. Dangerous pathogen consolidation and security in a single, safe facility were central to the biological partnership with Georgia, and over time the emphasis expanded to include enhanced disease surveillance as a key objective. This real-time awareness component will become an important technical advancement as the CTR program continues to grow.

Finding the right partners in the Georgian government was important. It was natural for the DOD to negotiate a framework agreement with the Georgian MOD, but during program implementation the Ministries of Health, Agriculture, and Education and Science played increasingly prominent roles. The multi-sectoral nature of this partnership made it important for the Georgian government to coordinate at a level above any single ministry, and key counterparts included the Prime Minister's Office. High-level engagement was essential to the success of such a large and complicated effort, and Senator Lugar's regular visits to Tbilisi provided invaluable access to Georgian presidents and prime ministers. During Senator Lugar's last trip to Georgia as a US Senator, President Mikheil Saakashvili generously named the central laboratory the Richard Lugar Center for Public Health Research.

In order to sustain the CTR's capacity-building approach in Georgia, there was the need for enduring strategic partners from US government institutions. Contractors could not provide this. We developed an innovative approach to long-term engagement, sustainment, and transparency by providing an enduring presence of researchers and health experts from the US Army Medical Research and Materiel Command and the US Centers for Disease Control and Prevention. Other vital partners included the World Health Organization and the European Union. The former has agreed to ensure the Lugar Center becomes a WHO Collaborating Center for Emerging Infectious Disease Surveillance, and the latter designated the Lugar Center a chemical, biological, radiological, and nuclear (CBRN) Center of Excellence.

The successful provision of this expertise to the Lugar Center, to which the CTR program made critical contributions, opened the door to work with the Georgian government to develop more creative approaches to threats beyond biological weapons. As a result, the Lugar Center now also provided the foundation for Georgia's national CBRN prevention, preparedness, and response capability. Thanks to this innovative approach in Georgia, CTR has made enhancing national and regional CBRN capacities a key component of recent work in the Asia-Pacific and the Middle East.

Real-time lessons from Libya and Syria

In 2014, the Motor Vessel (M/V) Cape Ray has been docked in Rota, Spain, awaiting transfer in Italy of Syria's most dangerous chemical agents for safe elimination. While there is still very challenging work to be done, the effort to safely remove and eliminate Syria's chemical weapons illustrates the value of relationships, and how bilateral partnerships developed at the working level can establish a foundation on which projects of global scale and importance can be developed years later.

Notably, in order to be prepared for the Syria challenge, the CTR program relied on lessons from its experience providing assistance in destroying the last of Gaddafi's chemical weapons stockpile in Libya. Critical to this project was the importance of both thinking big and thinking ahead. Bold endeavors are bound to be met with even greater doubts. For destroying Syria's chemical weapons, the CTR program faced three great doubts in our efforts to prepare the US Government for action: that the Syrian regime would never accede to the Chemical Weapons Convention (CWC); that the Russians would never work with us on this effort; and that it was an impossibly large task to get Syria's massive chemical stockpiles out in the midst of the country's civil war.

The CTR program had confronted similar doubts in Libya. There were grave concerns that Libya's infrastructure limitations and security challenges would never allow chemical weapons destruction to occur. Though it took significant effort, we assisted the Libyans in overcoming these challenges. This gave us even greater confidence that we needed to think big regarding the Syrian chemical weapons challenge.

First, the CTR program needed to convey that the scale of the challenge was manageable. Our experts believed that Syria's chemicals were primarily in bulk liquid form – not weaponized. Based on what we knew of the stockpile, we estimated that it could take as few as 200 truckloads to move the chemicals out of Syria.

Second, we needed to find a way to work together on a path to destroying Syria's chemical weapons program. The US Government began a confidential dialogue with the Russians to discuss the Syrian chemical weapons stockpile and options for how it could be destroyed if the opportunity presented itself. Participants in these discussions were many of same Russians and Americans who had partnered over the preceding two decades to safely eliminate former Soviet WMD through the CTR program. Over the course of a year, chemical weapons destruction experts from both countries developed what we called the "universal matrix," which identified the processes, personnel, and equipment needed to eliminate a chemical weapons stockpile.

This was a bold endeavor, and it paid off. Technical discussions and collaboration laid groundwork and helped build the trust needed to respond quickly after the US-Russia Framework for the Elimination of Syria's Chemical Weapons was finalized, and Syria acceded to the CWC.

Likewise, the DOD's rapid development of a transportable hydrolysis system demonstrates again that we were thinking big and thinking ahead. We created a system dedicated to anticipating needs and taking calculated risks in the commitment of resources. If we had not leaned forward on development of hydrolysis systems, we would not have had a solution to offer when the Syrians agreed to let the international community remove their chemical weapons.

The Syria chemical weapons elimination effort is ultimately an international mission that reflects a remarkable division of labor. Many of our international partners are participating and providing financial and in-kind assistance that is critical to the effort's success: Danish and Norwegian ships (with Finnish and British support) are removing chemical weapons materials from the Syrian port of Latakia. Russia and China are assisting with security for port loading operations. Italy has agreed to provide a port to allow transloading operations from the Danish cargo ship to the M/V Cape Ray. The United Kingdom has agreed to destroy nerve agent precursor chemicals through commercial incineration. Germany has agreed to destroy the by-product resulting from neutralization of the sulfur mustard agent. Additional countries have made generous financial contributions. Quite simply, this mission would not have a chance of succeeding without the contributions of our international partners.

The destabilizing effects of the Syrian civil war still worry Israel and Jordan greatly. However, their sense of relief at the elimination of the strategic threat presented by Syrian chemical weapons was palpable. The fact that Israel is no longer issuing gas masks to its citizens serves as a powerful validation of our hard work removing these hideous weapons.

Though this is an important achievement, we cannot afford to rest. We must look forward and think about what the Syria mission means for the future. Libya was practice for Syria, which is practice for North Korea. We need, always, to anticipate the next challenge and weigh the risks of inaction. Where would we be now if we had not assumed some risks in the planning and preparing for Syria?

Looking ahead

President Obama has correctly prioritized efforts to address the threat of WMD and the Defense Department is committed to developing and maintaining the capabilities necessary to counter this threat. Despite our best efforts, and the quality of our intelligence, we will not always be able to anticipate the next WMD challenge. It would not have been possible to predict that our experiences across the former Soviet Union would have been so important for our efforts to eliminate Syrian and Libyan chemical weapons. So, while we may think we have a good idea where tomorrow's threats will come from – and indeed we must work to anticipate and address these threats – we must also stand ready to improvise when confronted with unexpected challenges. The CTR program will continue to plan an invaluable role addressing WMD threats.

By applying its lessons and by investing in people and technologies required for effective threat reduction, the CTR model can be applied and expanded to new partners who can benefit from this type of cooperation. For example, the technology used in the AICMS project can be modernized to provide every nation with the capability to monitor and track not only nuclear weapons, but all nuclear material in use, storage, and transit across facilities. The CTR program can learn from its experience tackling chemical, biological, and nuclear threats individually by combining its approaches and developing an innovative, collective approach to all-hazards threat reduction. Relationships can and should be sustained and expanded to continue Senators Nunn and Lugar's vision of national security through partnership and cooperation. The Syrian crisis is an example of how the CTR program should not just be sustained, but strengthened and built upon as the United States and the international community face new and emerging threats.

Hopefully we can bring this effort in Syria to its successful completion. More importantly, though, we can also hope that the younger CTR practitioners involved in this effort will form the nucleus of a next generation of counter-WMD experts, and that the relationships they are developing every day to accomplish this difficult mission will become the foundation for productive collaboration over the next twenty years in pursuit of a world safe from the horrors of nuclear, chemical, and biological threats.

Notes

1. Hans Kristensen and Robert Norris, "Global Nuclear Weapons Inventories, 1945–2013," *Bulletin of Atomic Scientists*, Vol. 69, No 5 (September/October 2013), pp, 75–81, http://thebulletin.org/2013/september/global-nuclear-weapons-inventories-1945-2013. We owe words of gratitude to: Mr. William Moon (Program Manager, Global Nuclear Security Program, Cooperative Threat Reduction, Defense Threat Reduction Agency) for his service, subject matter expertise, and excellent storytelling; Christine Parthemore (Senior Advisor, Office of the Assistant Secretary of Defense for Nuclear, Chemical, and Biological Defense Programs), Will Bardenwerper (Advisor, Office of the Assistant Secretary of Defense for Nuclear, Chemical, and Biological Defense Programs), and Cameron Stanuch (Contractor, Office of Nonproliferation and International Security, National Nuclear Security Administration) for their service, excellent editorial skills and important perspectives.
2. Ibid.
3. Sam Nunn, "Moving Away from Doomsday and Other Dangers: The Need to Think Anew," speech at the National Press Club, Washington, DC, March 29, 2001, www.nti.org/media/pdfs/speech_samnunn_032901.pdf?_=1316466791.
4. The 1993 legislation signed by President William Clinton renamed the program to Cooperative Threat Reduction, stating that "This title [enacting this chapter] may be cited as the 'Cooperative Threat Reduction Act of 1993.'" See 22 USC § 5951 – Findings on cooperative threat reduction, http://uscode.house.gov/view.xhtml?req=granuleid:USC-prelim-title22-section5951&num=0&edition=prelim.
5. Government of Russia, Russkiy agentstvo po boyepripasam (Russian Munitions Agency), Khimicheskoye Oruzhiye (Chemical Weapons), www.munition.gov.ru/.
6. The regional and country-specific expansions are achieved through Secretary of Defense Determinations, which receive concurrence from the Secretary of State. The following are the dates and

regions for which the CTR Program received determinations: (1) Afghanistan and Pakistan on November 12, 2009; (2) Africa, China, India, and Iraq on December 14, 2010; (3) Southeast Asia on December 2, 2011; (4) Middle East on October 9, 2012; (5) Global Functional Determination for Nuclear and Radiological Material Transportation on May 2, 2013; (6) Global Functional Determination for WMD material disposition in May 21, 2013. The CTR program currently has active programs in: Afghanistan, Armenia, Azerbaijan, Burundi, Cambodia, China, Djibouti, Georgia, India, Indonesia, Iraq, Jordan, Kazakhstan, Kenya, Laos, Malaysia, Moldova, Pakistan, Philippines, Russia, Rwanda, South Africa, Tanzania, Thailand, Turkey, Uganda, Ukraine, Uzbekistan, and Vietnam.

7. The following section is based on information received during an author interview with a Defense Threat Reduction Agency representative on November 6, 2013.

8. Until recently, the 12th GUMO head held the rank of a three-star general and reported directly to the Russia President. The current chief of the 12th GUMO is Yuriy Grigoryevich Sych. He came on as chief with the rank of senior colonel and then was promoted to a one-star general. This is indicative of the realignment and reprioritization within the Russian Federation. For example, the previous three-star general 12th GUMO chiefs could approve CTR engagement activities. Currently, however, CTR engagements have to be sent up to the MOD for approval.

9. Kristensen and Norris, "Global Nuclear Weapons Inventories," pp. 75–81.

10. It is important to note that while this lesson-learned is focused on Russia, these programs were also implemented in other FSU states such as Belarus, Kazakhstan, Lithuania, Latvia, Ukraine, and Uzbekistan.

11. Jessica Stern, "US Assistance Programs for Improving MPC&A in the Former Soviet Union," *The Nonproliferation Review*, Vol. 3, No. 2 (Winter 1996), pp. 17–32.

12. Mark Hibbs, "Russia Improving Protection for Sensitive Nuclear Sites," *Nucleonics Week*, March 30, 1995, p. 12.

13. The Arzamas-16 project goals were to protect the lab against the insider threat. Scientists from Los Alamos National Labs developed a prototype with many different components, which provided a test bed for instruments and systems elements that were useful for various nuclear facilities. The Arzamas-16 lab scientists approved the prototype and installed thirty-nine similar integrated systems. In 1994 the lab-to-lab program also signed contracts with the Kurchatov Institute, Chelyabinsk-70, and the Institute of Physics and Power Engineering at Obninsk.

14. Ronald Augustson and John Phillips, as told to Debra Daugherty, "Russian-American MPC&A," *Los Alamos Science*, No. 24 (1996), pp. 72–86, www.fas.org/sgp/othergov/doe/lanl/pubs/00326622.pdf.

15. Stimson Center, "Materials Protection, Control, and Accounting (MPC&A), *Pragmatic Steps for Global Security*, The Stimson Center, 2013, www.stimson.org/materials-protection-control-and-accounting-mpca-/.

BIBLIOGRAPHY

Government documents and primary sources

Ahtisaari, Marti. "Report to the Secretary-General on Humanitarian Need in Kuwait and Iraq in the Immediate Post-Crisis Environment." UN Security Council, March 20, 1991, www.un.org/Depts/oip/background/reports/s22366.pdf.

Argentina, Brazil, ABACC, and IAEA. "Agreement between the Republic of Argentina, the Federal Republic of Brazil, the Brazilian-Argentine Agency for Accounting and Control of Nuclear Materials and the International Atomic Energy Agency for the Application of Safeguards (Quadripartite Agreement)." Signed December 13, 1991, www.abacc.org.br/?page_id=150&lang=en.

Aspin, Les. "The Defense Department's New Nuclear Counterproliferation Initiative." Address to the National Academy of Sciences, Washington, DC. December 7, 1993.

Australia Group. "Guidelines for Transfers of Sensitive Chemical or Biological Items." June 2012, www.australiagroup.net/en/guidelines.html.

Ban, Ki-moon. "The United Nations and Security in a Nuclear-weapon-free World." Speech delivered at the East-West Institute, New York, October 24, 2008, www.un.org/sg/statements/?nid=3493.

Baruch Plan. Presented to United Nations Atomic Energy Commission, June 14, 1946, www.atomic archive.com/Docs/Deterrence/BaruchPlan.shtml.

Blair, Dennis C. "Annual Threat Assessment of the Intelligence Community for the Senate Select Committee on Intelligence." Office of the Director of National Intelligence. February 12, 2009, www.intelligence.senate.gov/090212/blair.pdf.

Boucher, Richard. "North Korean Nuclear Program." United States Department of State, Press Statement. October 16, 2002, http://2001-2009.state.gov/r/pa/prs/ps/2002/14432.htm

Bunn, Matthew. "The Risk of Nuclear Terrorism and Next Steps to Reduce the Danger." Testimony before the Committee on Homeland Security and Governmental Affairs, US Senate, Washington, DC, April 2, 2008, http://belfercenter.ksg.harvard.edu/files/bunn-nuclear-terror-risk-test-08.pdf.

Bush, George W. "President Announces New Measures to Counter the Threat of WMD." Speech at the National Defense University, February 11, 2004, http://georgewbush-whitehouse.archives.gov/news/releases/2004/02/20040211-4.html

———. "Statement on the Next Steps in Strategic Partnership With India." January 12, 2004, www.gpo.gov/fdsys/pkg/WCPD-2004-01-19/pdf/WCPD-2004-01-19-Pg61-2.pdf.

———. "Remarks by the President to the People of Poland." Wawel Royal Castle, Krakow, Poland. May 31, 2003, http://georgewbush-whitehouse.archives.gov/news/releases/2003/05/20030531-3.html.

———. "President Speaks on War Efforts to Citadel Cadets." The Citadel, Charleston, South Carolina, December 11, 2001, http://georgewbush-whitehouse.archives.gov/news/releases/2001/12/2001 1211-6.html.

Clapper, James R. "Worldwide Threat Assessment of the US Intelligence Community." Senate Select Committee on Intelligence, January 29, 2014, www.dni.gov/files/documents/Intelligence %20Reports/2014%20WWTA%20%20SFR_SSCI_29_Jan.pdf.

Clinton, William J. Written Statement by the President, read by Robert Bell, "Press Briefing by Special Assistant to the President for Defense Policy. August 11, 1995." The American Presidency Project, www.presidency.ucsb.edu/ws/?pid=59461.

Cohen, William. "Transcript of News Briefing by Secretary of Defense William Cohen." December 19, 1998, www.defenselink.mil/transcripts/1998/t12191998_t1219fox.html.

Committee on Technical Issues Related to Ratification of the Comprehensive Nuclear Test Ban Treaty for the National Academy of Sciences. *Technical Issues Related to the Comprehensive Nuclear Test Ban Treaty*. Washington, DC: National Academy of Sciences, 2002, www.nap.edu/openbook.php?isbn= 0309085063.

Comprehensive Nuclear Test-Ban Treaty Organization. "Nuclear Testing 1945–Today." N.D., www.ctbto. org/nuclear-testing/history-of-nuclear-testing/nuclear-testing-1945-today/.

———. Preparatory Commission. "Comprehensive Nuclear Test-Ban Treaty." CBTBO, www.ctbto.org/fileadmin/content/treaty/treaty_text.pdf.

———. Preparatory Commission. "CTBT Treaty Text." www.ctbto.org/the-treaty/treaty-text/.

———. Preparatory Commission. "Concept for the Preparation and Conduct of the Next Integrated Field Exercise." CTBT/PTS/INF.1105. January 27, 2011.

———. Preparatory Commission. "Detection of Radioactive Gases Consistent with North Korean Test Underlines Strength of CTBTO Monitoring System." *CTBTO Spectrum*, No. 20 (July 2013), www.ctbto.org/fileadmin/user_upload/pdf/Spectrum/2013/Spectrum20_p26.pdf.

———. Preparatory Commission. "Final Declaration and Measures to Promote the Entry into Force of the Comprehensive Nuclear-Test-Ban Treaty." Report from the Conference on Facilitating the Entry into Force of the Comprehensive Nuclear-Test-Ban Treaty (New York). September 2013, www.ctbto.org/fileadmin/user_upload/Art_14_2013/Statements/Final_Declaration.pdf.

———. Preparatory Commission. "Report on the Conduct of the 2008 Integrated Field Exercise." CTBT/PTS/INF.1021. August 4, 2009.

———. Preparatory Commission. "Status of Signature and Ratification." CTBTO, www.ctbto.org/the-treaty/status-of-signature-and-ratification.

Council of the European Union. "Fight against the Proliferation of Weapons of Mass Destruction: EU Strategy against Proliferation of Weapons of Mass Destruction." Doc. no. 15708/03, December 10, 2003, www.consilium.europa.eu/showPage.aspx?id=718.

D'Agostino, Thomas P. "Testimony on US Strategic Posture before the House Armed Services Subcommittee, US House of Representatives." February 27, 2008, http://nnsa.energy.gov/media room/congressionaltestimony/02.27.08.

Director of Central Intelligence, *The 22 September 1979 Event*, Interagency Intelligence Assessment January 21, 1980, declassified June 2004, posted in the National Security Archive, George Washington University, www2.gwu.edu/~nsarchiv/NSAEBB/NSAEBB190/03.pdf.

Eisenhower, Dwight D. "Atoms for Peace." Address to the UN General Assembly, December 8, 1953, www.iaea.org/About/atomsforpeace_speech.html.

———. "Draft of the Presidential Speech Before the General Assembly of the United Nations." November 28, 1953, www.eisenhower.archives.gov/research/online_documents/atoms_for_peace/ Atoms_for_Peace_Draft.pdf.

European Union. "Joint Plan of Action." European External Action. November 24, 2013, http://eeas.europa.eu/statements/docs/2013/131124_03_en.pdf.

Federation of Electric Power Companies of Japan. "Japan's Nuclear Fuel Cycle is Poised for Completion." *Power Line*, Vol. 2, November 1998, www.fepc.or.jp/english/library/power_line/detail/02.

Fleischer, Ari. Press Briefing. The White House, Office of the Press Secretary. December 11, 2002, http://georgewbush-whitehouse.archives.gov/news/releases/2002/12/20021211-5.html.

Foreign and Commonwealth Office. "Lifting the Nuclear Shadow: Creating the Conditions for Abolishing Nuclear Weapons." Government of the United Kingdom. February 5, 2009, http://carnegieendowment.org/files/nuclear-paper.pdf.

Gandhi, Indira. "Non-Proliferation Treaty." Government of India. Office of the Prime Minister. April 5, 1968, http://meaindia.nic.in/pmicd.geneva/?50031138.

Ghandi, Rajiv. "Speech on Disarmament at the Opening Session of Six-Nation Five-Continent Peace Initiative." January 21, 1988, http://meaindia.nic.in/pmicd.geneva/?50031142.

Government of Brazil. Ministry of Foreign Affairs. "Nuclear Suppliers Group (NSG)." Press Release, No. 237, June 24, 2011.

Government of Georgia. Presentation at the International Conference on Illicit Trafficking Issues in the Black Sea Region, Chisinau, Moldova. November 7–8 , 2013.

Government of India. *Disarmament: India's Initiatives* (New Delhi: Ministry of External Affairs, External Publicity Division, 1988).

Government of Japan. Ministry of Foreign Affairs. "Joint Statement by the Leaders of Japan and the United States on Contributions to Global Minimization of Nuclear Material." The Hague Nuclear Security Summit (The Hague, Netherlands), March 24–25, 2014, www.mofa.go.jp/dns/n_s_ne/page18e_000059.html.

———. "National Defense Program Guidelines for FY 2014 and Beyond (Provisional Translation)." 2013, www.japanportal.jp/131227NDPG.pdf.

———. "National Security Strategy (Provisional Translation)." 2013, www.cas.go.jp/jp/siryou/131217 anzenhoshou/nss-e.pdf.

———. "Report on the Strategic Nuclear Forces of the Russian Federation Pursuant to Section 1240 of the National Defense Authorization Act for Fiscal Year 2012." www.fas.org/programs/ssp/nukes/nuclearweapons/DOD2012_RussianNukes.pdf.

———. "National Defense Program Guidelines for FY 2011 and Beyond (Provisional Translation)." (2010): www.tr.emb-japan.go.jp/T_06/files/National_Defense_Program_FY2011.pdf.

———. Ministry of Foreign Affairs. "Statement by Mr. Katsuya Okada, Minister for Foreign Affairs of Japan on the release of the US Nuclear Posture Review (NPR)." April 7, 2010, www.mofa.go.jp/announce/announce/2010/4/0407_01.html.

Government of Pakistan. Army Doctrine and Evaluation Directorate. "Pakistan Army Doctrine 2011: Comprehensive Response." December 2011, pp. 43–44.

———. Inter-Services Public Relations Directorate. "Press Release No. PR94/2011-ISPR." April 19, 2011, www.ispr.gov.pk/front/main.asp?o=t-press_release&id=1721.

Government of the People's Republic of China. "China's National Defense in 2010." March 2011, http://english.gov.cn/official/2011-03/31/content_1835499.htm.

Government of Russia. Russkiy agentstvo po boyepripasam (Russian Munitions Agency). Khimicheskoye Oruzhiye (Chemical Weapons). www.munition.gov.ru/.

Government of the United States of America and the Government of the Russian Federation. "Agreement between the Government of the United States of America and the Government of the Russian Federation Concerning the Management and Disposition of Plutonium Designated as No Longer Required for Defense Purposes and Related Cooperation, as Amended by 2010 Protocol." Signed on April 13, 2010, www.fissilematerials.org/library/PMDA2010.pdf.

Government of United Kingdom. Office of the Prime Minister. "UK–France Summit 2010 Declaration on Defence and Security Co-operation." Press Release. November 2, 2010, www.gov.uk/government/news/uk-france-summit-2010-declaration-on-defence-and-security-co-operation.

Hyde, Henry J. "United States-India Nuclear Cooperation." Sec. 104, January 3, 2006, www.gpo.gov/fdsys/pkg/BILLS-109hr5682enr/pdf/BILLS-109hr5682enr.pdf.

International Atomic Energy Agency. "Information Circulars: Documents, Numbers 501–550." IAEA website, www.iaea.org/Publications/Documents/Infcircs/Numbers/nr501-550.shtml.

———. "Power Reactor Information System (PRIS)." May 7, 2014, www.iaea.org/pris.

———. "Conclusion of Additional Protocols: Status as of 12 March 2014." IAEA website, www.iaea.org/safeguards/documents/AP_status_list.pdf.

———. "Energy, Electricity and Nuclear Power Estimates for the Period up to 2050." 2013 Edition, www-pub.iaea.org/MTCD/publications/PDF/RDS-1-33_web.pdf.

———. "IAEA Incident and Trafficking Database (ITDB): Incidents of nuclear and other radioactive material out of regulatory control—2013 Factsheet." IAEA Website, www-ns.iaea.org/downloads/security/itdb-fact-sheet.pdf.

———. "Objective and Essential Elements of a State's Nuclear Security Regime." *IAEA Nuclear Security Series*, No. 20, Vienna, Austria, 2013, www-pub.iaea.org/MTCD/Publications/PDF/Pub1590_web.pdf.

———. "Convention on the Physical Protection of Nuclear Material." December 17, 2013, www.iaea.org/Publications/Documents/Conventions/cppnm_status.pdf.

———. "Communication Received from the Permanent Mission of the United States of America to the International Atomic Energy Agency regarding Certain Member States' Guidelines for the Export of

Nuclear Material, Equipment and Technology." INFCIRC/254/Rev.11/Part 1, November 12, 2012, Paragraph 10, www.nuclearsuppliersgroup.org/A_test/doc/infcirc254r11p1.pdf.

———. *Regular Budget Appropriations for 2013.* GC(56)/RES/5, September 2012, www.iaea.org/About/Policy/GC/GC56/GC56Resolutions/English/gc56res-5_en.pdf.

———. "The Conceptualization and Development of Safeguards Implementation at the State Level." GOV/2013/38, Vienna. August 12, 2013, http://armscontrollaw.files.wordpress.com/2012/06/state-level-safeguards-concept-report-august-2013.pdf.

———. "Collaborative Projects: Proliferation Resistance and Safeguardability Assessment Tools (PROSA)." June 2012, www.iaea.org/INPRO/CPs/PROSA.

———. "INPRO Collaborative Project: Proliferation Resistance: Acquisition/Diversion Pathway Analysis (PRADA)." IAEA-TECDOC-1684. May 2012, www-pub.iaea.org/MTCD/publications/PDF/TE_1684_web.pdf.

———. "Energy, Electricity and Nuclear Power Estimates for the Period up to 2050." 2011 Edition, www-pub.iaea.org/MTCD/Publications/PDF/RDS1_31.pdf.

———. "Nuclear Security Recommendations on Physical Protection of Nuclear Materials Facilities." *IAEA Nuclear Security Series*, No. 13, Vienna, Austria, 2011, www-pub.iaea.org/books/IAEABooks/8629/Nuclear-Security-Recommendations-on-Physical-Protection-of-Nuclear-Material-and-Nuclear-Facilities-INFCIRC-225-Revision-5.

———. "Implementation of the NPT Safeguards Agreement and Relevant Provisions of Security Council Resolutions in the Islamic Republic of Iran, GOV/20011/65." November 8, 2011, www.iaea.org/Publications/Documents/Board/2011/gov2011-65.pdf.

———. "Evaluation Methodology for Proliferation Resistance and Physical Protection of Generation IV Nuclear Energy Systems." Revision 6, Generation IV, GIF/PRPPWG/2011/003, September 30, 2011, www.gen-4.org/gif/upload/docs/application/pdf/2013-09/gif_prppem_rev6_final.pdf.

———. "Communication received from the Permanent Mission of the Netherlands Regarding Certain Member States' Guidelines for the Export of Nuclear Material, Equipment and Technology." INFCIRC 254/Rev.10/Part I, July 26, 2011, www.iaea.org/Publications/Documents/Infcircs/2011/infcirc254r10p1.pdf.

———. "International Target Values 2010 for Measurement Uncertainties in Safeguarding Nuclear Materials." STR-368, Department of Safeguards, Vienna, Austria, November 2010, www.iaea.org/safeguards/documents/International_Target_Values_2010.pdf.

———. "Implementation of the NPT Safeguards Agreement and Relevant Provisions of Security Council Resolutions 1737 (2006), 1747 (2007), 1803 (2008) and 1835 (2008) in the Islamic Republic of Iran." Report by the Director General, February 18, 2010, www.iaea.org/Publications/Documents/Board/2010/gov2010-10.pdf.

———. "Facility Design and Plant Operation Features that Facilitate Implementation of IAEA Safeguards." SGCP-CCA, Report STR-360. February 2009, www.iaea.org/safeguards/documents/STR_360_external_version.pdf.

———. IAEA Illicit Trafficking Database (ITDB), Fact Sheet. Vienna, Austria. 2008, www.iaea.org/newscenter/features/radsources/pdf/fact_figures2007.pdf.

———. "Guidance for the Application of an Assessment Methodology for Innovative Nuclear Energy Systems: INPRO Manual – Safety of Nuclear Fuel Cycle Facilities." IAEA-TECDOC-1575 Rev. 1. November 2008, www.iaea.org/INPRO/publications/INPRO_Manual/TE_1575_CD/PDF/TE_1575_vol9_2008.pdf.

———. "Spent Fuel Reprocessing Options." IAEA-TECDOC-1587. August 2008, www-pub.iaea.org/MTCD/publications/PDF/te_1587_web.pdf.

———. "Implementation of the NPT Safeguards Agreement and Relevant Provisions of Security Council Resolutions 1737 (2006) and 1747 (2007) in the Islamic Republic of Iran, GOV/2007/58." November 15, 2007, http://iaea.org/Publications/Documents/Board/2007/gov2007-58.pdf.

———. "Nuclear Forensics Support, Reference Manual." *IAEA Nuclear Security Series*, No. 2, Technical Guidance, Vienna, Austria, 2006, pub.iaea.org/MTCD/publications/PDF/Pub1241_web.pdf.

———. "The Standard Text of Safeguards Agreements in Connection with the Treaty on the Non-Proliferation of Nuclear Weapons: Revision of the Standardized Text of the 'Small Quantities Protocol'." GOV/INF/276/Corr.1, February 28, 2006, http://ola.iaea.org/ola/documents/ginf276mod1corr1.pdf.

———. "The Standard Text of Safeguards Agreements in Connection with the Treaty on the Non-Proliferation of Nuclear Weapons." GOV/INF/276/Mod.1. February 21, 2006, http://ola.iaea.org/ola/documents/ginf276mod1.pdf.

———. "Implementation of the NPT Safeguards Agreement in the Islamic Republic of Iran, GOV/2006/14." February 4, 2006, www.iaea.org/Publications/Documents/Board/2006/gov2006-14.pdf.

———. "Multilateral Approaches to the Nuclear Fuel Cycle: Expert Group Report submitted to the Director General of the International Atomic Energy Agency." Infcirc/640, February 22, 2005, www.iaea.org/Publications/Documents/Infcircs/2005/infcirc640.pdf.

———. "Strengthening the Agency's Technical Co-operation Activities." GC(39)/RES/14. September 30, 2005, www.iaea.org/About/Policy/GC/GC39/Resolutions/gc39r14.html.

———. "Implementation of the NPT Safeguards Agreement in the Islamic Republic of Iran, GOV/2005/77." September 24, 2005, www.iaea.org/Publications/Documents/Board/2005/gov2005-77.pdf.

———. "Implementation of the NPT Safeguards Agreement in the Islamic Republic of Iran, GOV/2005/67." September 2, 2005, www.iaea.org/Publications/Documents/Board/2005/gov2005-67.pdf.

———. "Management of High-Enriched Uranium for Peaceful Purposes: Status and Trends." IAEA-TECDOC-1452, June 2005, pp. 16, 18, www-pub.iaea.org/mtcd/publications/pdf/te_1452_web.pdf.

———. "Implementation of the NPT Safeguards Agreement in the Islamic Republic of Iran, GOV/2004/83." November 15, 2004, http://iaea.org/Publications/Documents/Board/2004/gov2004-83.pdf.

———. "Implementation of the NPT Safeguards Agreement in the Islamic Republic of Iran, GOV/2004/60." September 1, 2004, www.iaea.org/Publications/Documents/Board/2004/gov2004-60.pdf.

———. "IAEA Welcomes US New Global Threat Reduction Initiative." IAEA Press Release, May 27, 2004, www.iaea.org/newscenter/news/2004/gtri_initiative.html.

———. "Implementation of the NPT Safeguards Agreement in the Islamic Republic of Iran, GOV/2003/75." November 10, 2003, http://iaea.org/Publications/Documents/Board/2003/gov2003-75.pdf.

———. "Implementation of the NPT Safeguards Agreement in the Islamic Republic of Iran, GOV/2003/40." June 6, 2003, http://iaea.org/Publications/Documents/Board/2003/gov2003-40.pdf.

———. "The Conceptual Framework for Integrated Safeguards." GOV/2002/8, February 8, 2002.

———. "Strengthening the Effectiveness and Improving the Efficiency of the Safeguards System and Application of the Model Additional Protocol." GC(45)/23, General Conference, 45th regular session, August 17, 2001, http://iaea.org/About/Policy/GC/GC45/GC45Documents/English/gc45-23_en.pdf.

———. "The Development of International Safeguards." GOV/INF/2000/26, November 17, 2000.

———. "Application of IAEA Safeguards in the Middle East." General Conference Decision, GC(44)/DEC/12. September 22, 2000, www.iaea.org/About/Policy/GC/GC44/GC44Decisions/English/gc44dec-12_en.pdf.

———. "The Development of International Safeguards." GOV/INF/2000/4, March 9, 2000.

———. "Communication Received from Certain Member States Concerning their Policies Regarding the Management of Plutonium." INFCIRC/549, March 16, 1998, www.iaea.org/Publications/Documents/Infcircs/1998/infcirc549.pdf.

———. "Model Protocol Additional to the Agreement(s) between State(s) and the International Atomic Energy Agency for the Application of Safeguards." INFCIRC/540 (Corrected), September 1997, www.iaea.org/Publications/Documents/Infcircs/1997/infcirc540c.pdf.

———. "Strengthening the Effectiveness and Improving the Efficiency of the Safeguards System." GC(40)/17, August 23, 1996, www.iaea.org/About/Policy/GC/GC40/Documents/gc40-17.html.

———. "Agreed Framework of 21 October 1994 Between the United States of America and the Democratic People's Republic of Korea, INFCIRC/457." November 2, 1994, www.iaea.org/Publications/Documents/Infcircs/Others/infcirc457.pdf.

———. "Strengthening the Effectiveness and Improving the Efficiency of the Safeguards System." Report by the Director General, GC(39)/17. August 22, 1995, www.iaea.org/About/Policy/GC/GC39/GC39Documents/English/gc39-17_en.pdf.

———. "Report by the Director General on the Implementation of the Resolution Adopted by the Board on 25 February 1993 and of the Agreement Between the Agency and the Democratic People's

Republic of Korea for the Application of Safeguards in Connection with the Treaty on the Non-Proliferation of Nuclear Weapons, GOV/2645." April 1, 1993, www.securitycouncilreport.org/atf/cf/%7B65BFCF9B-6D27-4E9C-8CD3-CF6E4FF96FF9%7D/Disarm%20GOV2645.pdf.

————. "Report on the Implementation of the Agreement Between the Agency and the Democratic People's Republic of Korea for the Application of Safeguards in Connection with the Treaty on the Non-Proliferation of Nuclear Weapons, GOV/2636." February 25, 1993, http://ahlambauer.files.wordpress.com/2013/03/gov2636.pdf.

————. "South Africa's Nuclear Capabilities." GC(XXXV)/RES/567. September 20, 1991, www.iaea.org/About/Policy/GC/GC35/GC35Resolutions/English/gc35res-567_en.pdf.

————. "Fourth NPT Review Conference." General Conference, Record of the 323rd Plenary Meeting, 34th Regular Session, September 17, 1990, GC(XXXIV)/OR.323. March 7, 1991, www.iaea.org/About/Policy/GC/GC34/GC34Records/English/gc34or-323_en.pdf.

————. "Fourth NPT Review Conference." GC(XXXIV)/INF/291, September 19, 1990, www.iaea.org/About/Policy/GC/GC34/GC34InfDocuments/English/gc34inf-291_en.pdf.

————. "Extracts Appearing in Fourth NPT Review Conference." NPT/CONF.IV/DC/l/Add.3(A), September 19, 1990, para. 28, www.iaea.org/About/Policy/GC/GC34/GC34InfDocuments/English/gc34inf-291_en.pdf.

————. "South Pacific Nuclear Free Zone Treaty." INFCIRC/331. February 1986, Articles 10–11, Annexes 3–4, www.iaea.org/Publications/Documents/Infcircs/Others/inf331.shtml.

————. "Report of the International Nuclear Fuel Cycle Evaluation." Vienna: IAEA, 1980.

————. "The Convention on the Physical Protection of Nuclear Material." Infcirc/274/Rev. 1, May 1980, www.iaea.org/Publications/Documents/Infcircs/Others/infcirc274r1.pdf.

————. "Communication Received from Certain Member States Regarding Guidelines for the Export of Nuclear Material, Equipment or Technology." INFCIRC/254, February 1978, www.iaea.org/Publications/Documents/Infcircs/Others/infcirc254.shtml.

————. "The Standard Text of Safeguards Agreements in Connection with the Treaty on the Non-Proliferation of Nuclear Weapons." GOV/INF/276. February 22, 1974, http://ola.iaea.org/ola/documents/GINF276.pdf.

————. "The Structure and Content of Agreements Between the Agency and States Required in Connection with the Treaty on the Non-Proliferation of Nuclear Weapons." INFCIRC/153 (Corrected), June 1972, www.iaea.org/Publications/Documents/Infcircs/Others/infcirc153.pdf.

————. "Treaty on the Non-Proliferation of Nuclear Weapons." INFCIRC/140, April 22, 1970, www.iaea.org/Publications/Documents/Infcircs/Others/infcirc140.pdf.

————. "The Agency's Safeguards System." INFCIRC/66/Rev.2. September 16, 1968, www.iaea.org/Publications/Documents/Infcircs/Others/infcirc66r2.pdf.

————. "Statute of the IAEA." October 23, 1956, www.iaea.org/About/statute.html.

————. "Factsheets and FAQs: Nuclear Non-Proliferation: Chronology of Key Events (July 1945–Present)." IAEA website, www.iaea.org/Publications/Factsheets/English/npt_chrono.html.

Joint Statement. "Strengthening Nuclear Security Implementation." Nuclear Security Summit, The Hague, the Netherlands, March 24–25, 2014, p. 3, www.nss2014.com/sites/default/files/downloads/strengthening_nuclear_security_implementation.pdf.

"Joint Statement of the 2014 Nuclear Industry Summit." 3rd Nuclear Industry Summit, Amsterdam, the Netherlands, March 23–25, 2014, p. 3, www.nss2014.com/sites/default/files/documents/nis2014-jointstatement_final.pdf.

Kansra, V.P. "Status of Power Reactor Fuel Reprocessing in India." International Atomic Energy Agency Advisory Group Meeting on Status and Trends in Spent Fuel Reprocessing. 1999, www.iaea.org/inis/collection/NCLCollectionStore/_Public/30/047/30047648.pdf.

Korean Peninsula Energy Development Organization. "Agreed Framework Between the United States of America and the Democratic People's Republic of Korea." October 21, 1994, www.kedo.org/pdfs/AgreedFramework.pdf.

Ledogar, Stephen J. "Statement By Ambassador Stephen J. Ledogar (Ret.), Chief US Negotiator of the CTBUT Prepared for the Senate Foreign Relations Committee Hearing on the CTBT." October 7, 1999, www.fas.org/nuke/control/ctbt/text/100799ledogar%20.htm.

McNamara, Robert S. "Memorandum for the President." February 12, 1963, declassified version, www.fas.org/man/eprint/dod1963.pdf.

Miki, Takeo, and Gerald R. Ford. "Japan-US Joint Announcement to the Press." Washington, August 6, 1975, www.ioc.u-tokyo.ac.jp/~worldjpn/documents/texts/JPUS/19750806.O1E.html.

Ministry of Foreign Affairs of Pakistan, Strategic Export Control Division. "Pakistan's Engagement with Multilateral Export Control Regimes." February 20, 2013, www.mofa.gov.pk/secdi

Missile Technology Control Regime. "Plenary Meeting of the Missile Technology Control Regime." Rome, Italy, October 14–18, 2013, www.mtcr.info/english/press/Italy2013.htm.v/pr-details.php?prID=1431.

———. "Guidelines for Sensitive Missile-Relevant Transfers." N.D., www.mtcr.info/english/guide text.htm

———. MTCR Annex Handbook. MTCR/TEM/2012/Annex, October 23, 2012, www.mtcr.info/english/annex.html.

National Intelligence Council. "Iran: Nuclear Intentions and Capabilities." Unclassified Executive Summary of a National Intelligence Estimate Office of the Director of National Intelligence, November 2007, www.dni.gov/files/documents/Newsroom/Reports%20and%20Pubs/20071203_ release.pdf.

National Research Council of the National Academies. *The Comprehensive Nuclear Test Ban Treaty: Technical Issues for the United States.* Washington, DC: The National Academies Press, 2012.

National Security Archive. "The Vela Incident: Nuclear Test or Meteoroid?" National Security Archive Electronic Briefing Book No. 190, May 5, 2006, www2.gwu.edu/~nsarchiv/NSAEBB/NSAEBB190.

Nitze, Paul H. "The START Treaty." Executive Report 102-53, Statement before the Senate Committee on Foreign Relations. September 18, 1992, Washington, DC, p. 27, www.congress.gov/cgi-bin/cpquery/?&sid=cp1067xg5W&refer=&r_n=sr043.106&db_id=106&item=&sel=TOC_83291&.

———. "The INF Treaty." Statement before US Congress, Senate Committee on Foreign Relations Senate Hearing 100-522, part 1, 100th Congress, 2nd Session, 1988, http://babel.hathitrust.org/cgi/pt?id=mdp.39015014752847.

North Atlantic Treaty Organization. "Deterrence and Defence Posture Review." Press Release, No. 063 (2012), www.nato.int/cps/en/natolive/official_texts_87597.htm?mode=pressrelease.

Nuclear Suppliers Group. "Public Statement (Final)." Plenary Meeting of the Nuclear Suppliers Group, Prague, Czech Republic, June 13–14, 2013, p. 1, www.nuclearsuppliersgroup.org/A_test/press/NSG%206%20PUBLIC%20STATEMENT%20HOD%20final.pdf.

———. "Updated Control Lists as Agreed by the 2013 Prague Plenary." N.D. www.nuclearsuppliers group.org/A_test/01-eng/13-list.php.

———. "Statement on Civil Nuclear Cooperation with India, Extraordinary Plenary Meeting." September 6, 2008. Attachment to IAEA, INFCIRC/734 (Corrected), September 19, 2008, www.iaea.org/Publications/Documents/Infcircs/2008/infcirc734c.pdf.

Obama, Barack. "Remarks by President Obama at the Brandenburg Gate, Berlin, Germany." The White House, Office of the Press Secretary. June 19, 2013, www.whitehouse.gov/the-press-office/2013/06/19/remarks-president-obama-brandenburg-gate-berlin-germany.

———. "Transcript of Obama's Speech in Berlin." June 19, 2013, http://blogs.wsj.com/washwire/2013/06/19/transcript-of-obamas-speech-in-berlin.

———. "Remarks by President Barack Obama, Hradcany Square, Prague, Czech Republic." The White House, Office of the Press Secretary. April 5, 2009, www.whitehouse.gov/the_press_office/Remarks-By-President-Barack-Obama-In-Prague-As-Delivered.

Organization for the Prohibition of Chemical Weapons. "Convention on the Prohibition of the Development, Production, Stockpiling and Use of Chemical Weapons and on their Destruction, July 29, 2005, rev." www.opcw.org/index.php?eID=dam_frontend_push&docID=6357.

Perino, Dana. "Statement by the White House Press Secretary on Syria and North Korea." April 24, 2008, www.cfr.org/syria/statement-white-house-press-secretary-syria-north-korea/p16102.

Reagan, Ronald. "Joint Statement on the Soviet-United States Summit Meeting." December 10, 1987, www.presidency.ucsb.edu/ws/?pid=33803.

Research Group on the Japan-US Alliance. "A New Phase in the Japan-US Alliance: The Japan US Alliance Toward 2020." *Institute for International Policy Studies Project Report*, 2009, www.iips.org/en/research/data/J-US-SEC2009e.pdf.

Rice, Condoleezza, Robert M. Gates, Taro Aso, and Fumio Kyuma. "Joint Statement of the Security Consultative Committee – Alliance Transformation: Advancing United States-Japan Security and Defense Cooperation." Washington, DC, May 1, 2007, www.mofa.go.jp/region/n-america/us/security/scc/pdfs/joint0705.pdf.

Russian Federal Inspectorate for Nuclear and Radiation Safety (Gosatomnadzor). "Anomalii v uchete i kontrole yadernykh materialov [Anomalies in Nuclear Materials Control and Accounting]." 29 August 2000.

Scott Kemp, R. "The Nonproliferation Emperor Has No Clothes. The Gas Centrifuge, Supply-Side Controls, and the Future of Nuclear Proliferation," *International Security*, Vol. 38, No. 4 (Spring 2014), pp. 39–78.

Singh, Manmohan. "PM's address at the Golden Jubilee function of the Department of Atomic Energy." Government of India. Office of the Prime Minister. October 23, 2004, http://pmindia.nic.in/speech-details.php?nodeid=31.

Special Advisor to the Director of Central Intelligence. "Comprehensive Report of the Special Advisor to the DCI on Iraq's WMD (Weapons of Mass Destruction)." September 30, 2004, www.cia.gov/library/reports/general-reports-1/iraq_wmd_2004.

Stussi, Jurg. "Historischer Abriss zur Frage einer Schweizer Nuklearbewaffnung [Historical Outline on the Question of Swiss Nuclear Armament]." (J. Wozniak, trans.) April 1996, http://nuclearweapon archive.org/Library/Swissdoc.html.

The Hague Code of Conduct against Ballistic Missile Proliferation (HCOC). HCOC Website. N.D., www.hcoc.at/.

The Hague Nuclear Security Summit Joint Communiqué, March 24, 2014. www.nss2014.com/sites/default/files/documents/the_hague_nuclear_security_summit_communique_final.pdf.

The White House. "Joint Statement by President Obama and Prime Minister Singh of India." November 8, 2010, www.whitehouse.gov/the-press-office/2010/11/08/joint-statement-president-obama-and-prime-minister-singh-india.

———. "President Announces New Measures to Counter the Threat of WMD." Washington, DC, February 11, 2004, http://georgewbush-whitehouse.archives.gov/news/releases/2004/02/20040211-4.html.

———. "National Security Council Memorandum: Agreed Definitions." US National Security Council, February 18, 1994.

Treaty for the Prohibition of Nuclear Weapons in Latin America and the Caribbean (Treaty of Tlatelolco). Art. I, http://opanal.org/opanal/Tlatelolco/Tlatelolco-i.htm.

United Nations, "2010 Review Conference of the Parties to the Treaty on the Non-Proliferation of Nuclear Weapons." NPT/CONF.2010/50 (Vol. I), New York, 2010, www.un.org/ga/search/view_doc.asp?symbol=NPT/CONF.2010/50(VOL.I).

———. "Principles and Objectives for Nuclear Non-Proliferation and Disarmament." NPT/CONF. 1995/32/Dec.2, September 17, 2008, www.un.org/disarmament/WMD/Nuclear/1995-NPT/pdf/NPT_CONF199501.pdf.

———. *United Nations Disarmament Yearbook, Vol. 30*. New York: United Nations, 2006.

———. "Official Records of the General Assembly, Fifty-fourth Session, Supplement No. 42(A/54/42)." 1999, www.opanal.org/Docs/Desarme/NWFZ/A54_42iAnnexI.pdf.

———. "Use of Mercenaries as a Means of Violating Human Rights and Impeding the Exercise of the Rights of Peoples to Self-determination." UN General Assembly A/52/112, annex, March 18, 1997, www.un.org/en/ga/search/view_doc.asp?symbol=A/RES/52/112&Lang=E.

———. "1995 Review and Extension Conference of the Parties to the Treaty on the Non-Proliferation of Nuclear Weapons." NPT/CONF.1995/32 (Part I), New York, 1995, www.un.org/disarmament/WMD/Nuclear/pdf/finaldocs/1995%20-%20NY%20-%20NPT%20Review%20Conference%20-%20Final%20Document%20Part%20I.pdf.

———. "UN Document S-10/2, Final Document of SSOD-1: Resolutions and Decisions of the Tenth Special Session of the General Assembly." May 23–June 30, 1978, www.un.org/disarmament/HomePage/SSOD/A-S-10-4.pdf

———. "UN Document A/10027/Add. 1, Comprehensive Study of the Question of Nuclear-Weapon-Free-Zones in All its Aspects." October 8, 1975, www.un.org/disarmament/HomePage/ODA Publications/DisarmamentStudySeries/PDF/A-10027-Add1.pdf.

———. "Treaty on the Nonproliferation of Nuclear Weapons." July 1, 1968, Art. III (b), www.un.org/en/conf/npt/2005/npttreaty.html.

———. "Statement by the Indian Representative (Husain) to the Eighteen Nation Disarmament Committee (ENDC): Non-proliferation of Nuclear Weapons." US Arms Control and Disarmament Agency, *Publication 46*. December 14, 1967; released July 1968, www.un.org/disarmament/publications/documents_on_disarmament/1967/DoD_1967.pdf.

———. "Final Verbatim Record of the Conference of the Eighteen-Nation Committee on Disarmament [Meeting 244]." ENDC/PV.244. Palais des Nations, Geneva, March 1, 1966, http://quod.lib.umich.edu/e/endc/4918260.0244.001.

———. "United States Memorandum Submitted to the First Committee of the General Assembly." UN Document A/C.l/783. January 12, 1957.

———. "Conference on the Statute of the International Atomic Energy Agency." Verbatim Record of the Seventh Plenary Meeting. September 27, 1956, www.iaea.org/inis/collection/NCLCollection Store/_Public/42/061/42061197.pdf.

———. "Protocol for the Prohibition of the Use in War of Asphyxiating, Poisonous or Other Gases, and of Bacteriological Methods of Warfare." Geneva, June 17, 1925, www.un.org/disarmament/WMD/Bio/pdf/Status_Protocol.pdf.

United Nations Agency for the Prohibition of Nuclear Weapons in Latin America and the Caribbean. "Comprehensive Study of the Question of Nuclear-Weapon-Free Zones in all its Aspects." U.N. General Assembly Resolution 3472 (XXX). December 11, 1975, www.un.org/disarmament/WMD/Nuclear/NWFZ.shtml.

United Nations Conference on Disarmament. "Report of Ambassador Gerald E. Shannon of Canada on Consultations on the most Appropriate Arrangement to Negotiate a Treaty Banning the Production of Fissile Material for Nuclear Weapons or Other Nuclear Explosive Devices." CD/1299. March 24 1995, www.fas.org/programs/ssp/nukes/armscontrol/shannon.html.

United Nations General Assembly. "Resolution A/RES/67/53." January 4, 2013, www.un.org/en/ga/search/view_doc.asp?symbol=A/RES/67/53.

———. "Consolidation of the Regime Established by the Treaty for the Prohibition of Nuclear Weapons in Latin America and the Caribbean (Treaty of Tlatelolco)." Resolution No. 58/31. November 20, 2000, https://gafc-vote.un.org/UNODA/vote.nsf/91a5e1195dc97a630525656f005b8adf/e9a22 d2025d8729385256dc20059fcc7?OpenDocument&ExpandSection=5.

———. "Review Conference of the Parties to the Treaty on the Nonproliferation of Nuclear Weapons." Final document. 2000, www.un.org/disarmament/WMD/Nuclear/NPT_Review_Conferences.shtml.

———. "Final Report of the 2000 Review Conference." Report from the 2000 Review Conference of the Parties to the Treaty on the Non-Proliferation of Nuclear Weapons (New York). April 24–May 19, 2000, www.un.org/disarmament/WMD/Nuclear/2000-NPT/2000NPTDocs.shtml.

———. "Decision 2: Principles and Objectives for Nuclear Non-Proliferation and Disarmament." NPT/CONF.1995/32. 1995 Review and Extension Conference of the Parties to the Treaty on the Non-Proliferation of Nuclear Weapons. New York, April 17–May 12, 1995, www.un.org/disarmament/WMD/Nuclear/1995-NPT/pdf/NPT_CONF199501.pdf.

———. "Decision 3: Extension of the Treaty on the Non-Proliferation of Nuclear Weapons." 1995 Review and Extension Conference of the Parties to the Treaty on the Non-Proliferation of Nuclear Weapons. New York, April 17–May 12, 1995, www.un.org/disarmament/WMD/Nuclear/1995-NPT/pdf/NPT_CONF199503.pdf.

———. "Resolution on the Middle East." NPT/CONF.1995/32. 1995 Review and Extension Conference of the Parties to the Treaty on the Non-Proliferation of Nuclear Weapons. New York, April 17–May 12, 1995, www.un.org/disarmament/WMD/Nuclear/1995-NPT/pdf/Resolution_MiddleEast.pdf.

———. "Resolution A/RES/48/75L." December 16, 1993.

———. "Establishment of a nuclear-weapon-free zone in the region of the Middle East." A/RES/46/30, 65th plenary meeting, December 6, 1991, www.un.org/documents/ga/res/46/a46r030.htm.

———. "Statement by Andrei A. Gromyko, Minister of Foreign Affairs of the USSR." Plenary Meeting of the Second Special Session of the United Nations General Assembly Devoted to Disarmament. June 12, 1982.

———. "Establishment of a Nuclear-weapon-free Zone in the Region of the Middle East." General Assembly Resolution 3263, 2309 plenary meeting, December 9, 1974, www.securitycouncilreport.org/atf/cf/%7B65BFCF9B-6D27-4E9C-8CD3-CF6E4FF96FF9%7D/Disarm%20ARES 3263%20%28XXIX%29.pdf.

———. "Convention on the Prohibition of the Development, Production and Stockpiling of Bacteriological (Biological) and Toxin Weapons and Their Destruction." March 26, 1975, www.un.org/disarmament/WMD/Bio/pdf/Text_of_the_Convention.pdf.

———. "Resolution 2758 (XXVI)." October 25, 1971, http://china.usc.edu/App_Images/1971-UN-China-seating.pdf.

———. "Treaty on the Non-Proliferation of Nuclear Weapons (NPT)." July 1, 1968, www.un.org/disarmament/WMD/Nuclear/NPTtext.shtml.

———. "Treaty for the Prohibition of Nuclear Weapons in Latin America." February 14, 1967, http://disarmament.un.org/treaties/t/tlatelolco/text.

———. "Resolution 1665 (XVI)." (Irish Resolution) December 4, 1961, http://daccess-dds-ny.un.org/doc/RESOLUTION/GEN/NR0/167/18/IMG/NR016718.pdf.

———. "Resolution 1652 (SVI)." November 24, 1961, http://daccess-dds-ny.un.org/doc/RESOLUTION/GEN/NR0/167/05/IMG/NR016705.pdf.

———. "Resolution 1148 (XII)." November 14, 1957, www.un.org/en/ga/search/view_doc.asp?symbol=A/RES/1148(XII)&Lang=E&Area=RESOLUTION.

United Nations Security Council. "Report of the Panel of Experts Established Pursuant to Resolution 1874 (2009)." S/2014/147. March 6, 2014, www.un.org/sc/committees/1718/poereports.shtml.

———. "Resolution 2094 (2013)." S/RES/2094 (2013), March 7, 2013, p. 4, www.un.org/en/ga/search/view_doc.asp?symbol=S/RES/2094(2013).

———. "Report of the Panel of Experts Established Pursuant to Resolution 1874 (2009)." S/2013/337. June 11, 2013, www.securitycouncilreport.org/atf/cf/%7B65BFCF9B-6D27-4E9C-8CD3-CF6E4FF96FF9%7D/s_2013_337.pdf.

———. "Resolution 1977 (2011)." S/RES/1977(2011), April 20, 2011, www.securitycouncilreport.org/atf/cf/%7B65BFCF9B-6D27-4E9C-8CD3-CF6E4FF96FF9%7D/CT%201540%20S%20RES%201977.pdf.

———. "Resolution 1929 (2010)." June 9, 2010, www.un.org/en/sc/documents/resolutions/2010.shtml.

———. "Resolution 1874 (2009)." S/RES/1874 (2009), June 12, 2009, www.un.org/en/ga/search/view_doc.asp?symbol=S/RES/1874(2009).

———. "Resolution 1718 (2006)." S/RES/1718 (2006), October 14, 2006, www.un.org/sc/committees/1718/.

———. "Resolution 1696 (2006)." July 31, 2006, www.un.org/News/Press/docs/2006/sc8792.doc.htm.

———. "Resolution 1540 (2004)." S/RES/1540 (2004), 495th meeting, April 28, 2004, http://daccess-dds-ny.un.org/doc/UNDOC/GEN/N04/328/43/PDF/N0432843.pdf.

———. "Resolution 1540 (2004)." S/RES/1540 (2004), 495th meeting, April 28, 2004, p. 3, www.un.org/en/ga/search/view_doc.asp?symbol=S/RES/1540%20(2004).

———. "Questions Relating to Measures to Safeguard Non-Nuclear-Weapon States Parties to the Treaty on the Non-Proliferation of Nuclear Weapons." UNSCR (1968), June 19, 1968, www.un.org/en/ga/search/view_doc.asp?symbol=S/RES/255(1968).

United States Arms Control and Disarmament Agency. *Arms Control and Disarmament Agreements: Texts and Histories of Negotiations*, 6th edition. Washington, DC: ACDA, 1990.

———. "International Negotiations on the Treaty on the Nonproliferation of Nuclear Weapons, Publication 48." Washington, DC: Government Printing Office, 1969.

———. "Brazilian Amendments to the Draft Nonproliferation Treaty." In *Documents on Disarmament 1967*, 546. Washington, DC: Government Printing Office, 1968.

———. "A Cutoff of Production of Fissionable Materials for Weapons Use with Demonstrated Destruction of Nuclear Weapons and Transfer of Fissionable Material Therefrom to Non-Weapons Uses." October 18, 1965, www2.gwu.edu/~nsarchiv/nukevault/ebb321/21.PDF.

United States Central Intelligence Agency. "Syria's Covert Nuclear Reactor at Al Kibar." video, April 25, 2008, www.youtube.com/watch?v=yj62GRd0Te8.

———. "Unclassified Report to Congress on the Acquisition of Technology Relating to Weapons of Mass Destruction and Advanced Conventional Munitions. 1 January – 30 June 2002." www.cia.gov/library/reports/archived-reports-1/jan_jun2002.html.

———. Office of the Director. "Nuclear Weapons Production in Fourth Countries: Likelihood and Consequences Number-100-6-57." June 18, 1957, declassified version, www2.gwu.edu/~nsarchiv/NSAEBB/NSAEBB155/prolif-2.pdf.

United States Congress. Senate Committee on Banking, Housing, and Urban Affairs. "P5 + 1 Interim Nuclear Agreement With Iran." 113th Congress, 1st Session, December 12, 2013.

———. House Committee on Foreign Affairs. "The Iran Nuclear Deal: Does It Further US National Security?" 113th Congress, 1st Session, December 10, 2013.

———. Senate Committee on Foreign Relations. *Enhancing Non-Proliferation Partnerships in the Black Sea Region: A Minority Staff Report*. Washington, DC: US Government Printing Office, 2011, http://wid.ap.org/documents/np-minority-report.pdf.

———. *Nuclear Forensics and Attribution Act*. H.R. 730, H.R. 730 (111th): Nuclear Forensics and Attribution Act, 111th Congress, 2009–2010, August 25, 2010, www.govtrack.us/congress/bills/111/hr730/text.

———. Senate Committee on Foreign Relations. "Legislative Activities Report." S. Rept. 111–12. 111th Congress, 1st Session, March 31, 2009.

———. Senate Committee on Foreign Relations. "Hearings on Sanctions Reform." 106th Congress, 1st Session, May 11, July 1, and July 21, 1999.

———. House Committee on International Relations. "Economic Sanctions and US Policy Interests." 105th Congress, 2nd Session, June 3, 1998

———. Senate. "Proceedings of the Senate Task Force on Economic Sanctions." 105th Congress, 2nd Session, September 1998, S. Doc. 105-26.

———. Office of Technology Assessment. *Nuclear Proliferation and Safeguards.* Washington, DC: OTA (1977): 1–270, www.princeton.edu/~ota/disk3/1977/7705/7705.PDF.

———. "Nuclear Regulatory Legislation." Atomic Energy Act of 1954 (PL 83–703), Sec.123. August 30, 1954, http://science.energy.gov/~/media/bes/pdf/nureg_0980_v1_no7_june2005.pdf.

United States Department of Defense. Office of the Secretary. "Military and Security Developments Involving the Democratic People's Republic of Korea 2013." Annual Report to Congress. March 5, 2014, www.defense.gov/pubs/North_Korea_Military_Power_Report_2013-2014.pdf.

———. "Task Force Report: Assessment of Nuclear Monitoring and Verification Technologies." Defense Science Board, Washington, DC, January 2014, www.acq.osd.mil/dsb/reports/NuclearMonitoring AndVerificationTechnologies.pdf.

———. "Report on Nuclear Employment Strategy of the United States Specified in Section 491 of 10 USC." Washington, DC: June 19, 2013, www.defense.gov/pubs/reporttoCongressonUSNuclear EmploymentStrategy_Section491.pdf.

———. Office of the Secretary. "Annual Report to Congress: Military and Security Developments Involving the People's Republic of China 2013." Department of Defense, May 2013, www.defense. gov/pubs/2013_china_report_final.pdf.

———. "Nuclear Posture Review Report." Washington, DC, April 2010, www.defense.gov/ npr/docs/2010%20Nuclear%20Posture%20Review%20Report.pdf.

———. Office of the Deputy Secretary. "Report on Activities and Programs for Countering Proliferation." Counter-Proliferation Program Review Committee. May 1995, www.dod.mil/ pubs/foi/International_security_affairs/other/766.pdf.

United States Department of Energy. National Nuclear Security Administration. "Global Threat Reduction Initiative." N.D., http://nnsa.energy.gov/aboutus/ourprograms/dnn/gtri.

———. National Nuclear Security Administration. "International Materials Protection and Cooperation." N.D., http://nnsa.energy.gov/aboutus/ourprograms/dnn/impc.

———. National Nuclear Security Administration. "Material Protection, Control and Accounting." N.D., http://nnsa.energy.gov/aboutus/ourprograms/dnn/impc/mpca.

———. National Nuclear Security Administration. "Megaports Initiative." N.D., http://nnsa.energy.gov/ aboutus/ourprograms/nonproliferation/programoffices/internationalmaterialprotectionandcoointer- nat/-5.

———. National Nuclear Security Administration. *Nuclear Weapons Stockpile Stewardship and Management Plan (for Fiscal Year 2014)*, http://nnsa.energy.gov/ourmission/managingthestockpile/ssmp.

———. "Report on Low Enriched Uranium for Naval Reactor Cores." Report to Congress, Office of Naval Reactors, January 2014.

———. National Nuclear Security Administration. "The Four Year Effort." YGG-13-0337. December 12, 2013, http://nnsa.energy.gov/sites/default/files/nnsa/12-13-inlinefiles/2013-12-12%204%20Year %20Effort.pdf.

———. National Nuclear Security Administration. "Under US-Russia Partnership, Final Shipment of Fuel Converted From 20,000 Russian Nuclear Warheads Arrives in United States and Will Be Used for US Electricity." Press Release, December 11, 2013, http://nnsa.energy.gov/mediaroom/ pressreleases/megatonstomegawatts.

———. National Nuclear Security Administration. "GTRI: Removing Vulnerable Civilian Nuclear and Radiological Material, Fact Sheet." October 31, 2013, http://nnsa.energy.gov/mediaroom/ factsheets/gtri-remove.

———. National Nuclear Security Administration. "Nuclear Test Readiness, Warheads, Nuclear Security, Workforce and Engineering." August 1, 2013.

———. "FY 2014 Congressional Budget Request: National Nuclear Security Administration." DOE/CF-0084, Vol. 1, April 2013, p. DN-5, http://energy.gov/sites/prod/files/2013/04/f0/ Volume1.pdf (accessed January 25, 2014).

———. National Nuclear Security Administration, Office of Nonproliferation and International Security. "Implementing Safeguards-by-Design at Gas Centrifuge Enrichment Plants." ORNL/TM-2012/364. September 2012, http://nnsa.energy.gov/sites/default/files/nnsa/11-12-multiplefiles/2012-11- 15%203%20NGSI%20SBD%20Guidance_GCEPs-final.pdf.

———. Office of the Inspector General. *Inquiry into the Security Breach at the National Nuclear Security Administration's Y-12 National Security Complex.* DOE/IG-0868, Washington, DC: DOE, August 2012, http://energy.gov/sites/prod/files/IG-0868_0.pdf.

———. National Nuclear Security Administration, Office of Nonproliferation and International Security.

———. "Nonproliferation Impact Assessment for the Global Nuclear Energy Partnership: Programmatic Alternatives (Draft)." December 2008. Executive Summary, http://nnsa.energy.gov/sites/default/files/nnsa/inlinefiles/GNEP_NPIA.pdf.

———. *Nonproliferation and Arms Control Assessment of Weapons-usable Fissile Material Storage and Excess Plutonium Disposition Alternatives.* Washington, DC. January 1997, www.ipfmlibrary.org/doe97.pdf.

United States Department of Homeland Security. "About the Domestic Nuclear Detection Office." N.D., www.dhs.gov/about-domestic-nuclear-detection-office.

———. "National Technical Nuclear Forensics Center." N.D., www.dhs.gov/national-technical-nuclear-forensics-center.

United States Department of State. "The Global Initiative to Combat Nuclear Terrorism." US Department of State website, N.D., www.state.gov/t/isn/c18406.htm.

———. "Mission Statement." Office of Cooperative Threat Reduction, N.D., www.state.gov/t/isn/58381.htm.

———. "Office of Cooperative Threat Reduction (ISN/CTR)." US Department of State Website. N.D., www.state.gov/t/isn/58381.htm.

———. "Ship Boarding Agreements." N.D., www.state.gov/t/isn/c27733.htm.

———. "US-India Civil Nuclear Cooperation." N.D., www.state.gov/p/sca/c17361.htm.

———. The EXBS Program." N.D., www.state.gov/t/isn/ecc/c27911.htm.

———. "New START Treaty Aggregate Numbers of Strategic Offensive Arms." Fact Sheet, Bureau of Arms Control, Verification, and Compliance. April 1 2014, www.state.gov/documents/organization/224449.pdf.

———. "Joint Statement on the Contributions of the Global Initiative to Combat Nuclear Terrorism (GICNT) to Enhancing Nuclear Security." Office of the Spokesperson, Washington, DC, March 20, 2014, www.state.gov/r/pa/prs/ps/2014/03/223761.htm.

———. "Adherence To and Compliance With Arms Control, Nonproliferation, and Disarmament Agreements and Commitments." July 2013, www.state.gov/documents/organization/212096.pdf.

———. "Proliferation Security Initiative 10th Anniversary High Level Political Meeting: Chairman's Summary." May 28, 2013, www.state.gov/t/isn/c10390.htm.

———. "Proliferation Security Initiative 10th Anniversary: Joint Statement on Strengthening Authorities for Action." May 28, 2013, www.state.gov/t/isn/jtstmts/211499.htm.

———. "Proliferation Security Initiative 10th Anniversary High-Level Political Meeting Outcomes." Media Note, May 28, 2013, www.state.gov/r/pa/prs/ps/2013/05/210010.htm.

———. "Report on Maintaining US-China Strategic Stability." International Security Advisory Board. October 26, 2012, www.state.gov/documents/organization/200473.pdf.

———. "Proliferation Security Initiative: Participants." November 20, 2012, www.state.gov/t/isn/c27732.htm.

———. "PSI-Endorsing States Undertake Effort to Build Critical Capabilities and Practices (CCP) for Interdicting WMD." Fact Sheet, Bureau of International Security and Nonproliferation. June 10, 2011, www.state.gov/t/isn/166732.htm.

———. "Agreement Between the Government of the United States of America and the Government of the Russian Federation Concerning the Management and Disposition of Plutonium Designated as No Longer Required for Defense Purposes and Related Cooperation as amended by the 2010 Protocol." April 13, 2010, www.state.gov/documents/organization/18557.pdf.

———. "Treaty Between the United States and the Russian Federation on Measures for the Further Reduction and Limitation of Strategic Offensive Arms." April 8, 2010, www.state.gov/documents/organization/140035.pdf.

———. "START Aggregate Numbers of Strategic Offensive Arms (as of July 1, 2009, compiled from individual data submissions of the Parties)." Fact Sheet. October 1, 2009, www.state.gov/t/avc/rls/130149.htm.

———. "Missile Technology Control Regime (MTCR)." Fact Sheet, Bureau of International Security and Nonproliferation. March 4, 2009, www.state.gov/t/isn/rls/fs/120017.htm.

———. "Agreement Between the Government of the United States of America and the Government of Belize Concerning Cooperation to Suppress the Proliferation of Weapons of Mass Destruction, Their

Delivery Systems, and Related Materials by Sea." January 20, 2009, http://2001-2009.state.gov/t/isn/trty/50809.htm.

———. "Adherence To and Compliance With Arms Control, Nonproliferation, and Disarmament Agreements and Commitments." August 2005, www.state.gov/documents/organization/52113.pdf.

———. "Proliferation Security Initiative: Chairman's Conclusions at the Fourth Meeting." October 10, 2003, www.state.gov/t/isn/rls/other/25373.htm.

———. "The National Security Strategy of the United States of America." September 2002, www.state.gov/documents/organization/63562.pdf

———. "Treaty Between the United States and the Russian Federation on Strategic Offensive Reductions." May 24, 2002, www.state.gov/t/avc/trty/127129.htm.

———. "Treaty Between the United States of America and the Union of Soviet Socialist Republics on Underground Nuclear Explosions for Peaceful Purposes (and Protocol Thereto)." December 11, 1990, www.state.gov/www/global/arms/treaties/pne1.html.

———. "United States Information Pertaining to the Treaty on the Non-Proliferation of Nuclear Weapons." Third Review Conference of the Parties to the Treaty on the Non-Proliferation of Nuclear Weapons. NPT/CONF/III/18, July 29, 1985, www.un.org/disarmament/WMD/Nuclear/pdf/finaldocs/1985%20-%20Geneva%20-%20NPT%20Review%20Conference%20-%20Final%20Document%20Part%20II.pdf.

———. "US and Soviet Statement of Data on the Numbers of Strategic Offensive Forces as of the Date of Signature of the Treaty." June 18, 1979, www.state.gov/t/isn/5195.htm.

———. "Treaty Between the United States of America and the Union of Soviet Socialist Republics on the Limitation of Underground Nuclear Weapons Tests (and Protocol Thereto) (TTBT)." July 3, 1974, www.state.gov/t/isn/5204.htm.

———. Office of the Historian. "The Acheson-Lilienthal & Baruch Plans, 1946." http://history.state.gov/milestones/1945-1952/baruch-plans.

———. "Report of Committee on Atomic Energy by a Board of Consultants. [The Acheson-Lilienthal Report]." Washington, DC, March 16, 1946, www.learnworld.com/ZNW/LWText.Acheson-Lilienthal.html.

United States Government Printing Office. *Enhancing Non-proliferation Partnerships in the Black Sea Region.* Washington, 2011, www.gpo.gov/fdsys/pkg/CPRT-112SPRT68115/html/CPRT-112SPRT68115.htm.

———. *A Report on the International Control of Atomic Energy, Prepared for the Secretary of State's Committee on Atomic Energy.* Washington, DC, March 16, 1946, http://universityhonors.umd.edu/HONR269J/archive/AchesonLilienthal.htm.

US National Aeronautics and Space Administration. "Schematic of Laser-Induced Breakdown Spectroscopy." NASA mission website, www.nasa.gov/mission_pages/msl/multimedia/pia15103_prt.htm.

United States White House, Office of the Press Secretary. "Summary of Technical Understandings Related to the Implementation of the Joint Plan of Action on the Islamic Republic of Iran's Nuclear Program." January 16, 2014, www.whitehouse.gov/the-press-office/2014/01/16/summary-technical-understandings-related-implementation-joint-plan-actio.

———. Office of the Press Secretary. "Fact Sheet: First Step Understandings Regarding the Islamic Republic of Iran's Nuclear Program." November 23, 2013, www.whitehouse.gov/the-press-office/2013/11/23/fact-sheet-first-step-understandings-regarding-islamic-republic-iran-s-n.

———. Office of the Press Secretary. "Work Plan of the Washington Nuclear Security Summit." April 13, 2010, www.whitehouse.gov/the-press-office/work-plan-washington-nuclear-security-summit.

———. Office of the Press Secretary. *The National Security Strategy of the United States of America.* March 16, 2006, http://nssarchive.us/NSSR/2006.pdf.

———. Office of the Press Secretary. "Proliferation Security Initiative: Statement of Interdiction Principles." Fact Sheet, Washington, DC, September 4, 2003, www.state.gov/t/isn/c27726.htm.

———. Office of the Press Secretary. "President Bush Delivers Graduation Speech at West Point." June 1, 2002, http://georgewbush-whitehouse.archives.gov/news/releases/2002/06/20020601-3.html.

———. Office of the Press Secretary. "President Delivers the State of the Union Address." January 29, 2002 www.whitehouse.gov/news/releases/2002/01/print/20020129-11.html.

———. Office of the Press Secretary. "President Speaks on War Effort to Citadel Cadets." December 11, 2001, http://avalon.law.yale.edu/sept11/president_115.asp.

News sources

ABC News
Aviation Week
Defense News
Financial Times
Haaretz,
Japan Times
Los Angeles Times
Novosti
PBS
Reuters
The Hindu
Wall Street Journal

Associated Press
BBC News
Der Spiegel
Foreign Policy
Harijan
Jerusalem Post
Namib Times
Nuclear News
Perspective (Russia)
Tehran Bureau
Times of India
Washington Post

Assyrian International News Agency
Defence News India
Economic Times
Global Security Newswire
Hürriyet Daily News
Korean Central News Agency
New York Times
Pakistan Today
Rahbord
The Diplomat
US News & World Report
Yomiuri Shimbun

Books, journal articles, and internet sources

Abe, Nobuyasu and Hirofumi Tosaki. "Untangling Japan's Nuclear Dilemma: Deterrence before Disarmament." In *Disarming Doubt: The Future of Extended Nuclear Deterrence in East Asia*, edited by Rory Medcalf and Fiona Cunningham, 19–46. Woollahra: Lowy Institute for International Policy, 2012.

Abraham, Itty. "The Ambivalence of Nuclear Histories." *Osiris*, Vol. 21, No. 1 (2006): 49–65, www.jstor.org/stable/10.1086/507135.

———. *Making of the Indian Atomic Bomb: Science, Secrecy and the Postcolonial State.* London: Zed Books, 1998.

Acronym Institute for Disarmament Diplomacy. "IAEA Resolution on Iran's 'non Compliance' with NPT Safeguards." September 24, 2005, www.acronym.org.uk/official-and-govt-documents/iaea-resolution-irans-non-compliance-npt-safeguards.

Acton, James M., *Silver Bullet? Asking the Right Questions about Conventional Prompt Global Strike.* Washington DC: Carnegie Endowment for International Peace, 2013.

———. *Deterrence during Disarmament: Deep Nuclear Reductions and International Security.* Abingdon: Rout-ledge for IISS, 2011.

Acton, James and Dan Joyner. "Iran Violated International Obligations on Qom Facility." Carnegie Endowment for International Peace. September 25, 2009, http://carnegieendowment.org/2009/09/25/iran-violated-international-obligations-on-qom-facility/6u2.

Adler, Emanuel. "The Emergence of Cooperation: National Epistemic Communities and the International Evolution of the Idea of Nuclear Arms Control." *International Organization*, Vol. 46, No. 1 (Winter 1992): 101–145, www.jstor.org/stable/2706953?.

Albright, David. "The Rocky Path to a Long-Term Settlement with Iran." *The Washington Post*, November 25, 2013, www.washingtonpost.com/opinions/reaching-a-final-iran-deal-will-be-a-tough-road/2013/11/25/dcc2f752-55ef-11e3-ba82-16ed03681809_story.html.

———. "Challenges Posed by North Korea's Weapon-grade Uranium and Weapon-grade Plutonium: Current and Projected Stocks." *38 North*. October 24, 2012, http://38north.org/2012/10/dalbright102312

———. *Peddling Peril: How the Secret Nuclear Trade Arms America's Enemies.* New York: Free Press, 2010.

———. "How Much Plutonium Does North Korea Have?" *Bulletin of the Atomic Scientists*, Vol. 50, No. 5 (September/October 1994): 46–53.

Albright, David and Kevin O'Neill. *Solving the North Korean Nuclear Puzzle.* Washington, DC: Institute for Science and International Security, 2000.

Albright, David and Robert Avagyan. "Recent Doubling of Floor Space at North Korean Gas Centrifuge Plant." ISIS Imagery Brief, Institute for Science and International Security. August 7, 2013, http://isis-online.org/uploads/isis-reports/documents/Yongbyon_fuel_facility_7Aug2013.pdf.

Albright, David and Serena Kelleher-Vergantini. "Changes Visible at Parchin Nuclear Site: Why Parchin Matters to a Final Deal." ISIS Report, Institute for Science and International Security. February 25, 2014, http://isis-online.org/isis-reports/detail/changes-visible-at-parchin-nuclear-site/8.

Albright, David and Christina Walrond. "North Korea's Estimated Stocks of Plutonium and Weapons-Grade Uranium." ISIS Report, Institute for Science and International Security. August 16, 2012, http://isis-online.org/uploads/isis-reports/documents/dprk_fissile_material_production_16Aug2012.pdf.

Albright, David and Olli Heinonen. "In Response to Recent Questionable Claims about North Korea's Indigenous Production of Centrifuges." ISIS Report, Institute for Science and International Security. October 18, 2013, http://isis-online.org/isis-reports/detail/in-response-to-recent-questionable-claims-about-north-koreas-indigenous-pro.

Albright, David, Olli Heinonen and Orde Kittrie. "Understanding the IAEA's Mandate in Iran: Avoiding Misinterpretations." Institute for Science and International Security. November 27, 2012, http://isis-online.org/uploads/isis-reports/documents/Misinterpreting_the_IAEA_27Nov2012.pdf.

Albright, David, Patrick Migliorini, Christina Walrond and Houston Wood. "Maintaining at Least a Six-Month Breakout Timeline: Further Reducing Iran's Near 20 Percent Stock of LEU." ISIS Report, Institute for Science and International Security. February 17, 2004, http://isis-online.org/uploads/isis-reports/documents/20_pct_stock_cap_17Feb2014-final.pdf.

Albright, David and Paul Brannan. *Taking Stock: North Korea's Uranium Enrichment Program* (Washington, DC: The Institute of Science and International Security, October 8, 2010), http://isis-online.org/uploads/isis-reports/documents/ISIS_DPRK_UEP.pdf.

———. "North Korean Site After Nuclear Test." ISIS Imagery Brief, Institute for Science and International Security. October 17, 2006, http://isis-online.org/uploads/isis-reports/documents/dprktestbrief17october2006.pdf.

Albright, David, Paul Brannan, Mark Gorwitz and Andrea Stricker. "ISIS Analysis of IAEA Iran Safeguards Report: Part II – Iran's Work and Foreign Assistance on a Multipoint Initiation System for a Nuclear Weapon." ISIS Report, Institute for Science and International Security. November 13, 2011, http://isis-online.org/isis-reports/detail/irans-work-and-foreign-assistance-on-a-multipoint-initiation-system-for-a-n/.

Allen, Craig H. *Maritime Counterproliferation Operations and the Rule of Law*. Praeger Security International Reports. Westport, CT: Praeger, 2007.

Allison, Graham. "The Red-Zone Theory of the Iran Nuclear Deal." *The Atlantic,* November 27, 2013, www.theatlantic.com/international/archive/2013/11/the-red-zone-theory-of-the-iran-nuclear-deal/281918/.

———. "Deterring Kim Jong Il." *Washington Post*, October 27, 2006, www.washingtonpost.com/wp-dyn/content/article/2006/10/26/AR2006102601254.html.

———. *Nuclear Terrorism: The Ultimate Preventable Catastrophe*. New York: Times Books, 2004.

Al-Zawahiri, Ayman. *Exoneration: A Treatise Exonerating the Community of the Pen and the Sword from the Debilitating Accusation of Fatigue and Weakness*. March 2008, translated at the Federation of American Scientists, www.fas.org/irp/dni/osc/exoneration.pdf.

Amies, Nick. "US Concerns Over Nuclear Smuggling Between Europe, North Africa." *Deutsche Welle*, May 10, 2011, www.dw.de/dw/article/0,,15434811,00.html.

Annan, Kofi. "A Global Strategy for Fighting Terrorism: Keynote Address to the Closing Plenary." The International Summit on Democracy, Terrorism and Security, Madrid, 2005, http://english.safe-democracy.org/keynotes/a-global-strategy-for-fighting-terrorism.html.

Anthony, Ian. "Multilateral Export Controls." *SIPRI Yearbook 2002: Armaments, Disarmament and International Security* (Oxford: Oxford University Press, 2002): 752–755.

Anthony, Ian and Sibylle Bauer. "Controls on Security-Related International Transfers." *SIPRI Yearbook 2009: Armaments, Disarmament and International Security* (Oxford: Oxford University Press, 2009): 459–481.

Anthony, Ian, Christer Ahlström and Vitaly Fedchenko. *Reforming Nuclear Export Controls: The Future of the Nuclear Suppliers Group*, SIPRI Research Report no. 22 (Oxford: Oxford University Press, 2007).

Arend, Anthony Clark. "International Law and the Preemptive Use of Military Force." *Washington Quarterly*, Vol. 26, No. 2 (Spring 2003): 89–103.

Arendt, Hannah. *Between Past and Future: Eight Exercises in Political Thought*. New York: Penguin Books, 1993.

———. *The Human Condition*. Chicago, IL: University of Chicago Press, 1958.

Arms Control Association. "Chronology of US-North Korean Nuclear and Missile Diplomacy." February 2014. www.armscontrol.org/factsheets/dprkchron

———. "History of Official Proposals on the Iranian Nuclear Issue." January 2014, www.armscontrol.org/factsheets/Iran_Nuclear_Proposals.

———. "Arms Control and Proliferation Profile: North Korea." April 2013. www.armscontrol.org/factsheets/northkoreaprofile

———. "Nuclear Weapons: Who Has What at a Glance." April 2013, www.armscontrol.org/factsheets/ Nuclearweaponswhohaswhat

———. "Nuclear-Weapon-Free Zones (NWFZ) At a Glance." September 2012, www.armscontrol.org/ factsheets/nwfz.

Ayazbekov, Anuar. "Kazakhstan's Nuclear Decision-Making 1991–1992." *Nonproliferation Review*, Vol. 21, No. 2 (June 2014): 149–168.

Baker, Peter and Dafna Linzer. "Diving Deep, Unearthing a Surprise." *The Washington Post*, December 8, 2007, www.washingtonpost.com/wp-dyn/content/article/2007/12/07/AR2007120702418.html.

Baram, Amatzia. "An Analysis of Iraqi WMD Strategy." *Nonproliferation Review*, Vol. 8, No. 2 (Summer 2001): 25–39, http://cns.miis.edu/npr/pdfs/82baram.pdf.

———. *Building Toward Crisis: Saddam Hussein's Strategy for Survival*. Washington, DC: Washington Institute for Near East Policy, 1998.

Barefield, J.E. II, S.M. Clegg, Loan A. Le and Leon Lopez. "Development of Laser Induced Breakdown Spectroscopy Instrumentation for Safeguards Applications." Paper presented at Preparing for Future Verification Challenges: Symposium on International Safeguards, International Atomic Energy Agency, Vienna, November 1–5, 2010, www.iaea.org/safeguards/Symposium/2010/Documents/Papers Repository/134.pdf.

Bari, Robert A. "Proliferation Resistance and Physical Protection (PR&PP) Evaluation Methodology: Objectives, Accomplishments and Future Directions." Proceedings of Global 2009, Paris, France, September 6–11, 2009, http://cybercemetery.unt.edu/archive/brc/20120621022022/http://brc.gov/ sites/default/filef/meetings/attachments/bari_9013-final.pdf.

Barletta, Michael. "The Military Nuclear Program in Brazil." CISAC Working Paper. Center for International Security and Cooperation. Stanford University. August 1997, http://iis-db.stanford.edu/ pubs/10340/barletta.pdf.

Bathke, Charles G., Bartley B. Ebbinghaus, Brad W. Sleaford, Richard K. Wallace, Brian A. Collins, Kevin R. Hase, Martin Robel, Gordon D. Jarvinen, Keith S. Bradley, John R. Ireland, M.W. Johnson, Andrew W. Prichard, and Brian W. Smith. "The Attractiveness of Materials in Advanced Nuclear Fuel Cycles for Various Proliferation and Theft Scenarios." *Nuclear Technology*, Vol. 179, No. 1 (July 2012): 5–30.

Baude, S. "HEU Seized in July 2001 in Paris: Analytical Investigations Performed on the Material." IAEA-CN-154/009, Proc. International Conference on Illicit Nuclear Trafficking: Collective Experience and the Way Forward, IAEA, Edinburgh. November 19–22, 2007.

Bauer, Sibylle. "Arms Trade Control Capacity Building: Lessons from Dual-Use Trade Controls." *SIPRI Insights on Peace and Security*, No. 2013/2 (March 2013), http://books.sipri.org/files/insight/SIPRI Insight1302.pdf.

———. "Developments in the Nuclear Suppliers Group." SIPRI Yearbook 2012: *Armaments, Disarmament and International Security* (Oxford: Oxford University Press, 2012): 376–386.

———. "Enhancing Export Control-Related CTR (Cooperative Threat Reduction) Programs: Options for the EU." Background Paper No. 6, Conference on Strengthening European Action on WMD Nonproliferation and Disarmament: How Can Community Instruments Contribute? Brussels, December 7–8, 2005, www.sipri.org/research/disarmament/dualuse/publications/papers_publications/BP6.

Bauer, Sibylle, Aaron Dunne and Ivana Mićić. "Strategic Trade Controls: Countering the Proliferation of Weapons of Mass Destruction." *SIPRI Yearbook 2011: Armaments, Disarmament and International Security* (Oxford: Oxford University Press, 2011): 441–443.

Beamont, Paul D. and Thomas Rubinsky. "An Introduction to the Issue of Nuclear Weapons in Latin America and the Caribbean." Background Paper, No. 2, Nuclear Weapons Project, International Law and Policy Institute. December 2012.

Beck, Michael and Seema Gahlaut. "Creating a New Multilateral Export Control Regime." *Arms Control Today*, Vol. 33, No. 3 (April 2003): 12–18, www.armscontrol.org/act/2003_04/beckgahlaut_apr03.

Bellucci, Jeremy J. and Antonio Simonetti. "Nuclear Forensics: Searching for Nuclear Device Debris in Trinitite-Hosted Inclusions." *Journal of Radioanalytical and Nuclear Chemistry*, Vol. 293, No. 1 (July 2012): 313–319, http://link.springer.com/article/10.1007%2Fs10967-012-1654-9.

Bergman, Eric A. and E. Robert Engdahl. "Analysis of the Location Capability of the International Monitoring System." ISS09 Conference, International Scientific Studies Project, Seismo-03/I section (Vienna, Austria). June 10–12, 2009, www.ctbto.org/fileadmin/user_upload/ISS_2009/Poster/SEISMO-03I%20%28US%29%20-%20Eric_Bergman%20and%20ER_Engdahl%20%28location%29.pdf.

Betts, Richard K. "The Lost Logic of Deterrence." *Foreign Affairs*, Vol. 92, No. 2 (March/April 2013): 87–99.

Beukes, Marshallino. "Uranium Theft Case Heads to Regional Court." *Namib Times*, September 6, 2013.

Bidwai, Praful and Achin Vanaik. *New Nukes: India, Pakistan and Global Disarmament*. New York: Olive Branch Press, 2000.

Bhabha, Homi J. and N.B. Prasad. *A Study of the Contribution of Atomic Energy to a Power Programme in India*. Proceedings of the Second United Nations International Conference on the Peaceful Uses of Atomic Energy. Geneva, 1958.

Bin, Li. "China." In *Country Perspectives on the Challenges to a Fissile Material (Cutoff) Treaty*. International Panel on Fissile Materials. Princeton University, 2008, pp. 7–13, http://fissilematerials.org/library/gfmr08 cv.pdf.

Blacker, Coit D. and Gloria Duffy,(eds), *International Arms Control: Issues and Agreements* (Palo Alto, CA: Stanford University Press, 1984), pp. 219–254.

Blechman, Barry M. "Extended Deterrence: Cutting Edge of the Debate on Nuclear Policy." Policy Forum Online 09-066A, August 13th, 2009, www.nautilus.org/publications/essays/napsnet/forum/2009-2010/09066Blechman.html/.

Boese, Wade. "NSG, Congress Approve Nuclear Trade with India." *Arms Control Today*, Vol. 38, No. 8 (October 2008): 27–28, www.armscontrol.org/act/2008_10/NSGapprove.

———. "Key US Interdiction Initiative Claim Misrepresented." *Arms Control Today*, Vol. 35, No. 5 (July–August 2005): 26–27, www.armscontrol.org/print/1848.

Bowen, Wyn Q. "Intelligence, Interdiction, and Dissuasion: Lessons from the Campaign against Libyan Proliferation." In *Over the Horizon Proliferation Threats*, edited by James J. Wirtz. and Peter R. Lavoy, 221–239. Palo Alto, CA: Stanford University Press, 2012.

———. "Libya, Nuclear Rollback, and the Role of Negative and Positive Security Assurances." In *Security Assurances and Nuclear Nonproliferation*, edited by Jeffrey W. Knopf, 89–110. Palo Alto, CA: Stanford University Press, 2012.

———. *Libya and Nuclear Proliferation: Stepping Back from the Brink*. London: Routledge, 2006.

Bracken, Paul. *Fire in the East: The Rise of Asian Military Power and the Second Nuclear Age*. New York: Harper Collins, 2009.

———. "The Structure of the Second Nuclear Age." *Orbis*, Vol. 47, No. 3 (Summer 2003): 399–413.

Braun, Chaim and Christopher F. Chyba. "Proliferation Rings: New Challenges to the Nuclear Nonproliferation Regime." *International Security*, Vol. 29, No. 2 (Fall 2004): 5–49.

Braut-Hegghammer, Malfrid. "Revisiting Osirak: Preventive Attacks and Nuclear Proliferation Risks." *International Security*, Vol. 36, No. 1 (Summer 2011): 101–132.

———. "Libya's Nuclear Turnaround: Perspectives from Tripoli." *Middle East Journal*, Vol. 62, No. 1 (Winter 2008): 55–72.

Brigagao, Clovis and Marcelo F. Valle Fonrouge. "A Regional Model of Confidence Building for Nuclear Security in Argentina and Brazil." *The International Journal of Peace Studies*, Vol. 3, No. 2 (July 1998), www.gmu.edu/programs/icar/ijps/vol3_2/Brigagao.htm.

Bromley, Mark and Paul Holtom. "Implementing an Arms Trade Treaty: Mapping Assistance to Strengthen Arms Transfer Controls." *SIPRI Insights on Peace and Security*, No. 2012/2 (July 2012), http://books.sipri.org/files/insight/SIPRIInsight1202.pdf.

Brown, Harold. "New Nuclear Realities." *The Washington Quarterly*, Vol. 31, No. 1 (Winter 2007–08): 7–22, http://home.comcast.net/~lionelingram/Nuclear_matters_08winter_brown.pdf.

Bundy, McGeorge, William J. Crowe, Jr and Sidney D. Drell, "Reducing Nuclear Danger." *Foreign Affairs*, Vol. 72, No. 2 (Spring 1993): 141–155.

Bunn, George. "The Legal Status of US Negative Security Assurances to Non-Nuclear Weapon States." *The Nonproliferation Review*, Vol. 4, No. 3 (Spring-Summer 1997): 1–17, http://cns.miis.edu/npr/pdfs/bunn43.pdf.

———. *Arms Control by Committee: Managing Negotiations with the Russians*. Palo Alto, CA: Stanford University Press, 1992.

Bunn, George and Roland Timerbaev. *Nuclear Verification Under the NPT: What Should It Cover – How Far May It Go?* Program for Promoting Nuclear Non-Proliferation, April 1994.

Bunn, Matthew. *Securing the Bomb 2010: Securing all Nuclear Materials in Four Years*. Cambridge, MA: Project on Managing the Atom, Belfer Center for Science and International Affairs, Harvard Kennedy School of Government and Nuclear Threat Initiative, April 2010, www.nti.org/media/pdfs/Securing_The_Bomb_2010.pdf.

———. *Securing the Bomb 2008*. Cambridge, MA: Project on Managing the Atom, Belfer Center for Science and International Affairs, Harvard Kennedy School of Government and Nuclear Threat Initiative, November 2008, www.nti.org/media/pdfs/Securing_The_Bomb_2008.pdf.

———. "Incentives for Nuclear Security." Proceedings of the 46th Annual Meeting of the Institute for Nuclear Materials Management, Phoenix, Arizona, July 10–14, 2005, Northbrook, IL: INMM, 2005, http://belfercenter.ksg.harvard.edu/files/inmm-incentives2-05.pdf.

———. "Proliferation-Resistance (and Terror-Resistance) of Nuclear Energy Systems." Lecture presented for "Nuclear Energy Economics and Policy Analysis." Managing the Atom Project, Harvard University, April 12, 2004, http://ocw.mit.edu/courses/nuclear-engineering/22-812j-managing-nuclear-technology-spring-2004/lecture-notes/lec17slides.pdf.

Bunn, Matthew and Anthony Wier. "Terrorist Nuclear Weapon Construction: How Difficult?" *Annals of the American Academy of Political and Social Science,* Vol. 607 (September 2006): 133–149.

Bunn, Matthew and Eben Harrell. *Threat Perceptions and Drivers of Change in Nuclear Security Around the World: Results of a Survey.* Cambridge, MA: Project on Managing the Atom, Harvard University, March 2014, http://belfercenter.ksg.harvard.edu/files/surveypaperfulltext.pdf.

———. *Consolidation: Thwarting Nuclear Theft.* Cambridge, MA: Project on Managing the Atom, Harvard University, March 2012, www.nuclearsummit.org/files/Consolidation_Thwarting_Nuclear_Theft.pdf.

Bunn, Matthew and Evgeniy P. Maslin. "All Stocks of Weapons-Usable Nuclear Materials Worldwide Must be Protected Against Global Terrorist Threats." *Journal of Nuclear Materials Management,* Vol. 39, No. 2 (Winter 2011): 21–27.

Bunn, Matthew, Martin Malin, Nickolas Roth and William H. Tobey. *Advancing Nuclear Security: Evaluating Progress and Setting New Goals.* Cambridge, MA: Project on Managing the Atom, Belfer Center for Science and International Affairs, Harvard Kennedy School, March 2014, http://belfercenter.ksg.harvard.edu/files/advancingnuclearsecurity.pdf.

Bunn, Matthew and Scott D. Sagan. *A Worst Practices Guide to Insider Threats: Lessons from Past Mistakes.* Cambridge, MA: American Academy of Arts and Sciences, April 2014, www.amacad.org/content/publications/publication.aspx?d=1425.

Bunn, Matthew, Steve Fetter, John Holdren and Bob van der Zwaan. "The Economics of Reprocessing vs. Direct Disposal of Spent Nuclear Fuel." *Nuclear Technology,* Vol. 150 (June 2005): 209–230.

Bunn, Matthew, Yuri Morozov, Rolf Mowatt-Larssen, Simon Saradzhyan, William H. Tobey, Viktor I. Yesin and Pavel S. Zolotarev. *The US-Russia Joint Threat Assessment of Nuclear Terrorism.* Cambridge, MA: Belfer Center for Science and International Affairs, Harvard Kennedy School, and Institute for US and Canadian Studies, June 2011, http://belfercenter.ksg.harvard.edu/publication/21087/.

Burgess, Stephen F. and Togzhan Kassenova. "The Rollback States: South Africa and Kazakhstan." In *Slaying the Nuclear Dragon. Disarmament Dynamics in the Twenty-First Century,* edited by Tanya Ogilvie-White and David Santoro, 85–117. Athens, GA: University of Georgia Press, 2012.

Burr, William. "'We can't go on the way we are': US Proposals for a Fissile Material Production Cutoff and Disarmament Diplomacy during the 1950s and 60s." National Security Archive. June 16, 2010, www2.gwu.edu/~nsarchiv/nukevault/ebb321.

Burr, William and Avner Cohen. "Israel's Secret Uranium Buy: How Argentina Fuelled Ben-Gurion's Nuclear Program." *Foreign Policy,* July 1, 2013, www.foreignpolicy.com/articles/2013/07/01/israels_secret_uranium_buy.

Burr, William and Hector L. Montford. "The Making of the Limited Test Ban Treaty 1958–1963." National Security Archive, August 8, 2003, www2.gwu.edu/~nsarchiv/NSAEBB/NSAEBB94/.

Burr, William and Jeffrey T. Richelson. "Whether to 'Strangle the Baby in the Cradle': The United States and the Chinese Nuclear Program, 1960–64." *International Security,* Vol. 25, No. 3 (Winter 2000/01): 54–99, http://belfercenter.ksg.harvard.edu/files/burr_and_richelson_winter_00_01.pdf.

Burt, Peter. "UK-France Nuclear Co-operation: The 'Teutates' Project." Presentation at Non-Proliferation Treaty PrepCom Meeting, April 23, 2013, http://nuclearinfo.org/sites/default/files/01%20NIS%20NPT%20presentation%20on%20Teutates%20project%20230413_0.pdf.

Bush, George W. *Decision Points.* New York: Crown, 2010.

Bush, Richard C. "The US Policy of Extended Deterrence in East Asia: History, Current Views, and Implications." Brookings Arms Control Series, No. 5, Brookings Institution, February 2011, www.brookings.edu/~/media/research/files/papers/2011/2/arms%20control%20bush/02_arms_control_bush.pdf.

Butler, Desmond. "Officials Say Crime Ring has Uranium." *Associated Press,* September 27, 2011, www.theguardian.com/world/feedarticle/9866962.

Calogero, Francesco. "Nuclear Terrorism." Nobel Peace Prize Centennial Symposium, Oslo, Norway, December 6–8, 2001, www.pugwash.org/september11/sept11-calogero.htm.

Carasales, Julio C. "The So-Called Proliferator That Wasn't: The Story of Argentina's Nuclear Policy." *Nonproliferation Review,* Vol. 6, No. 4 (Fall 1999): 51–64.

———. "The Argentine-Brazilian Nuclear Rapprochement." *The Nonproliferation Review*, Vol. 2, No. 3 (Spring-Summer 1995): 39–48, http://cns.miis.edu/npr/pdfs/carasa23.pdf.

Carlson, John. "Assessing and Minimizing Proliferation Risk." *International Luxembourg Forum*, forthcoming.

———. "Introduction to the Concept of Proliferation Resistance." ICNND Research Paper, No.8, revised June 3, 2009, http://a-pln.org/sites/default/files/apln-analysis-docs/Proliferation_Resistance.pdf.

Carter, Barry. *International Economic Sanctions: Improving the Haphazard US Legal Regime.* Cambridge: Cambridge University Press, 1988.

Center for Nonproliferation Studies. "Illicit Trafficking in Weapons-Usable Nuclear Material: Still More Questions than Answers." December 11, 2011, www.nti.org/analysis/articles/illicit-trafficking-weapons-useable-nuclear-material-still-more-questions-answers/.

Centre Virtuel de la Connaissance sur l'Europe. "The Rapacki Plan." February 14, 1958, www.cvce.eu/content/publication/2005/12/22/c7c21f77-83c4-4ffc-8cca-30255b300cb2/publishable_en.pdf.

Cha, Victor D. and David C. Kang. "The Debate over North Korea." *Political Science Quarterly*. Vol. 119, No. 2 (Summer 2004): 229–254.

———. *Nuclear North Korea: A Debate on Engagement Strategies.* New York: Columbia University Press, 2003.

Chinoy, Mike. *Meltdown: The Inside Story of the North Korean Nuclear Crisis.* New York: St Martin's Press, 2009.

Chivers, Daniel H., Bethany F. Lyles Goldblum, Brett H. Isselhardt and Jonathan S. Snider. "Before the Day After: Using Pre-Detonation Nuclear Forensics to Improve Fissile Material Security." *Arms Control Today*, Vol. 38, No. 6 (July/August 2008): 22–23, 25–28, www.armscontrol.org/act/2008_07-08/NuclearForensics.

Cirincione, Joseph. "A Global Assessment of Nuclear Proliferation Threats." Paper Prepared for the Weapons of Mass Destruction Commission. June 2004, www.blixassociates.com/wp-content/uploads/2011/03/No10.pdf.

Clary, Christopher and Mara E. Karlin. "The Pak-Saudi Nuke, and How to Stop It." *American Interest*, Vol. 7, No. 6 (July–August 2012): 24–30.

Clemens, Jr., Walter C. "North Korea's Quest for Nuclear Weapons: New Historical Evidence." *Journal of East Asian Studies*, Vol. 10, No. 1 (January–April 2010): 127–154.

Cohen, Avner. *Israel and the Bomb.* New York, NY: Columbia University Press, 1998.

Cohen, Avner and Marvin Miller. "Israel." In *Banning the Production of Fissile Materials for Nuclear Weapons: Country Perspectives on the Challenges to a Fissile Material (Cutoff) Treaty*, International Panel on Fissile Materials, Princeton University, September 2008, pp. 27-33, http://fissilematerials.org/library/FMCT-Perspectives.pdf.

Collina, Tom and Daniel Horner. "The South Asian Nuclear Balance: An Interview with Pakistani Ambassador to the CD Zamir Akram." *Arms Control Today*, Vol. 41, No. 10 (December 2011): 8–13, www.armscontrol.org/act/2011_12/Interview_With_Pakistani_Ambassador_to_the_CD_Zamir_Akram.

Corera, Gordon. *Shopping for Bombs, Nuclear Proliferation, Global Insecurity, and the Rise and Fall of the A.Q. Khan Network.* Oxford: Oxford University Press, 2006.

Cortright, David and George A. Lopez. *The Sanctions Decade: Assessing UN Strategies in the 1990s.* Boulder, CO: Lynne Rienner Publishers, Inc., 2000.

Cotta-Ramusino, Paolo and Maurizio Martellini. "Interview of Pakistan's former Director-General of the Strategic Plans Division, Khalid Kidwai." Landau Network-Centro Volta. February 2002, www.pugwash.org/september11/pakistan-nuclear.htm.

Council on Foreign Relations. "Obama's Speech in Prague on New START Treaty." April 8, 2010, www.cfr.org/proliferation/obamas-speech-prague-new-start-treaty-april-2010/p21849.

Craig, Campbell and Jan Ruzicka. "The Nonproliferation Complex." *Ethics & International Affairs*, Vol. 27, No. 3 (Fall 2013): 329–348.

Craig, Gordon A. and Alexander L. George. *Force and Statecraft: Diplomatic Problems of Our Time.* Oxford: Oxford University Press, 1983.

Dahlman, Ola, Jenifer Mackby, Svein Mykkeltveit and Hein Haak. *Detect and Deter: Can States Verify the Nuclear Test Ban?* Dordrecht, Netherlands: Springer, 2011.

Dahlman, Ola, Svein Mykkeltveit and Hein Haak. *Nuclear Test Ban – Converting Political Visions to Reality.* Dordrecht, Netherlands: Springer, 2009.

Dai, Xinyuan. *International Institutions and National Policies.* Cambridge: Cambridge University Press, 2007.

Daly, Sara, John Parachini and William Rosenau. *Aum Shinrikyo, al Qaeda, and the Kinshasa Reactor:*

Implications of Three Case Studies for Combating Nuclear Terrorism. Santa Monica, CA: RAND, 2005, www.rand.org/content/dam/rand/pubs/documented_briefings/2005/RAND_DB458.pdf.

Davenport, Kelsey. "WMD-Free Middle East Proposal at a Glance." Arms Control Association. July 2013, www.armscontrol.org/factsheets/mewmdfz.

Daugherty, Debra. "Russian-American MPC&A." *Los Alamos Science*, No. 24 (1996): 72–86, www.fas.org/sgp/othergov/doe/lanl/pubs/00326622.pdf.

Davis, Jay. "Post Detonation Nuclear Forensics." In *Nuclear Weapons Issues in the 21st Century*, edited by Pierce S. Corden, David Hafemeister and Peter Zimmerman, 206–209. AIP Conference Proceedings, Vol. 1596, AIP Publishing, 2014.

———. "Nuclear Forensics: A Capability We Hope Never to Use." APS Workshop on Nuclear Weapons Issues in the 21st Century, George Washington University, November 3, 2013, http://elliott.gwu.edu/sites/elliott.gwu.edu/files/downloads/events/4.8%20Davis%20slides.ppt.

Davis, Zachary. "The Yin and Yang of Strategic Transparency." in *Deterrence Stability and Escalation Control in South Asia*, edited by Michael Krepon and Julia Thompson, 175–186. Washington, DC: Henry L. Stimson Center, 2013.

Decker, Debra K. "Before the First Bomb Goes Off: Developing Nuclear Attribution Standards and Policies." Discussion Paper 2011-03, Belfer Center for Science and International Affairs, Harvard Kennedy School, Cambridge, Massachusetts, April 2011, http://belfercenter.ksg.harvard.edu/files/Decker_DP_2011_FINAL.pdf.

De Geera, Lars-Erik. "Radionuclide Evidence for Low-Yield Nuclear Testing in North Korea." *Science & Global Security*, Vol. 20, No. 1 (2012): 1–29.

Deming, Angus, Ron Moreau and David C. Marin. "Two Minutes over Baghdad." *Newsweek*, Vol. 97, No. 25 (June 22, 1981): 22.

DeThomas, Joseph. "Next Steps in Sanctions against Pyongyang." *38 North*. March 3, 2014, http://38north.org/2014/03/jdethomas030314.

Devenport, Kelsey. "India Moves Closer to Nuclear Triad." *Arms Control Today*, Vol. 42, No. 7 (September 2012): 32–33, http://armscontrol.org/act/2012_09/India-Moves-Closer-to-Nuclear-Triad.

Dobrianski, Paula and David Rivkin Jr. "Ukraine Must Wish it had Kept its Nukes." *USA Today*, March 6, 2004.

Dodge, Michaela. "US Nuclear Weapons in Europe: Critical for Transatlantic Security." Backgrounder No. 2875, Heritage Foundation, February 18, 2014, www.heritage.org/research/reports/2014/02/us-nuclear-weapons-in-europe-critical-for-transatlantic-security.

Dolgov, J., Y.K. Bibilashvili, N.A. Chorokhov, A. Schubert, G. Janssen, K. Mayer and L. Koch. "Installation of a Database for Identification of Nuclear Material of Unknown Origin." Proceedings of the 21st ESARDA Symposium, Sevilla, Spain, 1999, https://esarda.jrc.ec.europa.eu/index.php?option=com_jifile&filename=ZTNlNzRmMWI4YjkzZTIzNGRlZmI4MzI2MjU0NTJlYTA=.

Drell, Sidney D. and Raymond Jeanloz. "Nuclear Deterrence After Zero." Paper Presentation, Conference on Deterrence: Its Past and Future at the Hoover Institution. November 11, 2010, www.cna.org/sites/default/files/news/2011/Goodby_DeterrenceCONF_FINAL_SCRIBD.pdf.

Dunne, Aaron. "The Proliferation Security Initiative: Legal Considerations and Operational Realities." SIPRI Policy Paper no. 36. Stockholm: Stockholm International Peace Research Institute, May 2013.

Du Preez, Jean. "The Demise of Nuclear Negative Security Assurances." Article VI Forum, Ottawa, Canada, September 28, 2006, http://cns.miis.edu/programs/ionp/pdfs/visions_of_fission.pdf.

Du Preez, Jean and Thomas Maettig. "From Pariah to Nuclear Poster Boy: How Plausible Is a Reversal?." In *Forecasting Nuclear Proliferation in the 21st Century Vol. 2*, edited by William Potter and Gaukhar Mukhatzhanov, 302–336. Palo Alto, CA: Stanford University Press, 2010.

Durst, P.C., R. Wallace, I. Therios, M. H. Ehinger, R. Bean, D.N. Kovacic, A. Dougan, K. Tolk and B. Boyer. "Advanced Safeguards Approaches for New Reprocessing Facilities." Pacific Northwest National Laboratory, PNNL-16674. June 2007, www.pnl.gov/main/publications/external/technical_reports/pnnl-16674.pdf.

Edwards, Rob. "Three of Britain's nuclear warheads are being dismantled every year." August 11, 2013, www.robedwards.com/2013/08/three-of-britains-nuclear-warheads-are-being-dismantled-every-year.html.

Einhorn, Robert. "Understanding the Lessons of Nuclear Inspections and Monitoring in Iraq: A Ten-Year Review." Institute for Science and International Security. June 14, 2001, http://isis-online.org/einhorn/.

Einhorn, Robert J. and Gary Samore. "Ending Russian Assistance to Iran's Nuclear Bomb." *Survival*, Vol. 44, No. 2 (Summer 2002): 51–70.

Eisenstadt, Michael and Mehdi Khalaji. "Nuclear Fatwa: Religion and Politics in Iran's Proliferation Strategy." Washington Institute for Near East Policy. September 2011, www.washingtoninstitute.org/uploads/Documents/pubs/PolicyFocus115.pdf.

ElBaradei, Mohamed. Quoted in "World Institute for Nuclear Security (WINS) is Launched in Vienna; New Organization Will Strengthen Security for Nuclear Materials." Nuclear Threat Initiative. September 28, 2008, p. 2, www.nti.org/media/pdfs/release_WINS_092908.pdf?_=1316466791.

———. "Toward a Safer World." *The Economist*, Vol. 369 (October 18, 2003): 47–48, www.economist.com/node/2137602.

Federation of American Scientists. "Article I: Basic Obligations." *Article-by-Article Analysis of the Comprehensive Test Ban Treaty*, May 18, 2011, www.fas.org/nuke/control/ctbt/text/artbyart/index.html.

———. "Intermediate-Range Nuclear Forces." December 8, 1987, www.fas.org/nuke/control/inf/intro.htm.

———. "Memorandum of Understanding on the Establishment of the Data Base Relating to the Treaty between the United States of America and the Union of Soviet Socialist Republics on the Reduction and Limitation of Strategic Offensive Arms." November 1, 1978, www.fas.org/nuke/control/salt2/text/salt2-4.htm.

Feldman, Shai. "The Bombing of Osiraq – Revisited." *International Security*, Vol. 7, No. 2 (Fall 1982): 114–142.

Ferguson, Charles D., Tahseen Kazi and Judith Perera. "Commercial Radioactive Sources: Surveying the Risks." Occasional Paper No. 11, Center for Nonproliferation Studies, Monterey Institute of International Studies, Monterey, CA, January 2003, http://cns.miis.edu/opapers/op11/op11.pdf.

Fergusson, Ian and Paul K. Kerr. "US Export Control System and the President's Reform Initiative." Federation of American Scientists. CRS Report R41916. January 13, 2014, www.fas.org/sgp/crs/natsec/R41916.pdf.

Fetter, Steve. "Nuclear Archaeology: Verifying Declarations of Fissile Material Production." *Science and Global Security*, Vol. 3, No. 3–4 (1993): 237–259.

Financial Action Task Force. "High-risk and Non-cooperative Jurisdictions." February 2014, www.fatf-gafi.org/topics/high-riskandnon-cooperativejurisdictions.

———. "International Standards on Combating Money Laundering and the Financing of Terrorism and Proliferation: The FATF Recommendations." February 2012, www.fatf-gafi.org/media/fatf/documents/recommendations/pdfs/FATF_Recommendations.pdf.

Findlay, Trevor. *Beyond Nuclear Summitry: The Role of the IAEA in Nuclear Security Diplomacy After 2016*. Cambridge, MA: Project on Managing the Atom, Belfer Center for Science and International Affairs, Harvard Kennedy School, March 2014, http://belfercenter.ksg.harvard.edu/files/beyondnuclearsummitryfullpaper.pdf.

———. *Unleashing the Nuclear Watchdog: Strengthening and Reform of the IAEA*. Ontario: Canadian Center for Treaty Compliance, 2012, www.cigionline.org/sites/default/files/Unleashing_the_Nuclear_Watchdog.pdf.

Fitzpatrick, Mark. "The Surprisingly Good Geneva Deal." *Politics and Strategy Blog*. International Institute for Strategic Studies. November 25, 2013, www.iiss.org/en/politics%20and%20strategy/blogsections/2013-98d0/november-47b6/geneva-deal-0ef2.

Flournoy, Michèle A. "Implications for US Military Strategy." In *New Nuclear Nations: Consequences for US Policy*, edited by Robert D. Blackwill and Albert Carnesale, 135–161. New York: Council on Foreign Relations Press, 1993.

Ford, Christopher. "The NPT Regime and the Challenge of Shaping Proliferation Behavior." In *Over the Horizon Proliferation Threats*, edited by James J. Wirtz and Peter R. Lavoy, 179–204. Palo Alto, CA: Stanford University Press, 2012.

———. "Nuclear Weapons Reconstitution and its Discontents: Challenges of 'Weaponless Deterrence.'" In *Deterrence: Its Past and Future*, edited by George P. Shultz, Sidney D. Drell and James E. Goodby, 131–216. Stanford, CA: Hoover Institution Press, 2011.

———. "Misinterpreting the NPT." New Paradigms Forum. October 24, 2011, www.newparadigmsforum.com/NPFtestsite/?p=1100.

———. "Weapons Reconstitution and Strategic Stability." New Paradigms Forum. May 23, 2011, www.newparadigmsforum.com/NPFtestsite/?p=886.

———. "Nuclear Technology Rights and Wrongs: The Nuclear Nonproliferation Treaty, Article IV, and Nonproliferation." In *Reviewing the Nuclear Nonproliferation Treaty*, edited by Henry Sokolski, 237–384. Carlisle, PA: Strategic Studies Institute, 2010.

Frank, Jerome D. and John C. Rivard. "Antinuclear Admirals: An Interview Study." *Political Psychology*, Vol. 7, No. 1 (March 1986): 23–52, www.jstor.org/stable/3791155.

Freedman, Lawrence. "Disarmament and other Nuclear Norms." *Washington Quarterly*, Vol. 36, No. 2 (Spring 2013): 93–108.

———. "Framing Strategic Deterrence." *Royal United States Institute Journal*, Vol. 10, No. 4 (August 2009): 46–50.

Furukawa, Katsuhisa. "Japan's Nuclear Option." In *Over the Horizon Proliferation Threats*, edited by James Wirtz and Peter Lavoy, 13–32. Palo Alto, CA: Stanford University Press, 2012.

Garthoff, Raymond L. "Evaluating and Using Historical Hearsay." *Diplomatic History*, Vol. 14, No. 2 (April 1990): 223–230, http://onlinelibrary.wiley.com/doi/10.1111/j.1467-7709.1990.tb00086.x/abstract.

Gasner, Alex and Alexander Glasner. "Nuclear Archaeology for Heavy-Water-Moderated Plutonium Production Reactors." *Science & Global Security*, Vol. 19, No. 3 (2011): 223–233, http://scienceandglobalsecurity.org/archive/sgs19gasner.pdf.

Gavin, Francis J. *Nuclear Statecraft: History and Strategy in America's Atomic Age*. Cornell, NY: Cornell University Press, 2012.

———. "Nuclear Proliferation and non-proliferation during the Cold War." In *Cambridge History of the Cold War. Vol. 2: Crises and Détente*, edited by Melvyn Leffler and Odd Arne Westad, 395–416. Cambridge: Cambridge University Press, 2010.

George, Alexander. "Case Studies: The Method of 'Structured, Focused Comparison.'" In *Diplomacy: New Approaches in History, Theory and Policy,* edited by Paul Gordon Lauren, 43–68. New York: Free Press, 1979.

Gandhi, Mahatma. "Atom Bomb and Ahimsa." *Harijan*, July 7, 1946, http://meaindia.nic.in/pmicd.geneva/?50031131.

Gilinsky, Victor and Roger J. Mattson. "Did Israel Steal Bomb-grade Uranium from the United States?" *Bulletin of the Atomic Scientists,* April 17, 2014, thebulletin.org/did-israel-steal-bomb-grade-uranium-united-states7056.

———. "Revisiting the NUMEC Affair." *Bulletin of the Atomic Scientists*, Vol. 66, No. 2 (March 2010): 61–75.

Glaser, A. and S. Burger. "Verification of a Fissile Material Cutoff Treaty: The Case of Enrichment Facilities and the Role of Ultra-trace Level Isotope Ratio Analysis." *Journal of Radioanalytical and Nuclear Chemistry*, Vol. 280, No. 1 (April 2009): 85–90, http://link.springer.com/article/10.1007%2Fs10967-008-7423-0.

Glaser, Alexander and Frank von Hippel. "Thwarting Nuclear Terrorism." *Scientific American*, Vol. 294, No. 2 (February 2006): 56–63.

Glenn, L.A. and P. Goldstein. "Seismic Decoupling with Chemical and Nuclear Explosions in Salt." *Journal of Geophysical Research*, Vol. 99, No. B6 (June 1994): 11723–11730, http://onlinelibrary.wiley.com/doi/10.1029/94JB00497/abstract.

Gerami, Nima. "Leadership Divided? The Domestic Politics of Iran's Nuclear Debate." *Policy Focus*, No. 134, Washington Institute for Near East Policy. February 2014, www.washingtoninstitute.org/uploads/PolicyFocus134_Gerami-2.pdf.

Glitman, Maynard W. *The Last Battle of the Cold War: An Inside Account of Negotiating the Intermediate Range Nuclear Forces Treaty*. New York: Palgrave MacMillan, 2006.

Goldberg, Stephen, James Glasgow and James Malone, "'TRUST,' An Innovative Nuclear Fuel Leasing Arrangement." Presentation to the World Nuclear Fuel Cycle Conference (Helsinki, Finland). 18 April 2007, www.wnfc.info/proceedings/2007/presentations/goldberg_glasgow_maloneppt.pdf.

Goldblat, Jozef. "Nuclear-Weapon-Free Zones: A History and Assessment." *The Nonproliferation Review*, Vol. 4, No. 3 (Spring-Summer 1997): 18–32, http://cns.miis.edu/npr/pdfs/goldbl43.pdf.

Goldschmidt, Pierre. "Measures Needed to Strengthen the Nuclear Non-Proliferation Regime." In *NATO and the Future of the Nuclear Non-Proliferation Treaty*, edited by Joseph F. Pilat and David S. Yost, Occasional Paper no. 21. Rome: NATO Defense College, May 2007.

Goldstein, Lyle J. *Preventive Attack and Weapons of Mass Destruction: A Comparative Historical Analysis*. Palo Alto, CA: Stanford University Press, 2006.

Gompert, David and Phillip Saunders, *The Paradox of Power: Sino-American Strategic Restraints in an Age of Vulnerability*. Washington, DC: National Defense University Press, 2011.

Gordin, Michael. *Red Cloud at Dawn: Truman, Stalin, and the End of the Atomic Monopoly*. New York: Farrar, Straus, and Giroux, 2009.

Goto, Minoru. "Conceptual Design Study of High Temperature Gas-cooled Reactor for Plutonium

Incineration." IAEA Deep Burn Technical Meeting, Vienna, Austria. August 5–8, 2013, www.iaea.org/NuclearPower/Downloadable/Meetings/2013/2013-08-05-08-07-TM-NPTD/6_pu_incineration.pdf.

Graham, Thomas Jr., Leonor Tomero and Leonard Weiss. "Think Again: US-India Nuclear Deal." *Foreign Policy*, July 24, 2006, www.foreignpolicy.com/articles/2006/07/23/think_again_us_india_nuclear_deal.

Grand, Camille. "The Hague Code of Conduct: 10 years of Combating Ballistic Proliferation." *Non-Proliferation Monthly*, No. 74 (Special Issue, January 2013): 1, www.cesim.fr/documents/onp/eng/74.pdf.

Green, Michael and Katsuhisa Furukawa. "Japan: New Nuclear Realism." In *The Long Shadow: Nuclear Weapons and Security in 21st Century Asia*, edited by Muthiah Alagappa, 347–372. Palo Alto, CA: Stanford University Press, 2008.

Gregory, Shaun. "The Terrorist Threat to Nuclear Weapons in Pakistan." European Leadership Network, June 4, 2013, www.europeanleadershipnetwork.org/the-terrorist-threat-to-nuclear-weapons-in-pakistan_613.html.

Guarino, Douglas P. "Nuclear Security Program Review Complete, But Questions Remain." *Global Security Newswire*, March 7, 2013, www.nti.org/gsn/article/nonproliferation-program-review-complete-questions-remain.

Gujer, Eric. *Kampf an neuen Fronten*. Frankfurt am Main: Campus Verlag, 2006.

Gusterson, Hugh. "Nuclear Weapons and the Other in the Western Imagination." *Cultural Anthropology*, Vol. 14, No. 1 (February 1999): 111–143.

Ha, Young-sun. "Nuclearization of Small States and World Order: the Case of Korea." *Asian Survey*, Vol. 18, No. 11 (November 1978): 1134–1151.

Hanson, Marianne. "Advocating the Elimination of Nuclear Weapons: The Role of Key Individual and Coalition States." In *Slaying the Nuclear Dragon. Disarmament Dynamics in the Twenty-First Century*, edited by Tanya Ogilvie-White and David Santoro, 56–84. Athens, GA: University of Georgia Press, 2012.

Hansen, Nick. "Major Development: Reactor Fuel Fabrication Facilities Identified at Yongbyon Nuclear Complex." *38 North*. December 23, 2013, http://38north.org/2013/12/yongbyon122313.

Hansen, Nick and Jeffrey Lewis. "Satellite Images Show New Construction at North Korea's Plutonium Production Reactor: Rapid Start?" *38 North*. April 3, 2013, http://38north.org/2013/04/yongbyon040313.

Harrington de Santana, Anne I. "The Strategy of Nonproliferation: Maintaining the Credibility of an Incredible Pledge to Disarm." *Millennium*, Vol. 40, No.1 (August 2011): 3–19.

Harrison, Selig. "Did North Korea Cheat?" *Foreign Affairs*. Vol. 84. No. 1 (January/February 2005). pp. 99–110.

Healey, Denis. *The Time of My Life*. London: Michael Joseph, 1989.

Hecker, Siegfried. "A Return Trip to North Korea's Yongbyon Nuclear Complex." Center for International Security and Cooperation. November 20, 2010, http://iis-db.stanford.edu/pubs/23035/HeckerYongbyon.pdf.

———. "The Risks of North Korea's Nuclear Restart." *Bulletin of the Atomic Scientists*. May 12, 2009, http://thebulletin.org/risks-north-koreas-nuclear-restart.

Heinonen, Olli. "The North Korean Nuclear Program in Transition." *38 North*. April 26, 2012, http://38north.org/2012/04/oheinonen042612.

———. "North Korea's Nuclear Enrichment: Capabilities and Consequences." *38 North*. June 22, 2011, http://38north.org/2011/06/heinonen062211.

Helms, Jesse. "What Sanctions Epidemic?: US Business' Curious Crusade." *Foreign Affairs*, Vol. 78, No. 1 (January/February 1999): 2–8.

Hibbs, Mark. "Power Loop: China Provides Nuclear Reactors to Pakistan." *Jane's Intelligence Review*, December 30, 2013: 50–53, http://carnegieendowment.org/email/DC_Comms/img/JIR1401%20F3%20ChinaPak.pdf.

———. "The Plan for IAEA Safeguards." Carnegie Endowment for International Peace. November 20, 2012, http://carnegieendowment.org/2012/11/20/plan-for-iaea-safeguards/ekyb.

———. "The Unspectacular Future of the IAEA Additional Protocol." *Proliferation Analysis*. Carnegie Endowment for International Peace. April 26, 2012, http://carnegieendowment.org/2012/04/26/unspectacular-future-of-iaea-additional-protocol.

———. *The Future of the Nuclear Suppliers Group* (Washington, DC: Carnegie Endowment for International Peace, 2011).

———. "The Breach." *Foreign Policy*, June 4, 2010, www.foreignpolicy.com/articles/2010/06/04/the_breach.

———. "Russia Improving Protection for Sensitive Nuclear Sites." *Nucleonics Week*, March 30, 1995, pp. 12–13.

Hinderstein, Corey. *Cultivating Confidence: Verification, Monitoring, and Enforcement for a World Free of Nuclear Weapons.* Washington DC: Nuclear Threat Initiative, 2010.

Holloway, David. *Stalin and The Bomb.* New Haven, CT: Yale University Press, 1994.

Holmes, James and Toshi Yoshihara. "Thinking about the Unthinkable: Tokyo's Nuclear Option." In *Strategy in the Second Nuclear Age*, edited by Toshi Yoshihara and James Holmes, 115–132. Washington, DC: Georgetown University Press, 2012.

Horner, Daniel. "NSG Revises List, Continues India Debate." *Arms Control Today*, Vol. 43, No. 6 (July/August 2013): 36–37, www.armscontrol.org/act/2013_0708/NSG-Revises-List-Continues-India-Debate.

———. "NSG Revises Rules on Sensitive Exports." *Arms Control Today*, Vol. 41, No. 6 (July/August 2011): 29–30, www.armscontrol.org/act/2011_%2007-08/Nuclear_Suppliers_Group_NSG_Revises_Rules_Sensitive_Exports.

Hunter, Tom, Michael Anastasio and Georde Miller. "Tri-Lab Director's Joint Statement on the Nuclear Posture Review." Sandia National Laboratories, Press Release, April 9, 2010, https://share.sandia.gov/news/resources/news_releases/tri-lab-directors'-statement-on-the-nuclear-posture-review/#.U0v7utyXSZ8.

Hoodbhoy, Pervez (ed.), *Confronting the Bomb: Pakistani and Indian Scientists Speak Out.* Oxford: Oxford University Press, 2013.

Hufbauer, Gary Clyde, Jeffrey J. Schott, Kimberly Ann Elliott and Barbara Oegg. *Economic Sanctions Reconsidered.* 3rd Edition. Washington, DC: Peterson Institute for International Economics, 2007.

Hurtado de Mendoza, Diego. "Periferia y fronteras tecnológicas: Energía nuclear y dictadura militar en la Argentina (1976–1983)." *Revista Iberoamericana de Ciencia Tecnología y Sociedad*, Vol. 5, No. 13 (September 2009): 27–64.

Hymans, Jacques E.C. *Achieving Nuclear Ambitions: Scientists, Politicians and Proliferation.* Cambridge: Cambridge University Press, 2012.

———. "The Study of Nuclear Proliferation and Nonproliferation: Toward a New Consensus?" In *Forecasting Nuclear Proliferation in the 21st Century*, edited by William Potter and Gaukhar Mukhatzhanova, 13–37. Palo Alto, CA: Stanford University Press, 2010.

———. "When Does a State Become a 'Nuclear Weapons State?': An Exercise in Measurement Validation." In *Forecasting Nuclear Proliferation in the 21st Century*, edited by William Potter and Gaukhar Mukhatzhanova, 102–123. Palo Alto, CA: Stanford University Press, 2010.

———. *The Psychology of Nuclear Proliferation: Identity, Emotions and Foreign Policy.* Cambridge: Cambridge University Press, 2006.

———. "Of Gauchos and Gringos: Why Argentina Never Wanted The Bomb, and Why America Thought It Did." *Security Studies*, Vol. 10, No. 3 (Spring 2001): 153–185.

Ingram, Paul and Oliver Meier, (eds). "Reducing the Role of Tactical Nuclear Weapons in Europe: Perspectives and Proposals on the NATO Policy Debate." Report by the Arms Control Association and British American Security Information Council, May 2011, www.armscontrol.org/system/files/Tactical_Nuclear_Report_May_11.pdf.

Institute for Science and International Security. "Internal IAEA Information Links the Supreme Leader to 1984 Decision to Seek a Nuclear Arsenal." April 20, 2012, http://isis-online.org/uploads/isis-reports/documents/Khamenei_1984_statement_20April2012.pdf.

———. "Update on the Arak Reactor in Iran." ISIS Report. August 25, 2009, http://isis-online.org/uploads/isis-reports/documents/Arak_Update_25_August2009.pdf.

———. "ISIS Imagery Brief: Destruction at Iranian Site Raises New Questions About Iran's Nuclear Activities." ISIS Report. June 17, 2004, http://isis-online.org/isis-reports/detail/isis-imagery-brief-destruction-at-iranian-site-raises-new-questions-about-i/8.

International Civil Aviation Organization. "AVSEC Professional Management Course." N.D. www.icao.int/security/isd/avsecpmc/Pages/default.aspx.

———. "Convention on the Suppression of Unlawful Acts Relating to International Civil Aviation." September 10, 2010, www.icao.int/secretariat/legal/Docs/beijing_convention_multi.pdf.

International Framework for Nuclear Energy Cooperation. "IFNEC Reliable Nuclear Fuel Services Working Group (RNFSWG) Summary." February 24, 2013, www.ifnec.org/Meetings/RNFSWG Meetings.aspx.

————. "Membership." www.ifnec.org/About/Membership.aspx.

International Institute for Strategic Studies. "Anti-Access/Area Denial: Washington's Response." In *The Military Balance 2013*. London: International Institute for Strategic Studies, 2013.

————. "Illicit Trafficking in Radioactive Materials." In *Nuclear Black Markets: Pakistan, A.Q. Khan and the Rise of Proliferation Networks: A Net Assessment*, 119–138. London: International Institute for Strategic Studies, 2007.

————. "Nuclear Black Markets: Pakistan, A.Q. Khan and the Rise of Proliferation Networks." *IISS Strategic Dossier*, May 2, 2007, www.iiss.org/en/publications/strategic%20dossiers/issues/nuclear-black-markets—pakistan—a-q—khan-and-the-rise-of-proliferation-networks—-a-net-assessmen-23e1.

————. "Pakistan and North Korea: Dangerous Counter-Trades." *IISS Strategic Comments*, Vol. 8, No. 9 (November 2002), pp. 1–2, http://carnegieendowment.org/pdf/npp/Pakistan-and-North-Korea.pdf

International Law and Policy Institute. "An Introduction to the Issue of Nuclear Weapons in Southeast Asia." Background Papers, Nuclear Weapons Project. June 2013, http://nwp.ilpi.org/?p=2024.

International Maritime Organization. "Status of Conventions as at 28 February 2014." www.imo.org/About/Conventions/StatusOfConventions/Documents/status-x.xls.

————. "Adoption of the Final Act and Any Instruments, Recommendations and Resolutions Resulting from the Work of the Conference: Protocol of 2005 to the Convention for the Suppression of Unlawful Acts against the Safety of Maritime Navigation." International Conference on the Revision of the SUA Treaties. LEG/CONF.15/21. November 1, 2005, www.state.gov/t/isn/trty/81727.htm.

International Panel on Fissile Materials. "Global Fissile Material Report 2013: Increasing Transparency of Nuclear Warhead and Fissile Material Stocks as a Step toward Disarmament." Princeton University, October 2013, www.fissilematerials.org/library/gfmr13.pdf.

————. "UK nuclear warhead dismantlement program." August 26, 2013, fissilematerials.org/blog/2013/08/uk_nuclear_warhead_disman.html.

————. "India." February 4, 2013, www.fissilematerials.org/countries/india.html.

————. "Pakistan." February 3, 2013, www.fissilematerials.org/countries/pakistan.html.

————. "Global Fissile Material Report 2010: Balancing the Books: Production and Stocks." Princeton University Press, 2010, http://fissilematerials.org/library/gfmr10.pdf.

————. "Global Fissile Material Report 2009: A Path to Nuclear Disarmament." Princeton University, October 2009, www.fissilematerials.org/library/gfmr09.pdf.

————. *Country Perspectives on the Challenges to a Fissile Material (Cutoff) Treaty*. Princeton, NJ: Princeton University Press, 2008.

————. "Global Fissile Material Report 2008: Scope and Verification of a Fissile Material (Cutoff) Treaty." Princeton, NJ: Princeton University Press, 2008.

————. "Global Fissile Material Report 2007." Princeton University Press, 2007, http://fissilematerials.org/library/gfmr07.pdf.

————. "Global Fissile Material Report 2006." www.fissilematerials.org/ipfm/site_down/ipfmreport06.pdf.

International Uranium Enrichment Center. Mission Statement, http://eng.iuec.ru.

Jakobsen, Peter Viggo. "Reinterpreting Libya's WMD Turnaround – Bridging the Carrot-Coercion Divide." *Journal of Strategic Studies*, Vol. 35, No. 4 (August 2012): 489–512.

James Martin Center for Nonproliferation Studies. "Inventory of International Nonproliferation Organizations and Regimes." Monterey Institute of International Studies. May 10, 2013, http://cns.miis.edu/inventory/.

————. "NWFZ Clearinghouse." Monterey Institute of International Studies. April 28, 2010, http://cns.miis.edu/nwfz_clearinghouse.

Jasper, Ursula. *The Politics of Nuclear Non-Proliferation: A Pragmatist Framework for Analysis*. London: Routledge, 2013.

————. "Ambivalent Neutral: Rereading Switzerland's Nuclear History." *Nonproliferation Review*, Vol. 19, No. 2 (June 2012): 267–292.

Jentleson, Bruce and Christoper Whytlock. "Who Won Libya?: The Force-Diplomacy Debate and its Implications for Theory and Policy." *International Security*, Vol. 30, No. 3 (Winter 2005/2006): 47–86.

Jervis, Robert. "Getting to Yes with Iran: The Challenges of Coercive Diplomacy." *Foreign Affairs*, Vol. 92. No. 1 (January/February 2013): 105–115.

Johnson, Shirley. "Safeguards at Reprocessing Plants under a Fissile Material (Cutoff) Treaty." IPFM Research Report #6, International Panel on Fissile Materials, Princeton University Press, February 2009, http://fissilematerials.org/library/rr06.pdf.

Johnson, Shirley and Michael Ehinger. "Designing and Operating for Safeguards: Lessons Learned From the Rokkasho Reprocessing Plant (RRP)." Pacific Northwest National Laboratory, PNNL-19626. August 2010, www.pnl.gov/main/publications/external/technical_reports/pnnl-19626.pdf.

Johnson, Shirley, Mike Ehinger and Mark Schanfein. "Report on the NGS3 Working Group on Safeguards by Design for Aqueous Reprocessing Plants." PNNL-20226. February 2011, www.pnnl.gov/main/publications/external/technical_reports/PNNL-20226.pdf.

Jonas, David S., John Carlson and Richard S. Goorevich. "The NSG Decision on Sensitive Nuclear Transfers: ABACC and the Additional Protocol." *Arms Control Today*, Vol. 42, No. 9 (November 2012): 14–17, www.armscontrol.org/act/2012_11/The-NSG-Decision-on-Sensitive-Nuclear-Transfers-ABACC-and-the-Additional-Protocol.

Jonter, Thomas. *Explaining Nuclear Forbearance: Sweden and the Plans to Acquire Nuclear Weapons, 1945–1968.* Palo Alto, CA: Stanford University Press, forthcoming.

———. "The United States and Swedish Plans to Build the Bomb, 1945–68." In *Security Assurances and Nuclear Nonproliferation*, edited by Jeffrey W. Knopf, 219–245. Palo Alto, CA: Stanford University Press, 2012.

Joseph, Robert G. *Countering WMD: The Libyan Experience.* Fairfax, VA: National Institute Press, 2009.

Joyner, Daniel H. *Interpreting the Nuclear Non-Proliferation Treaty.* Oxford: Oxford University Press, 2011.

Kahneman, Daniel. *Thinking Fast and Slow.* New York: Penguin, 2011.

Kahneman, Daniel and Amos Tversky. "Choices, Values, and Frames." *American Psychologist*, Vol. 39, No. 4 (April 1984): 341–350.

Kamp, Karl-Heinz and Robertus Remkes. "Options for NATO Nuclear Sharing Arrangements." In *Reducing Nuclear Risks in Europe: A Framework for Action*, edited by Steve Andersen and Isabelle Williams, 13–32. Washington, DC: Nuclear Threat Initiative, 2011.

Kanga, Jungmin and Frank N. von Hippel. "U-232 and the Proliferation-Resistance of U-233 in Spent Fuel." *Science & Global Security*, Vol. 9, No. 1 (2001): 1–32.

Karp, Regina C. *Security without Nuclear Weapons?: Different Perspectives on Non-Nuclear Security.* Oxford: SIPRI, 1992.

Kaysen, Carl, Robert S. McNamara and George W. Rathjens. "Nuclear Weapons After the Cold War." *Foreign Affairs*, Vol. 70, No. 4 (Fall 1991): 95–110.

Keaney, Thamas A. and Eliot Cohen. *Revolution in Warfare? Air Power in the Persian Gulf.* Annapolis, MD: Naval Institute Press, 1995.

Keifer, Michael, Kurt Guthe and Thomas Scheber. *Assuring South Korea and Japan as the Role and Number of Nuclear Weapons are Reduced.* Ft. Belvoir: Defense Threat Reduction Agency, January 2011, www.nipp.org/Publication/Downloads/Downloads%202012/2011%20003%20Assuring%20ROK%20and%20Japan.pdf.

Kelly, James A. "US-East Asia Policy: Three Aspects." Remarks at the Woodrow Wilson Center. Washington, DC. December 11, 2002, http://2001-2009.state.gov/p/eap/rls/rm/2002/15875.htm.

Kemp, R. Scott. "A Performance Estimate for the Detection of Undeclared Nuclear-fuel Reprocessing by Atmospheric 85Kr." *Journal of Environmental Radioactivity*, Vol. 99, No. 8 (August 2008): 1341–1348.

Kennedy, Andrew B. "India's Nuclear Odyssey: Implicit Umbrellas, Diplomatic Disappointments, and the Bomb." *International Security*, Vol. 36, No. 2 (Fall 2011): 120–153.

Kerr, Paul K. "Iran's Nuclear Program: Tehran's Compliance with International Obligations." Congressional Research Service. March 31, 2009, www.fas.org/sgp/crs/nuke/R40094.pdf.

Kessler, Günther. *Proliferation-proof Uranium/Plutonium Fuel Cycles.* Karlsruhe, Germany: KIT Scientific Publishing, November 24, 2011.

Khan, Feroz. *Eating Grass: The Making of the Pakistani Bomb.* Palo Alto, CA: Stanford University Press, 2012.

Khan, Feroz and Gurmeet Kanwal. "Building Trust in South Asia through Cooperative Retirement of Obsolescent Missiles." Centre for Land Warfare Studies. September 4, 2011, www.claws.in/Building-Trust-in-South-Asia-through-Cooperative-Retirement-of-Obsolescent-Missiles-Gurmeet-Kanwal.html.

Kiernan, Kevin. "Why Do States Give Up Nuclear Arsenals?" *Bologna Center Journal of International Affairs*, Vol. 17 (2013), http://bcjournal.org/volume-11/why-do-states-give-up-nuclear-arsenals.html.

Kim, Duyeon. "Fact Sheet: North Korea's Nuclear and Ballistic Missile Programs." The Center for Arms Control and Non-Proliferation. July 2013, http://armscontrolcenter.org/issues/northkorea/articles/fact_sheet_north_korea_nuclear_and_missile_programs.

Kimball, Daryl G. "Is the NSG Up to the Task?" *Arms Control Today*, Vol. 40, No. 6 (July/August 2010): 4, www.armscontrol.org/act/2010_07/Focus.

Kimball, Daryl and Tom Collina. "Nuclear Weapons: Who Has What at a Glance." Arms Control Association. November 2013, www.armscontrol.org/factsheets/Nuclearweaponswhohaswhat.

Kissinger, Henry A. and Brent Scowcroft. "Nuclear Weapon Reductions Must Be Part of Strategic Analysis." *The Washington Post*, April 22, 2012, www.washingtonpost.com/opinions/nuclear-weapon-reductions-must-be-part-of-strategic-analysis/2012/04/22/gIQAKG4iaT_story.html.

Kissling, Claudia. *Civil Society and Nuclear Non-Proliferation: How Do States Respond?* Aldershot: Ashgate, 2013.

Klingner, Bruce. "Time to Go Beyond International North Korean Sanctions." *38 North*. April 29, 2014, http://38north.org/2014/04/bklingner042914.

Knopf, Jeffrey (ed.), *Security Assurances and Nuclear Nonproliferation*. Palo Alto, CA: Stanford University Press, 2012.

Krass, Allan, Peter Boskma, Boelie Elzen and Wim A. Smit. *Uranium Enrichment and Nuclear Proliferation*. London: Taylor & Francis, 1983.

Krepon, Michael and Julia Thompson. *Deterrence Stability and Escalation Control in South Asia*. Washington DC: Henry L. Stimson Center, 2013, www.stimson.org/images/uploads/research-pdfs/Deterrence_Stability_Dec_2013_web.pdf.

Kreps, Sarah E. and Matthew Fuhrmann. "Attacking the Atom: Does Bombing Nuclear Facilities Affect Proliferation? Targeting Nuclear Programs in War and Peace: A Quantitative Empirical Analysis, 1941–2000." *Journal of Conflict Resolution*, Vol. 54, No. 6 (December 2010): 831–859.

Krige, John. "The Proliferation Risks of Gas Centrifuge Enrichment at the Dawn of the NPT." *The Nonproliferation Review*, Vol. 19, No. 2 (July 2012): 219–227, www.tandfonline.com/doi/abs/10.1080/10736700.2012.690961#.UYswj7VBO4I.

Kristensen, Hans M. "US Nuclear Weapons in Europe. A Review of Post-Cold War Policy, Force Levels, and War Planning." National Resources Defense Council, February 2005, www.nrdc.org/nuclear/euro/euro.pdf.

Kristensen, Hans M. and Robert S. Norris. "US Nuclear Forces, 2014." *Bulletin of the Atomic Scientists*, Vol. 70, No. 1 (January/February 2014): 85–93.

———. "Global Nuclear Weapons Inventories, 1945–2013." *Bulletin of Atomic Scientists*, Vol. 69, No. 5 (September/October 2013): 75–81.

———. "Nuclear Notebook: Indian Nuclear Forces, 2012." *Bulletin of Atomic Scientists*, Vol. 68, No. 4 (July/August, 2012): 96–101, http://bos.sagepub.com/content/68/4/96.full.pdf+html.

———. "Pakistan's Nuclear Forces, 2011." *Bulletin of the Atomic Scientists*, Vol. 67, No. 4 (July/August 2011), http://bos.sagepub.com/content/67/4/91.full.pdf+html.

Kuno, Yusuke and J.S. Choi. *Nuclear Eye*, Vol. 55, No. 5 (2009): 59–62.

Kurosaki, Akira. *Kakuheiki to nichibei kankei: Amerika no kaku fukakusan gaikou to Nihon no sentaku, 1960–1976* [Nuclear Weapons and Japan-US Relations: US Nuclear Non-proliferation Policy and Japan's Choice, 1960–1976]. Tokyo: Yushisha, 2006.

Kutchesfahani, Sara Z. *Politics and the Bomb: The Role of Experts in the Creation of Cooperative Non-proliferation Agreements.* London: Routledge, 2013.

Kuzma, Heidi and Sheila Vaidya. "Data Mining." In *Science for Security*. Report from the International Scientific Studies Conference (Vienna, Austria), June 10–12, 2009, 47–53, www.ctbto.org/fileadmin/user_upload/pdf/ISS_Publication/Data_Mining_47-52.pdf.

Kuznetsov, V.M.. "Osnovnyye problemy i sovremennoye sostoyaniye bezopasnosti predpriyatiy yadernogo toplivnogo tsikla Rossiyskoy Federatsii." [Main Problems and Current State of Security of Nuclear Cycle Facilities in the Russian Federation] *AtomSafe*, www.atomsafe.ru, Moscow, 2001.

Kvaerna, Tormod, Frode Ringdahl, Johannes Schweitzer and Lyla Taylor. "Optimized Seismic Threshold Monitoring Part 1: Regional Processing." *Pure and Applied Geophysics*, Vol. 159, No. 5 (March 2002): 969–987.

Kyl, Jon. "Why We Need to Test Nuclear Weapons." Op-ed. *The Wall Street Journal*, October 20, 2009, http://online.wsj.com/news/articles/SB10001424052748704500604574483224117732120.

Kyl, Jon and Richard Perle. "Our Decaying Nuclear Deterrent." Op-ed. *The Wall Street Journal*, June 30, 2009, http://online.wsj.com/news/articles/SB124623202363966157.

Lal Bahadur Shastri. "Speech in the Lok Sabha on March 2, 1065, during the discussion on the President's Address." In *Selected Speeches of Lal Bahadur Shastri, June 11, 1964–January 10, 1966*. Ministry of Information and Broadcasting, 2007.

Langwiesche, William. *The Atomic Bazaar: The Rise of the Nuclear Poor*. New York: Farrar, Straus and Giroux, 2007.

Larsen, Jeffrey A. "NATO Counterproliferation Policy: A Case Study in Alliance Politics." Air Force Academy Institute for National Security Studies, Occasional Paper #17, November 1997, www.fas.org/irp/threat/ocp17.htm.

Lee, Rensselaer W. *Smuggling Armageddon: The Nuclear Black Market in the Former Soviet Union and Europe.* New York: St Martin's Griffin, 1999.

Lesniewski, Niels. "Schumer, Menedez Renew Calls for New Iran Sanctions." *#WGBD Blog,* Roll Call. November 24, 2013, http://blogs.rollcall.com/wgdb/schumer-menendez-renew-calls-for-new-iran-sanctions/.

Levi, Barbara, G. David, H. Albright and Frank von Hippel, "Stopping the Production of Fissile Materials for Weapons." *Scientific American,* Vol. 253, No. 3 (September 1985): 40–47.

Levi, Michael. *On Nuclear Terrorism.* Cambridge, MA: Harvard University Press, 2007.

Levite, Ariel. "Never Say Never Again: Nuclear Reversal Revisited." *International Security,* Vol. 27, No. 3 (Winter 2002/03): 59–88.

Lewis, Jeffrey. *The Minimum Means of Reprisal: China's Search for Security in the Nuclear Age.* Cambridge: MIT Press, 2007.

Liang, Xiaodon. "The Six-Party Talks at a Glance." Arms Control Association, May 2012, www.arms control.org/factsheets/6partytalks.

Lifton Robert J. and Richard Falk. *Indefensible Weapons: The Political and Psychological Case Against Nuclearism.* New York: Basic Books, 1991.

Lindsay, James M. and Ray Takeyh. "After Iran Gets the Bomb: Containment and Its Complications." *Foreign Affairs,* Vol. 89, No. 2 (March/April 2010): 33–49.

Litwak, Robert. S. *Outlier States: American Strategies to Change, Contain, or Engage Regimes.* Baltimore, MD and Washington, DC: Johns Hopkins University Press and Wilson Center Press, 2012.

———. *Regime Change: US Strategy through the Prism of 9/11.* Baltimore, MD and Washington, DC: Johns Hopkins University Press and Wilson Center Press, 2007.

———. *Rogue States and US Foreign Policy: Containment after the Cold War.* Washington, DC: Woodrow Wilson Center Press and Johns Hopkins University Press, 2000.

Luttwak, Edward N. "In a Single Night." *Wall Street Journal,* February 8, 2006, http://online.wsj.com/news/articles/SB113937026599968085.

Lyon, Rod. "The Challenges Confronting US Extended Nuclear Deterrence in Asia." *International Affairs,* Vol. 89, No. 4 (July 2013): 929–941.

Ma, Chunyan and Frank von Hippel. "Ending the Production of Highly Enriched Uranium for Naval Reactors." *The Nonproliferation Review,* Vol. 8, No. 1 (Spring 2001): 86–101, http://cns.miis.edu/npr/pdfs/81mahip.pdf.

Makino, Yoshihiro. "US Shows Nuclear Facilities to Reassure Japan, Allies on Deterrence." *Asahi Shimbun,* July 30, 2013, http://ajw.asahi.com/article/behind_news/politics/AJ201307300096.

Manyin, Mark. "Kim Jong-il's Death: Implications for North Korea's Stability and US Policy." Congressional Research Service. December 22, 2011, www.fas.org/sgp/crs/row/R42126.pdf.

May, Michael M., Reza Abedin-Zadeh, Donald A. Barr, Albert Carnesale, Philip E. Coyle, Jay Davis, Bill Dorland, Bill Dunlop, Steve Fetter, Alexander Glaser, Ian D. Hutcheon, Francis Slakey and Benn Tannenbaum. "Nuclear Forensics: Role, State of the Art, Program Needs." Report by the Joint Working Group of the American Physical Society Panel on Public Affairs and the American Association for the Advancement of Science, Center for Science, Technology and Security Policy, Washington, DC, February 2008, http://iis-db.stanford.edu/pubs/22126/APS_AAAS_2008.pdf.

Mayer, K., M. Wallenius and A. Schubert. "Data Interpretations in Nuclear Forensics." IAEA Nuclear Security Symposium, IAEA-CN-166/13, Vienna, Austria, March 30–April 3, 2009, www-pub.iaea.org/mtcd/meetings/PDFplus/2009/cn166/CN166_Presentations/Session%209/010%20Mayer.pdf.

Mayer, Klaus, Maria Wallenius and Zsolt Varga. "Nuclear Forensic Science: Correlating Measurable Material Parameters to the History of Nuclear Material." *Chemical Reviews,* Vol. 113, No. 2 (February 2013): 884–900.

Mazarr, Michael J. "The Notion of Virtual Arsenals." In *Nuclear Weapons in a Transformed World,* edited by Michael J. Mazarr, 3–33. New York: St Martin's Press, 1997.

———. *North Korea and the Bomb: A Case Study in Nonproliferation.* New York: St Martin's Press, 1995.

McCarthy, Timothy V. and Jonathan B. Tucker. "Saddam's Toxic Arsenal: Chemical and Biological Weapons in the Gulf Wars." In *Planning the Unthinkable: How New Powers Will Use Nuclear, Biological, and Chemical Weapons,* edited by Peter R. Lavoy, Scott D. Sagan and James J. Wirtz, 47–78. Ithaca, NY: Cornell University Press, 2000.

McGoldrick, Fred. *Limiting Transfers of Enrichment and Reprocessing Technology: Issues, Constraints. Options* (Cambridge, MA: Harvard Kennedy School, May 2011).

McGwire, Michael and Lee Butler. In *Alternative Nuclear Futures: The Role of Nuclear Weapons in the Post-Cold War World*, edited by John Baylis and Robert O'Neill. Oxford and New York: Oxford University Press, 2000.

McNamee, Terence. "Afrikanerdom and Nuclear Weapons: A Cultural Perspective on Nuclear Proliferation and Rollback in South Africa." PhD diss., London School of Economics and Political Science, 2002.

Mearsheimer, John. "The Case for a Ukrainian Nuclear Deterrent." *Foreign Affairs*, Vol. 72, No. 3 (Summer 1993): 50–66, http://johnmearsheimer.uchicago.edu/pdfs/A0020.pdf.

Medalia, Jonathan. "Comprehensive Nuclear Test-Ban Treaty: Background and Current Developments." Congressional Research Service, June 10, 2013, www.fas.org/sgp/crs/nuke/RL33548.pdf.

———. "North Korea's 2009 Nuclear Test: Containment, Monitoring Implications." Congressional Research Service, November 24, 2010, www.fas.org/sgp/crs/nuke/R41160.pdf.

Medcalf, Rory and Fiona Cunningham, (eds). *Disarming Doubt: The Future of Extended Nuclear Deterrence in East Asia*. Woollahra: Lowy Institute for International Policy, 2012.

Meier, Oliver. "Germany Opposes United States on China-Pakistan Nuclear Deal." *Arms Control Now*, Arms Control Association blog, June 21, 2011, http://armscontrolnow.org/2011/06/21/germany-opposes-united-states-on-china-pakistan-nuclear-deal/.

Meier, Oliver and Simon Lunn. "Trapped: NATO, Russia and the Problem of Tactical Nuclear Weapons." *Arms Control Today*, Vol. 44, No. 1 (January/February 2014): 18–24.

Mian, Zia and A.H. Nayyar. "Playing the Nuclear Game: Pakistan and the Fissile Material Cutoff Treaty." *Arms Control Today*, Vol. 40, No. 3 (April 2010): 17–24, www.armscontrol.org/act/2010_04/Mian.

Miller, Nicholas L. "Nuclear Dominoes: A Self-Defeating Prophecy?" *Security Studies*, Vol. 23, No. 1 (January–March 2014): 33–73.

Miller, Steven E. *Nuclear Collisions: Discord, Reform & the Nuclear Nonproliferation Regime*. Cambridge, MA: American Academy of Arts and Sciences, 2012.

Mohammadi, Mehdi. "Nuclear Case From Beginning to End in Interview With Dr Hasan Rowhani (Part 1): We Are Testing Europe." *Tehran Keyhan*. July 26, 2005, http://lewis.armscontrolwonk.com/files/2012/08/Rowhani_Interview.pdf.

Mohan, C. Raja. *India's Nuclear Diplomacy and the Global Order*. New Delhi: Academic Foundation, 2009.

Montgomery, Alexander H. "Stop Helping Me: When Nuclear Assistance Impedes Nuclear Programs." In *The Nuclear Renaissance and International Security*, edited by Adam Stulberg and Matt Fuhrmann, 177–202. Palo Alto, CA: Stanford University Press, 2013.

Montgomery, Alexander H. and Scott D. Sagan. "The Perils of Predicting Proliferation." *Journal of Conflict Resolution*, Vol. 53, No. 2 (April 2009): 302–328.

Moody, Kenton J., Ian D. Hutcheon and Patrick M. Grant. *Nuclear Forensics Analysis*. Boca Raton, FL: Taylor & Francis, 2005.

Moroney, Jennifer D.P., Aidan Kirby Winn, Jeffrey Engstrom, Joe Hogler, Thomas-Durell Young and Michelle Spencer. "Assessing the Effectiveness of the International Counterproliferation Program." RAND Corporation, 2001, www.rand.org/content/dam/rand/pubs/technical_reports/2011/RAND_TR981.pdf

Mousavian, Seyed Hussein. *The Iranian Nuclear Crisis: A Memoir*. Washington, DC: The Carnegie Endowment for International Peace, 2012.

Mowatt-Larssen, Rolf. "Al-Qaeda's Religious Justification of Nuclear Terrorism." Cambridge, MA: Belfer Center for Science and International Affairs, Harvard Kennedy School, November 12, 2010, http://belfercenter.ksg.harvard.edu/publication/20518/.

———. *Al Qaeda Weapons of Mass Destruction Threat: Hype or Reality?* Cambridge, MA: Belfer Center for Science and International Affairs, Harvard Kennedy School, January 2010, http://belfercenter.ksg.harvard.edu/files/al-qaeda-wmd-threat.pdf.

Müller, Harald. "A Nuclear Nonproliferation Test: Obama's Nuclear Policy and the 2010 NPT Review Conference." *Nonproliferation Review*, Vol. 18, No. 1 (March 2011): 219–236.

———. "The Exceptional End to the Extraordinary Libyan Quest." In *Nuclear Proliferation and International Security*, edited by Morton Bremer Maerli and Sverre Lodgaard, 73–95. London: Routledge, 2007.

———. "The 2005 NPT Review Conference: Reasons and Consequences of Failure and Options for Repair." Weapons of Mass Destruction Commission, Report No. 31, 2005, www.blixassociates.com/wp-content/uploads/2011/03/No31.pdf.

Müller, Harald and Andreas Schmidt. "The Little-Known Story of Deproliferation: Why States Give Up Nuclear Weapons Activities." In *Forecasting Nuclear Proliferation in the 21st Century*, edited by William Potter and Gaukhar Mukhatzhanova, 124–158. Palo Alto, CA: Stanford University Press, 2010.

Murphy, Jack, Ben Kohl, Jeff Stevens, Joe Bennett and H.G. Israelsson. "Exploitation of the IMS and Other Data for a Comprehensive, Advanced Analysis of the North Korean Nuclear Tests." Poster, CTBTO website, www.ctbto.org/fileadmin/user_upload/SandT_2011/posters/T2-P21%20B_Kohl%20 Exploitation%20of%20the%20IMS%20and%20other%20data%20for%20a%20comprehensive,%20adva nced%20analysis%20of%20the%20North%20Korean%20nuclear%20tests.pdf.

Musharraf, Pervez. *In the Line of Fire: A Memoir*. New York: Free Press, September 2006.

Mutimer, David. *The Weapon State: Proliferation and the Framing of Security.* Boulder, CO: Lynne Rienner, 2000.

Myre, Greg. "What if Ukraine Still Had Nuclear Weapons?" *National Public Radio*, March 10, 2014, www.npr.org/blog/parallels/2014/03/10/288572756/what-if-ukraine-still-had-nuclear-weapons.

Nanto, Dick K. and Emma Chanlett-Avery. "North Korea: Economic Leverage and Policy Analysis." Congressional Research Service. January 22, 2010, www.fas.org/sgp/crs/row/RL32493.pdf.

National Academy of Sciences and National Research Council. *Internationalization of the Nuclear Fuel Cycle: Goals, Strategies, and Challenges.* Washington, DC: The National Academies Press, 2009.

National Archives and Records Administration. "Atoms for Peace," www.eisenhower.archives.gov/ research/online_documents/atoms_for_peace.html.

National Institute for Defence Studies. *East Asian Strategic Review 2011.* Tokyo: Japan Times, 2011.

———. "Chapter 3: The Korean Peninsula: Emerging Prospects for Change." In *East Asian Strategic Review 2004.* Tokyo: *The Japan Times*, July 2004, www.nids.go.jp/english/publication/east-asian/pdf/ 2004/east-asian_e2004_03.pdf.

National Research Council. *The Comprehensive Nuclear Test Ban Treaty: Technical Issues for the United States.* Washington, DC: The National Academies Press, 2012.

———. *Nuclear Forensics: A Capability at Risk (Abbreviated Version).* Washington, DC: The National Academies Press, 2010.

Naval-Technology.com. "Indian Navy's K-15 SLBM successfully completes development trials." January 29, 2013, www.naval-technology.com/news/newsindian-navys-k-15-slbm-successfully-completes-development-trials.

Newhouse, John. *Cold Dawn: The History of SALT.* New York: Holt, Rinehart & Winston, 1973.

Newnham, Randall. "Carrots, Sticks and Bombs: The End of Libya's WMD Program." *Mediterranean Quarterly*, Vol. 20, No. 3 (Summer 2009): 77–94, www.cimicweb.org/cmo/libya/Documents/Security/ 20.3.2009.%20newnham%20libya%20wmd.pdf.

Niemeyer, S. and I. Hutcheon, "Forensic Analysis of a Smuggled HEU Sample Interdicted in Bulgaria." IAEA-CN-98/2/09 IA, www.iaea.org/inis/collection/NCLCollectionStore/_Public/33/057/ 33057956.pdf.

Nikitin, Mary Beth. "North Korea's Nuclear Weapons: Technical Issues." Congressional Research Service. April 3, 2013, www.fas.org/sgp/crs/nuke/RL34256.pdf.

———. "Proliferation Security Initiative (PSI)." Federation of American Scientists. CRS Report RL34327, Congressional Research Service. June 15, 2012, www.fas.org/sgp/crs/nuke/RL34327. pdf.

Niksh, Larry A. "North Korea's Nuclear Weapons Program." CRS Report IB91141, Congressional Research Service. November 5, 2003, www.nautilus.org/publications/books/dprkbb/ nuclearweapons/CRSIB91141_NKsNuclearWeaponsProgram.pdf.

Nishihara, Akie, *et al.* Atomic Energy Society of Japan. Hiroshima, September 2012.

Nonaligned Movement, "Working Paper Presented by the Group of Non-Aligned States Parties to the 2010 Review Conference of the Treaty on the Nonproliferation of Nuclear Weapons (NPT)." April 30, 2010, http://isis-online.org/uploads/conferences/documents/NAM_Working_Paper_for_2010_ NPT_RevCon_30April2010.pdf.

Nuclear Energy Study Group. "Nuclear Power and Proliferation Resistance: Security Benefits, Limiting Risk." American Physical Society Panel on Public Affairs, May 2005, www.aps.org/policy/reports/ popa-reports/proliferation-resistance/upload/proliferation.pdf.

Nuclear Power Plan Exporters' Principals of Conduct. "The Principals of Conduct." Brussels, Belgium, March 6, 2014, http://nuclearprinciples.org/the-principles.

———. "The Principles of Conduct: Nonproliferation and Safeguards," http://nuclearprinciples.org/ principle/nonproliferation-and-safeguards.

———. "South Korea: Overview." March 2014, www.nti.org/country-profiles/south-korea.

———. "Argentina." December 2013, www.nti.org/country-profiles/argentina/.

———. "North Korea." September 2013, www.nti.org/country-profiles/north-korea/nuclear/

———. "Experimental 25–30 MWe Light Water Reactor." *NTI.org.* April 16, 2013, www.nti.org/facilities/769/

———. "Libya Nuclear Chronology." February 2011, www.nti.org/media/pdfs/libya_nuclear.pdf?_=1316466791.

Nuclear Threat Initiative and Economist Intelligence Unit. *NTI Nuclear Materials Security Index: Building a Framework for Assurance, Accountability, and Action.* January 2012, www.nti.org/media/pdfs/NTI_Index_FINAL.pdf.

Nunn, Sam. "Moving Away from Doomsday and Other Dangers: The Need to Think Anew." Speech at the National Press Club, Washington, DC, March 29, 2001, www.nti.org/media/pdfs/speech_samnunn_032901.pdf?_=1316466791.

Nye, Jr., Joseph S. "Nuclear Learning and US-Soviet Security Regimes." *International Organization,* Vol. 41, No. 3 (Summer 1987): 371–402.

O'Connell, Mary Ellen. "The Myth of Preemptive Self-Defense." The American Society of International Law. Task Force On Terrorism Paper Series. Washington, DC, August 2002, http://cdm266901.cdmhost.com/cdm/ref/collection/p266901coll4/id/2944.

O'Neil, Andrew. *Asia, the US and Extended Nuclear Deterrence: Atomic Umbrellas in the Twenty-First Century.* Abingdon: Routledge, 2013.

———. "Extended Nuclear Deterrence in East Asia: Redundant or Resurgent?" *International Affairs,* Vol. 87, No. 6 (November 2011): 1439–1457.

Obama, Barack. "Renewing American Leadership." *Foreign Affairs,* Vol. 86, No. 4 (July/August 2007): 2–16, www.foreignaffairs.com/articles/62636/barack-obama/renewing-american-leadership.

Oberdorfer, Don. *The Two Koreas: A Contemporary History.* Reading, MA: Addison Wesley, 1997.

Oelrich, Ivan and Ivanka Barzashka. "Centrifuges and Nuclear Weapons Proliferation." Federation of American Scientists, N.D., www.fas.org/programs/ssp/nukes/fuelcycle/centrifuges/proliferation.html.

Ogilvie-White, Tanya. "Is There a Theory of Nuclear Proliferation?: An Analysis of the Contemporary Debate." *The Nonproliferation Review,* Vol. 4, No.1 (Fall 1996): 43–60, http://cns.miis.edu/npr/pdfs/ogilvi41.pdf.

Oh, Kongdan. "US-ROK: The Forgotten Alliance." Brookings East Asia Commentary, No. 22, Brookings Institution, October 2008, www.brookings.edu/research/opinions/2008/10/south-korea-oh.

Paine, Christopher E. and Thomas B. Cochran, "Nuclear Islands: International Leasing of Nuclear Fuel Cycle Sites to Provide Enduring Assurance of Peaceful Use." *The Nonproliferation Review,* Vol. 17, No. 3 (November 2010): 441–474, http://cns.miis.edu/npr/pdfs/npr_17-3_paine_cochran.pdf.

Painter, Daniel. "The Nuclear Suppliers Group at the Crossroads." *The Diplomat,* June 10, 2013, http://thediplomat.com/2013/06/the-nuclear-suppliers-group-at-the-crossroads/.

"Pakistan Secretly Transporting Uranium Ore from Afghanistan." BBC Summary of World Broadcasts, Part 1 The USSR; A. INTERNATIONAL AFFAIRS; 3. THE FAR EAST; SU/0213/A3/1, July 26, 1988.

Parker, Ann. "A Transparent Success: 'Megatons to Megawatts' Program." *Science and Technology Review,* Lawrence Livermore National Laboratory (April/May 2014): 16–19.

Parrish, Scott and William Potter. "Central Asian States Establish Nuclear-Weapon-Free Zone Despite US Opposition." Monterey Institute of International Studies. James Martin Center for Nonproliferation Studies. September 5, 2006, http://cns.miis.edu/stories/060905.htm.

Patti, Carlo. "Brazil in Global Nuclear Order." PhD dissertation in International Relations, Universitá degli Studi di Firenze, 2012.

———. "The Origins of the Brazilian Nuclear Program 1951–1955." *Cold War History,* forthcoming.

Paul, T.V. *Power Versus Prudence: Why Nations Forgo Nuclear Weapons.* Montreal: McGill-Queen's University Press, 2000.

Payne, Keith B. *The Fallacies of Cold War Deterrence and a New Direction.* Lexington, KY: The University Press of Kentucky, 2001.

Pelopidas, Benoît "The Oracles of Proliferation. How Experts Maintain a Biased Historical Reading that Limits Policy Innovation." *Nonproliferation Review,* Vol. 18, No.1 (March 2011): 297–314.

———. "La Couleur du Cygne Sud-Africain: Le Rôle des Surprises dans L'Histoire Nucléaire et les Effets d'une Amnésie Partielle. [The color of the South African swan: The role of surprises in nuclear history and the effects of a partial amnesia]." *French Yearbook of International Relations,* Vol. 11 (July 2010): 683–694.

————. *Renoncer à l'arme nucléaire. La séduction de l'impossible?* [Giving up nuclear weapons. The seduction of the impossible?]. Paris: Sciences Po University Press, Forthcoming.

————. *When Experts Back Policy Makers' Historical Memory and Biases: The Shared "Nuclear Proliferation Paradigm" in the US since the 1960s* (Unpublished manuscript).

Perkovich, George. *India's Nuclear Bomb: The Impact on Global Proliferation.* Berkeley, CA: University of California Press, 1999.

Perkovich, George and James M. Acton. *Abolishing Nuclear Weapons: A Debate.* Washington, DC: Carnegie Endowment, 2009.

Perkovich, George, Malcolm Chalmers, Steven Pifer, Paul Schulte and Jaclyn Tandler. "Looking Beyond the Chicago Summit: Nuclear Weapons in Europe and the Future of NATO." *The Carnegie Papers* (April 2012): 1–54, http://carnegieendowment.org/files/beyond_chicago_summit.pdf.

Perry, William J., James R. Schlesinger, *et al. America's Strategic Posture: The Final Report of the Congressional Commission on the Strategic Posture of the United States.* Washington, DC: United States Institute of Peace Press, 2009.

Peterson, Scott. "Stalled Nuclear Talks Fuel Sharp Exchange at Iran's Final Presidential Debate." *Christian Science Monitor.* June 8, 2013, www.csmonitor.com/World/Middle-East/2013/0608/Stalled-nuclear-talks-fuel-sharp-exchange-at-Iran-s-final-presidential-debate.

Philippe, Sébastien. "Safeguarding the Military Naval Nuclear Fuel Cycle." *Journal of Nuclear Materials Management,* Vol. 42, No. 3 (Spring 2014): 40–52.

Philippe, Sébastien and Alexander Glaser. "Nuclear Archaeology for Gaseous Diffusion Enrichment Plants." *Science & Global Security,* Vol. 22, No. 1 (2014): 27–49.

Pilat, Joseph F. (ed.), *Atoms for Peace: A Future after Fifty Years?* Baltimore, MD: Johns Hopkins University Press/Woodrow Wilson Center Press, 2007.

Podvig, Pavel. "Russia is Set to Produce New Highly-enriched Uranium." International Panel on Fissile Materials. June 1, 2012, http://fissilematerials.org/blog/2012/06/russia_to_resume_producti.html.

Pollack, Jonathan D. *No Exit: North Korea, Nuclear Weapons and International Security.* New York: Routledge, 2011.

Pollack, Jonathan D. and Mitchell B. Reiss. "South Korea: The Tyranny of Geography and the Vexations of History." In *The Nuclear Tipping Point: Why States Reconsider Their Nuclear Choices,* edited by Kurt M. Campbell, Robert J. Einhorn, Mitchell B. Reiss and Vartan Gregorian, 254–292. Washington, DC: Brookings Institution Press, 2004.

Pomeroy, George, Robert Bari, Edward Wonder, Michael Zentner, Eckhard Haas and Thomas Killeen. "Approaches to Evaluation of Proliferation Resistance Fundamentals for Future Nuclear Energy Systems." 49th Annual Meeting: Institute of Nuclear Materials Management (IMNN). Nashville, TN. July 13–17, 2008, www.iaea.org/INPRO/CPs/PRADA/approaches.pdf.

Porter, Theodore. *Trust in Numbers: The Pursuit of Objectivity in Science and Public Life.* Princeton, NJ: Princeton University Press, 1995.

Posen, Barry R. "US Security Policy in a Nuclear-Armed World or: What if Iraq had had Nuclear Weapons." *Security Studies,* Vol. 6. No. 3 (Spring 1997): 1–31.

Posner, Eric. "Should Ukraine have Kept its Nuclear Weapons?" ericposner.com, March 25, 2014, ericposner.com/should-ukraine-have-kept-its-nuclear-weapons.

Potter, William. "The NPT and the Sources of Nuclear Restraint." *Daedalus,* Vol. 139, No. 1 (Winter 2010): 68–81.

————. "The Politics of Nuclear Renunciation: The Cases of Belarus, Kazakhstan and Ukraine." *Stimson Center Occasional Paper,* No. 22, April 1995, http://cns.miis.edu/reports/pdfs/1995_potter_politics_of_nuclear_renunciation.pdf.

Potter, William C. and Gaukhar Mukhatzhanova. *Nuclear Politics and the Non-Aligned Movement: Principles vs Pragmatism.* Routledge, for the International Institute for Strategic Studies, Adelphi Series, Vol. 427 (2012).

———— (eds). *Forecasting Nuclear Proliferation in the 21st Century.* 2 Volumes. Palo Alto, CA: Stanford University Press, 2010.

————. "Forecasting Proliferation: The Role of Theory, an Introduction." In *Forecasting Nuclear Proliferation in the 21st Century,* edited by William Potter and Gaukhar Mukhatzhanova (Palo Alto, CA: Stanford University Press, 2010): 1–12.

Potter, William C. and Elena Sokova, "Illicit Nuclear Trafficking in the NIS: What's New? What's True?" *The Nonproliferation Review,* Vol. 9, No. 2 (Summer 2002): 112–120, http://cns.miis.edu/npr/pdfs/92potsok.pdf.

Press, Daryl G. *Calculating Credibility: How Leaders Assess Military Threats.* Ithaca, NY: Cornell University Press, 2005.

Purkitt, Helen H. and Stephen F. Burgess. *South African's Weapons of Mass Destruction.* Bloomington, IN: Indiana University Press, 2005.

Quinlan, Michael. "India-Pakistan Deterrence Revisited." *Survival,* Vol. 47, No. 3 (Autumn 2005): 103–116.

Ramaker, Jaap, Jenifer Mackby, Peter D. Marshall and Robert Geil. *The Final Test: A History of the Comprehensive Nuclear Test Ban Treaty Negotiations.* Vienna: Provisional Technical Secretariat of the Preparatory Commission of the Comprehensive Nuclear Test-Ban Treaty Organization, 2003.

Rauf, Tariq. "Realizing Nuclear Fuel Assurances: Third Time's the Charm." Carnegie International Non-Proliferation Conference, Washington, DC, June 24, 2007, www.carnegieendowment.org/files/fuel_assurances_rauf.pdf.

Rauf, Tariq and Zoryana Vovchok. "Fuel for Thought." *IAEA Bulletin,* Vol. 49, No. 2 (March 2008): 59–63, www.iaea.org/Publications/Magazines/Bulletin/Bull492/49204845963.pdf.

Reaching Critical Will. "Stockpiles or No Stockpiles." *CD Report.* March 12, 2013, http://reachingcritical will.org/disarmament-fora/cd/2013/reports/7501-stockpiles-or-no-stockpiles.

Redick, John R. "Tlatelolco and Regional Nonproliferation Initiatives." Agency for the Prohibition of Nuclear Weapons in Latin America and the Caribbean (OPANAL), 1995, www.opanal.org/Articles/cancun/can-Redick.htm.

———. "Nuclear Illusions: Argentina and Brazil." Occasional Paper No. 25, The Henry L. Stimson Center, December, 1995, www.acamedia.info/politics/IRef/StimsonC/redick.pdf.

———. "Latin America's Emerging Nonproliferation Consensus." *Arms Control Today,* Vol. 24, No. 2 (March 1994): 3–9.

Reiss, Mitchell B. "Strengthening Nonproliferation: The Path Ahead." In *Atoms for Peace: A Future after Fifty Years?,* Joseph F. Pilat (ed.), 43–44. Washington, DC and Baltimore, MD: Woodrow Wilson Center Press and John Hopkins University Press, 2007.

———. *Bridled Ambitions: Why Countries Constrain Their Nuclear Capabilities.* Washington DC: Woodrow Wilson Center Press, 1995.

———. *Without the Bomb: The Politics of Nuclear Nonproliferation.* New York: Columbia University Press, 1988.

Reiss, Mitchell B. and Harold Müller. (eds) *International Perspectives on Counterproliferaton.* Working Paper, No. 99. Washington, DC: Woodrow Wilson Center, Division of International Studies, January 1995.

Reiter, Dan. "Preventive Attacks Against Nuclear Programs and the 'Success' at Osiraq." *The Nonproliferation Review,* Vol. 12, No 2 (July 2005): 355–371.

Rennack, Dianne E. "Iran: US Economic Sanctions and the Authority to Lift Restrictions." Congressional Research Service. CRS Report R4331. February 14, 2014, www.fas.org/sgp/crs/mideast/R43311.pdf.

Richards, Paul. "Seismic Detective Work: CTBTO Monitoring System 'Very Effective' in Detecting North Korea's Third Nuclear Test." *CTBTO Spectrum,* No. 20 (July 2013): 22–25.

Richelson, Jeffrey. *Spying on the Bomb: American Nuclear Intelligence from Nazi Germany to Iran and North Korea.* New York: W.W. Norton & Co., 2007.

Ringbom, A., K. Elmgren, K. Lindh, J. Peterson, T. Bowyer, J. Hayes, J. McIntyre, M. Panisko and R. Williams. "Measurements of Radioxenon in Ground Level Air in South Korea Following the Claimed Nuclear Test in North Korea on October 9, 2006." ISS09 Conference (Vienna, Austria). June 10–12, 2009, www.ctbto.org/fileadmin/user_upload/ISS_2009/Poster/RN-26D%20%28Sweden%29%20-%20Anders_Ringbom%20etal.pdf.

Rivkin, Jr., David B. and Lee A. Casey. "From *The Bermuda* to *The So San.*" *National Review Online,* January 2, 2003, www.nationalreview.com/articles/205372/i-bermuda-so-san-i/david-b-rivkin-jr.

Roberts, Brad. "Extended Deterrence and Strategic Stability in Northeast Asia." NIDS Visiting Scholar Paper, National Institute for Defense Studies (Tokyo), No. 1 (August 9, 2013), www.nids.go.jp/english/publication/visiting/pdf/01.pdf.

Robel, Martin, Michael J. Kristo and Martin A. Heller. "Nuclear Forensic Inferences: Using Iterative Multidimensional Statistics." 50th INMM Annual Meeting, Tucson, Arizona, July 12–July 16, 2009, https://e-reports-ext.llnl.gov/pdf/374432.pdf.

Roberts, Guy B. "The Counterproliferation Self-help Paradigm: A Legal Regime for Enforcing the Norm Prohibiting the Proliferation of Weapons of Mass Destruction." *Denver Journal of International Law & Policy,* Vol. 27, No. 3 (June 1999): 483–529.

Rodriguez, C., A. Baxter, D. McEachern, M. Fikani and F. Venneri, "Deep-Burn: Making Nuclear Waste Transmutation Practical." *Nuclear Engineering and Design*, Vol. 222, Nos. 2–3 (June 2003): 1–19, www.researchgate.net/publication/222543918_Deep-Burn_making_nuclear_waste_transmutation_practical/file/79e41505a0eec467c5.pdf.

Rozen, Laura. "Three Days in March: New Details on How US, Iran Opened Direct Talks." *The Back Channel.* January 8, 2014, http://backchannel.al-monitor.com/index.php/2014/01/7484/three-days-in-march-new-details-on-the-u-s-iran-backchannel/.

Rublee, Maria Rost. *Nonproliferation Norms: Why States Choose Nuclear Restraint.* Athens, GA: University of Georgia Press, 2009.

Rühle, Michael. "Enlightenment in the Second Nuclear Age." *International Affairs*, Vol. 83, No. 3 (April 2007): 511–522.

Rumbaugh, Russell and Nathan Cohn. "Resolving Ambiguity: Costing Nuclear Weapons." Stimson Center. June 2012, Table 4, www.stimson.org/images/uploads/research-pdfs/RESOLVING_FP_4_no_crop_marks.pdf.

Russell, James A. "Extended Deterrence, Security Guarantees and Nuclear Weapons: US Strategic and Policy Conundrums in the Gulf." *Strategic Insights*, Vol. 8, No. 5 (December 2009): 17–26.

Rydell, Randy. "LOOKING BACK: Going for Baruch: The Nuclear Plan That Refused to Go Away." *Arms Control Today*, Vol. 36, No. 6 (June 2006): 45–48, www.armscontrol.org/print/2064.

Saalman, Lora. "Placing a Renminbi Sign on Strategic Stability and Nuclear Reductions." In *Strategic Stability: Contending Interpretations*, edited by Elbridge Colby and Michael Gerson, 343–382. Carlisle: Strategic Studies Institute and US Army War College Press, 2013.

———. "China and the US Nuclear Posture Review." *The Carnegie Papers* (February 2011): 1–62, http://carnegieendowment.org/files/china_posture_review.pdf.

Sagan, Scott D. "The Causes of Nuclear Proliferation." *Annual Review of Political Science*, Vol. 14 (2011): 225–244, www.annualreviews.org/doi/pdf/10.1146/annurev-polisci-052209-131042.

———. "Nuclear Latency and Nuclear Proliferation." In *Forecasting Nuclear Proliferation in the 21st Century*, edited by William Potter and Gaukhar Mukhatzhanova, 80–101. Palo Alto, CA: Stanford University Press, 2010.

———. "Rethinking the Causes of Nuclear Proliferation: Three Bomb Models in Search of a Bomb." In *The Coming Crisis: Nuclear Proliferation, US Interests, and World Order*, edited by Victor A. Utgoff, 17–50. Cambridge, MA: The MIT Press, 2000.

———. "Why do States Build Nuclear Weapons?: Three Models in Search of a Bomb." *International Security*, Vol. 21, No. 3 (Winter 1996/1997): 54–86, http://iis-db.stanford.edu/pubs/20278/Why_Do_States_Build_Nuclear_Weapons.pdf.

Sagan, Scott D. and Jane Vaynman. "Reviewing the Nuclear Posture Review." *Nonproliferation Review*, Vol. 18, No. 1 (March 2011): 17–37, www.tandfonline.com/doi/pdf/10.1080/10736700.2011.549169.

Saito, Masaki, V. Artisyuk, Y. Peryoga and K. Nikitin. "Advanced Nuclear Energy Systems for Protected Plutonium Production." International Conference on Innovative Technologies for Nuclear Fuel Cycles and Nuclear Power, Vienna, Austria. June 23–26, 2003, www.nr.titech.ac.jp/coe21/coe/results.html.

Samore, Gary. "Negotiating with Iran: Prospects and Problems." International Institute for Strategic Studies. March 10, 2014, www.iiss.org/en/events/events/archive/2014-0f13/march-a2fd/negotiating-with-iran-9999.

Samuel, Annie Tracy. "Revolutionary Guard is Cautiously Open to Nuclear Deal." *Iran Matters.* Belfer Center for Science and International Affairs, Harvard University. December 20, 2013, http://belfercenter.ksg.harvard.edu/publication/23779/revolutionary_guard_is_cautiously_open_to_nuclear_deal.html.

Samuels, Richard and James Schoff. "Japan's Nuclear Hedge: Beyond 'Allergy' and Breakout." In *Strategic Asia 2013–14: Asia in the Second Nuclear Age*, edited by Ashley Tellis, Abraham Denmark and Travis Tanner, 233–266. Washington, DC: National Bureau of Asian Research, 2013.

Sanger, David E. "In US, South Korean Makes Case for Nuclear Arms." *New York Times*, April 9, 2013, www.nytimes.com/2013/04/10/world/asia/in-us-south-korean-makes-case-for-nuclear-arms.html.

Sarma, N. and B. Banerjee. *Nuclear Power in India: A Critical History.* Rupa: New Delhi, 2008.

Satoh, Yukio. "Japan-US Alliance Cooperation in the Era of Global Nuclear Disarmament." In *The Japan-US Partnership Toward a World Free of Nuclear Weapons*, edited by Bryce Wakefield, Report of the Japan-US Join Public Policy Forum, Tokyo, October 21–22, 2009, 1–36. Washington, DC: Woodrow Wilson International Center for Scholars, 2010.

Scheinman, Adam M. "Calling for Action: The Next Generation Safeguards Initiative." *The Nonproliferation Review*, Vol. 16, No. 2 (July 2009): 257–267.

Scheinman, Lawrence. "Article IV of the NPT: Background, Problems, Some Prospects." The Weapons of Mass Destruction Commission, Paper No. 5, June 7, 2004, www.un.org/disarmament/education/wmdcommission/files/No5.pdf.

Schell, Jonathan. *The Abolition*. New York: Alfred A. Knopf, 1984.

Schneider, Barry R. *Future War and Counterproliferation: US Military Responses to NBC Proliferation Threats*. Westport, CT: Praeger, 1999.

Schneider, Mycle and Yves Marignac. *Spent Nuclear Fuel Reprocessing in France*. International Panel on Fissile Materials. Princeton University Press, April 2008, http://fissilematerials.org/library/rr04.pdf.

Schoff, James. "Changing Perceptions of Extended Deterrence in Japan." In *Strategy in the Second Nuclear Age*, edited by Toshi Yoshihara and James Holmes, 99–114. Washington, DC: Georgetown University Press, 2012.

Shultz, George P., William J. Perry, Henry A. Kissinger and Sam Nunn. "Steps in Reducing Nuclear Risks: The Pace of Nonproliferation Work Today Doesn't Match the Urgency of the Threat." *The Wall Street Journal*, March 2013, http://online.wsj.com/news/articles/SB10001424127887324338604578325912939001772.

———. "Deterrence in the Age of Nuclear Proliferation." *The Wall Street Journal*, March 2011, http://online.wsj.com/news/articles/SB10001424052748703300904576178760530169414.

———. "Toward a Nuclear-Free World." *Wall Street Journal*, January 15, 2008, http://online.wsj.com/news/articles/SB120036422673589947

———. "A World Free of Nuclear Weapons." *The Wall Street Journal*, July 4, 2007, http://online.wsj.com/news/articles/SB116787515251566636.

Serrano, Monica. "Common Security in Latin America-Treaty of Tlatelolco." Research Paper, University of London, 1992.

Sheets, Lawrence Scott and William J. Broad. "Smuggler's Plot Highlights Fear Over Uranium." *New York Times*, January 25, 2007, www.nytimes.com/2007/01/25/world/europe/25nuke.html.

Shelton, Christina. "The Roots of Analytic Failures in the US Intelligence Community." *International Journal of Intelligence and Counterintelligence*, Vol. 24, No. 4 (September 2011): 637–655.

Sigal, Leon V. *Disarming Strangers: Nuclear Diplomacy with North Korea*. Princeton, NJ: Princeton University Press, 1998.

Simpson, John. "The Role of Security Assurances in the Nuclear Nonproliferation Regime." In *Security Assurances and Nuclear Nonproliferation*, edited by Jeffrey Knopf, 57–88. Palo Alto, CA: Stanford University Press, 2012.

———. "Is the Nuclear Non-Proliferation Treaty Fit for Purpose?" Report for the United Nations Association of the UK, UNA-UK Briefing Report No. 1, August 2011, www.una.org.uk/sites/default/files/Is%20the%20Nuclear%20Non-Proliferation%20Treaty%20Fit%20For%20Purpose%20-%20Professor%20John%20Simpson.pdf.

Simpson, John and Jenny Nielsen. "The 2005 NPT Conference: Mission Impossible." *Nonproliferation Review*, Vol. 12, No. 2 (July 2006): 271–301.

Simpson, John and Matthew Harries. *NPT Briefing Book, 2014 Edition*. London and Monterey, CA: King's College London and Center for Nonproliferation Studies, 2014, www.kcl.ac.uk/sspp/departments/war studies/research/groups/csss/pubs/NPT-Briefing-Book-2014/NPT-Briefing-Book-2014.pdf.

Sloss, David. "Forcible Arms Control: Preemptive Attacks on Nuclear Facilities." *Chicago Journal of International Law*, Vol. 39, No. 54 (January 2003): 39–57.

Snow, Charles P. "The Moral Un-Neutrality of Science." *Science*, Vol. 133, No. 3448 (January 27, 1961): 255–262.

Sokov, Nikolai. "Ukraine: A Postnuclear Country." In *Forecasting Nuclear Proliferation in the 21st Century*, edited by William Potter and Gaukhar Mukhatzhanova, 255–284. Palo Alto, CA: Stanford University Press, 2010.

Solingen, Etel. *Sanctions, Statecraft and Nuclear Proliferation*. Cambridge: Cambridge University Press, 2012.

———. *Nuclear Logics: Contrasting Paths in East Asia and the Middle East*. Princeton, NJ: Princeton University Press, 2007.

Spector, Leonard S. *Going Nuclear*. Cambridge, MA: Ballinger, 1987.

Spektor, Mathias. "Explaining Brazil's Nuclear Behavior." Paper presented at the conference, "Uncovering the Sources of Nuclear Behavior: Historical Dimensions of Nuclear Proliferation." Zurich, Switzerland, June 18–20, 2010.

Squassoni, Sharon. "US-India Deal and Its Impact." *Arms Control Today*, Vol. 40, No. 6, (July/August 2010): 48–52, www.armscontrol.org/act/2010_07-08/squassoni.

————. "US Nuclear Cooperation with India: Issues for Congress." CRS Report for Congress. Congressional Research Service. July 29, 2005, www.fas.org/sgp/crs/row/RL33016.pdf.

Squassoni, Sharon and Fred McGoldrick, "Nonproliferation Policy towards North Korea." Nautilus Institute, November 24, 2009, http://nautilus.org/wp-content/uploads/2011/12/Squassoni McGoldrick.pdf.

Stanley, F.E. "A Beginner's Guide to Uranium Chronometry in Nuclear Forensics and Safeguards." *Journal of Analytical Atomic Spectrometry*, Vol. 27, No. 11 (November 2012): 1821–1830.

Stein, Aaron. "US-UAE Nuclear Cooperation." The Nuclear Threat Initiative, August 13, 2009, www.nti.org/analysis/articles/us-uae-nuclear-cooperation.

Stern, Jessica. "US Assistance Programs for Improving MPC&A in the Former Soviet Union." *The Nonproliferation Review*, Vol. 3, No. 2 (Winter 1996): 17–32.

Stevens, J.L., J.R. Murphy and N. Rimer. "Seismic Source Characteristics of Cavity Decoupled Explosions in Salt and Tuff." *Bulletin of the Seismological Society of America*, Vol. 81, No. 4 (August 1991): 1272–1291.

Stiler, Michael J. "US Nuclear Nonproliferation Policy in the North East Asia Region During the Cold War: the South Korea Case." *East Asia: An International Quarterly*, Vol.16, No. 3/4 (Autumn 1998): 41–79.

Stimson Center. "Materials Protection, Control, and Accounting (MPC&A)." Stimson Center. N.D., www.stimson.org/materials-protection-control-and-accounting-mpca-/.

Stocker, Jeremy. "The Strategy of Missile Defence: Defence, Deterrence and Diplomacy." *RUSI Journal*, Vol. 156, No. 3 (December 2011): 56–62.

Stockholm International Peace Research Institute. "SIPRI Statement on President Obama's Speech in Berlin." Press Release. June 19, 2013, www.sipri.org/media/pressreleases/2013/19-june-2013-sipri-statement-on-president-obama2019s-speech-in-berlin.

Sweetman, Bill. "Russia Develops Multiple Nuclear Systems." *Aviation Week*, November 11, 2013, http://aviationweek.com/awin/russia-develops-multiple-nuclear-systems.

Sykes, Lynn, R. "Dealing with Decoupled Nuclear Explosions under a Comprehensive Test Ban Treaty." In *Monitoring a Comprehensive Test Ban Treaty*, edited by Eystein S. Husebye and Anton M. Dainty, 247–393. Boston: Springer, NATO ASI Series, Vol. 303, 1996.

Sykes, Lynn R. and Göran Ekström. "Comparison of Seismic and Hydrodynamic Yield Determinations for the Soviet Joint Verification Experiment of 1988." *Proceedings of the National Academy of Science USA*, Vol. 86, No. 10 (May 1989): 3456–3460, www.pnas.org/content/86/10/3456.full.pdf+html.

Tagma, Halit M. "Realism at the Limits: Post Cold War Realism and Nuclear Rollback." *Contemporary Security Policy*, Vol. 31, No. 1 (April 2010): 165–188.

Takahashi, Sugio. "Ballistic Missile Defense in Japan: Deterrence and Military Transformation." *Asie. Visions*, No. 59/*Proliferation Papers*, No. 44 (December 2012): 7–27.

Takubo, Masafumi and Frank N. von Hippel. "Ending Reprocessing in Japan: An Alternative Approach to Managing Japan's Spent Nuclear Fuel and Separate Plutonium." International Panel on Fissile Material, Research Report No. 12, Princeton, New Jersey, November 2013, http://fissilematerials.org/library/rr12.pdf.

Talbott, Strobe. *Endgame: The Inside Story of SALT II* New York: Harper Colophon, 1979.

Tanaka, Satoru, Yusuke Kuno, *et al.* "A Study on the Establishment of an International Nuclear Fuel Cycle System for Asia." March 2013, www.flanker.n.t.u-tokyo.ac.jp/modules/labDownloads/.

Tape, James and Joseph Pilat. "Nuclear Safeguards and the Security of Nuclear Materials." In *Nuclear Safeguards, Security, and Nonproliferation; Achieving Security with Technology and Policy*, edited by James E. Doyle. Waltham, MA: Butterworth-Heinemann, 2008.

Tatsumi, Yuki. "Maintaining Japan's Non-Nuclear Identity: The Role of US. Security Assurances." In *Security Assurances and Nuclear Nonproliferation*, edited by Jeffery Knopf, 137–161. Palo Alto, CA: Stanford University Press, 2012.

Tazaki, Makiko and Yusuke Kuno. "The Contribution of Multilateral Nuclear Approaches (MNAs) to the Sustainability of Nuclear Energy." *Sustainability*, Vol. 4, No. 8 (August 2012): 1755–1775, www.mdpi.com/2071-1050/4/8/1755.

Tellis, Ashley, Abraham Denmark and Travis Tanner (eds), *Strategic Asia 2013–14: Asia in the Second Nuclear Age*. Washington, DC: National Bureau of Asian Research, 2013.

Tenet, George. *At the Center of the Storm: My Years at the CIA*. New York: HarperCollins, 2007.

Tertrais, Bruno. "Security Assurances and the Future of Proliferation." In *Over the Horizon Proliferation Threats*, edited by James J. Wirtz and Peter R. Lavoy, 240–265. Palo Alto, CA: Stanford University Press, 2012.

Tobey, William H. and Pavel Zolotarev. "The Nuclear Terrorism Threat." Pattaya, Thailand, January 13, 2014, http://belfercenter.ksg.harvard.edu/files/nuclearterrorismthreatthailand2014.pdf.

Tsuruoka, Michito. "Why the NATO Nuclear Debate is Relevant to Japan and Vice Versa." *Policy Brief* (Washington, DC: German Marshall Fund of the United States, October 2010): 1–5.

United States Enrichment Corporation, "Megatons to megawatts," www.usec.com/russian-contracts/megatons-megawatts.

Vaez, Ali and Karim Sadjadpour. *Iran's Nuclear Odyssey: Costs and Risks.* Washington, DC: Carnegie Endowment for International Peace, 2013.

Varga, Zsolt, Maria Wallenius and Klaus Mayer. "Age Determination of Uranium Samples by Inductively Coupled Plasma Mass Spectrometry Using Direct Measurement and Spectral Deconvolution." *Journal of Analytical Atomic Spectrometry,* Vol. 25, No. 12 (December 2010): 1958–1962.

Viski, Andrea. "The Revised Nuclear Suppliers Group Guidelines: A European Union Perspective." EU Non-proliferation Consortium, *Non-proliferation Papers,* No. 15 (May 2012), www.sipri.org/research/disarmament/eu-consortium/publications/nonproliferation-paper-15.

von Hippel, Frank. "Plutonium, Proliferation and Radioactive-Waste Politics in East Asia." Nonproliferation Policy Education Center. January 3, 2011, www.npolicy.org/article_file/von_Hippel_Paper.pdf.

———. "The Costs and Benefits of Reprocessing." In *Nuclear Power's Global Expansion: Weighing Its Costs and Risks,* edited by Henry Sokolski. Carlisle, PA: Strategic Studies Institute, 2010.

———. "South Korean Reprocessing: An Unnecessary Threat to the Nonproliferation Regime." *Arms Control Today,* Vol. 40, No. 3 (March 2010): 22–29, www.armscontrol.org/act/2010_03/VonHippel.

———. "Reprocessing Nuclear Fuel a Dangerous Option." *The Cap Times.* September 18, 2009. http://host.madison.com/news/opinion/column/guest/frank-von-hippel-reprocessing-nuclear-fuel-a-dangerous-option/article_0bd69b4a-a3d2-11de-bfd5-001cc4c03286.html.

von Hippel, Frank, Seyed Hossein Mousavian, Emad Kiyaei, Harold Feiveson and Zia Mian. "Fissile Material Controls in the Middle East: Steps toward a Middle East Zone Free of Nuclear Weapons and all other Weapons of Mass Destruction." International Panel on Fissile Materials, Princeton, October 2013, http://fissilematerials.org/library/rr11.pdf.

Wallenius, M., A. Morgenstern, C. Apostolidis and K. Mayer. "Determination of the Age of Highly Enriched Uranium." *Analytical and Bioanalytical Chemistry,* Vol. 374, No. 3 (October 2002): 379–384.

Waltz, Kenneth N. "Why Iran Should Get the Bomb: Nuclear Balancing Would Mean Stability." *Foreign Affairs,* Vol. 91, No. 4 (July/August 2012): 1–5.

Wang, Brian. "DUPIC Fuel Cycle: Direct Use of Pressurized Water Reactor Spent Fuel in CANDU." *Next Big Future.* April 15, 2009, http://nextbigfuture.com/2009/04/dupic-fuel-cycle-direct-use-of.html.

Way, Christopher and Jessica Weeks. "Making it Personal: Regime Type and Nuclear Proliferation." *American Journal of Political Science,* forthcoming; online version published November 20, 2013, http://onlinelibrary.wiley.com/doi/10.1111/ajps.12080/pdf.

Way, Lucan A. "Authoritarian State Building and the Sources of Regime Competitiveness in the Fourth Wave: The Cases of Belarus, Moldova, Russia and Ukraine." *World Politics,* Vol. 57, No. 2 (January 2005): 231–261.

Weaver, Angela. "IAEA Nuclear Fuel Bank: Where We Stand Today." Poniblogger's Blog. Center for Strategic and International Studies. July 11, 2013, https://csis.org/blog/iaea-nuclear-fuel-bank-where-we-stand-today.

Weiss, Leonard. "Israel's 1979 Nuclear Test and the US Cover-up." *Middle East Policy Journal,* Vol. 18, No. 4 (Winter 2011): 83–95.

Weiss, Thomas G., David Cortright, George A. Lopez, *et al. Political Gain and Civilian Pain: Humanitarian Impacts of Economic Sanctions.* Lanham, MD: Rowman & Littlefield, 1997.

Whun, Cheon Seong. "The Significance of Forming a ROK-US Extended Deterrence Policy Committee." *Online Series,* No. 10–39 (Seoul: Korea Institute for National Unification, 2010): 1–7.

WikiLeaks, "Cable 09WINDHOEK348." August 30, 2011, http://wikileaks.org.

Wilson, John L. and Xue Litai. *China Builds the Bomb.* Palo Alto, CA: Stanford University Press, 1988.

Wirtz, James J. "Conclusions." In *Security Assurances and Nuclear Nonproliferation,* edited by Jeffrey W. Knopf, 275–291. Palo Alto, CA: Stanford University Press, 2012.

Wirtz, James J. and Peter R. Lavoy. *Over the Horizon Proliferation Threats.* Palo Alto, CA: Stanford University Press, 2012.

Wit, Joel S., Daniel Poneman and Robert L. Gallucci. *Going Critical: The First North Korean Nuclear Crisis*. Washington, DC: Brookings Institution Press, 2004.

Wittner, Lawrence S. *Confronting the Bomb: A Short History of the World Nuclear Disarmament Movement*. Palo Alto, CA: Stanford University Press, 2009.

———. *The Struggle against the Bomb*. Palo Alto, CA: Stanford University Press, 2003.

Wohlstetter, Albert *et al*. *Moving Toward Life in a Nuclear Armed Crowd?* Report to the US Arms Control and Disarmament Agency. Los Angeles, CA: Pan Heuristics, 1976.

Wolfe, Thomas W. *The SALT Experience*. Cambridge, MA: Ballinger Publishing Co., 1979.

Wolfsthal, Jon. "The Intelligence 'Black Hole' over North Korea." Op-ed. *BBC NEWS*. July 17, 2003, http://news.bbc.co.uk/2/hi/asia-pacific/3073677.stm.

Wood, Thomas W., Bruce D. Reid, Christopher M. Toomey, Kannan Krishnaswami, Kimberly A. Burns, Larry O. Casazza, Don S. Daly and Leesa L. Duckworth. "The Future of Nuclear Archaeology: Reducing Legacy Risks of Weapons Fissile Material." *Science & Global Security*, Vol. 22, No. 1 (2014): 4–26.

Woods, Kevin M., David D. Palkki and Mark E. Stout (eds), *The Saddam Tapes: The Inner Workings of a Tyrant's Regime, 1978–2001*. Cambridge, MA: Cambridge University Press, 2011.

Woolfe, Amy. "Nuclear Weapons in the Former Soviet Union: Location, Command and Control." Congressional Research Service. November 27, 1996, www.fas.org/spp/starwars/crs/91-144.htm.

World Institute for Nuclear Security. "Global Needs Analysis for Nuclear Security Training." 2013, www.wins.org/files/wins_white_paper_global_needs_analysis_web.pdf.

World Nuclear Association. *World Uranium Mine Production*, July 2013, www.world-nuclear.org/info/Nuclear-Fuel-Cycle/Mining-of-Uranium/World-Uranium-Mining-Production/.

Wrobel, Paulo S. "From Rivals to Friends: The Role of Public Declarations in Argentina-Brazil Rapprochement." In *Declaratory Diplomacy: Rhetorical Initiatives and Confidence Building*, edited by Michael Krepon, Jenny S. Drezin and Michael Newbill. Washington, DC: Henry L. Stimson Center, 1999.

Wurst, Jim. "ElBaradei Calls for International Control of Nuclear Material Production." *Global Security Newswire*. November 4, 2003, www.nti.org/gsn/article/elbaradei-calls-for-international-control-of-nuclear-material-production-319.

Yadlin, Amos and Avner Golov, "If Attacked, How Would Iran Respond?" *INSS Strategic Assessment*, Vol. 16, No. 3 (October 2013): 7–21, www.inss.org.il/index.aspx?id=4538&articleid=5965.

Yanqiong, Liu and Liu Jifeng. "Analysis of Soviet Technology Transfer in China's Development of Nuclear Weapons." *Comparative Technology Transfer and Society*, Vol. 7, No. 1 (April 2009): 66–110.

Yeaw, Christopher, Andrew Erickson and Michael Chase. "The Future of Chinese Nuclear Policy and Strategy." In *Strategy in the Second Nuclear Age*, edited by Toshi Yoshihara and James Holmes, 53–80. Washington, DC: Georgetown University Press, 2012.

Yoshihara, Toshi and James Holmes (eds), *Strategy in the Second Nuclear Age: Power, Ambition and the Ultimate Weapon*. Washington, DC: Georgetown University Press, 2012.

Yost, David S. "US Extended Deterrence in NATO and North-East Asia." In *Perspectives on Extended Deterrence*. Research & Documents. Fondation pour la Recherche Stratégique (Paris), No. 3 (2010): 15–36, www.frstrategie.org/barreFRS/publications/rd/2010/RD_201003.pdf.

———. "Assurance and US Extended Deterrence in NATO." *International Affairs*, Vol. 85, No. 4 (2009): 755–780.

Yusuf, Moeed. "Predicting Proliferation: The History of the Future of Nuclear Weapons." *Brookings Foreign Policy Paper Series*, No. 11, January 2009, www.brookings.edu/research/papers/2009/01/nuclear-proliferation-yusuf.

Zaitseva, Lyudmila and Friedrich Steinhäusler. "Nuclear Trafficking Issues in the Black Sea Region." EU Non-Proliferation Consortium, Non-Proliferation Papers, No. 39, April 2014, www.nonproliferation.eu/documents/nonproliferationpapers/lyudmilazaitsevafriedrichsteinhausler53451ed0bbecb.pdf.

———. "Database on Nuclear Smuggling, Theft, and Orphan Radiation Sources (DSTO)." Division of Physics and Biophysics, University of Salzburg, Austria, January 2014.

Zanotti, Jim, Kenneth Katzman, Jeremiah Gertler and Steven A. Hildreth. "Israel: Possible Military Strike against Iran's Nuclear Facilities." Congressional Research Service, September 28, 2012, www.fas.org/sgp/crs/mideast/R42443.pdf.

Zelikow, Philip. "Offensive Military Options." In *New Nuclear Nations: Consequences for US Policy*, edited by Robert D. Blackwill and Albert Carnesale, 162–195. New York: Council on Foreign Relations Press, 1993.

Zhang, Baohui. "US Missile Defence and China's Nuclear Posture: Changing Dynamics of an Offence-Defence Arms Race." *International Affairs*, Vol. 87, No. 3 (May 2011): 555–569.

Zhang, Hui. "China's Nuclear Weapons Modernization: Intentions, Drivers, and Trends." Presentation, Institute for Nuclear Materials Management, 53rd Annual Meeting, Orlando. July 15, 2012, http://belfercenter.ksg.harvard.edu/files/ChinaNuclearModernization-hzhang.pdf.

Zhang, Hui and Frank von Hippel. "Using Commercial Imaging Satellites to Detect the Operation of Plutonium-Production Reactors and Gaseous-Diffusion Plants." *Science & Global Security*, Vol. 8, No. 3 (September 2000): 219–271.

INDEX

Caribbean, 9, 241, 246n13, 315n8, 317–19, 322, 325, 326n2,3,6,7, 334, 336n9
Carlson, John, 9–10, 387–90, 414n4
Carter, Jimmy, 292
Cartwright, James, 17–18
CBRN, *see* chemical, biological, radiological, and nuclear
CBW, *see* chemical or biological weapons
CCP, *see* Critical Capabilities and Practices
CD, *see* UN Conference on Disarmament
Central Asia, 241, 311–13, 316n20, 325
Central Asian NWFZ (CANWFZ), 241, 311–13
Central Intelligence Agency (CIA), 27n26, 231–2
C5, *see* five states of Central Asia
Chechen separatists, 25
chemical or biological weapons (CBW), 242
chemical, biological, radiological, and nuclear (CBRN), 462
Chemical Plants Complex (Dera Ghazi Khan), 88
Chemical Weapons Convention (CWC), 160, 181, 183n37, 207, 278–9, 332, 462–3
Cheney, Dick, 265
Chernobyl nuclear power plant, 367, 430–1, 449
Chile, 17, 316n24, 318–19, 321, 374n1
China, 6, 15–16, 19–24, 27n28, 42, 45, 56–66, 70, 73, 79–82, 86, 92–4, 99–104, 116, 136, 138, 144, 147, 154n14, 166, 171–3, 179–80, 188, 197–8, 200–3, 205, 209, 216, 219, 227–8, 230, 236, 240–1, 246n9, 267–9, 274n19, 282, 289, 302–5, 307, 310, 334, 359n3, 366–7, 371, 374, 377, 379, 381, 406, 413, 414n2,20, 443, 449, 463, 464n6; maritime assertiveness, 21; and other nuclear powers, 20–3; People's Republic of China (PRC), 116
CIA, *see* Central Intelligence Agency
CIRUS (Canada-India-Reactor-US), 99–101
CIS Collective Security Treaty (Tashkent Treaty), 312
The Citadel, 3
Clapper, James R., 30
Clinton, Bill, 101, 188, 190–1, 226–7, 230–3, 242, 294–5, 464n4
Clinton, Hillary, 311
CNC, *see* Computer Numerically Controlled
COEX, 391, 393
Cohen, William, 230, 237n25, 242
Cold War, 1, 8, 17, 22, 57, 59, 62–3, 113, 117–19, 121–2, 127, 160, 216–20, 241, 244, 248, 253, 306, 318, 455–6
Colombo Plan, 99
Common System of Accounting and Control of Nuclear Materials (SCCC), 321
Commonwealth of Independent States, 185
"comparative signatures," 250–1, 259–60
Comprehensive Iran Sanctions Accountability,

and Divestment Act of 2010, 282
Comprehensive Nuclear Test–Ban Treaty Organization (CTBTO), 172–3, 180, 191, 194n3; Executive Council (EC), 173, 177–8
Comprehensive Safeguards Agreement (CSAs), 17, 24, 145–53, 155n18
Comprehensive Test Ban Treaty (CTBT), 4, 6–7, 20, 100–2, 134–5, 137–8, 141n15, 171–81, 185–94, 257, 302, 312; amending, 191–2; Article XIV conference, 173; and disguising nuclear test yields, 188–9; and effective verification, 187–8; and entry into force, 180–1; key provisions of, 172–3; and monitoring, 174–7; negotiations, 172; and nonproliferation, 180; nuclear weapon testing, 171–2; and on–site inspections, 177–8; and other problems, 193–4; problems with, 190–1; and safety, 178–80; and testing treaties, 186–7; and verification, 173–4
Computer Numerically Controlled (CNC), 77
Conference on Disarmament (CD); *see* UN Conference on Disarmament
confidence and security building measures (CSBMs), 39
confidence–building measures (CBMs), 87, 94
Containment and Surveillance (C/S), 391
Convention on Early Notification of a Nuclear Accident, 311
Convention on the Physical Protection of Nuclear Material (CPPNM), 136, 422, 424, 427
Convention on the Suppression of Nuclear Terrorism, 136
Convention for the Suppression of Unlawful Acts Against
the Safety of Maritime Navigation (SUA) (Beijing Convention), 271, 273
Conventional Armed Forces in Europe Treaty, 293
conventional prompt global strike (CPGS), 65
Cooperative Threat Reduction (CTR), 3, 11, 136, 450, 455–64, 464n6, 465n8; and creativity, 459–60; and the future, 463–4; and history, 455–7; and innovation, 461–2; and Libya and Syria, 462–3; and patience and transparency, 457–9; and relationships, 460–1; and two decades of lessons learned, 457–62
counterproliferation, 5–8, 139, 226–36, 265–73, 277, 451; and conditions and constraints, 232–5; and deterrence by denial, 235; and future challenges, 235–6; and Gulf war, 230–1; historical cases of, 228–9; and Israeli raid on Iraq's Osiraq, 229; and Israeli raid on Syria's nuclear reactor, 231–2; and North Korea's nuclear program, 231; and Operation Desert Fox, 230–1; rise of, 226–8
CPGS, *see* conventional prompt global strike

model, 322–5; and processes and substance, 324–5; and Tlatelolco, 318–20

Lavisan–Shian, 44

Lawrence Livermore National Laboratory (US), 445–6

League of Arab States, 330–1, 335

Lebanon war (2006), 32

Lentini, Luca, 7–8

LEPs, *see* life–extension programs

LEU, *see* low–enriched uranium

LIBS, *see* laser induced breakdown spectrometry

Libya, 3–4, 9, 22, 24, 39, 58, 72, 75, 91, 93, 120–2, 135, 152, 216, 220, 222, 254, 268, 276–8, 283, 322, 337, 339, 341–3, 374n1, 449, 460, 462–4; and real time lessons, 462–3

life–extension programs (LEPs), 138, 179

Light–Water Reactors (LWRs), 73, 76, 252–3, 388–9, 392 Likud Party, 229

Limited Test Ban Treaty (LTBT), 290, 302, 308

Lisbon protocol of the START I Treaty, 294, 341

Lithuania, 414n20, 448, 465n10

Litwack, Robert S., 7

Lop Nor site, 99

Los Alamos National Laboratory, 11n1, 76, 139n1, 208, 460–1, 465n13

low–enriched uranium (LEU), 45, 76, 78, 202–3, 205–6, 209, 320, 372–3, 376, 379–80, 391, 395, 398–9, 411, 415, 442–52, 464

LTBT, *see* Limited Test Ban Treaty

Luch Scientific Production Association, 445

Lufthansa, 252

Lugar, Richard, 450, 455–6, 462, 464

LWR, *see* light–water reactors

M/V Light, 268

Macedonia, 163

MAD, *see* mutual assured destruction

Madero, Carlos Castro, 343

Maghreb sub–region, 39

Malawi, 449

Malaysia, 81, 267–73, 310, 464n6

Maldives, 39

Manhattan Project, 15, 358, 420

Mars rover, *Curiosity*, 208

Material Protection, Control, and Accounting (MPC&A) Programs, 11, 136, 450, 452, 459–60

Mayer, Klaus, 7–8

McNamara, Robert, 113

Medvedev, Dmitry, 179, 296, 301, 460

Megaports Initiative, 136

Menem, Carlos, 321

methodology, 5–11

MEWMDFZ, *see* Middle East Weapons of Mass Destruction Free Zone

Mexico, 115, 163, 274n19, 316n24, 318

Mian, Zia, 6–7

mid–range ballistic missiles (MRBM), 29

Middle East and North Africa (MENA), 28–39; and arms control, 38–9; and counterproliferation policies, 36; and diplomacy, 36; and extended deterrence, 37; and the Gulf cooperation Council States, 35; and Iran, 31–7; and Israeli nuclear policy, 30–1; and nuclear power, 30; and preemptive strikes, 37–8; and sanctions, 37

Middle East Nuclear Weapons Free Zone (MENWFZ), 24, 323

Middle East proliferation risks, 28–39

Middle East Resolution (1995), 330–1

Middle East Weapons of Mass Destruction Free Zone (MEWMDFZ), 131, 137, 313, 328–35; and Iran, 334–5; and long–standing interest, 328–31; and main undertakings, 332; modalities of, 331–3; and parties to the zone, 331–2; and peaceful nuclear cooperation, 333; and regional verification organization, 333; and security assurances, 333; and weapons banned, 332

Miki, Takeo, 57–8

Minatom, *see* Ministry of Atomic Energy

Ministry of Atomic Energy (Minatom), 445

Ministry of Defense (MOD) (Russian), 48–9, 301, 457

MIRVs, *see* multiple, independently targetable reentry vehicles

Missile Technology Control Regime (MTCR), 160–3, 166–7, 276, 278, 332

mixed oxide (MOX), 393

MNA Proposals from 2003 to the present, 398–9

MOD, *see* Ministry of Defense, Russian

model additional protocol, 150

Modi, Narendra, 22

Moldova, 19, 445–7, 451, 464n6

Morrocco, 39, 229

Moscow Treaty, *see* Strategic Offensive Reduction Treaty

Mossad, 229

MotorVessel (M/V) Cape Ray, 462

Moussa, Amr, 333

MOX, *see* mixed oxide

MPC&A, *see* Material Protection, Control, and Accounting Program

MRBM, *see* mid–range ballistic missiles

MT, *see* fissile material type

MTCR, *see* Missile Technology Control Regime

Mubarak, 22, 25, 313

Multilateral Enrichment Sanctuary Project (MESP), 399, 412

multilateral nuclear approaches (MNAs), 388, 394–6, 398–400

multinational approaches to the nuclear fuel cycle, 403–13; and black box technology, 413; and challenge to safeguards, 405–6; and civil nuclear programs, 404–6; and fuel bank

Wall Street Journal, 15–16, 291
Walrond, Christina, 76
WANO, *see* World Association of Nuclear Operators
War on Drugs, 452
Warsaw Pact, 1, 240
Washington Nuclear Security Summit (2010), 16
Wassenaar Arrangement on Export Controls for Conventional Arms and Dualuse Goods and Technologies (WA), 160–2, 332
weapons of mass destruction (WMD), 2, 8, 22, 28–30, 37–9, 50, 71, 79–82, 102–3, 131, 158–63, 221, 226–36, 265–73, 274n9, 276, 313, 328–35
Weapons of Mass Destruction Free Zone (WMDFZ), 313, 328, 331–3; modalities of, 331–3; *see* Middle East Weapons of Mass Destruction Free Zone
Weber, Andrew, 10–11
WINS Academy, 433–8
Wit, Joel S., 5–6
WMDFZ, *see* Weapons of Mass Destruction Free Zone
Woolf, Amy F., 8
Working Group for Aqueous Reprocessing Facilities, 391–2

World Association of Nuclear Operators (WANO), 431–3, 439
World Health Organization, 462
World Institute for Nuclear Security (WINS), 10, 385, 426, 433–9
World Nuclear Association (WNA), 398, 410
World War II, 15, 26n16, 106n2, 132, 358
WMD, *see* weapons of mass destruction
WNA, *see* World Nuclear Association
Y–12 nuclear facility, 424
"yellowcake" (uranium oxide concentrate), 449, 452
Yeltsin, Boris, 42, 294
Yemen, 39, 72, 265, 274n2,20, 374n1
Yerastov, V., 445
Yongbyon nuclear facility, 70–80, 120–1, 231–2, 255–6, 259
Yugoslavia, 283
Zaitseva, Lyudmila, 10
Zangger, Claude, 162
Zangger Committee, 162–3
Zarif, Javad, 46
Zone of Peace, Freedom and Neutrality (ZOPFAN), 310
ZOPFAN, *see* Zone of Peace, Freedom and Neutrality